T0143048

Recommendation Systems in Software Engineering

Martin P. Robillard • Walid Maalej •
Robert J. Walker • Thomas Zimmermann
Editors

Recommendation Systems in Software Engineering

 Springer

Editors
Martin P. Robillard
McGill University
Montréal, QC
Canada

Robert J. Walker
University of Calgary
Calgary, AB
Canada

Walid Maalej
University of Hamburg
Hamburg
Germany

Thomas Zimmermann
Microsoft Research
Redmond, WA
USA

ISBN 978-3-662-52404-6   ISBN 978-3-642-45135-5 (eBook)
DOI 10.1007/978-3-642-45135-5
Springer Heidelberg New York Dordrecht London

Printed on acid-free paper

Springer is part of Springer Science+Business Media (www.springer.com)

Preface

Software developers have always used tools to perform their work. In the earliest days of the discipline, the tools provided basic compilation and assembly functionality. Then came tools and environments that increasingly provided sophisticated data about the software under development. Around the turn of the millennium, the systematic and large-scale accumulation of software engineering data opened up new opportunities for the creation of tools that infer information estimated to be helpful to developers in a given context. This new type of software development tools came to be known as recommendation systems, in parallel with similar developments in other domains such as the e-commerce.

Recommendation systems in software engineering (RSSEs) share commonalities with conventional recommendation systems: mainly in their usage model, the usual reliance on data mining, and in the predictive nature of their functionality. Beyond these superficial traits, recommendation systems in software engineering are generally different from those in other domains. Traditional recommendation systems are heavily *user centric*. Users generally create the data items directly, e.g., in the form of ratings. An important challenge for traditional recommendation systems is to infer and model evolving user preferences and needs. In contrast, the major challenge for designing RSSEs is to automatically interpret the highly technical data stored in software repositories.

Realizing that some of the important knowledge that is necessary to build recommendation systems in a technical domain would not be readily found in existing books and other resources on conventional recommendation systems, we set about to capture as much of this knowledge as possible in this book.

About This Book

This book has been a community effort. Prospective authors submitted chapter proposals to an open call for contributions. The proposals and later the selected chapters were reviewed by the editors over four review iterations. In addition, the authors participating in this book were asked to review chapters by other contributors.

A unique aspect of this book was the RSSE Hamburg Meeting in April 2013. The contributing authors were invited to this 2-day event to present their chapter ideas, discuss the RSSE state of the art, and participate in editing and networking sessions. The meeting greatly helped to unify the presentation and content of this book and to further consolidate the RSSE community effort. The meeting has been part of a series of events that started with a workshop on software analysis for recommendation systems at McGill University's Bellairs Research Station in Barbados in 2008 and follow-up workshops at the ACM SIGSOFT International Symposium on the Foundations of Software Engineering in 2008 and at the ACM/IEEE International Conference on Software Engineering in 2010 and 2012. The last workshop in 2012 had over 70 participants, which shows a large interest in the topic.

Structure and Content

This book collects, structures, and formalizes knowledge on recommendation systems in software engineering. It adopts a pragmatic approach with an explicit focus on system design, implementation, and evaluation. The book is intended to complement existing texts on recommender systems, which cover algorithms and traditional application domains.

The book consists of three parts:

Part I: Techniques   This part introduces basic techniques for building recommenders in software engineering, including techniques not only to collect and process software engineering data but also to present recommendations to users as part of their workflow.

Part II: Evaluation   This part summarizes methods and experimental designs to evaluate recommendations in software engineering.

Part III: Applications   This part describes needs, issues, and solution concepts involved in entire recommendation systems for specific software engineering tasks, focusing on the engineering insights required to make effective recommendations.

Target Audience

The book contains knowledge relevant to software professionals and to computer science or software engineering students with an interest in the application of recommendation technologies to highly technical domains, including:

- senior undergraduate and graduate students working on recommendation systems or taking a course in software engineering or applied data mining;
- researchers working on recommendation systems or on software engineering tools;
- software engineering practitioners developing recommendation systems or similar applications with predictive functionality; and
- instructors teaching a course on recommendation systems, applied data mining, or software engineering. The book will be particularly suited to graduate courses involving a project component.

Website and Resources

This book has a webpage at rsse.org/book, which is part of the RSSE community portal rsse.org. This webpage contains free supplemental materials for readers of this book and anyone interested in recommendation systems in software engineering, including:

- lecture slides, datasets, and source code;
- an archive of previous RSSE workshops and meetings;
- a collection of people, papers, groups, and tools related to RSSE. Please contact any of the editors if you would like to be added or to suggest additional resources.

In addition to the RSSE community, there are several other starting points.

- The article "Recommendation Systems for Software Engineering," IEEE Software, 27(4):80–86, July–August 2010, provides a short introduction to the topic.
- The latest research on RSSE systems is regularly published and presented at the International Conference on Software Engineering (ICSE), International Symposium on the Foundations of Software Engineering (FSE), International Conference on Automated Software Engineering (ASE), Working Conference on Mining Software Repositories (MSR), and International Conference on Software Maintenance (ICSM).
- Many researchers working on RSSE systems meet at the International Workshop on Recommendation Systems for Software Engineering, which is typically held every other year.
- The ACM Conference on Recommender Systems (RecSys) covers recommender research in general and in many different application domains, not just software engineering.
- Several books on building conventional recommendation systems have been written. To get started, we recommend "Recommender Systems: An Introduction" (2010) by Jannach, Zanker, Felfernig, and Friedrich.

Acknowledgments

We are indebted to the many people who have made this book possible through their diverse contributions. In particular, we thank:

- The authors of the chapters in this book for the great work that they have done in writing about topics related to RSSEs and their timely and constructive reviews of other chapters.
- The Springer staff, in particular Ralf Gerstner, for their dedication and helpfulness throughout the project.
- The Dean of the MIN faculty and Head of Informatics Department at the University of Hamburg, for their financial and logistical support for the editing workshop, and Rebecca Tiarks and Tobias Roehm, for their help with the local organization of the workshop.
- The attendees at the past RSSE workshops, for their enthusiasm about the topic and their influx of ideas.
- The McGill Bellairs Research Institute, for providing an ideal venue for an initial workshop on the topic.

Montréal, QC, Canada   Martin P. Robillard
Hamburg, Germany   Walid Maalej
Calgary, AB, Canada   Robert J. Walker
Redmond, WA, USA   Thomas Zimmermann
October 2013

Contents

Part II   Evaluation

Part III   Applications

List of Contributors

Colin Atkinson Software-Engineering Group, University of Mannheim, Mannheim, Germany

Iman Avazpour Faculty of ICT, Centre for Computing and Engineering Software and Systems (SUCCESS), Swinburne University of Technology, Hawthorn, Australia

Gabriele Bavota University of Sannio, Benevento, Italy

Ayşe Bener Ryerson University, Toronto, ON, Canada

Markus Borg Department of Computer Science, Lund University, Lund, Sweden

Bora Çağlayan Boğaziçi University, Istanbul, Turkey

Gül Çalıklı Ryerson University, Toronto, ON, Canada

Carlos Castro-Herrera GOOGLE, Chicago, IL, USA

Jane Cleland-Huang School of Computing, DePaul University, Chicago, IL, USA

Paolo Cremonesi Politecnico di Milano, Milano, Italy

Andrea De Lucia University of Salerno, Fisciano, Italy

Daniel Diaz Université Paris 1 Panthéon-Sorbonne, Paris, France

Cosmin Dumitrescu Université Paris 1 Panthéon-Sorbonne, Paris, France

Alexander Felfernig Institute for Software Technology, Graz University of Technology, Graz, Austria

Thomas Fritz Department of Informatics, University of Zurich, Zurich, Switzerland

John Grundy Faculty of ICT, Centre for Computing and Engineering Software and Systems (SUCCESS), Swinburne University of Technology, Hawthorn, Australia

Lars Grunske Institute of Software Technology, Universität Stuttgart, Stuttgart, Germany

Negar Hariri School of Computing, DePaul University, Chicago, IL, USA

Kim Herzig Saarland University, Saarbrücken, Germany

Reid Holmes David R. Cheriton School of Computer Science, University of Waterloo, Waterloo, ON, Canada

Oliver Hummel Institute for Program Structures and Data Organization, Karlsruhe Institute of Technology, Karlsruhe, Germany

Laura Inozemtseva David R. Cheriton School of Computer Science, University of Waterloo, Waterloo, ON, Canada

Werner Janjic Software-Engineering Group, University of Mannheim, Mannheim, Germany

Michael Jeran Institute for Software Technology, Graz University of Technology, Graz, Austria

Miryung Kim The University of Texas at Austin, Austin, TX, USA

Angela Lozano ICTEAM, Université catholique de Louvain, Louvain-la-Neuve, Belgium

Walid Maalej Department of Informatics, University of Hamburg, Hamburg, Germany

Andrian Marcus Wayne State University, Detroit, MI, USA

Raúl Mazo Université Paris 1 Panthéon-Sorbonne, Paris, France

Na Meng The University of Texas at Austin, Austin, TX, USA

Kim Mens ICTEAM, Université Catholique de Louvain, Louvain-la-Neuve, Belgium

Tim Menzies Lane Department of Computer Science and Electrical Engineering, West Virginia University, Morgantown, WV, USA

Ayşe Tosun Mısırlı University of Oulu, Oulu, Finland

Bamshad Mobasher School of Computing, DePaul University, Chicago, IL, USA

Gail C. Murphy University of British Columbia, Vancouver, BC, Canada

Emerson Murphy-Hill North Carolina State University, Raleigh, NC, USA

Gerald Ninaus Institute for Software Technology, Graz University of Technology, Graz, Austria

Rocco Oliveto University of Molise, Pesche, Italy

Teerat Pitakrat Institute of Software Technology, Universität Stuttgart, Stuttgart, Germany

Florian Reinfrank Institute for Software Technology, Graz University of Technology, Graz, Austria

Stefan Reiterer Institute for Software Technology, Graz University of Technology, Graz, Austria

Romain Robbes Computer Science Department (DCC), University of Chile, Santiago, Chile

Martin P. Robillard McGill University, Montréal, QC, Canada

Per Runeson Department of Computer Science, Lund University, Lund, Sweden

Alan Said Centrum Wiskunde & Informatica, Amsterdam, The Netherlands

Camille Salinesi Université Paris 1 Panthéon-Sorbonne, Paris, France

Martin Stettinger Institute for Software Technology, Graz University of Technology, Graz, Austria

Domonkos Tikk Gravity R&D, Budapest, Hungary

Óbuda University, Budapest, Hungary

Burak Turhan University of Oulu, Oulu, Finland

Robert J. Walker Department of Computer Science, University of Calgary, Calgary, AB, Canada

Annie T.T. Ying McGill University, Montréal, QC, Canada

Andreas Zeller Saarland University, Saarbrücken, Germany

Chapter 1
An Introduction to Recommendation Systems in Software Engineering

Martin P. Robillard and Robert J. Walker

Abstract Software engineering is a knowledge-intensive activity that presents many information navigation challenges. Information spaces in software engineering include the source code and change history of the software, discussion lists and forums, issue databases, component technologies and their learning resources, and the development environment. The technical nature, size, and dynamicity of these information spaces motivate the development of a special class of applications to support developers: recommendation systems in software engineering (RSSEs), which are software applications that provide information items estimated to be valuable for a software engineering task in a given context. In this introduction, we review the characteristics of information spaces in software engineering, describe the unique aspects of RSSEs, present an overview of the issues and considerations involved in creating, evaluating, and using RSSEs, and present a general outlook on the current state of research and development in the field of recommendation systems for highly technical domains.

1.1 Introduction

Despite steady advancement in the state of the art, software development remains a challenging and knowledge-intensive activity. Mastering a programming language is no longer sufficient to ensure software development proficiency. Developers are continually introduced to new technologies, components, and ideas. The systems on

M.P. Robillard (✉)
McGill University, Montréal, QC, Canada
e-mail: martin@cs.mcgill.ca

R.J. Walker
University of Calgary, Calgary, AB, Canada
e-mail: walker@ucalgary.ca

M.P. Robillard et al. (eds.), *Recommendation Systems in Software Engineering*,
DOI 10.1007/978-3-642-45135-5_1, © Springer-Verlag Berlin Heidelberg 2014

which they work tend to keep growing and to depend on an ever-increasing array of external libraries and resources.

We have long since reached the point where the scale of the *information space*—facing a typical developer easily exceeds an individual's capacity to assimilate it. Software developers and other technical knowledge workers must now routinely spend a large fraction of their working time searching for information, for example, to understand existing code or to discover how to properly implement a feature. Often, the timely or serendipitous discovery of a critical piece of information can have a dramatic impact on productivity [6].

Although rigorous training and effective interpersonal communication can help knowledge workers orient themselves in a sea of information, these strategies are painfully limited by scale. Data mining and other knowledge inference techniques are among the ways to provide automated assistance to developers in navigating large information spaces. Just as recommendation systems for popular e-commerce Web sites can help expose users to interesting items previously unknown to them [15], recommendation systems can be used in technical domains to help surface previously unknown information that can directly assist knowledge workers in their task.

Recommendation systems in software engineering (RSSEs) are now emerging to assist software developers in various activities—from reusing code to writing effective bug reports.

1.2   Information Spaces in Software Engineering

When developers join a project, they are typically faced with a *landscape* [4] of information with which they must get acquainted. Although this information landscape will vary according to the organization and the development process employed, the landscape will typically involve information from a number of sources.

The project source code.   In the case of large software systems, the codebase itself will already represent a formidable information space. According to Ohloh.net, in October 2013 the source code of the Mozilla Firefox Web browser totaled close to 10 million lines written in 33 different programming languages. Understanding source code, even at a much smaller scale, requires answering numerous different types of questions, such as "where is this method called?" [19]. Answering such structural questions can require a lot of navigation through the project source code [11, 17], including reading comments and identifiers, following dependencies, and abstracting details.

The project history.   Much knowledge about a software project is captured in the version control system (VCS) for the project. Useful information stored in a VCS includes systematic code change patterns (e.g., files A and B were often changed together [22]), design decisions associated with specific changes (stored in commit logs), and, more indirectly, information about which developers have knowledge of which part of the code [13]. Unfortunately, the information contained in a VCS is not easily searchable or browsable. Useful knowledge must often be inferred from the VCS and other repositories, typically by using a combination of heuristics and data mining techniques [21].

Communication archives.   Forums and mailing lists, often used for informal communication among developers and other stakeholders of a project, contain a wealth of knowledge about a system [3]. Communication is also recorded in issue management systems and code review tools.

The dependent APIs and their learning resources.   Most modern software development relies on reusable software assets (frameworks and libraries) exported through application programming interfaces (APIs). Like the project source code itself, APIs introduce a large, heavily structured information space that developers must understand and navigate to complete their tasks. In addition, large and popular APIs typically come with extensive documentation [5], including reference documentation, user manuals, and code examples.

The development environment.   The development environment for a software system includes all the development tools, scripts, and commands used to build and test the system. Such an environment can quickly become complex to the point where developers perform suboptimally simply because they are unaware of the tools and commands at their disposal [14].

Interaction traces.   It is now common practice for many software applications to collect user interaction data to improve the user experience. User interaction data consists of a log of user actions as they visit a Web site or use the various components of the user interface of a desktop or mobile application [8]. In software engineering, this collection of usage data takes the form of the monitoring of developer actions as they use an integrated development environment such as Eclipse [10].

Execution traces.   Data collected during the execution of a software system [16, Table 3] also constitutes a source of information that can be useful to software engineers, and in particular to software quality assurance teams. This kind of dynamically collected information includes data about the state of the system, the functions called, and the results of computation at different times in the execution of the system.

The web.   Ultimately, some of the knowledge sought by or useful to developers can be found in the cloud, hosted on servers unrelated to a given software development project. For example, developers will look for code examples on the web [2], or visit the StackOverflow Questions-and-Answers (Q&A) site in the hopes of finding answers to common programming problems [12]. The problem with the cloud is that it is often difficult to assess the quality of the information found in some Web sites, and near impossible to estimate what information exists beyond the results of search queries.

Together, the various sources of data described above create the information space that software developers and other stakeholders of a software project will face. Although, in principle, all of this information is available to support ongoing development and other engineering activities, in reality it can be dispiritingly hard to extract the answer to a specific information need from software engineering data, or in some cases to even know that the answer exists. A number of aspects of software engineering data make discovering and navigating information in this domain particularly difficult.

1. The sheer amount of information available (the *information overload* problem), while not unique to software engineering, is an important factor that only grows worse with time. Automatically collected execution traces and interaction traces, and the cumulative nature of project history data, all contribute to making this challenge more acute.

2. The information associated with a software project is *heterogeneous*. While a vast array of traditional recommender systems can rely on the general concepts of *item* and *rating* [15], there is no equivalent universal baseline in software engineering. The information sources described above involve a great variety of information formats, including highly structured (source code), semi-structured (bug reports), and loosely structured (mailing lists, user manuals).

3. Technical information is highly *context-sensitive*. To a certain extent, most information is context-sensitive; for example, to interpret a restaurant review, it may be useful to know about the expectations and past reviews of the author. However, even in the absence of such additional context, it will still be possible to construct a coarse interpretation of the information, especially if the restaurant in question is either very good or very bad. In contrast, software engineering data can be devoid of meaning without an explicit connection to the underlying process. For example, if a large amount of changes are committed to a system's version control system on Friday afternoons, it could mean either that team members have chosen that time to merge and integrate their changes or that a scheduled process updates the license headers at that time.

4. Software data *evolves very rapidly*. Ratings for movies can have a useful lifetime measured in decades. Restaurant and product reviews are more ephemeral, but could be expected to remain valid for at least many months. In contrast, some software data experiences high *churn*, meaning that it is modified in some cases multiple times a day [9]. For example, the Mozilla Firefox project receives around 4,000 commits per month, or over 100 per day. Although not all software data gets invalidated on a daily basis (APIs can remain stable for years), the highly dynamic nature of software means that inferred facts must, in principle, continually be verified for consistency with the underlying data.

5. Software data is *partially generated*. Many software artifacts are the result of a combination of manual and automated processes and activities, often involving a complex cycle of artifact generation with manual feedback. Examples include the writing of source code with the help of refactoring or style-checking tools, the authoring of bug reports in which the output or log of a program is copied and pasted, and the use of scripts to automatically generate mailing list messages, for example, when a version of the software is released. These complex and

semiautomated processes can be contrasted, for example, with the authoring of reviews by customers who have bought a certain product. In the latter case, the process employed for generating the data is transparent, and interpreting it will be a function of the content of the item and the attributes of the author; the data generation process would not normally have to be taken into account to understand the review.

Finally, in addition to the challenging attributes of software engineering data that we noted above, we also observe that many problems in software engineering are not limited by data, but rather by computation. Consider a problem like *change impact analysis* [1, 20]: the basic need of the developer—to determine the impact of a proposed change—is clear, but in general it is impossible to compute a precise solution. Thus, in software engineering and other technical domains, guidance in the form of recommendations is needed not only to navigate large information spaces but also to deal with *formally undecidable problems*, or problems where no precise solutions can be computed in a practical amount of time.

1.3   Recommendation Systems in Software Engineering

In our initial publication on the topic, we defined a recommendation system for software engineering to be [18, p.81]:

> ...a software application that provides information items estimated to be valuable for a software engineering task in a given context.

With the perspective of an additional four years, we still find this definition to be the most useful for distinguishing RSSEs from other software engineering tools. RSSEs' focus is on providing *information* as opposed to other services such as build or test automation. The reference to *estimation* distinguishes RSSEs from fact extractors, such as classical search tools based on regular expressions or the typical cross-reference tools and call-graph browsers found in modern integrated development environments. At the same time, estimation is not necessarily *prediction*: recommendation systems in software engineering need not rely on the accurate prediction of developer behavior or system behavior. The notion of *value* captures two distinct aspects simultaneously: (1) novelty and surprise, because RSSEs support discovering new information and (2) familiarity and reinforcement, because RSSEs support the confirmation of existing knowledge. Finally, the reference to a specific *task* and *context* distinguishes RSSEs from generic search tools, e.g., tools to help developers find code examples.

Our definition of RSSEs is, however, still broad and allows for great variety in recommendation support for developers. Specifically, a large number of different information items can be recommended, including the following:

Source code within a project.   Recommenders can help developers navigate the source code of their own project, for example, by attempting to guess the areas of the project's source code a developer might need, or want, to look at.

Reusable source code.   Other recommenders in software engineering attempt to help users discover the API elements (such as classes, functions, or scripts) that can help to complete a task.

Code examples.   In some cases, a developer may know which source code or API elements are required to complete a task, but may ignore how to correctly employ them. As a complement to reading textual documentation, recommendation systems can also provide code examples that illustrate the use of the code elements of interest.

Issue reports.   Much knowledge about a software project can reside in its issue database. When working on a piece of code or attempting to solve a problem, recommendation systems can discover related issue reports.

Tools, commands, and operations.   Large software development environments are getting increasingly complex, and the number of open-source software development tools and plug-ins is unbounded. Recommendation systems can help developers and other software engineers by recommending tools, commands, and actions that should solve their problem or increase their efficiency.

People.   In some situations recommendation systems can also help finding the best person to assign a task to, or the expert to contact to answer a question.

Although dozens of RSSEs have been built to provide some of the recommendation functionality described above, no reference architecture has emerged to-date. The variety in RSSE architectures is likely a consequence of the fact that most RSSEs work with a dominant source of data, and are therefore engineered to closely integrate with that data source. Nevertheless, the major design concerns for recommendation systems in general are also found in the software engineering domain, each with its particular challenges.

Data preprocessing.   In software engineering, a lot of preprocessing effort is required to turn raw character data into a sufficiently interpreted format. For example, source code has to be parsed, commits have to be aggregated, and software has to be abstracted into dependency graphs. This effort is usually needed in addition to more traditional preprocessing tasks such as detecting outliers and replacing missing values.

Capturing context.   While in traditional domains, such as e-commerce, recommendations are heavily dependent on user profiles, in software engineering, it is usually the *task* that is the central concept related to recommendations. The *task context* is our representation of all information about the task to which the recommendation system has access in order to produce recommendations. In many cases, a task context will consist of a partial view of the solution to the task: for example, some source code that a developer has written, an element in the code that a user has selected, or an issue report that a user is reading. Context can also be specified explicitly, in which case the definition of the context becomes fused with that of a query in a traditional information retrieval system.

In any case, capturing the context of a task to produce recommendations involves somewhat of a paradox: the more precise the information available about the task is, the more accurate the recommendations can be, but the less likely the user can be expected to need recommendations. Put another way, a user in great need of guidance may not be able to provide enough information to the system to obtain usable recommendations. For this reason, recommendation systems must take into account that task contexts will generally be incomplete and noisy.

Producing recommendations. Once preprocessed data and a sufficient amount of task context are available, recommendation algorithms can be executed. Here the variety of recommendation strategies is only bounded by the problem space and the creativity of the system designer. However, we note that the traditional recommendation algorithms commonly known as collaborative filtering are only seldom used to produce recommendations in software engineering.

Presenting the recommendations. In its simplest form, presenting a recommendation boils down to listing items of potential interest—functions, classes, code examples, issue reports, and so on. Related to the issue of presentation, however, lies the related question of *explanation*: why was an item recommended? The answer to this question is often a summary of the recommendation strategy: "average rating," "customers who bought this item also bought," etc. In software engineering, the conceptual distance between a recommendation algorithm and the domain familiar to the user is often much larger than in other domains. For example, if a code example is recommended to a user because it matches part of the user's current working code, how can this matching be summarized? The absence of a universal concept such as ratings means that for each new type of recommendation, the question of explanation must be revisited.

1.4 Overview of the Book

In the last decade, research and development on recommendation systems has seen important advances, and the knowledge relevant to recommendation systems now easily exceeds the scope of a single book. This book focuses on the development of recommendation systems for technical domains and, in particular, for software engineering. The topic of recommendation systems in software engineering is broad to the point of multidisciplinarity: it requires background in software engineering, data mining and artificial intelligence, knowledge modeling, text analysis and information retrieval, human–computer interaction, as well as a firm grounding in empirical research methods. This book was designed to present a self-contained overview that includes sufficient background in all of the relevant areas to allow readers to quickly get up to speed on the most recent developments, and to actively use the knowledge provided here to build or improve systems that can take advantage of large information spaces that include technical content.

Part I of the book covers the foundational aspects of the field. Chapter 2 presents an overview of the general field of recommendation systems, including a presentation of the major classes of recommendation approaches: collaborative filtering, content-based recommendations, and knowledge-based recommendations. Many recommendation systems rely on data mining algorithms; to help readers orient themselves in the space of techniques available to infer facts from large data sets, Chap. 3 presents a tutorial on popular data mining techniques. In contrast, Chap. 4 examines how recommendation systems can be built without data mining, by relying instead on carefully designed heuristics. To-date, the majority of RSSEs have targeted the recommendation of source code artifacts; Chap. 5 is an extensive review of recommendation systems based on source code that includes many examples of RSSEs. Moving beyond source code, we examine two other important sources of data for RSSE: bug reports in Chap. 6, and user interaction data in Chap. 7. We conclude Part I with two chapters on human–computer interaction (HCI) topics: the use of developer profiles to take personal characteristics into account, in Chap. 8, and the design of user interfaces for delivering recommendations, in Chap. 9.

Now that the field of recommendation systems has matured, many of the basic ideas have been tested, and further progress will require careful, well-designed evaluations. Part II of the book is dedicated to the evaluation of RSSEs with four chapters on the topic. Chapter 10 is a review of the most important dimensions and metrics for evaluating recommendation systems. Chapter 11 focuses on the problem of creating quality benchmarks for evaluating recommendation systems. The last two chapters of Part II describe two particularly useful types of studies for evaluating RSSEs: simulation studies that involve the execution of the RSSE (or of some of its components) in a synthetic environment (Chap. 12), and field studies, which involve the development and deployment of an RSSE in a production setting (Chap. 13).

Part III of the book takes a detailed look at a number of specific applications of recommendation technology in software engineering. By discussing RSSEs in an end-to-end fashion, the chapters in Part III provide not only a discussion of the major concerns and design decisions involved in developing recommendation technology in software engineering but also insightful illustrations of how computation can assist humans in solving a wide variety of complex, information-intensive tasks. Chapter 14 discusses the techniques underlying the recommendation of reusable source code elements. Chapters 15 and 16 present two different approaches to recommend transformations to an existing codebase. Chapter 17 discusses how recommendation technology can assist requirements engineering, and Chap. 18 focuses on recommendations that can assist tasks involving issue reports, such as issue triage tasks. Finally, Chap. 19 shows how recommendations can assist with product line configuration tasks.

1.5 Outlook

As the content of this book shows, the field of recommendation systems in software engineering has already benefited from much effort and attention from researchers, tool developers, and organizations interested in leveraging large collections of software artifacts to improve software engineering productivity. We conclude this introduction with a look at the current state of the field and the road ahead.

Most of the work on RSSEs to-date has focused on the development of algorithms for processing software data. Much of this work has proceeded in the context of the rapid progress in techniques to mine software repositories. As a result, developers of recommendation systems in software engineering can now rely on a mature body of knowledge on the automated extraction and interpretation of software data [7]. At the same time, developments in RSSEs had, up to recently, proceeded somewhat in isolation of the work on traditional recommender systems. However, the parallel has now been recognized, which we hope will lead to a rapid convergence in terminology and concepts that should facilitate further exchange of ideas between the two communities.

Although many of the RSSEs mentioned in this book have been fully implemented, much less energy has been devoted to research on the human aspects of RSSEs. For a given RSSE, simulating the operation of a recommendation algorithm can allow us to record very exactly how the algorithm would behave in a large number of contexts, but provides no clue as to how users would react to the recommendations (see Part II). For this purpose, only user studies can really provide an answer. The dearth of user studies involving recommendation systems in software engineering can be explained and justified by their high cost, which would not always be in proportion to the importance of the research questions involved. However, the consequence is that we still know relatively little about how to best integrate recommendations into a developer's workflow, how to integrate recommendations from multiple sources, and more generally how to maximize the usefulness of recommendation systems in software engineering.

An important distinction between RSSEs and traditional recommendation systems is that RSSEs are task-centric, as opposed to user-centric. In many recommendation situations, we know much more about the task than about the developer carrying it out. This situation is reflected in the limited amount of personalization in RSSEs. It remains an open question whether personalization is necessary or even desirable in software engineering. As in many cases, the accumulation of personal information into a user (or developer) profile has important privacy implications. In software engineering, the most obvious one is that this information could be directly used to evaluate developers. A potential development that could lead to more personalization in recommender systems for software engineering is the increasingly pervasive use of social networking in technical domains. Github is already a platform where the personal characteristics of users can be used to navigate information. In this scenario, we would see a further convergence between RSSEs and traditional recommenders.

Traditional recommendation systems provide a variety of *functions* [15, Sect. 1.2]. Besides assisting the user in a number of ways, these functions also include a number of benefits to other stakeholders, including commercial organizations. For example, recommendation systems can help increase the number of items sold, sell more diverse items, and increase customer loyalty. Although, in the case of RSSEs developed by commercial organizations, these functions can be assumed, we are not aware of any research that focuses on assessing the nontechnical virtues of RSSEs. At this point, most of the work on assessing RSSEs has focused on the support they directly provide to developers.

1.6 Conclusion

The information spaces encountered in software engineering contexts differ markedly from those in nontechnical domains. Five aspects—quantity, heterogeneity, context-sensitivity, dynamicity, and partial generation—all contribute to making it especially difficult to analyze, interpret, and assess the quality of software engineering data. The computational intractability of many questions that surface in software engineering only add to the complexity. Those are the challenges facing organizations that wish to leverage their software data.

Recommendation systems in software engineering are one way to cope with these challenges. At heart, RSSEs must be designed to acknowledge the realities of the tasks, of the people, and of the organizations involved. And while developing effective RSSEs gives rise to new challenges, we have already learned a great deal about the techniques to create them, the methodologies to evaluate them, and the details of their application.

References

1. Arnold, R.S., Bohner, S.A.: Impact analysis: Towards a framework for comparison. In: Proceedings of the Conference on Software Maintenance, pp. 292–301 (1993). DOI 10.1109/ICSM.1993.366933
2. Brandt, J., Guo, P.J., Lewenstein, J., Dontcheva, M., Klemmer, S.R.: Two studies of opportunistic programming: Interleaving web foraging, learning, and writing code. In: Proceedings of the ACM SIGCHI Conference on Human Factors in Computing Systems, pp. 1589–1598 (2009). DOI 10.1145/1518701.1518944
3. Čubranić, D., Murphy, G.C., Singer, J., Booth, K.S.: Hipikat: A project memory for software development. IEEE Trans. Software Eng. 31(6), 446–465 (2005). DOI 10.1109/TSE.2005.71
4. Dagenais, B., Ossher, H., Bellamy, R.K., Robillard, M.P.: Moving into a new software project landscape. In: Proceedings of the ACM/IEEE International Conference on Software Engineering, pp. 275–284 (2010)
5. Dagenais, B., Robillard, M.P.: Creating and evolving developer documentation: Understanding the decisions of open source contributors. In: Proceedings of the ACM SIGSOFT International Symposium on Foundations of Software Engineering, pp. 127–136 (2010). DOI 10.1145/1882291.1882312
6. Duala-Ekoko, E., Robillard, M.P.: Asking and answering questions about unfamiliar APIs: An exploratory study. In: Proceedings of the ACM/IEEE International Conference on Software Engineering, pp. 266–276 (2012)
7. Hemmati, H., Nadi, S., Baysal, O., Kononenko, O., Wang, W., Holmes, R., Godfrey, M.W.: The MSR cookbook: Mining a decade of research. In: Proceedings of the International Working Conference on Mining Software Repositories, pp. 343–352 (2013). DOI 10.1109/MSR.2013.6624048

8. Hill, W.C., Hollan, J.D., Wroblewski, D.A., McCandless, T.: Edit wear and read wear. In: Proceedings of the ACM SIGCHI Conference on Human Factors in Computing Systems, pp. 3–9 (1992). DOI 10.1145/142750.142751

9. Holmes, R., Walker, R.J.: Customized awareness: Recommending relevant external change events. In: Proceedings of the ACM/IEEE International Conference on Software Engineering, pp. 465–474 (2010). DOI 10.1145/1806799.1806867

10. Kersten, M., Murphy, G.C.: Mylar: A degree-of-interest model for IDEs. In: Proceedings of the International Conference on Aspect-Oriented Software Deveopment, pp. 159–168 (2005). DOI 10.1145/1052898.1052912

11. Ko, A.J., Myers, B.A., Coblenz, M.J., Aung, H.H.: An exploratory study of how developers seek, relate, and collect relevant information during software maintenance tasks. IEEE Trans. Software Eng. **32**(12), 971–987 (2006). DOI 10.1109/TSE.2006.116

12. Kononenko, O., Dietrich, D., Sharma, R., Holmes, R.: Automatically locating relevant programming help online. In: Proceedings of the IEEE Symposium on Visual Languages and Human-Centric Computing, pp. 127–134 (2012). DOI 10.1109/VLHCC.2012.6344497

13. Mockus, A., Herbsleb, J.D.: Expertise Browser: A quantitative approach to identifying expertise. In: Proceedings of the ACM/IEEE International Conference on Software Engineering, pp. 503–512 (2002). DOI 10.1145/581339.581401

14. Murphy-Hill, E., Jiresal, R., Murphy, G.C.: Improving software developers' fluency by recommending development environment commands. In: Proceedings of the ACM SIGSOFT International Symposium on Foundations of Software Engineering, pp. 42:1–42:11 (2012). DOI 10.1145/2393596.2393645

15. Ricci, F., Rokach, L., Shapira, B.: Introduction to Recommender Systems Handbook. In: Ricci, F., Rokach, L., Shapira, B. (eds.) Recommender Systems Handbook, pp. 1–35. Springer, New York (2011). DOI 10.1007/978-0-387-85820-3_1

16. Robillard, M.P., Bodden, E., Kawrykow, D., Mezini, M., Ratchford, T.: Automated API property inference techniques. IEEE Trans. Software Eng. **39**(5), 613–637 (2013). DOI 10.1109/TSE.2012.63

17. Robillard, M.P., Coelho, W., Murphy, G.C.: How effective developers investigate source code: An exploratory study. IEEE Trans. Software Eng. **30**(12), 889–903 (2004). DOI 10.1109/TSE.2004.101

18. Robillard, M.P., Walker, R.J., Zimmermann, T.: Recommendation systems for software engineering. IEEE Software **27**(4), 80–86 (2010). DOI 10.1109/MS.2009.161

19. Sillito, J., Murphy, G.C., De Volder, K.: Asking and answering questions during a programming change task. IEEE Trans. Software Eng. **34**(4), 434–451 (2008). DOI 10.1109/TSE.2008.26

20. Weiser, M.: Program slicing. IEEE Trans. Software Eng. **10**(4), 352–357 (1984). DOI 10.1109/TSE.1984.5010248

21. Zimmermann, T., Weißgerber, P.: Preprocessing CVS data for fine-grained analysis. In: Proceedings of the International Workshop on Mining Software Repositories, pp. 2–6 (2004)

22. Zimmermann, T., Weißgerber, P., Diehl, S., Zeller, A.: Mining version histories to guide software changes. IEEE Trans. Software Eng. **31**(6), 429–445 (2005). DOI 10.1109/TSE.2005.72

Part I
Techniques

Chapter 2
Basic Approaches in Recommendation Systems

Alexander Felfernig, Michael Jeran, Gerald Ninaus, Florian Reinfrank, Stefan Reiterer, and Martin Stettinger

Abstract Recommendation systems support users in finding items of interest. In this chapter, we introduce the basic approaches of collaborative filtering, content-based filtering, and knowledge-based recommendation. We first discuss principles of the underlying algorithms based on a running example. Thereafter, we provide an overview of hybrid recommendation approaches which combine basic variants. We conclude this chapter with a discussion of newer algorithmic trends, especially critiquing-based and group recommendation.

2.1 Introduction

Recommendation systems [7,33] provide suggestions for items that are of potential interest for a user. These systems are applied for answering questions such as *which book to buy?* [39], *which website to visit next?* [49], and *which financial service to choose?* [19]. In software engineering scenarios, typical questions that can be answered with the support of recommendation systems are, for example, *which software changes probably introduce a bug?* [3], *which requirements to implement in the next software release?* [25], *which stakeholders should participate in the upcoming software project?* [38], *which method calls might be useful in the current development context?* [59], *which software components (or APIs) to reuse?* [45], *which software artifacts are needed next?* [40], and *which effort estimation methods should be applied in the current project phase?* [50]. An overview of the application of different types of recommendation technologies in the software engineering context can be found in Robillard et al. [53].

A. Felfernig (✉) • M. Jeran • G. Ninaus • F. Reinfrank • S. Reiterer • M. Stettinger
Institute for Software Technology, Graz University of Technology,
Inffeldgasse 16b/2, 8010 Graz, Austria
e-mail: alexander.felfernig@ist.tugraz.at; mjeran@ist.tugraz.at; gninaus@ist.tugraz.at;
florian.reinfrank@ist.tugraz.at; reiterer@ist.tugraz.at; mstettinger@ist.tugraz.at

M.P. Robillard et al. (eds.), *Recommendation Systems in Software Engineering*,
DOI 10.1007/978-3-642-45135-5_2, © Springer-Verlag Berlin Heidelberg 2014

The major goal of this book chapter is to shed light on the basic properties of the three major recommendation approaches of (1) collaborative filtering [12,26,36], (2) content-based filtering [49], and (3) knowledge-based recommendation [5, 16]. Starting with the basic algorithmic approaches, we exemplify the functioning of the algorithms and discuss criteria that help to decide which algorithm should be applied in which context.

The remainder of this chapter is organized as follows. In Sect. 2.2 we give an overview of collaborative filtering recommendation approaches. In Sect. 2.3 we introduce the basic concepts of content-based filtering. We close our discussion of basic recommendation approaches with the topic of knowledge-based recommendation (see Sect. 2.4). In Sect. 2.5, we explain example scenarios for integrating the basic recommendation algorithms into hybrid ones. Hints for practitioners interested in the development of recommender applications are given in Sect. 2.6. A short overview of further algorithmic approaches is presented in Sect. 2.7.

2.2   Collaborative Filtering

The item-set in our running examples is *software engineering-related learning material* offered, for example, on an e-learning platform (see Table 2.1). Each learning unit is additionally assigned to a set of categories, for example, the learning unit l_1 is characterized by Java and UML.

Collaborative filtering [12, 36, 56] is based on the idea of word-of-mouth promotion: the opinion of family members and friends plays a major role in personal decision making. In online scenarios (e.g., online purchasing [39]), family members and friends are replaced by the so-called *nearest neighbors* (NN) who are users with a similar preference pattern or purchasing behavior compared to the current user. Collaborative filtering (see Fig. 2.1) relies on two different types of *background data*: (1) a set of users and (2) a set of items. The relationship between users and items is primarily expressed in terms of *ratings* which are provided by users and exploited in future recommendation sessions for predicting the rating a user (in our case user U_a) would provide for a specific item. If we assume that user U_a currently interacts with a collaborative filtering recommendation system, the first step of the recommendation system is to identify the nearest neighbors (users with a similar rating behavior compared to U_a) and to extrapolate from the ratings of the similar users the rating of user U_a.

The basic procedure of collaborative filtering can best be explained based on a running example (see Table 2.2) which is taken from the software engineering domain (collaborative recommendation of learning units). Note that in this chapter we focus on the so-called memory-based approaches to collaborative filtering which—in contrast to model-based approaches—operate on uncompressed versions of the user/item matrix [4]. The two basic approaches to collaborative filtering are *user-based collaborative filtering* [36] and *item-based collaborative filtering* [54]. Both variants are predicting to which extent the active user would be interested in items which have not been rated by her/him up to now.

Table 2.1 Example set of software engineering-related learning units (LU). This set will be exploited for demonstration purposes throughout this chapter. Each of the learning units is additionally characterized by a set of categories (Java, UML, Management, Quality), for example, the learning unit l_1 is assigned to the categories Java and UML

Learning unit	Name	Java	UML	Management	Quality
l_1	Data Structures in Java	yes	yes		
l_2	Object Relational Mapping	yes	yes		
l_3	Software Architectures		yes		
l_4	Project Management		yes	yes	
l_5	Agile Processes			yes	
l_6	Object Oriented Analysis		yes	yes	
l_7	Object Oriented Design	yes	yes		
l_8	UML and the UP		yes	yes	
l_9	Class Diagrams		yes		
l_{10}	OO Complexity Metrics				yes

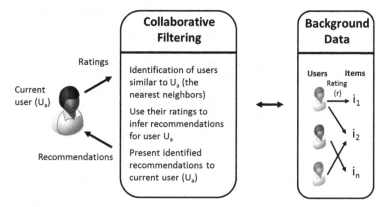

Fig. 2.1 Collaborative filtering (CF) dataflow. Users are rating items and receive recommendations for items based on the ratings of users with a similar rating behavior—the nearest neighbors (NN)

User-Based Collaborative Filtering. User-based collaborative filtering identifies the k-nearest neighbors of the active user—see Eq. (2.1)[1]—and, based on these nearest neighbors, calculates a prediction of the active user's rating for a specific item (learning unit). In the example of Table 2.2, user U_2 is the nearest neighbor ($k = 1$) of user U_a, based on Eq. (2.1), and his/her rating of learning unit l_3 will be taken as a prediction for the rating of U_a (rating = 3.0). The similarity between a user U_a (the current user) and another user U_x can be determined, for example, based on the Pearson correlation coefficient [33]; see Eq. (2.1), where LU_c is the set of items that have been rated by both users, r_{α,l_i} is the rating of user α for item l_i, and

---

[1]For simplicity we assume $k = 1$ throughout this chapter.

Table 2.2 Example collaborative filtering data structure (rating matrix): learning units (LU) versus related user ratings (we assume a rating scale of 1–5)

LU	Name	U_1	U_2	U_3	U_4	U_a
l_1	Data Structures in Java	5.0			4.0	
l_2	Object Relational Mapping	4.0				
l_3	Software Architectures		3.0	4.0	3.0	
l_4	Project Management		5.0	5.0		4.0
l_5	Agile Processes			3.0		
l_6	Object Oriented Analysis		4.5	4.0		4.0
l_7	Object Oriented Design	4.0				
l_8	UML and the UP		2.0			
l_9	Class Diagrams				3.0	
l_{10}	OO Complexity Metrics				5.0	3.0
average rating ($\overline{r_\alpha}$)		4.33	3.625	4.0	3.75	3.67

Table 2.3 Similarity between user U_a and the users $U_j \neq U_a$ determined based on Eq. (2.1). If the number of commonly rated items is below 2, no similarity between the two users is calculated

	U_1	U_2	U_3	U_4
U_a	–	0.97	0.70	–

$\overline{r_\alpha}$ is the average rating of user α. Similarity values resulting from the application of Eq. (2.1) can take values on a scale of $[-1, \ldots, +1]$.

$$\text{similarity}(U_a, U_x) = \frac{\sum_{l_i \in LU_c}(r_{a,l_i} - \overline{r_a}) \times (r_{x,l_i} - \overline{r_x})}{\sqrt{\sum_{l_i \in LU_c}(r_{a,l_i} - \overline{r_a})^2} \times \sqrt{\sum_{l_i \in LU_c}(r_{x,l_i} - \overline{r_x})^2}} \qquad (2.1)$$

The similarity values for U_a calculated based on Eq. (2.1) are shown in Table 2.3. For the purposes of our example we assume the existence of at least two items per user pair (U_i, U_j), for $i \neq j$, in order to be able to determine a similarity. This criterion holds for users U_2 and U_3.

A major challenge in the context of estimating the similarity between users is the *sparsity* of the rating matrix since users are typically providing ratings for only a very small subset of the set of offered items. For example, given a large movie dataset that contains thousands of entries, a user will typically be able to rate only a few dozens. A basic approach to tackle this problem is to take into account the number of commonly rated items in terms of a *correlation significance* [30], i.e., the higher the number of commonly rated items, the higher is the significance of

Table 2.4 User-based collaborative filtering-based recommendations (predictions) for items that have not been rated by user U_a up to now

	l_1	l_2	l_3	l_4	l_5	l_6	l_7	l_8	l_9	l_{10}
U_2	–	–	3.0	5.0	–	4.5	–	2.0	–	–
U_a	–	–	–	4.0	–	4.0	–	–	–	3.0
prediction(U_a, l_i)	–	–	3.045	–	–	–	–	2.045	–	–

the corresponding correlation. For further information regarding the handling of sparsity, we refer the reader to [30, 33].

The information about the set of users with a similar rating behavior compared to the current user (*NN*, the set of nearest neighbors) is the basis for predicting the rating of user U_a for an *item* that has not been rated up to now by U_a; see Eq. (2.2).

$$\text{prediction}(U_a, item) = \overline{r_a} + \frac{\sum_{U_j \in NN} \text{similarity}(U_a, U_j) \times (r_{j,item} - \overline{r_j})}{\sum_{U_j \in NN} \text{similarity}(U_a, U_j)} \quad (2.2)$$

Based on the rating of the nearest neighbor of U_a, we are able to determine a prediction for user U_a (see Table 2.4). The nearest neighbor of U_a is user U_2 (see Table 2.3). The learning units rated by U_2 but not rated by U_a are l_3 and l_8. Due to the determined predictions—Eq. (2.2)—item l_3 would be ranked higher than item l_8 in a recommendation list.

Item-Based Collaborative Filtering. In contrast to user-based collaborative filtering, item-based collaborative filtering searches for items (nearest neighbors—NN) rated by U_a that received similar ratings as items currently under investigation. In our running example, learning unit l_4 has already received a good evaluation (4.0 on a rating scale of 1–5) by U_a. The item which is most similar to l_4 and has not been rated by U_a is item l_3 (similarity(l_3, l_4) = 0.35). In this case, the nearest neighbor of item l_3 is l_4; this calculation is based on Eq. (2.3).

If we want to determine a recommendation based on item-based collaborative filtering, we have to determine the similarity (using the Pearson correlation coefficient) between two items l_a and l_b where U denotes the set of users who both rated l_a and l_b, r_{u,l_i} denotes the rating of user u on item l_i, and $\overline{r_{l_i}}$ is the average rating of the i-th item.

$$\text{similarity}(l_a, l_b) = \frac{\sum_{u \in U} (r_{u,l_a} - \overline{r_{l_a}}) \times (r_{u,l_b} - \overline{r_{l_b}})}{\sqrt{\sum_{u \in U} (r_{u,l_a} - \overline{r_{l_a}})^2} \times \sqrt{\sum_{u \in U} (r_{u,l_b} - \overline{r_{l_b}})^2}} \quad (2.3)$$

The information about the set of items with a similar rating pattern compared to the *item* under consideration is the basis for predicting the rating of user U_a for the *item*; see Eq. (2.4). Note that in this case *NN* represents a set of items already evaluated by U_a. Based on the assumption of $k = 1$, $prediction(U_a, l_3) = 4.0$, i.e., user U_a would rate item l_3 with 4.0.

$$\text{prediction}(U_a, item) = \frac{\sum_{it \in NN} \text{similarity}(item, it) \times r_{a,it}}{\sum_{it \in NN} \text{similarity}(item, it)} \qquad (2.4)$$

For a discussion of advanced collaborative recommendation approaches, we refer the reader to Koren et al. [37] and Sarwar et al. [54].

2.3 Content-Based Filtering

Content-based filtering [49] is based on the assumption of monotonic personal interests. For example, users interested in the topic *Operating Systems* are typically not changing their interest profile from one day to another but will also be interested in the topic in the (near) future. In online scenarios, content-based recommendation approaches are applied, for example, when it comes to the recommendation of websites [49] (news items with a similar content compared to the set of already consumed news).

Content-based filtering (see Fig. 2.2) relies on two different types of background data: (1) a set of users and (2) a set of categories (or keywords) that have been assigned to (or extracted from) the available items (item descriptions). Content-based filtering recommendation systems calculate a set of items that are most similar to items already known to the current user U_a.

The basic approach of content-based filtering is to compare the content of already consumed items (e.g., a list of news articles) with new items that can potentially be recommended to the user, i.e., to find items that are similar to those already consumed (positively rated) by the user. The basis for determining such a similarity are *keywords* extracted from the item content descriptions (e.g., keywords extracted from news articles) or *categories* in the case that items have been annotated with the relevant meta-information. Readers interested in the principles of keyword extraction are referred to Jannach et al. [33]. Within the scope of this chapter we focus on content-based recommendation which exploits item categories (see Table 2.1).

Content-based filtering will now be explained based on a running example which relies on the information depicted in Tables 2.1, 2.5, and 2.6. Table 2.1 provides an overview of the relevant items and the assignments of items to categories. Table 2.5 provides information on which categories are of relevance for the different users. For example, user U_1 is primarily interested in items related to the categories *Java* and *UML*. In our running example, this information has been derived from the rating matrix depicted in Table 2.2. Since user U_a already rated the items l_4, l_6, and l_{10} (see Table 2.2), we can infer that U_a is interested in the categories UML, Management, and Quality (see Table 2.5) where items related to the category UML and Management have been evaluated two times and items related to Quality have been evaluated once.

If we are interested in an item recommendation for the user U_a we have to search for those items which are most similar to the items that have already been consumed

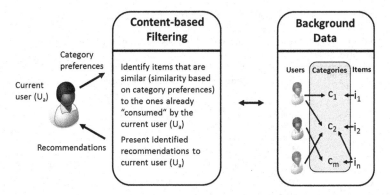

Fig. 2.2 Content-based filtering (CBF) dataflow. Users rate items and receive recommendations of items similar to those that have received a good evaluation from the current user U_a

Table 2.5 Degree of interest in different categories. For example, user U_1 accessed a learning unit related to the category *Java* three times. If a user accessed an item at least once, it is inferred that the user is interested in this item

Category	U_1	U_2	U_3	U_4	U_a
Java	3 (yes)			1 (yes)	
UML	3 (yes)	4 (yes)	3 (yes)	3 (yes)	2 (yes)
Management		3 (yes)	3 (yes)		2 (yes)
Quality				1 (yes)	1 (yes)

(evaluated) by the U_a. This relies on the simple similarity metric shown in Eq. (2.5) (the Dice coefficient, which is a variation of the Jaccard coefficient that "intensively" takes into account category commonalities—see also Jannach et al. [33]). The major difference from the similarity metrics introduced in the context of collaborative filtering is that in this case similarity is measured using keywords (in contrast to ratings).

$$\text{similarity}(U_a, item) = \frac{2 \times \text{categories}(U_a) \cap \text{categories}(item)}{\text{categories}(U_a) + \text{categories}(item)} \qquad (2.5)$$

2.4 Knowledge-Based Recommendation

Compared to the approaches of collaborative filtering and content-based filtering, *knowledge-based recommendation* [5, 14, 16, 23, 42] does not primarily rely on item ratings and textual item descriptions but on deep knowledge about the offered items. Such deep knowledge (semantic knowledge [16]) describes an item in more detail and thus allows for a different recommendation approach (see Table 2.7).

Table 2.6 Example of content-based filtering. User U_a has already consumed the items l_4, l_6, and l_{10}; see Table 2.2. The item most similar—see Eq. (2.5)— to the preferences of U_a is l_8 and is now the best recommendation candidate for the current user

LU	Rating of U_a	Name	Java	UML	Management	Quality	similarity(U_a, l_i)
l_1		Data Structures in Java	yes	yes			2/5
l_2		Object Relational Mapping	yes	yes			2/5
l_3		Software Architectures		yes			2/4
l_4	4.0	Project Management		yes	yes		–
l_5		Agile Processes		yes			2/4
l_6	4.0	Object Oriented Analysis		yes	yes		–
l_7		Object Oriented Design	yes	yes			2/5
l_8		UML and the UP		yes	yes		**4/5**
l_9		Class Diagrams		yes			2/4
l_{10}	3.0	OO Complexity Metrics				yes	–
U_a			yes	yes	yes		

Table 2.7 Software engineering learning units (LU) described based on *deep knowledge*: obligatory vs. nonobligatory (Oblig.), duration of consumption (Dur.), recommended semester (Sem.), complexity of the learning unit (Compl.), associated topics (Topics), and average user rating (Eval.)

LU	Name	Oblig.	Dur.	Sem.	Compl.	Topics	Eval
l_1	Data Structures in Java	yes	2	2	3	Java, UML	4.5
l_2	Object Relational Mapping	yes	3	3	4	Java, UML	4.0
l_3	Software Architectures	no	3	4	3	UML	3.3
l_4	Project Management	yes	2	4	2	UML, Management	5.0
l_5	Agile Processes	no	1	3	2	Management	3.0
l_6	Object Oriented Analysis	yes	2	2	3	UML, Management	4.7
l_7	Object Oriented Design	yes	2	2	3	Java, UML	4.0
l_8	UML and the UP	no	3	3	2	UML, Management	2.0
l_9	Class Diagrams	yes	4	3	3	UML	3.0
l_{10}	OO Complexity Metrics	no	3	4	2	Quality	5.0

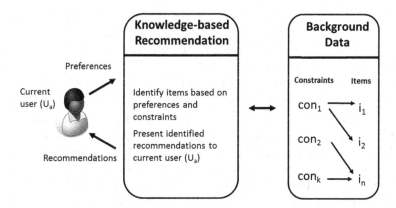

Fig. 2.3 Knowledge-based recommendation (KBR) dataflow: users are entering their preferences and receive recommendations based on the interpretation of a set of rules (constraints)

Knowledge-based recommendation (see Fig. 2.3) relies on the following background data: (a) a set of rules (constraints) or similarity metrics and (b) a set of items. Depending on the given user requirements, rules (constraints) describe which items have to be recommended. The current user U_a articulates his/her requirements (preferences) in terms of item property specifications which are internally as well represented in terms of rules (constraints). In our example, constraints are represented solely by user requirements, no further constraint types are included (e.g., constraints that explicitly specify compatibility or incompatibility relationships). An example of such a constraint is *topics = Java*. It denotes the fact that the user is primarily interested in Java-related learning units. For a detailed discussion of further constraint types, we refer the reader to Felfernig et al. [16]. Constraints are interpreted and the resulting items are presented to the user.[2] A detailed discussion of reasoning mechanisms that are used in knowledge-based recommendation can be found, for example, in Felfernig et al. [16, 17, 22].

In order to determine a recommendation in the context of knowledge-based recommendation scenarios, a *recommendation task* has to be solved.

Definition 2.1. A *recommendation task* is a tuple (R, I) where R represents a set of user requirements and I represents a set of items (in our case: software engineering learning units $l_i \in LU$). The goal is to identify those items in I which fulfill the given user requirements (preferences).

A solution for a recommendation task (also denoted as recommendation) can be defined as follows.

---

[2]Knowledge-based recommendation approaches based on the determination of similarities between items will be discussed in Sect. 2.7.

Definition 2.2. A *solution for a recommendation task* (R, I) is a set $S \subseteq I$ such that $\forall l_i \in S : l_i \in \sigma_{(R)} I$ where σ is the selection operator of a conjunctive query [17], R represents a set of selection criteria (represented as constraints), and I represents an item table (see, for example, Table 2.7). If we want to restrict the set of item properties shown to the user in a result set (recommendation), we have to additionally include projection criteria π as follows: $\pi_{(attributes(I))}(\sigma_{(R)} I)$.

In our example, we show how to determine a solution for a given recommendation task based on a conjunctive query where user requirements are used as selection criteria (constraints) on an item table I. If we assume that the user requirements are represented by the set $R = \{r_1 : semester \leq 3, r_2 : topics = \text{Java}\}$ and the item table I consists of the elements shown in Table 2.7, then $\pi_{(LU)}(\sigma_{(semester \leq 3 \wedge topics=\text{Java})} I) = \{l_1, l_2, l_7\}$, i.e., these three items are consistent with the given set of requirements.

Ranking Items. Up to this point we only know which items can be recommended to a user. One widespread approach to rank items is to define a utility scheme which serves as a basis for the application of multi-attribute utility theory (MAUT).[3] Alternative items can be evaluated and ranked with respect to a defined set of interest dimensions. In the domain of e-learning units, example interest dimensions of users could be *time effort* (time needed to consume the learning unit) and *quality* (quality of the learning unit). The first step to establish a MAUT scheme is to relate the interest dimensions to properties of the given set of items. A simple example of such a mapping is shown in Table 2.8. In this example, we assume that obligatory learning units (learning units that have to be consumed within the scope of a study path) trigger more time efforts than nonobligatory ones, a longer duration of a learning unit is correlated with higher time efforts, and low complexity correlates with lower time efforts. In this context, lower time efforts for a learning unit are associated with a higher utility. Furthermore, we assume that the more advanced the semester, the higher is the quality of the learning unit (e.g., in terms of education degree). The better the overall evaluation (*eval*), the higher the quality of a learning unit (e.g., in terms of the used pedagogical approach).

We are now able to determine the user-specific utility of each individual item. The calculation of *item* utilities for a specific user U_a can be based on Eq. (2.6).

$$utility(U_a, item) = \sum_{d \in Dimensions} contribution(item, d) \times weight(U_a, d) \quad (2.6)$$

If we assume that the current user U_a assigns a weight of 0.2 to the dimension *time effort* (weight(U_a, *time effort*) = 0.2) and a weight of 0.8 to the dimension *quality* (weight(U_a, *quality*) = 0.8), then the user-specific utilities of the individual items (l_i) are the ones shown in Table 2.9.

---

[3] A detailed discussion of the application of MAUT in knowledge-based recommendation scenarios can be found in Ardissono et al. [1] and Felfernig et al. [16, 18].

Table 2.8 Contributions of item properties to the dimensions *time effort* and *quality*

Item property	Time effort (1–10)	Quality (1–10)
obligatory = yes	4	-
obligatory = no	7	-
duration = 1	10	-
duration = 2	5	-
duration = 3	1	-
duration = 4	1	-
complexity = 2	8	-
complexity = 3	5	-
complexity = 4	2	-
semester = 2	-	3
semester = 3	-	5
semester = 4	-	7
eval = 0–2	-	2
eval = >2–3	-	5
eval = >3–4	-	8
eval = >4	-	10

Table 2.9 Item-specific utility for user U_a (i.e., utility(U_a, l_i)) assuming the personal preferences for *time effort* = 0.2 and *quality* = 0.8. In this scenario, item l_4 has the highest utility for user U_a

LU	Time effort	Quality	Utility
l_1	14	13	$2.8 + 10.4 = 13.2$
l_2	7	13	$1.4 + 10.4 = 11.8$
l_3	13	15	$2.6 + 12.0 = 14.6$
l_4	17	17	$3.4 + 13.6 = \mathbf{17.0}$
l_5	25	10	$5.0 + 8.0 = 13.0$
l_6	14	13	$2.8 + 10.4 = 13.2$
l_7	14	11	$2.8 + 8.8 = 11.6$
l_8	16	7	$3.2 + 5.6 = 8.8$
l_9	10	10	$2.0 + 8.0 = 10.0$
l_{10}	16	17	$3.2 + 13.6 = 16.8$

Dealing with Inconsistencies. Due to the logical nature of knowledge-based recommendation problems, we have to deal with scenarios where no solution (recommendation) can be identified for a given set of user requirements, i.e., $\sigma_{(R)} I = \emptyset$. In such situations we are interested in proposals for requirements changes such that a solution (recommendation) can be identified. For example, if a user is interested in learning units with a duration of 4 h, related to management, and a complexity level > 3, then no solution can be provided for the given set of requirements $R = \{r_1 : duration = 4, r_2 : topics = management, r_3 : complexity > 3\}$.

User support in such situations can be based on the concepts of conflict detection [34] and model-based diagnosis [13, 15, 51]. A conflict (or conflict set)

Fig. 2.4 Determination of the complete set of diagnoses (hitting sets) Δ_i for the given conflict sets $CS_1 = \{r_1, r_2\}$ and $CS_2 = \{r_2, r_3\}$: $\Delta_1 = \{r_2\}$ and $\Delta_2 = \{r_1, r_3\}$

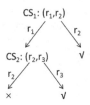

with regard to an item set I in a given set of requirements R can be defined as follows.

Definition 2.3. A *conflict set* is a set $CS \subseteq R$ such that $\sigma_{(CS)}I = \emptyset$. CS is *minimal* if there does not exist a conflict set CS' with $CS' \subset CS$.

In our running example we are able to determine the following minimal conflict sets CS_i: CS_1 : $\{r_1, r_2\}$, CS_2 : $\{r_2, r_3\}$. We will not discuss algorithms that support the determination of minimal conflict sets but refer the reader to the work of Junker [34] who introduces a divide-and-conquer-based algorithm with a logarithmic complexity in terms of the needed number of consistency checks.

Based on the identified minimal conflict sets, we are able to determine the corresponding (minimal) diagnoses. A diagnosis for a given set of requirements which is inconsistent with the underlying item table can be defined as follows.

Definition 2.4. A *diagnosis* for a set of requirements $R = \{r_1, r_2, \ldots, r_n\}$ is a set $\Delta \subseteq R$ such that $\sigma_{(R-\Delta)}I \neq \emptyset$. A diagnosis Δ is *minimal* if there does not exist a diagnosis Δ' with $\Delta' \subset \Delta$.

In other words, a diagnosis (also called a *hitting set*) is a minimal set of requirements that have to be deleted from R such that a solution can be found for $R - \Delta$. The determination of the complete set of diagnoses for a set of requirements inconsistent with the underlying item table (the corresponding conjunctive query results in $\emptyset$) is based on the construction of hitting set trees [51]. An example of the determination of minimal diagnoses is depicted in Fig. 2.4. There are two possibilities of resolving the conflict set CS_1. If we decide to delete the requirement r_2, $\sigma_{(\{r_1, r_3\})}I \neq \emptyset$, i.e., a diagnosis has been identified ($\Delta_1 = \{r_2\}$) and—as a consequence—all CS_i have been resolved. Choosing the other alternative and resolving CS_1 by deleting r_1 does not result in a diagnosis since the conflict CS_2 is not resolved. Resolving CS_2 by deleting r_2 does not result in a minimal diagnosis, since r_2 already represents a diagnosis. The second (and last) minimal diagnosis that can be identified in our running example is $\Delta_2 = \{r_1, r_3\}$. For a detailed discussion of the underlying algorithm and analysis we refer the reader to Reiter [51]. Note that a diagnosis provides a hint to which requirements have to be changed. For a discussion of how requirement repairs (change proposals) are calculated, we refer the reader to Felfernig et al. [17].

Table 2.10 Examples of hybrid recommendation approaches ($RECS$ = set of recommenders, s = recommender-individual prediction, score = item score)

Method	Description	Example formula
weighted	predictions of individual recommenders are summed up	$\text{score}(item) = \Sigma_{rec \in RECS}\, s(item, rec)$
mixed	recommender-individual predictions are combined into one recommendation result	$\text{score}(item) = \text{zipper-function}(item, RECS)$
cascade	the predictions of one recommender are used as input for the next recommender	$\text{score}(item) = \text{score}(item, rec_n)$ $\text{score}(item, rec_i) = \begin{cases} s(item, rec_1)\,, & \text{if } i = 1 \\ s(item, rec_i) \times \\ \quad \text{score}(item, rec_{i-1})\,, & \text{otherwise.} \end{cases}$

2.5   Hybrid Recommendations

After having discussed the three basic recommendation approaches of collaborative filtering, content-based filtering, and knowledge-based recommendation, we will now present some possibilities to combine these basic types.

The motivation for hybrid recommendations is the opportunity to achieve a better accuracy [6]. There are different approaches to evaluate the accuracy of recommendation algorithms. These approaches (see also Avazpour et al. [2] and Tosun Mısırlı et al. [58] in Chaps. 10 and 13, respectively) can be categorized into *predictive accuracy metrics* such as the mean absolute error (MAE), *classification accuracy metrics* such as precision and recall, and *rank accuracy metrics* such as Kendall's Tau. For a discussion of accuracy metrics we refer the reader also to Gunawardana and Shani [28] and Jannach et al. [33].

We now take a look at example design types of hybrid recommendation approaches [6, 33] which are *weighted*, *mixed*, and *cascade* (see Table 2.10). These approaches will be explained on the basis of our running example. The basic assumption in the following is that individual recommendation approaches return a list of *five* recommended items where each item has an assigned (recommender-individual) prediction out of $\{1.0, 2.0, 3.0, 4.0, 5.0\}$. For a more detailed discussion of hybridization strategies, we refer the reader to Burke [6] and Jannach et al. [33].

Weighted. Weighted hybrid recommendation is based on the idea of deriving recommendations by combining the results (predictions) computed by individual recommenders. A corresponding example is depicted in Table 2.11 where the

Table 2.11 Example of *weighted* hybrid recommendation: individual predictions are integrated into one score. Item l_8 receives the best overall score (9.0)

Items	l_1	l_2	l_3	l_4	l_5	l_6	l_7	l_8	l_9	l_{10}
$s(l_i, collaborative\ filtering)$	1.0	3.0	–	5.0	–	2.0	–	4.0	–	–
$s(l_i, content\text{-}based\ filtering)$	–	1.0	2.0	–	–	3.0	4.0	5.0	–	–
$score(l_i)$	1.0	4.0	2.0	5.0	0.0	5.0	4.0	**9.0**	0.0	0.0
$ranking(l_i)$	7	4	6	2	8	3	5	**1**	9	10

Table 2.12 Example of *mixed* hybrid recommendation. Individual predictions are integrated into one score conform the zipper principle (best collaborative filtering prediction receives score $= 10$, best content-based filtering prediction receives score $= 9$ and so forth)

Items	l_1	l_2	l_3	l_4	l_5	l_6	l_7	l_8	l_9	l_{10}
$s(l_i, collaborative\ filtering)$	1.0	3.0	–	5.0	–	2.0	–	4.0	–	–
$s(l_i, content\text{-}based\ filtering)$	–	1.0	2.0	–	–	3.0	4.0	5.0	–	–
$score(l_i)$	4.0	8.0	5.0	**10.0**	0.0	6.0	7.0	9.0	0.0	0.0
$ranking(l_i)$	7	3	6	**1**	8	5	4	2	9	10

individual item scores of a collaborative and a content-based recommender are summed up. Item l_8 receives the highest overall score (9.0) and is ranked highest by the weighted hybrid recommender.[4]

Mixed. Mixed hybrid recommendation is based on the idea that predictions of individual recommenders are shown in one integrated result. For example, the results of a collaborative filtering and a content-based recommender can be ranked as sketched in Table 2.12. Item scores can be determined, for example, on the basis of the zipper principle, i.e., the item with highest collaborative filtering prediction value receives the highest overall score (10.0), the item with best content-based filtering prediction value receives the second best overall score, and so forth.

Cascade. The basic idea of cascade-based hybridization is that recommenders in a pipe of recommenders exploit the recommendation of the upstream recommender as a basis for deriving their own recommendation. The knowledge-based recommendation approach presented in Sect. 2.4 is an example of a cascade-based hybrid recommendation approach. First, items that are consistent with the given requirements are preselected by a conjunctive query Q. We can assume, for example, that $s(item, Q) = 1.0$ if the item has been selected and $s(item, Q) = 0.0$ if the item has not been selected. In our case, the set of requirements $R = \{r_1 : semester \leq 3, r_2 : topics = Java\}$ in the running example leads to the selection of the items $\{l_1, l_2, l_7\}$. Thereafter, these items are ranked conform to

---

[4]If two or more items have the same overall score, a possibility is to force a decision by lot; where needed, this approach can also be applied by other hybrid recommendation approaches.

their utility for the current user (utility-based ranking U). The utility-based ranking U would determine the item order utility(l_1) > utility(l_2) > utility(l_7) assuming that the current user assigns a weight of 0.8 to the interest dimension *quality* (weight(U_a,*quality*) = 0.8) and a weight of 0.2 to the interest dimensions *time effort* (weight(U_a,*time effort*) = 0.2). In this example the recommender Q is the first one and the results of Q are forwarded to the utility-based recommender.

Other examples of hybrid recommendation approaches include the following [6]. *Switching* denotes an approach where—depending on the current situation—a specific recommendation approach is chosen. For example, if a user has a low level of product knowledge, then a critiquing-based recommender will be chosen (see Sect. 2.7). Vice versa, if the user is an expert, an interface will be provided where the user is enabled to explicitly state his/her preferences on a detailed level. *Feature combination* denotes an approach where different data sources are exploited by a single recommender. For example, a recommendation algorithm could exploit semantic item knowledge in combination with item ratings (see Table 2.7). For an in-depth discussion of hybrid recommenders, we refer the reader to Burke [6] and Jannach et al. [33].

2.6 Hints for Practitioners

In this section we provide several hints for practitioners who are interested in developing recommendation systems.

2.6.1 Usage of Algorithms

The three basic approaches of collaborative filtering, content-based filtering, and knowledge-based recommendation exploit different sources of recommendation knowledge and have different strengths and weaknesses (see Table 2.13). Collaborative filtering (CF) and content-based filtering (CBF) are easy to set up (only basic item information is needed, e.g., item name and picture), whereas knowledge-based recommendation requires a more detailed specification of item properties (and in many cases also additional constraints). Both CF and CBF are more adaptive in the sense that new ratings are automatically taken into account in future activations of the recommendation algorithm. In contrast, utility schemes in knowledge-based recommendation (see, for example, Table 2.9) have to be adapted manually (if no additional learning support is available [21]).

Serendipity effects are interpreted as a kind of accident of being confronted with something useful although no related search has been triggered by the user. They can primarily be achieved when using CF approaches. Due to the fact that content-based filtering does not take into account the preferences (ratings) of other users, no such effects can be achieved. Achieving serendipity effects for the users based on KBR is possible in principle, however, restricted to and depending on

Table 2.13 Summary of the strengths and weaknesses of collaborative filtering (CF), content-based filtering (CBF), and knowledge-based recommendation (KBR)

Property	CF	CBF	KBR
easy setup	yes	yes	no
adaptivity	yes	yes	no
serendipity effects	yes	no	no
ramp-up problem	yes	yes	no
transparency	no	no	yes
high-involvement items	no	no	yes

the creativity of the knowledge engineer (who is able to foresee such effects when defining recommendation rules). The *ramp-up problem* (also called the cold start problem) denotes a situation where there is the need to provide initial rating data before the algorithm is able to determine reasonable recommendations. Ramp-up problems exist with both CF and CBF: in CF users have to rate a set of items before the algorithm is able to determine the nearest neighbors; in CBF, the user has to specify interesting/relevant items before the algorithm is able to determine items that are similar to those that have already been rated by the user.

Finally, transparency denotes the degree to which recommendations can be explained to users. Explanations in CF systems solely rely on the interpretation of the relationship to nearest neighbors, for example, *users who purchased item X also purchased item Y*. CBF algorithms explain their recommendations in terms of the similarity of the recommended item to items already purchased by the user: *we recommend Y since you already purchased X which is quite similar to Y*. Finally—due to the fact that they rely on deep knowledge—KBR is able to provide deep explanations which take into account semantic item knowledge. An example of such an explanation is diagnoses that explain the reasons as to why a certain set of requirements does not allow the calculation of a solution. Other types of explanations exist: why a certain item has been included in the recommendation and why a certain question has been asked to the user [16, 24].

Typically, CF and CBF algorithms are used for recommending low-involvement items[5] such as movies, books, and news articles. In contrast, knowledge-based recommender functionalities are used for the recommendation of high-involvement items such as financial services, cars, digital cameras, and apartments. In the latter case, ratings are provided with a low frequency which makes these domains less accessible to CF and CBF approaches. For example, user preferences regarding a car could significantly change within a couple of years without being detected by the recommender system, whereas such preference shifts are detected by collaborative and content-based recommendation approaches due to the fact that purchases occur more frequently and—as a consequence—related ratings are available for the

---

[5]The impact of a wrong decision (selection) is rather low, therefore users invest less evaluation effort in a purchase situation.

recommender system. For an overview of heuristics and rules related to the selection of recommendation approaches, we refer the reader to Burke and Ramezani [9].

2.6.2 Recommendation Environments

Recommendation is an artificial intelligence (AI) technology successfully applied in different commercial contexts [20]. As recommendation algorithms and heuristics are regarded as a major intellectual property of a company, recommender systems are often not developed on the basis of standard solutions but are rather based on proprietary solutions that are tailored to the specific situation of the company. Despite this situation, there exist a few recommendation environments that can be exploited for the development of different recommender applications.

Strands is a company that provides recommendation technologies covering the whole range of collaborative, content-based, and knowledge-based recommendation approaches. MyMediaLite is an open-source library that can be used for the development of collaborative filtering-based recommender systems. LensKit [11] is an open-source toolkit that supports the development and evaluation of recommender systems—specifically it includes implementations of different collaborative filtering algorithms. A related development is MovieLens which is a noncommercial movie recommendation platform. The MovieLens dataset (user × item ratings) is publicly available and popular dataset for evaluating new algorithmic developments. Apache Mahout is a machine learning environment that also includes recommendation functionalities such as user-based and item-based collaborative filtering.

Open-source constraint libraries such as Choco and Jacop can be exploited for the implementation of knowledge-based recommender applications. WeeVis is a Wiki-based environment for the development of knowledge-based recommender applications—resulting recommender applications can be deployed on different handheld platforms such as iOS, Android, and Windows 8. Finally, Choicla is a group recommendation platform that allows the definition and execution of group recommendation tasks (see Sect. 2.7).

2.7 Further Algorithmic Approaches

We examine two further algorithmic approaches here: general critiquing-based recommendations and group recommendations.

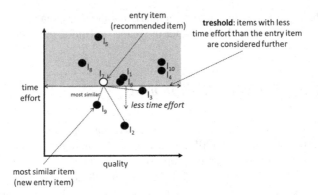

Fig. 2.5 Example of a critiquing scenario. The entry item l_7 is shown to the user. The user specifies the critique "less time effort." The new entry item is l_9 since it is consistent with the critique and the item most similar to l_7

2.7.1 Critiquing-Based Recommendation

There are two basic approaches to support item identification in the context of knowledge-based recommendation.

First, *search-based* approaches require the explicit specification of search criteria and the recommendation algorithm is in charge of identifying a set of corresponding recommendations [16,57] (see also Sect. 2.4). If no solution can be found for a given set of requirements, the recommendation engine determines diagnoses that indicate potential changes such that a solution (recommendation) can be identified. Second, *navigation-based* approaches support the navigation in the item space where in each iteration a reference item is presented to the user and the user either accepts the (recommended) item or searches for different solutions by specifying *critiques*. Critiques are simple criteria that are used for determining new recommendations that take into account the (changed) preferences of the current user. Examples of such critiques in the context of our running example are *less time efforts* and *higher quality* (see Fig. 2.5). Critiquing-based recommendation systems are useful in situations where users are not experts in the item domain and prefer to specify their requirements on the level of critiques [35]. If users are knowledgeable in the item domain, the application of search-based approaches makes more sense. For an in-depth discussion of different variants of critiquing-based recommendation, we refer the reader to [8, 10, 27, 41, 46, 52].

2.7.2 Group Recommendation

Due to the increasing popularity of social platforms and online communities, group recommendation systems are becoming an increasingly important technology

Table 2.14 Example of group recommendation: selection of a learning unit for a group. The recommendation (l_7) is based on the *least misery* heuristic

Items	l_1	l_2	l_3	l_4	l_5	l_6	l_7	l_8	l_9	l_{10}
alex	1.0	3.0	1.0	5.0	4.0	2.0	4.0	2.0	1.0	4.0
dorothy	5.0	1.0	2.0	1.0	4.0	3.0	4.0	2.0	2.0	3.0
peter	2.0	4.0	2.0	5.0	3.0	5.0	4.0	3.0	2.0	2.0
ann	3.0	4.0	5.0	2.0	1.0	1.0	3.0	3.0	3.0	4.0
least misery	1.0	1.0	1.0	1.0	1.0	1.0	**3.0**	2.0	1.0	2.0

[29, 44]. Example application domains of group recommendation technologies include tourism [47] (e.g., *which hotels or tourist destinations should be visited by a group?*) and interactive television [43] (*which sequence of television programs will be accepted by a group?*). In the majority, group recommendation algorithms are related to simple items such as hotels, tourist destinations, and television programs. The application of group recommendation in the context of our running example is shown in Table 2.14 (selection of a learning unit for a group).

The group recommendation task is to figure out a recommendation that will be accepted by the whole group. The group decision heuristics applied in the context is *least misery* which returns the lowest voting for alternative l_i as group recommendation. For example, the *least misery* value for alternative l_7 is 3.0 which is the highest value of all possible alternatives, i.e., the first recommendation for the group is l_7. Other examples of group recommendation heuristics are *most pleasure* (the group recommendation is the item with the most individual votes) and *majority voting* (the voting for an individual solution is defined by the majority of individual user votes: the group recommendation is the item with the highest majority value). Group recommendation technologies for high-involvement items (see Sect. 2.6) are the exception of the rule [e.g., 31, 55]. First applications of group recommendation technologies in the software engineering context are reported in Felfernig et al. [25]. An in-depth discussion of different types of group recommendation algorithms can be found in O'Connor et al. [48], Jameson and Smyth [32], and Masthoff [44].

2.8   Conclusion

This chapter provides an introduction to the recommendation approaches of collaborative filtering, content-based filtering, knowledge-based recommendation, and different hybrid variants thereof. While collaborative filtering-based approaches exploit ratings of nearest neighbors, content-based filtering exploits categories and/or extracted keywords for determining recommendations. Knowledge-based recommenders should be used, for example, for products where there is a need to encode the recommendation knowledge in terms of constraints. Beside algorithmic approaches, we discussed criteria to be taken into account when deciding about which recommendation technology to use in a certain application context. Furthermore, we provided an overview of environments that can be exploited for recommender application development.

References

1. Ardissono, L., Felfernig, A., Friedrich, G., Goy, A., Jannach, D., Petrone, G., Schäfer, R., Zanker, M.: A framework for the development of personalized, distributed web-based configuration systems. AI Mag. **24**(3), 93–108 (2003)
2. Avazpour, I., Pitakrat, T., Grunske, L., Grundy, J.: Dimensions and metrics for evaluating recommendation systems. In: Robillard, M., Maalej, W., Walker, R.J., Zimmermann, T. (eds.) Recommendation Systems in Software Engineering, Chap. 10. Springer, New York (2014)
3. Bachwani, R.: Preventing and diagnosing software upgrade failures. Ph.D. thesis, Rutgers University (2012)
4. Billsus, D., Pazzani, M.: Learning collaborative information filters. In: Proceedings of the International Conference on Machine Learning, pp. 46–54 (1998)
5. Burke, R.: Knowledge-based recommender systems. Encyclopedia Libr. Inform. Sci. **69**(32), 180–200 (2000)
6. Burke, R.: Hybrid recommender systems: Survey and experiments. User Model. User-Adapt. Interact. **12**(4), 331–370 (2002). DOI 10.1023/A:1021240730564
7. Burke, R., Felfernig, A., Goeker, M.: Recommender systems: An overview. AI Mag. **32**(3), 13–18 (2011)
8. Burke, R., Hammond, K., Yound, B.: The FindMe approach to assisted browsing. IEEE Expert **12**(4), 32–40 (1997). DOI 10.1109/64.608186
9. Burke, R., Ramezani, M.: Matching recommendation technologies and domains. In: Ricci, F., Rokach, L., Shapira, B., Kantor, P.B. (eds.) Recommender Systems Handbook, pp. 367–386. Springer, New York (2011). DOI 10.1007/978-0-387-85820-3_11
10. Chen, L., Pu, P.: Critiquing-based recommenders: Survey and emerging trends. User Model. User-Adapt. Interact. **22**(1–2), 125–150 (2012). DOI 10.1007/s11257-011-9108-6
11. Ekstrand, M.D., Ludwig, M., Kolb, J., Riedl, J.: LensKit: A modular recommender framework. In: Proceedings of the ACM Conference on Recommender Systems, pp. 349–350 (2011a). DOI 10.1145/2043932.2044001
12. Ekstrand, M.D., Riedl, J.T., Konstan, J.A.: Collaborative filtering recommender systems. Found. Trends Hum. Comput. Interact. **4**(2), 81–173 (2011b). DOI 10.1561/1100000009
13. Falkner, A., Felfernig, A., Haag, A.: Recommendation technologies for configurable products. AI Mag. **32**(3), 99–108 (2011)
14. Felfernig, A., Friedrich, G., Gula, B., Hitz, M., Kruggel, T., Melcher, R., Riepan, D., Strauss, S., Teppan, E., Vitouch, O.: Persuasive recommendation: Serial position effects in knowledge-based recommender systems. In: Proceedings of the International Conference of Persuasive Technology, *Lecture Notes in Computer Science*, vol. 4744, pp. 283–294 (2007a). DOI 10.1007/978-3-540-77006-0_34
15. Felfernig, A., Friedrich, G., Jannach, D., Stumptner, M.: Consistency-based diagnosis of configuration knowledge bases. Artif. Intell. **152**(2), 213–234 (2004). DOI 10.1016/S0004-3702(03)00117-6
16. Felfernig, A., Friedrich, G., Jannach, D., Zanker, M.: An integrated environment for the development of knowledge-based recommender applications. Int. J. Electron. Commerce **11**(2), 11–34 (2006a). DOI 10.2753/JEC1086-4415110201
17. Felfernig, A., Friedrich, G., Schubert, M., Mandl, M., Mairitsch, M., Teppan, E.: Plausible repairs for inconsistent requirements. In: Proceedings of the International Joint Conference on Artificial Intelligence, pp. 791–796 (2009)

18. Felfernig, A., Gula, B., Leitner, G., Maier, M., Melcher, R., Teppan, E.: Persuasion in knowledge-based recommendation. In: Proceedings of the International Conference on Persuasive Technology, *Lecture Notes in Computer Science*, vol. 5033, pp. 71–82 (2008). DOI 10.1007/978-3-540-68504-3_7

19. Felfernig, A., Isak, K., Szabo, K., Zachar, P.: The VITA financial services sales support environment. In: Proceedings of the Innovative Applications of Artificial Intelligence Conference, pp. 1692–1699 (2007b)

20. Felfernig, A., Jeran, M., Ninaus, G., Reinfrank, F., Reiterer, S.: Toward the next generation of recommender systems: Applications and research challenges. In: Multimedia Services in Intelligent Environments: Advances in Recommender Systems, *Smart Innovation, Systems and Technologies*, vol. 24, pp. 81–98. Springer, New York (2013a). DOI 10.1007/978-3-319-00372-6_5

21. Felfernig, A., Ninaus, G., Grabner, H., Reinfrank, F., Weninger, L., Pagano, D., Maalej, W.: An overview of recommender systems in requirements engineering. In: Managing Requirements Knowledge, Chap. 14, pp. 315–332. Springer, New York (2013b). DOI 10.1007/978-3-642-34419-0_14

22. Felfernig, A., Schubert, M., Reiterer, S.: Personalized diagnosis for over-constrained problems. In: Proceedings of the International Joint Conference on Artificial Intelligence, pp. 1990–1996 (2013c)

23. Felfernig, A., Shchekotykhin, K.: Debugging user interface descriptions of knowledge-based recommender applications. In: Proceedings of the International Conference on Intelligent User Interfaces, pp. 234–241 (2006). DOI 10.1145/1111449.1111499

24. Felfernig, A., Teppan, E., Gula, B.: Knowledge-based recommender technologies for marketing and sales. Int. J. Pattern Recogn. Artif. Intell. **21**(2), 333–354 (2006b). DOI 10.1142/S0218001407005417

25. Felfernig, A., Zehentner, C., Ninaus, G., Grabner, H., Maaleij, W., Pagano, D., Weninger, L., Reinfrank, F.: Group decision support for requirements negotiation. In: Advances in User Modeling, no. 7138 in Lecture Notes in Computer Science, pp. 105–116 (2012). DOI 10.1007/978-3-642-28509-7_11

26. Goldberg, D., Nichols, D., Oki, B., Terry, D.: Using collaborative filtering to weave an information tapestry. Comm. ACM **35**(12), 61–70 (1992). DOI 10.1145/138859.138867

27. Grasch, P., Felfernig, A., Reinfrank, F.: ReComment: Towards critiquing-based recommendation with speech interaction. In: Proceedings of the ACM Conference on Recommender Systems pp. 157–164 (2013)

28. Gunawardana, A., Shani, G.: A survey of accuracy evaluation metrics of recommendation tasks. J. Mach. Learn. Res. **10**, 2935–2962 (2009)

29. Hennig-Thurau, T., Marchand, A., Marx, P.: Can automated group recommender systems help consumers make better choices? J. Market. **76**(5), 89–109 (2012)

30. Herlocker, J., Konstan, J., Borchers, A., Riedl, J.: An algorithmic framework for performing collaborative filtering. In: Proceedings of the ACM SIGIR International Conference on Research and Development in Information Retrieval, pp. 230–237 (1999). DOI >10.1145/312624.312682

31. Jameson, A.: More than the sum of its members: Challenges for group recommender systems. In: Proceedings of the Working Conference on Advanced Visual Interfaces, pp. 48–54 (2004). DOI 10.1145/989863.989869

32. Jameson, A., Smyth, B.: Recommendation to groups. In: Brusilovsky, P., Kobsa, A., Nejdl, W. (eds.) The Adaptive Web: Methods and Strategies of Web Personalization, *Lecture Notes in Computer Science*, vol. 4321, Chap. 20, pp. 596–627. Springer, New York (2007). DOI 10.1007/978-3-540-72079-9_20

33. Jannach, D., Zanker, M., Felfernig, A., Friedrich, G.: Recommender Systems: An Introduction. Cambridge University Press, Cambridge (2010)

34. Junker, U.: QUICKXPLAIN: Preferred explanations and relaxations for over-constrained problems. In: Proceedings of the National Conference on Artifical Intelligence, pp. 167–172 (2004)

35. Knijnenburg, B., Reijmer, N., Willemsen, M.: Each to his own: How different users call for different interaction methods in recommender systems. In: Proceedings of the ACM Conference on Recommender Systems, pp. 141–148 (2011). DOI 10.1145/2043932.2043960

36. Konstan, J.A., Miller, B.N., Maltz, D., Herlocker, J.L., Gordon, L.R., Riedl, J.: GroupLens: Applying collaborative filtering to Usenet news.   Comm. ACM **40**(3), 77–87 (1997). DOI 10.1145/245108.245126

37. Koren, Y., Bell, R., Volinsky, C.: Matrix factorization techniques for recommender systems. Computer **42**(8), 30–37 (2009). DOI 10.1109/MC.2009.263

38. Lim, S., Quercia, D., Finkelstein, A.: StakeNet: Using social networks to analyse the stakeholders of large-scale software projects. In: Proceedings of the ACM/IEEE International Conference on Software Engineering, pp. 295–304 (2010). DOI 10.1145/1806799.1806844

39. Linden, G., Smith, B., York, J.: Amazon.com recommendations: Item-to-item collaborative filtering. IEEE Internet Comput. **7**(1), 76–80 (2003). DOI 10.1109/MIC.2003.1167344

40. Maalej, W., Sahm, A.: Assisting engineers in switching artifacts by using task semantic and interaction history. In: Proceedings of the International Workshop on Recommendation Systems for Software Engineering, pp. 59–63 (2010). DOI 10.1145/1808920.1808935

41. Mandl, M., Felfernig, A.: Improving the performance of unit critiquing. In: Proceedings of the International Conference on User Modeling, Adaptation, and Personalization, pp. 176–187 (2012). DOI 10.1007/978-3-642-31454-4_15

42. Mandl, M., Felfernig, A., Teppan, E., Schubert, M.: Consumer decision making in knowledge-based recommendation.   J. Intell. Inform. Syst. **37**(1), 1–22 (2010). DOI 10.1007/s10844-010-0134-3

43. Masthoff, J.: Group modeling: Selecting a sequence of television items to suit a group of viewers.   User Model. User-Adapt. Interact. **14**(1), 37–85 (2004). DOI 10.1023/B:USER.0000010138.79319.fd

44. Masthoff, J.: Group recommender systems: Combining individual models. In: Ricci, F., Rokach, L., Shapira, B., Kantor, P. (eds.) Recommender Systems Handbook, Chap. 21, pp. 677–702. Springer, New York (2011). DOI 10.1007/978-0-387-85820-3_21

45. McCarey, F., Ó Cinnéide, M., Kushmerick, N.: RASCAL: A recommender agent for agile reuse. Artif. Intell. Rev. **24**(3–4), 253–276 (2005). DOI 10.1007/s10462-005-9012-8

46. McCarthy, K., Reilly, J., McGinty, L., Smyth, B.: On the dynamic generation of compound critiques in conversational recommender systems.   In: Proceedings of the International Conference on Adaptive Hypermedia and Adaptive Web-Based Systems, *Lecture Notes in Computer Science*, vol. 3137, pp. 176–184 (2004)

47. McCarthy, K., Salamo, M., Coyle, L., McGinty, L., Smyth, B., Nixon, P.: Group recommender systems: A critiquing based approach. In: Proceedings of the International Conference on Intelligent User Interfaces, pp. 267–269 (2006). DOI 10.1145/1111449.1111506

48. O'Connor, M., Cosley, D., Konstan, J., Riedl, J.: PolyLens: A recommender system for groups of users. In: Proceedings of the European Conference on Computer Supported Cooperative Work, pp. 199–218 (2001). DOI 10.1007/0-306-48019-0_11

49. Pazzani, M., Billsus, D.: Learning and revising user profiles: The identification of interesting web sites. Mach. Learn. **27**(3), 313–331 (1997). DOI 10.1023/A:1007369909943

50. Peischl, B., Zanker, M., Nica, M., Schmid, W.: Constraint-based recommendation for software project effort estimation.   J. Emerg. Tech. Web Intell. **2**(4), 282–290 (2010). DOI 10.4304/jetwi.2.4.282-290

51. Reiter, R.: A theory of diagnosis from first principles.   Artif. Intell. **32**(1), 57–95 (1987). DOI 10.1016/0004-3702(87)90062-2

52. Ricci, F., Nguyen, Q.: Acqiring and revising preferences in a critiquing-based mobile recommender systems. IEEE Intell. Syst. **22**(3), 22–29 (2007). DOI 10.1109/MIS.2007.43

53. Robillard, M.P., Walker, R.J., Zimmermann, T.: Recommendation systems for software engineering. IEEE Software **27**(4), 80–86 (2010). DOI 10.1109/MS.2009.161

54. Sarwar, B., Karypis, G., Konstan, J., Riedl, J.: Item-based collaborative filtering recommendation algorithms. In: Proceedings of the International Conference on the World Wide Web, pp. 285–295 (2001). DOI 10.1145/371920.372071

55. Stettinger, M., Ninaus, G., Jeran, M., Reinfrank, F., Reiterer, S.: WE-DECIDE: A decision support environment for groups of users. In: Proceedings of the International Conference on Industrial, Engineering, and Other Applications of Applied Intelligent Systems, pp. 382–391 (2013). DOI 10.1007/978-3-642-38577-3_39
56. Takács, G., Pilászy, I., Németh, B., Tikk, D.: Scalable collaborative filtering approaches for large recommender systems. J. Mach. Learn. Res. **10**, 623–656 (2009)
57. Tiihonen, J., Felfernig, A.: Towards recommending configurable offerings. Int. J. Mass Customization **3**(4), 389–406 (2010). DOI 10.1504/IJMASSC.2010.037652
58. Tosun Mısırlı, A., Bener, A., Çağlayan, B., Çalıklı, G., Turhan, B.: Field studies: A methodology for construction and evaluation of recommendation systems in software engineering. In: Robillard, M., Maalej, W., Walker, R.J., Zimmermann, T. (eds.) Recommendation Systems in Software Engineering, Chap. 13. Springer, New York (2014)
59. Tsunoda, M., Kakimoto, T., Ohsugi, N., Monden, A., Matsumoto, K.: Javawock: A Java class recommender system based on collaborative filtering. In: Proceedings of the International Conference on Software Engineering and Knowledge Engineering, pp. 491–497 (2005)

Chapter 3
Data Mining

A Tutorial

Tim Menzies

Abstract Recommendation systems find and summarize patterns in the structure of some data or in how we visit that data. Such summarizing can be implemented by *data mining* algorithms. While the rest of this book focuses specifically on recommendation systems in software engineering, this chapter provides a more general tutorial introduction to data mining.

3.1 Introduction

A recommendation system finds and summarizes patterns in some structure (and those patterns can include how, in the past, users have explored that structure). One way to find those patterns is to use *data mining algorithms.*

The rest of this book focuses specifically on recommendation systems in software engineering (RSSEs). But, just to get us started, this chapter is a tutorial introduction to data mining algorithms:

- This chapter covers C4.5, K-means, Apriori, AdaBoost, kNN, naive Bayesian, CART, and SVM.
- Also mentioned will be random forests, DBScan, canopy clustering, mini-batch K-means, simple single-pass K-means, GenIc, the Fayyad–Irani discretizer, InfoGain, TF–IDF, PDDP, PCA, and LSI.
- There will also be some discussion on how to use the above for text mining.

T. Menzies (✉)
Lane Department of Computer Science and Electrical Engineering, West Virginia University, Morgantown, WV, USA
e-mail: tim@menzies.us

M.P. Robillard et al. (eds.), *Recommendation Systems in Software Engineering,*
DOI 10.1007/978-3-642-45135-5_3, © Springer-Verlag Berlin Heidelberg 2014

Data mining is a very active field. Hence, any summary of that field must be incomplete. Therefore this chapter ends with some suggested readings for those who want to read more about this exciting field.

Every learning method is biased in some way, and it is important to understand those biases. Accordingly, it is important to understand two biases of this chapter. Firstly, it will be the view of this chapter that *it is a mistake* to use data miners as black box tools. In that black box view, the learners are applied without any comprehension of their internal workings. To avoid that mistake, it is useful for data mining novices to reflect on these algorithms, as a menu of design options can be *mixed and matched and mashed-up* as required. Accordingly, where appropriate, this chapter will take care to show how parts of one learner might be used for another. Secondly, this chapter discusses *newer methods* such as CLIFF, WHERE, W2, and the QUICK active learner: work of the author, his collaborators, and/or his graduate students. Caveat emptor!

3.2 Different Learners for Different Data

Let us start at the very beginning (a very good place to start). When you read you begin with A-B-C. When you mine, you begin with data.

Different kinds of data miners work best of different kinds of data. Such data may be viewed as *tables* of *examples*:

- Tables have one column per *feature* and one row per example.
- The columns may be *numeric* (have numbers) or *discrete* (contain symbols).
- Also, some columns are *goals* (things we want to predict using the other columns).
- Finally, columns may contain *missing values*.

For example, in *text mining*, where there is one column per word and one row per document, the columns contain many missing values (since not all words appear in all documents) and there may be hundreds of thousands of columns.

While text mining applications can have many columns, *Big Data* applications can have any number of columns and millions to billions of rows. For such very large datasets, a complete analysis may be impossible. Hence, these might be sampled probabilistically (e.g., using the naive Bayesian algorithm discussed below).

On the other hand, when there are very few rows, data mining may fail since there are too few examples to support summarization. For such sparse tables, k-nearest neighbors (kNN) may be best. kNN makes conclusions about new examples by looking at their neighborhood in the space of old examples. Hence, kNN only needs a few (or even only one) similar examples to make conclusions.

If a table has no goal columns, then this is an *unsupervised* learning problem that might be addressed by (say) finding clusters of similar rows using, say, K-means or expectation maximization. An alternate approach, taken by the Apriori association rule learner, is to assume that every column is a goal and to look for what combinations of any values predict for any combination of any other.

If a table has one goal, then this is a *supervised* learning problem where the task is to find combinations of values from the other columns that predict for the goal values. Note that for datasets with one discrete goal feature, it is common to call that goal the *class* of the dataset.

For example, here is a table of data for a *simple data mining* problem:

outlook	temp	humidity	windy	play?
overcast	64	65	TRUE	yes
overcast	72	90	TRUE	yes
overcast	81	75	FALSE	yes
overcast	83	86	FALSE	yes
rainy	65	70	TRUE	no
rainy	71	91	TRUE	no
rainy	68	80	FALSE	yes
rainy	70	96	FALSE	yes
rainy	75	80	FALSE	yes
sunny	69	70	FALSE	yes
sunny	72	95	FALSE	no
sunny	75	70	TRUE	yes
sunny	80	90	TRUE	no
sunny	85	85	FALSE	no

In this table, we are trying to predict for the goal of play?, given a record of the weather. Each row is one example where we did or did not play golf (and the goal of data mining is to find what weather predicts for playing golf).

Note that temp and humidity are numeric columns and there are no missing values.

Such simple tables are characterized by just a few columns and not many rows (say, dozens to thousands). Traditionally, such simple data mining problems have been explored by C4.5 and CART. However, with some clever sampling of the data, it is possible to scale these traditional learners to Big Data problems [7, 8].

3.3 Association Rules

The *Apriori* learner seeks association rules, i.e., sets of ranges that are often found in the same row. First published in the early 1990s [1], Apriori is a classic recommendation algorithm for assisting shopper. It was initially developed to answer the *shopping basket* problem, i.e., "if a customer buys X, what else might they buy?"

Apriori can be used by, say, an online book store to make recommendations about what else a user might like to see. To use Apriori, all numeric values must be *discretized*, i.e., the numeric ranges replaced with a small number of discrete symbols. Later in this chapter, we discuss several ways to perform discretization but an $X\%$ *chop* is sometimes as good as anything else. In this approach, numeric feature values are sorted and then divided into X equal-sized bins. A standard default is $X = 10$, but the above table is very small, so we will use $X = 2$ to generate:

```
outlook  |      temp   |   humidity  | windy | play?
-------- |   --------- | ----------- | ----- | -----
overcast |   over 73.5 |   over 82.5 | FALSE |  yes
overcast |  up to 73.5 |  up to 82.5 | TRUE  |  yes
overcast |  up to 73.5 |   over 82.5 | TRUE  |  yes
overcast |   over 73.5 |  up to 82.5 | FALSE |  yes
rainy    |   over 73.5 |  up to 82.5 | FALSE |  yes
rainy    |  up to 73.5 |   over 82.5 | TRUE  |   no
rainy    |  up to 73.5 |  up to 82.5 | TRUE  |   no
rainy    |  up to 73.5 |   over 82.5 | FALSE |  yes
rainy    |  up to 73.5 |  up to 82.5 | FALSE |  yes
sunny    |   over 73.5 |   over 82.5 | TRUE  |   no
sunny    |   over 73.5 |   over 82.5 | FALSE |   no
sunny    |   over 73.5 |  up to 82.5 | TRUE  |  yes
sunny    |  up to 73.5 |   over 82.5 | FALSE |   no
sunny    |  up to 73.5 |  up to 82.5 | FALSE |  yes
```

In the discretized data, Apriori then looks for sets of ranges where the larger set is found often in the smaller. For example, one such rule in our table is:

```
play=yes ==> humidity=up to 82.5 & windy=FALSE
```

That is, sometimes when we play, humidity is high and there is no wind. Other associations in this dataset include:

```
humidity= up to 82.5 & windy=FALSE ==> play = no
humidity= over 82.5                ==> play = no
humidity= up to 82.5               ==> play = yes
temperature= up to 73.5            ==> outlook = rainy
outlook=overcast                   ==> play = yes
outlook=rainy                      ==> temperature = up to 73.5
play= yes                          ==> humidity = up to 82.5
play=no                            ==> humidity =  over 82.5
play=yes                           ==> outlook = overcast
```

Note that in association rule learning, the left- or right-hand side of the rule can contain one or more ranges. Also, while all the above are associations within our play data, some are much rarer than others. Apriori can generate any number of rules depending on a set of tuning parameters that define, say, the minimum number of examples needed before we can print a rule.

Formally, we say that an association rule learner takes as input D "transactions" of items I (e.g., see the above example table). As shown above, association rule learners return rules of the form $LHS \Rightarrow RHS$ where $LHS \subset I$ and $RHS \subset I$ and $LHS \cap RHS = \emptyset$. In the terminology of Apriori, an association rule $X \Rightarrow Y$ has *support s* if $s\%$ of D contains $X \wedge Y$, i.e., $s = \frac{|X \wedge Y|}{|D|}$, where $|X \wedge Y|$ denotes the number of transactions/examples in D containing both X and Y. The confidence c of an association rule is the percentage of transactions/examples containing X which also contain Y, i.e., $c = \frac{|X \wedge Y|}{|X|}$. As an example of these measures, consider the following rule:

```
play=yes ==> outlook = overcast
```

In this rule, $LHS = X = $ `play=yes` and $RHS = Y = $ `outlook=overcast`. Hence:

- support $= \frac{|X \wedge Y|}{|D|} = \frac{4}{14} = 0.29$
- confidence $= \frac{|X \wedge Y|}{|X|} = \frac{4}{9} = 0.44$.

Apriori was the first association rule pruning approach. When it was first proposed (1993), it was famous for its scalability. Running on a 33MHz machine with 64MB of RAM, Apriori was able to find associations in 838MB of data in under 100 s, which was quite a feat for those days. To achieve this, Apriori explored progressively larger combinations of ranges. Furthermore, the search for larger associations was constrained to smaller associations that occurred frequently. These *frequent itemsets* were grown incrementally and Apriori only explored itemsets of size N using items that occurred frequently of size $M < N$. Formally speaking, Apriori uses *support-based pruning*, i.e., when searching for rules with high confidence, sets of items $I_i, \ldots, I_k$ are examined only if all its subsets are above some minimum support value. After that, *confidence-based pruning* is applied to reject all rules that fall below some minimal threshold of adequate confidence.

3.3.1 Technical Aside: How to Discretize?

In the above example, we used a *discretization policy* before running Apriori. Such discretization is a useful technique for many other learning schemes (and we will return to discretization many times in this chapter).

For now, we just say that discretization need not be very clever [58]. For example, a 10 % chop is often as good as anything else (exception: for small tables of data like that shown above, it may be necessary to use fewer chops, just in case not enough information falls into each bin).

A newer method for discretization is to generate many small bins (e.g., 10 bins) then combine adjacent bins whose mean values are about the same. To apply this newer approach, we need some definition of "about the same" such as Hedges's test of Fig. 3.1.

3.4 Learning Trees

Apriori finds sets of interesting associations. For some applications this is useful but, when the query is more directed, another kind of learner may be more suited.

Hedges's test [28] explores two populations, each of which is characterized by its size, their mean, and standard deviation (denoted n, *mean*, and *sd*, respectively). When testing if these two populations are different, we need to consider the following:

- If the standard deviation is large, then this *confuses* our ability to distinguish the bins.
- But if the sample size is large then we can *attenuate* the effects of the large standard deviation, i.e., the more we know about the sample, the more certain we are of the mean values.

Combining all that, we arrive at an informal measure of the difference between two means (note that this expression weights *confusion* by how many samples are trying to confuse us):

```
attenuate = n1 + n2
confusion = (n1*sd1 + n2*sd2) / attenuate
delta = abs(mean1 - mean2) / confusion
```

A more formally accepted version of the above, as endorsed by Kampenes et al. [31], is the following. To explain the difference between the above expression and Hedges's test, note the following.

- This test returns true if the *delta* is less than some "small" amount. The correct value of "small" is somewhat debatable but the values shown below are in the lower third of the "small" values seen in the 284 tests from the 64 experiments reviewed by Kampenes et al.,
- A c term is added to handle small sample sizes (less than 20).
- Standard practice in statistics is to:

    - use $n - 1$ in standard deviation calculations; and
    - use variance sd^2 rather than standard deviation.

```
function hedges(n1,mean1,sd1, n2,mean2,sd2) {
    small     = 0.17 # for a strict test. for a less severe
          test, use 0.38
    m1        = n1 - 1
    m2        = n2 - 1
    attenuate = m1 + m2
    confusion = sqrt( (m1 * (sd1)^2 +  m2 * (sd2)^2) /
          attenuate)
    delta     = abs(mean1 - mean2) / confusion
    c         = 1 - 3/(4*(m1 + n1) - 1)
    return delta * c < small
}
```

Fig. 3.1 A tutorial on Hedges's test of the effect size of the difference between two populations [28, 31]

3.4.1 C4.5

The *C4.5* decision tree learner [50] tries to ignore everything except the minimum combination of feature ranges that lead to different *decisions*. For example, if C4.5 reads the raw golf data (from Sect. 3.2), it would focus on the play? feature. It would then report what other feature ranges lead to such playful behavior. That report would take the form of the following tree:

```
outlook = sunny
|    humidity <= 75: yes
|    humidity > 75: no
outlook = overcast: yes
outlook = rainy
|    windy = TRUE: no
|    windy = FALSE: yes
```

To read this decision tree, note that subtrees are indented and that any line containing a colon (:) is a prediction. For example, the top branch of this tree says: "If outlook is sunny and humidity $\leq$ 75 then we will play golf." Note that this decision tree does not include temp, i.e., the temperature. This is not to say that golf playing behavior is unaffected by cold or heat. Rather, it is saying that, for this data, the other features are more important.

C4.5 looks for a feature value that simplifies the data. For example, consider the above table with five examples of no playing of golf and nine examples of yes, we played golf. Note that the *baseline* distributions in the table are $p_1 = 5/14$ and $p_2 = 9/14$ for no and yes (respectively). Now look at the middle of the above tree, at the branch outlook = overcast. C4.5 built this branch since within that region, the distributions are very simple indeed: all the rows where the outlook is overcast have play? = yes. That is, in this subtree $p_1 = 0$ and $p_2 = 100\,\%$.

Formally, we say that decision tree learners look for splits in the data that reduce the diversity of the data. This diversity is measured by the entropy equation discussed in Fig. 3.2. For example, in the golf example, the relative frequency of each class was $p_1 = 5/14$ and $p_2 = 9/14$. In that case:
```
e = entropy([5/14, 9/14])
  = -5/14 * log2(5/14) - 9/14 *log2(9/14) = 0.94
```

For the subtree selected by outlook = overcast, where $p_1 = 0$ and $p_2 = 100\,\%$, we ignore the zero value (since there is no information there) and compute:
```
n1 = 4
e1 = entropy([1]) = -1 * log2(1) = 0
```

Note that for the subtree with five rows selected by outlook = sunny, there are two yes and one no. That is:
```
n2 = 5
e2 = entropy([2/5, 3/5]) = 0.97
```

Also, and for the subtree with five rows selected by outlook = rainy, there are three yes and two no. Hence:
```
n3 = 5
e3 = entropy([3/5, 2/5]) = 0.97
```

How to measure diversity? For numeric classes, it is customary to use standard deviation. However, for discrete classes, we need something else. To define such a diversity measure, we start with the following intuition:

- a population that contains only one thing is not diverse;
- a population that contains many things is more diverse.

Consider some sheep and cows in a barnyard, which we will represent as a piece of paper. Imagine that the animals do not like each other so they huddle in different corners. Say the sheep cover 10% of the yard and the cows cover 30%. To get some wool, we keep folding the piece of paper in half until we find all those sheep—a process we can represent mathematically as $\log_2(0.1)$. The same cost to find the cows takes $\log_2(0.3)$. The expected value of that search is the probability of each population times the cost of finding that population, i.e., $-1 \times (0.1 \times \log_2(0.1) + 0.3 \times \log_2(0.3))$. The logarithm of a probability less than one is negative so, by convention, we multiply by a minus sign. This informal example, while illustrative, has limitations (e.g., it ignores details like the 60% grass). The formal definition of symbol diversity comes from the famous information entropy expression of Shannon [55, 56]: $\text{entropy}([p_1, p_2, \ldots p_n]) = -\sum_i^n p_i \log_2(p_i)$. Shannon used entropy as a way to measure how much signal is in a transmission:

- A piece of paper that is full of only one thing has, by definition, one thing everywhere. In terms of the above discussion, this is the population that is not diverse.
- Such a piece of paper has no distinctions, i.e., no regions where one thing becomes another.
- Hence, to transmit that information takes zero bits since there is nothing to say.

Note that Shannon's equation captures this "zero bits" case. If you only have one thing then $n = 1$ and $p_1 = 1$ and entropy is zero: $\text{entropy}([1]) = 0$. On the other hand, as we increase diversity, the more bits are required to transmit that signal. For example, having three similar things is less diverse than having four or five similar things (as we might expect):

$$\text{entropy}([10, 10, 10]) = 1.58$$
$$\text{entropy}([10, 10, 10, 10]) = 2$$
$$\text{entropy}([10, 10, 10, 10, 10]) = 2.32$$

Fig. 3.2 A tutorial on measuring diversity using Shannon entropy [55, 56]

From the above, we can compute the expected value of the entropy after dividing the 14 rows in our table using the above tree:

```
n       = n1 + n2 + n3 = 14
expect = 4/14 * 0 + 5/14 * 0.97 + 5/14 * 0.97 = 0.65
```

That is, the above tree has simplified the data from e = 0.94 to the new expected value of 0.65.

3.4.2 CART

The *classification and regression tree* (CART) learner is another traditional learner first developed for simple data mining problems [6]. Like C4.5, CART has been a framework within which many researchers have proposed exciting new kinds of data miners (for example, the research on CART led to the invention of random forests, discussed below).

For certain classes of problem, CART is known to work as well as or better than more complex schemes [14]. The lesson here is that before rushing off to try the latest and greatest learner, it is worthwhile to spend some effort on simpler learners like CART and C4.5. At the very least, these simple learners will offer baseline results against which supposedly more sophisticated methods can be compared.

The entropy equation of C4.5 assumes that the goal class is discrete. The CART regression tree learner applies the same recursive split procedure of C4.5, but it assumes that the goal class is numeric. CART generates *regression trees* that look the same as decision trees but their leaves contain numeric predictions. For such numeric goals, we can measure the diversity of the class distribution using standard deviation.

For reasons of speed, it is useful to compute standard deviation using a single-pass algorithm. Suppose we have n measurements of numeric goals in a class distribution $x_1, x_2, x_3, \ldots$. If t is the sum of all the x_i variables and t_2 is the sum of the square of all the x_i variables, then $s = \text{stdev} = \sqrt{\frac{t_2 - (t^2/n)}{n-1}}$. Apart from the handling of the class variable, C4.5 and CART work in very similar ways: they try to split on all features, then they use the split that reduces diversity the most:

- C4.5 finds splits that divide the n *discrete* goals into n_i divisions, each with entropy e_i.
- CART finds splits that divide the n *numeric* goals into n_i divisions, each with standard deviation s_i.

Both algorithms then apply some weighted sum to compute the expected value of the split:

- C4.5: expected diversity $= \sum_i \frac{n_i}{n} \times e_i$;
- CART: expected diversity $= \sum_i \frac{n_i}{n} \times s_i$.

Once they find the feature that generates the split with the lowest diversity, they then apply that split and recurse on each division.

3.4.3 Hints and Tips for CART and C4.5

Any recursive algorithm such as CART (or C4.5) needs a stopping criterion; e.g., stop when there are less than M examples falling into each subtree.

- As M gets larger, it becomes harder to form new subtrees so the total tree size shrinks. That is, the tree becomes easier to read.
- As M gets smaller, it becomes easier for the learner to explore special cases within the data. That is, the predictions of the tree can become more accurate. Random forests, discussed below, use very small M values (e.g., $M = 2$).

For example, the *housing* dataset describes 506 houses from Boston. Each house is described in terms of 14 features (and the last feature "PRICE" is the target concept we seek to predict):

CRIM. Per capita crime rate by town.

ZN. Proportion of residential land zoned for lots over 25,000 square feet.

INDUS. Proportion of non-retail business acres per town.

CHAS. Charles River dummy variable (1 if the tract bounds the river, 0 otherwise).

NOX. Nitric oxides concentration (parts per 10 million).

RM. Average number of rooms per dwelling.

AGE. Proportion of owner-occupied units built prior to 1940.

DIS. Weighted distances to five Boston employment centers.

RAD. Index of accessibility to radial highways.

TAX. Full-value property-tax rate per $10,000.

PTRATIO. Pupil–teacher ratio by town.

B. $1000(B - 0.63)^2$ where B is the proportion of blocks by town.

LSTAT. Lower status of the population.

PRICE. Median value of owner-occupied homes.

With the default value of $M = 4$, CART generates a tree with 28 leaves. But with $M = 100$, we generate a much more readable and smaller tree with only 9 leaves. This tree is shown below:

```
STAT <= 9.725 :
|    RM <= 6.941 :
|    |    DIS <= 3.325 : PRICE = 27.4
|    |    DIS >  3.325 :
|    |    |    RM <= 6.545 : PRICE = 23.8
|    |    |    RM >  6.545 : PRICE = 26.8
|    RM >  6.941 : 36.0
LSTAT >  9.725 :
|    LSTAT <= 15 :
|    |    DIS <= 4.428 :
|    |    |    TAX <= 300 :   PRICE = 21.9
|    |    |    TAX >  300 :   PRICE = 20.3
|    |    DIS >  4.428 :   PRICE = 19.7
|    LSTAT >  15 :
|    |    CRIM <= 5.769 :   PRICE = 17.0
|    |    CRIM >  5.769 :   PRICE = 13.6
```

Any line containing a colon (:) is a prediction. For example, the top branch of this decision tree is saying: "If STAT < 9.725 and RM ≤ 6.941 and DIS ≤ 3.325 then PRICE $= 27.4$." The smaller tree, shown above, is less accurate than the tree grown with $M = 4$. However, the difference is not large:

- the predictions of the larger tree correlate with the actuals at $R^2 = 91\%$, and
- the smaller tree is nearly as accurate with $R^2 = 86\%$.

In the above, R^2 is a measure of how much one, say, class feature f is determined by another variable x. This is called the Pearson correlation coefficient[1] [45].

Note that the smaller tree is much easier to read and to understand while being nearly as accurate as the larger and more complex tree. When discussing a learned model with users, sometimes it is worth losing a few points in performance in order to display a smaller, more easily understood, tree. Note also that this trick of selecting M in order to balance performance vs readability can be applied to any tree learning procedure including CART or C4.5.

Finally, it is worth mentioning that tree learners often include a *post-pruning* step where the data miner experiments with removing subtrees. In this post-pruning, if the predictive power of the pruned tree is not worse than the original tree, then the pruner recurses on the reduced tree.

3.4.4 Random Forests

Traditional tree learners like CART and C4.5 cannot scale to Big Data problems since they assume that data is loaded into main memory and executed within one thread. There are many ways to address these issues such as the classic "peepholing" method of Catlett [8]. One of the most interesting, and simplest, is the *random forest* method of Breimann [7]. The motto of random forests is, "If one tree is good, why not build a whole bunch?" To build one tree in a random forest, pick a number m less than the number of features. Then, to build a forest, build many trees as follows:

1. select some subset d of the training data;
2. build a tree as above, but at each split, only consider m features (selected at random); and
3. do not bother to post-prune.

Finding the right d and m values for a particular dataset means running the forests, checking the error rates in the predictions, then applying engineering judgment to select better values. Note that d cannot be bigger than what can fit into RAM. Also, a useful default for m is the log of the number of features.

Random forests make predictions by passing test data down each tree. The output is the most common conclusion made by all trees.

Random forests have certain drawbacks:

- Random forests do not generate a single simple model that users can browse and understand. On the other hand, the forests can be queried to find the most important features (by asking what features across all the trees were used most as a split criteria).

---

[1]Given a mean value for x over n measurements $\bar{x} = \frac{1}{n} \sum_{i=1}^{n} x_i$, then the total sum of squares is $SS_{\text{tot}} = \sum_i (x_i - \bar{x})^2$ and the sum of squares of residuals is $SS_{\text{err}} = \sum_i (x_i - f_i)^2$. From this, the amount by which x determines f is $R^2 = 1 - (SS_{\text{err}}/SS_{\text{tot}})$.

- Some commonly used data mining toolkits insist that all the data load into RAM before running random forests.[2]

Nevertheless, random forests are remarkably effective:

- Random forests generate predictions that are often as good as, or better than, many other learners [7].
- They are fast. In [7], Breimann reports experiments where running it on a dataset with 50,000 cases and 100 variables, it produced 100 trees in 11 min on a 800MHz machine. On modern machines, random forest learning is even faster.
- They scale to datasets with very large numbers of rows or features: just repeatedly sample as much data as can fit into RAM.
- They extend naturally into cloud computing: just build forests on different CPUs.

Like C4.5 and CART, it might be best to think of random forests as a framework within which we can explore multiple data mining methods:

- When faced with data that is too big to process:

  - Repeat many times:
  - Learn something from subsets of the rows and features.

- Then make conclusions by sampling across that ensemble of learners.

As seen with random forests, this strategy works well for decision tree learning, but it is useful for many other learners as well (later in this chapter we discuss an analog of random forests for the naive Bayesian classifier).

Note that for this style of random learning to be practical, each model must be learned very fast. Hence, when building such a learner, do not "sweat the small stuff." If something looks tricky, then just skip it (e.g., random forests do not do post-pruning). The lesson of random forests is that multiple simple samples can do better than fewer and more complex methods. Don't worry, be happy.

A final note on random forests: they are an example of an *ensemble learning* method. The motto of ensemble learning is that if one expert is good, then many are better. While N copies of the same expert is clearly a waste of resources, N experts all learned from slightly different data can offer N different perspectives on the same problem. Ensemble learning is an exciting area in data mining—and one that has proved most productive. For example:

- The annual KDD-cup is an international competition between data mining research teams. All the first and second-placed winners for 2009–2011 used ensemble methods.
- In our own work, our current best-of-breed learner for effort estimation is an ensemble method [34].

Later in this chapter we will discuss other kinds of ensemble learners such as AdaBoost.

---

[2]But it should be emphasized that this is more an issue in the typical toolkit's implementation than some fatal flaw with random forests.

3.4.5   Applications of Tree Learning

C4.5 and CART are widely influential algorithms. The clarity and simplicity of this kind of learning has allowed many researchers to develop innovative extensions. In addition to random forests, those extensions include the following:

- The *Fayyad–Irani* discretizer [20] is a cut-down version of C4.5 that builds a tree from a single feature. The leaves of that tree are returned as the learned bins.
- The *InfoGain* feature selector [25] does not build trees. Rather, it acts like C4.5's first split when it conducts a what-if query over all features. InfoGain sorts the features by the entropy reduction that would result if the data was split on that data. A standard InfoGain algorithm requires discrete data and so is typically run over data that has been discretized by Fayyad–Irani.
- *Principal direction divisive partitioning* (PDDP) is a tree learner that splits on synthesized features [3]. At each level of the recursion, PDDP finds the eigenvectors of the correlation matrix of the data that falls into each sub-branch. Technically, this is a principal component analysis (PCA) that transforms the data to a new coordinate system such that the greatest variance by any projection of the data comes to lie on the first coordinate (called the first principal component).
- *WHERE* is a version of PDDP that uses the FASTMAP trick to find an approximation to the first component [40]. WHERE uses the Aha distance function (defined later in this chapter).
  - After picking any row X at random, WHERE finds the row *Right* that is furthest from X and then the row *Left* that is furthest from *Right*.
  - WHERE then projects all rows onto the line that runs from *Left* to *Right* by finding:
    1. the distance c between *Left* and *Right*; and
    2. for every row, the distance a and b to rows *Left* and *Right*.

    With that information, the projection of a row along the *Left* and *Right* line is $x = (a^2 + c^2 - b^2)/(2c)$.
  - WHERE finds the median x value, then splits the data above and below that split point. The algorithm then recurses on each split.

These variants can be much simpler than the standard C4.5 (or CART). For example:

- WHERE and PDDP can find much shallower trees than CART or C4.5. The reason for this is that if there exist N correlated features, then the principal component found by PCA (or the approximation found by WHERE) can model those N features with $M < N$ dimensions.
- WHERE runs much faster than PDDP. Finding the principal component takes polynomial time while WHERE's projections take linear time (only $4N$ distance measures between rows).
- InfoGain does not even have to model the recursive tree data structure. This algorithm is widely used in text mining since it runs in linear time and takes

Consider a two-column dataset where `column1` is the performance score of some learner and `column2` is the name of that learner. If we sort on `column1` then apply Fayyad–Irani, all the learners with the same scores will be grouped together in the one bin. The *best* learner is the most common learner found in the bin with greatest value.

Alternatively, consider a small modification of Fayyad–Irani, in which we recurse through a sorted list of buckets, sorted on their mean score. Each bucket contains all the performance scores on one learner. The first level split finds the index of the list that divides the buckets into two lists, which we will call `list1` and `list2`, that are up to and above the split:

- Let the mean of the performance scores in the entire list, `list1`, and `list2` be μ_0, μ_1, and μ_2 (respectively).
- Let the number of performance scores in `list1` and `list2` be n_1 and n_2 (respectively).
- A good split is the one that maximizes the expected value of the sum of squares of the mean differences before and after divisions. If $n = n_1 + n_2$ then that expected value is: $\frac{n_1}{n} \times \text{abs}(\mu_1 - \mu_0)^2 + \frac{n_2}{n} \times \text{abs}(\mu_2 - \mu_0)^2$.

This is the Scott–Knott procedure for ranking different treatments [53]. This procedure recurses, on the bins in each split, but only if some statistical test agrees that distributions in `list1` and `list2` are statistically different. This procedure is quite clever in that it can divide T treatments using $\log_2(T)$ comparisons. Mittas and Angelis [43] recommend using ANOVA to test if `list1` and `list2` are significantly statistically different. If the distributions are non-Gaussian, they also recommend applying the Bloom transform to the data as a preprocessor. It turns out that if we use the simpler Hedges procedure (described above), then the learners are grouped in the same way as using an ANOVA+Bloom test.

Fig. 3.3 A tutorial on using tree learners to rank treatments

very little memory. Hall and Holmes [25] comment that other feature selectors can be more powerful, but are slower and take more memory.

- Fayyad–Irani only needs to reason about two features at any one time (the numeric feature being discretized and the class feature). Hence, even if all the data cannot fit into RAM, it may still be possible to run Fayyad–Irani (and if memory problems persist, a simple preprocessor to the data that selects $X\%$ of the rows at random may suffice for learning the discretized ranges).

As an aside, this Fayyad–Irani discretizer is useful for more than just building decision trees. It is also useful a procedure for ranking performance results from different learners (see Fig. 3.3).

3.5 Naive Bayesian

When working with a new dataset, it is prudent to establish a *baseline* result using the most direct and simplest approach. Once that baseline performance is known, then it is possible to know how much more work is required for this data.

The most direct and simplest learning method discussed in this chapter is a *naive Bayesian* classifier. Despite the name, naive Bayesian classifiers are hardly "naive." In fact, they offer a range of important services such as learning from very large datasets, incremental learning, anomaly detection, row pruning, and feature pruning—all in near linear time (i.e., very fast). Better yet, as discussed below, implementing those services is trivially simple. The reason these classifiers are called "naive" is that they assume that, within one class, all features are statistically independent. That is, knowledge about the value of one feature does not tell us anything about the value of any other. So a naive Bayesian classifier can never look at a table of medical diagnoses to infer that `pulse=0` is associated with `temperature=cold`.

Proponents of tree learning would dispute this naive Bayesian assumption. They prefer algorithms like C4.5 or CART or random forests since tree learners always collect information in context: that is, all subtrees refer to data in the context of the root of that tree. Strange to say, naive Bayesian often performs as well as, or better than, decision tree learning—an observation that is carefully documented and explained by Domingos and Pazzani [15]. In short, they defined the volume of the zone where naive Bayesian classifiers would make a different decision to some optimal Bayesian classifier (one that knows about correlations between features). That zone is very small and grows vanishingly smaller as the number of features in the dataset increases. This is another way of saying that the space in which the naive Bayesian assumption is truly naive is quite tiny. This is very good news since it means that a naive Bayesian classifier can store data using a simple frequency table. Hence, a naive Bayesian classifier:

- has a tiny memory footprint;
- is very fast to training and very fast to make conclusions; and
- is simple to build.

Naive Bayesian classifiers use the famous Bayesian theorem to make predictions. Tables of data are separated into their various classes. Statistics are then collected for each class. For example, recall the `play?` data from Sect. 3.2. Here are the statistics for that data. Note that all these numbers are divided into the two class variables `play?=yes` and `play?=no`.

	outlook			temp			humidity	
	yes	no		yes	no		yes	no
sunny	2	3		83	85		86	85
overcast	4	0		70	80		96	90
rainy	3	2		68	65		80	70
	---	---		---	---		---	---
sunny	2/9	3/5	mean	73	74.6	mean	79.1	86.2
overcast	4/9	0/5	std dev	6.2	7.9	std dev	10.2	9.7
rainy	3/9	2/5						

	windy		play?	
	yes	no	yes	no
false	6	2	9	5
true	3	3		
	---	---	---	---
false	6/9	2/5	9/14	5/14
true	3/9	3/5		

Underneath each feature are some cumulative statistics. For example:

- The mean *humidity* is different for yes and no: 79.1 and 86.2 (respectively).
- overcast appears 4/9 times when we play and zero times when we do not play. That is, if in the future we see outlook=overcast, then it is far more likely that we play than otherwise (to be precise, it is infinitely more likely that we will play).

One way to view a naive Bayesian classifier is as a clustering algorithm where we have clustered together all things with the same class into the same cluster. When new data arrives we travel to every cluster and ask it to vote on "Does this look familiar to you?" And the cluster (class) that offers the most votes is used to make the prediction.

The voting procedure uses Bayes's rule: it says that our new belief in a hypothesis is the product of our old beliefs times any new evidence, i.e., *new* = *now* × *old*. As an aside: this simple equation hides a trick. If the test case (which is the *now* term in the above equation) has a missing feature, we just assume that it offers no evidence for a conclusion. Hence, we can just skip over that feature. Note that this is a much simpler scheme (to say the least) for handling missing values than other learners like C4.5. In C4.5, if a subtree starts with some feature that is missing in the test case, C4.5 then performs an intricate what-if query of all subtrees.

In Bayes's rule, the probability of a hypothesis H given evidence E is $\Pr(H|E) = \Pr(E|H) \times \Pr(H)/\Pr(E)$. In this expression:

- The $\Pr(E)$ term is the probability of the evidence. Since this is the same for each test case, it can be ignored (and a good thing too since it is very unclear how to calculate that term).
- The *old* term is the prior probability of the hypothesis, denoted $\Pr(H)$. This is just the frequency of each hypothesis. In our playing example, H is yes or no so $\Pr(\text{yes}) = 9/14$ and $\Pr(\text{no}) = 5/14$.
- The probability of the evidence given the hypothesis, denoted $\Pr(E|H)$, is looked up from the table of statistics. This is the *now* term.

For example, if we were told that tomorrow's forecast was for sun, the classes would offer the following votes on how likely it is that we would play or not:

- $\Pr(\text{yes}|\text{outlook=sunny}) = 2/9 \times 9/14 = 0.39$.
- $\Pr(\text{no}|\text{outlook=sunny}) = 3/5 \times 5/14 = 0.14$.

Since yes offers more votes, we would conclude that tomorrow we will play. Note that as more evidence arrives, the more information we can add to *now*. For example:

- Let the forecast be for sunshine, 66 degrees, 90 % humidity, and wind, i.e., $E =$ (outlook=sunshine, temp=66, humid=90, wind=true)
- To handle this conjunction, we multiply the individual probabilities:

$$\Pr(\text{yes}|E) = 2/9 * 0.0340 * 0.0221 * 3/9 * 9/14 = 0.000036$$

$$\Pr(\text{no}|E) = 3/5 * 0.0291 * 0.0380 * 3/5 * 5/14 = 0.000136 .$$

- To report the above, we normalized the probabilities:

$$\Pr(\text{yes}|E) = 0.00036/(0.00036 + 0.000136) = 21\,\%$$
$$\Pr(\text{no}|E) = 0.000136/(0.00036 + 0.000136) = 79\,\% .$$

- That is, for this forecast, no is offering more votes than yes. Hence, for this forecast, we would predict no.

The above calculation had some long decimal numbers (e.g., 0.0340). Where did these come from? Recall that temp=66 and for the class yes, the above table reports that the mean temperature was 73 degrees with a standard deviation of 6.2. How likely is 66 on a bell-shaped curve whose mean is 73 and whose standard deviation is 6.2? We say that:

- the closer we get to the mean value, the *higher* the likelihood;
- the greater the diversity in the data, the *lower* the likelihood of any one value.

Both these notions can be expressed in terms of a bell-shaped curve (also known as the normal or Gaussian distribution):

- This curve reaches maximum at the mean value.
- As the variance increases, the curve grows wider. Since the area under this probability curve must sum to one, the *wider* the curve, the *lower* the top-of-hill (where the mean is). That is, increasing diversity decreases our confidence in a particular value.

Hence, a standard naive Bayesian classifier uses a Gaussian probability distribution function to compute the likelihood of any particular number:

```
function gaussianPdf(mean, stdev, x) {
   return 1/(stdev * sqrt(2*pi)) * e ^ (-1*(x-mean)^2/(2*stdev*stdev))
}
print gaussianPdf(73, 6.2, 66)
==> 0.0340
```

Note that this calculation assumes that the underlying distribution is a bell-shaped Gaussian curve. While this can be a useful engineering approximation, it may not be true in many situations. Many Bayesian classifiers discretize their numerics before making predictions, thus avoiding the need for this Gaussian assumptions. A repeated result is that the performance of naive Bayesian is improved by discretization [16]. A standard discretizer is the Fayyad–Irani approach discussed in Sect. 3.4.5.

In 1999, NASA's $125M Mars climate orbiter burned up in the Martian atmosphere after
a mix-up in the units used to control the system.

- The problem was that meters were confused with feet and, as a result, the orbiter
  passed 60 km, not 150 km above the Martian atmosphere.
- The confusion in the units was apparent on-route to Mars—the spacecraft required
  unusually large course corrections.
- Sadly, the ground crew had no anomaly detector to alert them to how serious this
  deviation was from the craft's expected behavior.

In 2003, anomaly detection might have also saved the crew of the Columbia space shuttle.
On re-entry, a hypersonic shockwave entered a hole in the craft's wing and tore the craft
apart:

- The hole was formed when the shuttle was struck at launch by a block of frozen
  foam measuring 1200 in^3 and traveling at 477 mph (relative to the vehicle).
- Engineers concluded that such a strike was not hazardous using a program called
  CRATER. CRATER was trained on much smaller and much slower projectiles: a
  normal CRATER example was a 3 in^3 piece of debris traveling at under 150 mph.
- An anomaly detector could have alerted NASA to mistrust the engineers' conclusions since they were drawn from a region well outside of CRATER's certified expertise.

Fig. 3.4 High-profile disasters that might have been averted via anomaly detection

3.5.1 Bayesian and Anomaly Detection

If data miners are used for mission critical or safety critical applications, it is
important to understand when they cannot be trusted. This is the role of the anomaly
detector. Such detectors are triggered when a new example is outside the range of the
examples used to train the learner. Several recent high-profile disasters could have
been averted if anomaly detectors were running on learned models (see Fig. 3.4).
Anomaly detection is a very active area of research in data mining. For a detailed
survey, see Chandola et al. [9]. But to give the reader a sample of how to build an
anomaly detector, we mention here one anomaly detector that can be built using the
above Bayesian statistics table.

Farnstrom et al. [19] use a statistical approach to detect anomalies. Suppose we
have access to the above Bayesian statistics table:

- Read each row and replace its class value with some single symbol
  (e.g., global).
- For this global class, build the above Bayesian statistics table. With that table,
  compute the *suspect* region for each feature:

  - For numeric attributes, this region is outside the mean value plus or minus 1.96
    times the standard deviation (this corresponds to a 95 % confidence interval).
  - For discrete attributes, list all values that occur less than 5 % of the time in
    that row.

- When new data arrives, count how many times each feature falls into the suspect region. Reject any row that has more than n features with suspect values.[3]

The above shows how to detect anomalies—not what to do with them. This is a domain decision. One possibility is to store the anomalies in a bucket and, when that bucket gets too big, run a second learner just on those harder examples. For example, the trees generated by WHERE could be incrementally modified as follows:

- Build a tree from $X\%$ of the data.
- When new data arrives, push it down the tree to its nearest leaf cluster.
- At every level of that descent, check the *Left* and *Right* pairs. If the new instance falls outside the range *Left–Right*:

  - add the instance to a bucket of anomalies; and
  - mark which of *Left* and *Right* is closest to the anomaly.

- If the number of anomalies grows beyond some threshold, then rebuild any subtree with those anomalies. In that rebuild, use all the anomalies and any *Left* and *Right* row not marked by the last point.

Note that this approach implies we only need to rebuild parts of the tree, which is useful for any incremental learning scheme.

A more general version of this approach is the *AdaBoost* algorithm [21]. This is a *meta-learner* scheme, i.e., it can be applied to any learner (e.g., naive Bayesian, CART, C4.5, etc.). Like random forests, it is one of the most important ensemble methods, since it has a solid theoretical foundation, very accurate predictions, great simplicity (a few dozen lines of code to implement), and wide and successful applications. Also, this algorithm can "boost" the performance of a weak learner to a higher classification accuracy.

AdaBoost builds a sequence of T classifiers using some learner:

- To build a training set for classifier t, then for M times, sample with replacement from the dataset according to the D_t distribution described below.
- All $i \in m$ examples are given some weight. Initially that weight is $D_1(i) = \frac{1}{m}$. Subsequently, this weight is changed if classifier t incorrectly classifies example i.
- Examples with the greater weights are used with higher probability by the next classifier $t + 1$. That is, AdaBoost builds a sequence of classifiers $1, 2, \ldots, T$ each of which focuses on the examples that were problematic for classifier $t - 1$.

AdaBoost updates the weights as follows:

- Let $\epsilon_t = \frac{1}{m} \sum_i D_t(i)$ be sum of the weights of the examples with incorrect classifications made by classifier t_i.

---

[3]Note that Farnstrom et al. use $n = 1$ but this is a parameter that can be tuned. In the next section, we discuss incremental learners where, at least during the initial learning phase, all the data will be anomalous since this learner has never seen anything before. For learning from very few examples, n should be greater than one.

- Let $\beta_t = \epsilon_t / (1 - \epsilon_t)$.
- Let $D_{t+1} = \frac{D_t(i)}{Z_t} \gamma$ where:

  - $\gamma = \beta_t$ if i was correctly classified by classifier t. Otherwise $\gamma = 1$.
  - Z_t is a normalization constant such that $\sum D_{t+1}(i) = 1$.

To use this ensemble, each classifier $t = 1, 2, \ldots, T$ proposes its own classification c_t with weight $\log\left(\frac{1}{\beta_t}\right)$ (and AdaBoost returns the classification with the largest weighted vote).

3.5.2 Incremental Bayesian

Naive Bayesian is an excellent candidate for very large mining of very long streams of data. This is due to the fact that the working memory of a naive Bayesian classifier can be very small: a summary of the data seen so far and the next test case to classify. Such an incremental naive Bayesian classifier might work as follows: when a new test case arrives, classify it using the existing statistics; then (and only then) update the statistics with the new case. Some heuristics for incremental Bayesian learning include the following:

1. Use a learner that updates very fast. In this respect, a naive Bayesian classifier is a good candidate since its memory footprint is so small.
2. If the numerics in this domain do not conform to a Gaussian curve, use an incremental discretizer to convert the numbers to discrete values. Implementing such incremental discretizers is not a complex task [22].
3. If you use the Gaussian assumption, then be wary of floating point errors (particularly for very long data streams). Incrementally compute standard deviation using Knuth's method [32, p. 232].
4. To emulate something like a random forest ensemble, split the incoming data into 10 streams (each containing 90 % of the incoming data) and run a separate learner for each stream. Let each stream make a prediction and report the majority decision across all streams (perhaps weighted by accuracy performance statistic seen for all these learners). Note that since naive Bayesian has such a small footprint, then the memory overhead of running ten such classifiers is not excessive.
5. Skip any suspect examples (as defined by the Farnstrom et al. detector) or run the anomalies in their own separate stream.
6. Add an initial randomizer buffer that reads the input data in blocks of (say) 10,000 examples, then spits them out in a random order (for a linear-time randomizer, use the Fisher–Yates shuffle [17]. This random buffer minimizes *order effects* where the learned model is just some quirk of the ordering of the data. Also, this buffer is useful for collecting preliminary statistics on the data such as the minimum and maximum value of numeric values.
7. Do not trust the classifier until it has seen enough data. Experience with simple datasets is that the performance of incremental naive Bayesian classifiers plateaus

after a few hundred examples or less, but you need to check that point in your own data. In any case, it is wise to have some start-up period where classification is disabled.

8. To check for the performance plateau, divide the data into *eras* of, say, 100 examples in each era. Collect performance statistics across 10 streams. Compute the mean and standard deviation of accuracy in each era i. Declare a plateau if the performance of era $i + 1$ is about the same as era i (e.g., using Hedges's effect size rule shown above).

For some datasets, the number of examples needed to reach a plateau may be surprisingly brief. For example, certain defect datasets plateau after 100 (or less) examples [41]. Recent results with the QUICK *active learner* suggest that this can be reduced to even fewer if we intelligently select the next example for training. For example, in some software effort estimation datasets, we have plateaued after just a dozen examples, or even less [35].

3.5.3   *Incremental Learning and Dataset Shift*

Hand [26] warns that classifiers can make mistakes when their models become outdated. This can occur when some structure is learned from old data, then the data generating phenomenon changes. For example, software effort estimations trained on COBOL must be recalibrated if ever those programmers move to Javascript.

There are many ways to handle such *dataset shifts*; for a state-of-the-art report, see the work of Minku and Yao [42]. But just to describe a simple way to handle dataset shift, consider the incremental Bayesian classifier described above. In the following circumstances, a very simple dataset shift scheme can be applied:

- the number of examples required to reach the performance plateau is t_1;
- the rate of dataset shift is t_2;
- the data shifts at a slower rate than the time required to plateau, i.e., $t_1 < t_2$.

In this (not uncommon) situation, a data scientist (or a recommendation system) can handle dataset shift by running two learners: (1) an incremental Bayesian classifier (described above) and (2) any other learner they like (which, in fact, could also be a Bayesian classifier). While the performance plateau remains flat, the data scientist (or the recommendation system) can apply the other learner to all data seen to-date. But if the performance plateau starts changing (as measured by, say, Hedges's test of Fig. 3.1), then the data mining algorithm needs to dump the old model and start learning afresh.

3.6   Support Vector Machines

The learners discussed above try to find cuts between the features in tables of data that, say, predict for some class variable. An assumption of that approach is that the data divides nearly along the lines of the existing features. Sometimes, lining

Fig. 3.5 Data illustrating the
situation in which no split
exists parallel to the axes

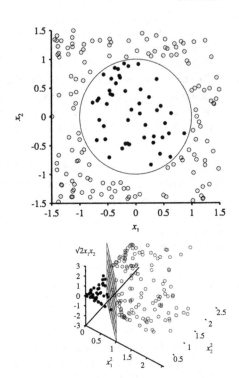

Fig. 3.6 Transforming the
data into different dimensions
can make the splits obvious
[reproduced from 51,
pp. 97–104]

up with the current features may not be the best policy. Consider the data shown in
Fig. 3.5: note that there is no simple split parallel to the x-axis or y-axis that best
separates the black and the white dots.

To solve this problem, we note that what looks complex in lower dimensions
can actually be simpler in higher dimensions. If we map the two-dimensional
points x_1, x_2 from the above figure into the three dimensions $\phi(x_1, x_2) \rightarrow (x_1^2, x_2^2, \sqrt{2}x_1x_2)$, we arrive at Fig. 3.6. Note that there now exists a hyperplane
that separates the black and white dots. Formally, ϕ is a "kernel function" that
transforms coordinates in one space into another. *Support vector machines* (SVMs)
are algorithms that can learn a hyperplane that separates classes in a hyper-
dimensional space [12] (for an example of such a hyperplane, see the rectangular
shape in Fig. 3.6). Combined with some kernel function ϕ, SVMs can handle
very complex datasets. Internally, SVMs are quadratic optimizers that search for
a hyperplane that best separates the classes. A maximum margin SVMs strives to
maximize the distance of this hyperplane to the *support vectors*, i.e., examples from
different classes that fall to either side of the hyperplane.

In the absence of expert knowledge, a *radial basis function* (RBF) is the usual
default kernel. For example, here is a simple Gaussian RBF: $\phi(r) = \exp(-(\varepsilon r)^2)$
(here, r is some distance of each example from an origin point where all values are
zero). Note that each kernel has a set of magic parameters that need to be tuned to
local domain. A standard architecture is to use some tuning learner to find the best
parameter settings—for example, when predicting software development effort,

Corazza et al. [11] use a Tabu search to learn the parameters for their radial bias function.

3.7 Pruning Data

In the previous section, we solved the data mining problem via *adding* dimensions. In this section, we explore another approach where we *delete* dimensions (i.e., the features) and/or rows in a dataset.

Many real-world datasets contain spurious, noisy, irrelevant, or redundant data. For this reason, it is often useful to strategically prune some of the training data. Many researchers report that it is possible to prune seemingly complex data since:

> ... the only reason any methods work in very high dimensions is that, in fact, the data are not truly high-dimensional. Rather, they are embedded in a high-dimensional space, but can be *efficiently summarized in a space of a much lower dimension* [38].

The rest of this section discusses two kinds of pruning: feature pruning and row pruning.

3.7.1 Feature Pruning

One advantage of tree learners over naive Bayesian classifiers is that the trees can be a high-level and succinct representation of what was learned from the data. On the other hand, the internal data structures of a Bayesian classifier are not very pleasant to browse. Many users require some succinct summary of those internals.

In terms of this chapter, dimensionality reduction means pruning some subset of the features in a table. Feature selection is an active area of data mining research. Two classic references in this area come from Kohavi and John [37] and Hall and Holmes [25]. A repeated result is that in many datasets, most features can be removed without damaging our ability to make conclusions about the data.

As to specific feature pruning methods, we will introduce them in three steps:

1. Near linear-time pruning methods such as InfoGain and CLIFF.
2. Polynomial-time pruning methods such as PCA and LSI.
3. Then, in Sect. 3.8, we will discuss other feature pruners especially designed for text mining such as stop lists, stemming, and TF–IDF.

For near linear-time pruning method, recall the InfoGain method discussed above in Sect. 3.4.5. After discretization, each feature can be scored by the entropy resulting for dividing the class variable into the discrete values for this feature (and better features have lower entropy, i.e., their values select for a smaller range of class values). For each feature, this process requires an $O(n \log(n))$ sort over all the features, but this is the slowest aspect of this feature selector. As to other near linear-time methods, recent results show that a Bayesian classifier can easily be converted into a feature pruner. We call this algorithm *CLIFF* [47]. It is detailed here as yet another example of what can be done with a supposedly "naive" Bayesian classifier.

Fig. 3.7 A dataset whose
first principal component is
not aligned with the Cartesian
axes

CLIFF discretizes all numeric data (using a 10 % chop) then counts how often
each discretized range occurs in each class.

```
Classes = all classes
for one in Classes:
  two = Classes - one
  c1  = |one|    # number of examples in class "one"
  c2  = |two|    # all other examples
  for f in features:
    ranges = discretized(f)
    for range in ranges:
        n1, n2 = frequency of range in one, two
    r1, r2 = n1/c1, n2/c2
    f.ranges[range].value[one] = r1*r1/(r1+r2)
```

The equation on the last row rewards ranges that are:

- more frequent in class one (this is the `r1*r1` term); and
- relatively more frequent in class one than in class two (this is in the fraction).

A range with high `value` is *powerful* in the sense that it is frequent evidence for
something that selects for a particular class. In CLIFF, we say that the *power of a
range* is the maximum of its `values` over all classes (as calculated by the above),
and the *power of a feature* is the maximum power of all its ranges. CLIFF can prune
features by discarding those with least power. Furthermore, within each feature, it
can prune ranges with lower power. CLIFF is very simple to implement. Once a
programmer has built a naive Bayesian classifier and a discretizer, CLIFF is 30 lines
or less in a high-level language such as Python. Our experience with this algorithm
is that it can convert large datasets into a handful of most powerful ranges that can
be discussed with a user.

Principal component analysis (PCA) [46] and *latent semantic indexing*
(LSI) [13] are examples of more complex polynomial methods, based on
synthesizing a small number of most-informative features. The key to this synthesis
is the *rotation* of the higher dimensions into lower dimensions. For example,
consider the data shown in Fig. 3.7. Clearly, for this data, the standard Cartesian
coordinate system is less informative than a new *synthesized* dimension that runs
through the middle of the data. Formally, we say that this two-dimensional data can
be approximated by a rotation into one-dimension along a synthesized dimension.
Such rotations are quite standard in software engineering. For example, Nagappan
et al. [44] use PCA to learn synthesized dimensions. When we applied their
technique to defect prediction, we found that we could find one simple rule within
24 features of a defect dataset: "`defective if domain1 greater than 0.317`."
Here, `domain1` is a dimension synthesized by PCA that is a linear combination of
the 24 features in the dataset:

```
domain1=0.241*loc+0.236*v(g) +0.222*ev(g)+0.236*iv(g) +
        0.241*n+0.238*v+0.086*l+0.199*d +0.216*i+0.225*e +
        0.236*b+0.221*t+0.241*loCode+0.179*loComment +
        0.221*loBlank+0.158*loCodeAndComment +0.163*uniqOp +
        0.234*uniqOpnd+0.241*totalOp+0.241*totalOpnd +
        0.236*branchCount
```

The important thing in this equation is the weights on the features. These weights range from 0.158 (for number of lines of code and comment) to 0.241 (for many things including the number of branches inside this code). That is, PCA is telling us that for the purposes of predicting defects, code branching is $\frac{0.241}{0.158} = 1.5$ more important than counts of lines of code and comment.

Under the hood, PCA builds N domains like the domain1 shown above using a matrix-oriented approach. Standard PCA uses the correlation matrix where cell i, j is the correlation between feature i and j. It then sorts the eigenvector of that matrix decreasing on their eigenvalue (so domain1, shown above, would have been the first eigenvector in that sort).[4]

LSI is another matrix-oriented method [13] for dimensionality reduction. LSI decomposes a matrix of data D into three matrices U, S, V which can be combined in order to regenerate D using $D = U S V^T$. The middle matrix S is special:

- The non-diagonal elements of S are zero.
- The diagonal elements of S are the weights of each feature.
- The rows of S are sorted in descending order by this weight.

A smaller dataset can now be generated by removing the k lowest rows in S and the k most right columns in V (i.e., that data relating to the least interesting features). We denote the truncated V matrix as V'. Now the document D_i can be described using the fewer number of features in V'_i.

3.7.2   Row Pruning

Science seeks general principles, i.e., a small number of factors that appear in many examples. For datasets that support such generality, we should therefore expect that a large number of rows are actual echoes of a smaller number of general principles.

Row pruning is the art of finding exemplars for those general principles. Just like with feature pruning, a repeated result is that most datasets can be pruned back to a small percentage of exemplars (also known as prototypes). For example, the prototype generators of Chang [10] replaced training sets of size (514, 150, 66) with prototypes of size (34, 14, 6) (respectively). That is, prototypes maybe as few as (7, 9, 9)% of the original data. If we prune a dataset in this way, then all subsequent reasoning runs faster. Also, performance quality can improve since we have removed strange outlier examples.

---

[4]It turns out that WHERE (described above in Sect. 3.4.5) is a heuristic method for finding the first domain of PCA. But while PCA takes polynomial time, WHERE runs in linear time. For more on the relationship of WHERE to PCA, see Platt [48].

There are many ways to do row pruning (also called instance selection). This is an active area of data mining [23]. For example, Hart [27] proposes an incremental procedure where, starting with a random selection of the data, if a new test case is misclassified, then it is deemed to be different to all proceeding examples. Hart recommends selecting just those novel instances. Kocaguneli et al. [33] prefer a clustering approach, followed by the deletion of all clusters that would confuse subsequent inference (i.e., those with the larger variance or entropy of any numeric or discrete class variable).

The methods of Hart and of Kocaguneli et al. are much slower than a newer methods based on CLIFF [47]. Recall that CLIFF finds *power* ranges, i.e., those ranges that tend to select for a particular class. If a row contains no power ranges, then it is not an interesting row for deciding between one class and another. To delete these dull rows, CLIFF scores and sorts each row by the product of the power of the ranges in that row. If then returns the top 10 % scoring rows. Note that this procedure runs in linear time, once the power ranges are known.

3.8   Text Mining

Up until now, this chapter has considered well-structured tables of examples. Most real-world data does not appear in such well-structured tables. One study concluded that:

- 80 % of business is conducted on unstructured information;
- 85 % of all data stored is held in an unstructured format (e.g., unstructured text descriptions);
- unstructured data doubles every 3 months.

That is, if we can tame the text mining problem, it would be possible to reason and learn from wide range of naturally occurring data.

Text mining data has a different "shape" than the tables of examples discussed above. Consider the text of this chapter. At the time of writing this sentence, it contains 1,574 unique words in 304 paragraphs and each line has 25 words (median). That is, if we represented this document as one example per paragraph, then:

- each row would be 1,574 features wide;
- each row would have entries for around 25 cells, which is another way of saying that this table would be $1 - \frac{25}{1574} = 98.4\%$ empty.

For such mostly empty datasets, before we can apply machine learning, we have to prune that empty space lest our learners get lost in all that nothingness.

That is, the essential problem of text mining is *dimensionality reduction*. There are several standard methods for dimensionality reduction such as *tokenization, stop lists, stemming, TF–IDF*.

Tokenization.   Tokenization replaces punctuation with spaces. Optionally, tokenizers also send all uppercase letters to lowercase.

Stopping. Stop lists remove "dull" words found in a "stop list" such as the following:

a	about	across	again	against
almost	alone	along	already	also
although	always	am	among	amongst
amongst	amount	an	and	another
any	anyhow	anyone	anything	anyway
anywhere	are	around	as	at
...	...	...	...	...

There are many online lists of stop words, but before you use one, you should review its contents. For example, the word "amount" is in the above stop list. However, in an engineering domain, the word "amount" might actually be vital to understanding the units of the problem at hand. Note also that stop world removal may be done in a procedural manner. For example, in one domain, we find it useful to stop all words less than four characters long.

Stemming. Stemming removes the suffixes of words with common meaning. For example, all these words relate to the same concept:

```
CONNECT
CONNECTED
CONNECTING
CONNECTION
CONNECTIONS.
```

The stemming algorithm of Porter [49] is the standard stemming tool. It repeatedly applies a set of pruning rules to the end of words until the surviving words are unchanged. The pruning rules ignore the semantics of a word and just perform syntactic pruning:

```
RULE                    EXAMPLE
----                    -------
ATIONAL  ->  ATE        relational     ->  relate
TIONAL   ->  TION       conditional    ->  condition
                        rational       ->  rational
ENCI     ->  ENCE       valenci        ->  valence
ANCI     ->  ANCE       hesitanci      ->  hesitance
IZER     ->  IZE        digitizer      ->  digitize
ABLI     ->  ABLE       conformabli    ->  conformable
ALLI     ->  AL         radicalli      ->  radical
ENTLI    ->  ENT        differentli    ->  different
ELI      ->  E          vileli         ->  vile
OUSLI    ->  OUS        analogousli    ->  analogous
IZATION  ->  IZE        vietnamization ->  vietnamize
ATION    ->  ATE        predication    ->  predicate
ATOR     ->  ATE        operator       ->  operate
ALISM    ->  AL         feudalism      ->  feudal
IVENESS  ->  IVE        decisiveness   ->  decisive
FULNESS  ->  FUL        hopefulness    ->  hopeful
OUSNESS  ->  OUS        callousness    ->  callous
ALITI    ->  AL         formaliti      ->  formal
IVITI    ->  IVE        sensitiviti    ->  sensitive
BILITI   ->  BLE        sensibiliti    ->  sensible
```

Porter's stemming algorithm has been coded in many languages and comes standard with many text-mining toolkits. The algorithm runs so quickly that there is little overhead in applying it.

TF–IDF. Term frequency—inverse document frequency (TF–IDF) is a calculation that models the intuition that jargon usually contains technical words that appear a lot, but only in a small number of paragraphs. For example, in a document describing a spacecraft, the terminology relating to the power supply may appear frequently in the sections relating to power, but nowhere else in the document.

Calculating TF–IDF is a relatively simple matter. Let t and d be the word and document of interest, respectively, and let D be the set of documents under consideration ($d \in D$). The *term frequency* (TF) of t in d is simply the count of occurrences of t in d; however, this will lead to a bias towards longer documents, so normalization by the frequency of the most common word in the document is standard. The *inverse document frequency* is the inverse ratio of the number of documents containing t to the total number of documents; in order to stop the inverse document frequency growing so large (for some entries) that it dominates all over entries, its logarithm is used:

$$\text{tf–idf}(t, d, D) = \frac{\text{TF}(t, d)}{\arg\max_{w \in d} \text{TF}(w, d)} \times \log\left(\frac{|D|}{|\{d \in D : t \in d\}|}\right).$$

There are three important aspects of TF–IDF that deserve our attention:

- It takes linear time to compute (so it scales to large datasets) and that computation is very simple to code (one implementation of the author, in a high-level scripting language, was less than 20 lines long).
- When applied to natural language texts, it is often than case that the majority of words have very low TF–IDF scores. That is, we just use the (say) 100 most important terms (as ranked by TF–IDF) then we can prune away vast numbers of uninformative words.

Other Text Mining Methods. The above sequence can be summarized as follows:

$$\textit{Tokenization} \rightarrow \textit{Stopping} \rightarrow \textit{Stemming} \rightarrow \textit{TF–IDF}$$

Note that this sequence takes linear time (so it scales to very large datasets). For complex domains, other methods may be required such as the InfoGain, PCA, and LSI methods discussed above. For example, a standard implementation is to use the V' matrix (from LSI) and find nearby words using cosine similarity, see Eq. (3.1).

3.9 Nearest-Neighbor Methods

Model-based methods such as decision tree learners first build some model (e.g., a decision tree), then use that model to reason about future examples.

Another approach is *instance-based reasoning* that reasons about new examples according to their nearest neighbors. This style of learning is called *lazy learning* since nothing happens until the new text example arrives. This lazy approach can be quite slow so it is customary to add a preprocessor step that clusters the data. Once those clusters are known, then it is faster to find similar examples, as follows:

- find the nearest cluster to the new test example;
- ignore everything that is not in that cluster; and
- find similar examples, but only looking in that cluster.

Clustering is an *unsupervised* learning algorithm in that, during clustering, it ignores any class feature. This is a very different approach to nearly all the algorithms above, which were *supervised*, i.e., they treated the class feature in a way that was special and different to all the other features. The only exception was Apriori that does not treat any feature different to any other (so it is *unsupervised*).

A core issue within clustering is how to measure the distance between rows of examples. For example, some use a kernel function to compute a weighted distance between rows. Much could be said on these more complex approaches but presenting that material would be a chapter all on its own. Suffice it to say that with a little column pruning, sometimes very simple functions suffice [35].

For example, consider the *overlap* defined for discretized data where the distance between two rows is the number of ranges that occur in both rows. Note that this *overlap* measure scales to very large datasets, using a reverse index that records what ranges occur in what rows. Given that reverse index, simple set intersection operators on the reverse index can then quickly find:

- if any two rows have no shared ranges (so distance = infinity);
- otherwise, the distance between two rows is the number of shared ranges.

This measure is used by McCallum et al. [39] in their work on canopy clustering (discussed below) and by the *W2* instance-based planner [5]. W2 accepts as input the *context* that is of interest to some manager, i.e., a subset of the data features that mention a subset of the feature ranges. W2 is discussed in Fig. 3.8.

Two other distance measures, which make more use of the specific distances between values, are the *cosine dissimilarity* and the *Minkowski distance*. Consider two rows in the database, x and y, with features $1, 2, 3, \ldots, f$. In cosine dissimilarity, the distance is least when the angle between two rows is zero. This can be calculated using the following equation:

$$\text{dist}(x, y) = 1 - \left(\frac{\sum_i x_i \, y_i}{\sqrt{\sum_i x_i^2} \, \sqrt{\sum_i y_i^2}} \right) \tag{3.1}$$

W2 is an example of nearest neighbor inference using a simple overlap distance measure:

- A manager might pose the question: "What is the best action for projects in which programmer capability equals low or very low and the database size is large or very large".
- W2 finds the K projects nearest this context (sorted by their overlap).
- Next, for the first time in all this processing, W2 looks at the class variable which might contain information (say) about the development time of the projects. It then divides the projects into the k_1 projects it likes (those with lowest development effort) and the k_2 is does not (and $K = k_1 + k_2$).
- Next, it sorts the ranges by the *value* of each range (as defined in the discussion on CLIFF in Sect. 3.7.1).
- Lastly, it conducts experiments where the first i items in that sorted range of values are applied to some holdout set.

As output, W2 prints its recommendations back to the manager. That manager gets a list of things to change in the project. That list contains the first i terms in the list of sorted items that select for projects in the hold out set with least (say) development time.

Fig. 3.8 A description of W2

The Minkowski distance is really a family of distance measures controlled by the variable p:

$$\text{dist}(x, y) = \left(\sum_i (w_i |x_i - y_i|^p) \right)^{1/p} \tag{3.2}$$

Here, w_i is the some weight given to each feature (the larger this weight, the more importance is given to that feature). At $p = 1$, this is the Manhattan (or city-block) distance. At $p = 2$, this is the standard Euclidean distance measure.

This Euclidean distance is used in the classic paper on instance-based reasoning by Aha et al. [2]. Their method allows us to handle missing data as well as datasets with both numeric and non-numeric features. This measure begins by normalizing all numerics min to max, 0 to 1. Such normalization has many benefits:

- Normalization lets us compare distances between numerics of different scale. To see why this is an issue, consider a database that lists rocket speeds and astronaut shoe sizes. Even if an astronaut shoe size increases by 50 % from 8 to 12, that difference would be lost when compared to rocket speeds (which can range from 0 to 41×10^6 meters per second). If we normalize all numerics zero to one, then a 100 % change in shoe size (that can range from 0 to 20) will not be lost amongst any changes to the rocket speed.
- Normalization let us compare distances between numeric and discrete features. Aha et al. offer the following distance measure for non-numerics: if two non-numeric values are the same, then their separation is zero; else, it is one. That is, the maximum difference for non-numerics is the same maximum difference for any normalized numeric value. If we combine numeric normalization with

the rule of Aha et al., then we can compare rows that contain numeric and non-numeric features.

Aha et al. also offer a method for handling missing data. The intuition behind this method is that if a value is missing, assume the worst case and return the maximum possible value. To implement that they recommend the following procedure when finding the difference between two values x_i and y_i from feature i:

- If both values are missing, return the maximum distance (assuming normalized data, then this maximum value is one).
- If the feature is non-numeric:
  - If one is absent, return one.
  - Else if the values are the same, return zero.
  - Else, return one.
- If the feature is numeric, then:
  - If only one value is present, then return the largest of 1 and that value.
  - Otherwise return $x_i y_i$.

Now that we can compute $x_i - y_i$, we can use the Euclidean measure:

$$\sqrt{\sum_i w_i (x_i - y_i)^2} \Big/ \sqrt{\sum_i w_i}$$

where w_i is some weight that defaults to one (but might otherwise be set by feature pruning tools described previously). Note that if we use normalized values for x_i and y_i, then this value returns a number in the range zero to one.

Note that for small datasets, it is enough to implement this distance function, without any clustering. The standard k-nearest neighbors algorithm generates predictions by finding the k rows nearest any new test data, then reporting the (say) median value of the class variable in that sample.

Returning now to clustering, this is a large and very active area of research [29, 30]. The rest of this chapter discusses a few fast and scalable clustering algorithms.

3.10   Some Fast Clustering Methods

DBScan [18] uses some heuristics to divide the data into neighborhoods. For all neighborhoods that are not clustered, it finds one with *enough* examples in an adjacent neighborhood (where *enough* is a domain-specific parameter). A cluster is then formed of these two neighborhoods, and the process repeats for any neighbors of this expanding cluster.

Canopy clustering [39] is a very fast distance measure used extensively at Google to divide data into groups of nearby items called *canopies*. Then it performs more elaborate (and more CPU expensive) analysis, but only within these canopies.

Farnstrom et al. [19] proposed a modification to the standard K-means algorithm. These modifications allow for incremental learning of clusters. In standard *K-means*, *K* rows are picked at random to be the centroids. All the other rows are then labeled according to which row is nearest. Each centroid is then moved to the middle of all the rows with that label. The process repeats until the centroid positions stabilize. Note that K-means can be slow since it requires repeated distance measurements between all centroids and all rows. Also, it demands that all the rows are loaded into RAM at one time. Farnstrom et al. fix both these problems with their *simple single-pass k-means* (SSK) algorithm:

- Work through the data in batches of size, say, 1 % (ideally, selected at random).
- Cluster each batch using K-means.
- For each new batch, call K-means to adjust the clusters from the last batch for the new data.
- New data is only added to the old clusters it is not anomalous (as defined by the Farnstrom et al. anomaly detector, mentioned above).
- In theory, this might result in some old centroid now having no data from the new 1 % of the data. In this case, a new centroid is created using the most distant point in the set of anomalous data (but in practice, this case very rarely happens).

Another fast clusterer based on K-means is *mini-batch K-means* [54]. Like SSK, this algorithm processes the data in batches. However, this algorithm is much simpler than SSK:

- Each centroid maintains a count v of the number of rows for which that centroid is the nearest neighbor.
- The data is read in batches of size M.
- The fewer the rows that used that centroid, the more it must be moved to a new position. Hence, after each batch has updated v:
  - Compute $n = 1/v$.
  - For each centroid:
    - Recall all rows r in the batch that found this centroid to be its nearest neighbor.
    - For each such row, move all values c in it towards r by an amount

$$(1 - n)c + nr$$

  (note that large v implies small n which translates to "do not move the heavily used centroids very much").

Sculley [54] reports that this approach runs orders of magnitude faster than standard k-means. Also, it is an incremental algorithm that only needs RAM for the current set of centroids and the next batch. But how to determine the right number of centroids? One method, which we adapt from the GenIc incremental cluster [24], is to pick a medium number of cluster; then, after each prune:

- Let each cluster contain c items.
- Find and delete the x dull centroids with $c/C \times N < \text{rand}()$, where C is the sum of all the c values from the N clusters.
- If $x > C/4$, then set x to $C/4$.
- Select any x rows at random and add them to the set of centroids. Note that this either replaces dull centroids or adds new centroids if we do not have enough.

Note that the Farnstrom et al. approach and mini-batch K-means satisfy the famous *Data Mining Desiderata* [4]. According to that decree, a scalable data miner has the following properties:

- It requires one scan (or less) of the database if possible: a single data scan is considered costly, early termination if appropriate is highly desirable.
- It is online "anytime" behavior: a "best" answer is always available, with status information on progress, expected remaining time, etc. provided.
- It is suspendible, stoppable, resumable; incremental progress saved to resume a stopped job.
- It has the ability to incrementally incorporate additional data with existing models efficiently.
- It works within confines of a given limited RAM buffer.
- It utilizes variety of possible scan modes: sequential, index, and sampling scans if available.
- It has the ability to operate on forward-only cursor over a view of the database. This is necessary since the database view may be a result of an expensive join query, over a potentially distributed data warehouse, with much processing required to construct each row (case).

Once the clusters are created, then it is not uncommon practice to apply a supervised learner to the data in each cluster. For example:

- *NBTrees* uses a tree learner to divide the data, then builds one naive Bayesian classifier for each leaf [36].
- WHERE applies the *principle of envy* to clustered data. Each cluster asks "who is my nearest cluster with better class scores than me?" Data mining is then applied to that cluster and the resulting rules are applied back to the local cluster [40]. WHERE built those rules using a more intricate version of W2, described above.

There are several advantages to intra-cluster learning:

- The learner runs on fewer examples. For example, WHERE builds a tree of clusters whose leaves contain the square root of the number of examples in the whole dataset. For any learner that takes more than linear time to process examples, running multiple learners on the square root of the data is faster than running one learner on all the data.

- The learner runs on a more homogeneous set of examples. To increase the reliability of the predictions from a data miner, it is useful to build the learner from similar examples. By learning on a per-cluster basis, a learner is not distracted by dissimilar examples in other clusters. In the case of WHERE, we found that the predictions generated per-cluster were much better than those found after learning from all the data (and by "better" we mean lower variance in the predictions and better median value of the predictions).

3.11 Conclusion

This chapter has been a quick overview of a range of data mining technology. If the reader wants to read further than this material, then the following material may be of interest:

- The Quora discussion list on data mining.
- The KDnuggets news list.
- The many excellent data mining texts such as Witten et al. [57] or all the learning-related sections of Russell and Norvig [52].
- The proceedings of the annual conferences, Mining Software Repositories and PROMISE.

Also, for a sample of data mining methods and applications to RSSEs, see the other chapters in this book.

References

1. Agrawal, R., Imieliński, T., Swami, A.: Mining association rules between sets of items in large databases. In: Proceedings of the ACM SIGMOD International Conference on Management of Data, pp. 207–216 (1993). DOI 10.1145/170035.170072
2. Aha, D.W., Kibler, D., Albert, M.K.: Instance-based learning algorithms. Mach. Learn. **6**(1), 37–66 (1991). DOI 10.1023/A:1022689900470
3. Boley, D.: Principal direction divisive partitioning. Data Min. Knowl. Discov. **2**(4), 325–344 (1998). DOI 10.1023/A:1009740529316
4. Bradley, P.S., Fayyad, U.M., Reina, C.: Scaling clustering algorithms to large databases. In: Proceedings of the International Conference on Knowledge Discovery and Data Mining, pp. 9–15 (1998)
5. Brady, A., Menzies, T.: Case-based reasoning vs parametric models for software quality optimization. In: Proceedings of the International Conference on Predictor Models in Software Engineering, pp. 3:1–3:10 (2010). DOI 10.1145/1868328.1868333
6. Breiman, L., Friedman, J.H., Olshen, R.A., Stone, C.J.: Classification and Regression Trees. Chapman and Hall/CRC, Boca Raton, FL (1984)
7. Breimann, L.: Random forests. Mach. Learn. **45**(1), 5–32 (2001). DOI 10.1023/A:1010933404324

8. Catlett, J.: Inductive learning from subsets, or, Disposal ofexcess training data considered harmful. In: Proceedings of the Australian Workshop on Knowledge Acquisition forKnowledge-Based Systems, pp. 53–67 (1991)
9. Chandola, V., Banerjee, A., Kumar, V.: Anomaly detection: A survey. ACM Comput. Surv. **41**, 15:1–15:58 (2009). DOI 10.1145/1541880.1541882
10. Chang, C.L.: Finding prototypes for nearest neighbor classifiers. IEEE Trans. Comput. **23**(11), 1179–1185 (1974). DOI 10.1109/T-C.1974.223827
11. Corazza, A., Di Martino, S., Ferrucci, F., Gravino, C., Sarro, F., Mendes, E.: How effective is tabu search to configure support vector regression for effort estimation? In: Proceedings of the International Conference on Predictor Models in Software Engineering, pp. 4:1–4:10 (2010). DOI 10.1145/1868328.1868335
12. Cortes, C., Vapnik, V.: Support-vector networks. Mach. Learn. **20**(3), 273–297 (1995). DOI 10.1023/A:1022627411411
13. Deerwester, S., Dumais, S., Furnas, G., Landauer, T., Harshman, R.: Indexing by latent semantic analysis. J. Am. Soc. Inform. Sci. **41**(6), 391–407 (1990). DOI 10.1002/(SICI)1097-4571(199009)41:6⟨391::AID-ASI1⟩3.0.CO;2-9
14. Dejaeger, K., Verbeke, W., Martens, D., Baesens, B.: Data mining techniques for software effort estimation: A comparative study. IEEE Trans. Software Eng. **38**, 375–397 (2012). DOI 10.1109/TSE.2011.55
15. Domingos, P., Pazzani, M.J.: On the optimality of the simple Bayesian classifier under zero-one loss. Mach. Learn. **29**(2–3), 103–130 (1997). DOI 10.1023/A:1007413511361
16. Dougherty, J., Kohavi, R., Sahami, M.: Supervised and unsupervised discretization of continuous features. In: Proceedings of the International Conference on Machine Learning, pp. 194–202 (1995)
17. Durstenfeld, R.: Algorithm 235: Random permutation. Comm. ACM **7**(7), 420 (1964). DOI 10.1145/364520.364540
18. Ester, M., Kriegel, H.P., Sander, J., Xu, X.: A density-based algorithm for discovering clusters in large spatial databases with noise. In: Proceedings of the International Conference on Knowledge Discovery and Data Mining, pp. 226–231 (1996)
19. Farnstrom, F., Lewis, J., Elkan, C.: Scalability for clustering algorithms revisited. SIGKDD Explor. Newslett. **2**(1), 51–57 (2000). DOI 10.1145/360402.360419
20. Fayyad, U.M., Irani, K.B.: Multi-interval discretization of continuous-valued attributes for classification learning. In: Proceedings of the International Joint Conference on Artificial Intelligence, pp. 1022–1029 (1993)
21. Freund, Y., Schapire, R.E.: A decision-theoretic generalization of on-line learning and an application to boosting. J. Comput. Syst. Sci. **55**(1), 119–139 (1997). DOI 10.1006/jcss.1997.1504
22. Gama, J., Pinto, C.: Discretization from data streams: Applications to histograms and data mining. In: Proceedings of the ACM SIGAPP Symposium on Applied Computing, pp. 662–667 (2006). DOI 10.1145/1141277.1141429
23. Garcia, S., Derrac, J., Cano, J.R., Herrera, F.: Prototype selection for nearest neighbor classification: Taxonomy and empirical study. IEEE Trans. Pattern Anal. Mach. Intell. **34**(3), 417–435 (2012). DOI 10.1109/TPAMI.2011.142
24. Gupta, C., Grossman, R.: GenIc: A single pass generalized incremental algorithm for clustering. In: Proceedings of the SIAM International Conference on Data Mining, pp. 147–153 (2004)
25. Hall, M.A., Holmes, G.: Benchmarking attribute selection techniques for discrete class data mining. IEEE Trans. Knowl. Data Eng. **15**(6), 1437–1447 (2003). DOI 10.1109/TKDE.2003.1245283
26. Hand, D.J.: Classifier technology and the illusion of progress. Stat. Sci. **21**(1), 1–14 (2006). DOI 10.1214/088342306000000060
27. Hart, P.: The condensed nearest neighbor rule. IEEE Trans. Inform. Theory **14**(3), 515–516 (1968). DOI 10.1109/TIT.1968.1054155
28. Hedges, L.V., Olkin, I.: Nonparametric estimators of effect size in meta-analysis. Psychol. Bull. **96**(3), 573–580 (1984)

29. Jain, A.K.: Data clustering: 50 years beyond K-means. Pattern Recogn. Lett. **31**(8), 651–666 (2010). DOI 10.1016/j.patrec.2009.09.011
30. Jain, A.K., Murty, M.N., Flynn, P.J.: Data clustering: A review. ACM Comput. Surv. **31**(3), 264–323 (1999). DOI 10.1145/331499.331504
31. Kampenes, V.B., Dybå, T., Hannay, J.E., Sjøberg, D.I.K.: A systematic review of effect size in software engineering experiments. Inform. Software Tech. **49**(11–12), 1073–1086 (2007). DOI 10.1016/j.infsof.2007.02.015
32. Knuth, D.E.: The Art of Computer Programming, vol. 2: Seminumerical Algorithms, 3rd edn. Addison-Wesley, Boston, MA (1998)
33. Kocaguneli, E., Menzies, T., Bener, A., Keung, J.: Exploiting the essential assumptions of analogy-based effort estimation. IEEE Trans. Software Eng. **28**(2), 425–438 (2012a). DOI 10.1109/TSE.2011.27
34. Kocaguneli, E., Menzies, T., Keung, J.: On the value of ensemble effort estimation. IEEE Trans. Software Eng. **38**(6), 1403–1416 (2012b). DOI 10.1109/TSE.2011.111
35. Kocaguneli, E., Menzies, T., Keung, J., Cok, D., Madachy, R.: Active learning and effort estimation: Finding the essential content of software effort estimation data. IEEE Trans. Software Eng. **39**(8), 1040–1053 (2013). DOI 10.1109/TSE.2012.88
36. Kohavi, R.: Scaling up the accuracy of naive-Bayes classifiers: A decision-tree hybrid. In: Proceedings of the International Conference on Knowledge Discovery and Data Mining, pp. 202–207 (1996)
37. Kohavi, R., John, G.H.: Wrappers for feature subset selection. Artif. Intell. **97**(1–2), 273–324 (1997). DOI 10.1016/S0004-3702(97)00043-X
38. Levina, E., Bickel, P.J.: Maximum likelihood estimation of instrinsic dimension. In: Saul, L.K., Weiss, Y., Bottou, L. (eds.) Advances in Neural Information Processing Systems 17, pp. 777–784. MIT Press, Cambridge, MA (2005)
39. McCallum, A., Nigam, K., Ungar, L.H.: Efficient clustering of high-dimensional datasets with application to reference matching. In: Proceedings of the ACM SIGKDD Conference on Knowledge Discovery and Data Mining, pp. 169–178 (2000). DOI 10.1145/347090.347123
40. Menzies, T., Butcher, A., Cok, D., Marcus, A., Layman, L., Shull, F., Turhan, B., Zimmermann, T.: Local vs. global lessons for defect prediction and effort estimation. IEEE Trans. Software Eng. **39**(6), 822–834 (2013). DOI 10.1109/TSE.2012.83
41. Menzies, T., Turhan, B., Bener, A., Gay, G., Cukic, B., Jiang, Y.: Implications of ceiling effects in defect predictors. In: Proceedings of the International Workshop on Predictor Models in Software Engineering (2008). DOI 10.1145/1370788.1370801
42. Minku, L.L., Yao, X.: DDD: A new ensemble approach for dealing with concept drift. IEEE Trans. Knowl. Data Eng. **24**(4), 619–633 (2012). DOI 10.1109/TKDE.2011.58
43. Mittas, N., Angelis, L.: Ranking and clustering software cost estimation models through a multiple comparisons algorithm. IEEE Trans. Software Eng. **39**(4), 537–551 (2012). DOI 10.1109/TSE.2012.45
44. Nagappan, N., Ball, T., Zeller, A.: Mining metrics to predict component failures. In: Proceedings of the ACM/IEEE International Conference on Software Engineering, pp. 452–461 (2006). DOI 10.1145/1134285.1134349
45. Pearson, K.: I. mathematical contributions to the theory of evolution—VII. on the correlation of characters not quantitatively measurable. Phil. Trans. Roy. Soc. Lond. Ser. A **195**, 1–47 & 405 (1900)
46. Pearson, K.: LIII. On lines and planes of closest fit to systems of points in space. Phil. Mag. **2**(11), 559–572 (1901). DOI 10.1080/14786440109462720
47. Peters, F., Menzies, T., Gong, L., Zhang, H.: Balancing privacy and utility in cross-company defect prediction. IEEE Trans. Software Eng. **39**(8), 1054–1068 (2013). DOI 10.1109/TSE.2013.6
48. Platt, J.C.: FastMap, MetricMap, and Landmark MDS are all Nyström algorithms. In: Proceedings of the International Workshop on Artificial Intelligence and Statistics, pp. 261–268 (2005)

49. Porter, M.F.: An algorithm for suffix stripping. Program Electron. Libr. Inform. Syst. **14**(3), 130–137 (1980). DOI 10.1108/eb046814

50. Quinlan, J.R.: C4.5: Programs for Machine Learning. Morgan Kaufmann, San Francisco (1993)

51. Russell, S.J., Norvig, P.: Artificial Intelligence: A Modern Approach, 2nd edn. Prentice Hall, Englewood Cliffs, NJ (2003)

52. Russell, S.J., Norvig, P.: Artificial Intelligence: A Modern Approach, 3rd edn. Prentice Hall, Englewood Cliffs, NJ (2009)

53. Scott, A.J., Knott, M.: A cluster analysis method for grouping means in the analysis of variance. Biometrics **30**(3), 507–512 (1974)

54. Sculley, D.: Web-scale k-means clustering. In: Proceedings of the International Conference on the World Wide Web, pp. 1177–1178 (2010). DOI 10.1145/1772690.1772862

55. Shannon, C.E.: A mathematical theory of communication. Bell Syst. Tech. J. **27**(3), 379–423 (1948a)

56. Shannon, C.E.: A mathematical theory of communication. Bell Syst. Tech. J. **27**(4), 623–656 (1948b)

57. Witten, I.H., Frank, E., Hall, M.A.: Data Mining: Practical Machine Learning Tools and Techniques, 3rd edn. Morgan Kaufmann, San Francisco, CA (2011)

58. Yang, Y., Webb, G.I.: Discretization for naive-Bayes learning: Managing discretization bias and variance. Mach. Learn. **74**(1), 39–74 (2009). DOI 10.1007/s10994-008-5083-5

Chapter 4
Recommendation Systems in-the-Small

Laura Inozemtseva, Reid Holmes, and Robert J. Walker

Abstract Many recommendation systems rely on data mining to produce their recommendations. While data mining is useful, it can have significant implications for the infrastructure needed to support and to maintain an RSSE; moreover, it can be computationally expensive. This chapter examines recommendation systems in-the-small (RITSs), which do not rely on data mining. Instead, they take small amounts of data from the developer's local context as input and use heuristics to generate recommendations from that data. We provide an overview of the burdens imposed by data mining and how these can be avoided by a RITS through the use of heuristics. Several examples drawn from the literature illustrate the applications and designs of RITSs. We provide an introduction to the development of the heuristics typically needed by a RITS. We discuss the general limitations of RITSs.

4.1 Introduction

Many recommendation systems rely on *data mining*, that is, attempting to discover useful patterns in large datasets. While such recommendation systems are helpful, it is not always practical to create, maintain, and use the large datasets they require. Even if this issue is resolved, data mining can be computationally expensive, and this may prohibit interactive use of the recommendation system during development. For these reasons, RSSE researchers have developed a number of *recommendation systems in-the-small* (RITSs): systems that base their recommendations on the

L. Inozemtseva (✉) • R. Holmes
David R. Cheriton School of Computer Science, University of Waterloo, Waterloo, ON, Canada
e-mail: lminozem@uwaterloo.ca; rtholmes@cs.uwaterloo.ca

R.J. Walker
Department of Computer Science, University of Calgary,Calgary, AB, Canada
e-mail: walker@ucalgary.ca

M.P. Robillard et al. (eds.), *Recommendation Systems in Software Engineering*,
DOI 10.1007/978-3-642-45135-5__4, © Springer-Verlag Berlin Heidelberg 2014

developer's immediate context, possibly using heuristics to compensate for the smaller amount of available data.

This chapter introduces this class of recommendation systems. Section 4.2 explains what recommendation systems in-the-small are by comparing a RITS with a system that uses data mining to generate its recommendations. Section 4.3 demonstrates the diversity of RITSs by introducing a few example systems from different application areas. Section 4.4 describes how the heuristics typically used in RITSs can be generated and the pros and cons of each method; we make the discussion more concrete by revisiting the recommendation systems discussed in Sect. 4.3. Section 4.5 discusses some of the limitations of this class of recommendation systems. Section 4.6 concludes the chapter and provides suggestions for further reading.

4.2   Recommendations with and without Data Mining

To illustrate the difference between RITSs and recommendation systems that use data mining to generate their recommendations, which we refer to as *data mining recommendation systems* (DMRSs), we examine a RITS and a DMRS that solve the same problem in different ways.

Consider the problem of finding code elements (functions, variables, etc.) that are relevant to a given task. This is an issue that software developers frequently face as they fix bugs, add new features, or perform other maintenance tasks. In fact, one study estimates that developers spend 60–90 % of their time reading and navigating code [3]. However, finding relevant code can be difficult. Basic lexical searches are one possible strategy, but are often insufficient since the developer may not know the correct search term to use. Even if the developer can find some of the relevant elements, it has been shown that it is difficult for a developer to faithfully find all dependencies from an entity [5]. A recommendation system that can suggest relevant code elements would therefore be helpful to developers.

Robillard [10] tackled this problem by developing a RITS called Suade. Suade takes as input a set of code elements that are known to be relevant to the developer's task and produces as output a ranked list of other code elements that are also likely to be relevant. Suade produces these recommendations by doing a localized analysis of the program's dependency graph to identify relevant elements. It does this in two steps. First, Suade builds a graph of the code elements in the project and the relationships that exist between them, such as function calls and variable accesses. When a developer initiates a query, Suade identifies elements in the graph that have a direct structural relationship to the known-relevant elements. It then uses two heuristics to rank the related elements from most to least likely to be relevant. We describe these heuristics in more detail in Sect. 4.3.

Though Suade builds a graph of relationships between code elements, it is a RITS because it does not generate recommendations by mining the full graph for patterns. Rather, it takes a small amount of localized information as input. The graph is only used to look up information about relationships; heuristics are used to rank the recommendations.

Zimmermann et al. [14] took a different approach and built a DMRS called eROSE (originally called ROSE). eROSE mines the project's version control system to identify program elements that are frequently changed together (in the same commit). This information is used to identify relevant elements, on the assumption that elements that changed together in the past will likely change together in the future. More specifically, when a developer modifies a program element e as part of a maintenance task, eROSE presents a list of other program elements that may need to be changed, ranked by how confident the system is about the necessity of the change. The confidence value for each recommended element e' is based on two factors: first, the number of times e and e' have occurred in the same commit in the past; and second, out of the total number of times e was changed in the past, the percentage of those times that e' also changed.

eROSE is a DMRS because it must mine a version control system to identify commits in order to produce a recommendation. Given that source code is updated incrementally, it may be possible for eROSE to update its database incrementally, but it is not possible to avoid data mining completely.

RITSs and DMRSs have different strengths. Data mining can reveal patterns that RITSs might miss. For example, eROSE's recommendations are not limited to source code: if a documentation file always appears in the same change set as a source code file, eROSE can identify that relationship. Suade cannot do this because it uses a graph of relationships that are specific to a programming language; while in principle it could be adapted to work for any programming language, this would require targeted development to accomplish.

That said, RITSs tend to be more lightweight and produce recommendations more quickly. In this case, eROSE is not particularly slow, and could be used interactively, but in general, mining a repository on every query can be computationally expensive and may not scale well to large projects. In addition, a repository of data must have been collected for the DMRS to mine. For eROSE, the history of commits must have been collected over time; when a project is new, there is no history and DMRSs can provide no help (this is known as the *cold start problem* [11]). A RITS is not subject to the cold start problem.

Figure 4.1 shows these differences diagrammatically. The general structure of the two diagrams is identical: the developer builds the recommendation system; then, the developer uses the recommendation system, issuing queries and receiving recommendations. The key difference is: for the RITS (on the left), the developer must determine one or more heuristics to build into the recommendation system before it can be used; for the DMRS (on the right), the recommendation system must mine its data source. If the data source is unchanging, the DMRS would not need to repeat the mining step in principle, but could simply make use of the patterns it had already detected; this is effectively a caching optimization.

Fig. 4.1 Flowcharts illustrating how recommendation systems are built and used. (**a**) Building and using a RITS. (**b**) Building and using a DMRS

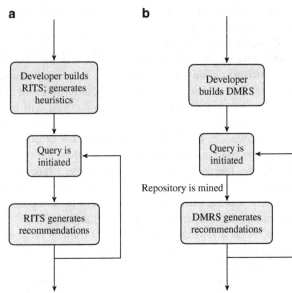

4.3   The Versatility of Recommendation Systems in-the-Small

In this section we demonstrate the versatility of recommendation systems in-the-small by describing several from the literature: Suade (in more detail); Strathcona; Quick Fix Scout; an unnamed Java method-name debugger; and YooHoo. These five tools illustrate the variety of tasks that RITSs can perform; they also provide an introduction to the development and inherent constraints of RITSs.

4.3.1   Suade: Feature Location

As noted above, Suade helps developers find code elements that are likely to be relevant to a particular task. It uses two heuristics to rank the results from most to least likely to be relevant. The first heuristic, which Robillard refers to as *specificity*,[1] considers how "unique" the relationship is between a given element and the known-relevant elements. Consider Fig. 4.2. Each node represents a code element. The shaded elements (D, E, and F) are known to be relevant to the current task, while the unshaded elements (A, B, and C) may or may not be relevant. Arrows represent a

---

[1]Not to be confused with the term that is synonymous with true negative rate.

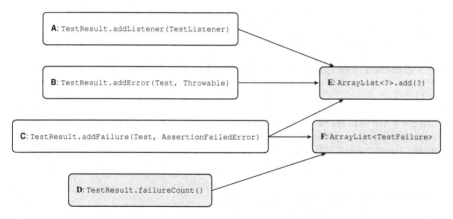

Fig. 4.2 An example showing specificity and reinforcement using relationships from JUnit's `TestResult` class. The *gray elements* are known to be relevant; the *white elements* are of unknown relevance. *Arrows* represent a *uses* relationship. C is both more specific and more reinforced than A and B

uses relationship; for example, the `addListener(TestListener)` method (node A) calls the `add(?)` method (node E). In this figure, node E has three neighbors of unknown relevance: A, B, and C. However, node F only has one neighbor of unknown relevance: C. C therefore has a more "unique" relationship with a known-relevant element than A or B do, so it will be given a higher specificity score. That is, Suade thinks C is more likely to be relevant to the current task than A or B.

The second heuristic, *reinforcement*, considers how many of the neighbors of a known-relevant element are also known to be relevant. In the figure, F has two neighbors, C and D. D is known to be relevant, so it seems likely that C is also relevant, since it is the "odd one out." Node E has three neighbors, and none of them are known to be relevant, so there is no particular reason to think any of the three are in fact relevant. Suade will therefore give C a higher reinforcement score than A or B. That is, Suade thinks C is more likely to be relevant to the current task than A or B.

The results of these two heuristics are combined so that an element that is both specific and reinforced is preferred to one that is specific but not reinforced or vice versa. Suade does not use a threshold value to limit the number of displayed results; all elements that are related to the known-relevant elements are shown to the developer in their ranked order.

Suade illustrates that RITSs can be used for code exploration and understanding tasks. Though RITSs use only the developer's context as input, they can identify useful information in other parts of the developer's project without mining its source code or associated metadata.

```
public class MyView extends ViewPart {
    public void updateStatus(String msg) {
        Action run = new Action("Run", IAction.AS_CHECK_BOX);
        ...
        IStatusLineManager.setMessage(msg);
    }
}
```

Listing 4.1 An example of a code snippet that could be submitted to Strathcona as a query. Strathcona will look for examples with similar structural properties; for example, methods in the corpus that also call `Action.Action(String, int)`

4.3.2 Strathcona: API Exploration

Holmes et al. [6] noted that developers sometimes have difficulty using unfamiliar APIs. These developers often look for examples of correct API usage to help them complete their tasks. Unfortunately, such examples are not always provided in the project documentation. The authors created a RITS called Strathcona to help developers locate relevant source code examples in a large code corpus. Queries are formed by extracting structural information from the developer's integrated development environment (IDE) and using this information to locate examples that have similar structure. Four heuristics are used to measure the structural similarity between the developer's code and a given example from the corpus. Like Suade, Strathcona uses a data repository but does not use data mining to find patterns in the repository; it simply looks up information about examples.

The two simplest heuristics locate examples that make the same method calls and field references as the query. For example, if the developer were to query Strathcona in a file containing the code snippet shown in Listing 4.1, the *calls* heuristic would locate all methods in the corpus that call `Action.Action(String, int)` and `IStatusLineManager.setMessage(String)`. If no method calls both of these methods, then methods that call one or the other would be returned. The *references* heuristic would locate all methods in the corpus that contain a reference to `Action.AS_CHECK_BOX`.

While these two simple heuristics excel at locating examples that use specific methods and fields, they are not good at identifying more general examples. Strathcona uses two additional heuristics to address this shortcoming. Rather than focusing on specific methods and fields, the *uses* heuristic looks at the containing types of the code elements (e.g., `IStatusLineManager`, `Action`, and `IAction` in Listing 4.1) and tries to find methods that use these types in any way. The *inheritance* heuristic also works more broadly, locating any classes that have the same parent classes as the query (e.g., classes that extend `ViewPart` for the query in Listing 4.1). These heuristics are more general than the previous two heuristics and usually match many more code examples.

Strathcona does not weight the heuristics; instead, every example is assigned a score that is the sum of the number of heuristics that it matched. The top ten examples are returned to the developer.

Strathcona illustrates that RITSs can be used for API exploration and code maintenance tasks. Even without data mining, RITSs can harness the knowledge of other programmers to help a developer write new code. In this case, Strathcona's heuristics allow it to find useful examples without mining the example repository.

4.3.3   Quick Fix Scout: Coding Assistance

The Eclipse IDE has many features to make development easier, one of which is quick fix suggestions. When a program has a compilation error, these suggestions allow developers to automatically perform tasks that may resolve the error. For example, if the developer types "public sTRING name," the dialog box will recommend changing "sTRING" to "String." Unfortunately, for more complex errors, the outcome of these quick fix tasks is unpredictable and may even introduce new errors. Muşlu et al. [8] created an Eclipse plugin called Quick Fix Scout that uses *speculative analysis* to recommend which quick fix to use. More precisely, it applies each quick fix proposal to a copy of the project, attempts to compile the resulting program, and counts the number of compilation errors. The plugin does this for each suggested quick fix and reorders the suggestions in the quick fix dialog so that the fixes that result in the fewest compilation errors are the top suggestions. Any two fixes that result in the same number of errors are kept in their original relative order. The heuristic used here is simply that fewer compilation errors are better.

Quick Fix Scout also augments the quick fix dialog box with the global best fix. Sometimes the best suggestion to fix a given compilation error is not found at the error location itself, but at some other program point. Quick Fix Scout checks all suggestions at all error locations to identify the best fix overall, rather than just at the individual program point queried by the developer. The global best fix is shown as the top suggestion in the Quick Fix Scout dialog box.

Quick Fix Scout illustrates that RITSs can help with the day-to-day work of development: their use of heuristics and small amounts of data make them fast enough to use interactively, which is not always the case for DMRSs. A DMRS developer would probably use static analysis for this application, while Quick Fix Scout can use the simpler "try it and see" approach.

4.3.4   A Tool for Debugging Method Names: Refactoring Support

Høst and Østvold [7] noted that Java programs are much more difficult to understand and maintain when the methods do not have meaningful names, that is, names that accurately describe what the methods do. As a concrete example, a method named `isEmpty` that returns a string is probably poorly named.

To address this, the authors developed a tool that automatically checks whether a given method's name matches its implementation. The authors used natural language program analysis on a large corpus of Java software to develop a "rule book" for method names, i.e., a set of heuristics that are built into the tool. To return to our previous example, a possible rule is that a method named is*Adjective*(...) should return a Boolean value. The tool compares the name of a method in the developer's program to its implementation using these rules and determines if it breaks the rules, which the authors call a *naming bug*. If a naming bug is present, the tool generates recommendations for a more suitable name. Specifically, it returns two suggestions: the (roughly speaking) most popular name that has been used for similar methods without resulting in a naming bug; and the name that is (again, roughly speaking) most similar to the current name that does not result in a naming bug. The tool does not use a threshold value when displaying results: it merely displays a list of methods that have naming bugs and two recommended replacement names for each one.

This tool illustrates that RITSs can support refactoring tasks. Moreover, they can obtain many of the benefits of data mining without using it online to generate recommendations. By using data mining to generate heuristics that are built into the tool, the recommendation system can produce better recommendations without the recurring cost of data mining.

4.3.5   YooHoo: Developer Awareness

One downside of relying on external libraries is that it can be hard for developers to keep apprised of when these libraries are updated. If a library is updated in a way that changes the API, the developer's program may stop working for users who have the new version of the library; the developer may not know about the problem until someone files an issue report. Holmes and Walker [4] noted that if developers wish to respond proactively to changes in libraries they depend on, they must constantly monitor a flood of information regarding changes to the deployment environment of their program. Unfortunately, the amount of information they must process leads to many developers giving up: rather than proactively responding to changes in the deployment environment, they respond reactively when an issue report is filed. The delay between the change occurring and the issue report being filed may exacerbate the problem and lower users' opinion of the product. In response, Holmes and Walker developed YooHoo, a tool that filters the flood of change events regarding deployment dependencies to those that are most likely to cause problems for a specific developer or project.

YooHoo has two components: *generic change analysis engines* (GCAs) and *developer-specific analysis engines* (DSAs). Each GCA is tied to a specific external repository and monitors changes that are made to that repository. When a developer starts using YooHoo, it automatically generates GCAs for all of the projects the developer depends on. These GCAs generate the flood of change events that may or may not be of interest to the developer.

DSAs are responsible for filtering the events captured by GCAs. YooHoo monitors the files in the developer's system to identify the set of files that the developer is responsible for. It then determines which external dependencies are used by those files so that it can limit the flood of change events to events coming from those dependencies. In addition, every event that comes from a relevant GCA is analyzed to gauge the severity of its impact on the developer's code. Events that might break the developer's code are shown, as are informational events such as updated documentation. All other events are discarded. This filtering process means the developer will see on the order of 1 % of the change events that occur, and most of them will be immediately relevant to the developer's work.

YooHoo illustrates that RITSs can be used for developer awareness and coordination tasks. Recommendation systems in-the-small have two advantages in this application area: they can generate recommendations quickly, and they are designed to make recommendations based on the developer's current context. They are therefore good at producing relevant recommendations for time-sensitive tasks. In YooHoo's case, its heuristics allow it to categorize change events quickly and with high accuracy. An alternative data mining approach to categorization would likely increase accuracy but at the price of speed.

4.4 Developing Heuristics

As we mentioned at the beginning of the chapter, recommendation systems in-the-small frequently use heuristics to compensate for having a limited set of raw data to base recommendations on. These heuristics can be developed by:

- using human intuition about the problem;
- using data mining during the development of the recommender to identify patterns that are built into the recommender as heuristics; or
- using machine learning to learn the heuristics during operation.

Combinations of these approaches can also be used; for instance, human intuition could be used to generate initial heuristics that are then refined by machine learning. Heuristics can also be combined, possibly with different weights assigned to each.

In this section, we discuss the advantages and disadvantages of these different methods of generating heuristics. We also discuss how the recommendation systems described in the previous section make use of these techniques.

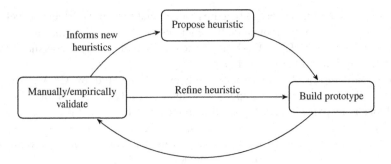

Fig. 4.3 The process that a recommendation system designer uses to develop the heuristics that the system will use

4.4.1 Human Intuition

When developing a RITS, the creators often use their intuition about the application domain to develop the heuristics that are built into the recommendation system. Figure 4.3 shows the general procedure for doing this. First, the recommendation system developer chooses some initial heuristics. The developer encodes these into the tool, tries it, and notes whether or not the recommendations are of satisfactory quality. The latter step might be done through manual inspection or empirical analysis. If the results are not satisfactory, the RITS developer can modify the existing heuristics, possibly by weighting them differently or using different threshold values. Alternatively, the developer can develop entirely new heuristics.

In the previous section, we saw three recommendation systems that use heuristics based on human intuition: Suade, Strathcona, and Quick Fix Scout. We examine in turn how the heuristics used by each were developed.

Suade's Heuristics

Suade's specificity and reinforcement heuristics are intuitive in the development setting. Specificity reflects the idea that if an element of unknown relevance has a unique relationship with an element that is known to be relevant, it is probably relevant itself. Reinforcement reflects the idea that if most of the elements in a group of structurally related elements are known to be relevant, then the rest of the elements in the group are probably relevant as well.

After building Suade around these heuristics, Robillard performed an empirical study on five programs to evaluate the heuristics. He chose a benchmark for each program by identifying a group of elements that had to be modified to complete a given task. The benchmarks were either generated for the study or reused from previous work. For each benchmark, the author generated a number of subsets of the known relevant elements, fed them into Suade, and verified that the other elements in the benchmark received high ratings.

Strathcona's Heuristics

The Strathcona system includes four heuristics that Holmes et al. believed would identify relevant source code examples. The authors began with two simple heuristics, but, finding them inadequate, added two more. The authors evaluated the heuristics with a small user study. They asked two developers to perform four tasks using Strathcona. For three of the tasks, Strathcona could identify relevant examples; the remaining task was deliberately chosen so that Strathcona could not help the developers. The developers were mostly successful at completing the tasks, though one developer did not finish the last task, and reported that Strathcona made the tasks easier. They also quickly realized that one of the tasks had no relevant examples, suggesting that Strathcona does not lead to wasted exploration time in the event that the example repository contains nothing relevant to the current task.

Quick Fix Scout's Heuristics

Quick Fix Scout relies on a simple heuristic: a fix that results in fewer compilation errors is better than one that results in more compilation errors. The way this is applied is trivial: try all fixes for a given error, count the number of remaining errors after the fix is applied, and sort the list to put the fix that resolves the most errors at the top. Quick Fix Scout also puts the global best fix at the top of every quick fix dialog box. This captures the intuitive knowledge that some faults manifest themselves as compilation errors in several program locations, so fixing the underlying fault can resolve several compilation errors at once.

Since it may be hard to believe that such a simple heuristic could be useful, the authors did a thorough evaluation of the tool. First, 13 users installed the plugin and used it for approximately a year. Second, the authors did a controlled study where 20 students performed 12 compilation-error removal tasks each, using either the regular quick fix dialog or Quick Fix Scout. The results from both studies suggest that Quick Fix Scout is helpful: feedback from the 13 long-term users was positive, and in the controlled study, students were able to perform compilation-error removal tasks 10 % faster.

Advantages and Disadvantages

The main advantage of relying on human intuition is that no dataset is needed. The only requirement is that the developer of the recommendation system should have sufficient knowledge of the application domain to generate heuristics and evaluate the correctness of the results. It is worth repeating that these heuristics are usually developed iteratively: as the results from one or more heuristics are examined, other heuristics are often introduced to either broaden or limit the results that are already identified. Domain knowledge is again necessary for this process.

Another advantage of these heuristics is that developers are often more willing to trust them, because they tend to be easy to understand and, obviously, intuitive to people who are familiar with the problem domain.

The main disadvantage of relying on human intuition is that it may not be correct. If this is the case, the recommendations will be poorer than they would be if a data-driven approach had been used instead. Even if the heuristics seem to work well, it is possible that better ones exist, but the recommendation designer stopped looking for them once a fairly good set had been identified.

4.4.2 Off-line Data Mining

At first glance, using data mining to generate heuristics may seem to contradict the theme of the chapter. However, there is an important distinction between using data mining off-line, while building the recommendation system, and using data mining online, as part of the recommendation system. In the first scenario, the developer constructing the recommendation system uses data mining on a large corpus of software projects to identify patterns. This information is then encoded as a heuristic in the recommendation system. The recommendation system itself does *not* perform data mining and does *not* update the heuristics: the heuristics are static. In the second scenario, the recommendation system itself mines a repository of some sort as part of its recommendation generation algorithm. This is the technique used by DMRSs and the one we wish to avoid, as it can be computationally expensive and requires maintenance of the data repository.

Using off-line data mining to generate heuristics is a way of getting some of the benefits of data mining without incurring the expenses of data mining each time we want a recommendation. We saw an example of this technique in the previous section: the tool of Høst and Østvold for debugging method names used a set of rules that were derived by performing natural language program analysis on a large corpus of Java programs. More precisely, the authors identified many attributes that methods can have, such as *returns type in name*, *contains loop*, and *recursive call*. They then used off-line data mining to establish statistical relationships between method names and these attributes; for instance, methods with the name get *Type*(...) nearly always have the attribute *returns type in name*. When a method in the developer's program breaks one of these rules—say, a method named getList that returns an object of type String—the recommendation system flags it as a naming bug. The authors did a small evaluation of their rules by running the tool on all of the methods in their Java corpus, randomly selecting 50 that were reported as naming bugs, and manually inspecting them. The authors found that 70 % of the naming bugs were true naming bugs, while the other 30 % were false positives.

Of course, this study is seriously limited, since the same corpus was used for both training and evaluating the tool, but it suggests the technique has promise.

The main advantage of off-line data mining is that if a sufficiently large and diverse repository is mined, the heuristics are likely to be more accurate and possibly more generalizable than heuristics generated with the other techniques.

The main disadvantage of this technique is that it is very susceptible to biased training data. If the repository being mined only contains software projects from, say, a particular application domain, the learned heuristics may not be applicable to other types of software projects and may lead to poor recommendations.

4.4.3 Machine Learning

The previous two heuristic generation techniques produce static heuristics. Since they cannot adapt to a developer's current context, recommendation systems that use static heuristics tend not to generalize as well; this can be mitigated by using machine learning to adapt the heuristics on the fly.

We saw an example of a RITS that uses machine learning in Sect. 4.3. YooHoo contains developer-specific analysis engines that filter the flow of incoming change events to those that are likely to impact a particular developer. This filtering relies on knowing which source files the developer owns, and since this changes over time, the developer-specific analysis engines (DSAs) must update themselves to match.

The authors evaluated the generated DSAs with a retrospective study that measured how well YooHoo compressed the flow of change events and whether it erroneously filtered important events. They found that YooHoo filtered out over 99 % of incoming change events, and on average 93 % of the impactful events remained after filtering; that is, YooHoo rarely erroneously filtered out impactful events.

The advantage of machine learning is that it may improve the quality of the recommendations, since the heuristics can evolve with the project. This also avoids one of the issues with using human intuition, where the human finds a "good enough" set of heuristics and stops trying to improve them. In addition, the recommendations will be pertinent to a greater variety of projects, since the heuristics were not developed with a particular (possibly biased) training set, and the heuristics can change to match the characteristics of a new project.

The main disadvantage of machine learning is that it can get bogged down in excess complexity in the data, identifying spurious relationships between variables. When it is fully automated (which is common), it cannot be combined with human analysis; when it is not fully automated, a developer has to be trained to interact with it and has to be willing to spend the time to do so. Machine learning also adds considerable complexity to the recommendation system's implementation, which may be undesirable for the sake of maintainability, runtime footprint, and error-proneness.

4.5 Limitations of Recommendation Systems in-the-Small

Given that recommendation systems in-the-small do not use data mining as they generate their recommendations, they cannot be used in application domains where it is necessary to identify patterns in large datasets. Consider code reuse: recommendation systems for this domain help developers reuse existing code components by locating potentially useful ones in a large component repository. The recommender must mine the component repository to obtain the information it needs to recommend components, so RITSs are not suitable for this domain. That said, there are still many areas where recommendation systems in-the-small are applicable and useful, as we saw in Sect. 4.3.

RITSs that do not use machine learning may not generalize well due to their reliance on static heuristics. If the training set does not include a variety of software systems, the RITS may produce poor recommendations when a developer tries to use it on a project that was not represented in the training set. Even if a developer's project is initially similar to one in the training set, if the project changes enough, the recommendations could degrade over time. Both of these issues can be addressed by updating the heuristics, either by incorporating machine learning or by manually updating them in each new version of the recommender.

Finally, RITSs cannot use information about non-localized trends to guide their recommendations. Since the recommendations are based on the developer's immediate context, they may not be as good as they could be if the recommender had access to information about the rest of the developer's system. Unfortunately, this is part of the fundamental trade-off between recommendation systems in-the-small and data mining recommendation systems.

4.6 Conclusion

Many recommendation systems use data mining in their recommendation generation algorithms, but this can be expensive and impractical. Recommendation systems in-the-small provide a lightweight alternative and can be used in many of the same application areas. This chapter described five recommendation systems in-the-small—Suade, Strathcona, Quick Fix Scout, the Java method debugger, and YooHoo—that show the diversity that RITSs can attain. However, these tools barely scratch the surface of what is possible with RITSs. Other works of possible interest include:

- SRRS [12], which helps the user choose an appropriate way of specifying the security requirements for their project;
- DPR [9], which recommends appropriate design patterns to help developers preserve their system's architectural quality; and
- The work by Bruch et al. [2], which compares data mining and non-data mining approaches to code completion recommendations.

RITSs often use heuristics to compensate for the smaller amount of data available to them, and we looked at three ways these heuristics can be generated: using human intuition, using off-line data mining, and using machine learning. We discussed some of the advantages and disadvantages of these different heuristic generation techniques. Readers who want to learn more about data mining may want to consult a textbook such as Tan et al. [13]; readers who want to use machine learning may be interested in Alpaydin [1].

Finally, we explored some limitations of recommendation systems in-the-small and some situations where they cannot be used. While RITSs are in some sense more limited than data mining recommendation systems, they are often easier to develop; they also tend to be easier to use and more responsive since there is no data repository to maintain. For these reasons, recommendation systems in-the-small will continue to hold a prominent position in the field of recommendation systems in software engineering. We encourage the reader to explore this interesting area.

References

1. Alpaydin, E.: Introduction to Machine Learning, 2nd edn. MIT Press, Cambridge, MA (2009)
2. Bruch, M., Monperrus, M., Mezini, M.: Learning from examples to improve code completion systems. In: Proceedings of the European Software Engineering Conference/ACM SIGSOFT International Symposium on Foundations of Software Engineering, pp. 213–222 (2009). DOI 10.1145/1595696.1595728
3. Erlikh, L.: Leveraging legacy system dollars for e-business. IT Prof. 2(3), 17–23 (2000). DOI 10.1109/6294.846201
4. Holmes, R., Walker, R.J.: Customized awareness: Recommending relevant external change events. In: Proceedings of the ACM/IEEE International Conference on Software Engineering, pp. 465–474 (2010). DOI 10.1145/1806799.1806867
5. Holmes, R., Walker, R.J.: Systematizing pragmatic software reuse. ACM Trans. Software Eng. Meth. 21(4), 20:1–20:44 (2012). DOI 10.1145/2377656.2377657
6. Holmes, R., Walker, R.J., Murphy, G.C.: Approximate structural context matching: An approach to recommend relevant examples. IEEE Trans. Software Eng. 32(12), 952–970 (2006). DOI 10.1109/TSE.2006.117
7. Høst, E.W., Østvold, B.M.: Debugging method names. In: Proceedings of the European Conference on Object-Oriented Programming, Lecture Notes in Computer Science, vol. 5653, pp. 294–317. Springer, New York (2009). DOI 10.1007/978-3-642-03013-0_14
8. Muşlu, K., Brun, Y., Holmes, R., Ernst, M.D., Notkin, D.: Speculative analysis of integrated development environment recommendations. In: Proceedings of the ACM SIGPLAN Conference on Object-Oriented Programming, Systems, Languages, and Applications, pp. 669–682 (2012). DOI 10.1145/2384616.2384665
9. Palma, F., Farzin, H., Guéhéneuc, Y.G., Moha, N.: Recommendation system for design patterns in software development: An [sic] DPR overview. In: Proceedings of the International Workshop on Recommendation Systems for Software Engineering (2012). DOI 10.1109/RSSE.2012.6233399
10. Robillard, M.P.: Topology analysis of software dependencies. ACM Trans. Software Eng. Meth. 17(4), 18:1–18:36 (2008). DOI 10.1145/13487689.13487691
11. Robillard, M.P., Walker, R.J., Zimmermann, T.: Recommendation systems for software engineering. IEEE Software 27(4), 80–86 (2010). DOI 10.1109/MS.2009.161

12. Romero-Mariona, J., Ziv, H., Richardson, D.J.: SRRS: A recommendation system for security requirements. In: Proceedings of the International Workshop on Recommendation Systems for Software Engineering (2008). DOI 10.1145/1454247.1454266
13. Tan, P.N., Steinbach, M., Kumar, V.: Introduction to Data Mining.   Addison-Wesley, Reading, MA (2005)
14. Zimmermann, T., Weißgerber, P., Diehl, S., Zeller, A.: Mining version histories to guide software changes. IEEE Trans. Software Eng. **31**(6), 429–445 (2005). DOI 10.1109/TSE.2005.72

Chapter 5
Source Code-Based Recommendation Systems

Kim Mens and Angela Lozano

Abstract Although today's software systems are composed of a diversity of software artifacts, source code remains the most up-to-date artifact and therefore the most reliable data source. It provides a rich and structured source of information upon which recommendation systems can rely to provide useful recommendations to software developers. Source code-based recommendation systems provide support for tasks such as how to use a given API or framework, provide hints on things missing from the code, suggest how to reuse or correct an existing code, or help novices learn a new project, programming paradigm, language, or style. This chapter highlights relevant decisions involved in developing source code-based recommendation systems. An in-depth presentation of a particular system we developed serves as a concrete illustration of some of the issues that can be encountered and of the development choices that need to be made when building such a system.

5.1 Introduction

In general, recommendation systems aid people to find relevant information and to make decisions when performing particular tasks. Recommendation systems in software engineering (RSSEs) [31] in particular are software tools that can assist developers in a wide range of activities, from reusing code to writing effective issue reports. This chapter's focus is on *source code based recommendation system (SCoReS)*, that is, recommendation systems that produce their recommendations essentially by analyzing the source code of a software system. Since programming lies at the heart of software development, it is no surprise that recommendation systems based on source code analysis are an important class of RSSEs.

K. Mens (✉) • A. Lozano
ICTEAM, Université catholique de Louvain, Louvain-la-Neuve, Belgium
e-mail: kim.mens@uclouvain.be; angela.lozano@uclouvain.be

M.P. Robillard et al. (eds.), *Recommendation Systems in Software Engineering*,
DOI 10.1007/978-3-642-45135-5_5, © Springer-Verlag Berlin Heidelberg 2014

Many current SCoReS are aimed at supporting the correct usage of application programming interfaces (APIs) [e.g., 9, 22, 39], libraries, or frameworks [e.g., 4]. They typically rely on a corpus of examples of known API usage, obtained by analyzing several applications that use a particular API. The recommendation tools that use this corpus often consist of a front-end embedded in the integrated development environment (IDE), and a back-end that stores the corpus. The front-end is in charge of displaying results and getting the right information from the IDE or development context in order to formulate appropriate queries. The back-end is in charge of producing results that match these queries and of updating the corpus. When a developer edits a program, the recommendation system can suggest how the API should be used, based on similar, previous uses of the API. Such recommendation systems can be considered as "smart" code completion tools. The match-making process typically uses information similar to that used by code completion tools, such as the type of the object expected to be returned and the type of the object from which the developer expects to access the required functionality.

In addition to this class of SCoReS, many other kinds of SCoReS can be distinguished, not only depending on the kind of recommendations they extract from source code or on what technique they use to do so, but also on the kind of design choices that went into building them. Although a wide variety of source code analysis techniques exists, and even though the information needs of developers when evolving their code have been identified [33], it is not always obvious how to leverage a particular technique into a successful recommendation tool. Even when the most appropriate technique is chosen that best suits the recommendation needs for a particular development task, there is no guarantee that it will lead to a successful recommendation tool. We do not claim to have discovered the philosopher's stone that will lead to successful recommendation tools that are adopted by a broad user base. We do argue that, when building a recommendation system, one needs to be aware of, and think carefully about, all relevant development choices and criteria, in order to be able to make educated decisions that may lead to better systems. All too often, development choices that may seem unimportant at first, when not thought about carefully, may in the end hinder the potential impact of a SCoReS.

The goal of this chapter is to present novices to the domain of source code-based recommendation systems a quick overview of some existing approaches, to give them a feeling of what the issues and difficulties are in building such systems, and to suggest a more systematic process to develop SCoReS. This process was distilled from a non-exhaustive comparison and classification of currently existing approaches, as well as from our own experience with building tools to support a variety of software development and maintenance tasks.[1]

---

[1] These tools range from source code querying tools like SOUL [26], over source code-based validation tools like IntensiVE [25] and eContracts [19], to source code mining and recommendation tools like Heal [5], Mendel [18], and MEnToR [20].

To achieve this goal, the chapter is structured as follows. After presenting a few concrete examples of SCoReS in Sect. 5.2, Sect. 5.3 lists the main decisions that need to be taken when developing such systems, suggests an order in which these development choices could be made, and illustrates this with different choices that have actually been made (whether explicitly or implicitly) by currently existing SCoReS—those introduced in Sect. 5.2 in particular. Being aware of the possible choices to make, as well as of the potential impact of those choices, is of key importance to novices in the area, so that they can make the right choices when building their own SCoReS. To illustrate this, Sect. 5.4 zooms in on a set of actual recommendation systems we built, highlighting the different design choices made or rejected throughout their development and evolution. We conclude the chapter and summarize its highlights in Sect. 5.5.

5.2   Selection of Source Code-Based Recommendation Systems

Before proposing our design process for SCoReS in the next section, we briefly present a selection of five recommendation systems that we use to illustrate the importance of certain design decisions. The selected systems are RASCAL, FrUiT, Strathcona, Hipikat, and CodeBroker. We selected these systems because they are complementary in terms of the covered design approaches.

5.2.1   RASCAL

RASCAL [23] is a recommendation system that aims to predict the next method that a developer could use, by analyzing classes similar to the one currently being developed. RASCAL relies on the traditional recommendation technique of collaborative filtering, which is based on the assumption that users can be clustered into groups according to their preferences for items. RASCAL's "users" are classes and the items to be recommended are methods to be called. The similarity between the current class and other classes is essentially based on the methods they call.

RASCAL is divided in four parts, in charge of different stages of the recommendation process. The first is the *active user*, which identifies the class that is currently being developed. Second is the *usage history collector*, which automatically mines a class–method usage matrix and a class–method order list (see Fig. 5.1) for all classes in a set of APIs. Each cell in the matrix represents the number of times a particular method is called by a class. Third is the *code repository*, which stores the data mined by the history collector. And fourth is the *recommender agent*, which recommends the next method for the user to call in the implementation of the method and class where the cursor is currently located. The recommender agent starts by locating classes similar to the one that is currently selected. The

Fig. 5.1 RASCAL database [23]. Reproduced with permission

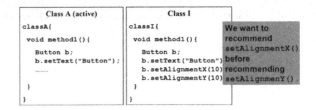

USERS	ITEMS				BookingGUI	User-Item Order List
	SetX()	SetY()	Copy()	Display()	SetX() Display() Display() Copy() SetX() Display()	
BookingGUI	2	0	1	3		
RemoteDB	1	0	2	1		
CompDlg	1	1	3	0		

User-Item Preference Database

Fig. 5.2 RASCAL recommendation ordering [23]. Reproduced with permission

Class A (active)	Class I	
classA{	classI{	We want to recommend setAlignmentX() before recommending setAlignmentY()
void method1(){	void method1(){	
Button b;	Button b;	
b.setText("Button");	b.setText("Button")	
....	b.setAlignmentX(10)	
	b.setAlignmentY(10)	
}	}	
}	}	

similarity between two classes is calculated by comparing the methods they call. The frequency with which a method is used is taken into account to identify significant similarities. Commonly used methods like toString() get lower weight than other methods when comparing two classes. As a concrete example, consider Fig. 5.2 illustrating a situation where, while implementing method1 in class A, a developer adds a call to method setText. To suggest other method calls to be added after this one, RASCAL looks at similar classes that contain a method calling setText, and then recommends the other method calls made by that method, in the same order as the appear in that method after its call to setText.

5.2.2 FrUiT

FrUiT [4] is an Eclipse plugin to support the usage of frameworks. FrUiT shows source code relations of the framework that tend to occur in contexts similar to the file that a developer is currently editing. Figure 5.3 shows a screenshot of FrUiT. The source code editor (1) determines the developer's context, in this case the file Demo.java. FrUiT's implementation hints for this file are shown (2) on a peripheral view in the IDE, and the rationale (3) for each implementation hint (e.g., "instantiate Wizard") is also shown. For each implementation hint, the developer can also read the Javadoc of the suggested class or method (4).

FrUiT's recommendations are calculated in three phases. First, FrUiT extracts structural relations from a set of applications using a given framework or API. These structural relations include *extends* (class A extends class B), *implements* (class A implements an interface B), *overrides* (class A overrides an inherited method m), *calls* (any of the methods of class A call a method m), and *instantiates* (a constructor of class B is invoked from the implementation of class A).

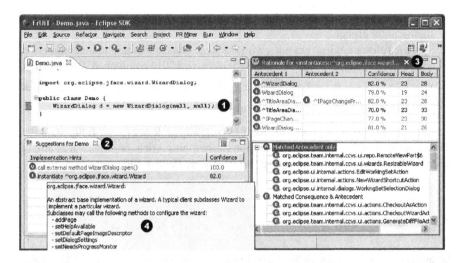

Fig. 5.3 A screenshot of FrUiT at work [4]. Reproduced with permission

Second, FrUiT uses association rule mining to identify structural relations that are common whenever the framework or API is used. Association rules are of the form:

$$antecedent \xrightarrow{\text{confidence}} consequent,$$

which can be interpreted as *if–then* rules. For instance, the rule

$$call : \mathrm{m} \xrightarrow{80\%} instantiate : \mathrm{B}$$

would mean that whenever an application using the framework calls the method m, it also tends to (in 80 % of the cases) call a constructor of class B. Notice that FrUiT also shows each of the cases in which the association rule holds or not (see bottom-right side of the IDE in Fig. 5.3). Given that association rule mining tends to produce a combinatorial explosion of results, it is necessary to filter the results to ensure that the tool produces only relevant information. FrUiT's filters include:

- *Minimum* support: there should be at least s cases for which the antecedent of the rule is true.
- *Minimum* confidence: the cases for which both the antecedent *and* the consequent of the rule are true over the cases for which the antecedent is true should be at least $c\%$.
- *Misleading rules*: whenever there are rules with the same consequent that have overlapping antecedents (e.g., $y \xrightarrow{c_1\%} z$ and $y \wedge x \xrightarrow{c_2\%} z$), the rule with the least prerequisites in the antecedent is preferred (i.e., $y \xrightarrow{c_1\%} z$), because the additional prerequisite for the antecedent (i.e., x) decreases the likelihood that z holds.
- Overfitting *rules*: even if in the case of the previous filter c_2 would be marginally greater than c_1, the rule with the more detailed antecedent would still be

rejected to keep the rule simpler, and because the increase in confidence is not significantly higher.

- Specific rules: imagine two rules with the same consequent and same confidence, whose antecedents are related by a third rule with 100 % confidence. For instance, $x \xrightarrow{c\%} z$, $y \xrightarrow{c\%} z$, and $y \xrightarrow{100\%} x$). Then the second rule can be discarded ($y \xrightarrow{c\%} z$) because it is already subsumed by the first one ($x \xrightarrow{c\%} z$).

In the third and final phase, for the file currently in focus of the Eclipse editor, FrUiT recommends all rules that mention in their antecedent or consequent any of the source code entities of the framework mentioned in that file.

5.2.3   Strathcona

Strathcona [13] is also an Eclipse plugin that recommends examples (see Fig. 5.4d) on how to complete a method that uses a third-party library. The user is supposed to highlight a source code fragment that uses the third-party library to ask Strathcona for examples that use the same functionality of the library (see Fig. 5.4a). The examples are taken from other applications using the same third-party library.

Strathcona works by extracting the *structural context* of source code entities. This structural context includes the method's signature, the declared type and parent type, the methods called, the names of fields accessed, and the types referred to by each method. The extracted structural context can be used in two ways: (1) as an automatic query that describes the source code fragment for which the developer requests support, and (2) to build a database containing the structural contexts of classes using the libraries that the tool supports. Relevant examples are located by identifying entities in Strathcona's database with a structural context similar to the one of the fragment being analyzed (see Fig. 5.4b,c). Similarity is based on heuristics that take into account entities extending the same types, calling the same methods, using the same types, and using the same fields. Entities in the result set that match more heuristics are ranked higher than those that match fewer ones.

5.2.4   Hipikat

Hipikat [7] helps newcomers to a software project to find relevant information for a maintenance task at hand. The idea behind Hipikat is to collect and retrieve relevant parts of the project's history based on its source code, email discussions, bug reports, change history, and documentation. Figure 5.5 shows a screenshot of Hipikat.

The main window in the IDE shows a bug report that the developer wants to fix (see Fig. 5.5a). Once the developer chooses "Query Hipikat" from the context menu, the tool will return a list of related artifacts. The artifacts related to the bug

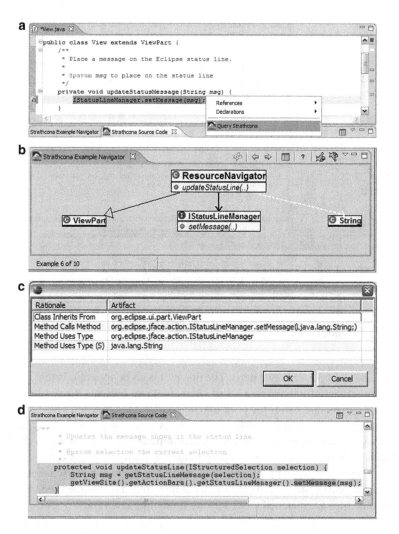

Fig. 5.4 Strathcona screenshots [13]. Reproduced with permission. (**a**) Querying Strathcona. (**b**) Graphical view of the recommended example, highlighting similarity with the queried code. (**c**) Explanation for the recommendation, as a list of structural facts matching the queried code. (**d**) Source code view of the recommended example

are shown in a separate view (see Fig. 5.5b). For each artifact found, Hipikat shows its name, type (webpage, news article, CVS revision, or Bugzilla item), the rationale for recommending it, and an estimate of its relevance to the queried artifact. Any of the artifacts found can be opened in the main window of the IDE to continue querying Hipikat, so the user can keep looking for solutions for problems similar to the one described in the bug report.

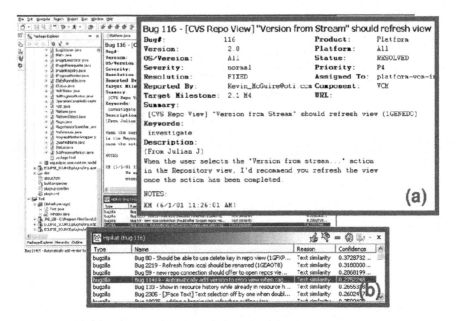

Fig. 5.5 A screenshot of Hipikat [7]. Reproduced with permission

Hipikat is composed of two parts. The first part is an Eclipse plugin that sends the query (by artifact of interest or a set of keywords) and presents the results (related artifacts). The second part is the back-end that builds a relationship graph of diverse software artifacts and calculates the artifacts relevant to the query. In contrast to the previously described SCoReS, Hipikat's recommendations are based on the links established between different artifacts and their similarity. The links are inferred by custom-made heuristics. For instance, bug report IDs are matched to change logs by using regular expressions on their associated message, and change time-stamps on source code files are matched to the closing time of bug reports.

5.2.5 CodeBroker

CodeBroker [38] recommends methods to call based on the comments and signature of the method where the developer's cursor is currently located. The goal of the system is to support the development of a new method by finding methods that already (partially) implement the functionality that the developer aims to implement.

CodeBroker is also divided in a front-end and a back-end. The front-end monitors the cursor, queries the back-end with relevant information from the current context, and shows the results. The back-end is divided in two parts: (1) a *discourse model* that stores and updates the comments and signatures of methods from a set of libraries, APIs, and frameworks to reuse, and (2) a *user model* to remove

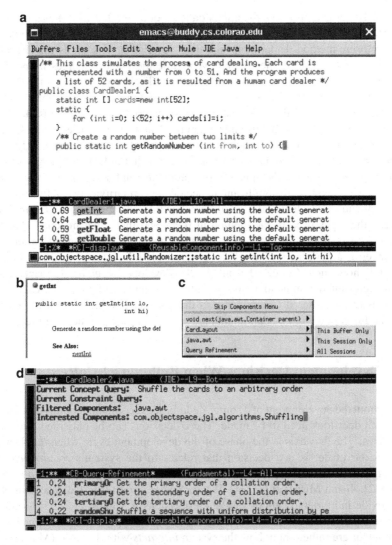

Fig. 5.6 Screenshots of CodeBroker [38]. Adapted with permission. (**a**) CodeBroker's recommended methods (first recommended method is selected). (**b**) Left-clicking on the selected recommendation shows the Javadoc of the method. (**c**) Right-clicking on the selected recommendation allows to remove it from the recommendation list or to refine the query. (**d**) Query refinement

methods, classes, or packages from the recommendation list, while remembering if the removal should be done for a session (irrelevant for the task) or for all sessions (irrelevant for the user, i.e., the developer is aware of the method and does not need to be reminded of it). For instance, Fig. 5.6c illustrates how it suffices to right click on a recommendation to be able to eliminate it from the recommendation list.

CodeBroker is a proactive recommendation tool integrated with the source code editor (emacs). That is, the tool proactively identifies the need for recommendations by monitoring method declarations and their description as soon as the developer starts writing them. This means that every time the cursor changes its position, it automatically queries the back-end repository. The query describes the method currently being developed in terms of the words used in its comments, of the words in its signature, and of the types used in its signature. This query aims at finding methods with similar comments and signatures. The technique used is the same as that used by basic text search engines—namely, latent semantic analysis (LSA)—which represents each method as a Boolean vector that indicates which words are mentioned by the method's signature or comments, and a vector of weights that indicates which words are significant, to decide the similarity between two methods of an application. The text search results are then filtered depending on the similarity between the types used in the method in focus and those that matched. As soon as there is a response for the query, matching methods are presented, ordered by relevance, in a peripheral view of the source code editor (see Fig. 5.6a). Finally, Fig. 5.6d shows how CodeBroker allows the developer to *guide* the back-end in finding relevant recommendations by adding the names of methods, classes, or packages to the Filtered Components so that they get excluded from the results, or to the Interested Components so that the search is limited to these entities.

5.3 Development Decisions When Building a SCoReS

Throughout the development of a source code-based recommendation system, many important decisions need to be made. These decisions can be classified along two main axes. The first axis is the phase of the development cycle when the decision needs to be made: is it a decision that relates to the system's *requirements*, to its *design*, to its actual *implementation*, or rather to its eventual *validation*? (Said et al. [32], Tosun Mısırlı et al. [34], Walker and Holmes [36], and Avazpour et al. [2] provide more details about validation decisions in Chaps. 11, 12, 13, and 10, respectively.) The other axis is whether these decisions apply to the recommendation *approach* or are rather about how the system *interacts* with the *user*. (Murphy-Hill and Murphy [29] provide more detail about user interaction in Chap. 9.) Table 5.1 summarizes these axes and the main classes of decisions that can be found along these axes.

5.3.1 Process

Assuming that we follow a traditional development cycle starting from the requirements down, the numbers in Table 5.1 suggest a possible process of how and when to make these decisions:

Table 5.1 Kinds of development decisions to be taken when building a SCoReS

	Requirements	Design	Implementation	Validation
Approach	1. Intent	3. Corpus	5. Method	7. Support
User interaction	2. HCI	4. General I/O	6. Detailed I/O	8. Interaction

1. Start by thinking about the system's **Intent** (see Sect. 5.3.2), which are all the decisions related to the *purpose* of the recommendation approach.
2. Then decide upon the **Human Computer Interaction** (see Sect. 5.3.3), that is, how the end-user (typically, a developer) is expected to interact with the SCoReS.
3. Once the functional and user interaction requirements have been decided upon, choose what **Corpus** (see Sect. 5.3.4) of data sources the system will use to provide its recommendations.
4. **General Input/Output** (see Sect. 5.3.5) decisions then refine the Human Computer Interaction decisions taken previously.
5. Now decide upon the details of the recommendation **Method** (see Sect. 5.3.6), that is, all details related to how the recommendation process is implemented.
6. Since the decisions of the previous step may shed more light on the **Detailed Input/Output** (see Sect. 5.3.7), next we can decide what precise information the approach requires as input and what and how it produces its output.
7. After having implemented the system, we need to choose how to validate it. On the approach axis, the main question is how well the system provides **Support** (see Sect. 5.3.8) for the tasks it aims to provide recommendations for.
8. On the user interaction axis, regarding the validation, some decisions need to be made on how to assess the **Interaction** (see Sect. 5.3.9) of different users with the SCoReS.

In the next subsections, we zoom in on each of these classes of decisions, one by one, providing examples taken from a selection of SCoReS approaches that we analyzed,[2] and the selected approaches presented in Sect. 5.2 in particular.

5.3.2   Intent

The *intent* decisions define the purpose of the system: who is the intended user, what tasks need to be supported by the system, what kind of cognitive support can it provide, what kind of information does it produce to support that task?

---

[2]Many approaches exist that extract relevant information for developers from source code. For the purpose of this chapter, we analyzed a non-exhaustive selection of approaches that call themselves or that have been cited by others as "recommendation systems." We further filtered this selection to those systems that rely explicitly on the source code to produce their recommendations, and privileged approaches published in well-known software engineering venues.

Intended User

Regarding the intended audience, first a decision should be made on the *role* of the expected users of the system. Although most SCoReS, such as those shown in Sect. 5.2, are targeted at developers, some others (whose supported task is not directly linked to modification requests) also consider other roles [1, 16]. German et al. [11] distinguish roles such as maintainers, reverse engineers, reengineers, managers, testers, documenters, or researchers. A second decision is related to the level of experience of the intended users. Whereas some recommendation systems make no assumptions about their users' levels of experience, others are targeted specifically at novices or experts in either the source code or the programming language being studied. For instance, Hipikat helps newcomers to a project, whereas CodeBroker can be personalized depending on the experience level of its users.

Supported Task

This decision is about what task the system aims to support. As already mentioned in Sect. 5.1, many SCoReS aim at supporting the correct *usage of APIs, libraries, or frameworks*. Others support *mappings* for API evolution [8] or for language migration [40]. Yet others recommend *code corrections* (source code entities that are associated to bugs) [5], *code to be reused* (methods to be reused that contain a functionality that needs to be implemented) like CodeBroker, *code changes* (source code entities impacted by the change of another source code entity) [41] or *code suggestions* (suggested changes to code entities to complete or standardize their implementation) [18, 20, 21]. Some SCoReS, like Hipikat, can support novices in *learning a new project*. Others provide relevant information that can help developers understand how certain concerns are implemented [12,30] or how certain bugs have been solved [1].

Cognitive Support

According to German et al. [11], another important decision is how recommendation systems support human cognition to achieve certain tasks. In other words, which questions about the task can the system help answering? Five categories of questions can be distinguished: *who, why, when, what,* and *how*.

Many systems aim at finding artifacts or source code entities relevant to developers to perform their task (i.e., they provide an answer to the question of *what* information is needed to complete the task) [7, 23].

The amount of information a system provides to explain its recommendations tends to depend on the context in which it is applied. Systems that offer API support and that act as a kind of code completion tool integrated with the IDE do not usually (need to) provide detailed information that could help a user evaluate the appropriateness of their recommendation. API support tools that are not embedded as code completion tools, on the other hand, do tend to provide diverse views that explain the rationale for each recommendation they propose. Nevertheless, the level of detail offered does not depend *only* on how the system is integrated with the IDE. While some SCoReS, like Hipikat and CodeBroker, provide information to explain *why* an entity is part of their recommendation set, others require the developer to figure out the rationale of the recommendation [12, 17, 30].

Another popular cognitive support provided by SCoReS, as exemplified by FrUiT and Strathcona, is information for developers on *how* to complete their task. The level of detail offered depends on the kind of support provided by the system. Systems with specific goals such as how to replace deprecated methods [8] or how to obtain an instance of a type from another instance of another type [9, 22] need to provide less background information on their recommendations than systems concerned with broader goals (e.g., how to complete a method [18, 20]), systems that require user input (e.g., how to map statements in a method [6]), or how to use an API method [4, 13].

Only a few systems provide support for answering questions about the reasons behind given implementation choices (why something is implemented in a certain way); the ones that are closest to supporting this proposition are those that look for information related to an artifact/entity [1, 12, 30] but the relation among those entities must still be discovered by the developer.

Similarly, few SCoReS seem to answer temporal questions (*when*), which is probably due to the fact that they often do not rely on change information. Such temporal information could however be useful for answering rationale questions, since it can uncover the trace behind a change.

Finally, SCoReS rarely permit to answer authorship (*who*) questions (a notable exception is DebugAdvisor [1]), due to the fact that the source code alone often does not have information on its author, unless complemented by other sources that do have this.

Proposed Information

This decision pertains to what kind of information a recommendation system proposes. The information proposed affects the usability of a recommendation.

Some recommendation systems propose concrete *actions* [3, 6, 9, 22, 39], that is, they not only advise *what* to do, but also *how* to do it. For most recommenders proposing actions, the only thing that remains to be done by users (typically developers) is to select the change that they judge adequate for the current context or task, and the system will perform it automatically (e.g., inserting a code snippet after the last statement added to the source code entity being implemented). Most systems providing API support or code completion propose actions as output.

Another common type of output, for example, in FrUiT, RASCAL, and Code-Broker, is *source code entities*—that is, *what* to change or use but not *how* to do it. Depending on the task at hand and the type of recommendation system, a further interpretation of the proposed results may then be required. For example, the recommendation system may propose to modify a particular source code entity in a very specific way, but the system's integration with the IDE may not be sophisticated enough to automate this action, thus requiring the user to perform this action manually.

Examples can help a user understand how a similar problem was solved in similar situations [13]. It is the user's job of deciding whether and which part of the example is relevant for the task at hand, and how to adapt the example to the current situation.

Finally, SCoReS can suggest related *software artifacts* (i.e., any by-product of the software development process that is not a source code entity) to help a developer in better understanding the implications of the task at hand [1, 7]. The usefulness and efficacy of these recommendations depend on the relevance of the information and links that the developer can abstract from the information the system proposes.

5.3.3   Human–Computer Interaction

After having focused on decisions related to the system's intent, the human–computer interaction must be considered. These decisions permit us to establish the expected interaction between a user and a SCoReS. They comprise the type of system, the type of recommendations generated, and the input expected of the user.

Type of System

A recommendation system can be an *IDE plugin*, a *standalone application*, or some other type such as a *command line* tool or an internal or external *domain-specific language* (DSL) to be used by the user of the system. Given that most of the SCoReS we analyzed are targeted at developers, they tend to be integrated with the development environment, as is the case with FrUiT, Hipikat, Strathcona, and CodeBroker. This choice allows for an easier detection of the user's context or activity, and sometimes easier access to the syntactic entities and relations being used in that context. Another alternative that is sometimes chosen for recommendation systems is to make them standalone applications, like RASCAL. Both standalone SCoReS and those integrated with the IDE tend to have a graphical interface. Programmatic SCoReS are seldom an implementation choice probably to reduce their intrusiveness.

Type of Recommender

This decision characterizes what *type* of recommender a SCoReS is: a "finder," an "advisor," or a "validator."

Some recommendation systems, such as Hipikat and Strathcona, are dedicated search engines that *find* relevant information for a particular task at hand. For example, Strathcona finds examples on how to use a given API, while Hipikat finds information related to a source code artifact, for instance, a change request. Other systems, such as FrUiT, RASCAL, and CodeBroker, focus on *advising* certain courses of action to the user. RASCAL, for example, recommends what method calls may need to be added. The advice produced may be sufficiently clear to end users only if it is part of their workflow, as is the case with code completion tools providing code suggestion to developers, or if the user knows exactly how to interpret the results produced by the recommendation system.

Yet other systems focus more on verifying or *validating* certain properties of the source code, such as adherence to certain conventions or design regularities [19,25].

An interesting observation is that it sometimes happens that developers misuse a SCoReS. For instance, if the methods recommended by some SCoReS often have words similar to those in the identifier or comments of the method currently being implemented, developers can be tempted into abusing the system as a kind of search tool, by changing the signature or comments of their methods to resemble the methods they anticipate to be within the APIs used. Such a case was reported in [38]. This change in the user's expected behavior (using the system as a finder rather than as a validator) could probably be explained by the fact that the developer found it frustrating to use the SCoReS due to repeated unsuccessful use because many of the anticipated methods did not exist in the APIs used. When building a SCoReS, being aware of the possibility of such abuses is important.

User Involvement

Another important choice that needs to be made is what kind of *user involvement* the SCoReS requires. For example, does it require manual input or does it require user involvement for filtering the output?

Usually, the input required for a SCoReS can be extracted automatically from the programming context. For instance, the method being implemented, the methods it has called so far, the types it has used so far, the order of the methods called, the last statement or identifier created, etc. Given that the majority of SCoReS only rely on the analysis of source-code entities related to the one being edited or selected, there is no need of manual input. However, if a SCoReS being developed requires data that cannot be extracted from the programming context, it is necessary to decide in which way the user will provide the information required. For instance, by using a query made by the user to select a set of seed entities [12] or by asking the user explicitly to provide the source and target for a mapping [6].

Another important choice to make is whether or not the user can or should filter out recommendations. This filtering can be done iteratively, like in FrUiT or CodeBroker, and/or from the group of final results, like in Strathcona, RASCAL, and CodeBroker. Interestingly, filtering of results can also be used to exclude the user's explicit input. For instance, CodeBroker eliminates results that the user knows by looking at their local history. Another interesting alternative to consider is allowing result filtering per user session or per module [38].

5.3.4 Corpus

Deciding on the *corpus* of a SCoReS amounts to deciding what data sources the system needs to provide its recommendations. The main source of information used by SCoReS is *program code*, yet it is sometimes complemented with additional sources of information such as change management or defect tracking repositories, informal communications, local history, etc. When combining several sources of data, it is also important to explicitly decide how these sources are to be correlated.

Program Code

A first important decision to make regarding the corpus is whether or not the system will calculate its recommendations based on the application on which a developer is currently *working*, as in Hipikat, or on an application that they are currently *using*, as in the other SCoReS we illustrated. The former set of systems build their corpus from the code of a *single application* (i.e., the one that is being built) while the latter build their corpus from the code of *multiple applications* (i.e., those that also use the application that is being used by the application being built).

This choice has repercussions on the techniques and methods that can be used to calculate recommendations, on storage requirements, and on their usefulness. SCoReS with a corpus based on *multiple applications* can use generic data analysis techniques, but require storage to hold the data collected previously and their recommendations are often restricted to the analysis of a specific library or framework. Therefore, their usefulness depends on the match between the APIs used by the user of the SCoReS and those available on the server. In contrast, SCoReS that analyze a *single application* do not need separate storage nor prefetched data, nevertheless they usually require specialized or heuristic-based data analysis techniques. These SCoReS are also well suited for closed source applications.

Complementary Information

In addition to source code or a source code repository, a recommendation system may also distill useful information from program execution traces [1], from version control systems [1, 7, 8, 41], from issue management systems [1, 7], from informal communication [7] transcripts between developers (taken from e-mail discussions, mailing lists, instant messages, discussion forums, etc.), or from the user's history by tracking and analyzing the user's navigation and edition behavior. Mylar [15] (later renamed Mylyn) provides an example of the latter by providing program navigation support that gives artifacts of more recent interest a higher relevance.

Correlated Information

All SCoReS that use data not originating from the source code correlate it to source code. Indeed, there is little added value of having several data sources if the system does not attempt to combine the sources into something that is more than the sum of its independent facts. A relevant decision to take is thus *how* to mix the information coming from program code with the information extracted from *complementary* sources. For example, author information and time-stamps of files in a CVS repository can be correlated to the source code contained in those files to infer what source code entities may have changed together [41], or the identifier of a bug report can be linked to the messages in CVS commits to locate the source code entities that were modified when fixing a bug [7].

5.3.5 General Input/Output

The general input/output decisions listed below define the interaction between a user and the recommendation system, and refine the human–computer interaction decisions discussed in Sect. 5.3.3.

Input Mechanism

A first decision regards whether or not the SCoReS infers its input from the currently active source code entity or artifact whenever the recommendation system is triggered. This decision depends on whether or not the information available from the source code development context is needed to calculate recommendations for the task to support. While most SCoReS infer their input implicitly from the current context or activity of the user, like in FrUiT, Strathcona, and RASCAL, others rely either partially or completely on the *user's input* to identify for which task or entity the recommendation is requested, like CodeBroker and Hipikat.

Nature of Input

The nature of the input directly affects the user's perception of how easy it is to use the system. The majority of SCoReS require as input (a fragment of) a *source code* to provide concrete recommendations regarding that source code, as in FrUiT or RASCAL. Other systems implicitly or explicitly take the users' *context* and *activity* into account in order to support them in that activity, like Strathcona or CodeBroker. Extracting the programming context is usually limited however to identifying the source code entity in focus or currently being used: only a few of the recommendation systems go beyond that. APIExplorer, for instance, finds source and target types in a code completion operation [9]. Finally, some systems take input under the form of a *natural language queries* [12], or other *non-code artifacts*, like in Hipikat.

Response Triggers

When building a SCoReS, one also needs to decide when the system should be *triggered* to calculate its recommendations. Recommendations can be calculated either upon *explicit request* by the user (known as reactive recommendations), as in FrUiT, Hipikat, Strathcona, and RASCAL, or proactively when a certain *contextual* situation occurs, such as saving a file. But even for those SCoReS that discover their input implicitly from the development environment, the request for calculating a recommendation typically remains explicit, except for a few systems like CodeBroker that *continuously* update their results. This design decision is related to whether the system's responses are considered as *intrusive* or not, in other words whether they interfere directly with how developers normally perform their tasks. Most SCoReS try to be not too intrusive by triggering responses only upon explicit request by the developer and by presenting the recommendations and their rationale in peripheral views and not in the main programming view.

Nature of Output

The nature of the output, too, may affect significantly the usability perception of a SCoReS. For example, for a source code fragment given as input, Strathcona provides similar source code examples to a developer. Each such example consists of three parts: a graphical UML-like overview illustrating the structural similarity of the example to the queried code fragment, a textual description of why the example was selected, and source code with structural details highlighted that are similar to the queried fragment.

There is no typical type of output for SCoReS. While some of them are restricted to deliver the information requested in some primitive *textual* description [4, 13, 22], others aim at integrating the recommendation into the IDE so it can be used as seamlessly as possible. This seamless information includes navigation and browsing aids such as: text links [18, 20]; clickable links as in FrUiT, Hipikat, Strathcona, and CodeBroker; *annotations or highlights* of relevant parts of the source code as in Strathcona and CodeBroker; or *graphical* notations as in Strathcona, for the results.

There are some missing opportunities at graphical outputs given that existing SCoReS tend to be limited to UML graphs, but the intermediate data representations used by the SCoReS (e.g., graphs, trees, vectors) so far have been neglected as a way to deliver the recommendations. We believe that, in some cases, presenting the recommendations in such a format, as opposed to presenting a mere list of recommendations, may provide a more intuitive way for the end-user to understand the results.

Type of Output

The usefulness of SCoReS also depends on the appropriateness of the output produced to the task to support. Examples of these outputs include existing *software artifacts* [1, 7] or *source code entities* relevant to the user's current task, *missing source code* entities or fragments [4, 18, 20], or suggestions for *mapping* entities (e.g., statements [6] or methods [8]). Existing relevant entities usually indicate other entities that were typically used or changed whenever the source code entity or entities given as input are used, for instance, methods to reuse [38], methods to change [41], the next method to call [3, 23], or a set of methods to call (as a list [12, 17, 30], as a sequence [37], using an example [13], or as a code snippet [9, 22]). Mappings indicate how to use or replace the components of one entity with the components of the other entity. And implementation suggestions indicate syntactic or structural relations that may have been forgotten in an entity's implementation (such as implementing an interface, calling a method, using a type, etc.).

5.3.6   Method

We now discuss all design choices specific to the software recommendation process.

Data Selection

Once the data to be used as input by a SCoReS is chosen (e.g., all applications that use a certain API), the developer of the SCoReS must decide on the level of detail in which the data will be collected. This decision affects which analyses are possible and which information will be available for the user of the SCoReS. As such, the data selected as relevant for the recommendations can provide a differentiating factor among similar SCoReS. It is therefore important to describe up front the rationale for the data to be collected, and in particular how it can be used to provide a useful recommendation, so that the appropriate level of granularity can be chosen. While a too coarse granularity may negatively affect the support the SCoReS aims to provide, there is no use in choosing too fine a granularity either.

Not surprisingly, when analyzing object-oriented source code, the preferred level of detail of most SCoReS seems to be at the level of *methods* [4, 13, 23, 38] and *relations between methods* (like call statements [4, 13, 23], overriding information [3], extends [3, 9, 13, 18, 20, 22], and implements [3, 22]). Nevertheless, *type information* like the return type of a method [9, 13, 22] or the type of its parameters [9, 13, 22] can be very useful to connect different source code entities as well. Tokens within the names of source code entities are another significant piece of information to consider [6, 12, 18, 20, 37–40] as a way to analyze the issues of diverse vocabulary to describe the same concept or feature, and to match the concrete concepts that developers use when dealing with modification requests versus the high-level concepts used when implementing reusable source-code entities. Other levels of source code information used include comments [38], files [1, 7, 41], types [9,17,22], fields [13,17,30,40], literals [39], signatures [38], contains/instantiates statements [3,4,6,9,13,17,18,20,22], access information [13,17,22,30,39], order of statements [23,37], and changes to source code [1,7,8,41].

Type of Analysis

The simplest kind of analyses are *textual approaches* that process raw source code directly. *Lexical approaches* or token-based techniques transform the code into a sequence of lexical tokens using compiler-style lexical analysis, as in Hipikat and CodeBroker. *Syntactic approaches* convert source code into parse trees or abstract syntax trees and perform their subsequent analyses on those trees, as in FrUiT, Strathcona, RASCAL, and CodeBroker too. *Semantics-aware approaches* perform their analysis at a more semantic level by relying, for example, on dynamic program analysis techniques [1].

Data Requirements

This decision defines any particular constraints on the data for the system to be able to work properly, such as the *programming paradigm* targeted by the system (e.g., object-oriented or procedural) or the *particular programming language* (e.g., Java, Smalltalk, C) supported by the system. This decision is usually taken for pragmatic reasons like being able to compare the results of a SCoReS with another one, which requires being able to analyze the same source code, or being able to use a certain auxiliary tool that can handle the data extraction or data processing.

The most common paradigm analyzed has been object-orientation [4, 13, 23], probably because it is more prevalent in current industrial practice, although a few are limited to the procedural paradigm [17]. However, many of the assumptions made for object-oriented code can be translated to procedural and vice versa. Java seems to be one of the languages most commonly supported by SCoReS [4, 7, 13, 23, 38]. Other languages tackled include C [17] and Smalltalk [18, 20, 21]. Although the choice of the actual implementation language may seem insignificant, dynamically typed languages like Smalltalk may make it easier to quickly prototype (recommendation or other) tools, but on the other hand dynamically typed languages cannot ensure all assumptions made for statically typed languages like Java, for instance, that a method signature can be uniquely linked to a type, that a method returns variables of a particular type, or that its parameters are of a particular type. Similarly, while the name of a method can indicate similar concerns in a language like Java, for languages like Smalltalk (where there is no difference between the name and the signature of a method) such indications are more difficult to validate.

In addition to the language, there may be *other* particular requirements on the data needed by the system, for instance, there should be sufficient example code available that uses a particular API, as is the case for Strathcona, for example.

Intermediate Data Representation

This decision concerns the actual acquisition of the raw data into the most appropriate format for facilitating further processing. Regarding this intermediate format, a SCoReS' designer can choose among *graph-based approaches* [1,9,12,17,22,30] by using, for example, program-dependence or call graphs, *tree-based approaches* [6] that reason about parse trees or other tree structures, approaches like RASCAL or CodeBroker that use *vectors or matrices* as intermediate representation, or *fact-based approaches* like FrUiT, Hipikat, or Strathcona, which organize their data as sets of logic or database facts. Yet other approaches may reason about metrics or simply about some *textual data. Hybrid* approaches combine several of these internal representations.

Graphs and fact bases seem to be among the most popular representations, probably because they provide flexible and well-known mechanisms to find interesting relations, and because these relations can be used to explain the rationale behind a recommendation. Vectors or matrix representations provide high-performance operations while keeping an exact account of the relevant facts. Textual and numeric representations seem less appropriate for SCoReS probably due to the lack of traceability they suffer from. Search-based techniques, for example, usually operate atop matrix or vector representations instead of text representations.

Analysis Technique

The next key decision is the choice of the actual algorithm or *technique* that produces relevant recommendations from the data extracted.

Traditional recommendation techniques are typically based on two sets: the *items* to recommend and the *users* of those items. Recommendation systems aim at matching users to items, by identifying the user's needs or preferences, and then locating the best items that fulfill those needs. To identify the user's need, recommendation techniques can take into account previous ratings of the current user (social tagging), demographic information, features of the items, or the fitness of the items to the current user. Once the matching is done, items can be prioritized by ratings of their users. The combination of these strategy results leads to different kinds of recommendation techniques. RASCAL is a typical example of a SCoReS that relies on a traditional recommendation technique. In Chap. 2, Felfernig et al. [10] provide a more elaborate discussion on traditional recommendation techniques.

In practice, however, unless a SCoReS recommends API calls (*items*) on a large and diverse set of example applications that use the API (*users*), it is often difficult for a SCoReS to rely on traditional recommendation techniques, because the likelihood of having enough users for a given source code entity is small. The most popular analysis techniques used by SCoReS therefore seem to be those that calculate similarities between the input and the rest of the entities analyzed, by using traditional *classification techniques* such as cluster analysis [3, 17, 37], association rule mining [4], and identification of frequent itemsets [3, 41]. Yet other approaches essentially rely on basic [22] or advanced [23, 38] *search techniques*, take inspiration from machine learning techniques or *logic reasoning* [5, 25, 26], or, like Hipikat and Strathcona, rely on heuristics. Heuristics are a popular choice because they can describe the expected similarity among entities that are not related by frequent relations. Among classification techniques, those that are resilient to minor exceptions (like frequent item-set analysis, or association rules) are privileged over those that take into account all information (like formal concept analysis) so that idiosyncratic characteristics that distinguish different source code entities do not disrupt the result. In Chap. 3, Menzies [28] provides a more elaborate discussion on data-mining techniques often used in software engineering and recommendation systems. In Chap. 4, Inozemtseva et al. [14] provide a more elaborate discussion on recommendation systems that rely on heuristics.

Filtering

Filtering (also known as data cleaning) aims to avoid the analysis of code entities that are likely to produce noise in the results (false positives or irrelevant/uninteresting recommendations). Many SCoReS use a two-phase filtering approach. The first phase finds entities or attributes related to the user context. Discarding information in this first phase is also known as *prefiltering*. Examples of prefiltering include using a blacklist of stop words, not including imported libraries, excluding system classes or generated code, etc. The second phase selects the most appropriate results from the first phase. Discarding information in this second phase is called *postfiltering*. Post-filtering aims at eliminating trivial, irrelevant, or wrong recommendations, ordering the remainder by relevance, and presenting only the most appropriate ones.

Filtering is usually done by comparing source code entities or other artifacts to the current context of the developer. This comparison can be done *by similarity* based on some measure of similarity [4, 7, 13, 23, 38], *by frequency* based on the number of occurrences as in FrUiT or Strathcona, or *by rating* based on some scoring mechanism as in CodeBroker or Strathcona. Both prefiltering and postfiltering can be done by using similarity, frequency, or rating information. Frequency is usually a proxy for rating[3] but frequencies tend to be preferred over ratings so that it is possible to provide recommendation even at early stages of the recommendation system (when no ratings have been given yet). Nevertheless, in

---

[3]If something is used by a lot of people, it may be a sign that people like it, and thus that it deserves a good rating.

order to use frequencies it is necessary to have several examples, and that might be one of the reasons for having API support as the preferred task supported by recommendation systems, at the expense of programming tasks and developer's questions [33] that might have more impact on their productivity. Another reason that might explain the few approaches using ratings is that early SCoReS reported them as being intrusive and a source of introducing noise [13]. Nevertheless, ratings can be a good way of collecting data on the usefulness of the approach and to move further toward using traditional recommendation techniques as opposed to mere mining techniques.

5.3.7   Detailed Input/Output

Decisions regarding the detailed input/output concern the detailed information that is required by the SCoReS (usually extracted from the developer's context or explicitly requested) as well as the quantity of results provided by the SCoReS.

Type of Input

In addition to the corpus (Sect. 5.3.4), the builder of a SCoReS needs to decide what additional information the system needs for its analysis. This decision is a refinement of the *input mechanism* and the *nature of the input* decisions described in Sect. 5.3.5.

Whereas some recommendation systems like Hipikat may start from a *search query* given by the user, others may start from a particular *source code entity* (partial implementations, as in Strathcona or RASCAL, or empty implementations, as in CodeBroker), *pairs of entities or artifacts* [6, 8, 9, 22] that need to be mapped in some way, or *sets of entities* [12, 30] that may together represent some higher-level concept.

If the user does not have a clear starting point, some systems allow finding it using any information that can be reached from the information provided, for instance, any identifier or literal in the file currently being edited.

Multiplicity of Output

The quantity of recommendations to be produced by a SCoReS should be chosen with care. Providing concise and accurate results is of utmost importance in the design of recommendation systems. Limiting the results to a reasonable set allows developers to evaluate their appropriateness and value and to choose or discard them accordingly. If a SCoReS produces a *single result* [6], this avoids the burden for the user to select the most relevant result, potentially at the risk of missing other relevant results. When *multiple results* [4, 7, 13, 23, 38] are returned, the burden of selecting the most appropriate ones can be reduced by *prioritizing* them rather than just showing an *unordered* list of results, so that the amount of time spent on evaluating recommendations to find a suitable one is minimized.

5.3.8 Support

This set of decisions focuses on aspects related to the suitability of the recommendations given by a SCoReS, with respect to the task it supports. It helps foresee ways to *validate* how *useful* or *correct* the system is.

Empirical Validation

If the builders of a SCoReS want to evaluate their system beyond example-based argumentation, it is important to decide what kind of empirical validations will be conducted to evaluate their system. Typical ways of validating a SCoReS are case studies (or in-depth analysis of particular applications) [12, 20, 30], benchmarks, and/or *comparisons* with other systems [3, 8, 12, 13, 17], automated simulation of usage of the system [13], comparing the system's results against some kind of *oracle or gold standard* [8, 18, 22], *controlled* experiments with dependent and independent variables [22, 38], or perhaps even a *validation with practitioners* [1,3,6,7,13,22,30, 38] or a field study. In Chaps. 10, 11, 12, and 13, Avazpour et al. [2], Said et al. [32], Walker and Holmes [36], and Tosun Mısırlı et al. [34] (respectively) provide more details on such validation issues.

The most common types of validation include analyzing how developers use the system, or comparison with similar systems. The majority of approaches choose open source systems for their validation. In such cases, it is essential to mention precisely the versions used, to allow for easy replicability of the results of the validation. Also consider whether or not to provide the corpus collected and the results obtained. Giving others access to this information allows them to validate and replicate each argumentation step, and facilitates the construction of benchmarks and simulations. It also offers the possibility to validate if the corpus was correctly built, and to identify differences between recommendations given by different SCoReS using the same corpus.

Usefulness

Validating how relevant a SCoReS is for the task it supports [4, 20, 38] can be done along three axes: assessing whether the SCoReS *enables users to complete a given task* satisfactorily [7, 13, 22], *faster* [22], or with *less intellectual effort*.

Most often, to validate their system, SCoReS builders only conduct a case study to argue how useful the recommendations provided by their system are, but refrain from performing a more *quantitative validation* to provide more empirical support for their claims. Nevertheless, regardless of the type of validation chosen, be aware of the requirements that entail a particular validation choice. For instance, being able to claim satisfactory task achievement requires an unambiguous specification of the task and when it is considered completed. Another example is the need for a valid proxy to assess claims (like intellectual effort). Finally, it is important to be aware that recommendations neglected by a user do not necessarily imply incorrect or invalid recommendations. From our analysis of existing SCoReS and their validation, we believe that there still remain a lot of opportunities for better assessment of the usefulness of recommendation systems.

Correctness

Regarding the quality of the results produced by a SCoReS, typical correctness measurements include precision (percentage of correct recommendations) [7,23,38] and recall (to what extent the recommendations found cover the recommendations needed) [7, 23, 38]. *Relevance* [7, 13, 38] could also be measured but is usually a subjective view of the user, and therefore difficult to gather automatically.

Notice that in order to measure precision or recall, it is necessary to establish *the* correct recommendations to compare against, for each user context. In practice, these ideal correct answers might be unattainable depending on the nature of the recommendations. Moreover, when conducting this type of validation, it is important to be able to argue that the user contexts analyzed are significant examples of typical user contexts.

5.3.9   Interaction

A final set of decisions focuses on how different types of users can interact with the SCoReS. The first type of users are the *developers* that will use the SCoReS as support for their work. Regarding this type of users, it is important to assess how easy it is for them to interact with the SCoReS (usability) and to what extent they can easily get hold of the SCoReS (availability). A second type of users are *researchers* that may want to compare their own approach with the SCoReS. These users are also concerned by the *system's availability* but more importantly by the *data availability* that would allow them to reproduce and compare results.

Usability

Regarding the usability of a SCoReS for its intended end-users (typically, developers), several criteria should be assessed carefully, such as the system's response time (is it sufficiently fast for practical usage?) [1, 6, 17], *conciseness* of the results (are the system's recommendations sufficiently succinct and relevant for the end-user to analyze and use?) [13, 22, 30], *ease of use* (is the system sufficiently easy to use by its intended audience?), and scalability (is the system capable of handling larger software systems?).

Measuring the usability of a SCoReS is not straightforward, however. The easier aspects of usability that could be assessed by measuring are its conciseness or its response time. However, even then, unless the SCoReS's measurements are compared against those of similar systems (which might not be possible), by themselves these measurements may not provide a significant argument to use the SCoReS.

System Availability

This decision describes under what form the system will be made available: as *source code* like with FrUiT, as *binaries* only [8, 9, 12, 30], by providing only a *description* of the system as for Hipikat and Strathcona, or keeping it *unavailable* like with RASCAL and CodeBroker. This decision may vary significantly depending on what the intended goal of the system builders is, for example, whether the SCoReS is a research prototype or a commercial system.

Availability of Recommendation Data

The last decision to consider is whether or not the empirical results of the validation of the SCoReS will be made available. Leaving all produced data public allows other researchers to reproduce the validation, and to compare results between systems. There are several levels of data availability to contemplate. The *corpus* [18] gathered or used by the SCoReS or the *results* [18] produced by the SCoReS on different subject systems could be published with the system or distributed upon request. Finally, the versions of the *subject systems* [4, 7, 13] analyzed could also be stored so that they could easily be used to create benchmarks or to compare the results already gathered for a given SCoReS with latter SCoReS (or future versions of the same SCoReS).

5.4 Building a Code-Based Recommendation System

Having elaborated in Sect. 5.3 on the decision process and design decisions involved in building SCoReS, in this section we walk through a set of SCoReS that we have built and discuss some of the design choices taken throughout their development and evolution. Figure 5.7 summarizes the history of these systems, starting from MEnToR [20] and Clairvoyant, both implemented in the Smalltalk language, via a first prototype of the Mendel system in Smalltalk [18], to its most recent

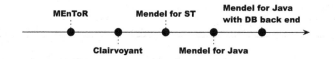

Fig. 5.7 From MEnToR to Mendel

reincarnations for the Java language (see decision 5c in Table 5.2). The case study serves a double purpose: it aims to illustrate the impact that certain design decisions can have but also serves as an illustration of an actual process of building SCoReS. Table 5.2 summarize the key decision choices for three of the systems in our case study (i.e., MEnToR and both the Smalltalk and Java implementation of Mendel). As we walk through the case study, we refer to these tables to highlight the key design choices made. For instance, decision 1a refers to the *Intended user* decision in the *Intent* category of Table 5.2 and we can observe that all systems we developed intend to provide support for software *developers or maintainers*.

The recommendation systems that we built are based on four initial assumptions. First, we assume that source code is the most reliable and most up to date artifact in the software development process. This first assumption motivated us to consider only program code as input (decision 4b) and no complementary information (decision 3b). Furthermore, our SCoReS are particular in the sense that they do not use a corpus consisting of multiple applications but focus on the application under analysis alone to provide their recommendations (decision 3a). Second, we assume that a lot of implicit and undocumented design knowledge somehow gets codified in the source code. More specifically, our third assumption is that they get encoded as coding idioms, naming conventions, and design patterns that tend to be adhered to more or less uniformly across the application code. We refer to such codified design knowledge in the code as "implementation regularities" (decision 1d). Our fourth assumption is then that understanding and maintaining those regularities consistent across the application (decision 1b) is beneficial to a program's comprehensibility and its evolution.

5.4.1   *MEnToR*

The first SCoReS we built upon these assumptions was called MEnToR (which stands for Mining Entities To Rules) [20, 21].

Requirements

MEnToR aims to provide support to make *developers or maintainers* (decision 1a) discover and *understand* relevant *implementation regularities* (decisions 1b and 1d). One problem is that given that implementation regularities are usually implicit, often

Table 5.2 Development decisions for three selected SCoReS

Decisions	MEnToR	Mendel for ST	Mendel for Java
1. Intent			
a. Intended user	Developers or maintainers		
b. Supported task	Understand implementation regularities	Provide code suggestions about implementation regularities	
c. Cognitive support	What are the design decisions hidden in the implementation?	How to implement/improve a source code entity?	
d. Proposed information	Implementation regularities		
2. Human Computer Interaction			
a.Type of system	IDE plugin		
b. Type of recommender	Finder	Advisor	
c. User involvement	Evaluation of final results	Selection of final results	
3. Corpus			
a. Program code	Single application		
b. Complementary information	None		
c. Correlated information	*(not applicable)*		
4. General Input/Output			
a. Input mechanism	User chooses the application to analyze	Implicit: source code entities opened in the IDE's editor	Implicit: source code entities selected in the IDE's editor
b. Nature of input	Source code		
c. Response triggers	Reactive	Proactive	Reactive
d. Nature of output	Textual description and UML-based visualization	Text links	
e. Type of output	Code regularities and entities that match them (or not)	Source code entities to add or modify	
5. Method			
a. Data selection	Identifiers, extends, implements	Identifiers, extends, implements, calls, types, signatures, Protocols[4]	Identifiers, fields declared, methods implemented, interfaces implemented, classes extended, types used, methods called, super calls, exceptions thrown, modifiers

(continued)

Table 5.2 (continued)

Decisions	MEnToR	Mendel for ST	Mendel for Java
b. Type of analysis	Syntactic and lexical		
c. Data requirements	Object-oriented/Smalltalk		Object-oriented/Java
d. Intermediate representation	Fact base		
e. Analysis technique	Association rule mining	Heuristics	
f. Filtering	By confidence, by support, using structural and heuristic filters	By similarity (family), by frequency (dominant/ recessive recommendations), by rating	By similarity (family) and by frequency (dominant/recessive recommendations)
6. Detailed Input/Output			
a. Type of input	Application to analyze	Source code entities in focus	
b. Multiplicity of output	Multiple results prioritized		
7. Support			
a. Empirical validation	Two case studies	Five comparisons against an oracle (simulation of SCoReS usage)	One comparison against an oracle (recommendations implemented during evolution of the subject system)
b. Usefulness	Less intellectual effort	Quantitative validations: complete code	
c. Correctness	Relevance	Precision and recall	
8. Interaction			
a. Usability	Concise results	Concise results, ease of use, scalability	
b. System availability	Unavailable	Source code	Unavailable
c. Data availability	None	Corpus, results, subject systems	Subject system

they are not perfectly adhered to. This observation led us to establish some initial requirements for MEnToR. First of all, the underlying mining technique chosen had to be robust toward slight deviations. A technique tolerant to irregularities but still capable of *finding* (decision 2b) relevant implementation regularities was necessary to reduce false positives and false negatives. Second, in order to be useful for developers, we wanted MEnToR's results to be concise (decision 8). Indeed,

---

[4]*Protocols* are tags used in Smalltalk to indicate the role of a method and can also be regarded as indicators of the interface that a method implements.

previous experiences with using techniques such as formal concept analysis to mine source code for regularities [24, 27, 35] taught us that due to redundancy and noise, the amount of results produced by such techniques was often too prohibitive to be usable in practice. Having few and unique results facilitates the adoption of the SCoReS by developers because it does not require much extra effort for analyzing the final results (decision 2c). Third, the result should indicate the intention or design decision behind the discovered regularities. The system needs to provide the developers with clues to let them understand the rationale of *why* certain source code entities are involved in some regularity (decision 1c).

Approach

To fulfill these requirements, MEnToR performs association rule mining (decision 5e) from diverse implementation characteristics (decision 5a) of the *application analyzed*, which is given as input by the user (decisions 4a and 6a). MEnToR's approach bears a lot of resemblance with FrUiT (see Sect. 5.2.2), which mines association rules that represent structural relations in the source code of applications that use a given framework.

A concrete example of a rule found by MEnToR is:

$$Id : \text{`Collection'} \xrightarrow{75\%} H : \texttt{SequenceableCollection}$$

which indicates that 75 % of the classes that have the keyword "Collection" in their name also belong to the hierarchy of class SequenceableCollection. Other characteristics taken into account (decision 5a) are the methods implemented. Note that, given that the set of classes that belong to the hierarchy of Sequenceable Collection and the set of classes that have the word "Collection" in their name overlap, the following association rule could be mined as well:

$$H : \texttt{SequenceableCollection} \xrightarrow{60\%} Id : \text{`Collection'}$$

However, to reduce redundancy in the results, after post-filtering (decision 5f) MEnToR would report only the first rule, because it has a higher confidence. Furthermore, in order to discover more high-level design decisions that are more concise (decision 8) and require less effort to understand (decision 7b), MEnToR also merges different association rules that affect an overlapping set of source code entities into single, higher-level, regularities. But before merging association rules into regularities, they are first filtered (decision 5f) to eliminate rules that are too trivial or that have too low confidence. An example of a trivial rule is that all classes in the hierarchy of a subclass are also in the hierarchy of its super-class, while a rule with low confidence represents either very few entities or has a minimal overlap between characteristics. MEnToR also filters other information that can produce noise before and after calculating the regularities. Before calculating association rules (prefiltering), MEnToR eliminates from the analysis source code entities that are likely to be too generic (like the class Object) as well as implementation characteristics that are very common (like the keyword "get" that appears in many method names). After calculating the regularities, MEnToR then prioritizes them (decision 6b) by amount of entities they cover, by amount of implementation characteristics shared by those entities, and by taking into account the rating given previously to the regularity by other developers.

MEnToR is implemented as an IDE plugin (decision 2a) that performs its analysis upon explicit request by the user (decision 4c). Every time a reported association rule or regularity is selected, MEnToR updates a view showing the source code entities that respect the rule, as well as some of those that do not respect it but should, together with the characteristics that those entities do and do not share (decision 4e). This view helps developers in better understanding the regularities and how well they are adhered to in the code. Although the discovered rules are essentially shown in textual format, they can also be visualized as a UML diagram that marks with different colors the entities that respect the rule and those that do not, thus giving a visual clue of the extent of the rule and its deviations (decision 4d).

Limitations

As useful as MEnToR could seem, after an initial validation on two case studies (decision 7a) we realized two main flaws of MEnToR. The first one was that it still required too much user involvement to evaluate the relevance of the discovered rules and regularities (decisions 2c and 7c). The system was showing relevant regularities to increase the user's awareness of hidden design decisions in the code, even if the user was already aware of those regularities and even if they were perfectly respected by the code (in practice, the user was often more interested in those entities that were breaking the rules). As such, the system was not giving actionable information to the user. For those cases where a regularity was not perfectly respected, even though the system highlighted those implementation characteristics that a source code entity was missing according to that regularity, the association rules were often too verbose and it was difficult for the user to assess how to use that information to improve code quality.

A second issue was that although MEnToR could show a developer whether or not a source code entity that was currently selected in the IDE lacked certain implementation characteristics, MEnToR did not cope well with the evolution of the application. Each time even a small change was made to the application, the fact base (decision 5d) of implementation characteristics could change and the association rule mining algorithm (as well as all subsequent processing) needed to be re-triggered for the entire application, possibly leading to slightly different rules and regularities.

To solve the first issue, we developed a new front-end for MEnToR called Clairvoyant. To solve the second issue, we developed an entirely new SCoReS using a different technique inspired by a closer analysis of MEnToR's results.

5.4.2 From MEnToR to Clairvoyant

Clairvoyant is a new front-end for MEnToR that, depending on the adherence of the source code entity in focus in the IDE to a rule, provides more actionable information to the developer. Rather than seeing association rules as implications, we can also regard them as overlapping sets of entities that satisfy different characteristics. For example, the association rule

$$Id : \text{`Collection'} \xrightarrow{75\%} H : \text{SequenceableCollection}$$

can be seen as two overlapping sets: the set of all classes that have the key-word 'Collection' in their name and the set of all classes in the hierarchy of SequenceableCollection, where 75 % of the entities in the first set also belong to the second set. We call the first set the *antecedent* of the rule, the second set its *consequent*, and the intersection of both sets the *matches*. Clairvoyant will flag an implementation characteristic as a likely *error* if the source code entity in focus is part of the antecedent but not part of the matches, as *satisfied* if the entity is part of the matching set, and as an implementation *suggestion* if the entity is part of the consequent but not part of the matches. Moreover, every time we click on a recommendation, Clairvoyant updates a view showing the matching source code entities as well as those that are in the antecedent but not in the consequent. Although Clairvoyant improved the appreciation of the system by developers, the fact that their changes were not reflected in the output of the system as soon as they made them, but still required the recalculation of all recommendations, made it an unrealistic system to support software developers and maintainers.

5.4.3 From Clairvoyant to Mendel

Mendel was developed to provide code suggestions about implementation reg-ularities (decision 1b) to developers or maintainers (decision 1a) continuously (decision 4c). That is, as soon as some code entity is changed, Mendel would update its recommendations. However, Mendel also aimed at tackling three shortcomings in the results proposed by Clairvoyant. A first shortcoming is the amount of noise produced. Although developers showed an interest in the suggestions and errors recommended by Clairvoyant, some rules are redundant. Often, Clairvoyant finds regularities that are very similar to, or even subsets of, other regularities. In such cases, it is difficult to choose automatically which of those regularities make more sense to recommend or which are most informative while minimizing noisy information. Noisy information could be caused, amongst others, by imple-mentation characteristics that are part of the regularity by accident, for example, because all entities sharing an important characteristic also happen to share a less relevant characteristic. What recommendation is perceived as "best" may vary from one developer to another. Second, some regularities are accidental (e.g., "accidental polymorphism" when a bunch of methods have the same name even though they do not implement a similar behavior) whereas others are essential and capture entities implementing a similar concept, naming and coding conventions, or important protocols and usage-patterns among entities. Third, the relevance of what implementation characteristics to consider may depend on the type of source code entity analyzed (e.g., reasoning in detail about the instructions contained in method bodies may be more relevant when providing method-level recommendations than when providing class-level recommendations).

To overcome some of these problems, we decided to build a new SCoReS called Mendel. Mendel is based on the concept of "family" of a source code entity. The concept of family aims at eliminating regularities found by chance. Entities belonging to a same family are more likely to share implementation characteristics that indicate essential design decisions. Given that many of the relevant regularities recommended by MEnToR/Clairvoyant described entities belonging to a same class hierarchy, we compute the family of class by taking the direct superclass of that selected class and return all of this superclass' direct subclasses, as well as the subclasses of these direct subclasses, except for the class analyzed (the class analyzed is excluded from the family). In other words, the family of a class is its siblings and nieces. The family of a method is defined as all methods with the same name that are in the family of its class.

The characteristics analyzed for a source code entity depend on its type. For methods, Mendel takes into account methods called, the method protocol, super-calls, referred types, and the AST structure. For classes, Mendel takes into account the keywords appearing in their name, implemented methods, and types used. These characteristics were chosen because they provide useful information to developers or maintainers to improve their code (decision 1c). Based on Mendel's metaphor of a family's genetic heritage, the characteristics of a source code entity are called *traits*. The traits chosen were not exhaustive and we aimed to explore different characteristics depending on the obtained results. Finally, the frequency of occurrence of an implementation characteristic in the family indicates the likelihood of that characteristic being relevant. Therefore, we call implementation characteristics shared by the majority of the family, the *dominant* traits of the family, while those that are shared by at least half of the members of the family (and that are not dominant) are called the *recessive* traits of the family. Dominant traits are shown as "must" recommendations while recessive traits are shown as "may" recommendations.

Both Mendel and Clairvoyant prioritize suggestions (decision 6b). The key suggestions in Mendel are the dominant traits, which correspond to the likely errors in Clairvoyant, while the recommendations with lower confidence are the recessive traits in Mendel, which correspond to the suggestions in Clairvoyant.

Mendel's initial validation consisted of simulating Mendel's usage with a partial implementation. For each source code entity (i.e., class or method), the simulator temporarily removed its implementation (leaving only an empty declaration), asked Mendel for recommendations, and compared Mendel's recommendation with the entity that was removed. We ran such a simulation over five open source systems of different domains (decision 7a) and showed that Mendel proposed a limited amount of recommendations that were calculated quickly in real time (decision 8). We also concluded that at least half of the proposed recommendations were correct, and that Mendel discovered 50–75 % of missing traits (decision 7c).

The concept of family had two purposes: reducing the set of entities analyzed to give a recommendation so that the system could be responsive to source code changes "on the fly" and reducing noise in the recommendations. As expected, Mendel's results are sensitive to the size of the family, which in turn depends on the depth and width of hierarchies in the analyzed software system. Moreover, manual inspection of some of the proposed recommendations indicated that the definition of family might not be the most appropriate one for all types of implementation characteristics.

We also did not manage to conduct a study with real developers, mainly because of the chosen programming language (decision 5c). Although in research labs where Mendel was conceived a few researchers were Smalltalk programmers and could thus have been invited as participants in a user study, it turned out that most of them had recently switched to another Smalltalk IDE (namely Pharo), making the first version of Mendel irrelevant (it was implemented in and integrated with VisualWorks Smalltalk). Therefore, Mendel was ported to Pharo. However, it then turned out that those developers who were willing to be part of our user study were working on very small Smalltalk applications only, which would have resulted into too small families without dominant traits. For these reasons, we decided to port Mendel to the Java programming language.

5.4.4 Porting Mendel from Smalltalk to Java

In addition to expanding the potential user base of our system (for purposes of validation, among others), our port of Mendel to Java had another goal. While porting it, we decided to extend it to be able to experiment with different alternative definitions of family, for recommending different implementation characteristics. For example, for a family of classes it could be more interesting to look at class-related characteristics such as inheritance, whereas for a family of methods it could be more interesting too look at method-related characteristics such as message sends. One of our master students thus implemented a prototype of an Eclipse plugin that supported several definitions of family, and storing the user rating of recommendations so that recommendations could be prioritized depending on how useful they had been for other developers.

As was already the case for the Smalltalk version, Mendel was designed to reduce the amount of computation needed for proposing recommendations and being capable of updating the recommendations "on the fly" as soon as any change took place in the source code. An important performance problem was encountered to conduct automated validations, however. In order to validate and compare the recommendations given by different family definitions, it would be necessary to calculate the implementation characteristics for each family member, for each family definition, for each source code entity, and this on each application analyzed. This approach proved to be very inefficient because it would recalculate the implementation characteristics several times for each source code entity. A more efficient approach therefore would be to calculate all implementation characteristics of each source code entity only once beforehand, and only then study the effect of choosing a different family definition. That was the motivation for implementing the latest version of Mendel: Mendel with a database storage back-end.

5.4.5   *Adding a Database Storage Back-End to Mendel*

Several existing Java code repositories were considered to study the effect of Mendel's family definitions on the quality of its recommendations. None of them, however, offered the level of detail Mendel required, while at the same time containing several versions of the code. The reason why we wanted to have several versions of the same systems being analyzed was because of the particular set-up of the validation we had in mind. Inspired by the kind of automated validation we conducted for the Smalltalk version of Mendel, we now wanted to validate whether a recommendation for a given source code entity in some version of a software system was relevant, not by first removing it and then checking it against itself, but rather by checking if it would actually be implemented in a later version of that system (and how many versions it took before that recommendation actually got implemented). To have the necessary information to conduct that experiment, we implemented another Eclipse plugin to gather all implementation characteristics of all source-code entities for all versions of all systems to be analyzed, and stored these as structural facts in a database. We then experimented with and compared different alternative definitions of families to assess if they gave rise to significant differences in precision and recall per type of implementation characteristic on which the family definition was based. Although more experimentation is still needed, partial results of this analysis indicate that the choice of family definition indeed affects the correctness of the results (depending on the type of recommended characteristic) and that families should probably not be described by a single implementation characteristic, but rather by a combination of different characteristics (as MEnToR's regularities did).

5.5   Conclusion

This chapter provided a brief overview of existing source code-based recommendation systems, including some we built. This overview illustrated the large variety of decision points and alternatives when building a source code-based recommendation system. We used this overview to highlight some of the key design decisions involved in building such systems. We organized these decisions along eight main categories, which were divided along two orthogonal dimensions. One dimension corresponds more or less to the development life cycle of the system, ranging from the elaboration of its requirements, through its design and implementation, to its validation. The other dimension focused either on the underlying approach or on how the user interacts with the system. Regarding the approach, the main categories of design decisions to address are related to the intent of the system, the corpus of data it uses to provide its recommendations, the underlying recommendation method it uses, and how to validate how well the system supports the task it aims to provide recommendations for. Regarding the user interaction, the design decisions that need to be taken involve how the end user is expected to interact with the system, at different levels of detail. We also suggested a waterfall-like process in which to address all these decisions, but this process should not be regarded as restrictive. The design decisions could be visited in any other order that best fits the needs of the system builder. Our main message, however, is that it is important to address all these design decisions carefully and up front because, as we had to learn, making the wrong decision can have a significant impact on the quality and perceived or actual usefulness of the developed system. This set of key design decisions can also offer a useful frame of reference against which to compare different systems, to understand why one system is better, worse, or simply different from another one, or to steer the development of one's own system to better suit certain needs. In any case, we hope that our set of design decisions and proposed process can be of use to guide unexperienced builders of source code-based recommendation systems in making them ask the right questions at the right time.

References

1. Ashok, B., Joy, J., Liang, H., Rajamani, S.K., Srinivasa, G., Vangala, V.: DebugAdvisor: A recommender system for debugging. In: Proceedings of the European Software Engineering Conference/ACM SIGSOFT International Symposium on Foundations of Software Engineering, pp. 373–382 (2009). doi: 10.1145/1595696.1595766
2. Avazpour, I., Pitakrat, T., Grunske, L., Grundy, J.: Dimensions and metrics for evaluating recommendation systems. In: Robillard, M., Maalej, W., Walker, R.J., Zimmermann, T. (eds.) Recommendation Systems in Software Engineering, Chap. 10. Springer, New York (2014)
3. Bruch, M., Monperrus, M., Mezini, M.: Learning from examples to improve code completion systems. In: Proceedings of the European Software Engineering Conference/ACM SIGSOFT International Symposium on Foundations of Software Engineering, pp. 213–222 (2009). doi: 10.1145/1595696.1595728
4. Bruch, M., Schäfer, T., Mezini, M.: FrUiT: IDE support for framework understanding. In: Proceedings of the Eclipse Technology eXchange, pp. 55–59 (2006). doi: 10.1145/1188835.1188847
5. Castro, S., De Roover, C., Kellens, A., Lozano, A., Mens, K., D'Hondt, T.: Diagnosing and correcting design inconsistencies in source code with logical abduction. Sci. Comput. Program. 76(12), 1113–1129 (2011). doi: 10.1016/j.scico.2010.09.001
6. Cottrell, R., Walker, R.J., Denzinger, J.: Semi-automating small-scale source code reuse via structural correspondence. In: Proceedings of the ACM SIGSOFT International Symposium

on Foundations of Software Engineering, pp. 214–225 (2008). doi: 10.1145/1453101.1453130
7. Čubranić, D., Murphy, G.C., Singer, J., Booth, K.S.: Hipikat: A project memory for software development. IEEE Trans. Software Eng. **31**(6), 446–465 (2005). doi: 10.1109/TSE.2005.71
8. Dagenais, B., Robillard, M.P.: Recommending adaptive changes for framework evolution. ACM Trans. Software Eng. Meth. **20**(4), 19:1–19:35 (2011). doi: 10.1145/2000799.2000805
9. Duala-Ekoko, E., Robillard, M.P.: Using structure-based recommendations to facilitate discoverability in APIs. In: Proceedings of the European Conference on Object-Oriented Programming, pp. 79–104 (2011). doi: 10.1007/978-3-642-22655-7_5
10. Felfernig, A., Jeran, M., Ninaus, G., Reinfrank, F., Reitererand, S., Stettinger, M.: Basic approaches in recommendation systems. In: Robillard, M., Maalej, W., Walker, R.J., Zimmermann, T. (eds.) Recommendation Systems in Software Engineering, Chap. 2. Springer, New York (2014)
11. German, D.M., Čubranić, D., Storey, M.A.D.: A framework for describing and understanding mining tools in software development. In: Proceedings of the International Workshop on Mining Software Repositories, pp. 7:1–7:5 (2005). doi: 10.1145/1082983.1083160
12. Hill, E., Pollock, L., Vijay-Shanker, K.: Exploring the neighborhood with Dora to expedite software maintenance. In: Proceedings of the IEEE/ACM International Conference on Automated Software Engineering, pp. 14–23 (2007). doi: 10.1145/1321631.1321637
13. Holmes, R., Walker, R.J., Murphy, G.C.: Approximate structural context matching: An approach to recommend relevant examples. IEEE Trans. Software Eng. **32**(12), 952–970 (2006). doi: 10.1109/TSE.2006.117
14. Inozemtseva, L., Holmes, R., Walker, R.J.: Recommendation systems in-the-small. In: Robillard, M., Maalej, W., Walker, R.J., Zimmermann, T. (eds.) Recommendation Systems in Software Engineering, Chap. 4. Springer, New York (2014)
15. Kersten, M., Murphy, G.C.: Mylar: A degree-of-interest model for IDEs. In: Proceedings of the International Conference on Aspect-Oriented Software Deveopment, pp. 159–168 (2005). doi: 10.1145/1052898.1052912
16. Li, Z., Zhou, Y.: PR-Miner: Automatically extracting implicit programming rules and detecting violations in large software code. In: Proceedings of the European Software Engineering Conference/ACM SIGSOFT International Symposium on Foundations of Software Engineering, pp. 306–315 (2005). doi: 10.1145/1081706.1081755
17. Long, F., Wang, X., Cai, Y.: API hyperlinking via structural overlap. In: Proceedings of the European Software Engineering Conference/ACM SIGSOFT International Symposium on Foundations of Software Engineering, pp. 203–212 (2009). doi: 10.1145/1595696.1595727
18. Lozano, A., Kellens, A., Mens, K.: Mendel: Source code recommendation based on a genetic metaphor. In: Proceedings of the IEEE/ACM International Conference on Automated Software Engineering, pp. 384–387 (2011). doi: 10.1109/ASE.2011.6100078
19. Lozano, A., Kellens, A., Mens, K.: Usage contracts: Offering immediate feedback on violations of structural source-code regularities. Sci. Comput. Program. (2013). Under review
20. Lozano, A., Kellens, A., Mens, K., Arévalo, G.: MEntoR: Mining entities to rules. In: Proceedings of the Belgian–Netherlands Evolution Workshop (2010a)
21. Lozano, A., Kellens, A., Mens, K., Arévalo, G.: Mining source code for structural regularities. In: Proceedings of the Working Conference on Reverse Engineering, pp. 22–31 (2010b). doi: 10.1109/WCRE.2010.12
22. Mandelin, D., Xu, L., Bodík, R., Kimelman, D.: Jungloid mining: Helping to navigate the API jungle. In: Proceedings of the ACM SIGPLAN Conference on Programming Language Design and Implementation, pp. 48–61 (2005). doi: 10.1145/1065010.1065018
23. McCarey, F., Ó Cinnéide, M., Kushmerick, N.: RASCAL: A recommender agent for agile reuse. Artif. Intell. Rev. **24**(3–4), 253–276 (2005). doi: 10.1007/s10462-005-9012-8
24. Mens, K., Kellens, A., Krinke, J.: Pitfalls in aspect mining. In: Proceedings of the Working Conference on Reverse Engineering, pp. 113–122 (2008). doi: 10.1109/WCRE.2008.10
25. Mens, K., Kellens, A., Pluquet, F., Wuyts, R.: Co-evolving code and design with intensional views: A case study. Comput. Lang. Syst. Struct. **32**(2–3), 140–156 (2006). doi: 10.1016/j.cl.2005.09.002

26. Mens, K., Michiels, I., Wuyts, R.: Supporting software development through declaratively codified programming patterns. Expert Syst. Appl. **23**(4), 405–431 (2002). doi: 10.1016/S0957-4174(02)00076-3
27. Mens, K., Tourwé, T.: Delving source code with formal concept analysis. Comput. Lang. Syst. Struct. **31**(3–4), 183–197 (2005). doi: 10.1016/j.cl.2004.11.004
28. Menzies, T.: Data mining: A tutorial. In: Robillard, M., Maalej, W., Walker, R.J., Zimmermann, T. (eds.) Recommendation Systems in Software Engineering, Chap. 3. Springer, New York (2014)
29. Murphy-Hill, E., Murphy, G.C.: Recommendation delivery: Getting the user interface just right. In: Robillard, M., Maalej, W., Walker, R.J., Zimmermann, T. (eds.) Recommendation Systems in Software Engineering, Chap. 9. Springer, New York (2014)
30. Robillard, M.P.: Topology analysis of software dependencies. ACM Trans. Software Eng. Meth. **17**(4), 18:1–18:36 (2008). doi: 10.1145/13487689.13487691
31. Robillard, M.P., Walker, R.J., Zimmermann, T.: Recommendation systems for software engineering. IEEE Software **27**(4), 80–86 (2010). doi: 10.1109/MS.2009.161
32. Said, A., Tikk, D., Cremonesi, P.: Benchmarking: A methodology for ensuring the relative quality of recommendation systems in software engineering. In: Robillard, M., Maalej, W., Walker, R.J., Zimmermann, T. (eds.) Recommendation Systems in Software Engineering, Chap. 11. Springer, New York (2014)
33. Sillito, J., Murphy, G.C., De Volder, K.: Asking and answering questions during a programming change task. IEEE Trans. Software Eng. **34**(4), 434–451 (2008). doi: 10.1109/TSE.2008.26
34. Tosun Mısırlı, A., Bener, A., Çağlayan, B., Çalıklı, G., Turhan, B.: Field studies: A methodology for construction and evaluation of recommendation systems in software engineering. In: Robillard, M., Maalej, W., Walker, R.J., Zimmermann, T. (eds.) Recommendation Systems in Software Engineering, Chap. 13. Springer, New York (2014)
35. Tourwé, T., Mens, K.: Mining aspectual views using formal concept analysis. In: Proceedings of the IEEE International Workshop on Source Code Analysis and Manipulation, pp. 97–106 (2004). doi: 10.1109/SCAM.2004.15
36. Walker, R.J., Holmes, R.: Simulation: A methodology to evaluate recommendation systems in software engineering. In: Robillard, M., Maalej, W., Walker, R.J., Zimmermann, T. (eds.) Recommendation Systems in Software Engineering, Chap. 12. Springer, New York (2014)
37. Xie, T., Pei, J.: MAPO: Mining API usages from open source repositories. In: Proceedings of the International Workshop on Mining Software Repositories, pp. 54–57 (2006). doi: 10.1145/1137983.1137997
38. Ye, Y., Fischer, G.: Reuse-conducive development environments. Automat. Software Eng. Int. J. **12**(2), 199–235 (2005). doi: 10.1007/s10515-005-6206-x
39. Zhang, C., Yang, J., Zhang, Y., Fan, J., Zhang, X., Zhao, J., Ou, P.: Automatic parameter recommendation for practical API usage. In: Proceedings of the ACM/IEEE International Conference on Software Engineering, pp. 826–836 (2012). doi: 10.1109/ICSE.2012.6227136
40. Zhong, H., Thummalapenta, S., Xie, T., Zhang, L., Wang, Q.: Mining API mapping for language migration. In: Proceedings of the ACM/IEEE International Conference on Software Engineering, vol. 1, pp. 195–204 (2010). doi: 10.1145/1806799.1806831
41. Zimmermann, T., Weißgerber, P., Diehl, S., Zeller, A.: Mining version histories to guide software changes. IEEE Trans. Software Eng. **31**(6), 429–445 (2005). doi: 10.1109/TSE.2005.72

Chapter 6
Mining Bug Data

A Practitioner's Guide

Kim Herzig and Andreas Zeller

Abstract Although software systems control many aspects of our daily life world, no system is perfect. Many of our day-to-day experiences with computer programs are related to software bugs. Although software bugs are very unpopular, empirical software engineers and software repository analysts rely on bugs or at least on those bugs that get reported to issue management systems. So what makes data software repository analysts appreciate bug reports? Bug reports are development artifacts that relate to code quality and thus allow us to reason about code quality, and quality is key to reliability, end-users, success, and finally profit. This chapter serves as a hand-on tutorial on how to mine bug reports, relate them to source code, and use the knowledge of bug fix locations to model, estimate, or even predict source code quality. This chapter also discusses risks that should be addressed before one can achieve reliable recommendation systems.

6.1 Introduction

A central human quality is that we can *learn from our mistakes*: While we may not be able to avoid new errors, we can at least learn from the past to make sure the same mistakes are not made again. This makes software bugs and their corresponding bug reports an important and frequently mined source for recommendation systems that make suggestions on how to improve the quality and reliability of a software project or process. To predict, rate, or classify the quality of code artifacts (e.g., source files or binaries) or code changes, it is necessary to learn which factors influence code quality. Bug databases—repositories filled with issue reports filed by end users and developers—are one of the most important sources for this data. These reports of open and fixed code quality issues make rare and valuable assets.

K. Herzig (✉) • A. Zeller
Saarland University, Saarbrücken, Germany
e-mail: herzig@cs.uni-saarland.de; zeller@cs.uni-saarland.de

M.P. Robillard et al. (eds.), *Recommendation Systems in Software Engineering*,
DOI 10.1007/978-3-642-45135-5__6, © Springer-Verlag Berlin Heidelberg 2014

In this chapter we discuss the techniques, chances, and perils of mining bug reports that can be used to build a recommender system that suggests quality. Such systems can predict the quality of code elements. This information may help to prioritize resources such as testing and code reviews. In order to build such a recommendation system, one has to first understand the available content of issue repositories (Sects. 6.2) and its correctness (Sect. 6.3). The next important step is to link bug reports to changes, in order to get a quality indicator, for example, a count of bugs per code artifact. There are many aspects that can lead to incorrect counts, such as bias, noise, and errors in the data (Sect. 6.4). Once the data has been collected, a prediction model can be built using code metrics (Sect. 6.5). The chapter closes with a hands-on tutorial on how to mine bug data and predict bugs using open-source data mining software (Sect. 6.6).

6.2   Structure and Quality of Bug Reports

Let us start with a brief overview discussing the anatomy and quality of bug reports. We will then present common practices on mining bug data along with a critical discussion on bug mining steps, their consequences, and possible impacts on approaches based on these bug mining approaches.

6.2.1   Anatomy of a Bug Report

In general, a bug report contains information about an *observed misbehavior* or *issue* regarding a software project. In order to fix the problem, the developer requires information to reproduce, locate, and finally fix the underlying issue. This information should be part of the bug report.

To provide some guidance and to enforce that certain information be given by a bug reporter, a bug report is usually structured as a *form* containing multiple required and optional fields. A bug report can thus be seen as a collection of *fields* dedicated to inform developers and readers about particular bug properties. The value of each field usually classifies the observed issue with respect to a given property or contributes to the description or discussion of the underlying issue. Figure 6.1 shows the structure of a typical bug report. Fields include the following:

- Information on the *product*, version, and *environment* tell developers on which project and in which environment the issue occurs.
- The *description* typically contains instructions to reproduce the issue (and to compare one's observations against the reported ones).
- Fields such as *issue type* (from feature request to bug report), *assignee*, and *priority* help management to direct which bug gets fixed by whom and when.

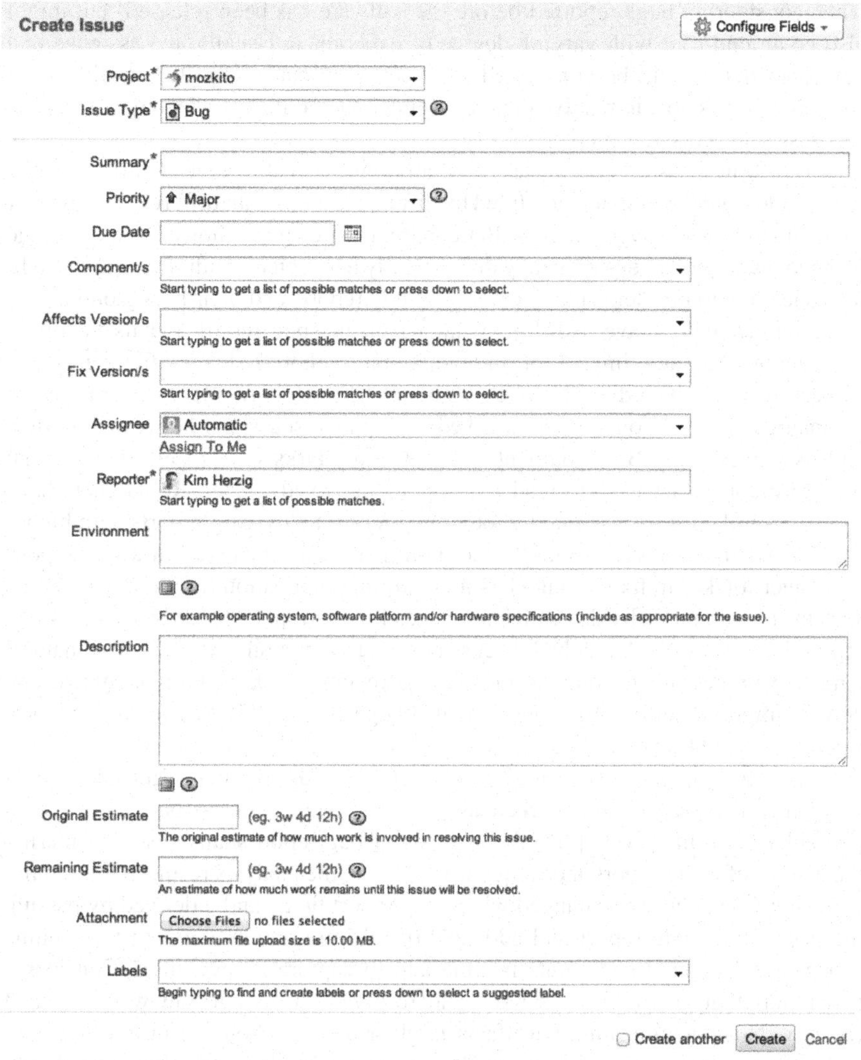

Fig. 6.1 Sample bug report and common bug report fields to be filled out when creating a new bug report

Typically, bug reports allow discussion about a particular issue. This discussion can but may not include the reporter. Comments on bug reports usually start with questions about an issue and the request of developers to provide additional information [15]. Later, many comments are dedicated to discussions between developers on possible fixes and solutions. This shows that bug-tracking systems should be seen primarily as a *communication platform*—first between bug *reporters* and *developers*, later between developers themselves. The reporter is usually the person that observed and reported the problem. She can be a developer (especially when considering bugs reported before the software has been released) but might also be an end-user with varying degree of experience. Usually, the assignee is a developer that should be considered an expert who can verify the validity of an issue and knows how to resolve the underlying issue or at least which developer the report should be assigned to.

When mining issue repositories, it is important to realize that the different bug report fields and their content are filled by different groups with different expertise or following different usage patterns. Bettenburg and Begel [8] showed that the usage of issue management systems may differ greatly between individual teams and subteams leading to problems in understanding bug reports and their background.

Individual fields have a different impact on the bug report and its handling. The importance and impact of individual bug report fields is frequently the subject of research studies. There exists a large degree of regularity on bug report summaries [35] and on questions asked in report discussions between reporters and assignees [15]. Bettenburg et al. [10] and Marks et al. [39] showed that well formulated and easy to read bug reports get fixed sooner. Researchers have shown a similar effect dedicated to other bug report fields. Bug reports with higher priority get fixed quicker [39, 46]; the more people are involved in a bug report, the longer it takes to fix the bug [1]—an important motivation for recommendation systems to automatically determine assignees for bug reports [3, 28, 40, 53]. As bug report descriptions and attached discussions contain natural text, the use of natural language processing becomes more and more important. Natural language can contain important information about related bug severity [37], bug reports [58, 64], affected code [34, 55], etc.

Bug reports evolve over time: Fields get updated, comments get added, and eventually they should be marked as resolved. Thus, mining bug reports at a particular point in time implies the analysis of bug report snapshots. Considering the history of a bug report and frequently updating the analysis results is important. Knowing when and who changed which bug report field can be derived by parsing the history of a bug report and adds additional information allowing to examine a bug report of previous points in time and to capture its evolution. Consider a bug report that got marked as fixed and resolved weeks ago but was reopened recently. Not updating mined artifacts might leave data sources in a misleading state: bug reports once marked as resolved and fixed might be reopened and should be considered unresolved until being marked as resolved again.

It is also common to use values of bug report fields as criteria to filter bug reports of particular interest. To determine code artifacts that were changed in order to fix a bug (see Sect. 6.4), bug data analysts usually consider only bug reports marked as fixed and resolved, or closed [4, 22, 69]. Reports with other statuses and resolutions indicate that the reported issue is either not addressed, has been reopened, or is invalid; thus, the set of changed artifacts is incomplete or might contain false positives. The priority field is often used to filter out trivial bug reports and to restrict the analysis to severe bug reports [18] while fields dedicated to project revisions are frequently used to distinguish between pre- and post-release bugs [12, 52, 69]—bugs filed before or after a product was released.

> When mining bug data,
>
> • Identify the semantics of the individual fields
> • Identify the individuals who fill out the fields
> • Use only reports that match your researches (e.g., closed and fixed bugs)

6.2.2 Influence of Bug-Tracking Systems

In general, all bug reports, independent from their origin, share the purpose of documenting program issues. But individual bug-tracking systems and development processes reflect and create *individual process patterns and philosophies*. Thus, it is important to understand that bug reports across different teams and projects should be considered different, although the differences can be small. But it is essential to identify these small differences as they are important to determine how bug reports get created, handled, used, and finally resolved. Thus, bug-tracking systems impact bug report content.

Depending on the goal of an issue repository analyst, bug-tracking and bug report differences might be relevant or irrelevant. In this section, we briefly discuss important aspects when targeting code quality-related recommendation systems:

Default Values. Creating a new bug report usually requires the bug reporter to fill out a form similar to the one shown in Fig. 6.1. These forms usually populate specific fields (e.g., bug type, bug severity) with default values. These values commonly reflect the typical setting or expected default setting but also help non-expert end-users to fill out all required fields. The drawback is that reporters tend to fill out only those fields that are required and not already set, thus default values can influence the values chosen by reporters [59]. Consequently, the configuration of the issue-tracking system defining which default values to be set may already impact the content of bug reports.

Report Types. Most bug-tracking systems allow not only bug reports but also other types of issues, such as feature requests, improvements, or tasks. Bug-tracking systems have different mechanisms to allow reporters to distinguish between these report types. A good example is the difference between Bugzilla and Jira, two commonly used bug tracking systems. In their standard configurations, Bugzilla supports only bug reports but allows the user to mark reports as enhancement requests using the severity field. In contrast, the Jira tracker not only supports bug and enhancement reports as full types but also offers report types like "task" and "improvement":

• To file an enhancement request instead of a bug report in Jira, the reporter has to set the field issue type accordingly.
• To perform the same task in Bugzilla, the reporter has to set the severity field choosing the value enhancement.

This unusual mechanism in Bugzilla has two consequences:

- To distinguish between bug reports and enhancement requests, we have to analyze the severity field and not the issue report type.
- Bugzilla does not allow the distinction between high and low severe enhancement requests.

This distinction between bug reports and enhancement requests might also leave many enhancement requests filed as bug reports. Unexperienced reporters might not know to use the severity field to file an enhancement request and relying on the default severity value will automatically mark a report as bug.

Ambiguous Terms.   Many fields offer ambiguous terms and vague definitions. In the default configuration, Bugzilla marks bug reports as enhancement requests using the severity field (see above). But the term "enhancement" is ambiguous. Fixing a bug can be seen as an enhancement or improvement but software repository analysts would like to see bug fixes being classified as "bug." It is up to the bug data analyst whether to mark Bugzilla enhancements as feature request, improvement, or any other issue report type. But no matter how he decides, he will most likely end up with noise due to misclassification.

Missing Fields.   Bug-tracking systems like Google tracker or SourceForge lack common bug report fields. These fields (e.g., report type, report priority, and affected product) are managed by *labels* instead of explicitly given fields. The advantage is that no default values exist. The disadvantage is that bringing Bugzilla and Google reports to a uniform object model requires detailed knowledge about possible fields and development processes. SourceForge also abandons the report type and forces projects to use different issue management system instances for different report types. While a bug is reported in the issue management system, feature requests are reported in a different tracker. Although an issue repository analyst can consider issue reports in a tracker to belong to the corresponding report type category, it complicates the process of turning a bug report into a feature request, or vice versa. A developer would have to delete the original report, file a new report and transfer properties, fields, and discussion—a process that can be considered to rarely happen. And even if developers would transfer reports between trackers, timestamp values would become unreliable.

Default field settings and predefined report structures impact mined bug data.

6.2.3   Peril of Duplicate Bug Reports

Once a software contains a bug, it is not unlikely that the issue is detected by multiple users. Although the underlying bug is the same, the user experience may vary—a bug can cause multiple crashes and failures. Consequently, it is not uncommon that a bug gets reported more than once. But are duplicate bug reports harmful? The answer to this question depends on the perspective.

Bettenburg et al. [11] showed that most developers do not consider duplicate bug reports as a serious problem pointing out that duplicate bug reports add additional bug description and details that help developers in their debugging process. Dhaliwal et al. [20] performed an empirical study of crash-reports and showed that grouping bug reports can effectively reduce the fix time of bugs by more than 5 %. In cases in which bug reports provide only high-level details about the issue, developers might benefit from additional reports providing additional details and thus help with progress on that particular issue. On the other hand, duplicate bug reports can cause unnecessary cost because detecting bug reports that should be considered duplicates can be expensive.

From an issue repository analyst's perspective, duplicate bug reports complicate the mining and in particular the analysis processes. Within an issue repository, duplicate bug reports are independent development artifacts. But for the purpose of analyzing bug reports, these independent artifacts should be marked as dependent. There exist a wide variety of approaches to automatically detect duplicate bug reports [56, 58, 62, 64]. Software repository analysts and developers can use these techniques to determine and validate duplicate bug reports. Once these bug reports are marked as duplicates, analysts face the problem of how to aggregate the information: should comments contained in different duplicate reports be seen as one larger discussion group? What priority or severity is to be assumed for a set of duplicate bug reports with different priority and severity values? Which report is the *master report* and should be treated as such [11, 58, 64]? Depending on the purpose of a study, the problem of duplicate bug reports is irrelevant and ignored. For example, when identifying the number of fixed bugs per source artifact, not dealing separately with duplicate bug reports may make sense because code changes and their commit messages refer to only one of the related reports. Thus, related and duplicate bug reports will not be associated with the corresponding code changes (see Sect. 6.4.1) causing no duplicate bug count.

> *Identify if and how duplicate issue reports should be handled.*

6.3 How Reliable Are Bug Reports?

Bug reports play an important role in software maintenance but also in recommendation systems related to code quality. Many mining approaches and recommendation systems are based on issue repositories in some way (e.g., [3, 10, 22, 69]), either as standalone artifact or as measurement for code quality. But how reliable are bug reports? The quality of bug reports is a frequent topic of research studies [9, 10, 22, 27]. Many of these studies show that bug reports often contain too little or incomplete information to reproduce and fix the reported issues. This raises further questions regarding the correctness of bug reports. If a bug report contains incomplete information, can we expect the data that is available to be correct? Antoniol et al. [2] and Herzig et al. [26] report that there exists a significant amount of incorrectly classified bug reports—reports marked as "bug" but not referring to any corrective maintenance task. Other fields in bug reports have been reported to contain many incomplete or even incorrect data.

The quality of bug reports is an issue not only in open-source projects. Aranda and Venolia [4] showed that even at industry "repositories hold incomplete or incorrect data more often than not." Bachmann and Bernstein [6] confirmed that data quality issues can be an impacting factor in industry datasets and presented a systematic investigation of software process data quality and measures project-specific characteristics that may be used to develop project-specific mining algorithms taking the individual characteristics of software project into account. In a similar study, Bernstein and Bachmann [7] also showed that "product quality—measured by number of bugs reported—is affected by process data quality measures."

6.3.1 Matter of Perspective

Many studies of bug report quality mention a gap between *reporters* and *developers* (at least in cases in which reporters are not developers themselves). We already discussed that the reputation of a reporter heavily impacts the probability that a report gets fixed [10,22,27]. Consequently, submitting bug reports seems to be more complicated than expected. Does a non-developer reporting a bug understand the differences between and the meanings of the required bug report fields? Reporters that are not developers are likely to be neither software nor development experts and thus might not know the difference between a bug and a documentation issue. For a user, a failure or unexpected behavior is a bug. But using the perspective of a user to determine the quality of the source code might cause mismatches. A user who observed bug stemming from outdated documentation does not refer to code issues, although the developer might have to change the documentation in the source file. Thus, mapping the source file change to the "bug" report and thus counting it as a bug fix introduces false bug identifications, because the source code in the source file is kept unchanged. However, since the user determines the issue report type when submitting the issue, the report is submitted as bug report and thus suggests a code issue.

The different perspective of reporters and developers might cause the reporter to select *wrong or misleading values* when filling out the bug report form. Herzig et al. [26] manually inspected over 7,000 bug reports of five open-source projects and found a significant amount of incorrectly classified issue reports. Table 6.1 shows their reclassification results for "bug" reports. Each column of Table 6.1 refers to the "bug" reports of one investigated open-source project. The rows of Table 6.1 represent the categories an issue report could be assigned to during manual

Table 6.1 Reclassification of reports originally filed as "bug". Taken from [26]

Classified category	HttpClient	Jackrabbit	Lucene	Rhino	Tomcat	Combined
bug	63.5%	75.1%	65.4%	59.2%	61.3%	66.2%
feature	6.6%	1.9%	4.8%	6.0%	3.1%	3.9%
documentation	8.7%	1.5%	4.8%	0.0%	10.3%	5.1%
improvement	13.0%	5.9%	7.9%	8.8%	12.0%	9.0%
refactoring	1.7%	0.9%	4.3%	10.2%	0.5%	2.8%
other	6.4%	14.7%	12.7%	15.8%	12.9%	13.0%
misclassifications	36.5%	24.9%	34.6%	40.8%	38.7%	33.8%

Table 6.2 Fractions of resolved issue reports whose type field got changed

	HttpClient	Jackrabbit	Lucene	Rhino	Tomcat	Combined
reports type changed	1/750	9/2413	1/2683	11/622	57/1242	79/7710
changed to bug	0	2/9	0	0	4/57	6/79
changed to non-bug	1/1	7/9	1/1	11/11	53/57	73/79
misclassified after type change [according to 25]	0	1/9	0	0/11	23/57	24/79

inspection. Thus, each cell of the table contains the proportion of original bug reports and the category these reports were assigned to during manual inspection. Between 6% and 13% of filed bug reports are improvement requests and up to 10% contain documentation issues. The fraction of bug reports containing feature requests lies between 2% and 7%. The striking number, however, is that on average 33.8% of reports filed against the investigated open-source projects are misclassified.

Herzig et al. [26] reported similar results for feature requests and improvement requests. Again, the reporter of a bug report might not know the difference between a bug, a feature (adding new functionality), or an improvement request (improving existing functionality)—even among developers, there exist different opinions on when a bug is a bug or when an improvement is a new feature.

Table 6.2 shows the number of issue reports for which the issue report type was changed at least once by a developer. Compared to the fraction of misclassified reports, this fraction is very low and lies between 0.04% for Lucene and 4.6% for Tomcat. Combining all five projects, the fraction of issue reports whose type was changed at least once lies at 1%—in contrast to the combined false classification rate of 30%. This evidence shows that developers rarely change the type of an issue report. Thus, bug data analysts should not rely on developers to detect and in particular to automatically correct issue report types. Interestingly, there exist many more issue reports being newly marked as non-bugs than reports moved from a non-bug category to "bug."

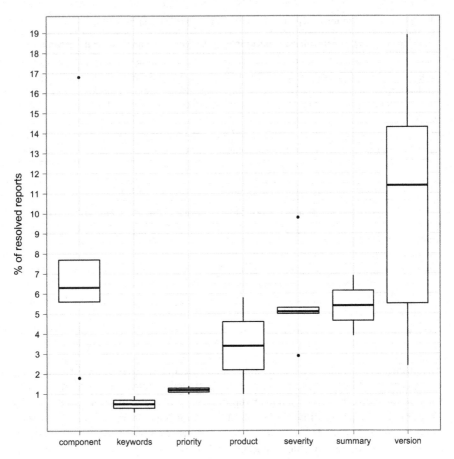

Fig. 6.2 Percent of resolved issue reports with respect to field changes. Priority, product, and summary only changed in Bugzilla tracker projects Rhino and Tomcat

How about other bug report fields? Figure 6.2 shows box plots that represent the fraction of reports for which the corresponding field was changed at least once. The box plot shows that at most 20 % of the resolved issue report fields get updated. Important fields like severity and priority (used to train recommendation systems on severe or important bugs only) are updated for 5 % of the issue reports.

We discuss the consequences of misclassified issue reports on quality-related models in Sect. 6.4.6.

If bugs are classified by reporters, check for possible misclassification.

6.3.2   Recommending Bug Report Fields

There exist multiple approaches to predict the correct values of issue report fields. Antoniol et al. [2] used linguistic data extracted from the issue report content to classify issue reports into bugs and non-bugs with a precision between 77 % and 82 %. Common keywords marking issue reports as bug reports are "exception," "fail," "npe" (null-pointer exception), or "error" [2].

Other studies have shown that it is also possible to predict the severity or priority of issue reports [37, 44, 67], who should be assigned [3, 28, 40, 53], and duplicate bug reports [56, 58, 62, 64]. These and other approaches can be used to verify the correctness of specific report field values but should be used with care to automatically correct issues regarding these fields. Most of these approaches are based on heuristics and should not be used as replacement for careful manual inspection. Manual inspection and quality assurance is key and should be conducted, at least on a significant sample.

It is possible to automatically correct misleading bug report fields.

6.4   Mapping Bug Data

As discussed, there exist many research studies and approaches targeting bug reports as standalone artifacts. Bug reports are key to software maintenance and therefore of great interest to software developers and managers. But in many software projects and companies, bug-tracking systems are separated from version control systems (VCS) and thus do not allow immediate reasoning about code quality and those artifacts that have shown to be defect prone. Thus, we need to relate bug reports with code changes. Once we are able to identify which code changes were made in order to fix which issue, we will be able to reason about code quality in detail, for example, identifying the most defect-prone source artifacts.

Although mapping bug reports to code changes is a common task when mining version archives, there exist surprisingly few fundamentally different mapping strategies and even less studies investigating the correctness of these mapping strategies and their impact on recommendation and prediction models based on these mappings. Recently, researchers investigated whether natural language processing and linguistic data can be used to improve existing mapping techniques. We discuss these approaches in Sect. 6.4.6. However, many mapping strategies are based on regular expressions searching for issue report references in version control commit messages and using a set of negative filters (e.g., bug to be closed and fixed or the bug report not to be marked as resolved before the code changes were committed) to eliminate obvious false positive mappings. But before discussing the consequences and issues regarding strategies to map bug reports and code changes, this section starts with an overview on how to map reported bugs to code changes.

6.4.1   Relating Bugs to Code Changes

Relating bug reports and code changes means finding references between artifacts contained in two separate archives. Fischer et al. [21] and Čubranić et al. [17] were among the first to search for references between code changes in VCSs and bug reports contained in issue-tracking systems. Their approach is straightforward. Commit messages of code changes may contain references to bug reports (e.g., "Fixes bug 7478" or simply "fixing #2367") that are easily found using *regular expressions*. The result is a set of pairs of bug reports and code changes for which the commit message of a code change is suspected to contain a reference of the corresponding bug report. But this set might also contain *false positive* relations. While regular expressions are excellent to detect patterns of text, they *ignore the context*. Thus, a regular expression like (bug|issue|fix):?\s*#?\s?(\d+) will match a commit message like "fixing copyright issue: 2002 → 2003." Clearly, the bug ID 2002 matched by the regular expression is referencing a date but not the bug report with the ID 2002. Thus, most bug data analysts apply a set of filters to prevent such false positives to be added to the final association set. Common filters are as follows:

Creation Order.   The bug report should have been created before the code change was applied.

Resolution Order.   The code change should be committed before the report was marked as "Resolved."

Authors.   The person who commits the change should be the same person who marks the report "Resolved" (there exist many development processes in which the fix requires review and the reviewer marks the report as "Resolved").

Software Version.   Filters might also consider the affected versions mentioned in the bug reports and the branch(es) where the code change was applied.

Bug ID Ranges.   Certain bug report ID ranges are more likely to introduce false positives as others (e.g., small bug IDs are likely to reference a year, date, build, or a line number instead of a report ID). Ignoring such references can be simple but requires software projects with a considerably higher number of reported bug reports than the chosen ignore-threshold or bug-tracking systems with a starting bug id above the threshold. The alternative is to mark these references for manual inspection—a very accurate but also very time-consuming process.

The used regular expressions and filters highly depend on the individual software project and the underlying development process. There may exist clear commit message formatting rules or none. Different projects use different bug report processes. For example, Jira bug reports usually start with a project identifier followed by a number (e.g., JRUBY-2002); this very simple difference can eliminate many false-positive mappings such as the confusion between year numbers and bug report IDs. Depending on these processes, their setups, and the development process, regular expressions and false positive filters should be changed, added, or removed. The overall approach described is illustrated in Fig. 6.3.

Fig. 6.3 Mapping bug reports to code changes using regular expressions

---

Mapping bugs to changes requires filtering, which is largely project-specific.

6.4.2 Relating Bugs to Code Artifacts

The result of the above-described mapping process is a set of pairs of bug reports associated with code changes. Each pair suggests that the bug report has been fixed or at least targeted in the associated code change. Assuming that our bug mapping strategy is perfect and thus introduces no false positives (see Sect. 6.4.3), we can use the pairs of bugs and changes to reason about code quality. Each code change touches a number of code artifacts. Mapping the fixed bug reports associated with code changes to those artifacts changed by the change, we can identify those bug reports whose resolution required a code artifact to be modified. Vice versa, for each code artifact we can list the bug reports that caused a change in the artifact. Similarly, we can also identify which developer applied changes required to fix which bug reports or VCS branches in which bug reports were fixed.

The bug report aggregation strategy works if the association between bug reports and code changes assigns each bug report to exactly one code change. But fixing bug reports can be a complicated and time-consuming task. It is common that there exist multiple code changes whose commit message claims to fix a bug report. Looking at commit messages only, it remains undecidable which code change contributes to the overall fix. The only thing we know is that the current last code change is likely to be the last fix and thus likely to be part of the final bug fix. But the contribution of the previous code changes associated to the same bug report remains undecidable. There are multiple possible contributions of these code changes: (a) the code change is part of the final fix but was incomplete, (b) the changes applied were completely reverted by later changes, or (c) the changes applied were partially reverted, thus the code change partially contributed to the final fix. Depending on the actual contribution of the individual code changes, we would have to consider a code change when aggregating quality data or not. To illustrate this, consider the following example (also shown in Fig. 6.4): There exist three code changes (CC_1, CC_2, CC_3) whose commit messages state that bug report #123 has been fixed. Code change CC_1 gets completely reverted by CC_2 that also applies a patch in $File_B$ that will be part of the initial fix. The changes applied by CC_2 to $File_C$ are again overwritten by changes applied in CC_3. Looking at the individual code changes,

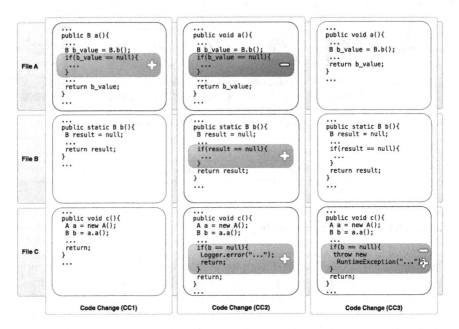

Fig. 6.4 Example of code changes overwriting each other. Which code change contributed to the overall fix?

it is clear that CC_1 does not contribute to the final fix whereas CC_2 and CC_3 do contribute. Thus, the bug report #123 required changes to the files $File_B$ and $File_C$ but not to $File_A$ although $File_A$ was changed twice.

Many studies and mining approaches do not consider source code analysis and patch aggregation when counting the number of applied fixes per source artifact (e.g., source files of binaries). Two frequently used heuristics are to use either the last code change only or to count the *distinct* number of bugs per changed code artifact. But both heuristics can be dangerous. The rationale behind using the last code change only is that the last change is very likely to contribute to the fix and thus proposes a low risk. But this rational assumes that the last applied change does not revert or clean up earlier unnecessary changes. In these cases, choosing the last code change selects exactly those code parts that should be considered as not changed. Counting the *distinct* number of bug reports per changed code artifact considers all applied changes but still does not identify code changes reverting earlier changes or cleaning up code. For code artifacts that are fixed and cleaned up, each bug ID is counted only once. But code artifacts being changes and later reverted will still be falsely associated to bug reports and thus considered being fixed, although the aggregated patch applied no semantical difference to the artifact. Consequently, there exists no heuristic to aggregate bug reports over a set of code changes without introducing mapping bias. The only safe way is to apply source code analysis and to aggregate the individual patches to create a final summarizing patch and to use this summary patch to detect changed source artifacts.

> *Mapping code changes to bug reports is a crucial but also error-prone task. It is very important to adjust mapping strategies to individual projects and to verify the correctness of the strategy.*

6.4.3 Mapping Bias

Although the described process of relating bug reports and code changes using regular expressions is frequently used in state-of-the-art research studies, there exists concerning evidence that such a simplistic process causes *mapping bias*—an inclination of mapping only bug reports and code changes that fulfill certain criteria. Even in realistic scenarios, data quality is low and some values are even missing [45]. This fact is confirmed by Liebchen and Shepperd [38] who surveyed hundreds of empirical software engineering papers to assess how studies manage data quality issues. Their result is alarming: "[...] only 23 out of the many hundreds of studies assessed, explicitly considered data quality" [38] and the issue of noise and missing data is not only limited to studies on relating bug data to code changes but also occurs in software engineering effort and cost estimation [48, 61]. In this section, we discuss error propagations and mapping limitations (the list is not complete) and their impact on quality datasets.

Unmapped Bug Reports

The first problem of any mapping strategy is that it will not find code changes that are bug fixes but state *no references to a bug report* or which state *references in an unrecognized format*. Using regular expressions to detect explicit bug report references (e.g., "1234" or "XSTR-1234") will not cover text references such as using the bug report title as commit message or phrasing the solution of a problem described in the bug report. Thus, regular expressions are too limited to cover all possible reference styles.

Bird et al. [12] showed that a selective mapping strategy, such as using only regular expressions, introduces mapping bias. The mapping strategy determines which bug reports and code changes get mapped and thus selects only those code changes and bug reports that reference each other using a specific manner. Bug reports and code changes using different, not handled, reference styles will be ignored. In their study, Bird et al. showed that certain bug types are over-represented leading to a biased quality dataset that "[...] threatens the effectiveness of processes that rely on biased datasets to build prediction models and the generalizable of hypotheses tested on biased data." This effect is not limited to open-source projects but also present in industrial setups enforcing strict development guidelines [54]. It seems clear that bug data analysts should act to reduce the amount of noise and bias introduced by mapping strategies. Possible solutions to this problem can be applied from two different sides of the problem: as pre- or post-processing steps.

Dealing with the problem as post-processing steps requires statistical methods to deal with the noise already introduced. Kim et al. [33] introduced a noise detection and elimination algorithm that eliminates data instances likely to be noise instances. Similarly, Cartwright et al. [16] used simple data imputation techniques to deal with the problem of missing data in software engineering datasets.

Dealing with the noise and bias problem from the other side, as preprocessing step, should be seen as a two-track challenge. Bug data analysts have to come up with less restrictive mapping strategies (see Sect. 6.4.6) that should be combined. On the other hand, software repository analysts have to deal with the data created by others. Empty commit messages or not-existing references cannot be overcome, no matter which strategy will be used. Thus, we also need better tool support allowing software developers to link artifacts with each other [14] and allowing repository analysts to create more reliable and less biased quality datasets.

Mismatched Timestamps

In Sect. 6.4.1, we also used a filtering pipeline to remove false-positive mappings such as bug reports closed before the fix was applied, or code changes applied before the bug report was filed. Some filters use timestamps to determine the order in which code changes and bug reports have been created, applied, and resolved. But timestamps should be handled with care, especially if we compare timestamps recorded by different systems and possibly on different machines and even time zones. A slight offset between timestamps in VCSs and the issue repositories can be fatal. A good example is the OpenBravo project. Their setup of VCS and issue management system showed a timestamp offset of multiple hours over a period of time. The effect is that when mining *OpenBravo* and mapping bug reports to code changes, the described filtering mechanism eliminated many true positive bug mappings. The problem is that many bug reports got created just hours before the actual fix was applied. But the time offset between both servers caused the creation time-stamp of the bug report to appear as being after the commit time-stamp of the actual, manually verified bug fix. Possible solutions would be to allow a certain time gap. But what is a good value for such a time gap? And should this time gap be applied to the complete dataset or only to a particular subset?

Similar problems occur when using timestamps to decide if a bug fix candidate was applied after the referenced bug report was recreated but before the bug was as marked as resolved. Kim and Whitehead showed that "bug fixes times in buggy files range from 100–200 days" [32]. Thus, using a time-based filtering mechanism might be of little help. A time period of 200 days is long and, in active software projects, we can expect many unrelated code changes to be submitted during such long time periods.

> Unmapped bug reports and mismatched time stamps can introduce bias in bug data.

6.4.4   Error Propagation: Misclassified Bug Reports

Section 6.3 already covered the issue of bug report reliability. In this paragraph, this discussion is continued since unreliable bug reports contribute to mapping bias. More specific, this section discusses the impact of misclassified issue reports when mapping issue reports to source code changes.

Herzig et al. [26] used the mapping strategy described in Sect. 6.4.1 to map bug reports to code changes, once including incorrectly classified bug report and once excluding these noise instances. The authors reported that for all five investigated open source projects, the percentage of misclassified bug reports that could be mapped to code changes and thus to code files lies above 20 %. Thus, more than 20 % of code changes marked as bug fix should not be marked as such since the bug report associated contained no bug description. Going one step further and counting the distinct number of bug reports fixed in a source file (see Sect. 6.4.2), the authors reported that on average 39 % of those source files being marked as having at least one bug never had a reported bug.

To give some more details on the differences between original and classified bug counts, Fig. 6.5 shows stacked bar plots displaying the distribution of bug count differences among source files. Each stacked bar contains intervals reflecting the difference between the original number of bug fixes (*num_original_bugs*) and the number of classified bug fixes (*num_classified_bugs*). A positive difference indicates that the number of defects fixed in the corresponding source files is actually lower. For files showing a negative difference, more defect fixes could have been found. While most files show no or only little changes to their bug count, there also exist files with large bug count differences. The number of files for which more bugs could have been found is marginal.

> *Misclassified reports can impact the bug count of source files and wrongly mark bug-free source files as being bug prone.*

6.4.5   Impact of Tangled Changes

The last important mapping bias source are simultaneously applied code changes that serve multiple development tasks (e.g., fixing a bug and cleaning up code or fixing a bug while implementing a new feature). We call these changes *tangled*. The problem is that it is hard for bug data analysts, mapping bug reports to code changes, to determine which code artifact changed in order to resolve either task. Which code artifacts were changed to fix the bug report and which code artifacts were changed to implement the new feature?

Kawrykow and Robillard [30] investigated over 24,000 code changes of seven open-source projects and showed that up to 15 % of method updates were due to *non-essential differences*. Later, Herzig and Zeller [25] manually inspected and

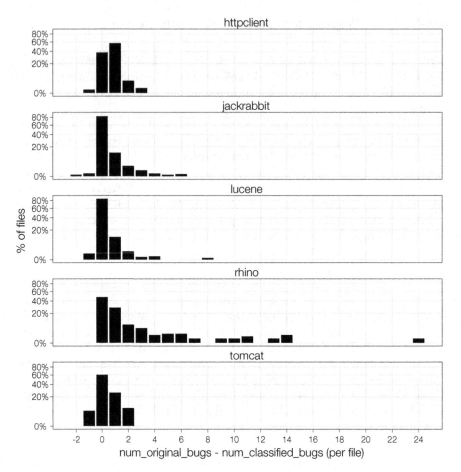

Fig. 6.5 Histograms showing the difference between the original number of bug fixes (*num_original_bugs*) and the number of classified bug fixes (*num_classified_bugs*) and their frequencies across all five projects

classified more than 7,000 code changes from five open-source projects and found that between 6 % and 15 % of all code changes, which contained references to at least one issue report, are tangled. Independently, Kawrykow and Robillard [30] and Herzig and Zeller [25] developed algorithms to separate tangled code changes from each other. The algorithm proposed by Kawrykow and Robillard identified non-essential changes allowing bug data analysts to map bug-fixing code changes only to essentially changed source artifacts. The algorithms proposed by Herzig and Zeller and a similar algorithm proposed by Herzig and Zeller [29] aim to untangle any multi-purpose code change into so-called code change partitions—subsets of applied code changes. Each such change partition contains those change operations likely belonging together. Thus, different change partitions are likely to contain change operations addressing different change purposes.

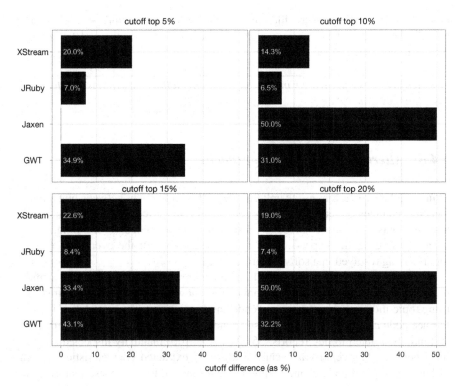

Fig. 6.6 The impact of tangled changes on bug-counting models represented by the percentage of the most defect-prone files that do not belong to this category because they were falsely associated with bug reports

But what is the impact of tangled changes on bug-counting models counting the number of distinct bug reports per source file? Herzig [24] showed this impact by using the untangling algorithm proposed by Herzig and Zeller [25]. He generated two datasets associating source files with the distinct number of bug reports whose resolution required the corresponding source file to change. One dataset contained the original bug fix count as discussed in Sect. 6.4.2. For the second bug count set, Herzig associated bug reports only to those code artifacts modified by change operations located in bug-fixing change partitions. He observed that between 10 % and 38 % of all source files were assigned a different bug count. Between 2 % and 7 % of files originally associated with at least one bug report had no bug associated after untangling. The impact on those files with the most bug counts is even worse. Herzig sorted source files decreasingly once by their original number of associated reports and once by their number of associated bug reports after untangling. He then used the symmetric difference between the two sets containing the corresponding top x% most defect-prone files. The results show that between 6 % and 50 % of the most defect-prone files do not belong to this category because they were falsely associated with bug reports. The detailed comparison results for all four open-source projects can be found in Fig. 6.6. Furthermore, Herzig showed that the Spearman rank correlations between the files remaining in the intersections of original and classified most defect-prone entities tends to be low: between 0.1 and 1 (median: 0.5; harmonic mean: 0.38).

Tangled changes can severely impact bug count models by associating bug fixes to files that never had a bug.

6.4.6 Alternative Mapping Approaches

Using regular expressions as the only strategy to find references between bug reports and code changes is clearly not good enough and is empirically proven to introduce mapping bias—the subset of bug reports that can be linked to bug-fixing code changes using regular expressions is not representative for the overall set of bug reports being resolved in a software project [12].

In recent years, more and more alternative approaches of finding such artifact references have been developed; Thomas [63] showed that there exists a trend in using topic modeling to trace source code and bug reports. Topic modeling is used to trace code artifacts and bug reports [5] and to specifically search for source files that may be related to bug reports [55]. Wu et al. [66] manually inspected explicit links between bug reports and change logs and extracted characteristic features of bug reports and code changes linking each other. Based on these features, the authors developed a prototype that "[...] automatically learns criteria of features from explicit links to recover missing links." Wu et al. also evaluated the impact of recovered links on software maintainability and defect prediction models and report that ReLink yields significantly better prediction accuracy when compared to traditional linking heuristics. Any mapping strategy linking bug reports and code changes that is not relying on developers to explicitly mention bug report identifiers when committing bug fixes or mentioning code change revisions when closing or resolving bug reports will help bridge the gap between those bug reports that can be linked to code changes and those that cannot be linked. Using natural language processing and topic modeling, we can rely on the individual software repository artifacts themselves.

The alternative to find links between bug reports and code changes retroactive during the mining processes are development environments that link artifacts already during the development process. Many commercial bug tracking, version control, and code review environments and tools follow this strategy. This does not only results in much more precise datasets that can be used to build recommendation systems, but also provides more detailed development information for actual developers, allowing them to instantly switch between development tools and thus navigate fluently through related artifacts. Prominent examples are the commercial tool series from Atlassian, or tools that support an automated mapping between code changes and bug reports based on usage data collections (e.g., Mylyn [31],

Palantír [60], Hipikat [17], Jazz, or Team Foundation Server). Systems like *Team Foundation Server* allow developers to attach related work items (e.g., bug reports) to code changes (and vice versa) using drag and drop. Thus, the developer does not have to manually add links to bug reports in her commit message but rather selects proposed artifacts (based on heuristics) or simply selects these artifacts from a given list of assigned tasks. Although such embedded mapping tools come with their own challenges (dummy bug reports created to commit or incomplete links between artifacts), these environments improve the linkage precision and number of artifacts that can be linked at all dramatically. Although such systems are very common in industry, they are rarely used in open-source projects. Thus, selecting the right project also requires investigating which tools and processes are used in the project.

> *There exist many approaches that may help to reduce bias in bug data. Using programming environments integrating version control systems and issue management systems can significantly improve mapping accuracy.*

6.5 Predicting Bugs

Knowing where bugs were fixed can be helpful and allows to review why artifacts were bug prone and which processes or circumstances led to these issues. Even more important, it allows to learn from these reviewed issues and to learn for future development. One way of leveraging past bugs is to estimate and predict future issues. Such bug prediction models have become popular in research and been adopted in industry. The number of publications on bug prediction models is too large to allow an extensive review of all approaches and findings. For a detailed review on different fault prediction studies in software engineering, we recommend the systematic literature review conducted by Hall et al. [23]. The authors provide answers to research questions: "How does context affect fault prediction?" "Which independent variables should be included in fault prediction models?" "Which modeling techniques perform best when used in fault prediction?" [23].

The goal of this section is to explain how to turn your own mined historic data into a bug prediction model. Along this path, analogous to the previous sections of this chapter, we discuss issues and pitfalls when training bug-prediction models.

6.5.1 Relating Bugs and Code Features

One application of *defect prediction models* is to support decisions on how to *allocate quality assurance resources*—for instance, which components to focus upon during reviewing and testing. The models can help by predicting the *number*

Table 6.3 Overall defect prediction model accuracy using different software measures on Windows Vista [adapted with permission from 50, 52]

Model	Precision	Recall
Change Bursts [52]	91.1%	92.0%
Organizational Structure [51]	86.2%	84.0%
Code Churn [49]	78.6%	79.9%
Code Complexity [41]	79.3%	66.0%
Social network measures [13]	76.9%	70.5%
Dependencies [68]	74.4%	69.9%
Test Coverage [47]	83.8%	54.4%
Pre-Release Defects	73.8%	62.9%

and sometimes the *location* of defects to be fixed in near future. This works because defects are not equally distributed across the code base; therefore, defect prediction models try to locate hot-spots in the system that are more defect prone than others.

Given a set of code artifacts, such a prediction model returns *risk factors* that indicate:

- The likelihood that a given artifact contains software defects (classification)
- Even more precisely, a number of expected defects to be found within the code artifact (prediction)

Most defect prediction models are based on *product metrics* (e.g., for each module, its domain or its code complexity) and *process metrics* (e.g., for each artifact, past defects found, or past changes applied). The model *correlates* these metrics with defect likelihood and can then be used to check new code artifacts expressed by their corresponding software metrics.

Over the years, researchers and engineers proposed hundreds of code metrics that can be used to build defect prediction models. The approach is always the same. The software metrics contains *meta-information* about each individual software artifact (e.g., lines of code per source file or number of authors that changed a source file) that describes code properties separating defect-prone code artifacts from artifacts that are not. The type of meta information can be arbitrary and can also describe process information (who developed the code how) or describe the dependencies between individual code artifacts (e.g., using call graphs). Table 6.3 summarizes the predictive power of post-release defect prediction models for Windows Vista categorized by the type of software metrics the models are based on. The differences in precision and recall measures show that the chosen set of software metrics heavily influences the prediction performance of the corresponding prediction model. Also note that these are numbers for the Microsoft's Windows Vista software product only. Switching to different software products in Microsoft or outside Microsoft might lead to different prediction performances and might also result in different rankings.

To allow machine-learning algorithms to learn which metrics correlate most with defect-prone source files, the dataset to train defect prediction models (and also to check their result and measure accuracy) requires a response or dependent variable

Table 6.4 Excerpt of an example metrics set combining network dependency metrics as described by Zimmermann and Nagappan [68] and the number of distinct bugs fixed per source file

filename	size	sizeOut	sizeIn	density	...	numBugs
optimizer/ClassCompiler.java	12	11	2	0.2651	...	1
optimizer/Codegen.java	30	29	2	0.1678	...	37
JavaAdapter.java	23	22	3	0.2094	...	11
ast/AstRoot.java	11	7	6	0.4	...	0
Parser.java	73	71	5	0.0778	...	33
ast/FunctionNode.java	20	7	17	0.2710	...	1
IRFactory.java	69	67	3	0.0837	...	23
CompilerEnvirons.java	14	5	11	0.2197	...	3
ObjToIntMap.java	15	3	13	0.2667	...	0
ast/ScriptNode.java	24	10	18	0.2536	...	0
ScriptRuntime.java	98	51	72	0.0842	...	41
IdFunctionCall.java	9	4	7	0.375	...	0
Scriptable.java	122	2	121	0.0529	...	0
IdFunctionObject.java	37	8	32	0.1876	...	0
Context.java	148	46	130	0.0484	...	19
ast/XmlString.java	6	4	3	0.4	...	0
ast/NodeVisitor.java	54	2	54	0.0527	...	0
ast/XmlFragment.java	8	4	5	0.3928	...	0
ast/AstNode.java	67	9	64	0.0961	...	1

The path prefix "/org/mozilla/javascript/" has been elided from each

that adds quality-related information per code artifact. Using the approach described in Sect. 6.4.2, we know which code changes fixed bug reports in which source files. Thus, we can count the distinct number of bugs fixed per source file and use this *bug count* as quality measurement—the more bugs were fixed, the lower the code quality. Source files without bug fixes have a *bug count* of zero.

The resulting dataset is a table-like data structure that associates each code artifact with a set of explanatory variables (metrics) and a dependent variable (number of recorded bug fixes). Table 6.4 shows an example dataset for the open-source project Rhino using **network dependency** metrics as described by Zimmermann and Nagappan [68] and the *bug count* metric as described earlier. The chosen code dependency network metric set is used exemplary and can be replaced or extended by any other metric set that can be collected for source files. For more details on the individual metrics, we refer the reader to the original dataset description [68]. The complete sample dataset as shown in Fig. 6.4 is available as a comma-separated text file (CSV) for download from http://rsse.org/book/c06/sampleset.csv.

In the next section, we use this dataset to model the relationship between the dependent variable and the explanatory variables using machine learners.

> *Relating software, history, or process metrics with bug fixes allows accurate bug prediction models to be built.*

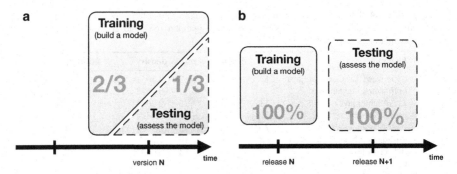

Fig. 6.7 (**a**) Random sampling or stratified random sampling splits one snapshot of a software project into 2/3 training and 1/3 testing parts. Performing multiple splits (holdouts) and reporting mean accuracy measures reduces sampling errors. (**b**) Using two releases or versions of one or different project histories is closest to what can be deployed in the real world where past project data is used to identify defect-prone entities in on-going or future releases

6.5.2   Training Prediction Models

To build and evaluate a bug prediction model, one needs a training and a testing set. Figure 6.7 shows two common approaches to train and test bug prediction models. Randomly splitting a single dataset into two subsets is frequently used if only one revision of a software project is available. The single dataset is split into a training set (usually containing two-thirds of the original set's artifacts) and into a testing set (see Fig. 6.7a). The intersection of the training and testing set is empty while the union of training and testing data matches the original dataset. Sampling datasets includes fuzziness: a single random sample can produce good results although the prediction model performs poorly on average. Thus, sampling is often combined with repeated holdout setups. Instead of splitting once, the dataset gets repeatedly split into training and testing subsets and for each cross-validation or holdout precision, recall, and accuracy are recorded. These measures correspond to the mean values over the corresponding set of performance holdouts.

The alternative of splitting one revision of a software project apart is to use two revisions of the software code base (see Fig. 6.7b). This method is commonly used to train and test prediction models based on releases. The earlier release serves as a training set while the other, later revision, is used to test the prediction model. Models are trained on revisions of different software projects. These forward or cross-release prediction setups are closest to what can be deployed in the real world where past project data is used to identify bug-prone entities in ongoing or future releases.

The training data will then be passed to a machine-learning algorithm (e.g., support vector machine). The resulting model will then accept new instances and returns a predicted value. Prediction models can either be trained as *classification* models or *regression* models. Classification models usually associate instances with a category (bug-prone or not bug-prone) while regression models predict the exact number of bugs to be expected in the corresponding code artifact. There are many statistical tools and algorithms on how to actually train machine learners for bug prediction purposes and there exist many different machine learners that can be used to predict bugs. Different models may assume different preconditions on the operation dataset and the predictive power of the models not only depends on the used metric sets but also on the machine learner used to predict bugs. In Chap. 3, Menzies [43] discusses this topic in more detail.

6.5.3 From Prediction to Recommendation

Many prediction models and their predicted values can be interpreted as recommendations. The predicted values estimate future events or future situations. This knowledge can be used to take action to support or work against a predicted trend or a predicted result. Bug prediction models predict the expected number of bugs to be fixed in code artifacts. Thus, the prediction results of these models can be used to determine those artifacts that should be tested or reviewed more carefully. Turning a prediction model into a recommendation system usually requires an interpretation of the predicted values and insights that allow to draw possible consequences for the software project.

Discussion the transformation between prediction to recommendation systems goes beyond the content of this chapter but will be discussed in later chapters.

> Just as data quality, the interpretation and consequences of predictor and recommendation models should be constantly questioned.

6.6 Hands-On: Mining Bug Repositories

After discussing the foundations (and perils!) of mining, let us now provide some hands-on experience. This section focuses on mining issue repositories, and the next one will focus on how to predict future bugs.

To mine issue repositories, we use the open-source, general purpose mining framework Mozkito. It provides the necessary extraction and parsing functionality required to bring bug reports into a uniform yet powerful format. Out of the box, Mozkito supports the open-source bug-tracking systems Bugzilla, Jira, Google Project Hosting, and others. Adding a new or customized connector requires the user to implement one interface.

The API of the uniform bug data model is shown in Fig. 6.8 as a UML class diagram. The user can decide whether to operate on an SQL database or to use Java objects and the Mozkito framework. The bug data model contains the most common bug report fields including attachments, discussions, and bug report history. For each bug report mined, Mozkito persists exactly one `Report` object in the database that can later be restored (see Step 3) and used for analysis purposes.

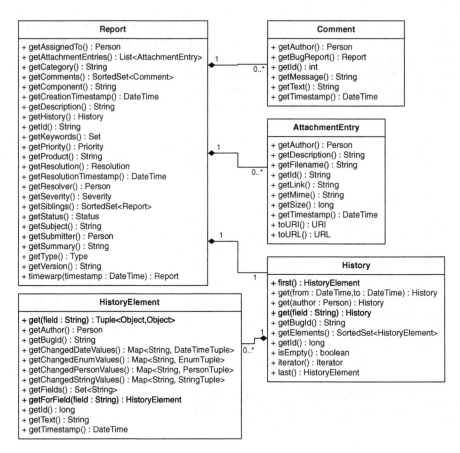

Fig. 6.8 Mozkito bug report model. The UML diagram lists only the most important methods

6.6.1   Step 1: Getting Mozkito

Mozkito is an open-source mining framework. For download and installing instructions, refer to the Mozkito website. To mine issue repositories, we use the Mozkito *issues* module. Once the Mozkito issues module is built (see Mozkito website for instructions), the Mozkito folder

```
mozkito-tools/mozkito-issues/target/
```

contains the executable jar file that can be used to mine issue repositories (referred to as mozkito-issues.jar for the sake of brevity):

```
mozkito-issues-<version>-jar-with-dependencies.jar[1]
```

---

[1]Replace <*version*> with the downloaded version number of Mozkito.

```
 1:  #### DATABASE PROPERTIES ####
 2:  database.host=localhost
 3:  database.driver=org.postgresql.Driver
 4:  database.name=moskito_rhino
 5:  database.user=<USER>
 6:  database.password=<PASSWD>
 7:  ############################
 8:  #### BUG TRACKER PROPERTIES ####
 9:  tracker.type=BUGZILLA
10:  bugzilla.overviewURI=https://bugzilla.mozilla.org/buglist.cgi
     ?product=Rhino
11:  tracker.uri=https://bugzilla.mozilla.org
```

Fig. 6.9 Mozkito-Issues configuration to mine the publicly available issue management system for the Mozilla product Rhino

6.6.2 Step 2: Mining an Issue Repository

To demonstrate how to use Mozkito-Issues to mine issue repositories, we will mine the publicly available issue management system of Mozilla and focus on project Rhino—a Javascript engine written in Java. The restriction to project Rhino is for demonstration purposes, only.

Mozkito-Issues can be configured using JVM arguments. To get a list of all available Mozkito arguments (required arguments will be marked) execute:

java -Dhelp -jar mozkito-issues.jar.

The configuration of Mozkito-Issues depends on the target bug-tracking system and the issue management system URL. Mozilla uses the bug-tracking system Bugzilla that can be accessed using the issue management system URL: https://bugzilla.mozilla.org. Figure 6.9 summarizes the used Mozkito arguments as Mozkito configuration file (<config_file>). To let Mozkito use the configuration file, simply start Mozkito specifying the *config* JVM argument:

java -Dconfig=<config_file> -jar mozkito-issues.jar.

Line 10 of the configuration (Fig. 6.9) specifies the target product (in our case Rhino). The configuration file also contains the required database connection properties that will be used to persist the uniform data format. The listed configuration requires a PostgreSQL database running on localhost. Most likely, these settings need to be adapted to fit a given environment (e.g., MySQL and different host name).

Depending on the size and speed of the issue repository, it may take several hours for Mozkito to fetch and mine all reports found in the target bug-tracking system. Once the mining process completed, the specified database should be populated with persisted Report instances (see Fig. 6.8), one for each bug report found in the mined bug-tracking system. Bug reports requiring additional permissions or that cause parsing errors will be dropped during the mining process.

```
 1  public int analysis() {
 2    int result = 0;
 3
 4    /*
 5     * please use the Mozkito documentation to see
 6     * how to create PersistenceUtil instances
 7     */
 8    final PersistenceUtil persistenceUtil =
 9      this.databaseArguments.getValue();
10
11    final Criteria<Report> loadCriteria =
12      persistenceUtil.createCriteria(Report.class);
13
14    final List<Report> allReports = persistenceUtil.load(
          loadCriteria);
15    for (final Report report : allReports) {
16      final History reportHistory = report.getHistory();
17
18      // we are only interested in HistoryElements
19      // changing the report type
20      final History reportTypeHistory = reportHistory.get("type");
21      if (!reportTypeHistory.isEmpty()) {
22         ++result;
23      }
24    }
25    return result;
26  }
```

Fig. 6.10 Sample source code analyzing the history of issue reports counting the number of reports for which at least one history entry changing the report type can be found

6.6.3   Step 3: Analyzing Bug Reports in Java

Once the content of the target issue management system is persisted, we can use Mozkito to analyze the mined issue reports. Figure 6.10 shows Java source code that loads the mined issue reports from the database and analyzes the report's history. The purpose of the program is to investigate for how many issue reports the report *type* was at least once changed. In other words, we want to analyze how many issue reports were filed as bug reports but resolved as feature or improvement request, or vice versa.

The PersistenceUtil class (line 8 in Fig. 6.10) of Mozkito can be used to load persisted objects from the database into your program.[2] Once we load the Report instances, we iterate over them (line 15) and check for the report history concerning the report type (lines 16 and 20). If this history of modifications applied to the report type is not empty (line 21), we find a report whose report type is changed at least once. We discussed the result of this particular analysis in Sect. 6.3.

---

[2]Please see the Mozkito documentation on how to create such a PersistenceUtil instance.

The presented sample code demonstrates how easy bug report analysis can be once we transformed the bug-tracking content into a uniform, persisted data format. You can use the code snippet presented in Fig. 6.10 as a blueprint to create your own issue report analysis.

6.6.4   Relating Bugs to Changes

As discussed in Sect. 6.4.1, there exist multiple strategies and approaches to map bug reports to code changes correctly and exhaustively. The general mining tool Mozkito ships with a number of state-of-the-art mapping techniques to associate bug reports with corresponding code changes. Discussing all strategies supported by and their possible combinations would exceed the scope of this chapter. Instead, this section explains how to use Mozkito to use the most common and simplest stand-alone strategy to efficiently map bug reports to code changes using regular expressions. The wiki pages of Mozkito provide a more detailed overview of built-in mapping strategies and instructions on how to perform these mappings. Please note that this mining step requires a mined VCS. Please read the corresponding wiki page (https://wiki.mozkito.org/x/FgAz) on how to mine VCSs using Mozkito.

Mozkito allows the user to combine multiple *mapping engines*. Each engine can be seen as a voter returning a confidence value for each pair of bug report and code change. The confidence value corresponds to the likelihood that the provided bug and change should be mapped to each other. To aggregate the different confidence values, we use a veto-strategy[3]—if the confidence value of one engine is below a certain threshold, the pair of report and change are not mapped to each other. In our case, we want to limit Mozkito to use the following engines:

Regular Expression Engine.   To search for explicit bug report references in commit messages.
Report Type Engine.   To consider only bug reports to be mapped (our goal is to map bugs to code changes).
Completed Order Engine.   To allow only a pair of associated reports and code changes for which the code change was applied before the report was marked as resolved.
Creation Order Engine.   To allow only a pair of associated reports and code changes for which the issue report was filed before the code change was applied.
Timestamp Engine.   To enforce that the associated report must be marked as resolved at most one day after the code change was committed.

To configure Mozkito to use exactly this set of engines, we have to add the following line to our already existing Mozkito configuration file (`<config_file>`):

---

[3] There exist more aggregation strategies. Please see the Mozkito manual for more details.

```
1.0  "({match}bug:?\\s*#?##ID##)" CASE_INSENSITIVE
1.0  "({match}bugs?:?\\s*(#?\\p{Digit}+,)*#?##ID##)"\
CASE_INSENSITIVE
1.0  "({match}https?://bugzilla.mozilla.org/show_bug.cgi\
\\?id=##ID##)" CASE_INSENSITIVE
1.0  "({match}#\\s?##ID##)" CASE_INSENSITIVE
1.0  "({match}BZ\\s?:?\\s*##ID##)" CASE_INSENSITIVE
1.0  "({match}fix\\s?:?\\s*##ID##)" CASE_INSENSITIVE
1.0  "({match}fixing\\s?:?\\s*##ID##)" CASE_INSENSITIVE
-100.0 "({match}test cases for") CASE_INSENSITIVE
-100.0 "({match} revert fix for") CASE_INSENSITIVE
```

Fig. 6.11 Sample <REGEX_FILE> specifying the regular expressions to be used to find bug report reference candidates in commit messages. Note that backslash characters must be escaped

```
mappings.engines.enabled=[RegexEngine, ReportTypeEngine, \
CompletedOrderEngine, CreationOrderEngine, TimestampEngine]

mappings.engines.reportType.type=BUG
mappings.engines.timestamp.interval="+1d 00h 00m 00s"
mappings.engines.RegexEngine.config=<REGEX_FILE>
```

The referenced regular expression file (<REGEX_FILE>) should contain the project-specific regular expressions Mozkito will use to match possible bug report references. The regular expression file can specify one expression per line including a confidence value to be returned if the regular expression matches (first number in line) and a specification whether Mozkito should treat the expression case sensitive or not. Mozkito iterates through all regular expressions in the <REGEX_FILE> from top to bottom and stops as soon as one regular expression matches. A typical regular expression file that can also be used for our Rhino project is shown in Fig. 6.11.

Once all the above-discussed lines are added to the Mozkito configuration file (<config_file>), the Mozkito mapping process can be started using the following command:

```
java -Dconfig=<config_file> -jar mozkito-mappings.jar⁴
```

> *There exist mining infrastructures allowing immediate mining actions. Using such infrastructures eases reproduction and allows comparison to other studies.*

Exporting Bug Count Per Source File

As a last step, we export the mapping between source files and bug reports into a comma-separated file that lists the distinct number of fixed bug reports per source file. To export the mapping we created above into a comma-separated bug count

---

[4]mozkito-issues-<version>-jar-with-dependencies.jar

file, we can use the built-in Mozkito tool mozkito-bugcount located in the folder `mozkito-tools/mozkito-bugcount/target/`. To export bug counts per source file, we execute the following command:

```
java -Dconfig=<config_file> -Dbugcount.granularity=file
   -Dbugcount.output=<csv_file> -jar mozkito-bugcount.jar⁵
```

where `<csv_file>` should point to a file path to which the bug count CSV file will be written.

In the next section, we use the `<csv_file>` to build a sample defect prediction model that can be used as basis for recommendation systems.

6.7 Hands-On: Predicting Bugs

After mining VCS and issue management system and after mapping bug reports with code changes, this section provides a hands-on tutorial on how to use the statistical environment and language R [57] to write a script that reads a dataset of our sample format (Fig. 6.4) as created in the previous section, performs a stratified repeated holdout sampling of the dataset, trains multiple machine learners on the training data before evaluating the prediction accuracy of each model using the evaluation measures precision, recall, and F-measure. Precision, recall, and f-measure are only one possibility to measure prediction or classification performance. Other performance measures include ROC curves [19] or even effort-aware prediction models [42].

The complete script containing all discussed R code snippets is available for download from http://rsse.org/book/c06/sample.R. The dataset we use for our example analysis below is also available for download from http://rsse.org/book/c06/sampleset.csv.

6.7.1 Step 1: Load Required Libraries

The script will use functionalities of multiple third-party libraries. The script will make heavy use of the *caret* [36] package for R. The last statement in the first R snippet below sets the initial random seed to an arbitrary value (we chose 1); this will make the shown results reproducible.

```
> rm(list = ls(all = TRUE))
> library(caret)
> library(gdata)
> library(plyr)
```

---

⁵mozkito-bugcount-*<version>*-jar-with-dependencies.jar

```
> library(reshape)
> library(R.utils)
> set.seed(1)
```

6.7.2   Step 2: Reading the Data

To load the sample dataset containing code dependency network metrics [68] and bug counts per source file (as described in Sect. 6.5.1 and shown in Fig. 6.4), we use the following snippet that reads the dataset directly over the Internet.

After execution, the variable data holds the dataset in a table-like data structure called data.frame. For the rest of the section, we assume that the column holding the dependent variables for all instances is called numBugs.

```
> data <- read.table(
+     http://rsse.org/book/c06/sampleset.csv,
+     header=T, row.names=1, sep=",")
```

We can now access the dataset using the data variable. The command below outputs the numBugs column for all 266 source files.

```
> data$numBugs
  [1]   1 37 11  0 33  1 23  3  0  0 41  0  0  0 19  0  0  0  1
 [20]   0  7  0  6  2  3 11  8  3 10  0  1 10  0  0  0  3  0 25
 [39]   5  1  1  0  3  0  1  3  2  2  1  0  0  0  0  2  0  0  1
 [58]   0  4  0  1  1  0  0  0 11  2  0 43  0  1  1  1  0  0  3
 [77]   0  0  0  4  1  0  2  0  2  0  0  0  0  3  0  0  0  0  0
 [96]   0  0  0  1  0  0  0  0  0  0  0  0  0  0  0  0  0  0  0
[115]   0  0  0  0  0  0  0  0  0  0  0  0  0  0  0  0  0  0  0
[134]   0  0  1  0  0  0  0  0  7  1  0  0  0  0  0  0  1 10  4
[153]   7  2  2  4  4  5  0  0  1  4  0  0  1  0  1  3  0  0  2
[172]   1  2  0  0  0  0  0  0  0  1  0  0  0  0  9  0  1  1  4
[191]   1  0  1  1  2  0  0 12  3 16  0  1  3  1  0  6  3  2  0
[210]   3  2  0  0  0  0  0 22  1  6  1  4  1  0  6  0  6  1  0
[229]   0  0  2  1  0  0  0  1  0  0  4  2  3  0  0  0  0  0  0
[248]   0  0  1  1  0  0  0  0  1  0  2  0  0  0  0  0  0  0  1
```

6.7.3   Step 3: Splitting the Dataset

First, we split the original dataset into training and testing subsets using stratified sampling—the ratio of files being fixed at least once in the original dataset is preserved in both training and testing datasets. This makes training and testing sets more representative by reducing sampling errors.

The first two lines of the R-code below are dedicated to separate the dependent variable from the explanatory variables. This is necessary since we will use only the explanatory variables to train the prediction models. In the third line, we then modify the dependent variable (column numBugs) to distinguish between code entities with bugs ("One") and without ("Zero"). Finally, we use the method createDataPartition to split the original datasets into training and testing sets (see Sect. 6.5.2). The training sets contain 2/3 of the data instances while the testing sets contain the remaining 1/3 of the data instances.

```
> dataX <- data[,which(!colnames(data) %in% c("numBugs"))]
> dataY <- data[, which(colnames(data) %in% c("numBugs"))]
> dataY <- factor(ifelse(dataY > 0, "One", "Zero"))
>
> inTrain <- createDataPartition(dataY, times = 1, p = 2/3)
>
> trainX <- dataX[inTrain[[1]], ]
> trainY <- dataY[inTrain[[1]]]
> testX <- dataX[-inTrain[[1]], ]
> testY <- dataY[-inTrain[[1]]]
```

After execution, the variable trainX holds the explanatory variables of all training instances while the variable trainY holds the corresponding dependent variables. Respectively, testX and testY contain the explanatory and dependent variables of all testing instances.

6.7.4   Step 4: Prepare the Data

It is always a good idea to remove explanatory variables that will not contribute to the final prediction model. There are two cases in which an explanatory variable will not contribute to the model.

1. If the variable values across all instances have zero variance (can be considered a constant)—the function call nearZeroVar(trainX) returns the array of columns whose values show no significant variance:

```
> train.nzv <- nearZeroVar(trainX)
> if (length(train.nzv) > 0) {
+       trainX <- trainX[, -train.nzv]
+       testX <- testX[, -train.nzv]
+ }
```

2. If the variable is correlated with other variables and thus does not add any new information—the function findCorrelation searches through the correlation matrix trainX and returns a set of columns that should be removed in order to reduce pair-wise correlations above the provided absolute correlation cutoff (here, 0.9):

```
> trainX.corr <- cor(trainX)
> trainX.highcorr <- findCorrelation(trainX.corr, 0.9)
> if (length(trainX.highcorr) > 0) {
+       trainX <- trainX[, -trainX.highcorr]
+       testX <- testX[, -trainX.highcorr]
+ }
```

Rescale the training data using the center to minimize the effect of large values on the prediction model by scaling the data values into the value range [0,1]. To further reduce the number of explanatory variables, you may also perform a principal component analysis—a procedure to determine the minimum number of metrics that will account for the maximum variance in the data. The function preProcess estimates the required parameters for each operation and predict .preProcess is used to apply them to specific datasets:

```
> xTrans <- preProcess(trainX, method = c("center", "scale"))
> trainX <- predict(xTrans, trainX)
> testX <- predict(xTrans, testX)
```

6.7.5   Step 5: Train the Models

This script will use several prediction models for the experiments: Support vector machine with radial kernel (svmRadial), logistic regression (multinorm), recursive partitioning (rpart), k-nearest neighbor (knn), tree bagging (treebag), random forest (rf), and naive Bayesian classifier (nb). For a fuller understanding of these models, we advise the reader to refer to specialized machine-learning texts such as Menzies [43] (Chap. 3) or Witten et al. [65].

```
> models <- c("svmRadial","multinom","rpart","knn","treebag",
+  "rf","nb")
```

Each model is optimized by the caret package by training models using different parameters (please see the caret manual for more details). "The performance of held-out samples is calculated and the mean and standard deviations is summarized for each combination. The parameter combination with the optimal re-sampling statistic is chosen as the final model and the entire training set is used to fit a final model" [36]. The level of performed optimization can be set using the *tuneLength* parameter. We set this number to five:

```
> train.control <- trainControl(number=2)
> tuneLengthValue <- 5
```

Using the train() function, we generate prediction models (called *fit*) and store these models in the list modelsFit to later access them to compute the prediction performance measures precision, recall, and accuracy:

```
> modelsFit <- list()
+
+ for(model in models){
+   print(paste("training",model," ..."))
+   fit <- train(trainX, trainY, method = model,
+     tuneLength = tuneLengthValue, trControl = train.control,
+     metric = "Kappa")
+   modelsFit[[model]] <- fit
+ }
```

6.7.6 Step 6: Make the Prediction

Using the function `extractPrediction()` we let all models predict the dependent variables of the testing set `testX`:

```
> pred.values <- extractPrediction(modelsFit, testX, testY)
> pred.values <- subset(pred.values, dataType == "Test")
> pred.values.split <- split(pred.values, pred.values$object)
```

After execution, the variable `pred.values.split` holds both the real and the predicted dependent variable values. To check the predicted values for any of the used models (e.g., `svmRadial`), we can access the variable `pred.values.split` as shown in the following text. The result is a list of observed (`obs` column) and predicted (`pred` column) values for each instance in the testing dataset. The result depends on the random split and thus may vary between individual experiments.

```
> pred.values.split$svmRadial
      obs  pred       model dataType     object
179   One  Zero   svmRadial      Test  svmRadial
180  Zero  Zero   svmRadial      Test  svmRadial
181  Zero  Zero   svmRadial      Test  svmRadial
182  Zero  Zero   svmRadial      Test  svmRadial
183  Zero  Zero   svmRadial      Test  svmRadial
184  Zero  Zero   svmRadial      Test  svmRadial
185   One  Zero   svmRadial      Test  svmRadial
186   One   One   svmRadial      Test  svmRadial
187   One   One   svmRadial      Test  svmRadial
188  Zero   One   svmRadial      Test  svmRadial
189   One   One   svmRadial      Test  svmRadial
190   One  Zero   svmRadial      Test  svmRadial
191   One   One   svmRadial      Test  svmRadial
192   One  Zero   svmRadial      Test  svmRadial
193  Zero  Zero   svmRadial      Test  svmRadial
```

6.7.7 Step 7: Compute Precision, Recall, and F-measure

The final part of the script computes precision, recall, and F-measure values for all models and stores these accuracy measures in a table-like data structure:

```
> getPrecision <- function(x) as.numeric(unname(x$byClass[3]))
> getRecall <- function(x) as.numeric(unname(x$byClass[1]))
> getFmeasure <- function(x, y) 2 * ((x * y)/(x + y))
>
> n.row = length(pred.values.split)
> results <- NULL
> results <- dataFrame(
+     colClasses = c(Model = "character", Precision = "double",
      Recall = "double", F.Measure = "double"), nrow = n.row)
> for (j in 1:length(pred.values.split)) {
```

```
+    conf.matrix <- confusionMatrix(pred.values.split[[j]]$pred,
+        pred.values.split[[j]]$obs, positive = "One")
+
+    precision <- getPrecision(conf.matrix)
+    if(is.na(precision)){ precision <- 0 }
+
+    recall <- getRecall(conf.matrix)
+    if(is.na(recall)){ recall <- 0 }
+
+    f.measure <- getFmeasure(precision, recall)
+    if(is.na(f.measure)){ f.measure <- 0+   }
+
+    results[j, 1] <- names(pred.values.split)[j]
+    results[j, 2:4] <- c(precision, recall, f.measure)
+ }
```

To print the prediction measures, we simply print the results table. That will print a table containing precision, recall, and F-measure values sorted by a machine-learning algorithm used for training and testing.

```
> print(results)
        Model Precision     Recall F.Measure
1         knn 0.6562500 0.5833333 0.6176471
2    multinom 0.7096774 0.6111111 0.6567164
3          nb 0.6571429 0.6388889 0.6478873
4          rf 0.7575758 0.6944444 0.7246377
5       rpart 0.5526316 0.5833333 0.5675676
6   svmRadial 0.7307692 0.5277778 0.6129032
7     treebag 0.8181818 0.7500000 0.7826087
```

The results show that using a tree bag model, we obtain a precision of 0.82, a recall of 0.75, and an F-measure of 0.78. The high precision value of 0.82 means that the tree bag model on average reports 18 % false positives—classifies code entities as having a bug although no bug was found. Similarly, the recall value of 0.75 implies that the model contains about 25 % false negatives—code entities classified as bug free but in which bugs have been fixed. Comparing this result with the overall defect prediction model accuracy measures on Windows Vista presented in Table 6.3 shows that the just-built classification model has comparable results to state-of-the-art defect prediction models (although trained and tested on a different project, using different metrics, and different granularity).

> *Ready-made scripts are available that predict and recommend future bugs.*

6.8 Conclusion

To err is human, but to learn from the past is human too. Mining issue repositories offer several opportunities to automate this learning process, producing recommendations that can help identify present bugs and avoid future bugs. Bug data is not without caveats, though. First, the data reflects specific users, tools, and processes, which should be identified to ensure proper interpretation of the results. Second, the data itself is frequently noisy or biased, which should also be taken into account, and where possible, reduced or eliminated. A bit of manual inspection and cross-checking can tremendously increase confidence in all automatic findings, and the future belongs to those who integrate automated tools into well-defined and systematic empirical investigations.

> *The central challenge of the future will be to combine both automatic and manual empirical bug analysis.*

Acknowledgments We thank Sascha Just and many anonymous reviewers for their work.

References

1. Anbalagan, P., Vouk, M.: On predicting the time taken to correct bug reports in open source projects. In: Proceedings of the IEEE International Conference on Software Maintenance, pp. 523–526 (2009). doi:10.1109/ICSM.2009.5306337
2. Antoniol, G., Ayari, K., Di Penta, M., Khomh, F., Guéhéneuc, Y.G.: Is it a bug or an enhancement?: a text-based approach to classify change requests. In: Proceedings of the IBM Centre for Advanced Studies Conference on Collaborative Research (2008). doi:10.1145/1463788.1463819
3. Anvik, J., Hiew, L., Murphy, G.C.: Who should fix this bug? In: Proceedings of the ACM/IEEE International Conference on Software Engineering, pp. 361–370 (2006). doi:10.1145/1134285.1134336
4. Aranda, J., Venolia, G.: The secret life of bugs: going past the errors and omissions in software repositories. In: Proceedings of the ACM/IEEE International Conference on Software Engineering, pp. 298–308 (2009). doi:10.1109/ICSE.2009.5070530
5. Asuncion, H.U., Asuncion, A.U., Taylor, R.N.: Software traceability with topic modeling. In: Proceedings of the ACM/IEEE International Conference on Software Engineering, vol. 1, pp. 95–104 (2010). doi:10.1145/1806799.1806817
6. Bachmann, A., Bernstein, A.: Software process data quality and characteristics: a historical view on open and closed source projects. In: Proceedings of the Joint ACM International Workshop on Principles of Software Evolution and ERCIM Workshop on Software Evolution, pp. 119–128 (2009). doi:10.1145/1595808.1595830
7. Bernstein, A., Bachmann, A.: When process data quality affects the number of bugs: correlations in software engineering datasets. In: Proceedings of the International Working Conference on Mining Software Repositories, pp. 62–71 (2010). doi:10.1109/MSR.2010.5463286
8. Bettenburg, N., Begel, A.: Deciphering the story of software development through frequent pattern mining. In: Proceedings of the ACM/IEEE International Conference on Software Engineering, pp. 1197–1200 (2013). doi:10.1109/ICSE.2013.6606677
9. Bettenburg, N., Just, S., Schröter, A., Weiß, C., Premraj, R., Zimmermann, T.: Quality of bug reports in Eclipse. In: Proceedings of the Eclipse Technology eXchange, pp. 21–25 (2007). doi:10.1145/1328279.1328284
10. Bettenburg, N., Just, S., Schröter, A., Weiss, C., Premraj, R., Zimmermann, T.: What makes a good bug report? In: Proceedings of the ACM SIGSOFT International Symposium on Foundations of Software Engineering, pp. 308–318 (2008). doi:10.1145/1453101.1453146

11. Bettenburg, N., Premraj, R., Zimmermann, T.: Duplicate bug reports considered harmful ... really? In: Proceedings of the IEEE International Conference on Software Maintenance, pp. 337–345 (2008). doi:10.1109/ICSM.2008.4658082
12. Bird, C., Bachmann, A., Aune, E., Duffy, J., Bernstein, A., Filkov, V., Devanbu, P.: Fair and balanced?: bias in bug-fix datasets. In: Proceedings of the European Software Engineering Conference/ACM SIGSOFT International Symposium on Foundations of Software Engineering, pp. 121–130 (2009). doi:10.1145/1595696.1595716
13. Bird, C., Nagappan, N., Gall, H., Murphy, B., Devanbu, P.: Putting it all together: using socio-technical networks to predict failures. In: Proceedings of the International Symposium on Software Reliability Engineering, pp. 109–119 (2009). doi:10.1109/ISSRE.2009.17
14. Bird, C., Bachmann, A., Rahman, F., Bernstein, A.: LINKSTER: enabling efficient manual inspection and annotation of mined data. In: Proceedings of the ACM SIGSOFT International Symposium on Foundations of Software Engineering, pp. 369–370 (2010). doi:10.1145/1882291.1882352
15. Breu, S., Premraj, R., Sillito, J., Zimmermann, T.: Information needs in bug reports: improving cooperation between developers and users. In: Proceedings of the ACM Conference on Computer Supported Cooperative Work, pp. 301–310 (2010). doi:10.1145/1718918.1718973
16. Cartwright, M.H., Shepperd, M.J., Song, Q.: Dealing with missing software project data. In: Proceedings of the IEEE International Symposium on Software Metrics, pp. 154–165 (2003). doi:10.1109/METRIC.2003.1232464
17. Čubranić, D., Murphy, G.C., Singer, J., Booth, K.S.: Hipikat: a project memory for software development. IEEE Trans. Software Eng. 31(6), 446–465 (2005). doi:10.1109/TSE.2005.71
18. D'Ambros, M., Lanza, M., Robbes, R.: An extensive comparison of bug prediction approaches. In: Proceedings of the International Working Conference on Mining Software Repositories, pp. 31–41 (2010). doi:10.1109/MSR.2010.5463279
19. Davis, J., Goadrich, M.: The relationship between precision–recall and ROC curves. In: Proceedings of the International Conference on Machine Learning, pp. 233–240 (2006). doi:10.1145/1143844.1143874
20. Dhaliwal, T., Khomh, F., Zou, Y.: Classifying field crash reports for fixing bugs: a case study of Mozilla Firefox (2011). doi:10.1109/ICSM.2011.6080800
21. Fischer, M., Pinzger, M., Gall, H.: Populating a release history database from version control and bug tracking systems. In: Proceedings of the IEEE International Conference on Software Maintenance, pp. 23–32 (2003). doi:10.1109/ICSM.2003.1235403
22. Guo, P.J., Zimmermann, T., Nagappan, N., Murphy, B.: Characterizing and predicting which bugs get fixed. In: Proceedings of the ACM/IEEE International Conference on Software Engineering, vol. 1, pp. 495–504 (2010). doi:10.1145/1806799.1806871
23. Hall, T., Beecham, S., Bowes, D., Gray, D., Counsell, S.: A systematic literature review on fault prediction performance in software engineering. IEEE Trans. Software Eng. 38(6), 1276–1304 (2012). doi:10.1109/TSE.2011.103
24. Herzig, K.: Mining and untangling change genealogies. Ph.D. thesis, Universität des Saarlandes (2013)
25. Herzig, K., Zeller, A.: The impact of tangled code changes. In: Proceedings of the International Working Conference on Mining Software Repositories, pp. 121–130 (2013)
26. Herzig, K., Just, S., Zeller, A.: It's not a bug, it's a feature: how misclassification impacts bug prediction. In: Proceedings of the ACM/IEEE International Conference on Software Engineering, pp. 392–401 (2013). doi:10.1109/ICSE.2013.6606585
27. Hooimeijer, P., Weimer, W.: Modeling bug report quality. In: Proceedings of the IEEE/ACM International Conference on Automated Software Engineering, pp. 34–43 (2007). doi:10.1145/1321631.1321639
28. Jeffrey, D., Feng, M., Gupta, R.: BugFix: a learning-based tool to assist developers in fixing bugs. In: Proceedings of the IEEE International Conference on Program Comprehenension, pp. 70–79 (2009). doi:10.1109/ICPC.2009.5090029
29. Kawrykow, D.: Enabling precise interpretations of software change data. Master's thesis, McGill University (2011)

30. Kawrykow, D., Robillard, M.P.: Non-essential changes in version histories. In: Proceedings of the ACM/IEEE International Conference on Software Engineering, pp. 351–360 (2011). doi:10.1145/1985793.1985842

31. Kersten, M.: Focusing knowledge work with task context. Ph.D. thesis, University of British Columbia, Vancouver (2007)

32. Kim, S., Whitehead, E.J.: How long did it take to fix bugs? In: Proceedings of the International Workshop on Mining Software Repositories, pp. 173–174 (2006). doi:10.1145/1137983.1138027

33. Kim, S., Zhang, H., Wu, R., Gong, L.: Dealing with noise in defect prediction. In: Proceedings of the ACM/IEEE International Conference on Software Engineering, pp. 481–490 (2011). doi:10.1145/1985793.1985859

34. Kimmig, M., Monperrus, M., Mezini, M.: Querying source code with natural language. In: Proceedings of the IEEE/ACM International Conference on Automated Software Engineering, pp. 376–379 (2011). doi:10.1109/ASE.2011.6100076

35. Ko, A.J., Myers, B.A., Chau, D.H.: A linguistic analysis of how people describe software problems. In: Proceedings of the IEEE Symposium on Visual Languages and Human-Centric Computing, pp. 127–134 (2006). doi:10.1109/VLHCC.2006.3

36. Kuhn, M.: caret: classification and regression training. Version 4.76, R package (2011). URL http://cran.r-project.org/web/packages/caret/caret.pdf. [retrieved 9 October 2013]

37. Lamkanfi, A., Demeyer, S., Soetens, Q.D., Verdonck, T.: Comparing mining algorithms for predicting the severity of a reported bug. In: Proceedings of the European Conference on Software Maintenance and Reengineering, pp. 249–258 (2011). doi:10.1109/CSMR.2011.31

38. Liebchen, G.A., Shepperd, M.: Data sets and data quality in software engineering. In: Proceedings of the International Workshop on Predictor Models in Software Engineering, pp. 39–44 (2008). doi:10.1145/1370788.1370799

39. Marks, L., Zou, Y., Hassan, A.E.: Studying the fix-time for bugs in large open source projects. In: Proceedings of the International Conference on Predictor Models in Software Engineering, pp. 11:1–11:8 (2011). doi:10.1145/2020390.2020401

40. Matter, D., Kuhn, A., Nierstrasz, O.: Assigning bug reports using a vocabulary-based expertise model of developers. In: Proceedings of the International Working Conference on Mining Software Repositories, pp. 131–140 (2009). doi:10.1109/MSR.2009.5069491

41. McCabe, T.J.: A complexity measure. IEEE Trans. Software Eng. 2(4), 308–320 (1976). doi:10.1109/TSE.1976.233837

42. Mende, T., Koschke, R.: Effort-aware defect prediction models. In: Proceedings of the European Conference on Software Maintenance and Reengineering, pp. 107–116 (2010). doi:10.1109/CSMR.2010.18

43. Menzies, T.: Data mining: a tutorial. In: Robillard, M., Maalej, W., Walker, R.J., Zimmermann, T. (eds.) Recommendation Systems in Software Engineering. Springer, Berlin (2014)

44. Menzies, T., Marcus, A.: Automated severity assessment of software defect reports. In: Proceedings of the IEEE International Conference on Software Maintenance, pp. 346–355 (2008). doi:10.1109/ICSM.2008.4658083

45. Mockus, A.: Missing data in software engineering. In: Shull, F., Singer, J., Sjøberg, D. (eds.) Guide to Advanced Empirical Software Engineering, pp. 185–200. Springer, London (2008). doi:10.1007/978-1-84800-044-5_7

46. Mockus, A., Fielding, R.T., Herbsleb, J.D.: Two case studies of open source software development: Apache and Mozilla. ACM Trans. Software Eng. Methodol. 11(3), 309–346 (2002). doi:10.1145/567793.567795

47. Mockus, A., Nagappan, N., Dinh-Trong, T.T.: Test coverage and post-verification defects: a multiple case study. In: Proceedings of the International Symposium on Empirical Software Engineering and Measurement, pp. 291–301 (2009). doi:10.1109/ESEM.2009.5315981

48. Myrtveit, I., Stensrud, E., Olsson, U.H.: Analyzing data sets with missing data: an empirical evaluation of imputation methods and likelihood-based methods. IEEE Trans. Software Eng. 27(11), 999–1013 (2001). doi:10.1109/32.965340

49. Nagappan, N., Ball, T.: Use of relative code churn measures to predict system defect density. In: Proceedings of the ACM/IEEE International Conference on Software Engineering, pp. 284–292 (2005). doi:10.1145/1062455.1062514

50. Nagappan, N., Ball, T.: Evidence-based failure prediction. In: Oram, A., Wilson, G. (eds.) Making Software: What Really works,and Why we believe it, pp. 415–434. O'Reilly Media, Sebastopol (2010)

51. Nagappan, N., Murphy, B., Basili, V.: The influence of organizational structure on software quality: an empirical case study. In: Proceedings of the ACM/IEEE International Conference on Software Engineering, pp. 521–530 (2008). doi:10.1145/1368088.1368160

52. Nagappan, N., Zeller, A., Zimmermann, T., Herzig, K., Murphy, B.: Change bursts as defect predictors. In: Proceedings of the International Symposium on Software Reliability Engineering, pp. 309–318 (2010). doi:10.1109/ISSRE.2010.25

53. Nagwani, N.K., Verma, S.: Predicting expert developers for newly reported bugs using frequent terms similarities of bug attributes. In: Proceedings of the International Conference on ICT and Knowledge Engineering, pp. 113–117 (2012). doi:10.1109/ICTKE.2012.6152388

54. Nguyen, T.H.D., Adams, B., Hassan, A.E.: A case study of bias in bug-fix datasets. In: Proceedings of the Working Conference on Reverse Engineering, pp. 259–268 (2010). doi:10.1109/WCRE.2010.37

55. Nguyen, A.T., Nguyen, T.T., Al-Kofahi, J., Nguyen, H.V., Nguyen, T.N.: A topic-based approach for narrowing the search space of buggy files from a bug report. In: Proceedings of the IEEE/ACM International Conference on Automated Software Engineering, pp. 263–272 (2011). doi:10.1109/ASE.2011.6100062

56. Prifti, T., Banerjee, S., Cukic, B.: Detecting bug duplicate reports through local references. In: Proceedings of the International Conference on Predictor Models in Software Engineering, pp. 8:1–8:9 (2011). doi:10.1145/2020390.2020398

57. R Development Core Team: R: A Language and Environment for Statistical Computing. R Foundation for Statistical Computing, Vienna (2010)

58. Runeson, P., Alexandersson, M., Nyholm, O.: Detection of duplicate defect reports using natural language processing. In: Proceedings of the ACM/IEEE International Conference on Software Engineering, pp. 499–510 (2007). doi:10.1109/ICSE.2007.32

59. Samuelson, W., Zeckhauser, R.: Status quo bias in decision making. J. Risk Uncertain. 1, 7–59 (1988). doi:10.1007/BF00055564

60. Sarma, A., Noroozi, Z., van der Hoek, A.: Palantír: raising awareness among configuration management workspaces. In: Proceedings of the ACM/IEEE International Conference on Software Engineering, pp. 444–454 (2003). doi:10.1109/ICSE.2003.1201222

61. Strike, K., El Emam, K., Madhavji, N.: Software cost estimation with incomplete data. IEEE Trans. Software Eng. 27(10), 890–908 (2001). doi:10.1109/32.935855

62. Sun, C., Lo, D., Khoo, S.C., Jiang, J.: Towards more accurate retrieval of duplicate bug reports. In: Proceedings of the IEEE/ACM International Conference on Automated Software Engineering, pp. 253–262 (2011). doi:10.1109/ASE.2011.6100061

63. Thomas, S.W.: Mining software repositories using topic models. In: Proceedings of the ACM/IEEE International Conference on Software Engineering, pp. 1138–1139 (2011). doi:10.1145/1985793.1986020

64. Wang, X., Zhang, L., Xie, T., Anvik, J., Sun, J.: An approach to detecting duplicate bug reports using natural language and execution information. In: Proceedings of the ACM/IEEE International Conference on Software Engineering, pp. 461–470 (2008). doi:10.1145/1368088.1368151

65. Witten, I.H., Frank, E., Hall, M.A.: Data Mining: Practical Machine Learning Tools and Techniques, 3rd edn. Morgan Kaufmann, San Francisco (2011)

66. Wu, R., Zhang, H., Kim, S., Cheung, S.C.: ReLink: recovering links between bugs and changes. In: Proceedings of the European Software Engineering Conference/ACM SIG-SOFT International Symposium on Foundations of Software Engineering, pp. 15–25 (2011). doi:10.1145/2025113.2025120

67. Yu, L., Tsai, W.T., Zhao, W., Wu, F.: Predicting defect priority based on neural networks. In: Proceedings of the International Conference on Advanced Data Mining and Applications. Lecture Notes in Computer Science, vol. 6441, pp. 356–367 (2010). doi:10.1007/978-3-642-17313-4_35
68. Zimmermann, T., Nagappan, N.: Predicting defects using network analysis on dependency graphs. In: Proceedings of the ACM/IEEE International Conference on Software Engineering, pp. 531–540 (2008). doi:10.1145/1368088.1368161
69. Zimmermann, T., Premraj, R., Zeller, A.: Predicting defects for Eclipse. In: Proceedings of the International Workshop on Predictor Models in Software Engineering, pp. 9:1–9:7 (2007). doi 10.1109/PROMISE.2007.10

Chapter 7
Collecting and Processing Interaction Data for Recommendation Systems

Walid Maalej, Thomas Fritz, and Romain Robbes

Abstract Traditional recommendation systems in software engineering (RSSE) analyze artifacts stored in large repositories to create relevant recommendations. More recently, researchers have started exploring interaction data as a new source of information—moving closer to the creation and usage of the artifacts rather than just looking at the outcome. In software engineering, interaction data refers to the data that captures and describes the interactions of developers with artifacts using tools. For instance, the interactions might be the edits or selections that affect specific source code entities or webpages (artifacts) using an integrated development environment or a web browser (tools). Interaction data allows to better investigate developers' behaviors, their intentions, their information needs, and problems encountered, providing new possibilities for precise recommendations. While various recommendation systems that use interaction data have been proposed, there is a variety in the data being collected, the way the data is collected, and how the data is being processed and used. In this chapter, we survey and summarize the major approaches for RSSEs that create recommendations based on interaction data. Along with this, we propose a conceptual framework for collecting and processing interaction data for the purpose of recommendation.

W. Maalej (✉)
Department of Informatics, University of Hamburg, Hamburg, Germany
e-mail: maalej@informatik.uni-hamburg.de

T. Fritz
Department of Informatics, University of Zurich, Zurich, Switzerland
e-mail: fritz@ifi.uzh.ch

R. Robbes
Computer Science Department (DCC), University of Chile, Santiago, Chile
e-mail: rrobbes@dcc.uchile.cl

M.P. Robillard et al. (eds.), *Recommendation Systems in Software Engineering*,
DOI 10.1007/978-3-642-45135-5_7, © Springer-Verlag Berlin Heidelberg 2014

7.1   Introduction

Online retailers such as amazon.com or booking.com use data on how their users interact with the websites to automatically recommend potentially interesting items. A common scenario is "other users who looked at these products considered buying these products too. . . " Similarly, search portals aggregate the web navigation history into a user profile to improve the relevance of search results [7].

Software engineering researchers also started looking into using developers' interaction data to make a variety of recommendations. The idea is that single interactions such as document selections, code changes, command executions, or web searches allow for a better understanding of a developer's work and thus for more fine-grained and precise recommendations. Conventional software repositories such as version control systems provide only aggregated, high-level information on a developer's work.

For example, a developer might work all day to fix a bug. While the version control system only stores the few code changes committed at the end of the day, the developer did a lot more than just perform the committed changes. For instance, the developer might have used the debugger to reproduce the bug, navigated through other parts of the code, read documentation, run tests, or performed web searches to get help. A more fine-grained tracking of interaction data can be used to reflect the problems encountered by the developers and eventually recommend relevant documents, actions, people, or even pieces of code.

The ability to monitor almost every single interaction of a developer with modern tools, in particular within the integrated development environment (IDE), provides new and manifold opportunities for recommendation systems. Many recommendation systems in software engineering (RSSEs) that use interaction data have been proposed. For instance, Mylyn [13] tracks the selections and edits of source code artifacts to filter most relevant artifacts for the current task. Other systems use the interaction data to suggest reusable pieces of code [33], predict defects [16], raise awareness amongst developers [6], or prevent conflicts in teams [15].

These recommendation systems vary mainly along the types of interaction data gathered, the artifacts concerned by the interaction, as well as how the interaction history is collected, aggregated, and used to recommend information of interest. In this chapter, we describe the general principles for collecting and processing interaction data for the purpose of recommendation. Along with this, we survey and summarize major approaches for RSSE that are based on interaction data.

The remainder of this chapter is structured as follows. Section 7.2 presents three tools that use interaction data in order to support developers in their daily work. Section 7.3 defines interaction data, its main concepts, and granularity levels. Section 7.4 proposes a general framework for creating interaction data collection tools. Section 7.5 summarizes the main approaches to *process* interaction data, including the sessionization, filtering, and aggregation of interaction events. Section 7.6 discusses the main usage scenarios addressed by RSSEs that use interaction data: productivity and awareness. Finally, Sect. 7.7 presents the main challenges in the field and sketches future research directions.

7.2 Examples

After summarizing early foundational work, we present three tools that use interaction data to support developers in their work: Mylyn, Switch, and OCompletion.

7.2.1 Early Work

Many recommendation systems that collect and use interaction data are based on early work from the human–computer interaction community. Hill et al. [12] monitored edits, selections, and scrolls to compute "edit wear" and "read wear" metrics of documents. Edit wear measures how often a given line in a document was edited, while the read wear measures how often it was read. The idea was derived from the wear in physical objects, which gets visible due to interactions with the objects. Similarly, the edit and read wear are shown in the scroll bar of the document, allowing to spot which parts of the document were changed and read most frequently. Wexelblat and Maes [39] presented a tool for tracking interactions with web documents to support navigation. The goal was to capture and reuse navigation patterns of webpages to make new web investigations on similar topics more efficient. The collected information can be displayed as a map of webpages, showing how often a page was visited.

In the software engineering community, DeLine et al. [3] proposed TeamTracks, a tool that reuses the read wear metaphor to filter the list of artifacts displayed in the IDE. The tool monitors the previous transitions between source code files to recommend related files when a file is browsed. Evaluation studies showed that the tool helped developers in program comprehension tasks. The tool also helped experienced developers, working on large systems, to remember related artifacts to the one they are currently browsing. Singer et al. [38] proposed a similar tool, which recommends files to developers during maintenance tasks. The assumption is that files involved in *short navigation cycles* are related. A repository of association rules is built based on the observed cycles and is mined thereafter to recommend files related to those currently being browsed.

7.2.2 Mylyn

Mylyn is one of the most popular software productivity tools that uses interaction data. Mylyn is a plugin for the Eclipse IDE that allows users to focus only on the code elements that are relevant for their current tasks. For this Mylyn maintains for each task a "task context," which consists of the interaction data for that task. Based on this interaction data, Mylyn calculates a degree of interest (DOI) value for each code element [13]. This value represents the interest of a developer in the element

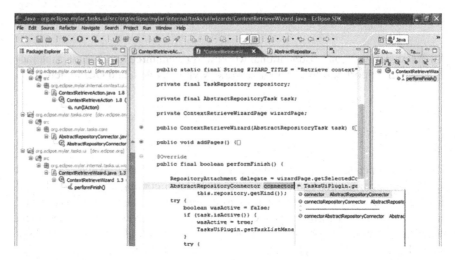

Fig. 7.1 Mylyn uses interaction data to recommend source code artifacts relevant for the current task

for the given task. Whenever a developer selects or edits an element in the IDE, the element's DOI value increases accordingly. At the same time, the DOI values of other elements decrease over time since interaction with them lies further back in the past. This recency aspect of DOI allows for the model to adapt to changing interest. Mylyn uses these DOI values to determine, filter, and highlight the most relevant code elements for a task at hand to counteract the information overload developers face in their IDE with the thousands of code elements that are usually displayed for a single project. When using Mylyn, only the elements with a DOI value exceeding a certain threshold are shown in the IDE (see Fig. 7.1).

7.2.3 OCompletion

OCompletion [33] improves code completion tools based on a fine-grained analysis of previous edit interactions. When a developer is typing the beginning of a long method name, code completion tools generate suggestions to help the developer complete the name, making it easier and faster to complete the method name, and avoiding spelling mistakes. In many cases, however, the list of suggestions is long and ordered alphabetically, making it time consuming for the developer to go through the list and find the relevant suggestion.

OCompletion addresses this issue by analyzing the changes made during the development session. It prioritizes the suggestions based on the recency of fine-grained interactions a developer previously had with the code. This approach makes it possible to have a short and accurate list of relevant suggestions instead of long lists (see Fig. 7.2).

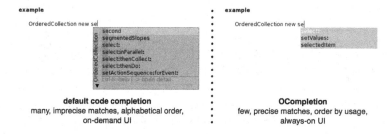

Fig. 7.2 OCompletion uses interaction data to recommend code completions

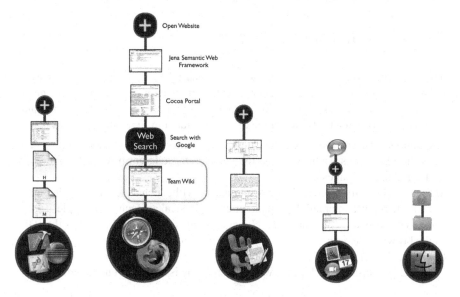

Fig. 7.3 Switch! uses interaction data to recommend the artifact needed next

7.2.4 Switch!

Developers work with a variety of tools and artifacts, not just the IDE or artifacts within the IDE. For instance, developers frequently consult API documentation on the web, communicate with other developers via email or chat, and use specifications, diagrams, and plans best viewed and changed with specific tools. Often there are dependencies between the various artifacts that require the developer to switch back and forth between the artifacts to complete a given task.

Switch! [23] is a recommendation system that automatically infers these dependencies based on the sequence of interaction events and the types of artifacts. Unlike Mylyn and OCompletion, Switch! gathers the interactions a developer has with all tools in an operating system. Switch! uses the interaction data to create a reactive graphical interface (see Fig. 7.3) that allows developers to quickly switch to the artifacts that they will most probably need next.

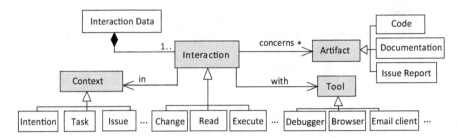

Fig. 7.4 The main concepts of interaction data

7.3 What Is Interaction Data?

Interaction data refers to a record of the actions taken by a user (in our case a software developer) with a tool. These actions are usually performed in a context, such as a specific task. Interaction data typically involves four types of data: interactions, artifacts, tools, and contexts, as illustrated in Fig. 7.4.

Interactions. The actions (i.e., the interaction events) taken by a developer, such as the clicks of specific buttons, the changes to code entities, or the views of documentation pages.

Artifacts. The entities a developer is interacting with, such as a source code entity, an issue report, an email document, or even physical artifacts and people.

Tools. The software application developers use during their work, such as the IDE, the browser, the issue tracking system, or the email client.

Contexts. The circumstances in which the developer is performing an interaction, such as the task a developer is working on or the issue being encountered.

7.3.1 Interactions

Interaction data is typically recorded as a stream of interactions or interaction events. Each interaction event denotes a single interaction a developer performs on an artifact using a tool. For example, a developer might open a source code entity using an editor, run a specific test case within a testing tool, edit a requirement using a text editor, or change a release plan using an issue management system. For this chapter, we focus on interactions that are observable on a developer's computer. However, a more general definition could capture any interaction a developer has with any virtual or physical artifact, including calling a customer over the phone, taking notes on a piece of paper, or drawing a model on a whiteboard.

In the following, we introduce common types of interaction events. This list is by no means exhaustive. It is rather open-ended and only intends to give an idea of the possibilities.

Select. A select interaction refers to the explicit selection of an artifact by a developer, such as selecting a specific class in the IDE, a particular issue report in the issue management system, or a particular tab in the web browser.

Edit. An edit refers to the creation, removal, or modification of an artifact by a developer. While on a fine granular level each individual keystroke might be recorded as a separate event, on a higher granular level, an edit event might represent the whole modification (e.g., to a source code element, a part of a document, or a package).

Read. A read interaction represents the developer acquiring the information in an artifact. This typically involves selecting the artifact and scrolling its content.

Open and Close. An open or a close event refers to the explicit opening or closing of an artifact, such as opening a file from disk, the attachment of an email, or accessing a website. Open and close can also concern a tool such as opening the email client or the web browser.

Reference. A reference event represents the indirect usage of a specific artifact, for example, through importing a library or calling a method in a source code.

IDE Command. IDEs offer a variety of commands to the users, each with a specific semantic and functionality. A command interaction refers to a developer executing one of these commands in the IDE. The exact set of possible commands depends on the specific IDE used and its plugins. Commands are typically grouped into user interface menus, including the following:

Debugging. A debugging command refers to specific debug actions, such as "set breakpoint," "step over," "inspect," "change variable," etc.

Versioning. These refer to specific commands in the versioning system, for example, "checkin," "checkout," "synchronize," etc.

Issue tracking. These refer to commands in the issue-tracking system such as "create a bug report," "close a bug report," "add a comment," etc.

Refactoring. These commands include common refactoring operations such as "rename," "move method," "extract method," etc.

Testing. These commands refer to the running and managing of test cases.

Text Input. A text input event refers to a user entering text into a specific field to perform a command. Examples are web searches, IDE searches, or rename commands. These interactions have a different semantic than edit events and are therefore often treated differently.

Use. This is a general type of interaction, which might, for example, concern tools or applications, such as using a debugger, or using an email client.

Other. Finally, there are commands specific to applications other than an IDE, such as starting a chat session, sending an email, or playing a video file. These are similar to the IDE commands in the sense that they are an open set of actions that may vary from user to user, from platform to platform, and even from application version to application version.

Interaction events depict a certain interest of a developer in the concerned artifact. Depending on the type, an event might indicate a different degree of interest in the artifact. For example, an edit event might indicate a higher interest in a source code method than a selection of the same method [14].

7.3.2 Artifacts

Developer interactions affect various types of artifacts. The artifacts range from source code entities (such as classes and methods), to models, documentation pages, and emails. Artifacts vary in their level of granularity. For instance, a developer might open a whole class file in a code editor, then select a single method therein, then change one call to another method, and then interact with a code navigation tool to navigate to the called method.

One of the most common types of artifacts used in RSSEs are source code artifacts, that is, the entities that a software system is composed of. Recorded artifacts may range from packages or binaries at a higher-level, down to files, classes, modules, methods, procedures, attributes, variables, and even individual expressions or statements, depending on the purpose of recommendations. For instance, while Mylyn stops at the method and variable level, OCompletion distinguishes interaction events at the code statement level.

In addition to source code entities, recommendation systems might also monitor developer interactions with other project artifacts, such as bug reports, test cases, documentation, build and configuration files, models of the system, and requirement specifications. More and more websites are also considered as very important artifacts in software development and the interaction with them reveal information about the developers' interests, their intent, or their problems encountered. These websites range from online API documentation, over question and answer websites, such as StackOverflow, to the results of web or code searches. From the perspective of developers, we can distinguish between two types of artifacts: documents that can be read and edited by the people (such as text documents, images, or videos) and binaries that can be executed or used.

7.3.3 Tools

Tools are the software applications developers interact with to perform their work. These tools might run as a separate process in the operating system or as a specific plugin in the IDE, such as plugins for source code analysis, for version control systems, or bug-tracking systems. Tools might also be remote applications, which are accessed, for example, via a web browser or a console. An example of such a remote tool is the Bugzilla issue-tracking system, which is typically used through the web browser. External tools that are often outside of the IDE but still important to a developer's work include web browsers, email clients, instant messaging, video-conferencing platforms, design tools, or requirement tools.

Typically, a specific artifact type is accessed and maintained by a specific tool type [17]. For example, editors and debuggers are used to manipulate source code. Diagramming and visualization tools are used to create and maintain models. Issue-tracking systems are used to gather and process issue reports. Finally, email clients and chat programs are used to share information and coordinate work. Some recommendation systems collect interaction data from a single tool. A more sophisticated recommendation system should take into account the variety of tools that developers use.

7.3.4 Context

Context is a loosely defined term and can refer to manifold concepts, such as artifacts related to the one the developer is interacting with all the way to the mood of the developer. We define the context of a developer's interaction as to the conditions or circumstances in which the developer interacts with an artifact. Context allows to better understand why certain interactions happened. For instance, a text input interaction might be part of a refactoring command, which might be part of a task to clean up the code.

For any interaction there is some context, for example, the preceding interactions that are relevant for the current interaction or some more abstract goal or intention of the developer. This context can be used to interpret developers' interactions and provide better recommendations. However, not all types of context are easily *observable*. For instance, if a developer accidentally hits a keyboard button when trying to catch a fly, the reason for the accidental edit would in most cases not be recorded and thus relevant context will be missing.

The context of an interaction can be on multiple levels of granularity, such as a developer's interaction preceding the event, a higher-level activity, or the more abstract task a developer is working on. Typically, higher-level context information is interpreted by processing interaction data, as described in Sect. 7.5. Common kinds of context that are of interest to recommendation systems are (a) the concrete *tasks* or *intentions* the developer is having (e.g., fixing a specific bug) and (b) a recurrent activity or situation in the developer's work (e.g., encountering a problem versus applying a solution).

Tasks and Intentions. In software engineering, a task is commonly defined as an atomic and well-defined work assignment for a project participant or a team [2, 14]. A task includes a description and an assignee; it typically includes a duration and time frame. Tasks describe what developers should do. An example of a task is "Task #123: implement the XML Export Feature" assigned to Alice or "Weekly integration test for web server" assigned to Bob. Recommendation systems like Mylyn [14] associate every interaction event with a specific task, which has been previously activated by the developer (to express that this task is being worked on). The interaction data associated to a task is called task context. It is used to provide recommendations tightened to that task—for example, the most relevant artifacts, the related bug reports, or the people who should work on the task.

A significant amount of developers' work is rather informal and thus not always associated to specific predefined tasks. Maalej [17] previously found that about half of developer interactions are not related to specific tasks. This kind of context is called intention [18]. It refers to the mental state that underpins the user interactions but is not necessarily stated explicitly, for example, "explore a new API," "assist a colleague," or "fix the discovered but unreported bug." There are several approaches that aim at detecting and describing the intention of the user [e.g., 18, 37]. However, most of them are still exploratory and experimental.

Activities and Situations. Activities are coarser-grained types of interactions, typically referring to a class or a set of interaction events. Examples of activities include navigating, coding, testing, debugging, specifying, planning, documenting, designing, amongst others. An activity typically includes more than one interaction event and lasts for at least a few minutes. Activities are often part of a task. For instance, in fixing a bug, developers might navigate through the code; once they find the right code, they make changes to it and then test it. Activities can also be more coarse-grained, for instance, if two tasks are about *documenting* two parts of a user interface. Activities reveal a recurrent development situation with well-defined semantics. They are interesting for recommendation systems to suggest items typically relevant in such situations.

Other types of situations include the "phases" of a task or the "states" in a mental model of the developer. For example, a typical change task includes an initiation phase, a concept location phase, and an impact analysis phase [30]. Phases might also be oriented toward a problem-solution cycle, such as locate cause, search solution, and test solution [34]. The better these concepts can be automatically inferred from a developer's interaction, the more precise the recommendations based on interaction data might become and the broader the approaches might become.

7.3.5 Interaction Granularity

Interaction data might include various levels of abstractions, often called *granularity levels* or granularity spectrum [35]. For instance, to perform a refactoring, a developer might have to enter text or edit and select parts of the code in between. In this case, the refactoring event represents a higher-level of granularity than the edit and select events.

All types of interaction data including interaction events, artifacts, tools, and contexts present different levels of granularity. For instance, an interaction event might be a step-in or a debugging event. An artifact involved in the interaction might be a package, a class, a method, a section, or even a single line in a document. A tool might be the whole IDE such as Eclipse or a single plugin in the IDE. Finally, a context might be the task activated by the developer, a certain release, or the current project phase. Typically, interaction data with a low level of granularity can be collected programmatically, while interaction data with a higher level of granularity needs to be inferred by processing the low-level data. One way to more formally describe the granularity levels of interaction data is to use ontologies [e.g., 21].

From the perspective of a developer, interactions with input devices such as mouse clicks and keystrokes represent the lowest level of granularity. An interaction with a single widget of the user interface, such as entering text in a text field or clicking a button, represents a higher level of granularity. A single widget interaction consists of multiple interactions with the hardware periphery such as multiple key presses on the keyboard to enter text in a text field. More precise information about the interaction can be derived at the widget level, since clicked widgets typically are associated with a name and a given purpose. For example, a mouse click can now be identified as pressing a button to create a project or the selection of a window part. The next level of granularity is an aggregation of several single widget interactions, for example, creation of a new project using an IDE wizard. Finally, several single-widget or multiple-widget interactions can represent a user activity such as refactoring the code, which in turn is a step of a task.

7.4   Collecting Interaction Data

Researchers and tool vendors have proposed several approaches to collect developers' interaction data, including the following:

- Eclipse usage data collector [http://www.eclipse.org/epp/usagedata/]
- Mylyn monitor [14]
- SpyWare, to record fine-grained code changes [32]
- Teamweaver, to record interactions with tools inside and outside the IDE [19]

In the following, we discuss the general procedure underlying these approaches. While different recommendation systems require different types and granularity levels on developers' interactions, they are generally all comprised of three parts: a monitor with a set of listeners (also called sensors), a component to generate interaction events, and a component to log these events and enable their processing. Figure 7.5 shows the general procedure for collecting interaction data.

7.4.1   Monitoring Developers' Interactions

The monitoring component varies depending on the tools, the artifacts, and the interactions that should be collected. While some approaches might, for example, only monitor coarse-grained IDE actions, others monitor every single keystroke. In general, the monitoring component manages several listeners, which are also

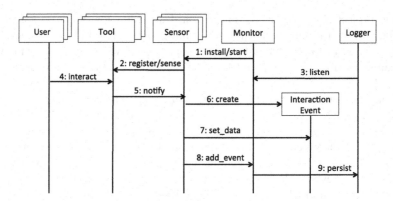

Fig. 7.5 Main components for collecting interaction data with a simplified flow

called sensors [19]. These sensors instrument the work environment, such as the tool, the IDE, or the operating system where the relevant events are triggered. The sensors continuously monitor their targets and whenever a new and relevant interaction happens, they collect the necessary information such as the name of artifacts concerned, its type, or the duration of the interaction.

The implementation of the sensors is often specific to the type and the technology of the tool being instrumented. For example, sensors might operate on the operating systems or the virtual machines level. These offer interfaces to listen to particular types of events such as opening a file with a tool. The Microsoft Windows operating system, for example, provides hooks, while OS X offers an Apple Script interface to implement such functionality. Also the Java virtual machine and the Eclipse runtime environment provide libraries to observe the interactions with the user interface elements. In addition, program-monitoring and tracing frameworks (such as DTrace or SystemTap) are deeply integrated into the operating system and execution environments with the purpose of tracing program execution that can provide further information on interactions. Sensors might also operate on the application level. This is particularly convenient if the application provides means for installing the sensors as plugins. Sensors should generally provide an interface to install/uninstall and active/deactivate them. This allow the users to have the full control and reduces the privacy concerns for collecting interaction data.

7.4.2 Generating Interaction Events

Once the sensor has captured an interaction, it generates an interaction event. Most commonly, an interaction event is composed of the following information:

- Type of event, for example, a select event or an edit event
- Timestamp denoting when the event occurred

```
<pre:e1 rdf:type interaction:JavaElementChange />
<pre:e1 interaction:hasTimeStamp 1222002002 />
<pre:e1 interaction:hasDuration 200 />
<pre:e1 interaction:concerns pre:java?name=myMethod />
<pre:java?name=myMethod rdf:type artefact:Method />
<pre:java?name=myMethod artefact:partOf pre:java?name=myProject.
   myClass />
```

Fig. 7.6 Example of an XML representation of interaction data

- Duration or end time of the event
- Artifact concerned by the interaction, for example, setName() or "Issue #234"
- Type of artifact concerned by the interaction, for example, a method or a bug report
- Tool used to perform this interaction

An example of an XML representation of interaction data is shown in Fig. 7.6. In addition, the generated event might contain information on the context, such as the task of which the event is a part. All of this information is gathered by the component and aggregated in a newly generated interaction event.

7.4.3 Logging Interaction Data

The final component is a logger that persists the generated interaction events. Different approaches use different techniques for the logging with respect to compression and the segmentation of the data. Mylyn, for instance, collects a set of interaction events and compresses them by collapsing similar events into one. This approach minimizes the use of disk space and write operations. However, it makes it difficult to recover the exact sequence of interaction events (see Sect. 7.5.4). In addition, Mylyn logs the interaction data related to the task a developer is working on in a so-called task context. Task contexts then provide a means to easily recover all interactions for a specific task. Other approaches log interaction events sequentially into a file without compressing or segmenting it in any particular way. Additional processing steps applied to the log file later can then also help to recover task boundaries (see Sect. 7.5.1).

The logging component might be on the developer's machine [14] or on a server [28]. Typically, the interaction logger provides additional functionality such as the obfuscation of the data to reduce the risks of misusing it or the archiving of the data to reduce its size. Evaluations have shown that, for a tool like Mylyn, the size of a log file for the interaction data of a full workday typically includes 1–10 MB of data [14].

7.5 Processing Interaction Data

Interaction data in its raw form is usually not what is needed. For recommendation purposes, further processing of the collected data is often necessary. We discuss common data-processing approaches and summarize pitfalls that should be avoided when processing interaction data. Processing interaction data is an active research field. Other approaches might emerge in the future.

7.5.1 Sessionization of Interaction Events

The raw interaction data is typically in the form of a stream of events, which might need to be split into individual sessions. We call this process *sessionization* of events. Ideally, the developers will explicitly define the start and end of a session, for example, to indicate what task they are working on. For example, Mylyn users can sessionize their work by explicitly activating and deactivating a specific task from the task list. However, since developers typically work on different tasks in parallel and frequently change their focus back and forth [29], they might not be willing to invest extra effort to indicate when they start and finish a specific work, or might simply forget to do this. The problem of sessionization is also present in conventional repository mining. It has been shown that developers occasionally perform several tasks in one commit, as discussed by Herzig and Zeller [11] in Chap. 6.

To identify sessions retrospectively, there are several approaches or heuristics that might be considered:

- Several empirical studies have shown that work sessions with a particular goal in mind typically last between 30 and 90 min [20].
- Period of sustained inactivity, that is, consecutive events that are separated by large amounts of time, can be used to split the stream of events into sessions. The threshold of 1 h has shown good results, that is, less than a lunch break or a meeting, but more than a coffee break.
- Shorter interruptions can be detected as well, and processed accordingly. The process is similar, only the threshold retained is lower (e.g., 5 min).
- Specific events represent strong indicators for switching the work session, such as a committing event, starting a new tool, or viewing the task list or the issue-management system.
- Individual work sessions can be focused on one task or be composed of several tasks. Several sessionization algorithms defined in the literature are based on time information and the artifacts that constitute the task [e.g., 29, 37, 41].
- Some tasks are too large to be finished in one development session. In this case, sessions that involve related artifacts may be linked together, forming a "macro-session" if the entities in common between both sessions are above a certain threshold.

7.5.2 Filtering of Events

Depending on the goal of the recommendation system, some events might be undesirable and considered as noise. These events must be detected and removed. Examples of these events include the following:

- "Transient changes" are changes that do not survive a development session, for instance, when a developer inserts debugging statements in the code in order to find a bug and removes them once the bug is fixed. Other examples are errors in the code (incorrect method calls) that are corrected later in the session. Transient changes strongly depend on the usage scenario of the interaction data. These events might be irrelevant in specific cases but relevant in other situations.
- Events that are not originating from the developer but rather from the tools that the developer is using may need to be treated separately. For instance, changes occurring from a refactoring tool do not represent developer interactions. Using these changes to evaluate the performance of code completion algorithms would misrepresent them. Changes performed by tools are performed much faster than changes performed by developers, making it possible to mark them as such (e.g., a rename refactoring will change the name of a method, and update all references to it in rapid succession, on the order of milliseconds).
- "Bulk events," for example, events of type "selection," may originate from selections of many artifacts in the IDE. If the developer selects all the classes in a given package, they may be marked as individually selected, yielding a very large number of selection events in a short time.

Filtering is performed when the spurious events are deemed to be irrelevant for the task at hand. In that case, events are simply removed from the stream of events.

7.5.3 Aggregation of Events and Inference of Context Information

Recommendation systems in software engineering might also aggregate interaction events to infer a higher level of granularity (see Sect. 7.3.5). A typical purpose is to infer the current task or situation of the developer from the low-level interaction events. We distinguish between three major aggregation approaches: semantic approaches, heuristic-based approaches, and probabilistic approaches (i.e., using machine learning).

Semantic approaches use a type hierarchy (i.e., a specific taxonomy) to aggregate interactions or artifacts to a higher-level type in the hierarchy [19, 23]. For instance, observed "step-in" and "step-out" events have "debugging" as the common higher-level type and can thus be aggregated into a more general debugging interaction. Similarly, a "method" and a "class" are subtypes of the higher-level type "code." The two events "edit the method X" and "edit the class Y" can be aggregated to "edit the code X and Y." The interaction and artifact taxonomies might also define cross-relationships to allow for reasoning. For example, the interaction type "implement" might be associated with the artifact type "method," whereas the type "specify" is associated with the artifact type "class." From observing an "implement" event that concerns an artifact of type "class," we can infer that the event is of type "specify." The main disadvantage of taxonomy-based approaches is the maintenance of the taxonomy, which is difficult and time consuming. Moreover, interaction types can have multiple higher-level types (i.e., multiple inheritance). It is thus nontrivial to navigate the taxonomy up and down to select the right type.

Similar semantic approaches without taxonomies aggregate interactions concerning the same artifact or the artifacts concerned by the same type of interaction. For instance, in Mylyn multiple events concerning the same code entity are sometimes represented as an aggregated event with a start date, an end date, and a number of events (i.e., the total number of events between the first and the last, both included). Similarly, the events originating from the clicks on items of the same menu (e.g., view, edit, or debug) can also be aggregated to an event describing that menu. Finally, all edit events that concern methods of the same class can be aggregated to an edit of that class.

Heuristic-based approaches typically use assumptions and metrics to aggregate events and infer context. For instance, the DOI model underlying Mylyn aggregates all the events concerning an artifact and compute an interest value that is updated over time based on the recency of the interaction [14]. Similarly, the defect prediction approach of Lee et al. [16] computes a variety of metrics over session data, aggregating interactions in one development session. These metrics then serve as input to a metric-based defect prediction model. Likewise, the Robbes and Lanza [31] classification of development sessions to one of five categories is based on metrics. Finally, Ying and Robillard [40] suggest to use the interaction style (i.e., the distribution over time) of the edit events to determine whether the developer is working on an enhancement task, minor, or major bugs fixes. Development sessions consisting of Edit-Last events are most likely enhancement tasks. Edit-First interaction style is most likely an indicator for minor bug fixes while Edit-Throughout is an indicator for major bug fixes. In general, the *duration*, the *recency*, the *type*, and the *frequency* of interaction events can reveal "important" context. Heuristics based on these features can be used to label sets of events in a developer session.

Finally, *probabilistic approaches* might use data mining and machine-learning algorithms (such as those introduced in Chap. 3 [26]) to aggregate interaction data. Generally, these approaches try to identify in the interaction history recurrent patterns, which characterize specific situations. When these patterns are observed in future interaction data, the system predicts the situation with a certain probability. For example, RSSEs might define the set of development situations to be inferred. In a training phase, the system learns the probability to move between two situations when certain interaction events occur. This can be, for example, to move from a testing to a debugging situation when a "read error message" event occurs. Later, the RSSE infers the current situation based on the observed events. Roehm and Maalej [34] suggested a similar approach using a hidden Markov model. Other machine-learning approaches such as time series analysis, or frequent itemset mining might also be used.

7.5.4 Pitfalls When Processing Interaction Data

Processing the interaction data can make it more useful to the recommendation task at hand, but certain pitfalls have to be kept in mind:

Over-processing. Each processing step may introduce noise. Algorithms detecting patterns in the data rarely have perfect precision and recall, especially algorithms that rely on thresholds: slight changes to the threshold return different results for borderline cases. Therefore, composing processing steps can potentially compound the inherent imprecisions of each algorithm. We recommend double-checking the results with care and if possible using a semi-automatic approach that corrects wrong processing results.

Destructive Operations. When aggregating events, we recommend keeping the original data intact as much as possible, as it is hard to predict what information will be needed. When the Spyware tool detects a refactoring operation, it creates an aggregated refactoring event, but keeps the actual changes as a part of this event in case a future RSSE need consult this data. Mylyn's aggregation of events loses detail on the specific interactions so that only the start and end time of a sequence of interaction is known, but the timestamps of intermediate events is removed. This makes it difficult for other approaches that need a full sequential list of interaction events to use the Mylyn monitor. As a workaround, Ying and Robillard [40] assumed that the intermediate events were equally distributed between the first and the last timestamp.

Tool Limitations. Data recorded about what the developer is doing may still be inaccurate. Each interaction data collection tool has issues that should be known to avoid false interpretations (e.g., that a very large number of artifacts are manually inspected by developers in a large amount of time). When using existing monitoring tools, we recommend to carefully review the data produced by the tool, in order to have a clear understanding of what kind of events are producing what kind of data. If possible, the data should be preprocessed to attenuate data quality issues.

Developer Inactivity. Developer inactivity is hard to assess, as it may simply be due to missing interaction data. For instance, the IDE sensor may not register any activity because the developer is browsing the web or because the developer is carefully reading a visible piece of code on the screen. Treating these moments as breaks in the work may introduce imprecisions.

7.6   Using Interaction Data

In this section, we discuss scenarios where interaction data can be used to provide recommendations to developers. We focus on approaches to increase developers' productivity and to support awareness and collaboration amongst development teams.

7.6.1   Productivity

Interaction data can be used to improve developers' productivity. Current approaches can be grouped into four main scenarios: (1) reducing information overload and helping developers to focus, (2) recommending a particular piece of information that is needed in the current task and that will help in satisfying developers' information needs, (3) suggesting a relevant source code, and (4) predicting a particular project metric, such as the bug-proneness of a module.

Mylyn [14] aims to *reduce information overload* for developers by optimizing the user interface of the Eclipse IDE (see Sect. 7.2). The core idea is that only a subset of all code artifacts in large software projects is relevant for working on a given task. Thus, Mylyn hides or blurs code artifacts that are less relevant. The tool collects all interaction events that a developer performs while working on a task and calculates a "DOI" value for each code element. This value reflects a certain interest level of the developer in this code element. The DOI assumes that the more frequent and more recent an element is interacted with, the more interesting it is to the developer for the current task at hand. The DOI value is then interpreted to visually indicate task-related files in the IDE. Kersten and Murphy [14] evaluated the influence of Mylyn on the personal productivity of developers by calculating the edit ratio of 16 subjects with and without using Mylyn. The edit ratio is the relative amount of edit versus select interactions for a certain period of time. The authors found that Mylyn significantly increased the edit ratios of their subjects, on average by 50 %. Mylyn is already part of the most common distribution of the Eclipse IDE and is being used by a large population of software developers.

Reverb [36] is a tool that recommends *websites including relevant information* for developers based on the code they are currently editing. The tool assumes that people often revisit the same websites and take into account two kinds of interactions: a developer's web browser history and the editor window the user is currently interacting with in the IDE. Any website a developer visits for at least 5 s is considered relevant and therefore indexed. When a developer interacts with the Java code editor in the IDE, Reverb extracts the Abstract Syntax Tree elements from the currently visible source code in the editor and queries the developer's browser history with these code elements. An evaluation showed that 51 % of code-related revisits can be predicted by Reverb, which reduces the time developers need to find and open the website needed. Murphy-Hill et al. [27] introduced a similar approach based on very fine grained interaction data for improving developers' fluency by recommending specific commands in the IDE that might save time and of which the developer might not be aware of.

Since *code completion tools* are commonly used by developers, we can assume that increasing their accuracy will increase the productivity of the developers. Robbes and Lanza [33] evaluated using fine-grained change interactions to improve the accuracy of code completion tools. The authors used a large data set including a list of fine-grained changes performed by developers while working on tasks in their IDE. From this data set, the insertions of method calls and class names are identified. When detecting such an insertion, the code completion engine is simulated, as if the developer was asking for a code completion. The code completion engine returns an ordered list of recommendations for the completed identifier. The proposals of the completion engine are compared with the actual identifier that is included in the sequence of prerecorded changes. The authors found that the default algorithms ordered their recommendations alphabetically, which yielded very poor accuracy. Ordering the suggestions based on their usage recency gave much better results, increasing the score fivefold.

Finally, Lee et al. [16] investigated developers' interaction history for *defect prediction*. Based on select and edit interaction events, they define 56 micro-interaction patterns. In an experiment, they compared the predictive power for regression and classification of these patterns against source code and history metrics. The authors show that micro-interaction patterns can improve upon existing defect prediction models based on source code or history metrics. For example, the pattern "NumLowDOIEdit" representing the number of edit events with a low DOI value, that is, editing a code element that one has not interacted with a lot before, has the highest power to predict a defect.

7.6.2 Awareness and Collaboration

"Awareness is the understanding of the activities of others, which provides a context for the own activity" [4]. Interaction data is being used to provide awareness to developers, mainly answering questions such as "who is working on what." Approaches for awareness vary depending on the granularity of the interaction data (from very fine-grained code edits to more coarse-grained file changes), the type of artifacts the awareness is provided for (such as project code or work items), and the kind of information visualizations being provided.

To provide team awareness and avoid conflicts, FastDash [1] visualizes where people are interacting with files in a project. This approach collects two kinds of data: (a) active file actions that are based on developers' interactions with the Visual Studio IDE, such as opening, editing, or debugging files, and (b) source repository actions, such as which files are checked out by whom. The interaction data is collected on a server and visualized in a dashboard, which presents the project files in a tree map and annotates files with which developers are currently interacting.

Seesoft [5] is a similar recommendation tool for creating awareness in software projects. It colors each line of code in the IDE according to the recency of its last change: the recently changed lines are colored in red, older lines in dark blue. The interaction used in this approach is limited to the changes that people made to the code in the source code repository.

More recently, Fritz et al. [6] suggested the Degree-of-knowledge model to recommend expert developers for parts of the code. This approach uses authorship and interaction data to characterize a developer's knowledge of the source code. The degree-of-knowledge model predicts for each code element a developer who should know most about it. In addition, Fritz et al. showed how this model could be used to recommend bug reports that might be of interest to a developer.

7.7 Challenges and Future Directions

The field of collecting and processing interaction data for the purpose of recommendation is relatively new. Despite recent advances, there are scientific and technical challenges as well as promising usage scenarios left for future research.

7.7.1 Challenges

Efficient, Integrated, Non-intrusive Instrumentation. The first step in implementing recommendation systems that use interaction data is instrumenting the work environments of developers and (in particular cases) end users. To this end, a question about the efficiency and intrusiveness of data collection arise, that is, how data can be collected without disturbing the user's workflow. Moreover, the integration of the context monitoring into heterogeneous tools and applications poses an additional engineering challenge on how various workplaces (including heterogeneous tools, information, and activities) can be instrumented and observed. This leads to the question of whether such instrumentation can be *systematically* integrated into (or offered by) underlying frameworks such as graphical user interfaces, accessibility libraries, operating systems, middleware, and execution environments.

Representation of Interaction Data. The usefulness of interaction data depends on the specific scenario for which it is used. In some cases, fine-grained interaction data and artifacts are needed. In other cases, higher-level interaction events and context information are more useful. This makes the general modeling and representation of interaction data for recommendation systems a difficult endeavor.

The representation of interaction data and its context has more complicated requirements than the representation of simple logs, for example, a web server traffic log. Interaction data should be represented efficiently and should allow for eventually unknown queries and processing. The following questions arise: How can we represent interaction data to enable reasoning, semantic interpretation, and querying? Which representations allow for a flexible and accurate comparison of similar contexts? What should be observed and what not? What should be rather processed?

Sessionization of Interaction Events. A central research issue for using interaction data in RSSEs and more generally building context aware systems is the sessionization of the event stream (see Sect. 7.5). Sessionization is a complex problem since people frequently switch their focus and intentions. Interruptions and new thoughts lead to context overlaps. Sessionization packages interaction data and context information that belongs together. The question is thus: How can we precisely sessionize interaction data? How can a context switch be detected? How can we automatically detect and classify users' intentions to well-defined types, for example, based on the meaning of interaction events (such as testing, debugging, or releasing context)?

Context Prediction and Comparison. Raw interaction data includes a lot of noise because of the large amount of *potentially useful* information that can be collected. Interaction data should be processed and aggregated, its information ranked, and new knowledge about the context derived out of it. The following questions arise: How can we aggregate interaction data for different levels of granularity (different situations require different levels of details)? How can short-term context such as the current intention and long-term context such as the profile and preference of the developers be predicted based on observed interaction? How can aggregated context be compared and decomposed if more details are needed?

Privacy Protection. Recommendation systems based on interaction data collect numerous, possibly sensitive information about the user. This raises privacy concerns, since information can be abused, misinterpreted, or even sold for marketing agencies. For example, the interaction data of a developer can be misused by the employer to measure and compare the productivity of the developers. The questions are: what are acceptable trade-offs for RSSE users? How can we protect users' privacy while collecting their sensitive information? How can we ensure the principle minimality, that is, ensure to collect only the minimally required set of information? The more difficult question is: how can we ensure that currently anonymized interaction data will not reveal sensitive information in the future, for example, if combined with other data about the user collected from different sources (e.g., other RSSEs)?

7.7.2 Future Scenarios

Proactive Knowledge Capturing, Sharing, and Access. Interaction data includes useful knowledge, for example, on how a problem has been solved by a developer [10]. If filtered and aggregated accurately, such data will represent experience description, that can be populated in wikis or used to recommend solution alternatives when similar problems are encountered. It is useful, for example, to capture information on where developers looked for help while having similar bugs, or what they did to fix it [9]. Similarly, reuse scenarios such as component integration or API reuse require significant background knowledge [8]. In such scenarios, useful information includes how other developers proceeded in the reuse, how they instantiated a particular API, where they looked for help, and where they started. Such experiences are typically lost or scattered across private documents.

Knowledge sharing can be made more precise and efficient by supporting the role of knowledge producers [9]. Future recommendation systems can actively capture the experiences of developers by observing interaction data and encouraging them to share certain information with certain team members [10], for example, asking to share a webpage that a developer extensively used to solve a certain problem.

Future recommendation systems can also automatically identify links between artifacts, for example, source code, created and documentation useful to understand it. For example, while implementing a change request, a developer might check the issue tracker, read the customer's email, browse a forum discussion, reuse a new library, and change several pieces of source code. The ticket, the discussion, the email, and the library can be linked and later traced to the changes and resulting versions. Linking changes to their context enables developers to trace these changes and understand them in the future [17]. These links simplify the information retrieval based on available information (e.g., the customer's email instead of the version number).

User Involvement and Continuous Requirements Engineering. In modern product development, the user feedback and the user acceptance of the product are essential for market success [25]. Current requirement engineering practices are characterized by a communication gap between users and developers [24]. The context that underlies the user feedback is either gathered asynchronously or submitted with the wrong level of detail.

Observing the interaction data of users can make user feedback a first order concern in software engineering. Software systems would observe how their users use certain features, their problem situations, their workplaces, and workflows. Such information facilitates continuous, semi-automatic communication between users and developers. Problems or bugs will be reproduced and understood faster, and wrong requirements corrected and elaborated remotely. This increases the quality of user input and the efficiency of requirements and maintenance processes. This would also enable users to bring their innovations and become a "collaborator" in the project [22], as their interaction data can be used to systematically evaluate particular software features (e.g., in a new release), how they are used, and why they are used in that way—promoting a deeper understanding of the user's needs.

7.8 Conclusion

In software engineering, interaction data captures the *interaction* of developers with *tools* to perform specific work and includes information about the *artifacts* being concerned by the interaction. Interaction data might also contain information about the *context* in which the interaction occurred (e.g., the task at hand, the intention in mind, or the problem being encountered). Current RSSEs using interaction data focus on increasing developers' productivity by, for instance, filtering irrelevant information or predicting reusable code, as well as creating awareness by, for instance, showing who is working on which artifact or recommending experts.

In this chapter, we discussed means to represent and collect interaction data for recommendation systems. Collecting this data typically requires installing monitors and sensors that listen to user interactions in the target applications and thereof create a log of interaction events. Furthermore, we discussed some of the major goals and challenges of processing interaction data, including the filtering of noise, the aggregation of events, the sessionization of event steams, and the inference of higher-level context. Although there have been considerable advances in the field in past years, there are still many open challenges for using interaction data in recommendation systems. These challenges include the efficient instrumentation and privacy concerns for interaction data. Potentially useful future scenarios include the extraction of knowledge and experience from the interaction data and the collection and processing of usage data software at runtime.

Acknowledgments We are grateful to Tobias Roehm, Zardosht Hodaie, and the reviewers for their constructive feedback on this chapter. We also thank Bernd Brügge and Bashar Nuseibeh for the comments on early versions of this work. The first author is supported by the EU research projects MUSES (grant FP7-318508).

References

1. Biehl, J.T., Czerwinski, M., Smith, G., Robertson, G.G.: FASTDash: A visual dashboard for fostering awareness in software teams. In: Proceedings of the ACM SIGCHI Conference on Human Factors in Computing Systems, pp. 1313–1322 (2007). doi:10.1145/1240624.1240823
2. Bruegge, B., Dutoit, A.: Object-Oriented Software Engineering, 3rd edn. Prentice Hall, Englewood Cliffs (2009)
3. DeLine, R., Czerwinski, M., Robertson, G.G.: Easing program comprehension by sharing navigation data. In: Proceedings of the IEEE Symposium on Visual Languages and Human-Centric Computing, pp. 241–248 (2005). doi:10.1109/VLHCC.2005.32
4. Dourish, P., Bellotti, V.: Awareness and coordination in shared workspaces. In: Proceedings of the ACM Conference on Computer Supported Cooperative Work, pp. 107–114 (1992). doi:10.1145/143457.143468
5. Eick, S.G., Steffen, J.L., Sumner, E.E. Jr.: Seesoft: a tool for visualizing line oriented software statistics. IEEE Trans. Software Eng. **18**(11), 957–968 (1992). doi:10.1109/32.177365
6. Fritz, T., Ou, J., Murphy, G.C., Murphy-Hill, E.: A degree-of-knowledge model to capture source code familiarity. In: Proceedings of the ACM/IEEE International Conference on Software Engineering, vol. 1, pp. 385–394 (2010). doi:10.1145/1806799.1806856

7. Google Official Blog: Personalized search for everyone. http://googleblog.blogspot.de/2009/12/personalized-search-for-everyone.html (2009). Retrieved 9 Oct 2013
8. Griss, M.L.: Software reuse: objects and frameworks are not enough. Technical Report HPL-95-03, Hewlett Packard Laboratories (1995)
9. Happel, H.J.: Social search and need-driven knowledge sharing in Wikis with Woogle. In: Proceedings of the International Symposium on Wikis and Open Collaboration, pp. 13:1–13:10 (2009). doi:10.1145/1641309.1641329
10. Happel, H.J., Maalej, W.: Potentials and challenges of recommendation systems for software development. In: Proceedings of the International Workshop on Recommendation Systems for Software Engineering, pp. 11–15 (2008). doi:10.1145/1454247.1454251
11. Herzig, K., Zeller, A.: Mining bug data: a practitioner's guide. In: Robillard, M., Maalej, W., Walker, R.J., Zimmermann, T. (eds.) Recommendation Systems in Software Engineering. Springer, Berlin (2014)
12. Hill, W.C., Hollan, J.D., Wroblewski, D.A., McCandless, T.: Edit wear and read wear. In: Proceedings of the ACM SIGCHI Conference on Human Factors in Computing Systems, pp. 3–9 (1992). doi:10.1145/142750.142751
13. Kersten, M., Murphy, G.C.: Mylar: a degree-of-interest model for IDEs. In: Proceedings of the International Conference on Aspect-Oriented Software Development, pp. 159–168 (2005). doi:10.1145/1052898.1052912
14. Kersten, M., Murphy, G.C.: Using task context to improve programmer productivity. In: Proceedings of the ACM SIGSOFT International Symposium on Foundations of Software Engineering, pp. 1–11 (2006). doi:10.1145/1181775.1181777
15. Lanza, M., Hattori, L., Guzzi, A.: Supporting collaboration awareness with real-time visualization of development activity. In: Proceedings of the European Conference on Software Maintenance and Reengineering, pp. 202–211 (2010). doi:10.1109/CSMR.2010.37
16. Lee, T., Nam, J., Han, D., Kim, S., In, H.P.: Micro interaction metrics for defect prediction. In: Proceedings of the European Software Engineering Conference/ACM SIGSOFT International Symposium on Foundations of Software Engineering, pp. 311–321 (2011). doi:10.1145/2025113.2025156
17. Maalej, W.: Task-first or context-first?: Tool integration revisited. In: Proceedings of the IEEE/ACM International Conference on Automated Software Engineering, pp. 344–355 (2009). doi:10.1109/ASE.2009.36
18. Maalej, W.: Intention-Based Integration of Software Engineering Tools. Verlag Dr. Hut, München (2010)
19. Maalej, W., Happel, H.J.: A lightweight approach for knowledge sharing in distributed software teams. In: Proceedings of the International Conference on Practical Aspects of Knowledge Management. Lecture Notes in Computer Science, vol. 5345, pp. 14–25 (2008). doi:10.1007/978-3-540-89447-6_4
20. Maalej, W., Happel, H.J.: From work to word: how do software developers describe their work? In: Proceedings of the International Working Conference on Mining Software Repositories, pp. 121–130 (2009). doi:10.1109/MSR.2009.5069490
21. Maalej, W., Happel, H.J.: Can development work describe itself? In: Proceedings of the International Working Conference on Mining Software Repositories, pp. 191–200 (2010). doi:10.1109/MSR.2010.5463344
22. Maalej, W., Pagano, D.: On the socialness of software. In: Proceedings of the IEEE International Conference on Dependable, Autonomic and Secure Computing, pp. 864–871 (2011). doi:10.1109/DASC.2011.146
23. Maalej, W., Sahm, A.: Assisting engineers in switching artifacts by using task semantic and interaction history. In: Proceedings of the International Workshop on Recommendation Systems for Software Engineering, pp. 59–63 (2010). doi:10.1145/1808920.1808935
24. Maalej, W., Happel, H.J., Rashid, A.: When users become collaborators: towards continuous and context-aware user input. In: Companion to the ACM SIGPLAN Conference on Object-Oriented Programming, Systems, Languages, and Applications, pp. 981–990 (2009). doi:10.1145/1639950.1640068

25. McKeen, J.D., Guimaraes, T.: Successful strategies for user participation in system development. J. Manag. Inf. Syst. **14**(2), 133–150 (1997)
26. Menzies, T.: Data mining: a tutorial.   In: Robillard, M., Maalej, W., Walker, R.J., Zimmermann, T. (eds.) Recommendation Systems in Software Engineering. Springer, Berlin (2014)
27. Murphy-Hill, E., Jiresal, R., Murphy, G.C.: Improving software developers' fluency by recommending development environment commands. In: Proceedings of the ACM SIGSOFT International Symposium on Foundations of Software Engineering, pp. 42:1–42:11 (2012). doi:10.1145/2393596.2393645
28. Pagano, D., Juan, M.A., Bagnato, A., Roehm, T., Bruegge, B., Maalej, W.: FastFix: monitoring control for remote software maintenance. In: Proceedings of the ACM/IEEE International Conference on Software Engineering, pp. 1437–1438 (2012). doi:10.1109/ICSE.2012.6227076
29. Parnin, C., Rugaber, S.: Resumption strategies for interrupted programming tasks.   In: Proceedings of the IEEE International Conference on Program Comprehenension, pp. 80–89 (2009). doi:10.1109/ICPC.2009.5090030
30. Rajlich, V.: Software Engineering: The Current Practice. CRC, West Palm Beach (2012)
31. Robbes, R., Lanza, M.: Characterizing and understanding development sessions. In: Proceedings of the IEEE International Conference on Program Comprehenension, pp. 155–166 (2007). doi:10.1109/ICPC.2007.12
32. Robbes, R., Lanza, M.: SpyWare: a change-aware development toolset. In: Proceedings of the ACM/IEEE International Conference on Software Engineering, pp. 847–850 (2008). doi:10.1145/1368088.1368219
33. Robbes, R., Lanza, M.: Improving code completion with program history. Autom. Software Eng. Int. J. **17**(2), 181–212 (2010). doi:10.1007/s10515-010-0064-x
34. Roehm, T., Maalej, W.: Automatically detecting developer activities and problems in software development work. In: Proceedings of the ACM/IEEE International Conference on Software Engineering (2012). doi:10.1109/ICSE.2012.6227104
35. Roehm, T., Gurbanova, N., Bruegge, B., Joubert, C., Maalej, W.: Monitoring user interactions for supporting failure reproduction. In: Proceedings of the IEEE International Conference on Program Comprehenension, pp. 73–82 (2013)
36. Sawadsky, N., Murphy, G.C., Jiresal, R.: Reverb: recommending code-related web pages. In: Proceedings of the ACM/IEEE International Conference on Software Engineering, pp. 812–821 (2013). doi:10.1109/ICSE.2013.6606627
37. Shen, J., Irvine, J., Bao, X., Goodman, M., Kolibaba, S., Tran, A., Carl, F., Kirschner, B., Stumpf, S., Dietterich, T.G.: Detecting and correcting user activity switches: algorithms and interfaces.   In: Proceedings of the International Conference on Intelligent User Interfaces, pp. 117–126 (2009). doi:10.1145/1502650.1502670
38. Singer, J., Elves, R., Storey, M.A.D.: NavTracks: supporting navigation in software maintenance. In: Proceedings of the IEEE International Conference on Software Maintenance, pp. 325–334 (2005). doi:10.1109/ICSM.2005.66
39. Wexelblat, A., Maes, P.: Footprints: history-rich tools for information foraging. In: Proceedings of the ACM SIGCHI Conference on Human Factors in Computing Systems, pp. 270–277 (1999). doi:10.1145/302979.303060
40. Ying, A.T.T., Robillard, M.P.: The influence of the task on programmer behaviour.   In: Proceedings of the IEEE International Conference on Program Comprehenension, pp. 31–40 (2011). doi:10.1109/ICPC.2011.35
41. Zou, L., Godfrey, M.W.: An industrial case study of Coman's automated task detection algorithm: what worked, what didn't, and why. In: Proceedings of the IEEE International Conference on Software Maintenance, pp. 6–14 (2012). doi:10.1109/ICSM.2012.6405247

Chapter 8
Developer Profiles for Recommendation Systems

Annie T.T. Ying and Martin P. Robillard

Abstract Developer profiles are representations that capture the characteristics of a software developer, including software development knowledge, organizational information, and communication networks. In recommendation systems in software engineering, developer profiles can be used for personalizing recommendations and for recommending developers who can assist with a task. This chapter describes techniques for capturing, representing, storing, and using developer profiles.

8.1 Introduction

Recommendation systems in software engineering (RSSEs) seek to assist individuals in performing software engineering tasks. In many situations, useful recommendations will be independent from the developer involved in the task. For example, a recommendation to inspect a file for faults that is based on code churn metrics [37] will be the same for everyone. However, there are also situations where the relevance and quality of a recommendation will be impacted by the personal characteristics of the developer performing the task.

Consider a system that recommends elements from an application programming interface (API) that could be used to implement some functionality. A developer chooses a descriptive name for the method (e.g.,"sortRecords()"), enters some comments that describe its purpose, and the recommendation system outputs one or more potentially useful API elements, such as the sort method from a library. At first glance this sounds like a great system, until we realize that the library sort method gets recommended every time we implement some sorting functionality. Here the recommendation system makes the assumption that the recommended API elements are unknown to the developer, who must discover them to carry

A.T.T. Ying (✉) • M.P. Robillard
McGill University, Montréal, QC, Canada
e-mail: annie.ying@cs.mcgill.ca; martin@cs.mcgill.ca

M.P. Robillard et al. (eds.), *Recommendation Systems in Software Engineering*,
DOI 10.1007/978-3-642-45135-5_8, © Springer-Verlag Berlin Heidelberg 2014

out the task. For this idea to work properly, the recommendation system must be able to reason about what API elements might already be known to a developer. The functionality described above was first implemented by a system called CodeBroker [54]. One of the prominent features of CodeBroker is that it could personalize the recommendations by storing a model of the user's knowledge of an API, to avoid recommending methods known to the user.

In the context of recommendation systems, personalization is the delivery of different information (i.e., recommendations) depending on the target user [1, 13, 15, 19]. The concept of personalization is pervasive in many application domains for recommendation systems. For example, Netflix's personalized movie recommender is responsible for as much as 60% of its movie rentals [40]; Google search engine has provided personalized search results at since least 2009 [16]. Outside the context of recommendation systems, more complex personalization approaches involving personalizing the delivery of the content have found success in domains such as intelligent tutoring systems [47], natural language dialog systems [51], and adaptive hypermedia [48]. Despite its successful use in commercial systems, personalization is not yet widely supported in the software engineering domain.

Customization is often considered to be a type of manual personalization. In customizable systems, users have the ability to build their own profiles by specifying preferences, typically from a list of options [15]. Systems that support customization are usually called adaptable systems. An example of an adaptable system is MyYahoo!: Users of MyYahoo! can adjust what type of content they prefer to see displayed in their homepage (e.g., type of news articles, stock prices), as well as how the content should be organized. In software engineering, the IBM Rational Application Developer provides an example of a customizable system. This system is a development environment built on top of the Eclipse integrated development environment (IDE) that allows users to specify roles, such as "Java developer" and "Web developer." These roles simplify the user interface for each role by limiting the number of available features [12].

The techniques needed to support customization within an application are well understood. In the simplest case, customization can be implemented through a simple key-value property mechanism. For this reason, this chapter focuses instead on adaptive systems that can personalize recommendations automatically, typically based on inferred user characteristics.

Beyond modeling the technical knowledge of a developer, as in the case of CodeBroker, RSSEs can take into account other characteristics of developers. These include not only basic information maintained by their employer (such as demographic information) but also more complex structures that capture their communication network. In the personalization community, a representation that captures these types of personal characteristics is called a *user profile* or a *user model* [1, 13, 15, 19].

In software engineering, models of developer characteristics are not only useful for personalizing recommendations: they are also the basis for producing recommendations *about* developers. For example, Expertise Recommender [32] can discover and recommend developers who have the most expertise on a given module by analyzing the change history of a system under development. In the case of such expert-finding tools, the developer characteristics stored and analyzed by the system under development are not necessarily those of the developer *using* the recommendation system (as in the case of personalization). For this reason, we use the term *developer profile* to refer to a collection of information about a developer, to avoid the overly restrictive focus on users.

In this chapter, we describe a collection of techniques that can be used to build developer profiles. We begin with a discussion of the potential applications of developer profiles in software engineering, illustrated with a description of their use in three different systems (Sect. 8.2). We follow with a presentation and discussion of the techniques necessary to collect and store different types of information about developers. Section 8.3 focuses on modeling software development knowledge and Sect. 8.4 discusses organizational information and communication networks. In Sect. 8.5, we discuss general issues related to the maintenance and storage of developer profiles. We conclude in Sect. 8.6 with a short discussion of the risks and limitations of developer profiles in RSSEs.

8.2 Applications of Developer Profiles

The two main areas of application for developer profiles in RSSEs are to *personalize recommendations* and to *recommend developers*.

8.2.1 *Personalizing Recommendations*

We return to CodeBroker, the RSSE introduced in Sect. 8.1, to illustrate how capturing a model of a developer's knowledge supports adaptive recommendations.

CodeBroker [54] facilitates code reuse by recommending Java methods that can be used to complete a task. Figure 8.1 shows the system operating within Emacs. The figure shows the Java source code written by a developer in the process of implementing randomization functionality in a card game. Specifically, the developer has just finished typing in the signature of the getRandomNumber method, preceded by some descriptive comments. At that point the developer moves beyond the method signature (see the cursor in Fig. 8.1), and CodeBroker automatically generates recommendations (bottom view in Fig. 8.1). The top recommendation is a method named getLong from the Randomizer class. This API method generates a random number between two given long integers, essentially the functionality and signature the programmer is about to implement. Here the programmer is obviously unaware of this API method. The recommendation is useful because it saves the overhead of reimplementing getRandomNumber.

To produce recommendations, CodeBroker considers terms in the comments and method signature and uses information retrieval techniques to match them

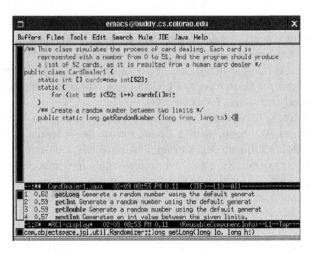

Fig. 8.1 CodeBroker recommendations in Emacs [reproduced with permission, from 53]

- java.applet
  - Applet
    · getParameterInfo (**added by Jeff at Thu 2 08:30:10 2000**)
- java.io
  - File
    · exists (Thu Nov 2 08:35:49 2000, Nov 2 08:15:10 2000, Nov 2 08:10:22 2000)
    · isAbsolute (Thu Nov 2 09:36:31 2000, Nov 2 09:19:15 2000)
  - CharArrayWriter
    · toCharArray (**added by Jeff at Thu 2 09:00:11 2000**)
- java.net (**added by Jeff at Thu 2 09:15:11 2000**)

Fig. 8.2 An example developer profile in CodeBroker [53]. The *top-level bullets* indicate the Java package, the *second-level bullets* indicate the classes in the corresponding package, and the *third-level bullets* the methods in the class

with methods of the Java Development Kit API. However, in this context, reuse recommendations are only useful if they support the discovery of new API methods.

To avoid generating useless and distracting recommendations for methods already known, CodeBroker maintains a developer profile that captures the API methods estimated to be known by a developer and removes from the recommendation list any method found in the developer profile.

A developer profile in CodeBroker initially contains the methods used by the developer. As the developer types in more code, the profile is automatically updated. Figure 8.2 shows an example of a developer profile in CodeBroker. The profile includes two methods of the `java.io.File` class that were automatically included through code analysis. In addition, the developer ("Jeff") complemented the profile by specifying that he had knowledge of the whole Java package `java.net` as well as the individual methods `getParameterInfo` and `toCharArray`. As this example

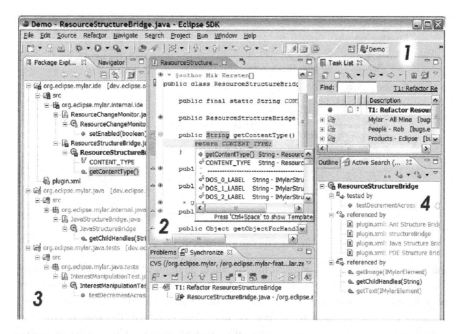

Fig. 8.3 Mylyn in action in the Eclipse IDE [reproduced with permission, from 23]

shows, manual adjustments to the profile can be done at various levels of granularity (e.g., entire packages or classes).

CodeBroker uses developer profiles to provide filtering on a list of API elements recommended for reuse. The concept of information filtering is taken further in Mylyn [23], a tool that adapts the user interface of Eclipse to the present needs of a developer by hiding information (code elements) that have not been accessed recently and by emphasizing the parts of the user interface that are more likely to be accessed.

Figure 8.3 shows Mylyn in action as part of a scenario originally described by Kersten and Murphy [23]. Mylyn adapts various views in Eclipse (e.g., the Package Explorer: Fig. 8.3, item 3) to only show the information relevant to the current task. The task the developer is working on is entitled "Task-1: Refactor ResourceStructureBridge" (marked with a solid dot in the Task List view in Fig. 8.3, item 1).

Mylyn adapts the user interface based on the developer's interaction history in the IDE. Program elements that are accessed more often and more recently as part of a task have higher importance, called degree-of-interest (DOI). For example, in a view that displays the system structure (Fig. 8.3, item 3), the only artifacts visible are the ones Mylyn estimated to be relevant. This view also marks the most relevant artifacts in bold.

In Mylyn, the structure that stores relevant elements and their corresponding DOI is called a *task context*. A user can also manually increase or decrease the DOI of

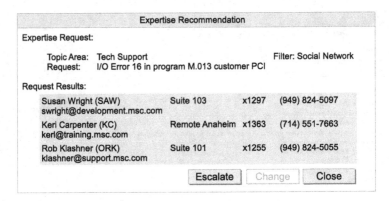

Fig. 8.4 An example of interface to present expertise recommendations based on Expertise Recommender [32]

the elements in a task context, resulting in direct changes to the model. We consider that task contexts are a form of developer profile that captures the immediate interest of a developer involved in a task. In addition to adapting the user interface, task contexts can also be used to restore the resources visible in the user interface at a different point in time, for example after an interruption. The developer profile used in Mylyn is task oriented and does not capture information beyond the current task.

8.2.2 Recommending Developers

Recommendation systems in software engineering can also be used to help locate individuals with a certain expertise. The problem of identifying who has the right expertise has become increasingly important given the ubiquity of large and distributed teams [17]. For these types of recommendation systems, developer profiles constitute the data items in the knowledge base used to produce recommendations. These systems are exemplified by Expertise Recommender [32].

Expertise Recommender was designed to help technical support personnel get in contact with the people best able to solve customer support requests. Figure 8.4 shows a list of recommendations produced by Expertise Recommender. In this scenario, a technical support representative fielded a support call from a customer and entered the request "I/O Error 16 in program M.013 customer PCI" with, among others, the value "Social Network" as a filter.

In Expertise Recommender, recommendations are derived from various filtering heuristics applied to a *profile database*. In principle the profile database can capture any kind of developer information available in an organization. In the example described by McDonald and Ackerman [32], the profile database is populated from two basic data sources: the version control system (VCS) for the software and the issue repository.

The issue repository is used to search for technical support personnel who had solved problems with the description similar to the input query. In our example scenario, the query includes three pieces of key information: the module name "M.013," the customer name "PCI," and the problem description "I/O Error 16." Each of the three pieces of information would trigger a separate search for past problems that match the information. The recommendation is the technical support personnel who solved the past problems that best matched the three pieces of information. In addition, Expertise Recommender supports another mode ("Change History" rather than "Tech Support") which uses source file contributions from commits and the proximity in the organization of the expert requester.

The Expertise Recommender architecture does not explicitly capture the concept of a developer profile as an explicit data structure. Instead, various optimizations are used, such as database indexes and maps. We can nevertheless consider that a developer profile in Expertise Recommender implicitly captures, in addition to basic contact information, a list of modules and a term vector that contains the important words in the description of all the issues solved by a developer. This observation illustrates the important point that developer profiles are conceptual entities that do not need to be explicitly represented as a unit in the implementation of the RSSE.

An interesting note about Expertise Recommender is that the recommendations produced take into account the characteristics of the user of the system. The "filter" parameter allows the results to be filtered according to two values: "Department" and "Social Network." The "Department" value returns developers ranked according to how close they are to the user of the system in terms of the official organizational structure (e.g., it prioritizes developers in the same department). "Social Network" instead prioritizes developers who are the closest in an ad hoc social network that takes additional personal relations into account. The developers of Expertise Recommender argue that this personalization feature helps distinguish their system as a recommendation system, in contrast to a more traditional information retrieval system. In the context of this chapter, we note that this feature makes Expertise Recommender an example of a system that uses developer profiles both as knowledge base elements and as a means to personalize the recommendations.

8.3 Development Knowledge

Software development knowledge is the knowledge developers have about both the system(s) they are working on and their general software development experience. Software development knowledge is usually derived *implicitly* rather than by explicitly asking a developer to provide it. This process requires an RSSE to infer the development knowledge from various actions performed by the developer. These actions are typically captured by three types of artifacts: change logs stored in a VCS, interaction traces collected by an IDE, and records stored in an issue tracking system. Sections 8.3.1–8.3.3 discuss these three data sources used for inferring development knowledge. We follow with a brief discussion of how certain types of software development knowledge can also be collected by *explicitly* asking the developer (Sect. 8.3.4). We present several common representations for software development knowledge in Sect. 8.3.5.

8.3.1   Version Control System Data

Version control system data typically refers to commits obtained from source code revision repositories, including the traditional ones such as SVN and CVS and, more recently, distributed repositories such as Git. There are several ways to use VCS data to infer development knowledge.

One heuristic is to assume that a developer changing a particular part of the source code has knowledge in that part of the code. One can find out who changed which lines of code by looking at the commit logs from a VCS. This heuristic is derived from the so-called *Line 10 rule* observed in a field study [32]: when a developer wanted to know who had the expertise for a particular part of the code, say line 10 of a particular file, the developer would consult the VCS commit log to see who was the last person changing line 10.[1] Expertise Recommender [32] uses this idea to recommend developers who have the expertise for a software module. Each developer profile includes the list of modules that a particular developer has last changed. Expertise Recommender takes a textual query as input and identifies all of the program modules mentioned. The list of recommendations are all the individuals who have modified a module mentioned in the query, ranked by recency of the last change by an individual.

The Line 10 heuristic is useful to infer knowledge about the source code being developed and when the change history of the source code is available. However, this heuristic would not work for estimating expertise about API elements, or about parts of the code for which change history is not available. For example, CodeBroker personalizes recommendations by filtering out recommendations that contain API elements known to the user. If a developer has used the Java API method addElement from java.util.Vector, CodeBroker would not recommend this API method. For this type of filtering to work, an RSSE must model the developer's knowledge of the API by analyzing which API elements are used in the code.

Extracting which API elements (e.g., methods) are used (e.g., called) from commits is a technical challenge. Identifying which method a developer is using in the code requires determining the type bindings of object variables that are the target of methods. This task is normally handled by compilers. However, in the context of

---

[1]Using data from older VCSes requires mapping lines to high-level program elements such as methods. For more information about this step, readers can refer to Zimmermann and Weißgerber [58].

Fig. 8.5 An incomplete Java program demonstrating the difficulty to extract information about method calls (example adopted from work by Dagenais and Hendren [10, pp. 1–2])

```
1  import p.;
2
3  class B {
4    void main() {
5      A a = new A();
6      a.p1 = "hello";
7      a.dd(a.p1);
8      a.remove(a.p1);
9    }
10 }
```

Fig. 8.6 The part of the program missing in the incomplete program demonstrated in Fig. 8.5 (example adopted from work by Dagenais and Hendren [10, pp. 1–2])

```
package p;

public class A {
  String p1;
  void add(Object o) {}
  void remove(Object o) {}
}
```

a commit, resolving type bindings is technically challenging because commits from a VCS are generally a subset of the whole program, possibly without the necessary dependency information for the usual type binding resolution to work. Even when one has access to the source code and the dependencies of the whole program, it may not be practical to compile a snapshot of the whole program for every commit. One technique that can infer type bindings from commits is partial program analysis (PPA) [10].

For example, suppose that a developer added one line of source code (line 7) to class B in Fig. 8.5. For the purpose of building the developer profile, we want to know which method is called at line 7 so that we can store this information in the developer profile. A syntactic analysis of only the code shown in Fig. 8.5 can only tell us that a method named add with one parameter is called at line 7, but not which class declares add nor the type of the parameter. This is especially problematic when multiple classes declare methods with the name add and one parameter. Improving upon pure syntactic analysis, PPA infers that method add(String) is called by looking at the string in the assignment in line 5. This inference is not strictly correct: in this example, apparently, class A (Fig. 8.6) only has one method named add with one parameter, add(Object) (line 13); thus, the inference is more specific than the one provided by syntactic analysis on the full program consisting of classes A and B.

Besides the actual code location and the methods that are called at the location, additional method calls in the code lines above and below a changed line can also be considered for inclusion in a developer profile [28]. For example, if a developer changed line 7 in the code in Fig. 8.5, we could also infer that the developer also knows the method remove at line 8. Textual terms extracted from commit messages and the actual commit have been used as a surrogate of expertise for the purpose of bug triage [31]. Terms extracted from the commit are taken from the identifiers and the comments of the code. Bug triage is a process necessary in many open source projects that maintain an issue tracking system. This triage process can become a resource-intensive task when a significant number of incoming bug reports are filed by outsiders because a project member has to determine whether an incoming bug report is valid and, if so, who should be assigned to the task of fixing the bug.

8.3.2 Interaction History Data

The second type of data one can mine to capture a developer's technical knowledge is interaction history. Interaction history refers to a sequence of events initiated by actions performed by a user with a tool. In Chap. 7, Maalej et al. [29] provide a detailed discussion on interaction history. We show how an RSSE adapts its output to individual users by looking at Mylyn [23]. Mylyn adapts various views in Eclipse to only show the information relevant to the current task. Mylyn harnesses interaction history involving software artifacts recorded in an IDE as a surrogate of relevance to the task.

In Mylyn, some events are the direct result of a developer's interaction with program artifacts. These events include *selections* (such as selecting a Java method and viewing its source) and *edits*. Other events are caused by indirect interactions. For example, when refactoring a class `ResourceStructureBridge` to a different name in Eclipse, Eclipse will update the name of the classes referencing the renamed class. Each of the referencing classes results in an indirect event called *propagation*. As part of this refactoring, Mylyn also tracks the actual rename operation in Eclipse, called a *command* event in Mylyn. Table 8.1 shows the events corresponding to this refactoring operation, as part of the task "Task-1: Refactor `ResourceStructureBridge`" first described in Sect. 8.2. The columns with a name prefixed with "Event" denote pieces of information captured in a Mylyn event and the column "Developer action" describes the event. For simplicity, we use an event number instead of the timestamp of an event (the column named "Event #"). The column "Event origin" refers to the tool associated with the event recorded and the column "Event target(s)" refers to the software artifacts associated with the event. Event 1 corresponds to the developer selecting the class. Events 2–6 correspond to the propagation and command events resulting from the rename operation.

Another example of an indirect event is when the developer selects the `get` `ContentType` method (Fig. 8.3, item 2). For each structural parent of the method (its class, source file, package, source folder, and project), Mylyn creates a propagation event. These propagation events cause the structural parents to become relevant and, therefore, visible in the Package Explorer (Fig. 8.3, item 3).

In addition to changes and navigation to code elements, a wide range of other interactions can be observed in an IDE. In the web domain, researchers have found that linger time and amount of scrolling can be useful indicators of interest [1]. Evidence to this effect is mixed in the software engineering domain [11, 44]: To determine whether source files visited by a user are relevant for the task, Mylyn [23] uses how frequently and recently a program element is being accessed, but not how long a developer stays on a program element nor how much a developer scrolls

Table 8.1 Sample events in the interaction history captured by Mylyn (table adopted from the work by Kersten and Murphy [23])

Developer action	Event #	Event kind	Event origin	Event target(s)
select RSB	1	selection	Package Explorer	class
rename RSB	2–5	propagation	Package Explorer	source file, package source folder, project
rename RSB	6	command	Rename refactoring	class

"RSB" is short for "ResourceStructureBridge"

within a program element, as its means for retaining source files visited by a user as relevant for the task. A separate study found that scrolling does not indicate interest or importance of the element, but rather an indication that the developer is lost [44].

Navigating to a code element and checking in changes to a VCS can imply different levels of familiarity on the source code. Fritz et al. [14] found that initial authorship of a code element is the strongest factor for predicting the correct level of source code familiarity (compared to subsequent authorship, navigating to the code element, and intermediate editing of the code element). Robbes and Lanza [43] compared algorithms making use of various types of implicit data, interaction history, and commits, in terms of their predictability of the next change.

8.3.3 Issue Tracking System Data

The third type of data source that can reveal development knowledge is issue tracking systems. Issue tracking systems refer to systems that maintain lists of issues such as software bugs. In Chap. 6, Herzig and Zeller [18] provide some practical advice in mining bug reports. In open source projects, issue tracking systems allow users to report bugs directly to the open source developers. Many commercial software organizations use issue tracking systems as an internal medium for coordinating software testers, developers, and managers in reporting, prioritizing, and discussing issues. Another type of issue tracking systems keeps track of technical support call tickets in a call center.

Expertise Recommender [32] identifies technical support personnel who can resolve a customer support request. The design was motivated by a field study [32] on the process for identifying which of the technical support staff can solve a technical call. The heuristic is to find similar technical calls completed in the past, by first querying the support database and then determining which of the results were similar to the current problem.

For each technical support staff member, Expertise Recommender builds an entry in the profile database using three pieces of information from the technical support problems resolved by the given person: the problem description, the customer, and the module responsible for the problem. These three fields are used to build three term vectors that characterize a staff member. A term vector's dimensions are textual terms, and the value of a dimension is the number of times a term appears in the past problems resolved by the staff member. In Chap. 3, Menzies [33] explains the concept of term vectors in more detail.

In the scenario described in Sect. 8.2, the customer "PCI" complained in the call that the system has a file error "I/O Error 16" in the module called "M.013." The representative taking the call was familiar with the module in general, but was unsure why this particular customer was experiencing the file error. For this representative's profile, the customer vector's "PCI" dimension would have value 0 because the representative had not dealt with the customer "PCI" before, while the module vectors "M.013" dimension would have a positive value because the representative had dealt with the module in previous problems. On the other hand, the top personnel recommended in Fig. 8.4, Susan Wright, most likely had positive values for the customer vector's dimension for "PCI," the module vector's dimension for "M.013," and the problem description's dimension for "I/O Error 16."

In Expertise Recommender, a term vector is normalized using a master term vector which represents the total number of times a term is used in the entire problem database. Other technical challenges in dealing with textual terms include building a thesaurus and handling misspellings and abbreviations.

8.3.4 Explicit Data Collection

The data collection strategies presented above estimate development knowledge using heuristics applied to various data sources. A more direct way to obtain development knowledge is to explicitly ask the developer to provide the information. In e-commerce, data provided explicitly usually comes in the form of user ratings. A classical example is the Netflix movie recommendation system. For the Netflix system to provide useful recommendations, users have to first explicitly provide examples of movies they like or dislike in a scale of one to five stars.

Besides the fact that explicit data collection imposes a burden on the user and may not scale in many situations, a problem with manually generated profiles is that users may not have the ability to evaluate their own expertise. Because of these two problems, it may not be practical for RSSEs to ask a developer to provide the level of expertise for each individual item.

Instead of solely depending on explicit information, RSSEs can elicit information from the user to complement the implicitly captured information. To reduce the effort from the user, explicit information can be collected at a *coarse-grained* level, where a user indicates a large group of items (in contrast to a fine-grained approach, where a user provides information for individual items). CodeBroker, described in Sect. 8.2, allows a user to manually adjust the developer profile. Developers can do so by specifying that they have knowledge at a coarse-grained level, for example, on a whole Java package `java.net` in the developer profile demonstrated in Fig. 8.2.

In terms of the quality of data obtained explicitly versus implicitly, in the web domain, conclusions have shifted over time. Earlier opinions suggested that implicitly collected data was of lower quality than explicitly collected data [21]. More recent studies provide a more positive perspective on the usefulness of implicitly collected data [49, 52]. There is not as much investigation in software engineering. Fritz et al. [14] investigated two types of implicitly collected information—interaction history and commits from a VCS—to construct a model of a developer's familiarity with a given code element. The study shows that data from the commits from VCS is a better indicator than interaction history when inferring a developer's familiarity to a code element.

8.3.5   Representation

The simplest way to represent *what* a developer knows is to list the signature of the program elements a developer has knowledge of, without distinguishing the *extent* of the knowledge. For example, CodeBroker's user profile (Fig. 8.2) includes the list of method signature for all of the methods in a developer profile, organized in terms of enclosing class and package. CodeBroker does not model the extent of the knowledge but implicitly assumes that a developer has the same knowledge on every method listed in the developer profile.

This assumption is not always appropriate. In Expertise Browser, a tool analogous to Expertise Recommender, the developer profile is also a list of what is called *experience atoms*: locations of source code checked in by a developer [35]. Expertise Browser keeps counts of how many times a particular line of source code has been modified by a developer. These experience atoms can be used to reason about the expertise of a person, or aggregated to reason about the expertise of an organization. These counts can also be used to rank recommendations for the most expert developer on a given part of the code.

The assumption of Expertise Browser is that each use of a program element increases the extent of the knowledge equally. However, different weighting schemes can also be considered for this purpose. For example, the frequency counts can be normalized by the global counts computed on all individuals. The intuition is that common methods such as List.add would get less weight because they are used many times by many individuals, whereas rarer methods would get a higher weight. The extent of the knowledge can also be affected by how recently the developer acquired the knowledge. This idea is discussed in the profile maintenance section (Sect. 8.5).

A developer profile is not limited to the program elements that a developer interacted with directly, but can also represent *relationships* between program elements. In Mylyn, indirect events such as the propagation event in Table 8.1 represent relationships among program elements. However, Mylyn does not store these relationships in a persistent task context. An in-memory task context graph representing these program elements and relationships is constructed by processing the events in the persisted task context. The benefit of this approach is that the task context can be shared with other developers. When loaded on another developer's workspace, the graph can be adjusted to adapt to the program elements and relationships present in the other developer's workspace. When reconstructing the in-memory representation on another developer's workspace, additional interaction history incurred by the other developer can also augment the representation.

The weighting for each element in the task context, called DOI, is derived from the frequency and recency of the events in the interaction history. The frequency is the number of interaction events that refer to the element as a target. Each type of event has a different scaling factor, resulting in different weightings for different kinds of interactions. Old events are weighted less because of a decay function, as discussed in Sect. 8.5. The DOI of a relation, consisting of a source and a target element, is computed using the same DOI algorithm, by means of the relation's target element.

Instead of capturing a list of program elements, it is also possible to aggregate the knowledge they represent by using term vectors that represent a normalized version of the frequency of individual terms used in software development artifacts authored or changed by a developer [31]. Vector-based user profiles thus refer to the representation popular in information retrieval for textual documents: a document is represented as a vector of n dimensions, where the dimensions correspond to n indexed textual terms[2] in the corpus of documents. For example, instead of containing a list of methods a developer has used, a developer profile could contain a method-by-term matrix where every row represents a method and every column, a term in the vocabulary of all terms in the signatures of methods in a program (assuming method identifiers are tokenized, e.g., by relying on the camel case convention). It is also possible for the term vectors to capture information in the source code of the method, their comments, etc. In Chap. 3, Menzies [33] dives deeper into information retrieval.

This approach is used by a bug triage recommendation system where a user profile is the text extracted from the most recently fixed bug reports [3]. Each vector in the profile contains text converted from free-form text in the summary and description of a report. A value in the vector indicates the frequency of a particular term, normalized by the length of the bug report, total intra-document frequency, and inter-document frequency. Another bug triage recommendation system also used a vector representation, not to model the text from bug report but terms extracted from the source code changes by a given developer [31]. A value in a vector is the term frequency present in a source code change.

More sophisticated representations and algorithms have been explored in domains outside software engineering, for example, in adaptive educational systems and personalized information retrieval. A survey by Steichen et al. [48] provides an overview.

---

[2]Terms are typically tokens from document corpus, stemmed or not depending on the application, after removing stop words and non-alphabetic tokens [30].

8.4 Organizational Information and Communication Networks

To make recommendations in a software engineering context, it is also possible to leverage data about the position of developers in their organization, or information about their communication networks. Organizational information includes characteristics such as a developer's position in the organization, the management structure, and a developer's role in the software development process. Developers' communication networks are the graphs that model their various interactions with other people for work purposes.

Organizational information and communication networks can play various roles in RSSEs, from being the central data source used to generate recommendation to serving as a filter for recommendations generated in some other way. For example, organizational information can be used as the basis for predicting fault-prone modules [38], Expertise Browser allows users to explore recommended experts by organizational structure [35], and Expertise Recommender offers the capability to filter its recommendations to only show those in the social network [32].

8.4.1 Data Collection

Organizational information can normally be obtained from sources such as company organization directories and software project management servers. A standard protocol for accessing and maintaining a company organizational directory is the Lightweight Directory Access Protocol (LDAP). Such a directory typically contains the geographical location and the position of an employee. Many company directories are built on an LDAP server as the back-end and use the LDAP's query facility. A example query that such company directories support is to find all employees located in a particular city and have a particular role (e.g., "software developer"). RSSE designers can use the query facility to obtain organizational information.

Software development roles can be implicitly mined from an integrated software development management platform, such as IBM Rational Team Concert [8]. Team Concert allows a software development team to create and specify roles. This information can be obtained from the Java API of Team Concert.

Developers' communication networks can be inferred directly from communication media such as emails and IRC chat logs, for example by drawing edges between senders and receivers. Communication networks can also be built from a variety of other sources, depending on what can be considered to constitute evidence of communication. Sources such as VCSes and issue tracking systems can be used as an indicator of interaction by considering that developers are related if they have been involved with the same issue. Involvement can be specified as a subset of any of the possible ways for a developer to be associated with a bug report, including fixing the bug described in the issue report, being CCed (carbon-copied) on emails related to the issue, or providing comments on the issue [2].

Two important technical challenges when building communication networks from VCS data and emails are *linking* bug reports with the source code artifacts that solve them, and *de-aliasing* different email addresses that may be associated with the same person. Unless sufficient care is taken to control imprecision in the linking and email aliases, these issues can introduce a significant amount of noise in the resulting networks. Bird et al. [5] offer an in-depth discussion of the problem of linking bug reports to the corresponding fixes [4]. For email de-aliasing, one algorithm found to work well is to group email addresses using a clustering algorithm. (In Chap. 6, Herzig and Zeller [18] provide more information about clustering algorithms in general.) The clustering algorithm requires a similarity function that returns a similarity value between any pair of email addresses. The output of the algorithm are groups of email addresses; the email addresses in a group are predicted to be associated with the same individual.

STeP_IN is an example of RSSE that relies on organizational data and communication networks [55]. STeP_IN recommends relevant experts and artifacts based on information obtained from VCSes, issue tracking systems, and a communication network derived from email archives. One unique feature of STeP_IN is that instead of simply capturing communication relationships, STeP_IN also models how likely it is that the person being recommended wishes to be involved in the communication. Specifically, STeP_IN captures the concept of *obligation*, to avoid one constantly asking help from a particular colleague, or to avoid one only asking help but never helping others. In STeP_IN, a user can explicitly change the preference value describing whether to be involved in an interaction with a particular colleague.

8.4.2 Representation

A communication network is a graph that can simply be represented as an $n \times n$ adjacency matrix, where n is the number of nodes in the graph and a value of 1 in a cell ij represents an arc between nodes i and j (and 0 otherwise).

Coordination requirements illustrate how a matrix representation of developer characteristics can be employed to compute derived information about developers. Coordination requirements represent a type of recommendation, namely, information about who a developer should coordinate with to best complete the work [7].

Conceptually, the approach uses two input matrices:

1. a *file authorship matrix* (a developer by file matrix), where a cell ij indicates the number of times a developer i has committed to a file j; and
2. a *file dependency matrix* (a file by file matrix), where a cell ij (or ji) indicates the number of times the files i and j have been committed together.

The approach computes coordination requirement through two matrix multiplications (Fig. 8.7). The first product multiplies the file authorship matrix and the file

$$
d_1 \begin{bmatrix} \cdot & \cdot & \cdot & \cdot & \cdot \\ \end{bmatrix} \overset{f_1\ f_2\ f_3\ f_4\ f_5}{}
$$

$$
\begin{array}{c} \\ d_1 \\ d_2 \\ d_3 \end{array}
\overset{\textstyle f_1\ f_2\ f_3\ f_4\ f_5}{\begin{bmatrix} \cdot & \cdot & \cdot & \cdot & \cdot \\ \cdot & \cdot & \cdot & \cdot & \cdot \\ \cdot & \cdot & \cdot & \cdot & \cdot \end{bmatrix}}
\begin{array}{c} f_1 \\ f_2 \\ f_3 \\ f_4 \\ f_5 \end{array}
\overset{\textstyle f_1\ f_2\ f_3\ f_4\ f_5}{\begin{bmatrix} \cdot & \cdot & \cdot & \cdot & \cdot \\ \cdot & \cdot & \cdot & \cdot & \cdot \\ \cdot & \cdot & \cdot & \cdot & \cdot \\ \cdot & \cdot & \cdot & \cdot & \cdot \\ \cdot & \cdot & \cdot & \cdot & \cdot \end{bmatrix}}
\begin{array}{c} f_1 \\ f_2 \\ f_3 \\ f_4 \\ f_5 \end{array}
\overset{\textstyle d_1\ d_2\ d_3}{\begin{bmatrix} \cdot & \cdot & \cdot \\ \cdot & \cdot & \cdot \\ \cdot & \cdot & \cdot \\ \cdot & \cdot & \cdot \\ \cdot & \cdot & \cdot \end{bmatrix}}
= \begin{array}{c} d_1 \\ d_2 \\ d_3 \end{array}
\overset{\textstyle d_1\ d_2\ d_3}{\begin{bmatrix} \cdot & \cdot & \cdot \\ \cdot & \cdot & \cdot \\ \cdot & \cdot & \cdot \end{bmatrix}}
$$

Fig. 8.7 Dimensions of the input matrices and the final matrix representing coordination requirements

$$
\begin{array}{c} \\ d_1 \end{array}
\overset{\textstyle f_1\ f_2\ f_3\ f_4\ f_5}{\begin{bmatrix} \cdot & \cdot & \cdot & \cdot & \cdot \\ \end{bmatrix}}
\begin{array}{c} f_1 \\ f_2 \\ f_3 \\ f_4 \\ f_5 \end{array}
\overset{\textstyle f_1\ f_2\ f_3\ f_4\ f_5}{\begin{bmatrix} \cdot & \cdot & \cdot & \cdot & \cdot \\ \cdot & \cdot & \cdot & \cdot & \cdot \\ \cdot & \cdot & \cdot & \cdot & \cdot \\ \cdot & \cdot & \cdot & \cdot & \cdot \\ \cdot & \cdot & \cdot & \cdot & \cdot \end{bmatrix}}
\begin{array}{c} f_1 \\ f_2 \\ f_3 \\ f_4 \\ f_5 \end{array}
\overset{\textstyle d_1\ d_2\ d_3}{\begin{bmatrix} \cdot & \cdot & \cdot \\ \cdot & \cdot & \cdot \\ \cdot & \cdot & \cdot \\ \cdot & \cdot & \cdot \\ \cdot & \cdot & \cdot \end{bmatrix}}
= d_1
\overset{\textstyle d_1\ d_2\ d_3}{\begin{bmatrix} \cdot & \cdot & \cdot \end{bmatrix}}
$$

Fig. 8.8 Dimensions of the input and the coordination requirements for a given developer d_1

dependency matrix, resulting in a developer by file matrix. This matrix represents the set of files a developer should be aware of given the files the developer has committed and the relationships of those files with other files in the system. To obtain a representation of coordination requirements (a developer by developer matrix), the approach then multiplies the first product with the transpose of the file authorship matrix. This final product is a matrix where a cell ij (or ji) represents the amount of shared expertise of developers i and j. More precisely, the matrix describes the extent to which developer i committed files that share commit-relationships with files committed by developer j.

Emergent Expertise Locator is a recommendation system that builds on the concept of coordination requirements [34]. To construct a profile specific to a given developer d, Emergent Expertise Locator constructs the coordination requirements on the fly, focusing on the current developer. As a result, the product is a vector that represents the coordination requirements relevant to the given developer (see Fig. 8.8).

8.5 Profile Maintenance and Storage

A number of design decisions can impact developer profiles and their use in RSSEs. This section discusses two important design dimensions for RSSEs using developer profiles: profile maintenance and profile storage. Profile maintenance concerns whether an RSSE can adapt a developer profile over time. This issue is referred to as *adaptivity* by the user modeling and recommendation system community [20, 36]. Profile storage is concerned with which component of an RSSE the profile is constructed and stored.

8.5.1   Adapting Developer Profiles

The simplest approach to profile maintenance is to keep the profile static. When using implicitly gathered data, the user profile is based on the entire available data at the time of the profile construction. For example, usage expertise can be mined from the entire change history of a system [45]. However, in any high-churn situation, static user profiles will quickly get out of date. There are two ways to improve upon static profiles.

First, in a system that builds developer profiles in a batch mode, the profiles can be manually adapted by requiring the user to specify which time period corresponds to the current experience [35]. In such cases we would consider the profiles to be *adaptable*.

Second, in more dynamic systems, another strategy is to ask the user to set some parameters that guide the adaptation of the user profile. In Mylyn [23] for example, a developer needs to explicitly declare the current task, so that the Mylyn monitor can identify the boundary of the interaction history that belongs to the current task context. This design decision is a result from the user study performed on an earlier version of Mylyn [22]: that version of Mylyn did not have the notion of tasks. The user profile was built from a single stream of interaction history, where the relative importance of older interaction history decayed automatically.

The motivation for asking a programmer to explicitly declare which task the programmer is working on is that programmers tend to switch between multiple tasks. This semiautomated approach to user profiling helps to make the profiles partly adaptive. Some work has been proposed to support the identification of task boundaries. The SpyWare tool displays a visualization and identifies sessions of work based on several measures including the number of edits per minute [42]. Coman and Sillitti [9] proposed an approach to segment development sessions.

The problem of automatically detecting parts of the interaction history that belongs to a task remains a hard problem [53], but its solution would eventually make user profiles completely adaptive. The following section presents additional strategies for achieving adaptive developer profiles.

The most straightforward way for an RSSE to adapt a developer profile is through a fixed time window. The notion of time can be defined either as the usual elapsed clock time [3], or in terms of a fixed number of events in the interaction history [46, 50].

Different strategies are possible for eliminating data outside a time window of interest. The simplest is obviously to delete older events. However, when developer profiles associate data with a degree of association (in contrast to a binary, in-or-out, model of what pieces of information are associated with a developer), it is also possible to decay the association of older elements. For example, Mylyn uses a decay function for program elements in a task context. In Mylyn, the decay is proportional to the total number of events associated with the task. As another example, Matter et al. [31] employed a 3 % weekly decay on VCS commits used for building a developer profile; this decay provides the optimal level of accuracy in the bug triage predictions.

8.5.2 Storing Developer Profiles

A major design decision for storing developer profiles is whether to store them on server components (e.g., in the back-end tier in a multi-tier architecture), or in the client component used directly by users.

Developer profiles based on information mined from server repositories tend to be stored on servers. Such repositories include VCSes and issue tracking systems as discussed in Sect. 8.3. Systems that employ profiles based on organizational information and communication networks need information about multiple users [7, 17, 39]. Such systems typically require a server-based approach. The STeP_IN system models a software project as a server-based project memory with relations between artifacts and their socio-technical links with developers [56].

A major concern with the collection and storage of developer information in a server is privacy. In RSSEs, privacy is a concern especially when data is collected implicitly (e.g., interaction history) and stored on a server. A simple solution is to allow a user to disable the data collection. For example Mylyn, which monitors a developer's interaction history, has a "silent activity mode" [22]. However, since tools like Mylyn base their recommendations on interaction history, disabling the collection of interaction history completely renders the tool useless. RSSE designers interested in other ways to respect privacy can consult research [e.g., 6, 24–26] on privacy-preserving personalization and recommendation systems.

In storing interaction history on the server, Mylyn [23] is somewhat of an exception. Typically, interaction history is stored in the client side, not only because of privacy reasons but also because of the voluminous nature of raw interaction history. Conceptually, the interaction history is a sequence of ordered events. If storing interaction history on the server is important, data compression strategies must be considered. For example, Mylyn does not record all user actions. Most of the events involving the same program element used in the same way are aggregated. When such an aggregation happens, the event data stores two timestamps instead of one: the timestamp of the first event and the timestamp of the last event being aggregated. Mylyn stores task contexts offline as a compact representation of the interaction history in an XML file in the client side [23]. Such an XML file is designed to be uploaded with the corresponding task, a bug report, or a feature request, if the user chooses to share a task context. One advantage of this client-based approach is the portability of task contexts as they can be used by other tools and analyses [27, 57].

Systems that support customization (see Sect. 8.1) usually employ developer profiles on the client side. In the web domain, websites such as MyYahoo! store customization information in cookies, pieces of data sent from a website and stored in the user's web browser [20]. Analogously, in software engineering, UI customization information is typically stored as an individual's local settings.

8.6   Conclusion

In our daily interactions, many of us have already been immersed in adaptive recommendation systems as we browse results from a search engine, choose a book to purchase online, or decide on a movie. These systems implement a type of personalization. Adaptive recommendations are constructed based on a user's interest represented by a user model. In the context of RSSEs, developer profiles support not only the adaptive recommendations *to* developers but also the ability to generate recommendation *about* developers.

In this chapter, we reviewed the techniques necessary for constructing developer profiles employed by adaptive recommendation systems for software engineering. Developer profiles can capture a wide range of characteristics about developers including their development knowledge, organizational information, and communication networks.

Many of the issues discussed in this chapter overlap with other aspects of RSSEs. Version control systems, interaction history, and issue tracking systems are the key data sources for generating developer profiles, but they are also used for generating many different types of recommendations, as discussed in Chaps. 6, 18, 7, and 5. Designing developer profiles that accurately and reliably capture the true characteristics of a developer is an empirical endeavor that will require much experimentation (Chaps. 10–13). The concept of personalization is also intimately tied with usability issues (Chap. 9). Readers interested in the general area of personalization can consult several surveys [1, 15, 19, 20, 36, 48].

Even though personalization can be effective in supporting developers in their information acquisition tasks, there are concerns that adaptive systems can be too personal, up to a point where individuals are segregated into information silos, by not making available information that is available to others [40]. In the context of software engineering, a developer may discover information that is irrelevant to the current task but may increase the developer's overall knowledge and appreciation of the project. Recommendation systems that focus developers' information discovery too narrowly may negatively impact the developer's overall performance, even if they successfully support them for individual tasks. An RSSE recommending only relevant parts of the code to examine for the current task will not allow such serendipitous opportunities beneficial beyond the current task. Similarly, an expert-finding tool cannot provide all the information that would be gathered through impromptu water-cooler conversations. From the technical point of view, Ricci et al. [41] suggest to use active learning, which "allows the system to actively influence the items the user is exposed to [...], as well as by enabling the user to explore his/her interests freely."

When we consider the individual developer receiving recommendations from
RSSEs, they inevitably have differences in experience, ability, and needs. In cases
where a recommendation depends on the individual receiving the recommendation,
using developer profiles in RSSEs should then contribute to improving the quality
of recommendations, ideally without stifling the developer's freedom to explore and
discover.

Acknowledgments We are grateful for the help from the following people and organizations:
Christoph Treude helped us greatly improve the structure of the chapter since early on and provided
us comments on a previous draft. Ben Steichen acted as a reviewer external to software engineering,
provided us with his expert advice on user modeling, and gave us numerous pointers to work in the
user modeling community. The editors of this book provided guidance and feedback throughout
the whole writing process. Mik Kersten and Yunwen Ye kindly allowed us to reproduce figures
from their respective theses. Finally, NSERC and McGill have provided financial support.

References

1. Anand, S., Mobasher, B.: Intelligent techniques for web personalization. In: Revised Selected
Papers of the IJCAI Workshop on Intelligent Techniques for Web Personalization. Lecture
Notes in Computer Science, vol. 3169, pp. 1–36 (2005). doi:10.1007/11577935_1
2. Anvik, J., Murphy, G.C.: Determining implementation expertise from bug reports. In:
Proceedings of the International Workshop on Mining Software Repositories (2007).
doi:10.1109/MSR.2007.7
3. Anvik, J., Murphy, G.C.: Reducing the effort of bug report triage: Recommenders for
development-oriented decisions. ACM Trans. Software Eng. Methodol. **20**(3), 10:1–10:35
(2011). doi:10.1145/2000791.2000794
4. Bachmann, A., Bird, C., Rahman, F., Devanbu, P., Bernstein, A.: The missing links: bugs
and bug-fix commits. In: Proceedings of the ACM SIGSOFT International Symposium on
Foundations of Software Engineering, pp. 97–106 (2010). doi:10.1145/1882291.1882308
5. Bird, C., Gourley, A., Devanbu, P., Gertz, M., Swaminathan, A.: Mining email social networks.
In: Proceedings of the International Workshop on Mining Software Repositories, pp. 137–143
(2006). doi:10.1145/1137983.1138016
6. Canny, J.: Collaborative filtering with privacy. In: Proceedings of the IEEE Symposium on
Security and Privacy, pp. 45–57 (2002). doi:10.1109/SECPRI.2002.1004361
7. Cataldo, M., Wagstrom, P.A., Herbsleb, J.D., Carley, K.M.: Identification of coordination
requirements: Implications for the design of collaboration and awareness tools. In: Proceedings
of the ACM Conference on Computer Supported Cooperative Work, pp. 353–362 (2006).
doi:10.1145/1180875.1180929
8. Cheng, L.T., de Souza, C.R.B., Hupfer, S., Patterson, J., Ross, S.: Building collaboration into
IDEs. ACM Queue **1**(9), 40–50 (2003). doi:10.1145/966789.966803
9. Coman, I.D., Sillitti, A.: Automated identification of tasks in development sessions. In:
Proceedings of the IEEE International Conference on Program Comprehenension, pp. 212–217
(2008). doi:10.1109/ICPC.2008.16
10. Dagenais, B., Hendren, L.: Enabling static analysis for partial Java programs. In: Proceedings
of the ACM SIGPLAN Conference on Object-Oriented Programming, Systems, Languages,
and Applications, pp. 313–328 (2008). doi:10.1145/1449955.1449790
11. de Alwis, B., Murphy, G.C.: Using visual momentum to explain disorientation in the Eclipse
IDE. In: Proceedings of the IEEE Symposium on Visual Languages and Human-Centric
Computing, pp. 51–54 (2006). doi:10.1109/VLHCC.2006.49

12. Findlater, L., McGrenere, J., Modjeska, D.: Evaluation of a role-based approach for customizing a complex development environment. In: Proceedings of the ACM SIGCHI Conference on Human Factors in Computing Systems, pp. 1267–1270 (2008). doi:10.1145/1357054.1357251
13. Fischer, G.: User modeling in human–computer interaction. User Model. User-Adapt. Interact. 11(1), 65–86 (2001). doi:10.1023/A:1011145532042
14. Fritz, T., Ou, J., Murphy, G.C., Murphy-Hill, E.: A degree-of-knowledge model to capture source code familiarity. In: Proceedings of the ACM/IEEE International Conference on Software Engineering, vol. 1, pp. 385–394 (2010). doi:10.1145/1806799.1806856
15. Gauch, S., Speretta, M., Chandramouli, A., Micarelli, A.: User profiles for personalized information access. In: Brusilovsky, P., Kobsa, A., Nejdl, W. (eds.) The Adaptive Web: Methods and Strategies of Web Personalization. Lecture Notes in Computer Science, vol. 4321, Chap. 2, pp. 54–89. Springer, Berlin (2007). doi:10.1007/978-3-540-72079-9_2
16. Google Official Blog: Personalized search for everyone. URL http://googleblog.blogspot.de/2009/12/personalized-search-for-everyone.html (2009). Retrieved 9 Oct 2013
17. Herbsleb, J.D.: Global software engineering: the future of socio-technical coordination. In: Proceedings of the Future of Software Engineering, pp. 188–198 (2007). doi:10.1109/FOSE.2007.5
18. Herzig, K., Zeller, A.: Mining bug data: a practitioner's guide. In: Robillard, M., Maalej, W., Walker, R.J., Zimmermann, T. (eds.) Recommendation Systems in Software Engineering. Springer, Berlin (2014)
19. Jameson, A.: Adaptive interfaces and agents. In: Sears, A., Jacko, J.A. (eds.) The Human-Computer Interaction Handbook: Fundamentals, Evolving Technologies and Emerging Applications, 2nd edn., pp. 433–458. CRC Press, West Palm Beach (2008)
20. Keenoy, K., Levene, M.: Personalisation of web search. In: Proceedings of the IJCAI Workshop on Intelligent Techniques for Web Personalization. Lecture Notes in Computer Science, vol. 3169, pp. 201–228 (2005). doi:10.1007/11577935_11
21. Kelly, D., Teevan, J.: Implicit feedback for inferring user preference: a bibliography. ACM SIGIR Forum 37(2), 18–28 (2003). doi:10.1145/959258.959260
22. Kersten, M., Murphy, G.C.: Mylar: A degree-of-interest model for IDEs. In: Proceedings of the International Conference on Aspect-Oriented Software Development, pp. 159–168 (2005). doi:10.1145/1052898.1052912
23. Kersten, M., Murphy, G.C.: Using task context to improve programmer productivity. In: Proceedings of the ACM SIGSOFT International Symposium on Foundations of Software Engineering, pp. 1–11 (2006). doi:10.1145/1181775.1181777
24. Kobsa, A.: Privacy-enhanced personalization. Commun. ACM 50(8), 24–33 (2007). doi:10.1145/1278201.1278202
25. Kobsa, A.: Privacy-enhanced web personalization. In: Brusilovsky, P., Kobsa, A., Nejdl, W. (eds.) The Adaptive Web: Methods and Strategies of Web Personalization, Chap. 21, pp. 628–670. Springer (2007). doi:10.1007/978-3-540-72079-9_21
26. Lam, S.K.T., Frankowski, D., Riedl, J.: Do you trust your recommendations?: an exploration of security and privacy issues in recommender systems. In: Proceedings of the International Conference on Emerging Trends in Information and Communication Security. Lecture Notes in Computer Science, vol. 3995, pp. 14–29 (2006). doi:10.1007/11766155_2
27. Lee, T., Nam, J., Han, D., Kim, S., In, H.P.: Micro interaction metrics for defect prediction. In: Proceedings of the European Software Engineering Conference/ACM SIGSOFT International Symposium on Foundations of Software Engineering, pp. 311–321 (2011). doi:10.1145/2025113.2025156
28. Ma, D., Schuler, D., Zimmermann, T., Sillito, J.: Expert recommendation with usage expertise. In: Proceedings of the IEEE International Conference on Software Maintenance, pp. 535–538 (2009). doi:10.1109/ICSM.2009.5306386
29. Maalej, W., Fritz, T., Robbes, R.: Collecting and processing interaction data for recommendation systems. In: Robillard, M., Maalej, W., Walker, R.J., Zimmermann, T. (eds.) Recommendation Systems in Software Engineering. Springer, Berlin (2014)

30. Manning, C.D., Raghavan, P., Schutze, H.: Introduction to Information Retrieval. Cambridge University Press, Cambridge (2008)
31. Matter, D., Kuhn, A., Nierstrasz, O.: Assigning bug reports using a vocabulary-based expertise model of developers. In: Proceedings of the International Working Conference on Mining Software Repositories, pp. 131–140 (2009). doi:10.1109/MSR.2009.5069491
32. McDonald, D.W., Ackerman, M.S.: Expertise recommender: a flexible recommendation system and architecture. In: Proceedings of the ACM Conference on Computer Supported Cooperative Work, pp. 231–240 (2000). doi:10.1145/358916.358994
33. Menzies, T.: Data mining: a tutorial. In: Robillard, M., Maalej, W., Walker, R.J., Zimmermann, T. (eds.) Recommendation Systems in Software Engineering. Springer, Berlin (2014)
34. Minto, S., Murphy, G.C.: Recommending emergent teams. In: Proceedings of the International Workshop on Mining Software Repositories, pp. 5:1–5:8 (2007). doi:10.1109/MSR.2007.27
35. Mockus, A., Herbsleb, J.D.: Expertise browser: a quantitative approach to identifying expertise. In: Proceedings of the ACM/IEEE International Conference on Software Engineering, pp. 503–512 (2002). doi:10.1145/581339.581401
36. Montaner, M., López, B., De La Rosa, J.L.: A taxonomy of recommender agents on the internet. Artif. Intell. Rev. 19(4), 285–330 (2003). doi:10.1023/A:1022850703159
37. Nagappan, N., Ball, T.: Use of relative code churn measures to predict system defect density. In: Proceedings of the ACM/IEEE International Conference on Software Engineering, pp. 284–292 (2005). doi:10.1145/1062455.1062514
38. Nagappan, N., Murphy, B., Basili, V.: The influence of organizational structure on software quality: an empirical case study. In: Proceedings of the ACM/IEEE International Conference on Software Engineering, pp. 521–530 (2008). doi:10.1145/1368088.1368160
39. Ohira, M., Ohsugi, N., Ohoka, T., Matsumoto, K.: Accelerating cross-project knowledge collaboration using collaborative filtering and social networks. In: Proceedings of the International Workshop on Mining Software Repositories, pp. 15:1–15:5 (2005). doi:10.1145/1083142.1083163
40. Pariser, E.: The Filter Bubble: What the Internet Is Hiding from You. Penguin Press HC, New York (2011)
41. Ricci, F., Rokach, L., Shapira, B.: Introduction to Recommender Systems Handbook. In: Ricci, F., Rokach, L., Shapira, B. (eds.) Recommender Systems Handbook, pp. 1–35. Springer, Berlin (2011). doi:10.1007/978-0-387-85820-3_1
42. Robbes, R., Lanza, M.: Characterizing and understanding development sessions. In: Proceedings of the IEEE International Conference on Program Comprehension, pp. 155–166 (2007). doi:10.1109/ICPC.2007.12
43. Robbes, R., Lanza, M.: Improving code completion with program history. Autom. Software Eng. Int. J. 17(2), 181–212 (2010). doi:10.1007/s10515-010-0064-x
44. Robillard, M.P., Coelho, W., Murphy, G.C.: How effective developers investigate source code: an exploratory study. IEEE Trans. Software Eng. 30(12), 889–903 (2004). doi:10.1109/TSE.2004.101
45. Schuler, D., Zimmermann, T.: Mining usage expertise from version archives. In: Proceedings of the International Workshop on Mining Software Repositories, pp. 121–124 (2008). doi:10.1145/1370750.1370779
46. Singer, J., Elves, R., Storey, M.A.D.: NavTracks: supporting navigation in software maintenance. In: Proceedings of the IEEE International Conference on Software Maintenance, pp. 325–334 (2005). doi:10.1109/ICSM.2005.66
47. Sleeman, D., Brown, J.S.: Intelligent Tutoring Systems. Academic, New York (1982)
48. Steichen, B., Ashman, H., Wade, V.: A comparative survey of personalised information retrieval and adaptive hypermedia techniques. Inf. Process. Manag. 48(4), 698–724 (2012). doi:10.1016/j.ipm.2011.12.004
49. Teevan, J., Dumais, S.T., Horvitz, E.: Personalizing search via automated analysis of interests and activities. In: Proceedings of the ACM SIGIR International Conference on Research and Development in Information Retrieval, pp. 449–456 (2005). doi:10.1145/1076034.1076111

50. Viriyakattiyaporn, P., Murphy, G.C.: Improving program navigation with an active help system. In: Proceedings of the IBM Centre for Advanced Studies Conference on Collaborative Research, pp. 27–41 (2010). doi:10.1145/1923947.1923951
51. Wahlster, W., Kobsa, A.: User models in dialog systems. In: Kobsa, A., Wahlster, W. (eds.) User Models in Dialog Systems, Symbolic Computation, Chap. 1, pp. 4–34. Springer, Berlin (1989). doi:10.1007/978-3-642-83230-7_1
52. White, R.W., Ruthven, I., Jose, J.M.: Finding relevant documents using top ranking sentences: an evaluation of two alternative schemes. In: Proceedings of the ACM SIGIR International Conference on Research and Development in Information Retrieval, pp. 57–64 (2002). doi:10.1145/564376.564389
53. Ye, Y.: Supporting component-based software development with active component repository systems. Ph.D. thesis, Department of Computer Science, University of Colorado, Boulder (2001)
54. Ye, Y., Fischer, G.: Supporting reuse by delivering task-relevant and personalized information. In: Proceedings of the ACM/IEEE International Conference on Software Engineering, pp. 513–523 (2002). doi:10.1145/581339.581402
55. Ye, Y., Yamamoto, Y., Nakakoji, K.: A socio-technical framework for supporting programmers. In: Proceedings of the European Software Engineering Conference/ACM SIGSOFT International Symposium on Foundations of Software Engineering, pp. 351–360 (2007). doi:10.1145/1287624.1287674
56. Ye, Y., Yamamoto, Y., Nakakoji, K., Nishinaka, Y., Asada, M.: Searching the library and asking the peers: learning to use Java APIs on demand. In: Proceedings of the International Symposium on Principles and Practice of Programming in Java, pp. 41–50 (2007). doi:10.1145/1294325.1294332
57. Ying, A.T.T., Robillard, M.P.: The influence of the task on programmer behaviour. In: Proceedings of the IEEE International Conference on Program Comprehension, pp. 31–40 (2011). doi:10.1109/ICPC.2011.35
58. Zimmermann, T., Weißgerber, P.: Preprocessing CVS data for fine-grained analysis. In: Proceedings of the International Workshop on Mining Software Repositories, pp. 2–6 (2004)

Chapter 9
Recommendation Delivery

Getting the User Interface Just Right

Emerson Murphy-Hill and Gail C. Murphy

Abstract Generating a useful recommendation is only the first step in creating a recommendation system. For the system to have value, the recommendations must be delivered with a user interface that allows the user to become aware that recommendations are available, to determine if any of the recommendations have value for them and to be able to act upon a recommendation. By synthesizing previous results from general recommendation system research and software engineering recommendation system research, we discuss the factors that affect whether or not a user considers and accepts recommendations generated by a system. These factors include the ease with which a recommendation can be understood and the level of trust a user assigns to a recommendation. In this chapter, we will describe these factors and the opportunities for future research towards helping getting the user interface of a recommendation system just right.

9.1 Introduction

Recommendation systems in software engineering (RSSEs) can be divided into two parts: the backend that decides what to recommend and the frontend that delivers the recommendation. In this chapter, we refer to the developer for whom a recommendation is aimed as the user. *Toolsmiths*, those developers who design and build RSSEs, often focus on the backend, because one clearly has to have something good to recommend before presenting it to the user.

E. Murphy-Hill (✉)
North Carolina State University, Raleigh, NC, USA
e-mail: emerson@csc.ncsu.edu

G.C. Murphy
University of British Columbia, Vancouver, BC, Canada
e-mail: murphy@cs.ubc.ca

M.P. Robillard et al. (eds.), *Recommendation Systems in Software Engineering*,
DOI 10.1007/978-3-642-45135-5_9, © Springer-Verlag Berlin Heidelberg 2014

Less attention is paid to the user interface than the backend. A toolsmith has
many options when choosing a user interface for an RSSE. The first iteration of an
RSSE is typically what is easiest to implement, so that is what toolsmiths pick for
their first implementation of an RSSE as a demonstration of feasibility, yet never get
around to improving the user interface. One could make the case that the reason so
few RSSEs have been adopted by the software engineering community is because
toolsmiths have spent so little time thinking about the user interface. But let us
examine the case of one particular recommendation system outside the domain
of software engineering, a case that suggests that the user interface does indeed
matter.

Consider Clippy, a user interface agent that recommended new tools to Microsoft
Word users. Clippy had a reasonably good recommendation algorithm, backed up
by significant empirical research [16]. For example, Clippy would recommend
that users try Word's letter template, which may have saved the user a significant
amount of time. However, Clippy was often disliked, even hated, by his user base,
enough so that it was listed by Time magazine on its 50 worst inventions list. Why?
Many retrospectives pin the blame on the user interface, such as the indictment of
Whitworth [49] that Clippy was not sufficiently polite.

Although RSSEs do not have such a famous example, the lesson is clear—
the user interface matters. The user interface mechanisms for auto-complete and
variable renaming, which are invoked with a simple keystroke in an editor, are
examples of successful user interfaces for RSSEs, as evidenced by the fact that
most integrated development environments provide convenient mechanisms for
toolsmiths to implement them. However, this does not necessarily mean that these
two mechanisms are the appropriate mechanisms for all information presented by
RSSEs. For example, we have argued that for smell detectors [27], a user interface
based on underlining code that is potentially involved in a smell is inappropriate,
because code smells, such as Long Method [12], are not binary, but are instead
matters of degree. Furthermore, even for RSSEs with a firmly entrenched user
interface, such as code completion, that brings up an overlay in the code editor, it
is not clear that the current user interfaces are the *best* mechanisms to represent
recommended information—perhaps they are simply the mechanisms to which
people are most accustomed.

Other communities have likewise realized the importance of user interfaces.
For example, collaborative filtering-based recommendation systems, such as
GroupLens [18], have seen increasing attention paid to the user interface in recent
years. Konstan and Riedl [19] refer to a turning point when it became evident that
the evaluation and design of the user experience for a recommendation systems
was as important as ensuring the underlying algorithms were accurate. Work on
the user experience in the collaborative filtering community focuses on such aspects
as personalization, ratings, and privacy. RSSEs typically use algorithms that are
less personalized and thus our focus in this chapter is on different factors than are
reported on in the collaborative filtering-based recommendation community.

In this chapter, we first discuss several factors that affect a user's likelihood to be
receptive to a recommendation. Next, we discuss the space of options a toolsmith

has when creating an RSSE user interface and discuss some of the advantages and disadvantages of those options. Then, we review some techniques toolsmiths can use in the design and evaluation of the user interface of an RSSE.

9.2 Presenting Recommendations

The user interface of an RSSE must present recommendations in a manner that allows users to consider acting upon the recommendations. Presenting the recommendations requires a user interface of some kind. The toolsmith must make many choices when designing the user interface for a recommender. We describe five factors the toolsmith must consider: understandability, transparency, assessability, trust, and timing. As we describe the factors, we provide examples of RSSE user interfaces that have made different choices. We also describe how the factors interact.

9.2.1 Understandability

Understandability refers to whether a user is able to determine *what* a recommender is suggesting. There are two primary dimensions to understandability: *obviousness* and *cognitive effort*. These two dimensions are independent. A user interface can be nonobvious, but once learned, may require significantly less cognitive effort.

The obviousness dimension describes how easy or hard it is for a user to recognize the kind of recommendation being provided. What a recommendation is may be readily apparent to a user. For instance, a duplicate bug recommender [e.g., 14] that brings up other bug reports from the same project when a new report is being considered provides a recommendation that is obvious for the user: the recommended bugs are in a style and form that a user immediately recognizes as a bug report. When a recommendation is obvious, little or no training is needed to describe what the recommendation is to a user. At the other end of the scale, a recommender that suggests properties of an artifact may require more training. For example, StenchBlossom [27] displays information about design defects in a users' code by displaying a visualization that the user must explore and interpret in order to comprehend.

The effort dimension describes how much cognitive effort is required to understand the meaning of the recommendation when it is presented. A recommendation for which the cognitive effort is at-a-glance will be easy for a user, once trained, to recognize the meaning. For example, the size of a petal in StenchBlossom maps to "how bad" a problem is, and users can simply glance at the visualization to interpret it, once they have trained themselves to interpret it. As an example at the other end of the scale, if a user is recommended a source code element, such as a method, which may be related to a current element being edited [8], the cognitive effort to understand the meaning of the recommendation may be much higher.

How can a toolsmith improve understandability in their system? Nielsen [30] provides several heuristics for user interface design, three of which are applicable for understandability in RSSEs. The first is "match between system and the real world," which suggests that the system should use words, phrases, and concepts that the user has likely encountered previously. The second is "consistency and standards," which suggests that the system should follow conventions and not make the user wonder whether two words or concepts mean the same thing. The third is "help and documentation," which suggests that the system should be usable without help, but help should be provided when required in a searchable, task-focused, concrete, and minimal manner.

9.2.2 Transparency

In addition to understanding what a recommendation is, a user must be able to determine *why* the recommendation is being provided. Similar to other earlier works [e.g., 41], we refer to this factor as *transparency*.

Transparency is related to rationale. If it is clear why a recommendation is being given, the transparency is high. Using our example of a duplicate bug recommender, it may be straightforward to provide transparency if the recommendation is based on similarity of text by reporting a percentage of similarity or by indicating stack traces that match exactly.

When a recommendation is based on more than a simple measure, describing the rationale for the recommendation may be more difficult. For example, a recommender that suggests a likely more efficient command to use in a development environment may require more substantial text or pictures to explain how the new command replaces other commands. For example, the user interface for the Spyglass system [47], which provides command recommendations, shows the user a rationale that describes the intended action, such as intending to navigate a call relationship between two specific points in the code, and the various ways of invoking the more efficient recommended command, such as using a call graph tool through a keyboard shortcut or a menu item.

When transparency is low and rationale is needed, the content and presentation of the rationale can have an effect on the user's perception of the recommender, such as the user's trust in the system [43]. The user modeling and collaborative-filtering recommendation communities have performed many studies into the effect of different styles of explanation on user behavior [e.g., 25].

How can a toolsmith improve transparency in their system? In general, the more information that the system can provide about the rationale for a recommendation, the better. This information is generally available to the underlying RSSE algorithm, and transparency is merely a matter of providing it to the user. However, the challenge is doing it in a way that remains understandable. In the field of general recommender systems, Ozok et al. [35] advise concrete explanations, such as "People who use X also use Y," over abstract ones, such as "You may also like Y."

9.2.3 Assessability

Once a user understands what a recommendation is and why it is being provided, there is still a need to *assess* whether or not a recommendation is relevant and is one that a user wants to take action upon.

Recommendations provided in software development typically require higher assessment than those provided in consumer-oriented domains. For instance, recommending a related news article to a user [18] may be assessable in a split second; does the title of the article appear interesting? In contrast, recommending a potential duplicate bug report requires gaining an understanding of the recommended report and comparing that against the new report: a cognitively challenging task. If seven potential duplicates are presented to the user, at least six comparisons are needed with substantial cognitive shifting between each comparison.

There is a spectrum of assessability in software engineering recommenders. At one end of the spectrum, it may be relatively easy for a user of Reverb [39], which recommends a webpage the user has previously visited relevant to code currently being edited, to determine if the webpage is of use for the current task. The assessment in this case may be simple because the user may recall the webpage from previous interactions. At the other end of the spectrum, it may be difficult for a user of Fishtail [38], which recommends a likely relevant but not necessarily previously visited webpage, to determine if the webpage is useful as it may take them significant time and effort to read through the recommended page. In general, the longer it takes a user to assess a recommendation, the higher the cost of false positives and the more a recommender needs to be accurate.

Assessability is related to, but different from, understandability and transparency. Easy to use and transparent recommendations may be more likely to be easy to assess. A recommendation of a webpage that a user has previously visited when they previously edited code may be easy to understand, transparent, and easy to assess. However, a recommendation can be easy to understand and transparent yet hard to assess. The difficulty of assessing the duplicate bugs outlined above is an example of this case. More difficult to understand and less transparent recommendations may be acceptable, if once the recommendations are assessed they are almost always applicable. For instance, a highly accurate duplicate bug recommender may be acceptable and considered useful and efficient to a user.

How can a toolsmith improve assessability in their system? If a recommendation is an alternative to what the user already has already done (such as recommending a duplicate bug report), the system should make it easy for the user to compare the existing item and the recommended item. In the duplicate bug report example, the system can highlight the salient differences between bug reports. If multiple comparisons are necessary, a higher level difference summary may be appropriate.

In general, the system can make it easy for the user to assess the value of a recommendation by comparing the recommendation against the alternatives with respect to the user's values.

9.2.4 Trust

Even if a recommendation is understandable, transparent, and assessable, a user must trust the recommendation to be of benefit in the way the recommender system implies. The need to establish trust varies with the level of commitment that the user needs to make with using a recommender. At one end of the spectrum, an RSSE that makes a recommendation to change a user's code and that will make the change automatically requires a significant amount of trust. If the automatic change were to introduce a subtle bug, the user may not recognize it until long into the future, and it may take a significant amount of time to track down and fix. On the other hand, an RSSE that auto-completes a method name may not require much trust from a user, because if users do not like the chosen method, they simply delete the identifier immediately.

Trust is especially important in RSSEs that necessitate behavior changes on the part of the user. For example, we have previously created an RSSE that recommends integrated development environment tools to users [47]. Such RSSEs might recommend, for example, that a user use a "Call Hierarchy" tool in an integrated development environment such as Eclipse, rather than using multiple invocations of a "Find References" command. Even though the RSSE provided high levels of transparency, which can help build trust [36], users found the recommendations hard to trust.

So, how can a toolsmith enable the user to trust their system?

Build it   Start with a small, modest recommendation before making more substantial recommendations. Although, to our knowledge, user interfaces in RSSEs have not allowed users to provide explicit feedback, such feedback has been shown to increase trust in other recommender systems [29].

Borrow it   Borrow trust from someone or something that already has it, such as a colleague of the user. For example, rather than saying "when making this change, you could also look at class X," instead say that "when making similar changes, your colleague Bill often looks at class X."

Fake it   Because humans are social creatures, they are influenced by social cues, cues that could be leveraged to improve recommendation acceptance. Cialdini [5] gives six principles of persuasion that could be leveraged in RSSEs: reciprocity, commitment and consistency, social proof, authority, liking, and scarcity. For example, a toolsmith could use authority in the RSSE by appealing to the fact that the recommendation is derived from Ph.D. work that has analyzed millions of lines of source code. The principles of Cialdini have been used successfully outside of software engineering to improve recommendations [7].

9.2.5 *Distraction*

When should an RSSE make a recommendation? Many types of RSSEs make recommendations when the user explicitly asks for it; in these cases, the answer is clear—deliver the recommendation when it is asked for. For RSSEs where the tool needs to take the initiative, the answer is less clear.

For some RSSEs, delivering a recommendation in the middle of a user's work is critical. For example, BeneFactor can suggest that a user complete a manual refactoring by using a tool [13]. In this case, the longer the RSSE waits to make the recommendation, the less time the user will save in taking the recommendation. If the user completes the refactoring manually, the recommendation has lost its value.

There are downsides to delivering early (and potentially frequent) recommendations as delivering a recommendation in the middle of a user's task may be distracting. That is, the cost of the interruption may outweigh the benefit that the recommendation brings, assuming the user even realizes that benefit.

How can a toolsmith reduce distraction in their system? Several user interface techniques have been proposed to help balance the need for timely recommendations with the need to avoid distracting users. One is the use of negotiated interruption [24], which informs the user that a recommendation is available without forcing the user to acknowledge it immediately. Annotations (Sect. 9.3.1) are one implementation of negotiated interruptions—the user can easily ignore or defer the recommendations that these affordances contain.[1] Another is the use of attention-sensitive alerting [16], where the recommender system tries to infer when the user is not in the middle of an important task. Carter and Dewan [4] have created such a system that gives help to developers when it detects that they are stuck. Adamczyk and Bailey [1] provide a good overview of techniques designed to reduce distraction in general human–computer interaction that can be applied to RSSEs.

9.3 Strategies Used in RSSE User Interfaces

Many existing ways to present recommendations exist. We divide this presentation into two parts: getting the user's attention (Sect. 9.3.1) and providing further information (Sect. 9.3.2).

9.3.1 *Interfaces for Getting Users' Attention*

As we hinted at earlier, how contact is initially made between a user and an RSSE is one major user interface decision when designing an RSSE. One of the

---

[1]We use the term *affordance* from the human–computer interaction field to refer to "the actionable properties between the world and an actor" [34].

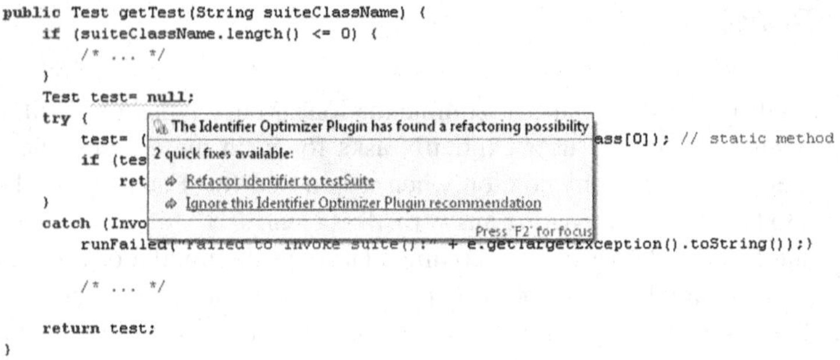

```
public Test getTest(String suiteClassName) {
    if (suiteClassName.length() <= 0) {
        /* ... */
    )
    Test test= null;
    try {
        test= (                                                              ass[0]); // static method
        if (tes   2 quick fixes available:
            ret      Refactor identifier to testSuite
    )              Ignore this Identifier Optimizer Plugin recommendation
    catch (Invo                                        Press 'F2' for focus
        runFailed("failed to invoke suite()" + e.getTargetException().toString());)

        /* ... */

    return test;
}
```

The Identifier Optimizer Plugin has found a refactoring possibility

Fig. 9.1 An example of an annotation (reproduced from Thies and Roth [42] under a Creative Commons Attribution license). Here, an information popup is shown after the mouse has hovered over the annotation

major distinctions is reactive versus proactive initiation [51]. Reactive initiation means that when users are ready to receive a recommendation, they ask the tool for it. Proactive initiation does not require the user's invocation; instead, the tool makes a recommendation when it is programmed to do so, perhaps at a scheduled time or perhaps because of some event. Schafer et al. [40] call this distinction "automatic" versus "manual" recommendations. Elsewhere, systems implemented with proactive initiation have also been called "active help systems" [9].

Not all user interfaces fit cleanly into these two categories. For example, Quick Fix Scout piggybacks quick-fix recommendations on top of an existing recommender's user interface [26]; the user does not have to explicitly ask for a recommendation from Quick Fix Scout, but neither is one offered at a particular time.

Proactive recommendations tend to be appropriate whenever a recommendation is timely, that is, it may significantly improve the task that the user is doing at the time the recommendation is made. Reactive recommendations tend to be appropriate when the delivery of a recommendation does not impact a time-sensitive task and when communication of a recommendation requires significant time.

Reactive recommendations tend to be easier to implement; the toolsmith provides a button or hotkey, and users invoke it when they want a recommendation. Finding such a button or a hotkey can be a challenge for the user [28]. There is a significant challenge, however, in designing and implementing a proactive initiation recommendation system. In the subsections in this section, we discuss several existing user interfaces for facilitating proactive initiation.

Annotations. Annotations are markup on program text that associate a particular recommendation with the segment of text that they are displayed on. Annotations are often represented as squiggly underlines or highlights. Figure 9.1 shows an example built by Thies and Roth [42], where a yellow underlining of the code test = null is augmented by a text hover, providing additional information.

The advantage of annotations is that they are often familiar interfaces for software developers, and many integrated development environments make it easy to implement them. They also appear in a convenient location whenever a recommendation is associated with a specific code location, so that when developers look at the code, they are likely to notice the recommendation. For example, in Fig. 9.1, the annotations work well because the recommendation speaks to the variable declaration on which the annotation is displayed.

However, annotations are not well suited for some situations: when recommendations occur *frequently* in source code, or when they are *soft, imprecise,* or *overlapping*. Frequent annotations are those that would be scattered all over the code, overloading the user to the point of ignoring the recommendations or turning them off. For example, Fowler suggests that comments are indicators of poor design [12], but an RSSE that annotated all comments would be excessive. Soft recommendations are those that require human judgment, such as what it means for a method to be "too long" [12]. Imprecise recommendations are those that could reasonably be placed on multiple points in code; for example, a recommendation that coupling should be reduced between classes could as easily be annotated on the referencing class as the referenced class. Overlapping recommendations are those that would overlap if the source code were annotated; for example, if multiple tools all annotated the same expression, at a glance the developer would not be able to distinguish one annotation from multiple annotations.

A special type of annotation is what might be called "document splits," where information is inserted between lines in a document. Figure 9.2 shows an example, where line numbers are shown along the left-hand side; between some lines, information about variable values is displayed. Document splits not only can display more information initially than other kinds of annotations but also may be significantly more distracting because they distort a user's documents.

Icons. Icons are small graphic images that appear in a development environment. Icons are typically displayed on the periphery of the user's workspace, sometimes as markers in the gutter of an editor. Figure 9.3 shows an example of the BeneFactor tool [13] recommending that the developer should use a refactoring tool.

Icons share many of the advantages and disadvantages of annotations, but because icons do not occupy the same screen space as code, icons may be less noticeable than annotations when the user does not happen to glance towards them.

Affordance Overlays. Affordance overlays are annotations that appear on top of user interface affordances, such as files in a browser or items in a dropdown menu. For example, Fig. 9.4 shows a set of task contexts, where one source code file is overlaid with a rounded rectangle, for the purpose of offering the user a recommendation that this is the file they should look at next.

Affordance overlays are well suited to recommendation contexts where a recommendation is frequent or constant and where the existing development environment's user interface should be as unperturbed as possible. Affordance overlays

```
                                          4:     int result;
                                          5:   } EXPR, *PEXPR;
                                          6:
                                          7:   #define ADD  1
                                          8:   #define SUB  2
 :                                        9:   #define MULT 3
 1:  typedef struct _EXPR{                10:  #define DIV  4
 2:    int oper;                          11:
 3:    int op1, op2;                      12:  void Eval(PEXPR e)
 4:    int result;                        13:  {
 5:  } EXPR, *PEXPR;                       14:    int op, a1, a2, res;
 6:                                        15:
 7:  void Eval(PEXPR e)                    16:
 8:  {                                     17:    op = e->oper;
 9:                                             [e = 8482, e->oper = 3, op = 3]
10:    if (e->oper == 1)                  18:    a1 = e->op1;
       [e->oper = 3, e = 8482]                 [a1 = -914, e = 8482, e->op1 = -914]
11:    {                                  19:    a2 = e->op2;
12:       e->result = e->op1 + e->op2;         [a2 = 0, e = 8482, e->op2 = 0]
13:    }                                  20:    res = -1;
14:    else if (e->oper == 2)                  [res = -1]
       [e = 8482, e->oper = 3]            21:
15:    {                                  22:    switch (op)
16:       e->result = e->op1 - e->op2;         [op = 3]
17:    }                                  23:    {
18:    else                               24:      case ADD:
19:    {                                  25:        res = a1 + a2; break;
20:       e->result = -1;                 26:      case SUB:
       [e = 8482, e->result = -1]         27:        res = a1 - a2; break;
21:    }                                  28:      case MULT:
22:  }                                    29:        res = a1 * a2; break;
23:                                            [a2 = 0, a1 = -914, res = 0]
24:                                       30:      default: break;
                                          31:    }
                                          32:    e->result = res;
                                              [e->result = 0, res = 0, e = 8482]
                                          33:  }
                                          34:
                                          35:
```

Fig. 9.2 An example of a document split from the SymDiff tool (reproduced from Lahiri et al. [20] under a Creative Commons Attribution license)

```
printArea.x = (fullWidth - (allBoxesWidth + sizeAccess.x + textPadding)) / 2;
printArea.width = sizeAccess.x;
sp.printString(e.gc, printArea, 0);
```

Fig. 9.3 An example of an icon (at left) from the BeneFactor tool (reproduced from Ge et al. [13] under a Creative Commons Attribution license)

may not work well in high-stakes situations, when a user missing a recommendation would have a significant impact.

Popup. Popup (or toaster) recommendations are those that appear in a new user interface layer when a recommendation is made, on top of an existing user interface. Popups may force the user to acknowledge them, or may disappear after some amount of time. Figure 9.5 shows a basic popup that Carter and Dewan [4] used for helping software developers when they get stuck. Popups not only typically disappear after a few seconds but also have various degrees of ephemerality, from disappearing completely to leaving behind an affordance (such as an icon) that the user can invoke to retrieve the recommendation after the popup itself has disappeared.

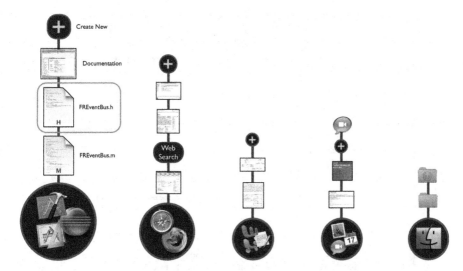

Fig. 9.4 An example of an overlay from the Switch! user interface (reproduced from Maalej and Sahm [22] under a Creative Commons Attribution license)

Fig. 9.5 An example of a popup (reproduced from Carter and Dewan [4] under a Creative Commons Attribution license)

Popups may work well in situations where getting the user's attention to deliver a recommendation is a high priority and when recommendations are infrequent. Popups may not work well when the likelihood of the user taking the recommendation is low.

Dashboard. A dashboard is a user interface affordance where recommendations are made to users in a fixed, known location on the screen, typically on the periphery of the user's vision, allowing the user to glance at recommendations frequently and with low commitment. Like the dashboard on a car, RSSE dashboards typically integrate recommendations of different types or from different sources. Figure 9.6 shows an example of a dashboard, StenchBlossom, which continuously displays information about multiple code smells while the developer works.

Dashboards may work well in situations where recommendations are continuous and pervasive. They may not work well when a user does not have the screen real estate to spare to the dashboard.

Email Notification. Email notifications are those that are delivered via email, rather than into an integrated development environment. One example is email notifications delivered by the Coverity static analysis tool [6], which can notify developers of potential defects via email.

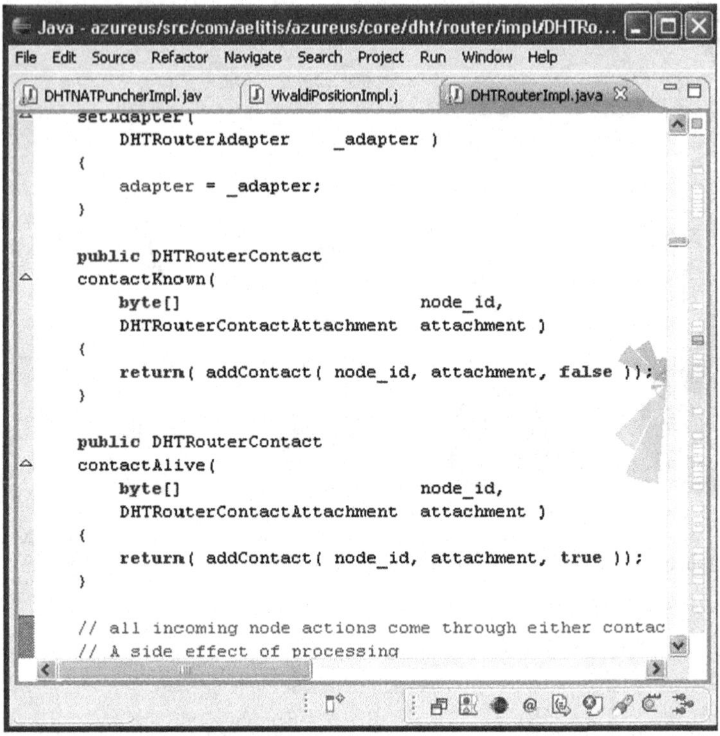

Fig. 9.6 An example of a visualization of code smells, where each "petal" represents the magnitude of a single code smell in the code on the screen [27]. For example, the bottom-most petal indicates a strong Large Class smell [12]

Email notifications may work well in situations where every recommendation should be considered by a user, and in situations where collaborating with outside entities (such as project managers) may be essential when a developer deals with a recommendation. Because users may be notified about new emails according to their email client preferences, email notifications are a way to provide the user with enhanced customizability and workflows. Since email is asynchronous, email may not work well in situations where recommendations must be handled immediately.

9.3.2 Descriptive User Interface Options

Beyond making initial contact with a user, toolsmiths often want their recommendation systems to provide additional information to a user. Since providing such information in the initial contact may be overwhelming, toolsmiths can employ progressive disclosure [31] to give the user more information. As we discuss in the following subsections, broadly speaking, this information can be conveyed

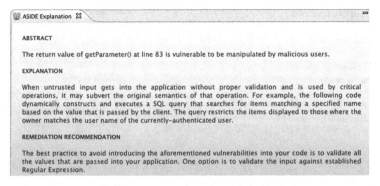

Fig. 9.7 An example of a textual description from the ASIDE tool (reproduced from [52] under a Creative Commons Attribution license)

in a textual way, as a transformation, or as a visualization. These user interface options for providing recommendation descriptions are equally appropriate for both proactive and reactive recommender systems.

Textual. A textual description is one that explains a recommendation in text. Textual descriptions can be enhanced by using markup, visual emphasis, and a tabular format. Figure 9.7 gives an example of a textual description from the ASIDE security tool, which explains why a developer should fix an input vulnerability. Many other tools provide textual descriptions, including the tool of Niu et al. [33] for recommending conflict resolution, the Example Overflow tool [53] that recommends relevant source code, and the Seahawk tool [2] that recommends relevant answers from a question and answer site.

Textual descriptions may be appropriate when a recommendation requires significant context and rationale. However, textual descriptions may not be appropriate when users have little time to read the text.

Transformative. Transformative recommendations are those that show the user the impact of taking a recommendation. The impact might be what happens when a tool is invoked or when code is changed. Figure 9.8 shows an example where a refactoring is recommended. Before this screenshot was taken, the developer had cut the code

```
int string_size = string.length();
size += string_size;
```

out of the `for` loop and had begun typing `findSize` into that loop. The recommendation system, WitchDoctor, then recommended that the developer create a new method with the cut code using the appropriate parameters and return value. The recommendation is made in a transformative way, because the gray code (i.e., "size =", "(size, string);", etc.) previews what would happen if the user accepts the recommendation. A more conventional implementation of transformative recommendations might simply show a preview of a change in a separate

Fig. 9.8 An example of a transformative recommendation from the WitchDoctor tool (reproduced from [11] under a Creative Commons Attribution license)

```
public static int fullSize()
{
    int size = 0;

    for(String s : list)
    {
        size = findSize(size, s);
    }

    return size;
}

public static int findSize(int size, String s)
{
    int string_size = s.length();
    size += string_size;
    return size;
}
```

window or popup. ChangeCommander [10] is an example of a recommendation system that takes this approach. A similar approach would be to allow the recommender system to make a code change, but then allow the developer to undo that change.

Transformative recommendations may work well in situations where the consequence of a recommendation is known. They may not work so well in situations where the consequence takes a significant amount of time for the user to understand, since the user must essentially reverse engineer the transformation to understand the problem that it solved.

Visualization. Visualizations convey recommendations in a graphical way. Figure 9.9 shows a visualization of callers and callees in a piece of software. Trumper and Dollner [46] provide an overview of visualization techniques for RSSEs.

Visualizations may work well when recommendations are indirect and require a software developer's judgment. In essence, visualizations collect and display information, with the hope that the developer will take action based on the information that the RSSE provides. This is contrast to many textual recommendations, which precisely tell the developer what to do.

In this section, we have discussed several user interfaces that toolsmiths can use to present their recommendations. However, we do not want the reader to treat this list as exhaustive—our opinion is that novel user interfaces may better fit the needs of users. Such novel interfaces may completely discard our list of user interfaces, or combine them in a novel way.

The user interfaces presented in this section may seem to be intuitively related to the dimensions we describe in the prior section, but we view the two as orthogonal issues. For example, one might assume that a popup user interface is more distracting than an affordance overlay. However, the fact that many popups appear distracting is inessential to that user interface; a toolsmith can reduce the distraction of popups by using techniques such as gradual fading and more intelligent timing.

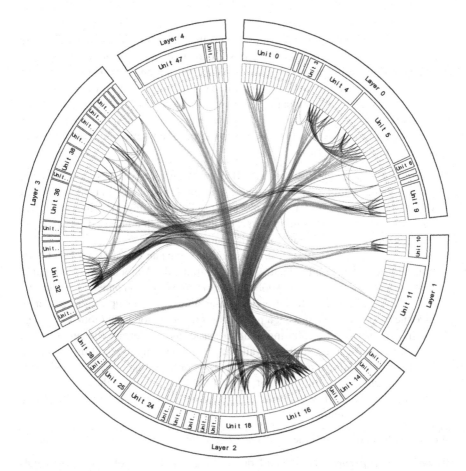

Fig. 9.9 An example of a visualization from a call tree (reproduced from Holten [15] under a Creative Commons Attribution license)

9.4   Conclusion

In this chapter we have provided a review of some desirable properties of RSSEs and a variety of user interfaces to help implement those properties. When toolsmiths have an idea for a user interface, how do they design the user interface that is going to deliver recommendations in an effective way? Here, we provide some practical advice on how to do so.

First, toolsmiths should determine their level of commitment to producing the right user interface. At one end of the spectrum, if the toolsmiths were just creating a proof-of-concept, the most convenient user interface may suffice—including not having a user interface at all. For example, WitchDoctor [11] recommends refactorings, but it was evaluated without actually showing the RSSE to developers, and thus a user interface was not necessary to demonstrate effectiveness. At the other end of the spectrum, if a toolsmith wants the tool to be widely adopted by the user community, a stronger commitment is needed in creating the user interface.

Second, a toolsmith should choose a strategy for creating a good user interface that is congruent with the level of commitment. Typically, such a strategy involves two symbiotic parts: design (creating the user interface) and evaluation (determining the goodness of the user interface). Below, we describe several strategies for performing design and evaluation. With a low level of commitment, here are a few appropriate design strategies:

Use another interface for inspiration.   If a user interface was designed to solve one problem, a tool that needs to solve a similar problem may be designed with a similar interface. For example, because both compiler warnings and static analysis warnings serve similar purposes, annotations that are used for compiler warnings may be appropriate for static analysis warnings.

Mockups.   Mockups allow an RSSE designer to create an initial idea for an RSSE user interface, then communicate that idea graphically. A mockup may be created using Microsoft PowerPoint, Adobe Fireworks, or simply on paper. For example, the authors of WitchDoctor provided a user interface mockup in their paper to give the reader an idea of what a practical implementation might look like [11].

Cognitive walkthroughs.   Starting with a basic user interface design (e.g., a mockup), a toolsmith can then "walk through" how a user would use it for the first time by creating a number of scenarios. By pretending to use the design for each scenario, a toolsmith can determine for which scenarios the user interface appears to work well. Wharton et al. [48] provide an overview of the cognitive walkthrough procedure.

With a low level of commitment, here are a few appropriate evaluation strategies:

Wizard Of Oz experiments.   Wizard of Oz experiments provide a way for toolsmiths to evaluate the user interface of RSSEs without implementing the RSSE fully; instead, the toolsmith manually provides fake (but useful) recommendations directly through the user interface. Maulsby et al. [23] provide an introduction to the approach.

Heuristic evaluation.   A heuristic evaluation is a way to evaluate RSSE user interfaces by having a panel of experts analyze a user interface by comparing its features to a set of known good usability heuristics. Nielsen and Molich [32] provide an overview.

With a high level of commitment, appropriate design strategies include those that fall under the heading of requirements elicitation and analysis. Indeed, a toolsmith can treat RSSEs like any piece of software, and design RSSEs using methodologies such as Participatory Design or Joint Application Design [3]. Evaluation strategies with high levels of commitment include:

A/B testing.   This type of evaluation, more commonly found in web design, gives one sample of users one user interface, and another sample of users a slightly different user interface [17]. Across both samples, a toolsmith measures an outcome of interest, such as the number of recommendations taken.

Controlled experiments. In controlled experiments, different user interfaces to RSSEs are given to different groups of people and some outcome is measured, but external variables (such as task) are controlled for [50]. As with A/B testing, a toolsmith measures some outcome of interest, and results are compared between groups. However, non-comparative controlled experiments can also be conducted when no reasonable point of comparison exists.

Case studies. Case studies are like controlled experiments, except they are not conducted in controlled conditions, but instead are conducted in a user's usual workspace, which improves their generalizability [37]. Data can be collected through a number of means, such as remote instrumentation or by asking users to keep journals.

In addition to the reference given above, Toleman and Welsh [44] provide a more in-depth overview of evaluating design choices. LaToza and Myers [21] provide an overview of the software engineering design process, much of which is applicable to RSSEs. In Chap. 13, Tosun Mısırlı et al. [45] also discuss an end-to-end design and evaluation approach called a field study.

Getting the user interface right takes time and effort, but it is also a necessary step in creating a successful recommendation system for software engineering. In this chapter, we have outlined factors that a toolsmith should consider when building a user interface for an RSSE, have provided examples of choices the toolsmith can make, and have described how user interfaces for RSSEs can be progressively designed and evaluated.

References

1. Adamczyk, P.D., Bailey, B.P.: If not now, when?: The effects of interruption at different moments within task execution. In: Proceedings of the ACM SIGCHI Conference on Human Factors in Computing Systems, pp. 271–278 (2004). doi: 10.1145/985692.985727
2. Bacchelli, A., Ponzanelli, L., Lanza, M.: Harnessing Stack Overflow for the IDE. In: Proceedings of the International Workshop on Recommendation Systems for Software Engineering, pp. 26–30 (2012). doi: 10.1109/RSSE.2012.6233404
3. Carmel, E., Whitaker, R.D., George, J.F.: PD and joint application design: A transatlantic comparison. Commun. ACM **36**(6), 40–48 (1993). doi: 10.1145/153571.163265
4. Carter, J., Dewan, P.: Design, implementation, and evaluation of an approach for determining when programmers are having difficulty. In: Proceedings of the ACM Conference on Computer Supported Cooperative Work, pp. 215–224 (2010). doi: 10.1145/1880071.1880109
5. Cialdini, R.B.: Influence: Science and Practice, 4th edn. Allyn and Bacon, London (2000)
6. Coverity: Effective management of static analysis vulnerabilities and defects (2011). URL http://www.coverity.com/library/pdf/effective-management-of-static-analysis-vulnerabilities-and-defects.pdf. [retrieved 9 October 2013]
7. Cremonesi, P., Garzotto, F., Turrin, R.: Investigating the persuasion potential of recommender systems from a quality perspective: An empirical study. ACM Trans. Interact. Intell. Syst. **2**(2), 11:1–11:41 (2012). doi: 10.1145/2209310.2209314

8. DeLine, R., Czerwinski, M., Robertson, G.G.: Easing program comprehension by sharing navigation data. In: Proceedings of the IEEE Symposium on Visual Languages and Human-Centric Computing, pp. 241–248 (2005). doi: 10.1109/VLHCC.2005.32

9. Fischer, G., Lemke, A., Schwab, T.: Active help systems. In: Readings on Cognitive Ergonomics: Mind and Computers, Lecture Notes in Computer Science, vol. 178, pp. 115–131 (1984). doi: 10.1007/3-540-13394-1_10

10. Fluri, B., Zuberbühler, J., Gall, H.C.: Recommending method invocation context changes. In: Proceedings of the International Workshop on Recommendation Systems for Software Engineering, pp. 1–5 (2008). doi: 10.1145/1454247.1454249

11. Foster, S.R., Griswold, W.G., Lerner, S.: WitchDoctor: IDE support for real-time auto-completion of refactorings. In: Proceedings of the ACM/IEEE International Conference on Software Engineering, pp. 222–232 (2012). doi: 10.1109/ICSE.2012.6227191

12. Fowler, M.: Refactoring: Improving the Design of Existing Code. Addison-Wesley, Boston, MA (1999)

13. Ge, X., DuBose, Q.L., Murphy-Hill, E.: Reconciling manual and automatic refactoring. In: Proceedings of the ACM/IEEE International Conference on Software Engineering, pp. 211–221 (2012). doi: 10.1109/ICSE.2012.6227192

14. Hiew, L.: Assisted detection of duplicate bug reports. Master's thesis, The University Of British Columbia (2006)

15. Holten, D.: Hierarchical edge bundles: Visualization of adjacency relations in hierarchical data. IEEE Trans. Visual. Comput. Graph. 12(5), 741–748 (2006). doi: 10.1109/TVCG.2006.147

16. Horvitz, E., Jacobs, A., Hovel, D.: Attention-sensitive alerting. In: Proceedings of the Conference on Uncertainty in Artificial Intelligence, pp. 305–313 (1999)

17. Kohavi, R., Longbotham, R., Sommerfield, D., Henne, R.M.: Controlled experiments on the web: Survey and practical guide. Data Min. Knowl. Discov. 18(1), 140–181 (2009). doi: 10.1007/s10618-008-0114-1

18. Konstan, J.A., Miller, B.N., Maltz, D., Herlocker, J.L., Gordon, L.R., Riedl, J.: GroupLens: Applying collaborative filtering to Usenet news. Commun. ACM 40(3), 77–87 (1997). doi: 10.1145/245108.245126

19. Konstan, J.A., Riedl, J.: Recommender systems: From algorithms to user experience. User Model. User-Adapt. Interact. 22(1–2), 101–123 (2012). doi: 10.1007/s11257-011-9112-x

20. Lahiri, S., Hawblitzel, C., Kawaguchi, M., Rebêlo, H.: SymDiff: A language-agnostic semantic diff tool for imperative programs. In: Proceedings of the International Conference on Computer Aided Verification, *Lecture Notes in Computer Science*, vol. 7358, pp. 712–717 (2012). doi: 10.1007/978-3-642-31424-7_54

21. LaToza, T.D., Myers, B.A.: Designing useful tools for developers. In: Proceedings of the ACM SIGPLAN Workshop on Evaluation and Usability of Programming Languages and Tools, pp. 45–50 (2011). doi: 10.1145/2089155.2089166

22. Maalej, W., Sahm, A.: Assisting engineers in switching artifacts by using task semantic and interaction history. In: Proceedings of the International Workshop on Recommendation Systems for Software Engineering, pp. 59–63 (2010). doi: 10.1145/1808920.1808935

23. Maulsby, D., Greenberg, S., Mander, R.: Prototyping an intelligent agent through Wizard of Oz. In: Proceedings of the ACM SIGCHI Conference on Human Factors in Computing Systems, pp. 277–284 (1993). doi: 10.1145/169059.169215

24. McFarlane, D.C., Latorella, K.A.: The scope and importance of human interruption in human–computer interaction design. Hum. Comput. Interact. 17(1), 1–61 (2002). doi: 10.1207/S15327051HCI1701_1

25. McSherry, D.: Explanation in recommender systems. Artif. Intell. Rev. 24(2), 179–197 (2005). doi: 10.1007/s10462-005-4612-x

26. Muşlu, K., Brun, Y., Holmes, R., Ernst, M.D., Notkin, D.: Speculative analysis of integrated development environment recommendations. In: Proceedings of the ACM SIGPLAN Conference on Object-Oriented Programming, Systems, Languages, and Applications, pp. 669–682 (2012). doi: 10.1145/2384616.2384665

27. Murphy-Hill, E., Black, A.P.: An interactive ambient visualization for code smells. In: Proceedings of the ACM Symposium on Software Visualization, pp. 5–14 (2010). doi: 10.1145/1879211.1879216
28. Murphy-Hill, E., Murphy, G.C.: Peer interaction effectively, yet infrequently, enables programmers to discover new tools. In: Proceedings of the ACM Conference on Computer Supported Cooperative Work, pp. 405–414 (2011). doi: 10.1145/1958824.1958888
29. Nass, C.I., Yen, C.: The Man Who Lied to his Laptop: What Machines Teach Us about Human Relationships. Current Hardcover, New York (2010)
30. Nielsen, J.: Ten Usability Heuristics. Alertbox (2005). URL. http://www.useit.com/alertbox/20030825.html. [last accessed on 11/14/05]
31. Nielsen, J.: Progressive disclosure (2006). URL http://www.nngroup.com/articles/progressive-disclosure/. [retrieved 9 October 2013]
32. Nielsen, J., Molich, R.: Heuristic evaluation of user interfaces. In: Proceedings of the ACM SIGCHI Conference on Human Factors in Computing Systems, pp. 249–256 (1990). doi: 10.1145/97243.97281
33. Niu, N., Yang, F., Cheng, J.R.C., Reddivari, S.: A cost-benefit approach to recommending conflict resolution for parallel software development. In: Proceedings of the International Workshop on Recommendation Systems for Software Engineering, pp. 21–25 (2012). doi: 10.1109/RSSE.2012.6233403
34. Norman, D.A.: Affordance, conventions, and design. Interactions 6(3), 38–43 (1999). doi: 10.1145/301153.301168
35. Ozok, A.A., Fan, Q., Norcio, A.F.: Design guidelines for effective recommender system interfaces based on a usability criteria conceptual model: Results from a college student population. Behav. Inform. Tech. 29(1), 57–83 (2010). doi: 10.1080/01449290903004012
36. Pu, P., Chen, L.: Trust building with explanation interfaces. In: Proceedings of the International Conference on Intelligent User Interfaces, pp. 93–100 (2006). doi: 10.1145/1111449.1111475
37. Runeson, P., Höst, M.: Guidelines for conducting and reporting case study research in software engineering. Empir. Software Eng. 14(2), 131–164 (2009). doi: 10.1007/s10664-008-9102-8
38. Sawadsky, N., Murphy, G.C.: Fishtail: From task context to source code examples. In: Proceedings of the Workshop on Developing Tools as Plug-ins, pp. 48–51 (2011). doi: 10.1145/1984708.1984722
39. Sawadsky, N., Murphy, G.C., Jiresal, R.: Reverb: Recommending code-related web pages. In: Proceedings of the ACM/IEEE International Conference on Software Engineering, pp. 812–821 (2013). doi: 10.1109/ICSE.2013.6606627
40. Schafer, J.B., Konstan, J., Riedi, J.: Recommender systems in e-commerce. In: Proceedings of the ACM Conference on Electronic Commerce, pp. 158–166 (1999). doi: 10.1145/336992.337035
41. Sinha, R., Swearingen, K.: The role of transparency in recommender systems. In: Extended Abstracts of the ACM SIGCHI Conference on Human Factors in Computing Systems, pp. 830–831 (2002). doi: 10.1145/506443.506619
42. Thies, A., Roth, C.: Recommending rename refactorings. In: Proceedings of the International Workshop on Recommendation Systems for Software Engineering, pp. 1–5 (2010). doi: 10.1145/1808920.1808921
43. Tintarev, N., Masthoff, J.: Evaluating the effectiveness of explanations for recommender systems : Methodological issues and empirical studies on the impact of personalization. User Model. User-Adapt. Interact. 22(4–5), 399–439 (2012). doi: 10.1007/s11257-011-9117-5
44. Toleman, M.A., Welsh, J.: Systematic evaluation of design choices for software development tools. Software Concepts Tool 19(3), 109–121 (1998)
45. Tosun Mısırlı, A., Bener, A., Çağlayan, B., Çalıklı, G., Turhan, B.: Field studies: A methodology for construction and evaluation of recommendation systems in software engineering. In: Robillard, M., Maalej, W., Walker, R.J., Zimmermann, T. (eds.) Recommendation Systems in Software Engineering, Chap. 13. Springer, New York (2014)
46. Trumper, J., Dollner, J.: Extending recommendation systems with software maps. In: Proceedings of the International Workshop on Recommendation Systems for Software Engineering, pp. 92–96 (2012). doi: 10.1109/RSSE.2012.6233420

47. Viriyakattiyaporn, P., Murphy, G.C.: Improving program navigation with an active help system. In: Proceedings of the IBM Centre for Advanced Studies Conference on Collaborative Research, pp. 27–41 (2010). doi: 10.1145/1923947.1923951
48. Wharton, C., Rieman, J., Lewis, C., Polson, P.: The cognitive walkthrough method: A practitioner's guide. In: Nielsen, J., Mack, R.L. (eds.) Usability Inspection Methods, pp. 105–140. Wiley, New York (1994)
49. Whitworth, B.: Polite computing. Behav. Inform. Tech. **24**(5), 353–363 (2005). doi: 10.1080/01449290512331333700
50. Wohlin, C., Runeson, P., Host, M., Ohlsson, M.C., Regnell, B., Wesslen, A.: Experimentation in Software Engineering. Springer, New York (2012). doi: 10.1007/978-3-642-29044-2
51. Xiao, J., Catrambone, R., Stasko, J.: Be quiet?: Evaluating proactive and reactive user interface assistants. In: Proceedings of the IFIP TC13 International Conference on Human–Computer Interactaction, vol. 3, pp. 383–390 (2003)
52. Xie, J., Lipford, H., Chu, B.T.: Evaluating interactive support for secure programming. In: Proceedings of the ACM SIGCHI Conference on Human Factors in Computing Systems, pp. 2707–2716 (2012). doi: 10.1145/2207676.2208665
53. Zagalsky, A., Barzilay, O., Yehudai, A.: Example Overflow: Using social media for code recommendation. In: Proceedings of the International Workshop on Recommendation Systems for Software Engineering, pp. 38–42 (2012). doi: 10.1109/RSSE.2012.6233407

Part II
Evaluation

Chapter 10
Dimensions and Metrics for Evaluating Recommendation Systems

Iman Avazpour, Teerat Pitakrat, Lars Grunske, and John Grundy

Abstract Recommendation systems support users and developers of various computer and software systems to overcome information overload, perform information discovery tasks, and approximate computation, among others. They have recently become popular and have attracted a wide variety of application scenarios ranging from business process modeling to source code manipulation. Due to this wide variety of application domains, different approaches and metrics have been adopted for their evaluation. In this chapter, we review a range of evaluation metrics and measures as well as some approaches used for evaluating recommendation systems. The metrics presented in this chapter are grouped under sixteen different dimensions, e.g., correctness, novelty, coverage. We review these metrics according to the dimensions to which they correspond. A brief overview of approaches to comprehensive evaluation using collections of recommendation system dimensions and associated metrics is presented. We also provide suggestions for key future research and practice directions.

10.1 Introduction

Due to the complexity of today's software systems, modern software development environments provide recommendation systems for various tasks. These ease the developers' decisions or warn them about the implications of their decisions. Examples are code completion, refactoring support, or enhanced search capabilities

I. Avazpour (✉) • J. Grundy (✉)
Faculty of ICT, Centre for Computing and Engineering Software and Systems (SUCCESS),
Swinburne University of Technology, Hawthorn, Australia
e-mail: iavazpour@swin.edu.au; jgrundy@swin.edu.au

T. Pitakrat (✉) • L. Grunske (✉)
Institute of Software Technology, Universität Stuttgart, Stuttgart, Germany
e-mail: teerat.pitakrat@informatik.uni-stuttgart.de; lars.grunske@informatik.uni-stuttgart.de

M.P. Robillard et al. (eds.), *Recommendation Systems in Software Engineering*,   245
DOI 10.1007/978-3-642-45135-5_10, © Springer-Verlag Berlin Heidelberg 2014

during specific maintenance activities. In recent years, research has produced a
variety of these recommendation systems and some of them have similar intentions
and functionalities [24, 60]. One obvious question is, therefore, how can we assess
quality and how can we benchmark different recommendation systems?

In this chapter, we provide a practical guide to the commonly used quantitative
evaluation techniques used to compare recommendation systems. As a first step,
we have identified a set of dimensions, e.g., the correctness or diversity of the
results that may serve as a basis for an evaluation of a recommendation system. The
different dimensions will be explained in detail and different metrics are presented
to measure and quantify each dimension. Furthermore, we explore interrelationships
between dimensions and present a guide showing how to use the dimensions in an
individual recommendation system validation.

The rest of the chapter is organized as follows: Sect. 10.2 introduces the
evaluation dimensions for recommendation systems and presents common metrics
for them. Section 10.3 explores relationships between the different dimensions.
Section 10.4 provides a description of some evaluation approaches and their
practical application and implications. Finally, conclusions are drawn in Sect. 10.5.

10.2 Dimensions

The multi-faceted characteristics of recommendation systems lead us to consider
multiple dimensions for recommender evaluation. Just one dimension and metric
for evaluating the wide variety of recommendation systems and application domains
is far too simplistic to obtain a nuanced evaluation of an approach as applied to a
particular domain.

In this chapter, we investigate a variety of dimensions that may be used to play
a significant role in evaluating a recommendation system. We list these dimensions
below according to our view of their relative evaluative importance, along with the
characteristics that each dimension is used to measure. Some of these dimensions
describe qualitative characteristics while others are more quantitative.

Correctness.   How close are the recommendations to a set of recommendations
   that are assumed to be correct?
Coverage.   To what extent does the recommendation system cover a set of items
   or user space?
Diversity.   How diverse (dissimilar) are the recommended items in a list?
Trustworthiness.   How trustworthy are the recommendations?
Recommender confidence.   How confident is the recommendation system in its
   recommendations?
Novelty.   How successful is the recommendation system in recommending items
   that are new or unknown to users?
Serendipity.   To what extent has the system succeeded in providing surprising yet
   beneficial recommendations?

Table 10.1 Categorization of dimensions

Recommendation-centric	User-centric	System-centric	Delivery-centric
Correctness	Trustworthiness	Robustness	Usability
Coverage	Novelty	Learning rate	User preference
Diversity	Serendipity	Scalability	
Recommender confidence	Utility	Stability	
	Risk	Privacy	

Utility. What is the value gained from this recommendation for users?

Risk. How much user risk is associated in accepting each recommendation?

Robustness. How tolerant is the recommendation system to bias or false information?

Learning rate. How fast can the system incorporate new information to update its recommendation list?

Usability. How usable is the recommendation system? Will it be easy for users to adopt it in an appropriate way?

Scalability. How scalable is the system with respect to number of users, underlying data size, and algorithm performance?

Stability. How consistent are the recommendations over a period of time?

Privacy. Are there any risks to user privacy?

User preference. How do users perceive the recommendation system?

We have grouped these dimensions into four broad categories, depending on different aspects of the recommendation system they address: *recommendation-centric*, *user-centric*, *system-centric*, and *delivery-centric*. Table 10.1 summarizes how each of the above dimensions can be grouped inside each category.

Recommendation-centric dimensions primarily assess the recommendations generated by the recommendation system itself: their coverage, correctness, diversity and level of confidence in the produced recommendations. On the other hand, user-centric dimensions allow us to assess the degrees to which the recommendation system under evaluation fulfills its target end-user needs. This includes how trustworthy are the recommendations produced, degree of novelty, whether serendipitous recommendations are a feature, the overall utility of the recommendations from the users' perspective, and risks associated with the recommendations produced, again from the users' perspective. System-centric dimensions in contrast principally provide ways to gauge the recommendation system itself, rather than the recommendations or user perspective. These include assessment of the robustness of the recommendation system, its learning rate given new data, its scalability given data size, its stability under data change, and degree of privacy support in the context of shared recommendation system datasets. Finally, delivery-centric dimensions primarily focus of the recommendation system in the context of use, including its usability (broadly assessed) and support for user configuration and preferences.

The following subsections describe each of these dimensions in detail.

10.2.1 Correctness

In order to be of real value, recommendation systems must provide useful results that are close to users' interests, intentions, or applications, without overwhelming them with unwanted results. A key measure of this is the *correctness* of the set of recommendations produced. Correctness provides a measure of how close the recommendations given to a user are to a set of expected predefined, or assumed correct, recommendations. This predefined set of correct recommendations is sometimes referred to as the *gold standard*. The correctness of a recommendation may refer to its alignment with a benchmark (e.g., each recommended link is in the predefined set of correct links), or how well it adheres to desired qualities (e.g., an increase in developer productivity).

Depending on the type of recommendations the system is generating, different methods can be used for measuring correctness. A recommender might predict how users rate an item, the order (ranking) of most interesting to least interesting items for a user in a list, or which item (or list of items) is of interest to the user. In the following subsections, we describe the most commonly used metrics for evaluating recommendation approaches for correctness in each scenario.

Predicting User Ratings

If the recommendations produced are intended to predict how users rate items of interest, then *root-mean-squared-error* (RMSE) or *mean absolute error* (MAE) metrics are often used [e.g., 6,34,42,66,75]. When calculating RMSE, the difference between actual user ratings and predicted ratings (often called the *residual*) should be determined. If r_{ui} is the actual rating of user u for item i, and $\hat{r}_{ui}$ is the predicted value, $(\hat{r}_{ui} - r_{ui})$ is the residual of the two ratings. Depending on whether the recommendation system has over- or under-estimated the rating, residuals can be positive or negative. RMSE can be calculated by squaring the residuals, averaging the squares, and taking the square root, as follows:

$$\text{RMSE}(T) = \sqrt{\frac{\Sigma_{(u,i) \in T} (\hat{r}_{ui} - r_{ui})^2}{N}} .$$

MAE, on the other hand, measures the average absolute deviation of predicted ratings from user ratings:

$$\text{MAE}(T) = \frac{\Sigma_{(u,i) \in T} |\hat{r}_{ui} - r_{ui}|}{N} ,$$

where T is the test set of user item pairs (u, i) and N is the number of all ratings. All individual residuals in MAE are equally weighted while in RMSE large errors get penalized more than small errors. This is because the errors are squared before they are averaged. Therefore, if large errors are undesirable, RMSE is a more suitable metric than MAE. Lower values of both RMSE and MAE indicate greater correctness. RMSE is generally larger than or equal to the MAE. If both metrics are equal, then all errors have the same magnitude.

Both RMSE and MAE can be normalized according to the rating range to represent scaled versions of themselves:.

$$\text{normalized RMSE}(T) = \frac{\text{RMSE}(T)}{r_{\max} - r_{\min}} \, ,$$

$$\text{normalized MAE}(T) = \frac{\text{MAE}(T)}{r_{\max} - r_{\min}} \, .$$

If the items to be tested represent an unbalanced distribution, RMSE and MAE can be used in averaged form, depending on the evaluation (e.g., per-user or per-item). If the RMSE of each item can be calculated separately, then the average of all calculated RMSEs represents the average RMSE of the recommendation system.[1]

Example. ▷ Consider the problem of ranking Java files returned by a recommendation system for code search. Assume three files are recommended to a user with predicted ratings of 3, 5, 5 in a 1–5 scale scoring system while the actual ratings provided by the user are 4, 3, 5 respectively. The above metrics can be calculated as follows.

$$\text{RMSE} = \sqrt{\frac{(3-4)^2 + (5-3)^2 + (5-5)^2}{3}} \approx 1.291 \, ,$$

$$\text{MAE} = \frac{(3-4) + (5-3) + (5-5)}{3} \approx 0.334 \, ,$$

$$\text{normalized RMSE} = \frac{\text{RMSE}}{5-1} \approx 0.323 \, ,$$

$$\text{normalized MAE} = \frac{\text{MAE}}{5-1} \approx 0.08 \, .$$

◁

Ranking Items

Ranking measures are used when an ordered list of recommendations is presented to users according to their preferences. This order can be the most important, or "most relevant," items at the top and the least important, or "least relevant" items at the bottom. For example, when recommending links between architecture documents

---

[1]Editors' note: This is the notion of macroevaluation; compare microevaluation.

and code artifacts in a source code traceability recommendation system, the most closely related links should be shown first. Similarly, when recommending code snippets for reuse from a source code repository in a code reuse recommendation system, the code snippet most appropriate to the current reuse context should be shown first.

When checking for correctness of ranking measures, if a reference ranking (benchmark) is available, the correctness of the ranking can be measured by the *normalized distance-based performance measure* (NDPM) [79]. The value returned by NDPM is between 0 and 1 with any acceptable ranking having a distance of 0. A ranking farthest away from an ideal ranking would have a normalized distance of 1.

NDPM penalizes a contradicting prediction twice as much as when it does not predict an item in the ranking. It also does not penalize the system for ranking one item over another when they have ties. Having a tie in some situations, however, indicates that the value of the tied items is equal to the user. Therefore, ranking one item higher than the other in a tie will produce inaccurate ranking. In situations where ties between recommended items are to be considered, rank correlation measures, such as Spearman's ρ [74] or Kendall's τ can be used [30, 31].

For some cases, the position of recommended items in the list is important for the application of the recommendation. For example, in a software documentation retrieval environment, since all documentation artifacts are not of equal relevance to their users, highly relevant documents, or document components, should be identified and ranked first for presentation [28]. Therefore, the correctness of an item in the ranking list should be weighted by its position in the ranking. A frequently used metric for measuring ranking correctness, considering item ranking position, is the *normalized discounted cumulative gain* (NDCG). It is calculated based on measuring the *discounted cumulative gain* (DCG) and then comparing that to the ideal ranking. DCG measures the correctness of a ranked list based on the relevance of items discounted by their position in the list. Higher values of NDCG indicate better ranked lists and therefore better correctness. Various approaches have been introduced to optimize NDCG and ranking measures. Examples of these approaches can be found in Weimer et al. [78] and Le and Smola [41].

Recommending Interesting Items

If a recommendation system is providing the items that users may like to use, a common approach to evaluate it is to use classification metrics like precision, recall (also called true positive rate), accuracy, false positive rate, and specificity (also called true negative rate). These metrics have been used excessively across different domains [e.g., 15, 17, 18, 43, 47, 80] to classify recommendations into groups, as indicated by Table 10.2. Once the categories are defined, these metrics can be calculated as follows:

Table 10.2 Categorization of all possible recommendations (also called the confusion matrix)

	Recommended	Not Recommended	Total
Used	true positives (TP)	false negatives (FN)	Total Used
Not Used	false positives (FP)	true negatives (TN)	Total Not Used
Total	Total Recommended	Total Not Recommended	Total

$$\text{precision} = \frac{TP}{TP + FP}$$

$$\text{recall} = \frac{TP}{TP + FN}$$

$$\text{accuracy} = \frac{TP + TN}{TP + TN + FP + FN}$$

$$\text{false positive rate} = \frac{FP}{FP + TN}$$

$$\text{specificity} = \frac{TN}{FP + TN} = 1 - \text{false positive rate}$$

When testing for these metrics offline and on test data, a common assumption is that items that the user has not selected are uninteresting, or useless, to other users. This assumption can often be incorrect [70]. A user might not select an item because they are not aware of such an item. Therefore, there can be a bias in the categories defined by Table 10.2. Also, there exists an important tradeoff between these metrics when measuring correctness. For instance, allowing for a longer list of recommendations improves recall but is likely to reduce precision. Improving precision often worsens recall [63]. The **F-measure** is the harmonic mean of precision and recall, calculated as follows:

$$F = 2 \times \frac{\text{precision} \times \text{recall}}{\text{precision} + \text{recall}}$$

It is also important to mention the cost associated with identifying false positives (FP) and false negatives (FN). For example, it could be relatively easier to identify FP for a user. If this is the case, calculating recall would be less costly and hence more preferred than precision. The F-measure assumes an equal cost for both FP and FN.[2]

Sometimes it is desirable to provide multiple recommendations to users. In this case, these metrics can be altered to provide correctness measured for the number of items being provided to user. For example, consider a code completion

---

[2]Editors' note: The general F-measure allows for unequal but specific costs.

recommender that can recommend hundreds of items while the user is typing program code. Showing one item at a time would be too limited; similarly, showing all recommendations would not be useful. If for each recommendation five items are shown to the user, to calculate the precision of this code completion recommender for example, precision at 5 can be used.

If using recommendations over a range of recommendation list lengths, one can plot precision versus recall (the precision–recall curve) or true-positive rate versus false-positive rate (the receiver operating characteristic, or ROC, curve) [26]. Both curves measure the proportion of preferred items that are actually recommended. Precision–recall curves emphasize the proportion of recommended items that are preferred while ROC curves emphasize the items that are not preferred but are recommended.

Example. ▷ Assume that an application programming interface (API) function list contains 100 items in total, and 20 of them are of interest to a certain user in an API reuse recommendation system. Given that the user is presented with a list of ten recommended items, with six being of interest and four otherwise, the precision, recall, and F-measure metrics can be calculated as follows:

$$TP = 6, \ FP = 4, \ FN = 14, \ TN = 76 \ ;$$

$$\text{precision} = \frac{6}{6+4} = 0.6 \ ,$$

$$\text{recall} = \frac{6}{6+14} = 0.3 \ ,$$

$$\text{false positive rate} = \frac{4}{4+76} = 0.05 \ ,$$

$$\text{specificity} = \frac{76}{4+76} = 0.95 \ ,$$

$$\text{accuracy} = \frac{6+76}{6+76+4+14} = 0.82 \ ,$$

$$F = 2 \times \frac{0.6 \times 0.3}{0.6+0.3} = 0.4 \ .$$

◁

10.2.2 Coverage

Recommendation systems make recommendations by searching available information spaces. This recommendation is not always possible, for example when new items or users are introduced, or insufficient data is available for particular items or users. *Coverage* refers to the proportion of available information (items, users) for which recommendations can be made.

Consider a code maintenance recommendation system that guides developers on where to look in a large code base to apply modifications [e.g., 59]. If such a recommender is not capable of covering the whole codebase at hand, developers might not be able to find the actual artifact that requires alteration. Hence, the information overload problem and complexity of finding faults in the codebase will still exist to a greater or lesser degree. Sometimes this is acceptable, such as when alternative techniques, like visualization, can assist users. Sometimes this is unacceptable, for example when the search space is too large for developers or important parts of the code base remain un-searched, thus hindering maintenance effort.

Coverage usually refers to *catalog coverage* (item-space coverage) or *prediction coverage* (user-space coverage) [26]. Catalog coverage is the proportion of available items that the recommendation system recommends to users. Prediction coverage refers to the proportion of users or user interactions that the recommendation system is able to generate predictions for.

A straightforward way to measure catalog coverage is by calculating the proportion of items able to be recommended in a single recommendation session where multiple recommender algorithms would be executed a number of times. Therefore, if the set of items recommended to a user over a particular recommendation session is S_r and S_a is the set of all available items, catalog coverage can be calculated as follows:

$$\text{catalog coverage} = \frac{|S_r|}{|S_a|}.$$

The items available for recommendation may not all be of interest to a user. Consider a recommendation system that finds relevant expertise to perform a collaborative software engineering task [e.g., 50]. In such a system, if users are looking for expertise in file processing for a Java-based project, recommending an expert in Prolog will not be useful and should be filtered out. Ge et al. propose *weighted* catalog coverage for balancing the decrease in coverage by usefulness for users [20]:

$$\text{weighted catalog coverage} = \frac{|S_r \cap S_s|}{|S_s|}.$$

where S_s is the set of items that are considered useful to users.

Similar to catalog coverage, prediction coverage can be calculated by measuring the ratio of the number of users for whom a prediction can be made, to the total number of users:

$$\text{prediction coverage} = \frac{|S_p|}{|S_u|}.$$

Accordingly, by considering the usefulness of recommended items for the user as a function $f(x)$ we obtain:

$$\text{weighted prediction coverage} = \frac{\Sigma_{i \in S_p} f(i)}{\Sigma_{j \in S_u} f(j)}.$$

Ge et al. suggest using correctness and novelty metrics to calculate the usefulness function $f(x)$ and the set of useful items S_s.

Situations where a new item is added to the system and sufficient information (like ratings by other users for that item) does not yet exist is referred to as the *cold start problem*. Cold start can also refer to situations where new users have joined the system and their preferences are not yet known. For example, consider a recommendation system that recommends solutions to fixing a bug similar to DebugAdvisor [5]. In such a recommender the developer submits a query describing the defect. The system then searches for bug descriptions, functions, or people that can help the developer fix the bug. If the bug, or a similar bug, has not been previously reported, there is no guarantee that the returned results will help resolve the situation. Similarly, if the system has been newly implemented in a development environment with few bug reports or code repositories, the recommendation would not be very helpful.

Cold start is seen more often in collaborative filtering recommenders as they rely heavily on input from users. Therefore, these recommenders can be used in conjunction with other non-collaborative techniques. Such a hybrid mechanism was proposed by Schein et al. [67], in which they used two variations of ROC curves to evaluate their method, namely global ROC (GROC) and customer ROC (CROC). GROC was used to measure performance when the recommender is allowed to recommend more often to some users than others. CROC was used to measure performance when the system was constrained to recommend the same number of items to each user.

10.2.3 Diversity

In some cases, having similar items in a recommendation list does not add value from the users' perspectives. The recommendations will seem redundant and it takes longer for users to explore the item space. For example, in an API recommendation system, showing two APIs with the same non-functional characteristics may not be useful unless it helps users gain confidence in the recommendation system. Showing two APIs with (say) diverse performance, memory overheads, and providers could be more desirable for the developer.

A recommendation list should display some degree of diversity in the presented items. Candillier et al. [11] performed a case study on recommending documents to users in which they showed that users prefer a system providing document diversity. This allows users to get a more complete map of the information.

Diversity could be also considered to be the opposite of similarity. If items presented to users are too similar, they do not present diverse items and so may not be of interest. Thus, Smyth and McClave [73] defined diversity in a set of items, $c_1 \ldots c_n$, as the average dissimilarity between all pairs of items in the itemset:

$$\text{diversity}(c_1, \ldots, c_n) = \frac{2}{n(n-1)} \sum_{i=1}^{n} \sum_{j=i}^{n} (1 - \text{similarity}(c_i, c_j)) \, ,$$

where *similarity* is calculated by the weighted-sum metric for item c and target query t:

$$\text{similarity}(t, c) = \frac{\sum_{i=1}^{n} \omega_i \, \text{sim}(t_i, c_i)}{\sum_{i=1}^{n} \omega_i} \, ,$$

and where $\text{sim}(t, c)$ can be a similarity heuristic based on sum, average, or minimum or maximum distance between item pairs, and ω is the associated weight.

Since, in a fixed size recommendation list, improving diversity results in sacrificing similarity, a strategy that optimizes this similarity–diversity tradeoff is often beneficial. Thus, a quality metric was introduced to combine both diversity and similarity [73]:

$$\text{quality}(t, c, R) = \text{similarity}(t, c) \times \text{relative diversity}(c, R) \, .$$

This basically specifies that the quality of item c is proportional to its similarity with the current target query t, and to the diversity of c relative to those items so far selected $R = \{r_1, \ldots, r_m\}$. This notion of relative diversity can be defined as:

$$\text{relative diversity}(c, R) = \begin{cases} 0 \, , & \text{if } R = \emptyset \\ \frac{1}{m} \sum_{i=1}^{m} (1 - \text{similarity}(c, r_i)), & \text{otherwise} \, . \end{cases}$$

To measure diversity in a recommendation list, an alternative approach is to compute the distance of each item from the rest of the list and average the result to obtain a diversity score. For such an average, however, a random recommender may also produce diverse recommendations. Therefore, this needs to be accompanied by some measure of precision. Plotting precision–diversity curves helps in selecting the algorithm with the dominating curve [70]. Having correctness metrics combined with diversity has an added advantage, as correctness metrics do not take into account the entire recommendation list. Instead, they consider the correctness of individual items. For instance, the *intra-list similarity* metric can help to improve the process of topic diversification for recommendation lists [81]. In this way, the returned lists can be checked for intra-list similarity and altered to either increase or decrease the diversity of items on that list as desired or required. Increasing diversity this way has been shown to perform worse than unchanged lists, according to correctness measures, but users preferred the altered lists [45].

Diversity of rating predictions can be measured by well-known diversity measures being used in ensemble learning [37]. These approaches try to increase diversity for returned classification of individual learning algorithms in order to improve the overall performance. For example, Q-statistics can be used to find diversity between two recommender algorithms. Q-statistics are based on a modified confusion matrix, confronting two classifiers as correctly classified versus incorrectly classified. As a result, the confusion matrix displays the overlap of those itemsets. Q-statistic measures are then defined to combine the elements in the modified confusion matrix, ultimately arriving at a measure for the diversity of the two recommender algorithms. Kille and Albayrak [32] used this approach and introduced a *difficulty* measure to help with personalizing recommendations per user. They measured a user's difficulty by means of the diversity of rating predictions (RMSE) and item rankings (NDCG), and used diversity metrics by pairwise Q-statistics to fit the item ranking scenario.

Lathia et al. [40] introduced a measure of diversity for recommendations in two lists of varying lengths. In their approach, given two sets L_1 and L_2, the items of L_2 that are not in L_1 are first determined as their set theoretic difference. Then, the diversity between the two lists (at depth N) is defined as the size of their set theoretic difference over N. This way, diversity returns 0 if the two lists are the same, and 1 if the two lists are completely different at depth N.

10.2.4 Trustworthiness

A recommendation system is expected to provide trustworthy suggestions to its users. It has been shown that perceived usefulness correlates most highly with *good* and *useful* recommendations [71]. If the system is continuously producing incorrect recommendations, users' trust in the recommender will be lost. Lack of trustworthiness will encourage users to ignore recommendations and so decrease the usefulness of the recommendation system. For example, in an IDE being used for a refactoring scenario, a wrong suggestion made by the refactoring task recommender may adversely impact large amounts of application code. If users of such a refactoring recommendation system use a faulty recommendation and experience the consequences, they will be less likely to use it again.

Some users will not build trust in the recommendations unless they see a well-known item, or an item they were already aware of, being recommended [71]. Also, explanations regarding how the system comes up with its recommendations can encourage users to use them and build trust [72, 77].

A common approach to measure trust is to ask users in a user study whether the recommendations are reasonable [7, 14, 25]. Depending on the usage scenario of the recommendation system, it might be possible to check how frequently users use recommendations, to gain understanding of their trust [52]. For example, in a code reuse recommender, how often the user selects and applies one of the recommended code snippets. Or similarly, how often do users select recommendations of a code completion recommender.

10.2.5   Recommender Confidence

Recommender confidence is the certainty the system has in its own recommendations or predictions. In online scenarios, it is possible to calculate recommender confidence by observing environmental variables. For example, a refactoring recommendation system can build confidence scores by observing how frequently users use and apply suggested refactoring recommendations to their application.

Some prediction models can be used in calculating confidence scores. For example, Bell et al. [6] used a neighborhood-aware similarity model that considers similarities between items and users for generating recommendations. In their model, a recommendation that maximizes the similarity between the item being recommended and similar items, and the user to whom a recommendation is to be presented and similar users, defines the most suitable recommendation. They showed how such a metric can help identify most suitable recommendations, according to RMSE of the predicted rating and the user's true rating.

Cheetham and Price [13] provided an approach for calculating confidence in case-based reasoning (CBR) systems. They proposed to identify multiple indicators such as "sum of similarities for retrieved cases with best solution" or "similarity of the single most similar case with best solution." Once possible indicators are defined, their effect on the CBR process was determined using "leave-one-out" testing. Finally, they used Quinlan's C4.5 algorithm [56] on the leave-one-out test results to identify indicators that are best at determining confidence.

Recommender confidence scores can be used in the form of confidence intervals [e.g., 61] or by the probability that the predicted value is true [70]. Also, they have been used in hybrid recommendation systems for switching between recommender algorithms [8].

10.2.6   Novelty

A *novel* recommendation is one that the users did not know about. Novelty is very much related to the emotional response of users to a recommendation; as a result, it is a difficult dimension to measure [45].

A possible approach for building a novel recommender is to remove items that the user has already rated or used before in a recommendation list. If this information is available, novelty of the recommender can be measured easily by comparing recommendations against already used or rated recommendations. This requires keeping user profiles so that it is possible to know which user chose and rated which items. User profiles can then be used to calculate the set of familiar items. For example, CodeBroker [80] is a development environment that promotes reuse by enabling software developers to reuse available components. It integrates a *user model* for capturing methods that the developer already knows and thus does not need to be recommended again.

An alternative approach for measuring novelty is to count the number of popular items that have been recommended [70]. This metric is based on the assumption that highly rated and popular items are likely to be known to users and therefore not novel [48]. A good measure for novelty might be to look more generally at how well a recommendation system made the user aware of previously unknown items that subsequently turn out to be useful in context [26].

10.2.7   Serendipity

Serendipity by definition is "the occurrence and development of events by chance in a happy or beneficial way" [54]. In the context of recommendation systems this has been referred to as an unexpected and fortuitous recommendation [45]. Serendipity and novelty are different considering the fact that there is an element of correctness present in serendipity, which prevents random recommenders from being serendipitous. Novel unexpected items may, or may not, turn out to be serendipitous. While a random recommender may be novel, if a surprising recommendation does not have any utility to the user it will not be classified as serendipitous, but rather as erroneous and distracting. Therefore it is required that correctness and serendipity be balanced and considered together [70].

Like novelty, to have a serendipitous recommender, similar recommendations should be avoided since their expected appearance in the list will generally not benefit the user [45]. Therefore, user profiles or an automatic or manual labeling of pairs of similar items can help filter out similar items. The definition of this similarity, however, should be dependent on the context in which the recommender is being used. For example, an API recommender presenting completely unusable APIs in the current code context is highly unlikely to promote serendipitous reuse. A document recommender, showing unlikely but still possibly related artifacts in a traceability recommender, may very well present the user with serendipitously useful artifacts.

Ratability is a feature defined in accordance to serendipity. It is considered mostly in machine learning approaches. Given that the system has some understanding of the user profile, the ratability of a recommended item to a user is the probability that the item will be the next item the user will consume [45]. It is assumed that items with higher ratability are the items that the user has not consumed yet but is likely to use in future, or the items the user has consumed but have not been added to the user profile [44]. In other words, ratability defines the *obviousness* of a "user rating an item." Since machine-learning approaches calculate the probability of the item being chosen next, if the recommendation system is using a leave-one-out approach to train the learning procedure, it is possible to calculate the ratability based on that probability.

10.2.8 Utility

Utility is the value that the system or user gains from a recommendation. For example, PARSEWeb [76] aims to help developers find sequences of method calls on objects of a specific type. This helps to match an object with a specific method sequence. In that context, the evaluation can be based on the amount of time saved for finding such a method sequence using recommendations. Therefore, the value of a correct recommendation is based on the utility of that item. A possible evaluation in this context is to consider utility from a cost/benefit ratio analysis [26].

It is noteworthy that precision cannot measure the true usefulness of a recommendation. For example, recommending an already well-known and used API call, document link, code snippet, data map or algorithm will increase precision but has very low utility [48] since such an item will probably already be known to the user. On the other hand, for memory-intensive applications, it is sometimes beneficial to recommend well-known items. Thus, it is fair to align the recommender evaluation framework with utility measures in real world applications rather than overalign for correctness.

Depending on the application domain of the recommendation system, the utility of a recommendation can be specified by the user (e.g., in user-defined ratings) or computed by the application itself (e.g., profit-based utility function) [1]. The utility might be calculated by observing subsequent actions of the user, for example, interacting with the recommendation or using recommended items.

For some applications, the position of a recommendation in a list is a deciding factor. For example, RASCAL [43] uses a recommender agent to track usage histories of a group of developers and recommends components that are expected to be needed by individual developers. The components that are believed to be most useful to current developers will appear first in the recommendation list. If we assume that there is a higher chance for developers to choose a recommendation among top recommended items rather than exploring the whole list, the utility of each recommendation is then the utility of the recommended item in relation to its position in the list of recommendations [70].

10.2.9 Risk

Depending on where the recommendation system is being used and what its application domain is, the recommendations can be associated with various potential risks. For example, recommending a list of movies to watch is usually less risky than recommending refactoring solutions in complex coding situations (unless the movies might include inappropriate material for some audiences). Therefore, high-risk recommendation systems must obey a set of constraints on a valid solution. This is because false positive recommendations are less tolerable and users must be more convinced to use a recommendation [9].

Consequently, users may approach risk differently. For example, different users might be prepared to tolerate different levels of risk. One user might prefer using a component which is no longer maintained but has all required features. Another user might prefer a component that has less features but is under heavy development. In such cases, a standard way to evaluate risk is to consider utility variance in conjunction with the measures of utility and parameterize the degree of risk that users will tolerate, in the evaluation [70].

Another aspect of risk involves privacy. If the system is working according to user profiles, collecting information from users to create that profile introduces the risk of breaching users' privacy [57]. Therefore, it should be ensured that users are aware and willing to take that risk. For example, when recommending developers based on expertise for outsourcing tasks, many other factors will also need to be considered. Privacy will be discussed more in Sect. 10.2.15.

10.2.10 Robustness

Robustness is the ability of a recommendation system to tolerate false information intentionally provided by malicious users or, more commonly, to tolerate mistaken information accidentally provided by users. Mistakes made by users may include asking recommender to analyze documents in incorrect formats, mistakenly rating items, making mistakes in the user profile specification, and using the recommender in the wrong context or for the wrong tasks.

In order to evaluate the robustness of a system against attacks, O'Mahony et al. [53] compared prediction ratings before and after false information is provided and analyzed the prediction shift that reflects how the prediction changed afterwards. The prediction shift of item i (Δi) and its average $(\overline{\Delta i})$ can be defined as:

$$\Delta i = \sum_{u \in U} \frac{\hat{\hat{r}}_{ui} - \hat{r}_{ui}}{|U|} \,, \tag{10.1}$$

$$\overline{\Delta i} = \sum_{i \in I} \frac{\Delta i}{|I|} \,,$$

where $\hat{r}$ and $\hat{\hat{r}}$ are the predicted ratings before and after false information (respectively), U is a set of users, and I is a set of items.

A large shift, however, may not always affect performance of the system if the false information does not alter the items recommended to users. This situation may occur if actual rating of particular items are ranked so low that the mistakes still cannot push them to the top of recommended items. Many studies [e.g., 49,64,69] have also discussed and employed other metrics, including *average hit ratio* and *average rank*, to evaluate robustness. Average hit ratio measures how effective the misleading information is to push items into a recommended list while average rank measures the drop of item ratings outside the recommended list. Hit ratio and rank for item i, and their averages, can be defined as:

$$\text{hit ratio}(i) = \sum_{u \in U} \frac{H_{ui}}{|U|},$$

$$\text{rank}(i) = \sum_{u \in U} \frac{\text{rank}^*(u, i)}{|U|},$$

$$\text{average hit ratio} = \sum_{i \in I} \frac{\text{hit ratio}(i)}{|I|}, \text{ and}$$

$$\text{average rank} = \sum_{i \in I} \frac{\text{rank}(i)}{|I|},$$

where H_{ui} is 1 if item i appears in the list of recommended items of user u and 0 otherwise. The operator $\text{rank}^*(u, i)$ returns the position of item i in the unrecommended list of user u sorted in a descending order.

10.2.11 Learning Rate

Learning rate is the speed at which a recommendation system learns new information or trends and updates the recommended item list accordingly. A system with high learning rate will be able to adapt to new user preferences or interests of existing users to provide useful recommendations within a short period of learning time. For example, an API recommendation system may have a high learning rate if every time a user rates a recommended item the ranking index and calculations are immediately updated. In comparison, a code recommendation system may have a low learning rate if the indexing of the code repository can only be undertaken sporadically due to high overheads.

Although a fast learning rate can cope with quick shifts in trends, it may also give up some prediction correctness since the new trend that the system recommends might not perfectly match a user's interests. A slow learning rate can also affect the system utility if it fails to catch up with trends and cannot provide a new set of useful recommendations.

The evaluation of learning rate can be done by measuring (1) the time that takes the system to regain its prediction correctness when user interests drift, (2) the time to reach a certain level of correctness for new users, or (3) the prediction correctness that the system can achieve within a limited learning time. Koychev and Schwab [35] measured and plotted the prediction correctness of a recommendation system over time and assessed how fast their algorithm adapted to changes. To evaluate the learning rate for new users, Rashid et al. [58] evaluated different algorithms that learn user preferences during the sign-up process. Each algorithm presents users with a list of initial items to be rated and learns from the given ratings. After the sign-up process and the learning phase is completed, predictions for other items are made and the accuracies of the algorithms are measured and compared.

10.2.12   Usability

In order for recommendation systems to be effective, their target end users must be able to use them in appropriate ways. They must also adhere to the general principles of usability. They must be effective, efficient, and provide some degree of satisfaction for their target end users [51].

Recommendation systems typically manifest in some way via a user interface. The contents presented by this user interface play an important role in acceptance of the recommendation [55]. This user interface may simply be an in situ suggestion to the user in the containing application. More commonly, a list of recommendations, often ranked, is provided to the user on demand. Additionally, many recommendation systems require configuration parameters, user preferences, and some form of user profile to be specified. All of these interfaces greatly impact on the usability of the recommendation system as a whole. For example, presenting the user with an overwhelmingly large list of unranked or improperly ordered items is ineffective and inefficient. Presenting the user with very complicated or hard to understand information is also ineffective and impacts satisfaction. Satisfaction and efficiency are reduced if users are not allowed to interact with recommended items, for example go to target document adversely, or if the system is slow in producing a set of recommendations. These factors of recommendation systems are generally evaluated through user studies [55, 71, 72].

10.2.13   Scalability

One of the most important goals of a recommendation system is to provide online recommendations for users to navigate through a collection of items. When the system scales up to the point where there are thousands of components, bug reports, or software experts to be recommended, the system must be able to process and make each recommendation within a reasonable amount of time. If the system cannot otherwise handle a large amount of data, other dimensions will have to be compromised. For instance, the algorithm might generate recommendations based on only a subset of items instead of using the whole database. This reduces the processing time but consequently also reduces its coverage and correctness. Many examples exist of recommendation systems that work well on small datasets but struggle with large item sets or large numbers of users. These include most early API and code recommenders, many existing code or database search and rank result recommenders and complex design or code refactoring recommenders.

The scalability problem can be divided into two parts: (1) the training time of the recommendation algorithm and (2) the performance of the system or throughput when working with a large item database. The time that is required to train the algorithm can be evaluated by training different algorithms with the same dataset or by training them until they reach the same level of prediction correctness [21, 29]. The performance of the system can be evaluated in terms of *throughput*— the number of recommendations that the system can generate per second [16,23,65]. Performance (in terms of number of recommendations) can also adversely impact the usability of the recommendation system as response time may become too slow to be effective for its users.

10.2.14   Stability

Stability refers to the prediction consistency of the recommendation system over a period of time, assuming that new ratings or items added during that period are in agreement with the ones already existing in the system. A stable recommender can help increase user trust as users will be presented with consistent predictions. The prediction that changes and fluctuates frequently can cause confusion to the users and, consequently, distrust in the system.

Stability can be measured by comparing a prediction at a certain point in time with a point when new ratings are added. Adomavicius and Zhang [2, 3] carried out a stability evaluation by training the recommendation algorithm with the existing ratings and making a first prediction. After new ratings during the next period are added, the algorithm is retrained with this new dataset. It then makes a second prediction. Similar to robustness, the prediction shift (10.1) can be calculated after a new set of ratings are added.

10.2.15   Privacy

Recommendation systems often record and log user interaction into historical user profiles. This helps personalize recommendations and improve understanding of user needs. Recording this information introduces a potential threat to users' privacy. Therefore, some users might request their personal data to be kept private and not disclosed. To secure data, some approaches have proposed cryptographic solutions, or removing the single trusted party having access to the collected data [e.g., 4, 12].

Despite these efforts, it has been demonstrated that it is possible to infer user histories by passively observing a recommender's recommendations [10].

Indeed, introducing a metric for measuring privacy is a difficult task. A feasible approach is to measure how much information has been disclosed to third parties as used in web browsing scenarios [36]. The *differential privacy* measure is a privacy definition based on similar principles [19]. It indicates that the output of a computation should not permit the inference of any record's presence in, or absence from, the computation's input. The definition is as follows. Consider a randomized function $\mathcal{K}$ with its input as the dataset and its output as the released information. Also consider datasets D_1 and D_2 differing on at most one element. Then function $\mathcal{K}$ gives ϵ-differential privacy if, for all $S \subseteq \text{range}(\mathcal{K})$:

$$\Pr[\mathcal{K}(D_1) \in S] \leq \exp(\epsilon) \times \Pr[\mathcal{K}(D_2) \in S] . \tag{10.2}$$

In the context of recommendation systems, however, privacy should be measured in conjunction with correctness since keeping information from the system, or third party recommendation system, has a direct effect on correctness of the recommendation system. This difference can be shown by plotting correctness against the options available for preserving privacy. For example, McSherry and Mironov [46] demonstrated their privacy preserving application by plotting RMSE versus differential privacy.

There are still open questions and areas to explore regarding how privacy can affect recommendation systems and how to measure its effects [39]. Consider multi-user and multi-organizational situations such as open source applications where API, bug triage, code reuse, document/code trace, and expertise recommenders may share repositories. Capturing user recommender interactions may enhance recommender performance for all of these domains, however, exposing the recommended items, user ratings and recommender queries all have the potential to seriously compromise developer and organizational privacy.

10.2.16   User Preferences

We have presented a number of measures to evaluate the performance of recommendation systems. The bottom line of any recommendation system evaluation is the perception of the users of that system. Therefore, depending on application domain, an effective evaluation scenario could be to provide recommendations regarding the selection of algorithms and ask users which one they prefer. Moreover, it has been shown that some metrics (although useful for comparison) are not good measures of user preference. For example, what MAE measures and what really matters to users contrast since, due to the decision supportive nature of recommendation systems, the exact predicted value is of far less importance to a user than the fact that an item is recommended [39]. A number of recent document/code link recovery recommenders incorporate concurrently used algorithms that generate multiple sets of recommendations that can be presented either separately or combined. Many systems allow users to configure the presentation of results, ranking scales, filters on results, number of results provided, and relative weighting of multiple item features.

It should be taken into consideration, however, that user preferences are not binary values. Users might prefer one algorithm to another [70]. Therefore, if testing user preferences regarding a group of algorithms, a non-binary measure should be used before the scores are calibrated [33]. Also, new users should be separated in the evaluation from more experienced users. New users may need to establish trust and rapport with a recommender before taking advantage of the recommendations it offers. Therefore, they might benefit from an algorithm which generates highly ratable items [45].

10.3 Relation Between Dimensions

To have an effective evaluation, relationships between dimensions should also be considered. These relationships describe whether changing a dimension affects other dimensions. We have captured these relationships in Table 10.3, depicting the relationships between dimensions for overall performance of the recommendation system. Each cell in this table depicts relationships between one dimension when compared to another. If changes to a dimension are in accordance with another dimension, i.e., if improving that dimension improves the other, it has been shown by ⊙. If a dimension tends to adversely impact another, it is shown as a ×. Dimensions that tend to be independent are shown with blank cells. Below we summarize some of these recommender dimension interrelations that are not already mentioned in previous sections.

Coverage can directly affect correctness, since the more data available for generating recommendations, the more meaningful the recommendations are. Hence correctness increases with increasing coverage [22]. Coverage is also closely related to serendipity. Not every increase in coverage increases serendipity; however, an increase in serendipity will lead to higher catalog coverage. On the other hand, greater correctness dictates more constraints and therefore decreases serendipity [20]. The same is true for risk, i.e., if recommendations are being used in high risk environments, more constraints should be considered. This decreases serendipity, novelty, and diversity but increases correctness, trust, and utility.

High usability increases the amount of trust that users have in the recommendation system, especially when recommendations are transparent and accompanied by explanations. Improving privacy forces recommendation systems to hide some user data and hence affects the correctness of the recommendation.

Novel recommendations are generally recommendations that are not known to the user. It is not always a requirement for a novel recommendation to be accurate. Improving novelty by introducing randomness may decrease correctness. Also, improving novelty by omitting well-known items will affect correctness. Therefore, increasing novelty may decrease correctness. The same is true for diversity.

Table 10.3 Relationships between metrics

Metric	User preference	Correctness	Coverage	Confidence	Trustworthiness	Novelty	Serendipity	Diversity	Utility	Risk	Robustness	Privacy	Usability	Stability	Scalability	Learning rate
User preference	-	×	⊙		⊙				⊙				⊙	⊙		
Correctness	×	-	⊙		⊙	×	×	×	⊙	⊙	×	×			⊙	⊙
Coverage	⊙	⊙	-			⊙	⊙	⊙	⊙		×				⊙	
Confidence				-												
Trustworthiness	⊙	⊙			-					⊙	⊙		⊙	⊙		
Novelty		×	⊙			-	⊙	⊙			×		⊙			
Serendipity		×	⊙		⊙		-	⊙			×		⊙			
Diversity		×	⊙		⊙	⊙		-			×					
Utility	⊙	⊙	⊙						-		⊙					⊙
Risk		⊙			⊙	×	×	×	⊙	-	⊙	⊙				
Robustness		×			⊙				⊙		-			⊙		×
Privacy		×	×						⊙			-				
Usability	⊙				⊙	⊙	⊙						-			
Stability	⊙				⊙						⊙			-		
Scalability		⊙	⊙												-	
Learning rate		⊙							⊙		×					-

⊙ indicates a direct relationship, while ⊗ indicates an adverse relationship

Scalability and learning rate directly affect correctness since improving them allows faster adaptation of new items and users, thus resulting in better correctness. Improving scalability at the same time also improves coverage.

Improving robustness prevents mistaken information from affecting recommendations and hence improves user trust [38]. It will, however, result in true recommendations being adopted more slowly, therefore reducing short-term correctness.

It is noteworthy that from the metrics presented in this table, risk could have been categorized separately. Regardless of how the recommendation system performs, risks involved with the application are the same, i.e., although having a better performing recommendation system helps to minimize the risk associated with "selecting a recommendation," it does not change the fact that risks for that particular application exist in general.

The true relationships between metrics are more nuanced than can be represented in a two-dimensional table. For example, improving coverage directly improves correctness and increasing novelty might improve coverage. Thus, improving novelty can be considered to indirectly improve correctness, contradicting the table. Therefore, a better framework or standard for understanding these relationships is needed and should be considered for future research.

Table 10.4 Summary of metrics

Dimension	Metric/Technique	Type(s)
Correctness	*Ratings*: root-mean-square-error, normalized RMSE, mean absolute error, normalized MAE *Ranking*: normalized distance-based performance measure, Spearman's ρ, Kendall's τ, normalized discounted cumulative gain *Classification* : precision, recall, false positive rate, specificity, F-measure, receiver operating characteristic curve	quantitative
Coverage	catalog coverage, weighted catalog coverage, prediction coverage, weighted prediction coverage	quantitative
Diversity	diversity measure, relative diversity, precision–diversity curve, Q-statistics, set theoretic difference of recommendation lists	quantitative
Trustworthiness	user studies	qualitative
Confidence	neighborhood-aware similarity model, similarity indicators	qualitative/quantitative
Novelty	comparison of recommendation lists and user profiles, counting popular items	qualitative/quantitative
Serendipity	comparison of recommendation lists and user profiles, ratability	qualitative/quantitative
Utility	profit-based utility function, study user intention, user studies	qualitative/quantitative
Risk	depends on application and user preference	qualitative
Robustness	prediction shift, average hit ratio, average rank	quantitative
Learning rate	correctness over time	quantitative
Usability	user studies (survey, observation, monitoring)	qualitative/quantitative
Scalability	training time, recommendation throughput	quantitative
Stability	prediction shift	quantitative
Privacy	differential privacy, RMSE vs. differential privacy curve	qualitative/quantitative
User preference	user studies	qualitative/quantitative

10.4   Evaluation Approaches and Frameworks

Table 10.4 summarizes the set of evaluation metrics and technique dimensions described earlier according to their corresponding dimension and type(s). Some of the dimensions are qualitative assessments while others are quantitative.

The most basic evaluation of a recommendation system is to use just one or two metrics covering one or two dimensions. For example, one may choose to evaluate and compare a recommender using correctness and diversity dimensions. When possible, the selected dimensions can be plotted to allow better analysis.

The selection of dimensions can be chosen according to a particular recommender application. As mentioned in Sect. 10.3, however, there is always a tradeoff present between the dimensions of a recommendation system that should be considered when evaluating the effectiveness of recommendation systems. Also, the multi-faceted characteristics of these systems, and unavailability of a standard framework for evaluation, and in many case suitable performance benchmarks, has directly affected the evaluation of different systems by dimensions. In addition, many metrics require significant time and effort to properly design experiments, and to capture and analyze results. Availability of end users, suitable datasets, suitable reference benchmarks, and multiple implementations of different approaches are all often challenging issues.

However, some new approaches are beginning to emerge to help developers and users decide between different recommender algorithms and systems. An example of this is an approach that helps users define which metrics can be used for evaluation of the recommendation system at hand [68]. It proposes to consider evaluation goals to ensure the selection of an appropriate metric. An analysis of a collection of correctness metrics is provided as evidence regarding how different goals can affect the outcome of the evaluation.

Hernández del Olmo and Gaudioso [27] propose an objective-based framework for the standardization of recommendation system evaluations. Their framework is based on the concept that a recommendation system is composed of interactive and non-interactive subsystems (called *guides* and *filters* respectively). The guide decides when and how each recommendation is to be shown to users. The filter selects interesting items to recommend. Accordingly, a performance metric P has been introduced as the quantification of the final performance of a recommendation system over a set of sessions. P is defined as the number of selected relevant recommendations that have been followed by the user over a recommendation session.

A more recent approach introduced a multi-faceted model for recommender evaluation that proposes evaluation along three axis: users, technical constraints, and business models [62]. This approach considers user, technical, and business aspects together and evaluates the recommender accordingly. However, considerable further work is needed to enable detailed evaluation of recommendation system against many of the potential metrics itemized in Table 10.4.

10.5   Conclusion

In this chapter, we have presented and explained a range of common metrics used for the evaluation of recommendation systems in software engineering. Based on a review of current literature, we derived a set of dimensions that are used to evaluate an individual recommendation system or in comparing it against the current state of the art. For the dimensions, we have provided a description as well as a set of commonly used metrics and explored relationships between the dimensions.

We hope that our classification and description of this range of available evaluation metrics will help other researchers to develop better recommendation systems. We also hope that our taxonomy will be used to improve the validation of newly developed recommendation systems and clearly show in specific ways how a new recommendation system is better than the current state of the art. Finally, the content of this chapter can be used by practitioners in understanding the evaluation criteria for recommendation systems. This can thus improve their decisions when selecting a specific recommendation system for a software development project.

References

1. Adomavicius, G., Tuzhilin, A.: Toward the next generation of recommender systems: a survey of the state-of-the-art and possible extensions. IEEE Trans. Knowl. Data Eng. **17**(6), 734–749 (2005). doi:10.1109/TKDE.2005.99
2. Adomavicius, G., Zhang, J.: Iterative smoothing technique for improving stability of recommender systems. In: Proceedings of the Workshop on Recommendation Utility Evaluation: Beyond RMSE. CEUR Workshop Proceedings, vol. 910, pp. 3–8 (2012a)
3. Adomavicius, G., Zhang, J.: Stability of recommendation algorithms. ACM Trans. Inform. Syst. **30**(4), 23:1–23:31 (2012b). doi:10.1145/2382438.2382442
4. Aïmeur, E., Brassard, G., Fernandez, J.M., Onana, F.S.M.: Alambic: a privacy-preserving recommender system for electronic commerce. Int. J. Inf. Security **7**(5), 307–334 (2008). doi:10.1007/s10207-007-0049-3
5. Ashok, B., Joy, J., Liang, H., Rajamani, S.K., Srinivasa, G., Vangala, V.: DebugAdvisor: a recommender system for debugging. In: Proceedings of the European Software Engineering Conference/ACM SIGSOFT International Symposium on Foundations of Software Engineering, pp. 373–382 (2009). doi:10.1145/1595696.1595766
6. Bell, R., Koren, Y., Volinsky, C.: Modeling relationships at multiple scales to improve accuracy of large recommender systems. In: Proceedings of the ACM SIGKDD Conference on Knowledge Discovery and Data Mining, pp. 95–104 (2007). doi:10.1145/1281192.1281206
7. Bonhard, P., Harries, C., McCarthy, J., Sasse, M.A.: Accounting for taste: using profile similarity to improve recommender systems. In: Proceedings of the ACM SIGCHI Conference on Human Factors in Computing Systems, pp. 1057–1066 (2006). doi:10.1145/1124772.1124930
8. Burke, R.: Hybrid web recommender systems. In: Brusilovsky, P., Kobsa, A., Nejdl, W. (eds.) The Adaptive Web: Methods and Strategies of Web Personalization. Lecture Notes in Computer Science, vol. 4321, pp. 377–408. Springer, New York (2007). doi:10.1007/978-3-540-72079-9_12
9. Burke, R., Ramezani, M.: Matching recommendation technologies and domains. In: Ricci, F., Rokach, L., Shapira, B., Kantor, P.B. (eds.) Recommender Systems Handbook, pp. 367–386. Springer, New York (2011). doi:10.1007/978-0-387-85820-3_11
10. Calandrino, J.A., Kilzer, A., Narayanan, A., Felten, E.W., Shmatikov, V.: "You might also like": privacy risks of collaborative filtering. In: Proceedings of the IEEE Symposium on Security and Privacy, pp. 231–246 (2011). doi:10.1109/SP.2011.40
11. Candillier, L., Chevalier, M., Dudognon, D., Mothe, J.: Diversity in recommender systems: bridging the gap between users and systems. In: Proceedings of the International Conference on Advances in Human-Oriented and Personalized Mechanisms, Technologies, and Services, pp. 48–53 (2011)
12. Canny, J.: Collaborative filtering with privacy. In: Proceedings of the IEEE Symposium on Security and Privacy, pp. 45–57 (2002). doi:10.1109/SECPRI.2002.1004361

13. Cheetham, W., Price, J.: Measures of solution accuracy in case-based reasoning systems. In: Proceedings of the European Conference on Case-Based Reasoning. Lecture Notes in Computer Science, vol. 3155, pp. 106–118 (2004). doi:10.1007/978-3-540-28631-8_9

14. Cramer, H., Evers, V., Ramlal, S., Someren, M., Rutledge, L., Stash, N., Aroyo, L., Wielinga, B.: The effects of transparency on trust in and acceptance of a content-based art recommender. User Model. User-Adap. Interact. **18**(5), 455–496 (2008). doi:10.1007/s11257-008-9051-3

15. Čubranić, D., Murphy, G.C., Singer, J., Booth, K.S.: Hipikat: a project memory for software development. IEEE Trans. Software Eng. **31**(6), 446–465 (2005). doi:10.1109/TSE.2005.71

16. Das, A.S., Datar, M., Garg, A., Rajaram, S.: Google news personalization: scalable online collaborative filtering. In: Proceedings of the International Conference on the World Wide Web, pp. 271–280 (2007). doi:10.1145/1242572.1242610

17. De Lucia, A., Fasano, F., Oliveto, R., Tortor, G.: Recovering traceability links in software artifact management systems using information retrieval methods. ACM Trans. Software Eng. Methodol. **16**(4), 13:1–13:50 (2007). doi:10.1145/1276933.1276934

18. Dolques, X., Dogui, A., Falleri, J.R., Huchard, M., Nebut, C., Pfister, F.: Easing model transformation learning with automatically aligned examples. In: Proceedings of the European Conference on Modelling Foundations and Applications. Lecture Notes in Computer Science, vol. 6698, pp. 189–204 (2011). doi:10.1007/978-3-642-21470-7_14

19. Dwork, C.: Differential privacy: a survey of results. In: Proceedings of the International Conference on Theory and Applications of Models of Computation. Lecture Notes in Computer Science, vol. 4978, pp. 1–19 (2008). doi:10.1007/978-3-540-79228-4_1

20. Ge, M., Delgado-Battenfeld, C., Jannach, D.: Beyond accuracy: evaluating recommender systems by coverage and serendipity. In: Proceedings of the ACM Conference on Recommender Systems, pp. 257–260 (2010). doi:10.1145/1864708.1864761

21. George, T., Merugu, S.: A scalable collaborative filtering framework based on co-clustering. In: Proceedings of the IEEE International Conference on Data Mining (2005). doi:10.1109/ICDM.2005.14

22. Good, N., Schafer, J.B., Konstan, J.A., Borchers, A., Sarwar, B., Herlocker, J., Riedl, J.: Combining collaborative filtering with personal agents for better recommendations. In: Proceedings of the National Conference on Artificial Intelligence and the Conference on Innovative Applications of Artificial Intelligence, pp. 439–446 (1999)

23. Han, P., Xie, B., Yang, F., Shen, R.: A scalable P2P recommender system based on distributed collaborative filtering. Expert Syst. Appl. **27**(2), 203–210 (2004). doi:10.1016/j.eswa.2004.01.003

24. Happel, H.J., Maalej, W.: Potentials and challenges of recommendation systems for software development. In: Proceedings of the International Workshop on Recommendation Systems for Software Engineering, pp. 11–15 (2008). doi:10.1145/1454247.1454251

25. Herlocker, J.L., Konstan, J.A., Riedl, J.: Explaining collaborative filtering recommendations. In: Proceedings of the ACM Conference on Computer Supported Cooperative Work, pp. 241–250 (2000). doi:10.1145/358916.358995

26. Herlocker, J.L., Konstan, J.A., Terveen, L.G., Riedl, J.T.: Evaluating collaborative filtering recommender systems. ACM Trans. Inform. Syst. **22**(1), 5–53 (2004). doi:10.1145/963770.963772

27. Hernández del Olmo, F., Gaudioso, E.: Evaluation of recommender systems: a new approach. Expert Syst. Appl. **35**(3), 790–804 (2008). doi:10.1016/j.eswa.2007.07.047

28. Järvelin, K., Kekäläinen, J.: Cumulated gain-based evaluation of IR techniques. ACM Trans. Inform. Syst. **20**(4), 422–446 (2002). doi:10.1145/582415.582418

29. Karypis, G.: Evaluation of item-based top-N recommendation algorithms. In: Proceedings of the International Conference on Information and Knowledge Management, pp. 247–254 (2001). doi:10.1145/502585.502627

30. Kendall, M.G.: A new measure of rank correlation. Biometrika **30**(1–2), 81–93 (1938)

31. Kendall, M.G.: The treatment of ties in ranking problems. Biometrika **33**(3), 239–251 (1945)

32. Kille, B., Albayrak, S.: Modeling difficulty in recommender systems. In: Proceedings of the Workshop on Recommendation Utility Evaluation: Beyond RMSE. CEUR Workshop Proceedings, vol. 910, pp. 30–32 (2012)
33. Kitchenham, B.A., Pfleeger, S.L.: Principles of survey research. Part 3: constructing a survey instrument. SIGSOFT Software Eng. Note. **27**(2), 20–24 (2002). doi:10.1145/511152.511155
34. Koren, Y., Bell, R., Volinsky, C.: Matrix factorization techniques for recommender systems. Computer **42**(8), 30–37 (2009). doi:10.1109/MC.2009.263
35. Koychev, I., Schwab, I.: Adaptation to drifting user's interests. In: Proceedings of the Workshop on Machine Learning in the New Information Age, pp. 39–46 (2000)
36. Krishnamurthy, B., Malandrino, D., Wills, C.E.: Measuring privacy loss and the impact of privacy protection in web browsing. In: Proceedings of the Symposium on Usable Privacy and Security, pp. 52–63 (2007). doi:10.1145/1280680.1280688
37. Kuncheva, L.I., Whitaker, C.J.: Measures of diversity in classifier ensembles and their relationship with the ensemble accuracy. Mach. Learn. **51**(2), 181–207 (2003). doi:10.1023/A:1022859003006
38. Lam, S.K., Riedl, J.: Shilling recommender systems for fun and profit. In: Proceedings of the International Conference on the World Wide Web, pp. 393–402 (2004). doi:10.1145/988672.988726
39. Lam, S.K.T., Frankowski, D., Riedl, J.: Do you trust your recommendations?: an exploration of security and privacy issues in recommender systems. In: Proceedings of the International Conference on Emerging Trends in Information and Communication Security. Lecture Notes in Computer Science, vol. 3995, pp. 14–29 (2006). doi:10.1007/11766155_2
40. Lathia, N., Hailes, S., Capra, L., Amatriain, X.: Temporal diversity in recommender systems. In: Proceedings of the ACM SIGIR International Conference on Research and Development in Information Retrieval, pp. 210–217 (2010). doi:10.1145/1835449.1835486
41. Le, Q.V., Smola, A.J.: Direct optimization of ranking measures. Technical Report (2007) [arXiv:0704.3359]
42. Massa, P., Avesani, P.: Trust-aware recommender systems. In: Proceedings of the ACM Conference on Recommender Systems, pp. 17–24 (2007). doi:10.1145/1297231.1297235
43. McCarey, F., Ó Cinnéide, M., Kushmerick, N.: RASCAL: a recommender agent for agile reuse. Artif. Intell. Rev. **24**(3–4), 253–276 (2005). doi:10.1007/s10462-005-9012-8
44. McNee, S.M.: Meeting user information needs in recommender systems. Ph.D. thesis, University of Minnesota (2006)
45. McNee, S.M., Riedl, J., Konstan, J.A.: Being accurate is not enough: how accuracy metrics have hurt recommender systems. In: Extended Abstracts of the ACM SIGCHI Conference on Human Factors in Computing Systems, pp. 1097–1101 (2006). doi:10.1145/1125451.1125659
46. McSherry, F., Mironov, I.: Differentially private recommender systems: building privacy into the net. In: Proceedings of the ACM SIGKDD Conference on Knowledge Discovery and Data Mining, pp. 627–636 (2009). doi:10.1145/1557019.1557090
47. Melnik, S., Garcia-Molina, H., Rahm, E.: Similarity flooding: a versatile graph matching algorithm and its application to schema matching. In: Proceedings of the International Conference on Data Engineering, pp. 117–128 (2002). doi:10.1109/ICDE.2002.994702
48. Meyer, F., Fessant, F., Clérot, F., Gaussier, E.: Toward a new protocol to evaluate recommender systems. In: Proceedings of the Workshop on Recommendation Utility Evaluation: Beyond RMSE. CEUR Workshop Proceedings, vol. 910, pp. 9–14 (2012)
49. Mobasher, B., Burke, R., Bhaumik, R., Williams, C.: Toward trustworthy recommender systems: an analysis of attack models and algorithm robustness. ACM Trans. Inter. Tech. **7**(4), 23:1–23:38 (2007). doi:10.1145/1278366.1278372
50. Mockus, A., Herbsleb, J.D.: Expertise Browser: a quantitative approach to identifying expertise. In: Proceedings of the ACM/IEEE International Conference on Software Engineering, pp. 503–512 (2002). doi:10.1145/581339.581401
51. Nielsen, J.: Usability Engineering. Morgan Kaufmann Publishers Inc., San Francisco, CA, USA (1993)

52. O'Donovan, J., Smyth, B.: Trust in recommender systems. In: Proceedings of the International Conference on Intelligent User Interfaces, pp. 167–174 (2005). doi:10.1145/1040830.1040870
53. O'Mahony, M., Hurley, N., Kushmerick, N., Silvestre, G.: Collaborative recommendation: a robustness analysis. ACM Trans. Inter. Tech. **4**(4), 344–377 (2004). doi:10.1145/1031114.1031116
54. Oxford Dictionaries: Oxford Dictionary of English. 3rd edn. Oxford: Oxford University Press, UK (2010)
55. Ozok, A.A., Fan, Q., Norcio, A.F.: Design guidelines for effective recommender system interfaces based on a usability criteria conceptual model: results from a college student population. Behav. Inf. Technol. **29**(1), 57–83 (2010). doi:10.1080/01449290903004012
56. Quinlan, J. R.: C4.5: Programs for Machine Learning. Morgan Kaufmann Publishers Inc., San Francisco, CA, USA (1993)
57. Ramakrishnan, N., Keller, B.J., Mirza, B.J., Grama, A.Y., Karypis, G.: Privacy risks in recommender systems. IEEE Internet Comput. **5**(6), 54–62 (2001). doi:10.1109/4236.968832
58. Rashid, A.M., Albert, I., Cosley, D., Lam, S.K., McNee, S.M., Konstan, J.A., Riedl, J.: Getting to know you: learning new user preferences in recommender systems. In: Proceedings of the International Conference on Intelligent User Interfaces, pp. 127–134 (2002). doi:10.1145/502716.502737
59. Robillard, M.P.: Topology analysis of software dependencies. ACM Trans. Software Eng. Methodol. **17**(4), 18:1–18:36 (2008). doi:10.1145/13487689.13487691
60. Robillard, M.P., Walker, R.J., Zimmermann, T.: Recommendation systems for software engineering. IEEE Software **27**(4), 80–86 (2010). doi:10.1109/MS.2009.161
61. Rubens, N., Kaplan, D., Sugiyama, M.: Active learning in recommender systems. In: Ricci, F., Rokach, L., Shapira, B., Kantor, P.B. (eds.) Recommender Systems Handbook, pp. 735–767. Springer, New York (2011). doi:10.1007/978-0-387-85820-3_23
62. Said, A., Tikk, D., Shi, Y., Larson, M., Stumpf, K., Cremonesi, P.: Recommender systems evaluation: a 3D benchmark. In: Proceedings of the Workshop on Recommendation Utility Evaluation: Beyond RMSE. CEUR Workshop Proceedings, vol. 910, pp. 21–23 (2012)
63. Salfner, F., Lenk, M., Malek, M.: A survey of online failure prediction methods. ACM Comput. Surv. **42**(3), 10:1–10:42 (2010). doi:10.1145/1670679.1670680
64. Sandvig, J.J., Mobasher, B., Burke, R.: Robustness of collaborative recommendation based on association rule mining. In: Proceedings of the ACM Conference on Recommender Systems, pp. 105–112 (2007). doi:10.1145/1297231.1297249
65. Sarwar, B., Karypis, G., Konstan, J., Riedl, J.: Application of dimensionality reduction in recommender system: a case study. Technical Report 00-043, Department of Computer Science & Engineering, University of Minnesota (2000)
66. Sarwar, B., Karypis, G., Konstan, J., Riedl, J.: Item-based collaborative filtering recommendation algorithms. In: Proceedings of the International Conference on the World Wide Web, pp. 285–295 (2001). doi:10.1145/371920.372071
67. Schein, A.I., Popescul, A., Ungar, L.H., Pennock, D.M.: Methods and metrics for cold-start recommendations. In: Proceedings of the ACM SIGIR International Conference on Research and Development in Information Retrieval, pp. 253–260 (2002). doi:10.1145/564376.564421
68. Schroder, G., Thiele, M., Lehner, W.: Setting goals and choosing metrics for recommender system evaluation. In: Proceedings of the Workshop on Human Decision Making in Recommender Systems and User-Centric Evaluation of Recommender Systems and Their Interfaces. CEUR Workshop Proceedings, vol. 811, pp. 78–85 (2011)
69. Seminario, C.E., Wilson, D.C.: Robustness and accuracy tradeoffs for recommender systems under attack. In: Proceedings of the Florida Artificial Intelligence Research Society Conference, pp. 86–91 (2012)
70. Shani, G., Gunawardana, A.: Evaluating recommendation systems. In: Ricci, F., Rokach, L., Shapira, B., Kantor, P.B. (eds.) Recommender Systems Handbook, pp. 257–297. Springer, New York (2011). doi:10.1007/978-0-387-85820-3_8

71. Simon, F., Steinbrückner, F., Lewerentz, C.: Metrics based refactoring. In: Proceedings of the European Conference on Software Maintenance and Reengineering, pp. 30–38 (2001). doi:10.1109/.2001.914965
72. Sinha, R., Swearingen, K.: The role of transparency in recommender systems. In: Extended Abstracts of the ACM SIGCHI Conference on Human Factors in Computing Systems, pp. 830–831 (2002). doi:10.1145/506443.506619
73. Smyth, B., McClave, P.: Similarity vs. diversity. In: Proceedings of the International Conference on Case-Based Reasoning. Lecture Notes in Computer Science, vol. 2080, pp. 347–361 (2001). doi:10.1007/3-540-44593-5_25
74. Spearman, C.: The proof and measurement of association between two things. Am. J. Psychol. 15(1), 72–101 (1904). doi:10.2307/1412159
75. Su, X., Khoshgoftaar, T.M.: A survey of collaborative filtering techniques. Adv. Artif. Intell. 2009, 421425:1–421425:19 (2009). doi:10.1155/2009/421425
76. Thummalapenta, S., Xie, T.: PARSEWeb: a programmer assistant for reusing open source code on the web. In: Proceedings of the IEEE/ACM International Conference on Automated Software Engineering, pp. 204–213 (2007). doi:10.1145/1321631.1321663
77. Tintarev, N., Masthoff, J.: A survey of explanations in recommender systems. In: Proceedings of the IEEE International Workshop on Web Personalisation, Recommender Systems and Intelligent User Interfaces, pp. 801–810 (2007). doi:10.1109/ICDEW.2007.4401070
78. Weimer, M., Karatzoglou, A., Le, Q.V., Smola, A.: CoFi^{RANK}: maximum margin matrix factorization for collaborative ranking. In: Proceedings of the Annual Conference on Neural Information Processing Systems, pp. 222–230 (2007)
79. Yao, Y.Y.: Measuring retrieval effectiveness based on user preference of documents. J. Am. Soc. Inform. Sci. Technol. 46(2), 133–145 (1995). doi:10.1002/(SICI)1097-4571(199503)46:2⟨133::AID-ASI6⟩3.0.CO;2-Z
80. Ye, Y., Fischer, G.: Reuse-conducive development environments. Automat. Software Eng. Int. J. 12(2), 199–235 (2005). doi:10.1007/s10515-005-6206-x
81. Ziegler, C.N., McNee, S.M., Konstan, J.A., Lausen, G.: Improving recommendation lists through topic diversification. In: Proceedings of the International Conference on the World Wide Web, pp. 22–32 (2005). doi:10.1145/1060745.1060754

Chapter 11
Benchmarking

A Methodology for Ensuring the Relative Quality of Recommendation Systems in Software Engineering

Alan Said, Domonkos Tikk, and Paolo Cremonesi

Abstract This chapter describes the concepts involved in the process of benchmarking of recommendation systems. Benchmarking of recommendation systems is used to ensure the quality of a research system or production system in comparison to other systems, whether algorithmically, infrastructurally, or according to any sought-after quality. Specifically, the chapter presents evaluation of recommendation systems according to recommendation accuracy, technical constraints, and business values in the context of a multi-dimensional benchmarking and evaluation model encompassing any number of qualities into a final comparable metric. The focus is put on quality measures related to recommendation accuracy, technical factors, and business values. The chapter first introduces concepts related to evaluation and benchmarking of recommendation systems, continues with an overview of the current state of the art, then presents the multi-dimensional approach in detail. The chapter concludes with a brief discussion of the introduced concepts and a summary.

A. Said (✉)
Centrum Wiskunde & Informatica, Amsterdam, The Netherlands
e-mail: alan@cwi.nl

D. Tikk
Gravity R&D, Budapest, Hungary

Óbuda University, Budapest, Hungary
e-mail: domonkos.tikk@gravityrd.com; domonkos.tikk@nik.uni-obuda.hu

P. Cremonesi
Politecnico di Milano, Milano, Italy
e-mail: paolo.cremonesi@polimi.it

M.P. Robillard et al. (eds.), *Recommendation Systems in Software Engineering*,
DOI 10.1007/978-3-642-45135-5_11, © Springer-Verlag Berlin Heidelberg 2014

11.1 Introduction

Benchmarking is a structural approach to quality engineering and management [7]; essentially it is a comparison process aimed at finding the best practice for a given well-specified problem. The concept of benchmarking originated in optimizing business processes by investigating and analyzing industry standards, comparing them to the one applied in the investigator's own organization, and creating an implementation plan with predefined goals and objectives to improve the quality and performance of the evaluated process. In the last few decades, benchmarking has also become very popular in scientific research and software engineering, driven by the need to identify best-in-class approaches or algorithms for scientific problems, and to facilitate various stages of the software development lifecycle, including automated code-testing [18].

The process of traditional benchmarking is built up from the following steps: (1) design and target specification, (2) data collection, (3) evaluation and analysis, and (4) implementation of improvements. Scientific benchmarking, on the other hand, mainly focuses on providing a means for comparison and exploration of novel ideas on a dataset collected for the given purpose,[1] and puts less emphasis on the implementation of the improvements in an industrial environment.

Due to their origins in the research community, recommendation systems are primarily evaluated using accuracy-oriented metrics, such as precision, recall, root-mean-squared error, etc. [22]. As a typical example, we refer to the Netflix Prize competition [31] (see more details in Sect. 11.2). However, these measures only represent one type of performance, namely the objective recommendation accuracy, not taking into consideration software engineering and business aspects, technical constraints, and subjective user-centric values, thus creating an unbalanced focus on only one dimension of the evaluation spectrum. This lack of balance makes benchmarking of recommendation systems in different domains and settings difficult, if not impossible. The business and technical constraints are largely neglected in traditional algorithmic evaluation [22]. Even in cases where multi-objective evaluation is applied, the evaluation often focuses only on recommendation accuracy [e.g., 24]. The broadly accepted philosophy is that the higher the accuracy (or lower the error) metrics are, the better the recommendation system performs [22]. In order to objectively estimate the utility of a recommendation system, from all perspectives, the complete spectrum of recommendation quality should be evaluated, especially in contexts where accuracy is not necessarily the ultimate goal.

In real-world scenarios, business- and technology-centered measures are just as important, if not more so, than accuracy alone. An evaluation model incorporating all three values was presented by Said et al. [37]. This model, if applied in the context of a real-world, market-driven recommendation system, simplifies the

---

[1] See for example the UCI Machine Learning Repository that contains a large selection of machine learning benchmark datasets. Recommendation-system-related benchmark datasets can also be found in KONECT, e.g., under category ratings.

algorithm-to-algorithm comparison of recommendation systems. Especially from a software engineering perspective, evaluating technical constraints is particularly important in order to create a well-functioning system.

Throughout this chapter, we use the evaluation model outlined by Said et al. [37] to discuss and reason whether the most important challenges are related to large-scale, real-time, business-driven, or highly accurate recommendations. The context of the recommendation is often related to the setting in which the recommendation is to be presented, and to what quality is important in the specific setting. For instance, below we present a few examples where recommendation systems can be (and often are) deployed, and, given the diversity of the services, where the sought-after qualities in each service need not to be the same.

Video/Music-on-Demand. Video-on-demand (VOD) and music-on-demand (MOD) are services where multimedia content is provided to the users on request; examples of these include Netflix and Spotify. The difference from other media, e.g., radio or live TV, is the user-driven availability of the content. This instant availability of content creates a certain context in which the recommendations are most often consumed directly and not stored for later viewing, listening, etc. Additionally, there is a business context in which a specific item might be a preferred recommendation from the provider based on infrastructure, revenue, or other factors. It should however still represent a suitable recommendation from the user's perspective.

Linear TV. In linear (or traditional) television (TV) where the delivery of content is driven by one provider to a large audience without any personalization, the selection of items is limited and quickly changing. In this context, it is imperative for the recommendation system to adapt to the currently available items. However, the user- and business-focused aspects should not be overlooked as the utility of quickly updating but poorly performing recommendation systems is low both for the user and for the service operator.

Webshop. In a webshop setting, the user- and business-focused aspects of recommendations might be different, since users seek quality products at low prices, while the business is focusing on maximizing the revenue/profit per user visit. The latter could potentially be achieved by recommending quality and more expensive/larger margin products. Therefore the utility of the recommender is different for the two aspects, which may necessitate the implementation of a recommendation algorithm that trades off between the different goals.

News Portal. On a news portal, users seek interesting content to read, and their "currency" is the time they spend on the site, visit frequency, and the number of pages visited. Since users' browsing time is usually limited per visit, the quality of recommendations, and therefore the user satisfaction and loyalty is often mirrored in increased visit frequency [28]. On the service provider's end, the business goal is to increase the total number of page views, since the ad display-based business model scales with page views. Alternatively, pay-per view or subscriber content could provide an additional revenue stream; in such a case the recommender algorithm should also identify those users that are willing to pay for the content. An additional user-focused quality measure is the diversity of the recommendation that also requires good adaptability from the recommendation system to capture, in real-time, the user's actual interest.

Internet Marketplaces. On Internet marketplaces, such as auction sites (e.g., eBay) or classified media sites (e.g., leboncoin, craigslist), the perceived quality of recommendations from the user depends on how quickly the algorithm can adapt to the actual need of the visit. On the business side, it is important to keep users engaged and active in using the service while being able to sell value-added services for advertisers/sellers. Therefore the recommendation algorithm should again trade off between user satisfaction and the site's business goals.

The requirements on the recommendation algorithms deployed in each example are clearly different; the implication that follows is that they should also be evaluated differently. The multidimensional evaluation model presented in this chapter allows for this, while still keeping a reasonable means of comparison.

11.2 Benchmarking and Evaluation Settings

We explain the process of benchmarking based on the Netflix Prize (NP) example, which is by far the most widely known benchmarking event and dataset for recommendation systems. Recall that the benchmarking process has the following steps: (1) design and target specification, (2) data collection, (3) evaluation and analysis, and (4) implementation of improvements.

Netflix initiated the contest in order to improve their in-house recommendation system—called Cinematch—that provides movie recommendations to their customers. Although the ultimate goal of Netflix was to improve or replace Cinematch with a recommendation system that would provide more satisfactory recommendations to the end-users and thus improve their business,[2] they selected a less sensitive and essentially simpler task as a proxy to benchmark algorithms of the participants.

At Netflix, users can express their movie preferences by rating movies on a 1–5 scale. The aim of the competition was to improve the prediction accuracy of user ratings, that is, participants in the competition had to create algorithms to predict a set of unreported user ratings (called the Qualifying set), using a set of reported user ratings (called the Training set). Netflix released a large rating dataset (for comparison to other datasets, see Table 11.1) as follows [43] (see Fig. 11.1 for an overview). Netflix selected a random subset of users from their entire customer base

---

[2]Better recommendations postpone or eliminate the *content glut effect* [32]—a variation on the idea of information overload—and thus increases customer lifetime, which is translated into additional revenue of Netflix's monthly plan based subscription service.

Table 11.1 Benchmark datasets for recommendation tasks. Starred datasets contain implicit ratings; density is given as a percentage

Name	Domain	Events	Users	Items	Density
Jester	jokes	4,136,360	73,421	100	56.34
Book-crossing	book	1,149,780	278,858	271,379	0.001
MovieLens 100k	movie	100,000	943	1682	6.30
MovieLens 1M	movie	1,000,000	6040	3900	4.25
MovieLens 10M	movie	10,000,000	71,567	10,681	1.31
Netflix	movie	100,480,507	480,189	17,7	1.17
CAMRa2010 (Moviepilot)	movie	4,544,409	105,137	25,058	0.002
CAMRa2011 (Moviepilot)	movie	4,391,822	171,67	29,974	0.001
CAMRa2010 (Filmtipset time)	movie	5,862,464	34,857	53,6	0.003
CAMRa2010 (Filmtipset social)	movie	3,075,346	16,473	24,222	0.008
Last.fm 1K*	music	19,150,868	992	176,948	10.91
Last.fm 360K*	music	17,559,530	359,347	294,015	0.016
Yahoo Music (KDD Cup 2011)	music	262,810,175	1,000,990	624,961	0.042
Mendeley*	publications	4,848,724	50	3,652,285	0.002
LibimSeTi	dating	17,359,346	135,359	168,791	0.076
Delicious	tags	420,000,000	950	132,000,000	$3 \cdot 10^{-6}$
Koders-log-2007	code search	5M + 5M	3,187,969	see note 5	see note 5

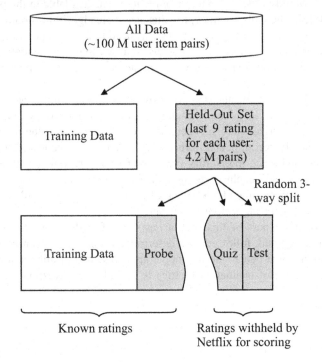

Fig. 11.1 The benchmark dataset of the Netflix Prize [adapted from 6]

with at least 20 ratings in a given period. A *Hold-Out set* was created from the 9 most recent ratings of each of these users,[3] consisting of about 4.2 million ratings. The remaining data formed the Training set. The ratings of the Hold-Out set were split randomly into three subsets of equal size: Quiz, Test, and Probe. The Probe set was released with ratings, primarily to allow the competitors to self-evaluate their algorithms, although they also used this data for training purposes in submitting the final predictions. The Quiz and Test sets formed the Qualifying set for which the actual ratings were withheld in order to evaluate competitors. The Quiz/Test split of the Qualifying set was unknown to the public. Netflix adopted root-mean-squared error (RMSE) as their evaluation measure to compare the algorithms. Participants had to submit only the predictions on the Qualifying set, not their algorithms. The organizers returned the RMSE of the submissions on the Quiz set, which is also reported on a public leaderboard. The RMSE on the Test set was withheld by Netflix, in order to retain some data for which competitors were unable to adjust their algorithms.

In 2009, the 1 million dollar prize was awarded to an ensemble algorithm, which successfully outperformed Cinematch by more than 10 % at RMSE. However, in the end the ensemble was not deployed by Netflix; one of the reasons behind this was simply that it would not scale-up to the amount of data available in the production environment [2]. The inability to deploy this ensemble algorithm should serve as a motivation as to why recommendation systems need to be evaluated in terms other than recommendation accuracy only. Because real-world recommendation systems are software tools, considering software engineering related parameters at their evaluation is essential.

Other benchmarking events, organized by academia and industry—e.g., KDD Cup 2011 [25], various installations of the ECML/PKDD Discovery Challenge, the Overstock RecLab Prize, etc.—all focused on one dimension of the recommendation quality, namely, recommendation accuracy. Even though a considerable amount of time has passed since the Netflix Prize competition, recommendation systems are still evaluated and benchmarked in a similar fashion. Recent examples of this include the 2013 Recommender Systems Challenge where again only RMSE was used for comparing the algorithms to one another.

In the remaining part of this section, aspects of traditional evaluation (e.g., accuracy) are presented, followed by a description on how these can be applied in the multi-dimensional benchmarking model also presented in this section. A more in-depth perspective of evaluation metrics is provided by Avazpour et al. [3] in Chap. 10.

---

[3]The date-based partition of the NP dataset into Training/Testing sets reflects the original aim of recommendation systems, which is the prediction of future interest of users from their past ratings/activities.

11.2.1   Datasets

Traditional evaluation of recommendation systems (based on accuracy metrics) requires a dataset on which the recommendation algorithms can be trained and validated. These range from user–item interaction datasets used for item recommendation, e.g., the Netflix Prize dataset, to more engineering-focused datasets containing API changes across versions of software or source code search queries and downloads, e.g., the Koders-log [4]. Table 11.1 shows some of the most common datasets used for these purposes together with their domains and sizes.[4]

Looking at attributes such as **density**, it is reasonable to believe that recommendation accuracy results on (for example) the Jester dataset are not directly comparable to (for example) the Delicious dataset. Similarly, comparing the scalability or speed of an algorithm using the Movielens 100k dataset and the KDD Cup 2011 dataset would not be fair either.[5]

11.2.2   Toolkits

When benchmarking recommendation algorithms, one of the aspects that affects factors such as **scalability** or even the accuracy of the system is the implementation of the algorithm itself. There exist several open source frameworks that are commonly used in research and industry; some of these are specialized on one or a few specific algorithms or recommendation contexts, whereas others provide very broad machine learning (ML) and natural language processing (NLP) libraries.

Table 11.2 shows some of the most common recommendation frameworks currently available together with their specific features.[6] Even though most of these frameworks have similar implementations of the most common algorithms (e.g., k-nearest neighbors [15]), due to the differences of the implementation languages, running time and memory usage may vary even if the same datasets, algorithms, and hardware are used.

11.2.3   Accuracy and Error Metrics

Traditional metrics measure concepts related to dataset-specific factors; often these are measures found in or based on similar concepts in statistics, radiology,

---

[4]Additional recommendation datasets can be found at the Recommender Systems Wiki.

[5]Due to the different context of this dataset, no number of items is given as the dataset instead contains two sets of event types (*search* and *download*). A density cannot be calculated as there is no fixed set of items.

[6]See mloss.org for additional general ML software and the Recommender Systems Wiki for recommendation-specific software.

Table 11.2 Common frameworks used for recommendation both in research and production systems

Name	License	Language	Type
CofiRank	MPL	C++	collaborative filtering
Crab	BSD	Python	recommendation
EasyRec	GPL v2	Java	recommendation
GraphLab	Apache 2.0	C++	high performance computation
Lenskit	LGPL v2.1	Java	recommendation
Mahout	Apache 2.0	Java	general ML
MyMediaLite	GPL	C# & Java	recommendation
PREA	BSD	Java	CF algorithms
Python-recsys	N/A	Python	recommendation
RapidMiner	AGPL	Java	ML, NLP & data mining
Recommendable	MIT	Ruby	recommendation
Recommender 101	Custom	Java	recommendation
Recommenderlab	GPL v2	R	recommendation
Svdfeature	Apache 2.0	C++	matrix factorization
Waffles	LGPL	C++	ML and data mining

medicine, etc. [21]. We overview a few such metrics here; for a more complete overview of recommendation evaluation measures, see Chap. 10 [3].

Classification Accuracy

Classification accuracy metrics measure to what extent a recommendation system is able to correctly classify items as interesting or not. Examples are precision and recall, which require the ratings to be mapped onto a binary relevance scale (relevant vs. not relevant). The number of recommendations returned by the recommender algorithm relates to precision and recall. Recall is typically used with a fixed number of recommended items (5–50); this setting reflects the online usage, when users receive a limited number of recommendations during a visit. Other classification accuracy metrics are the mean average precision [41], the receiver operating characteristic (ROC) curve, area under curve (AUC) [22], customer ROC (CROC) [40], etc.

Predictive Accuracy Metrics

Predictive accuracy metrics measure how a recommendation system can predict the ratings of users. Since rated items have an order, predictive accuracy metrics can also be used to measure a system's ability to rank items. The mean absolute error (MAE) and the root-mean-squared error (RMSE) are widely used metrics, and several variants of these exist. Several authors [9, 22] report that predictive accuracy metrics are not always appropriate: errors in the recommendation systems' predicted ratings only affect the user when it results in erroneously classifying an interesting item as not interesting or vice versa.

Coverage Metrics

Coverage metrics measure the percentage of items for which the recommendation system can make predictions or recommendations [48]. A recommendation system cannot always generate a prediction since there might be insufficient data. There are two types of coverage identified by Herlocker et al. [22]: *prediction coverage*, the percentage of items in the input domain of the recommendation system for which it is able to make recommendations; and *catalog coverage*, the percentage of items in the output range of the recommendation system that it will ever present within a recommendation. A higher coverage means that the system is able to support decision making in more situations. Coverage cannot be considered independently from accuracy: a recommendation system can possibly achieve high coverage by making spurious predictions, but this has repercussions on accuracy.

Confidence Metrics

Confidence metrics measure how certain the recommendation system is about the accuracy of the recommendations. Extremely large or small predictions are often based on a small number of user ratings (i.e., high accuracy, low confidence). As the number of ratings grows, the prediction will usually converge to the mean (i.e., low accuracy, high confidence). Recommendation systems have different approaches to deal with confidence. Either they discard items with a confidence level that is below a certain threshold or display the confidence of a recommendation to the user. There is no general consensus on how to measure recommendation system confidence, since classical metrics based on statistical significance tests cannot be easily applied to all the algorithms [29].

Learning Rate Metrics

Many recommendation systems incorporate algorithms that gradually become better in recommending items. For instance, collaborative filtering (CF) algorithms are likely to perform better when more ratings are available. The learning rate measures the recommendation system's ability to cope with the cold start problem, i.e., how much historical data is needed before an algorithm can produce "good" recommendations. Three different types are overall learning rate, per item learning rate, and per user learning rate. Though the cold start problem is widely recognized by researchers, the evaluation of a recommendation system's learning rate has not yet been extensively covered in the literature and no specific metrics exist [39].

Diversity Metrics

Diversity of items in a recommendation list is an important factor for the usefulness of a recommendation. For instance, a user watching the first episode of the film "The Lord of the Rings" might receive recommendations for the sequel movies, which may be considered trivial. According to Ziegler et al. [48], diversity has a large effect on the usefulness of recommendation lists and therefore there is the need to define an intra-list similarity metric. The intra-list similarity metric is a measure for the diversity of a recommendation list.

Novelty and Serendipity Metrics

A recommendation system can produce highly accurate recommendations, have reasonably good coverage and diversity, and still not satisfy a user if the recommendations are trivial [44]. Novelty and serendipity are two closely related dimensions for non-obviousness [22]. Serendipity is the experience of discovering an unexpected and fortuitous item. This definition contains a notion of unexpectedness, i.e., the novelty dimension. Novelty and serendipity metrics thus measure the non-obviousness of recommendations and penalize "*blockbuster*" (i.e., common or popular) recommendations. The few existing suggestions on how to measure novelty and serendipity are limited to on-line analysis [14, 35].

User Satisfaction Metrics

In our context, *user satisfaction* is defined as the extent to which a user is supported in coping with the information overload problem.[7] This is a somewhat vague aspect and therefore it is difficult to measure [14,35]. All the previously defined metrics can support and/or inhibit user satisfaction to some extent. Studies that investigated user satisfaction with respect to recommendation systems are scarce, mainly because of the difficulties in performing on-line testing [35].

11.2.4   One-Dimensional Evaluation

Traditional recommendation system benchmarking commonly evaluates only one dimension of the recommender, i.e., quantitative recommendation accuracy. Moreover, even traditional recommendation accuracy driven evaluation may have

---

[7]Editors' note: More broadly, recommendation systems in software engineering do not only or always deal with the information overload problem [46]; thus, the definition of user satisfaction needs to be broadened in such situations.

Table 11.3 A user–item matrix divided into a training set (the top half) and a test set (the bottom half)

	u_1	u_2	u_3	u_4	u_5
i_1	1	1	0	0	1
i_2	1	0	1	1	1
i_3	0	0	0	1	0
i_4	1	0	1	0	1
i_5	0	0	1	1	0
i_6	0	0	0	1	0

drawbacks when applied together with an improper evaluation setting. To illustrate this we focus on the context of user-centric evaluation in a traditional user–item interaction scenario.

Consider this top-n recommendation example. We have a user-item interaction matrix, as shown in Table 11.3. The table shows a matrix of 5 users and 6 items and their interactions, where each one represents an interaction (rating, purchase, etc.), and each zero the lack thereof.

The training/test split is illustrated by the line in the middle of the table. In this case, a traditional evaluation approach will only recognize item i_6 as a true positive recommendation for user u_4 and item i_5 for users u_3 and u_4. Users u_1, u_2 and u_5 will not have any true positive recommendations since they have not interacted with any of the items. The evaluation does not consider that the items might actually be liked by the user, if recommended in a real-world situation.

Traditional evaluation estimates the users' taste by analyzing their histories of item interactions, e.g., items they have rated, purchased, or otherwise consumed. This type of evaluation models the accuracy of the recommender algorithm, to a certain point [22]. In order to further estimate the quality from the user's perspective, a different set of metrics and evaluational concepts need to be considered instead.

11.2.5 Multi-dimensional Evaluation and Benchmarking

In any real-world application, recommendation systems should simultaneously satisfy (1) functional requirements that relate to qualitative assessment of recommendations, and (2) non-functional requirements that are specified by the technological parameters and business goals of the service. These requirements have to be evaluated together: without the ability to provide sufficiently accurate recommendations, no recommendation system can be valuable. Since bad quality recommendations will have an adverse effect on customer retention and user loyalty, they ultimately will not serve the business goal of the service (see Sect. 11.2.5). Similarly, if the recommendation system does not scale well with the characteristics of a service, and is not able to provide recommendation in real time (the response

Fig. 11.2 The three primary
dimensions of the
multi-dimensional evaluation
approach

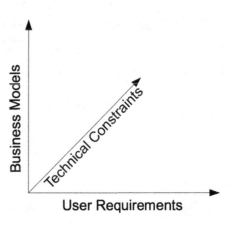

time depends on the virtue of the service, but usually ranges within 10–1,000 ms),
neither users nor service provider benefit from the recommender. Consequently, a
tradeoff between these types of requirements is necessary for an impartial and comprehensive evaluation (and if needed, benchmarking) of real-world recommender
solutions.

The three primary dimensions of the multi-dimensional evaluation approach [37]
are shown in Fig. 11.2.

User Aspects

From the user perspective, the benefits of recommendation systems lie in their
persuasiveness, i.e., their capability to influence a user's attitude, decisions, or
behavior. By making it easy to access information, and by tailoring the content
offered, a recommender can affect a user's attitude positively toward the application,
and make their relationship with the system more trustful. According to the user's
tasks, recommendations may have different goals. The goal could, for instance,
be to reduce information overload, facilitate search and exploration, and identify
interesting items, increasing the quality and decreasing the time of the decision-
making process. Increased trust and confidence in the service could also be key
factors [23].

Perception of quality is a broad concept commonly discussed in topics ranging
from e-business, where Lai [27] developed methods and instruments for measuring the perceived quality of electronic services among employees of several
international electronic services; to e-learning, where Sumner et al. [42] identified
educators' expectations and requirements on educational systems; to information
quality, where Goh et al. [19] compared perceptions of the users' engagement in
a mobile game, etc. These works show that, in the context of recommendation
systems, perception of quality is not only dependent on the accuracy of the
recommendation but also on other, domain-dependent, factors.

Different ways of presenting recommendations can also result in different perceptions based on cultural settings. This has been shown in different contexts, e.g., Chen and Pu [11] show this within a user study ($n = 120$) on participants from a "western culture" and participants from an "oriental culture" that was performed in order to evaluate, among other issues, the perceived quality of an organizational recommendation system. The study showed that even though cultural differences do not affect the complete spectrum of perception-related concepts, the perceived quality in one out of two presentation formats did differ significantly between the cultures. Similar concepts in information interaction were studied by Barber and Badre [5], showing that some design elements in websites are perceived differently across cultures.

Similarly Cremonesi et al. [13] compared the quality of recommendation algorithms in seven different systems by means of a user study ($n = 210$). The three principal findings were that (1) non-personalized recommendation algorithms provided for high user satisfaction, although with low utility; (2) content-based algorithms performed on par with, or better than, collaborative filtering-based recommendation algorithms; and (3) traditional accuracy metrics (recall and fallout) did not approximate the perceived quality very well.

It seems clear that the user's perception of the recommender does not need to be tied to the actual measured performance of the recommendation algorithm. Instead, the context of the recommendation dictates how it will be perceived by the end user. It is for this reason that the user aspects need to be prioritized, in contexts where they are important. Recommendation accuracy, in its traditional sense, is only important in some of these contexts. Others can stipulate that the recommendation accuracy can very well be low, as long as other factors attain desired levels.

Business Aspects

The business model is the method that allows a company to generate revenue and to sustain itself. Different business models may lead to different requirements in terms of expected added value from a recommendation system. Examples of business requirements include: increased profit, increased revenues, increased user retention and user loyalty. For instance, in a pay-per-view video-on-demand business model (see Sect. 11.1), the goal of the recommendation system may be to increase sales of movies that allow the company to maximize revenues (e.g., movies with the largest cost and/or margin). However, in subscriber-based video-on-demand business model, the driving forces for a company may be the desire to get users to return to the service in the future, i.e., increase user retention and customer lifetime; a typical showcase where recommendation systems help is outlined by Dias et al. [16].

One can also differentiate between recommendation scenarios when the recommendation system has direct effect on the revenue generated or the influence is rather indirect. Typical examples of the first case include webshop recommendation and video-on-demand recommendation. There, the process of converting a recommendation to an actual purchase usually contains multiple steps, and the recommendations should be both relevant and persuasive for successful purchase conversion. First, the user should click on the recommended product, then add it to the cart, and finally confirm the purchase at the checkout.[8] Accordingly, the success of recommendation is measured and evaluated in each step, since the user can churn at any stage of the purchase process. First, the click-through rate (CTR) of the recommendations is measured: the ratio of successful recommendation box displays, i.e., when the user clicks on a recommended content compared to the total number of recommendation box displays. Second, the conversion rate is measured: the ratio of recommended content views that result in a purchase (Fig. 11.3).

In other recommendation scenarios, for instance in video streaming and "tube" sites like YouTube, or in news websites, the goal of the recommendation system is to keep the users on-site by providing relevant, perhaps also serendipitous and usually novel content for them. The business model of such sites is usually advertising and page view driven: the more page views attained, the more advertising surface can be sold, hence increasing the revenue of the site. Page views can be increased primarily in each user visit, or by increasing the frequency of user visits. Consequently, the primary business evaluation metric is the CTR of recommendations, and additionally the average page views per visit, average user page per days/months, or return frequency of users.

Video streaming sites like Hulu may also sell advertising units within the content: depending on the placement of the advertisement, one can talk about pre-, mid-, and post-roll advertisements (i.e., temporally relative to when the actual content is shown). In such cases, the success of recommendations can be also quantified by the average video watch length compared to the total video length, or by the number of in-video ad views achieved by the recommendations. Therefore, successful recommendations should not just have an interesting and appealing title or thumbnail image, but their content should also be relevant for the user.

CTR measured on recommendation boxes is higher than the conversion rate of the entire recommendation conversion chain. As the conversion rate rather evaluates the overall success of the whole system and since many factors independent from the quality of recommendations may be influential, the CTR on the recommendation boxes should be considered as the direct success measure of the recommendations themselves [e.g., 33]. The influence of relevant and persuasive recommendations, however, reaches beyond the first clicks and result in higher conversion rate as well. Interestingly, Zheng et al. [47] showed that empirical CTR values and the relevance of recommendations are not consistent; thus, using only CTR as the ultimate metric for online evaluation of recommendation systems may be biased and restrictive. They also suggest that optimizing recommendations based on normalized Google distance [12] may be a better proxy for evaluating

---

[8]In some webshop implementations, clicking on a recommended content can directly add the content to the cart, thus reducing the number of steps and simplifying the purchase process.

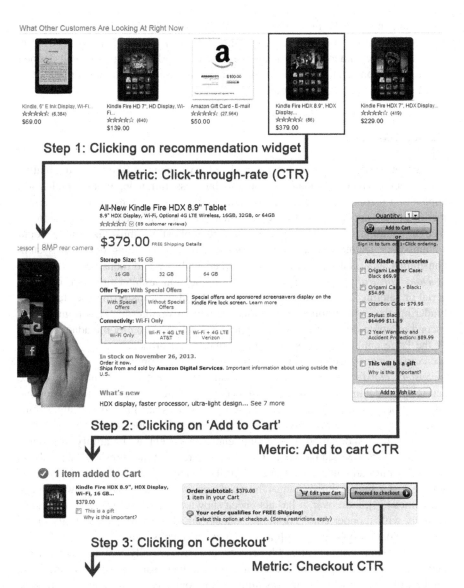

Fig. 11.3 CTR and conversion rate. In this case the conversion rate is calculated as the product of the three metrics: CTR, add-to-cart CTR, and checkout CTR

recommendation relevance than CTR, since the latter is biased by content popularity.

Ideally, the evaluation metrics for business aspects should correlate and be consistent with traditional offline evaluation metrics as discussed above. However, both research from academia and practitioners from industry realize the gap between offline and online evaluation settings [20]. With sales and profitability as the obvious common baseline denominator, the specific core metrics for real-world application are use-case dependent, while academic research tends to focus on well-defined recommendation related problems that can be assessed by standard offline error based or information retrieval metrics.

Technical Aspects

In addition to user-centric and business-related requirements that relate to qualitative assessment of recommendations and the business rationale, in any real-world application recommendation systems should equally meet non-functional requirements that are specified by the technological parameters. The choice of candidate recommendation systems for specific real-life applications must take into account a number of technical requirements and constraints including data and system constraints, as well as reactivity, scalability, adaptability, and robustness.

Data constraints derive from the communication architecture. For instance, aerial or satellite TV services lack a return channel for transferring user feedback, hindering the application of traditional collaborative filtering algorithms. As a second example, linear TV services typically lack good-quality metadata because of the large amount of video content produced and broadcast every day. In this scenario, content-based filtering techniques could not be applied.

System constraints derive from hardware and/or software limitations in the service provider infrastructure. For instance, in a mobile TV scenario, the processing and memory capacity in the users' hand-held devices are limited and algorithms requiring significant computation or storage on the client side cannot be applied.

Reactivity is understood in a recommendation system as the ability to provide good quality recommendations in real-time where the time threshold depends on the application area use case, typically in the range of 10–1,000 ms. In an online setting, fast response time is a must, because web users do not tolerate slow webpage load times [30]; moreover, it has also been shown that load performance correlates strongly with shopper conversion and bounce rate. Therefore, the reactivity of the recommendation system also influences the its business success.

Although non-origin content (third party services, typically analytics, advertising and social network plug-ins) accounts for an increasing portion of the total fetched objects and bytes, interestingly, their contribution to page load time is minimal [8], which explains the popularity of using third party recommendation systems provided by specific vendors. Recommendations are typically displayed asynchronously to prevent slowing down loading of the main content; however, this can only be a partial remedy, when the entire page content is personalized, such as location-based and personalized news aggregator services [38].

Quick response time is less critical for batch recommendation tasks, like personalized newsletter generation, when a large number of recommendations should be provided for many users.

Summarizing, reactivity of online recommendation systems is measured by performance indicators including but not limited to average response time, and response rate exceeding the time threshold is measured.

Scalability of recommendation systems is generally understood as the ability to provide good quality recommendations independently of the size of the dataset and its primary dimensions (number of user and items), its growth, and the dynamic of the growth. Scalability requirements can be further broken down into model initialization and maintenance-related (training and updates) and online-operation-related parts. By the former is meant the ability to process extremely large, potentially heterogeneous datasets at the system initialization and recurrent system update phases (including model building if necessary) using computational resources linearly scalable with the data size. The latter is meant as the ability to serve large amounts of parallel recommendation requests in real time (see also reactivity) without significant degradation in recommendation quality. In other words, online scalability extends the concept of reactivity for many simultaneous user accesses.

The online scalability of initialized recommendation systems can be validated through stress-tests where recommendation requests are sent in scalable multi-thread configuration, and scalability performance indicators—e.g., recommendation throughput, response success rate, fallback response—are measured.

These requirements are particularly strict in linear TV applications, where millions of TV viewers are used to a very responsive interface. In this scenario, there is the need to use recommender algorithms able to run (and make efficient usage of all resources) on a multi-processor and multi-node distributed environment. As shown by Takács et al. [43], memory-based collaborative filtering algorithms may fall short in this scenario.

Adaptability of recommendation systems is the ability to react to changes in user preferences, content availability and contextual parameters. Adaptability is crucial to overcome the cold start problem. Adaptive recommender algorithms are able to capture new users' preferences after the first few interactions, and thus the quality of recommendations is improved by each user click. Analogously, adaptive item modeling is of particular importance for new items, since integrating user feedback on new items may improve recommendation quality significantly, when metadata is not sufficient for appropriate item modeling [34]. Therefore adaptability can be measured as the recommendation quality for new users and on new items. Adaptability to changes in user preferences and content availability can also be measured by systematic synthetic tests populating users and/or items incrementally to the recommendation systems. Similarly, adaptability to changes in contextual parameters will be tested by varying certain contextual parameters of recommendation requests.

Robustness *requirements* are necessary to create high-quality recommendation services, able to work in case of data corruption or component failure in a distributed environment. Such a situation may equally arise during system initialization and operational phases. These requirements are typically translated into the need for fault-tolerant recommenders able to run on high-availability clustered systems, using, for instance, fallback components in case of system failures and including algorithmic solutions that are stable against missing or corrupted data [1].

11.2.6 When to Benchmark and When to Evaluate

In the context of this chapter, the difference between benchmarking a recommendation system and evaluating it is based on the expected outcome of the process. Evaluation is traditionally used in order to estimate the quality of a single system, i.e., using the same recommendation context, datasets, and implementation frameworks. An example of this is when tuning an algorithm to either higher accuracy, lower running time, or any other sought-after value. Benchmarking on the other hand is applied in order to compare systems not necessarily deployed in the same environment, e.g., the previously mentioned Netflix Prize. Benchmarking allows a system-to-system comparison between not only different algorithmic implementations, but across various datasets, frameworks and recommendation contexts—provided a benchmarking protocol is defined, e.g., when benchmarking a single evaluational aspect, a protocol for the evaluation metric is specified and used across different systems.

In terms of recommendation accuracy, a benchmarking protocol might specify what measures, metrics, data splits (training/validation sets) and other relevant factors to use in order to allow for a fair comparison (e.g., see Fig. 11.1). Similarly, for multi-dimensional benchmarking, it is imperative to specify such a benchmarking protocol in order to ensure a fair and accurate comparison. In this context, the protocol should include the dimensions to measure, how these should be measured (e.g., specifying metrics, how datasets should be prepared, etc.), and how the final benchmark score should be calculated in order to allow for a simple means of comparison. In benchmarking events such as the Netflix Prize or the KDD Cup, the benchmarking protocol was given by the organizers; when running a stand-alone benchmark, the protocol needs to be defined such that it meets the purpose of the comparison. An example of this is presented below.

11.3 Benchmarking Example

As discussed above, the process of benchmarking a recommendation system should be dependent on the use case it is deployed in. This applies to any measurable attribute that is to be benchmarked, whether speed, or recommendation accuracy. Failure in doing so could potentially prove detrimental to the overall quality of the recommendation system.

This section illustrates the application of the proposed benchmarking model. Three different recommendation approaches are evaluated and benchmarked, each having a different characteristic, and each showing the value of a multi-dimensional evaluation approach.

11.3.1 Evaluation Setting

In order to comprehensively evaluate a recommendation system f, multiple objectives need to be taken into consideration. In the scope of this chapter, these objectives come from the three dimensions: user aspects, business aspects, and technical constraints. Each of these is represented by some evaluation metric $E_i(f)$.

For the sake of convenience, we assume that all evaluation metrics are formulated as utility functions, which we want to maximize. We define the multi-objective evaluation function E by

$$\mathbf{E}(f) = \begin{bmatrix} E_1(f) \\ E_2(f) \\ \vdots \\ E_p(f) \end{bmatrix}, \tag{11.1}$$

where $\mathbf{E}(f)$ is a vector of evaluation metrics $E_i(f)$ and p is the number of evaluation metrics. This setting corresponds to the three-dimensional benchmarking model presented in this chapter.

The question to be answered is as follows: Suppose that we have a set of two recommendation systems, f and f'. Which of these systems is more suitable to deploy in our context, as defined by the multi-objective evaluation function $\mathbf{E}$?

The field of multi-objective optimization suggests several approaches to this question [e.g., 17,45,49]. In order to keep the example evaluation below simple, we present one common approach: weighting. This is done by combining the evaluation metrics E_i into one single, weighted, global evaluation criterion:

$$U(f) = \mathbf{w}^T \mathbf{E}(f) = \sum_i w_i E_i(f), \tag{11.2}$$

where $\mathbf{w}$ is a column vector and $w_i \geq 0$ are weights specifying the importance of the evaluation metric E_i. Using the utility function U, a recommendation system f is seen to perform better than f', if $U(f) > U(f')$. It is however crucial that the choice of evaluation metrics E_i and weights w_i are problem-dependent design decisions: each recommendation system needs to have these specified based on its context, the users' context, and the business context, i.e., a benchmarking protocol.

11.3.2 Benchmarking Experiment

In this benchmarking experiment, we demonstrate multi-objective evaluation of three recommendation algorithms, each tuned to a specific recommendation quality. The algorithms are:

- **k-nearest neighbors (kNN)** is a traditional recommendation algorithm widely-used for recommendation in a wide variety of settings. kNN recommends items that are preferred by users similar to oneself, i.e., one's neighbors. This can however cause low diversity due to effects of popularity, e.g., highly rated popular movies are often recommended to very many users [10].
- **k-furthest neighbors (kFN)** is an algorithm that turns the kNN algorithm inside-out and recommends items that are disliked by users dissimilar to oneself. The algorithm is specifically tuned to deliver more diverse recommendations, e.g., those that traditional recommendation algorithms fail to recommend, while still keeping the recommendations personalized [36].
- **Random (Rnd)** is a random recommender. This recommender is non-personalized, simply recommending a random selection of the items available. The benefit of this algorithm is its constant speed, i.e., independent of the numbers of users or items. The random recommender has an obvious inherent component of diversity and novelty, although with random accuracy, which is presumably low.

For each of the three axis, the following data is available: (1) business axis: the users' intention to return to the site; (2) user axis: the usefulness of the recommendations; and (3) technology axis: the computation time required to calculate recommendations. The data is based on a user study ($n = 132$). The study was set up as a simple movie recommender (described in detail by Said et al. [36]) where users would rate a number of movies and receive recommendations based on the input. The above three recommendation algorithms were employed.

For the business and user axes, upon receiving a set of 10 recommended movies users were asked whether they would consider using the system again (intention of return), and whether the recommendations were useful (usefulness of recommendation). Answers to the questionnaire amount to ratings normalized to a scale from 0 (not appropriate) to 1 (highly appropriate). Based on these data, we selected the following evaluation metrics:

- $E_b(f)$ measures the average intention of return of f;
- $E_u(f)$ measures the average usefulness of f; and
- $E_t(f)$ measures the utility of the average computation time t_f required by f according to

$$E_t(f) = \frac{a}{1 + \exp\left(\frac{t_f}{T} - 1\right)}, \tag{11.3}$$

where $T = 30$ is the maximum time considered as acceptable, and a is a factor scaling $E_t(f)$ to 1 if $t_f = 0$. The evaluation metric E_t is one at $t_f = 0$ and approaches zero with increasing computation time.

According to (11.2), we combine the evaluation metrics to a utility function of the form

Table 11.4 Utility values $U(f)$ for different weights **w**. The maximum accepted time is $T = 30\,s$

	kNN	kFN	Rnd
$E_u(f)$	0.53	0.52	0.44
$E_b(f)$	0.56	0.51	0.36
$E_t(f)$	0.80	0.80	0.99
$U(f)$ with $\mathbf{w} = (0.\bar{3}, 0.\bar{3}, 0.\bar{3})$	0.63	0.61	0.60
$U(f)$ with $\mathbf{w} = (0.6, 0.3, 0.1)$	0.57	0.55	0.47
$U(f)$ with $\mathbf{w} = (0.3, 0.6, 0.1)$	0.58	0.54	0.43
$U(f)$ with $\mathbf{w} = (0.1, 0.1, 0.8)$	0.75	0.74	0.87

$$U(f) = w_b\, E_b(f) + w_u\, E_u(f) + w_t\, E_t(f)\,. \tag{11.4}$$

The choice of **w** is shown in Table 11.4.

11.3.3 Results

The utility values for different weights **w** (shown in Table 11.4) show that kNN attains better values than kFN for two out of three evaluation metrics (E_b and E_u) and ties in one (E_t). As a consequence, the utility value U of kNN is always equal to or better than the one of kFN regardless of how the weights are chosen. In multi-objective optimization, we say that kNN is Pareto-superior to kFN [26]. As expected, when business- and user-requirements are preferred, kNN and kFN outperform the random recommender. In a use case where computation time is the most critical constraint, the random recommender outperforms the others solely based on the speed of the recommendation. In a scenario where all three axes are equally important, kNN performs best.

The results illustrate that an appropriate choice of evaluation metrics, as well as weight parameters, are critical issues for the proper design of a utility function and benchmarking protocol. This design process is highly domain- and problem-dependent. Once a proper utility function has been set up, the performance of different recommender algorithms can be objectively compared. Since current state-of-the-art recommendation methods are often optimized with respect to a single recommendation accuracy metric, introducing multi-objective evaluation functions from the different contexts of a deployed recommendation system sets the stage for constructing recommendation algorithms that optimize several individual evaluation metrics without simultaneously worsening another.

11.4   Discussion

The concepts related to evaluation, and specifically to multi-dimensional evaluation presented in this chapter provide a motivation as to why (and how) recommendation systems can be evaluated and compared to each other across different domains, datasets, and contexts—as long as the evaluation and benchmarking protocols are specified. The creation of these protocols, and specifically the combination (weights) of the dimensions of the evaluation are however not entirely trivial and need to be chosen with the recommendation requirements in mind. When these are provided, the overall quality of the recommendation system can be estimated and compared toward other recommendation algorithms, no matter the datasets, contexts, and other system-specific deployment aspects.

Benchmarking protocols need to accurately reflect the expectations and constraints of the benchmark, such as the domains in which the recommendation systems are deployed (e.g., products, code) and other aspects related to the environment in which the recommendation systems live (e.g., framework, memory, CPU). An accurate benchmarking protocol needs to be based on a thorough analysis or empirical studies of the needs and priorities of the context in which a recommendation system is to be deployed.

It should be noted that a simple one-dimensional evaluation approach will in most cases be sufficient to tune a recommendation algorithm and estimate its quality. The added cost (in terms of development) of a benchmarking protocol that can estimate the in situ quality of an algorithm could potentially be higher than an in-place evaluation of said algorithm. However, when comparing multiple algorithms across a variety of systems, the accumulated cost will likely be lower when using benchmarking protocols than performing in situ evaluation of each candidate algorithm.

11.5   Conclusion

In this chapter, we have introduced concepts related to evaluation and benchmarking of recommendation systems, e.g., reactivity, scalability, adaptability, business values, etc. The combination of these concepts allows for a cross-system comparison of recommendation systems in order to find the most suitable recommendation algorithm for a specific recommendation context. Combined, the concepts create a benchmarking model—a protocol—that can be tuned to the specific use case of the recommender in order to accurately reflect the system's quality.

Additionally, the chapter surveyed benchmarking events such as the Netflix Prize, which set the standard for recommendation system evaluation during the last decade. Moreover, an overview of common datasets and frameworks for recommendation and evaluation was provided in order to show factors that can affect evaluation, e.g., data sparsity, size, and implementation differences across programming languages. Following this, the chapter introduced aspects of recommendation system evaluation related to the technical constraints and business values in a deployed system, e.g., the importance of rapidly changing recommendations in a system with ephemeral items (live TV), or the importance of delivering the right recommendation not only from the user's perspective but also from the provider's (Internet marketplaces). These factors, even though seldom used for evaluation, define whether a recommendation system will be able to perform adequately in its deployed context or not.

Finally, the chapter introduced a multi-dimensional benchmarking model that allows for a comparison of recommendation systems across domain-, dataset-, and recommendation-contexts. The model takes into consideration not only traditional evaluation methods (accuracy, rating prediction error), but also any number of factors from other domains (business and technical) in order to create a simple comparable value encompassing all relevant evaluational aspects and domains.

The model allows a comparison of the qualities of recommendation systems deployed in different domains, using different datasets and having different requirements by using a tailored benchmarking protocol.

Acknowledgments The authors would like to thank Martha Larson from TU Delft, Brijnesh J. Jain from TU Berlin, and Alejandro Bellogín from CWI for their contributions and suggestions to this chapter.

This work was partially carried out during the tenure of an ERCIM "Alain Bensoussan" Fellowship Programme. The research leading to these results has received funding from the European Union Seventh Framework Programme (FP7/2007-2013) under grant agreement no. 246016.

References

1. Adomavicius, G., Zhang, J.: Stability of recommendation algorithms. ACM Trans. Inform. Syst. **30**(4), 23:1–23:31 (2012). doi:10.1145/2382438.2382442
2. Amatriain, X., Basilico, J.: Netflix recommendations: Beyond the 5 stars (Part 1)—The Netflix tech blog. URL http://techblog.netflix.com/2012/04/netflix-recommendations-beyond-5-stars. html (2012) Accessed 9 October 2013
3. Avazpour, I., Pitakrat, T., Grunske, L., Grundy, J.: Dimensions and metrics for evaluating recommendation systems. In: Robillard, M., Maalej, W., Walker, R.J., Zimmermann, T. (eds.) Recommendation Systems in Software Engineering, Chap. 10. Springer, New York (2014)
4. Bajracharya, S.K., Lopes, C.V.: Analyzing and mining a code search engine usage log. Empir. Software Eng. **17**(4–5), 424–466 (2012). doi:10.1007/s10664-010-9144-6
5. Barber, W., Badre, A.: Culturability: The merging of culture and usability. In: Proceedings of the Conference on Human Factors & the Web, Basking Ridge, NJ, USA, 5 June 1998
6. Bell, R., Koren, Y., Volinsky, C.: Chasing $1,000,000: How we won the Netflix Progress Prize. ASA Stat. Comput. Graph. Newslett. **18**(2), 4–12 (2007)
7. Boxwell Jr., R.J.: Benchmarking for Competitive Advantage. McGraw-Hill, New York (1994)
8. Butkiewicz, M., Madhyastha, H.V., Sekar, V.: Understanding website complexity: Measurements, metrics, and implications. In: Proceedings of the ACM SIGCOMM Conference on Internet Measurement, pp. 313–328, Berlin, Germany, 2 November 2011. doi:10.1145/2068816.2068846

9. Carenini, G.: User-specific decision-theoretic accuracy metrics for collaborative filtering. In: Proceedings of the International Conference on Intelligent User Interfaces, San Diego, CA, USA, 10–13 January 2005

10. Celma, Ò., Lamere, P.: If you like the Beatles you might like …: A tutorial on music recommendation. In: Proceedings of the ACM International Conference on Multimedia, pp. 1157–1158. ACM, New York (2008). doi:10.1145/1459359.1459615

11. Chen, L., Pu, P.: A cross-cultural user evaluation of product recommender interfaces. In: Proceedings of the ACM Conference on Recommender Systems, pp. 75–82, Lousanne, Switzerland, 23–25 October 2008. doi:10.1145/1454008.1454022

12. Cilibrasi, R.L., Vitányi, P.M.B.: The Google similarity distance. IEEE Trans. Knowl. Data Eng. **19**(3), 370–383 (2007). doi:10.1109/TKDE.2007.48

13. Cremonesi, P., Garzotto, F., Negro, S., Papadopoulos, A.V., Turrin, R.: Looking for "good" recommendations: A comparative evaluation of recommender systems. In: Proceedings of the IFIP TC13 International Conference on Human–Computer Interactaction, Part III, pp. 152–168, Lisbon, Portugal, 5–9 September 2011. doi:10.1007/978-3-642-23765-2_11

14. Cremonesi, P., Garzotto, F., Turrin, R.: Investigating the persuasion potential of recommender systems from a quality perspective: An empirical study. ACM Trans. Interact. Intell. Syst. **2**(2), 11:1–11:41 (2012). doi:10.1145/2209310.2209314

15. Desrosiers, C., Karypis, G.: A comprehensive survey of neighborhood-based recommendation methods. In: Ricci, F., Rokach, L., Shapira, B., Kantor, P.B. (eds.) Recommender Systems Handbook, pp. 107–144. Springer, Boston (2011). doi:10.1007/978-0-387-85820-3_4

16. Dias, M.B., Locher, D., Li, M., El-Deredy, W., Lisboa, P.J.G.: The value of personalised recommender systems to e-business: A case study. In: Proceedings of the ACM Conference on Recommender Systems, pp. 291–294, Lousanne, Switzerland, 23–25 October 2008. doi:10.1145/1454008.1454054

17. Ehrgott, M., Gandibleux, X. (eds.): Multiple Criteria Optimization: State of the Art Annotated Bibliographic Surveys. Kluwer, Boston (2002). doi:10.1007/b101915

18. Fraser, G., Arcuri, A.: Sound empirical evidence in software testing. In: Proceedings of the ACM/IEEE International Conference on Software Engineering, pp. 178–188, Zurich, Switzerland, 2–9 June 2012. doi:10.1109/ICSE.2012.6227195

19. Goh, D., Razikin, K., Lee, C.S., Chu, A.: Investigating user perceptions of engagement and information quality in mobile human computation games. In: Proceedings of the ACM/IEEE-CS Joint Conference on Digital Libraries, pp. 391–392, Washington, DC, USA, 10–14 June 2012. doi:10.1145/2232817.2232906

20. Gomez-Uribe, C.: Challenges and limitations in the offline and online evaluation of recommender systems: A Netflix case study. In: Proceedings of the Workshop on Recommendation Utility Evaluation: Beyond RMSE, *CEUR Workshop Proceedings*, vol. 910, p. 1 (2012)

21. Gunawardana, A., Shani, G.: A survey of accuracy evaluation metrics of recommendation tasks. J. Mach. Learn. Res. **10**, 2935–2962 (2009)

22. Herlocker, J.L., Konstan, J.A., Terveen, L.G., Riedl, J.T.: Evaluating collaborative filtering recommender systems. ACM Trans. Inform. Syst. **22**(1), 5–53 (2004). doi:10.1145/963770.963772

23. Hu, R.: Design and user issues in personality-based recommender systems. In: Proceedings of the ACM Conference on Recommender Systems, pp. 357–360, Barcelona, Spain, 26–30 Septembert 2010. doi:10.1145/1864708.1864790

24. Jambor, T., Wang, J.: Optimizing multiple objectives in collaborative filtering. In: Proceedings of the ACM Conference on Recommender Systems, pp. 55–62, Barcelona, Spain, 26–30 Septembert 2010. doi:10.1145/1864708.1864723

25. Koenigstein, N., Dror, G., Koren, Y.: Yahoo! music recommendations: Modeling music ratings with temporal dynamics and item taxonomy. In: Proceedings of the ACM Conference on Recommender Systems, pp. 165–172, Chicago, IL, USA, 23–27 October 2011. doi:10.1145/2043932.2043964

26. Kung, H.T., Luccio, F., Preparata, F.P.: On finding the maxima of a set of vectors. J. ACM **22**(4), 469–476 (1975). doi:10.1145/321906.321910

27. Lai, J.Y.: Assessment of employees' perceptions of service quality and satisfaction with e-business. In: Proceedings of the ACM SIGMIS CPR Conference on Computer Personnel Research, pp. 236–243, Claremont, CA, USA, 13–15 April 2006. doi:10.1145/1125170.1125228

28. Liu, J., Dolan, P., Pedersen, E.R.: Personalized news recommendation based on click behavior. In: Proceedings of the International Conference on Intelligent User Interfaces, pp. 31–40, Hong Kong, China, 7–10 February 2010. doi:10.1145/1719970.1719976

29. McNee, S., Lam, S.K., Guetzlaff, C., Konstan, J.A., Riedl, J.: Confidence displays and training in recommender systems. In: Proceedings of the IFIP TC13 International Conference on Human–Computer Interactaction, pp. 176–183, Zurich, Switzerland, 1–5 September 2003

30. Nah, F.F.H.: A study on tolerable waiting time: How long are Web users willing to wait? Behav. Inform. Technol. 23(3), 153–163 (2004). doi:10.1080/01449290410001669914

31. Netflix Prize: The Netflix Prize rules (2006). URL http://www.netflixprize.com/rules. Accessed 9 October 2013

32. Perry, R., Lancaster, R.: Enterprise content management: Expected evolution or vendor positioning? Tech. rep., The Yankee Group (2002)

33. Peška, L., Vojtáš, P.: Evaluating the importance of various implicit factors in E-commerce. In: Proceedings of the Workshop on Recommendation Utility Evaluation: Beyond RMSE, *CEUR Workshop Proceedings*, vol. 910, pp. 51–55, Dublin, Ireland, 9 September 2012

34. Pilászy, I., Tikk, D.: Recommending new movies: Even a few ratings are more valuable than metadata. In: Proceedings of the ACM Conference on Recommender Systems, pp. 93–100, New York, NY, USA, 23–25 October 2009. doi:10.1145/1639714.1639731

35. Pu, P., Chen, L., Hu, R.: A user-centric evaluation framework for recommender systems. In: Proceedings of the ACM Conference on Recommender Systems, pp. 157–164, Chicago, IL, USA, 23–27 October 2011. doi:10.1145/2043932.2043962

36. Said, A., Fields, B., Jain, B.J., Albayrak, S.: User-centric evaluation of a K-furthest neighbor collaborative filtering recommender algorithm. In: Proceedings of the ACM Conference on Computer Supported Cooperative Work, pp. 1399–1408, San Antonio, TX, USA, 23–27 February 2013. doi:10.1145/2441776.2441933

37. Said, A., Tikk, D., Shi, Y., Larson, M., Stumpf, K., Cremonesi, P.: Recommender systems evaluation: A 3D benchmark. In: Proceedings of the Workshop on Recommendation Utility Evaluation: Beyond RMSE, *CEUR Workshop Proceedings*, vol. 910, pp. 21–23, Dublin, Ireland, 9 September 2012

38. Sarwat, M., Bao, J., Eldawy, A., Levandoski, J.J., Magdy, A., Mokbel, M.F.: Sindbad: A location-based social networking system. In: Proceedings of the ACM SIGMOD International Conference on Management of Data, pp. 649–652, Scottsdale, AZ, USA, 20–24 May 2012. doi:10.1145/2213836.2213923

39. Schein, A.I., Popescul, A., Ungar, L.H., Pennock, D.M.: Methods and metrics for cold-start recommendations. In: Proceedings of the ACM SIGIR International Conference on Research and Development in Information Retrieval, pp. 253–260, Tampere, Finland, 11–15 August 2002. doi:10.1145/564376.564421

40. Schein, A.I., Popescul, A., Ungar, L.H., Pennock, D.M.: CROC: A new evaluation criterion for recommender systems. Electron. Commerce Res. 5(1), 51–74 (2005). doi:10.1023/B:ELEC.0000045973.51289.8c

41. Schütze, H., Silverstein, C.: Projections for efficient document clustering. In: Proceedings of the ACM SIGIR International Conference on Research and Development in Information Retrieval, pp. 74–81, Philadelphia, PA, USA, 27–31 July 1997. doi:10.1145/258525.258539

42. Sumner, T., Khoo, M., Recker, M., Marlino, M.: Understanding educator perceptions of "quality" in digital libraries. In: Proceedings of the ACM/IEEE-CS Joint Conference on Digital Libraries, pp. 269–279, Houston, Texas, USA, 27–31 May 2003. doi:10.1109/JCDL.2003.1204876

43. Takács, G., Pilászy, I., Németh, B., Tikk, D.: Scalable collaborative filtering approaches for large recommender systems. J. Mach. Learn. Res. 10, 623–656 (2009)

44. Terveen, L., Hill, W.: Beyond recommender systems: Helping people help each other. In: Carroll, J.M. (ed.) Human–Computer Interaction in the New Millennium. Addison-Wesley, New York (2001)
45. Van Veldhuizen, D.A., Lamont, G.B.: Multiobjective evolutionary algorithms: Analyzing the state-of-the-art. Evol. Comput. **8**(2), 125–147 (2000). doi:10.1162/106365600568158
46. Walker, R.J.: Recent advances in recommendation systems for software engineering. In: Proceedings of the International Conference on Industrial Engineering and Other Applications of Applied Intelligent Systems, *Lecture Notes in Computer Science*, vol. 7906, pp. 372–381. Springer, Heidelberg (2013). doi:10.1007/978-3-642-38577-3_38
47. Zheng, H., Wang, D., Zhang, Q., Li, H., Yang, T.: Do clicks measure recommendation relevancy?: An empirical user study. In: Proceedings of the ACM Conference on Recommender Systems, pp. 249–252, Barcelona, Spain, 26–30 September 2010. doi:10.1145/1864708.1864759
48. Ziegler, C.N., McNee, S.M., Konstan, J.A., Lausen, G.: Improving recommendation lists through topic diversification. In: Proceedings of the International Conference on the World Wide Web, pp. 22–32, Chiba, Japan, 10–14 May 2005. doi:10.1145/1060745.1060754
49. Zitzler, E., Deb, K., Thiele, L.: Comparison of multiobjective evolutionary algorithms: Empirical results. Evol. Comput. **8**(2), 173–195 (2000). doi:10.1162/106365600568202

Chapter 12
Simulation

A Methodology to Evaluate Recommendation Systems in Software Engineering

Robert J. Walker and Reid Holmes

Abstract Scientists and engineers have long used simulation as a technique for exploring and evaluating complex systems. Direct interaction with a real, complex system requires that the system be already constructed and operational, that people be trained in its use, and that its dangers already be known and mitigated. Simulation can avoid these issues, reducing costs, reducing risks, and allowing an imagined system to be studied before it is created. The explorations supported by simulation serve two purposes in the realm of evaluation: to determine whether and where undesired behavior will arise and to predict the outcomes of interactions with the real system. This chapter examines the use of simulation to evaluate recommendation systems in software engineering (RSSEs). We provide a general model of simulation for evaluation and review a small set of examples to examine how the model has been applied in practice. From these examples, we extract some general strengths and weaknesses of the use of simulation to evaluate RSSEs. We also explore prospects for making more extensive use of simulation in the future.

12.1 Introduction

The creation and study of simulations is a traditional activity performed by scientists and engineers, aimed at understanding something about the "real world," in which the real world is too complex, too expensive, or too risky to directly understand well [29]. Consider two examples: a computer program that forecasts the weather and a wind tunnel containing a scale model of an airplane. In weather forecasting,

R.J. Walker (✉)
Department of Computer Science, University of Calgary, Calgary, AB, Canada
e-mail: walker@ucalgary.ca

R. Holmes
David R. Cheriton School of Computer Science, University of Waterloo, Waterloo, ON, Canada
e-mail: rtholmes@cs.uwaterloo.ca

M.P. Robillard et al. (eds.), *Recommendation Systems in Software Engineering*,
DOI 10.1007/978-3-642-45135-5_12, © Springer-Verlag Berlin Heidelberg 2014

predictions about the weather are needed in advance in order to plan; while an unexpected rainy weekend is unpleasant, imagine an unexpected hurricane arriving. In the wind tunnel, avionics engineers can measure properties of a proposed airplane's performance; this avoids the high cost of constructing a prototype real airplane, avoids the risk to a real test pilot's life, and avoids the necessity of locating the precise physical conditions somewhere in the real world that are of interest.

Essentially, a simulation is an imitation of the functioning of one system by the functioning of another, typically simpler one; a simulation involves executing a model of behavior with specific inputs to obtain the resulting outputs. In other words, we seek to abstract away those details of the real system that are too complex or that otherwise are not considered important for what is being studied.

The word "simulation" can refer to the general, abstract idea ("simulation is a common methodology"); a specific instance in which the methodology is applied ("the simulation was conducted as follows"); and a particular execution of a specific model ("we observed interesting phenomena recorded during the third simulation"). Some research fields differentiate *simulation modeling* [6, 11, 29] as the activity that creates the static model that is then dynamically driven to produce the results, i.e., during the "simulation." While in principle this overloading of the term can confuse the reader, the context in which the term is used generally disambiguates the meaning.

Simulation is performed for three main purposes: (1) to estimate the answer to a problem whose exact computation would be too expensive to solve directly; (2) to explore the range of behaviors attainable from the model for a set of inputs that are representative in some sense; or (3) to predict a set of outputs that can then be compared against reality, for the sake of evaluating the model. Cases 2 and 3 involve evaluation and will be most pertinent to this chapter.

For recommendation systems in software engineering (RSSEs), few authors [5, 15, 23, 36] make mention of the term "simulation," often referring to their studies as simply "experiments" or "evaluations" [4, 12, 13, 18, 19, 21, 37]. An *evaluation* involves an examination of something to assess its merits. An *experiment* involves following a disciplined procedure to test a hypothesis, usually under controlled conditions. A simulation involves imitating the behavior of some process, usually for the purpose of study. Thus, experiments and simulations can be used in evaluation, and simulations can be used in order to conduct experiments. But a simulation need not involve experimentation (an exploration does not involve testing a hypothesis) nor even an evaluation (watching an animated simulation may be simply aesthetically pleasing).

Perceptions of the value of simulation can color the accepted usage of the term. For example, some disciplines make a distinction between "the use of computer techniques to perform calculations, on the one hand, and [proper] computer simulation, on the other" [16, p. 128]. Winsberg [35] claims that two characteristics distinguish "mere number crunching" from "true simulation":

1. the use of a variety of techniques to draw inferences from the numbers; and
2. the application of expertise and judgment to decide which results are reliable.

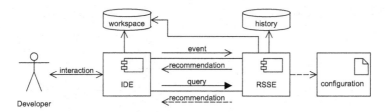

Fig. 12.1 A model of a typical RSSE

The essential point is to say that the algorithmic production of data does not imbue it with validity [2, p. 67]: garbage-in/garbage-out. A serious simulation must be designed with careful consideration of its underlying model and choice of inputs; triangulation of the results—in which different methodologies are applied to address a research question—is most likely to ensure that they are meaningful [8].

The remainder of the chapter is structured as follows. Section 12.2 describes a general model for the use of simulation in evaluating RSSEs. Section 12.3 describes examples from the RSSE literature that have made use of simulation for evaluation, focusing specifically on that use, and referring to our general model. Section 12.4 summarizes the lessons learned.

12.2   A General Model of Simulation for Evaluation of RSSEs

RSSEs come in many varieties, with differing characteristics, differing purposes, and differing design decisions [26, 27]. Nevertheless, consider the model shown in Fig. 12.1, which represents a common arrangement in many RSSEs. In it, a developer interacts with an integrated development environment (IDE) in order to perform development tasks. This interaction may explicitly involve asking the RSSE for recommendations (query/response), or the developer's activities may cause events to be reported to the RSSE, which in turn can cause changes to occur in the IDE (to announce recommendations). During these activities, the IDE will typically interact with some internal representation of the programs and other artifacts upon which it operates (the "workspace," which may include a version control system or other repositories); some RSSEs will also directly access this representation. Many RSSEs are configurable in some form, which we represent as an artifact upon which the RSSE depends. Furthermore, the RSSE may record and later utilize a history of information: for example, past decisions by this developer or decisions by others.

This is a potentially complex situation. The workspace and history can be large and can differ significantly between organizations; the human developer can be unpredictable; the IDE can contain bugs. Simulation can most obviously be used here in two ways: to determine how the developer will react to certain situations and to determine how the RSSE will react to certain situations. Unlike other simulation contexts (like the wind tunnel or in weather forecasting), we will typically have

Fig. 12.2 A generic model
for the typical simulation
scenario for an RSSE

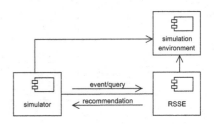

the RSSE already in hand, so the simulation will either involve (a) constructing
an artificial workspace/history/configuration in order to see how the developer
will react or (b) imitating the developer and the environment around the RSSE to
examine how the RSSE behaves.

As a standard means of simplifying the situation, we note that the RSSE receives
inputs and produces outputs, but that the real sources and sinks of that data can
be imitated; this results in the generic simulation model of Fig. 12.2. In it, the
developer is removed along with the IDE to be replaced with a *simulator* that
generates events/queries and receives responses (likely recording these somehow);
in practice, the simulator is simple and may not even be automated. A *simulation
environment* for an RSSE is a combination of workspace, history, and configuration,
appropriate for the particular RSSE being studied. Note that this generic simulation
model will work for RSSEs that are not well described by the model of Fig. 12.1; its
only assumption is that the RSSE takes input (explicit and/or implicit) and produces
output.

This model is analogous to the standard model of *unit testing*, in which a
software unit of functionality (e.g., a class) provides an interface that can be
called, that can have data passed to it, that returns output, and that may depend
on other units of functionality; we want to isolate the unit of interest, and so the
other units that it depends upon are eliminated in favor of ones constructed to
collect information and/or to return specific values to the unit under test. These
replacement dependencies are often called *stubs* (they come in many varieties each
using different names).

The RSSE is analogous to the unit under test, the simulator is the driver, and
the simulation environment is the stub that replaces the other dependencies of the
RSSE. Different scenarios can be explored by adjusting the content of the simulator
and simulation environment. As with choosing the extent of a given unit in unit
testing, the researcher can adjust the boundary between the RSSE and the simulation
environment to achieve different purposes: for example, one might choose to have
the RSSE construct and modify a real history over an extended interaction sequence,
rather than just initializing a synthetic history directly.

An alternative simulation scenario makes sense in some settings (see Fig. 12.3).
In this scenario, the RSSE is not present, but the researcher wants to evaluate
the reaction of the developer to potential recommendations, possibly derived from
data previously collected from them. In this case, the RSSE itself is simulated: its
recommendations may be computed offline or synthesized and can be presented

Fig. 12.3 A generic model for an alternative simulation scenario for an RSSE

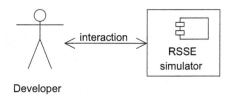

Developer

directly by a human being, as a paper prototype, or as a mocked-up program. This case is not currently common in the RSSE literature, but it is not unknown in other areas—so-called **Wizard of Oz experiments** [17] are one variation on this idea.

Given either of these setups, it is necessary to determine with what inputs the simulation will be driven and what to do with the outputs that result. Ultimately, these decisions are important and should be based on the purposes for conducting the specific simulation. The chapter henceforth focuses on the case where the RSSE's context is being imitated (as per Fig. 12.2).

12.2.1 Inputs and Outputs

Let V be the set of possible simulation environments for a specific RSSE. In addition, let Q be the set of possible queries on the RSSE. Then the set I of possible inputs will be $I \subseteq Q \times V$ (it is a subset because not all queries may be possible for all simulation environments). Furthermore, let R be the set of possible recommendations that the RSSE could possibly produce, and let M be the set of meta-results (like the time needed to perform its calculations) that are not derivable from R. Then the set O of possible outputs from the RSSE will be $O \subseteq R \times M \times V$, where V is included as the RSSE could modify the simulation environment. Thus, we can see the RSSE as defining a function $f : Q \times V \mapsto R \times M \times V$. For most RSSEs, the input space and output space will be too large to evaluate exhaustively; even sampling thoroughly such a large space will be infeasible in general [31].

While the need to abstract away from the full input and output spaces ought to be obvious, there is the danger of oversimplification that can lead to poor generalizability and questionable meaningfulness [9, 32]. The inputs tried and outputs obtained ought to comprise a **representative sample** of the possible inputs and outputs—that is, the results ought to generalize to the full space, or at least the subset of that space that is considered most important. There are three basic approaches to obtain representative samples. (1) Consider the full input space abstractly, without concern for the relative likelihood that a given query will occur in practice. (2) Consider the intended application, where we have knowledge or assumptions of realistic inputs and can judge whether a given input is likely. (3) Select inputs so that the resulting outputs are representative of the output space, which can require either that the function f be invertible or that a search process be followed to find an input that can obtain a given output. Hybrid approaches between the three basic ones are also conceivable. In general, the desire is to sample more heavily those regions of the full (input or output) space that are more likely to occur in practice. But sometimes, the researcher is interested in determining the overall characteristics of the space, such as whether problematic states can ever result.

Simulations of RSSEs often consist of multiple trials of single-step simulations: each trial i consists of selecting $q_i \in Q$ and $v_i \in V$ to obtain $r_i \in R$, $m_i \in M$, and $v_i' \in V$. But it is also possible to have each trial involve multiple steps, where $v_{i,j}$ is $v_{i,j-1}'$ obtained from the previous step. In this way, emergent behavior of an RSSE that alters its environment can be investigated; this is obviously only of interest where $v_{i,j} \neq v_{i,j-1}'$ for at least some trials. Whether single-step or multiple-step trials make more sense depends greatly on the characteristics of the specific RSSE and the purpose of the simulation. In practice, many RSSEs do not directly modify their environment, although they are used within environments that change over time, for example, where a version control system tracks code modifications and the RSSE uses this information.

12.2.2 Characterizing the Results

How a researcher should characterize the results of simulation trials depends on what the purpose is for conducting them. Such purposes could involve (1) description of individual results without reference to an external notion of what would be good; (2) indication of under what conditions certain classes of results occur; or (3) assessment of the quality of the results.

As an example of simple, descriptive summarization, if the execution time of the RSSE is to be described, standard descriptive statistics will often suffice (i.e., minimum, maximum, mean, standard deviation), but sometimes, a graphical plot of the execution time may be better—especially if the researcher has noticed that the execution time appears to have a relationship with other factors. These kinds of characterizations depend heavily on the numeric nature of the (meta-)data being characterized and are not appropriate for categorical data, in particular, which is what a recommendation would typically consist of.

Simulation can also be used to explore the behavior of the RSSE without concern about the "correctness" of its recommendations. This can be appropriate in situations where the general properties of the RSSE's behavior, relative to the inputs, are of interest. For example, if one wished to determine under what input conditions the RSSE would provide no recommendations, simulation could be used to probe the input space to address the question. In practice, such questions are usually supplementary to asking about the "correctness" of the recommendations.

In many settings, we want to assess the quality of the resulting recommendations. Quality is an imprecise term that may possess both objective and subjective elements; as a result, different stakeholders can have significantly different opinions about the quality of a recommendation. Consider that the needs of a novice are often very different from those of an expert: the same recommendation given to each would likely attain different opinions as to its quality. Furthermore, users' needs depend heavily on the context of their applications: in some contexts, incorrect recommendations would be disastrous; in others, recommending all possible answers is irrelevant as long as a single expected recommendation is actually recommended; in yet others, the order of individual recommendations will matter.

In the typical RSSE simulation scenario, a key purpose is to avoid the use of collecting subjective assessments and the complications outlined in the previous paragraph, so some means of determining the "right answer" (i.e., the *expected recommendation*) is needed that would be expected to be recommended by an ideal oracle with perfect knowledge (see Sect. 12.2.2); this can then be used to assess the objective aspect of the quality. Expected recommendations are often derived from data collected from the real world; note that this does not automatically mean that the expected recommendations are objectively "correct" though (see Sect. 12.2.2). A variety of measures are available to characterize the objective quality, with varying levels of detail and appropriateness (see Sect. 12.2.2). But one must be careful: this purely quantitative approach to assessing quality may not result in an accurate reflection of the user experience. Ultimately, human-participant studies are needed to determine whether the quantitative analysis of quality agrees with the reality; this would be a form of triangulation.

In Chaps. 11, 13, and 9, Said et al. [28], Tosun Mısırlı et al. [33], and Murphy-Hill and Murphy [24] (respectively) expand on the idea of a more complete evaluation of an RSSE, often involving real developers.

Determining Expected Recommendations

Most commonly, it is the quality of the RSSE's recommendations that is to be evaluated; this requires knowing, assuming, or otherwise estimating the expected recommendations. With a given expected recommendation for a given input, the researcher can compare the RSSE's actual recommendation against the expected recommendation for the given input.

It is generally problematic to determine the expected recommendations. In many situations, it is impossible or impractical to automatically generate the expected recommendations; otherwise, the RSSE would use that algorithm and the "RSSE" would no longer qualify as a recommendation system (instead it would compute the correct answer). There are three possibilities for determining expected recommendations: (1) asking human participants for their assessments; (2) using a variety of other automated approaches comparatively; or (3) using data collected previously from the real world.

Human participants from an appropriate population (e.g., students, experts, etc.) can be asked to either provide the correct answers or judge whether the RSSE's answers are correct. When the definition of correctness is dependent on the context of the task for which recommendations are being produced, it is important that the participants understand the context of the task in order to make such judgments. Detailed instruction and training exercises with feedback are common techniques for ensuring that participants have a common understanding of the tasks to be performed. It is also important that the study design avoid the participants' biases: their tendency to assume that the recommendations are correct, or their wish to provide the answers that they assume are desired by the experimenters. Ideally, the experimenters should avoid giving any hint of their own opinions and avoid indicating whether the RSSE being studied is their own. When the definition of correctness being used is subjective, the human participants will tend to differ in their opinions. Often, the majority opinion is interpreted to be the expected recommendation (particularly for categorical data); other options include using the average (for numerical data) or allowing multiple possible expected recommendations. But when participants' opinions differ, there exists a threat to validity of the results: it may be that the experimenters failed to instruct the participants sufficiently, or that the task is too subjective. Minor variations in opinions are often ignored without serious problems. But even when participants' opinions agree, there is no guarantee that no threat to validity exists; it could be that all the participants share the same bias, and so a systematic error exists in the experiment. In either case, it is best practice to be explicit that the threat exists.

Attempting to estimate the expected recommendation on the basis of other automated approaches (e.g., other RSSEs) is fraught with danger. First, if based on published results of the other approaches' application to the same data, there is a strong chance that the current RSSE will have been developed with the knowledge of those results—it has been overfitted to this data. Second, triangulation of other RSSEs' recommendations is no guarantee of the correctness of those other RSSEs nor of their "averaged" results; a researcher will be biased in evaluating novel recommendations not in the union of the recommendations from the other RSSEs (see previous paragraph). As argued in the literature [3,7], although determining the ground truth for expected recommendations may be costly, reference to the ground truth is the only way that an evaluation of quality can approach a lack of bias.

Real Data

For many RSSEs, the researcher can take advantage of some sort of real-world data in producing the set of queries and/or the simulation environment. For example, a repository of open-source programs can serve either to produce queries that ask about source constructs or as the simulated workspace from which the RSSE will draw its knowledge. If a reasonable argument can be made that the data thus used is representative, or at least not a bad representation of other inputs (because it is not too trivial, too large, or too biased in some way), such real data can often avoid the high costs and questionable validity of constructing that data artificially.

For some RSSEs, a repository of data is available that contains both examples of real queries and the corresponding examples of expected recommendations; that is, the repository D consists of pairs $d_i = (q_i, e_i)$ of queries q_i and corresponding expected recommendations e_i. (Note that the generality of these extracted examples is dependent on the representativeness of the source of the data, too.) If the RSSE need not draw upon a workspace or history, each query q_i from the repository can be posited to the RSSE, and its actual recommendation a_i can be compared against the expected recommendation e_i. If the RSSE does need to draw upon a workspace or history, it is important to separate the data used for querying from the data used to form the workspace or history—otherwise, the RSSE would already have access to the expected answer for that query, which will generally not be a representative simulation situation. The typical approach to this process divides the real data into a training set and an evaluation set. When this process is repeated with k different partitions (often chosen at random) and measures of quality are averaged over each, it is called a k-fold cross-validation [22]. In many RSSE situations, a truly random partition of the data cannot be chosen, but instead all data before a given point (for example, a particular timestamp) are used as the training set, and the remaining k data items are used for the evaluation set; this is called k-tail evaluation [21].

It is possible to draw both the queries and the simulation environment's data from the same data items, but this is necessarily a tricky proposition. Given a data item $e_i \in D'$ that will ultimately serve as an expected recommendation, one can construct its corresponding query q_i by extracting a subset of the information from e_i. If that set of information is too perfect, this will not be a fair evaluation. Thus, the researcher must define a transformation $\mathscr{T} : D' \to Q$ that will obfuscate the original identity of e_i from the RSSE. For example, elements can be removed from the set of extracted information, elements can be added to it, or elements can be modified to hide their nature. The details of fair and appropriate transformations depend heavily upon the application context, the design of the RSSE, and the research questions being addressed. A researcher can expect to have difficulty convincing reviewers that the chosen transformation is not biased.

Evaluating the Objective Aspect of Quality

Researchers are often interested in the objective quality of the recommendations produced by an RSSE. As discussed above, a careful choice of the inputs (both queries and simulation environment) is important to obtain meaningful results, and availability of the expected recommendations is needed for the sake of evaluating the quality. But in the absence of perfect agreement or perfect disagreement between the actual and expected recommendations, one needs a way to assess the quality. This is often done with measures borrowed from the field of information retrieval, but several aspects of their use is important to note: (a) there are many such measures available with differing strengths and weaknesses; (b) summarizing a set of observations of agreements/disagreements between actual and expected recommendations necessarily eliminates information—the fewer in quantity that the resulting summary measurements are, the more information that has been lost; (c) the measurements are correct only for the specific inputs and outputs for the RSSE, and these will generalize to other situations only if the inputs were representative of those other situations; and thus (d) comparing two RSSEs requires that the same measures be used on each, and that they be collected in identical situations.

A useful notion in evaluating quality is the **confusion matrix**, shown below:

		Expected	
		Yes	No
Actual	*Yes*	TP	FP
	No	FN	TN

For any given item, the two dimensions represent what the expected recommendation is (either "Yes," it is in the set of interest, or "No," it is not) and what the actual recommendation from a given RSSE and simulation environment was. Where the expected and actual recommendations agree, we have a *true* recommendation from the RSSE—either a true positive (TP) or true negative (TN); in case of disagreement, we have a *false* recommendation from the RSSE—either false positive (FP) or false negative (FN). Typical RSSEs will provide multiple recommendations in a given situation, so each recommendation in the set can then be classified within a confusion matrix; this results in a four-valued characterization of the quality of that recommendation.

Often, people use a characterization of quality with fewer values, in which the confusion matrix is reduced to other measures [34]—for example, the **precision and recall**, or just the **F-measure** (the harmonic mean of the precision and recall). To summarize the overall quality of recommendations from a set of trials, one can either populate a single confusion matrix (called **microevaluation**) or use a means of summarizing the individual quality measures [30] (called **macroevaluation**): for example, a simple approach is to take the mean over the individual measures.

One can introduce schemes to weight certain cells in the confusion matrix, allowing us to account for contexts in which, say, false positives are problematic. Such a scheme ought to possess some a priori justification, such as empirical knowledge of the application context, in order to achieve construct validity [10, 20].

Variations on the standard idea of the confusion matrix are possible. For example, one can use matrices with higher dimensionality in order to simultaneously compare multiple RSSEs with expected recommendations. One can allow more than two outcomes: some RSSEs are explicit about recommending to do something, recommending not to do something, or making no recommendation [e.g., 15]. One can permit the confusion matrix cells to represent **fuzzy sets**: the probable count of cases that fall within a cell. For example, recommendations often come with **confidence** values attached to them that can be interpreted as the probability that the recommendation is right. Each cell of the confusion matrix would then be a sum of the probabilities of the recommendations that fall therein.

In Chap. 10, Avazpour et al. [1] expand on the notion of quality, exploring a variety of other measures.

12.3 Experience with Simulation to Evaluate RSSEs

We proceed to examine four papers from the literature on RSSEs that have applied simulation for the sake of evaluation. These four papers use simulation in different problem contexts and in different ways; common strengths and weaknesses of simulation for evaluation can be seen from these. Section 12.3.1 examines eROSE (originally called ROSE) [37]; its evaluation solely involved simulation, derived from data collected in industrial version control systems. Section 12.3.2 examines Strathcona [15]; its evaluation used simulation only to generalize the results from its formal experiments. Section 12.3.3 examines Gilligan+Suade [12]; its evaluation made heavy use of simulation, derived from data previously collected during a formal experiment. Section 12.3.4 examines an unnamed approach for recommending development environment commands [23]; its design started from a simulation, derived from data collected from actual industrial use of an IDE. It is particularly interesting as it is a rare case in which the RSSE itself was simulated.

Only enough detail is provided to describe the application problem addressed and the solution pursued in order to contextualize the use of simulation in the evaluation of the research. In addition, each subsection attempts to emphasize the evaluation problem that the research attempted to address through simulation, details of the simulation procedure followed, and threats to the validity of the results as reported by the authors of each paper.

12.3.1 Recommending Programmatic Entities to Change: eROSE

Real software systems tend to be large and complex. As a result, developers can have trouble recognizing dependencies between different parts of a system: in some cases, they fail to see explicit dependencies due to excess visual noise from other code; in other cases, the dependencies are too subtle to easily detect. As a result, when the developer modifies one part of their system, they are liable to overlook other parts that should also be changed. Automated analyses of the control- and data-flow within the system can help in some cases, but undecidability can limit the effectiveness of such analyses.

The Recommendation System

Instead of analyzing the structure or runtime of the program to look for dependencies, past human experience can be leveraged as recorded in a version control system. By detecting that two (or more) entities have tended to change together in the past, the hypothesis is that they are likely to change together again in the future.

Thus, in detecting the fact that a developer has modified one or more entities in the program, recommendations for other entities to change can also be made. This is the premise of the eROSE tool [37].

eROSE mines the history to locate commits: sets of changes simultaneously submitted, where a change consists of a change type and an entity. Commits must be inferred, particularly for repositories using CVS (which versions only individual files, and so groups of files simultaneously submitted can be detected only indirectly). Furthermore, entities are considered the same (and hence two versions of the same entity) if and only if their names (or signatures, for methods) and the names of their structural ancestors are identical. The presence of two (or more) changes occurring frequently enough together leads eROSE to infer a rule that a change to one entity likely ought to be accompanied with a change to that (or those) other entities. CVS supports branching to allow independent development paths of different variants of a system; in some cases, changes within a branch are merged back into the main trunk, resulting in apparent commits involving very large numbers of entities. eROSE heuristically ignores commits that involve too many entities, in order to avoid considering merges.

In general eROSE takes a set of changed entities as the query from the developer's IDE, mines for rules involving those entities, and makes recommendations about other entities to investigate. For each recommendation it indicates two measures of relevance: the confidence, representing the frequency with which the rule has applied previously for equivalent queries, and the *support count*, indicating how many cases have gone into constructing the rule.

The Evaluation Problem

eROSE operates by finding other entities to recommend once the developer has made a change to a system. If real developers were provided with eROSE while they performed change tasks, very little empirical data would be collected relative to the large amount of time required to conduct the experiments. Furthermore, eROSE has many aspects that could be and were evaluated, including: the length of history to be analyzed; the kind of scenario in which it is being applied; the kinds of changes to be analyzed from history; the minimum thresholds of confidence and support count at which to make a recommendation; and the specific system to which it is being applied. Simulation is a promising methodology to apply here in order to assess a wide variety of situations at relatively low cost.

How Simulation Was Used

A set of industrial software systems, each with an available change history, were selected. The general simulation procedure that was used followed four steps: (1) a time-limited portion of the history was designated as the training set to be mined by eROSE (the training set formed the simulation environment V); (2) the remainder of the history was used to collect a set of commits T; (3) each commit $t \in T$ was partitioned into a query q and an expected recommendation e; and (4) eROSE was given each query, and the actual recommendation was compared against the expected recommendation.

Several variations on this general procedure were followed. In particular, the manner of partitioning the commits into queries and expected recommendations was varied according to three conjectured usage scenarios.

1. *Navigation* involved the simulated developer making a single change and recommending to them a set of other changes. For each commit t_i, $|t_i|$ distinct queries q_j were formed such that $|q_j| = 1$.
2. *Error prevention* involved the simulated developer making a set of changes but missing one. Again, $|t_i|$ distinct queries were formed, but each one contained the entirety of the commit except for one change; hence, each $q_j = t_i - \{e_j\}$ for some unique e_j.
3. *Closure* involved checking that eROSE would not recommend additional changes when the whole commit was used as the query. This involved one query for each commit, for which $e_i = \emptyset$.

The general simulation procedure was then followed for several cases.

- The effects, on the quality of eROSE's results, of selecting thresholds for confidence and support count were explored for each of the usage scenarios. For each scenario, different levels were selected representing the appropriate trade-off between precise recommendations (few wrong recommendations) and complete recommendations (few missing, correct recommendations). This can be seen as a configuration phase.
- With the preferred settings for a given usage scenario in place, the quality of eROSE's results was then evaluated for that scenario.
- The effects of the level of granularity of the entities being analyzed and reported were considered. The configurations from the previous item were repeated, but for which the entities were considered only in terms of files, rather than individual functions or variables. The quality of eROSE's results was then evaluated and compared against those from the previous item.
- The effects of restricting changes to consider only alteration ("maintenance") events, as opposed to addition or deletion of entities, were considered. Two conditions were compared: where only maintenance events were considered, and where all change events were considered. The navigation scenario with its preferred configuration was again used to instantiate the general procedure.
- The effects of differentiating the kinds of change events, as opposed to treating them all as generic change events, were considered. The configuration from the previous item, in which all change events were considered was used again; this time, two conditions varied this configuration: whether the kinds of change events were differentiated or not.
- The effects of the duration of the project's history were considered on the quality of the recommendations, both in terms of looking at the intervals from the project

start until a set of specific moments and in terms of looking at the intervals of a specific length prior to a set of specific moments. This investigation was restricted to two projects.

Reported Threats to Validity

Zimmermann et al. [37] report four possible threats to validity in their work on eROSE. (1) More than 100,000 commits on eight large open-source systems were studied. Although these systems differ in terms of domain (and likely also in terms of development processes, design issues, etc.), the results may not be representative of all systems. This issue plagues much research in software engineering, regardless of methodology applied or problem context investigated. (2) Transactions do not record ordering information about individual changes. Zimmermann et al. express concern that different frequencies for specific orderings of changes could affect results for the navigation and error prevention usage scenarios. (3) Transactions are not assessed for their quality. Any commit that is not filtered out by the branch-merging heuristic is used by eROSE. This is potentially problematic since developers sometimes make bad decisions, and so the expected recommendations extracted from the history would differ from the true expected recommendations. But since bad decisions will make their way into the version control system far less frequently than good decisions, the effect on the expected recommendations is likely small. (4) There is a difference between a recommendation being correct and it being useful. Assessing the usefulness of recommendations would require a different methodology to be applied.

12.3.2 Recommending Usage Examples for an API: Strathcona

Developers frequently make use of libraries and frameworks to create software applications. Libraries and frameworks provide application programming interfaces (APIs) specifically for this purpose. For nontrivial cases, understanding how to correctly utilize an API can be difficult: particular subtypes must be provided, particular objects must be created, and particular methods must be called in particular orders. Examples are often used by developers to understand usage scenarios for APIs, but this requires (a) that the examples exist and (b) that the developer know how to locate the appropriate example for their needs.

The Recommendation System

To overcome these weaknesses, a recommendation system can be created that allows the developer to specify the kind of example of interest. Many forms of specification are possible, but few are developer-centric, placing a high burden on the developer to be precise and accurate. Instead, the fact that the developer is specifically trying to interact with the API means that they will have a partial implementation of what interests them, a *skeleton*. This skeleton may not even compile, but hopefully describes certain details of the interaction that matter to the developer. Furthermore, for many APIs, source code already exists that uses it in some form. By extracting information from the skeleton and looking for existing source code that also contains (some of) the same information, we can hope to provide meaningful examples to the developer.

This is the basic idea behind the Strathcona example recommendation system [15]. Strathcona utilizes only the structural facts it locates in the skeleton (the developer's class containing the skeleton, plus the skeleton's supertypes; types used in the skeleton; methods called), but this is often enough to locate even uncommon examples. Strathcona was configured to weigh the importance of particular facts; these heuristics were determined over time with informal experimentation.

The Evaluation Problem

Many aspects of Strathcona could be and were evaluated. For example, user studies were conducted to determine whether developers would be able to interpret and utilize the recommended examples. The generalizability of these studies was of concern: they were expensive and focused on a small set of tasks that (while of differing levels of complexity) were not definable as representative of all possible tasks. In particular, to reduce variability between subjects, skeletons were provided to the participants.

How Simulation Was Used

In order to generalize from these user studies, a simulation was conducted to evaluate Strathcona's ability to return appropriate examples given varying skeletons.

The general simulation procedure consisted of four steps: (1) code fragments of between 10 and 20 lines in length were selected at random from the repository that Strathcona was using (these were the expected recommendations); (2) the set of structural facts used by Strathcona were extracted from the selected code fragment (with references eliminated to entities that would easily identify examples, such as private methods); (3) subsets of these filtered structural facts were selected to form queries; and (4) it was recorded whether the Strathcona server was able to locate the target answer amongst the top ten matches.

The general procedure was followed in two variations: (1) all subsets of the structural facts were used, even when these were clearly generic (e.g., calls to methods on string) and (2) the structural facts were restricted to eliminate those that were deemed generic, then all subsets of the restricted structural facts were used. The purpose of the second variation was to determine how many important facts needed to be known by a developer in order to locate the target answer.

A graph was provided for each of the two variations, in which the number of facts in the query was plotted against the occurrence rate of the target answer, for each of the (four) randomly selected code fragments.

Reported Threats to Validity

Although the simulation part of the evaluation was conducted by Holmes et al. specifically to address threats to validity arising in other parts of their evaluation, the simulation itself possessed three reported threats to validity. (1) It is unknown if the queries (which are the essence of what is extracted from the skeletons) that are successful in actually recommending the expected recommendation are representative of the queries that a developer would form in practice. (2) The examples selected for the simulation all contained slightly fewer than the average number of structural facts. It is unknown if this biased the results in a serious way. (3) The simulation focused on the APIs provided by the Eclipse IDE. Although the paper describes informal experience with other APIs, it is possible that the results are not representative of general APIs.

12.3.3 Recommending Dependency Treatments During Reuse: Gilligan+Suade

While software reuse has long been pursued for its potential benefits for productivity and quality, traditional approaches require that the needed form of reuse of functionality be predicted ahead of time and be explicitly designed for. When unpredicted reuse scenarios occur, developers will often pursue a *pragmatic* process of reuse, involving copying and modifying the source code that provides their needed functionality.

During such a task, the developer attempts to balance the desire to reuse as much code as possible that implements the desired functionality, with the desire to avoid reusing as much irrelevant code as possible. A pragmatic reuse task involves the developer navigating the source code for potential reuse, following dependencies between elements, and considering the cost of eliminating each element versus the (future) cost of retaining each element. The Gilligan tool [14] allows the developer to record their decisions about whether to retain or eliminate elements while investigating the functionality to be reused; the result is a plan about the pragmatic reuse task that can be semiautomatically enacted at any point, and atomically undone if the results are unsatisfactory, to be revised when necessary.

The process of creating a pragmatic-reuse plan is an iterative one in which the goal is to find the ideal dependencies at which to "cut away" unwanted functionality while minimizing the effort required to repair or replace the resulting dangling references. This is a complex decision process hampered by four factors: cutting a given dependency may eliminate relevant functionality; cutting a given dependency may incur high costs to repair the resulting dangling reference; *not* cutting a given dependency may fail to eliminate irrelevant functionality; and not cutting a given dependency may force us to cut a dependency in an even worse situation. Analyzing the possibilities requires both local and nonlocal reasoning to determine good dependencies at which to cut. Gilligan does not directly aid in making these decisions, but only in recording them and analyzing whether the overall plan is complete.

The Recommendation System

Developers are generally good at local reasoning about repairing dangling references, and low-cost analyses are unlikely to improve upon the manual approach. In contrast, nonlocal reasoning on the dependency graph is much more difficult as standard tools provide at most localized views of this information. An opportunity exists for a recommendation system that draws on knowledge of transitive dependencies and a model of cost and relevance to suggest where good or bad cuts could be made. This is the central idea of the Gilligan+Suade tool [12].

Gilligan+Suade takes a partial pragmatic-reuse plan and the dependency graph of the system from which functionality is to be reused; it makes recommendations to cut dependencies (*reject* the depended upon entity) or not to cut dependencies (*accept* the depended upon entity). For a given depended upon entity, it may make no recommendation about its treatment. The recommendations are revised as the developer makes additional decisions or revises previous decisions.

These recommendations are based on two heuristic measures for each entity: its *structural relevance* [25] and its *reuse cost*. The structural relevance (as defined by the Suade tool [25]) is based on heuristics that attempt to characterize the local shape of the dependency graph; dependencies from elements that possess fewer dependencies are each deemed more relevant, and dependencies back to entities already marked as being reused are also deemed more relevant. The reuse cost is based on the number of descendants of a given entity in the dependency graph, weighted by the length of the shortest path to each of them.

The Evaluation Problem

Human participant studies involving the performance of pragmatic reuse tasks are expensive to design and run, as the tasks cannot be trivial if they are to be meaningful. A set of such experiments had been conducted previously [14] during which interaction data from developers' actions with Gilligan were recorded. Rather than repeat such actual experiments again, it was desired to make use of the recorded data. A recommendation system for these decisions had been specifically requested by the study participants to enhance the usefulness of Gilligan.

How Simulation Was Used

Two simulation phases were performed. In the first phase, each experimental session was replayed by executing the developer's decisions in chronological order, in order to reconstruct the partial pragmatic-reuse plans at each moment. The recommendations that would have been displayed by Gilligan+Suade were computed for each instant at which a decision was actually made.

The sessions for which the data was reused ultimately resulted in successful pragmatic-reuse plans; "correct" decisions were deemed to be those for which at least 75 % of the developers agreed, and these were treated as the expected recommendation in each situation. Each actual recommendation was thus compared against the expected recommendation and the developer's immediate decision, which they sometimes changed (even multiple times) later. The quality of the recommendations was reported in terms of agreement or disagreement with the expected recommendations; the presence of the cases where no recommendation was made inhibited the use of standard quality measures.

The second simulation phase was performed because the authors perceived that the behavior of an actual developer in performing a pragmatic reuse task could be quite different in the presence of the RSSE: the results of the first simulation phase might have had little external validity. The second phase thus involved one of the authors (Holmes) using Gilligan+Suade to repeat the experimental tasks to see how it would affect his decision behavior and whether the tasks would still be successful.

Holmes spent little effort confirming cases with recommendations and never disagreed with these, but focused carefully on the (minority of) cases where no recommendation was forthcoming. The result was successful completion of both tasks according to the criteria of the original human-participant experiment, but at the cost of a small expansion of the code having been reused.

Reported Threats to Validity

Holmes et al. [12] explained that their rationale for conducting the second phase of the simulation was the concern that the presence of the recommendation system could have affected the developer actions enough to have invalidated the use of the recorded data. Nevertheless, the second phase of the simulation involved only one author following a largely mechanical procedure in order to gain confidence that the results were promising. This involved a small set of tasks that may not have been representative of all tasks, by a "participant" who possessed a biased perspective.

12.3.4   *Recommending Development Environment Commands*

IDEs have grown increasingly complex. With their increased usage and increased ease of extension, a plethora of tools have been added to them. While the existence of the right tool for a given task is of benefit to the developer performing that task, that benefit can be realized only if the developer is aware of the existence of the tool, of how the tool can be activated, and of how to use the tool. At some point, tools become hard to find within an IDE because of their large numbers: this is the proverbial "finding a needle in a haystack." If the developer knows that the tool exists, simple navigation strategies like searching and browsing will likely suffice to find it. But if the developer is unaware that a tool exists, that a better tool exists than the one they are using, or that a simpler command exists for activating that tool, they will not even know to perform a search or browse.

The Recommendation System

When a developer learns how to make use of a tool, their initial attempts can be awkward and inefficient; upon discovering a more effective approach, they abandon their original style of usage for the one that they see as better. This gives rise to a detectable pattern over time. Patterns of interaction by the current developer can be compared to such patterns from other developers. If those other developers eventually abandoned a style of usage that the current developer is also following, the improved style of usage adopted by those others can be recommended to the current developer. This is the premise of the work of Murphy-Hill et al. [23]. Their proposed recommendation system is proactive: it observes the developer's interactions with an IDE and makes recommendations when it can.

The Evaluation Problem

Murphy-Hill et al. were in possession of a large repository of data concerning developers' interactions with an IDE. Their problem was to decide on an algorithm (out of eight possibilities postulated) that would most effectively leverage this data to recommend novel commands to developers and, ultimately, to determine whether such a recommendation system would be useful in practice.

How Simulation Was Used

Two simulations were performed. The initial phase involved an automated simulation in which k-tail evaluation (see Sect. 12.2.2) over the data repository was performed. The second phase involved a human participant-based evaluation of the usefulness of a set of recommendations; this also was essentially a simulation. Both simulations focused on commands in the Eclipse IDE (e.g., commands involving the use of CVS; commands involving the editing and refactoring of Java source code).

For the automated simulation, the general procedure was as follows. The data repository was factored into interaction histories for individual developers. For a given value of k, the last k commands discovered by each developer was determined, by detecting the first occurrence of each command in the interaction history for a given developer. (Developers without k command discovery events were immediately eliminated from consideration.) The full interaction history for a developer prior to the first of the k command-discovery events formed the simulated history (i.e., training set) for the recommendation system. The expected recommendations would then be the k commands themselves. The recommendation system was configured in turn with each of the postulated algorithms. The authors chose to suppress cases where one or more of the algorithms were unable to deliver recommendations, for example, due to insufficient history in the training set.

Three variations on this generic procedure were followed. The standard variation is as described above; it assumes that the first use of a given command led to the developer deeming the command to be useful. Examination of the interaction histories indicated that, in some cases, the command was not repeated again, and so the assumption of usefulness was likely not correct. This led to two other variations: (1) k-tail multi-use, in which commands that are not repeated are ignored and do not contribute to the k commands sought and (2) k-tail multi-session, in which commands that are not repeated in different development sessions are ignored and do not contribute to the k commands sought. (The multi-session variation is strictly more conservative than the multiuse variation.)

For the simulation involving human participants, a set of recommendations was generated from the dataset by each algorithm and for each participant. Two populations of participants were sampled: experts and novices. Each recommendation was presented verbally to a participant who was asked to rate the novelty of the command and to explain the rationale for this rating.

Reported Threats to Validity

Murphy-Hill et al. [23] report one key threat to validity for the automated simulation: the inability to determine whether the recommendations were actually useful, since the expected recommendations were constructed by inferring behaviors in the previously recorded interaction traces. For the simulation involving human participants, they report one other key threat: the fact that the recommendations were delivered to participants by a human experimenter could have influenced the participant to be more willing to accept them; an automated RSSE would likely find more resistance from its users.

12.4 Lessons Learned

Every nontrivial empirical study necessarily has some weaknesses: the space to be explored is effectively infinite, while a study must be finite. Nevertheless, each of the studies described in the previous section points to issues about which we need to worry and strategies that we can apply to address these. We discuss here four lessons we can learn from these studies.

12.4.1 Triangulation

One convenient but misguided interpretation of the papers described in the previous section would be that simulations suffice for evaluation, and that through the use of simulation, one can avoid user studies altogether. But simulations can only be as good as the model, assumptions, and data that go into them. While being careful in designing and running a simulation can go a long way towards the validity of its results, this is not enough to ensure that some issue has not been overlooked.

Every empirical methodology has inherent strengths and weaknesses; this is equally true of simulation. The strengths can be eroded by a poor study design, and the weaknesses can be mitigated in some circumstances. Triangulation is an approach in which multiple evaluations are conducted, each using different methods and/or on different data sources in order to improve the generalizability of the findings. When the threats to validity of the individual evaluations differ and the results support the same conclusion, the threats are mitigated overall.

In the works on Strathcona, Gilligan+Suade, and the approach of Murphy-Hill, we see that simulation was used in combination with other studies for the sake of triangulation. Sometimes simulation was used to mitigate the threats accrued from other evaluations (in the case of Strathcona); sometimes simulation was used as the first step in collecting evidence before a human-participant study was conducted (in the other two cases).

In the work on eROSE, triangulation consisted of repeating the same kind of study on multiple software systems and performing different kinds of study to evaluate different aspects of the approach. Zimmermann et al. point out that their methodology was unable to address the actual usefulness of the recommendations, and further, that their study could be affected by bad developer decisions recorded in history. The purpose of their study was to examine how often eROSE could produce correct recommendations; there is no obvious alternative means to obtain a set of expected recommendations for simulation purposes. Further triangulation involving user studies could help to mitigate these threats, but the contribution of their work was already large, so it is not surprising that this last step was not taken.

It would be wrong to think that the authors of the work on eROSE chose the wrong path for triangulation. In the other three papers, the overall study was smaller and less thorough, sometimes necessitated by the available data source from which to extract expected recommendations. In the end, it is easy to say, "they should have done more studies"; it is much harder to judge when this demand is excessive. Further studies beget further studies; such is the nature of science. We all have limited resources to expend; how best to make use of those resources depends on our goals and how important the answers are. As an area matures, it is natural for reviewers to expect stronger results.

12.4.2 Quality of Real Data

The availability of real-world data with which to evaluate or populate a simulation is an important factor in pursuing a simulation. As such, it is natural to believe that whatever real-world data one has in possession will be good enough. Much of science revolves around this fact: all real data is imperfect.

Most data that is used in evaluating or driving a simulation has been automatically recorded by some program. All programs contain bugs. Any useful program will execute on a real computer; real computers contain bugs. Humans make mistakes, and this can affect the quality of any data that was written down by a human.

All real data was recorded in a real setting. Particular people doing particular things in a particular context and at a particular time. In using this data for other purposes, one has to assume that differences between the original setting and the setting being simulated are not significant, but this assumption can be false.

Sometimes the real data does not provide the information that is desired. In the case of eROSE, Zimmermann et al. tell us that they would have liked to know about the order in which entities were changed, but that this was not recorded and no inference could be made to recover this information. There is no obvious way to overcome this limitation, but it is also unclear that the limitation would be a significant one, so following a more expensive route to collect this data might be unwarranted.

In the case of the work by Murphy-Hill et al., the recommendations were not received by the participants as well as had been predicted by the initial simulation. The data quality could have been an issue. Murphy-Hill et al. assumed that evidence of learning commands could be inferred from the available interaction traces; they were surprised to find that some participants claimed that they were already using recommended commands, as a recommendation should not happen in that situation. Either the data was wrong, their tool contained bugs, or the participants' claims were false—all problematic cases to deal with. There is no obvious way that they could have avoided this issue a priori. Perhaps with further study, the nature of the issue will be discovered as well as how it can be avoided. Another potential issue was that there could have been a time gap between when the trace data was recorded, and when the recommendations were made; in this time gap, the developers could have discovered the command and started to use it. Ensuring that the data being leveraged is very fresh and that it contains all of the participant's interactions would be about the only way to avoid this, but could be difficult to enforce in most studies.

12.4.3 The Importance and Dangers of Assumptions

We all make assumptions. Sometimes we are aware of our assumptions, and sometimes we make them implicitly. Assumptions are absolutely needed when the evidence available does not permit inference. But obviously, assumptions can be wrong. When assumptions are explicit, one needs to decide whether it is worthwhile to invest time into testing them. When assumptions are implicit, they cannot be directly tested, so triangulation in general is the best means to discover any consequences arising from false ones.

In the case of eROSE, assumptions were made about its usage scenarios. These were necessary to drive the simulations; they were presumably derived from the experience of Zimmermann et al. rather than actual data. While these assumptions appear reasonable, there is no guarantee that they would really occur in practice or that other important scenarios would not occur. This is an inherent weakness of the methodology used that could only be mitigated through other methodologies or other data sources containing direct evidence of such usage scenarios.

In the case of Strathcona, the sensitivity of the approach to the amount of input facts was assessed through simulation. The simulation attempted to use as queries all subsets of facts of a small set of examples. This implicitly assumes that these queries are representative of what developers would typically provide. Perhaps a better design would have been to non-exhaustively select subsets of facts from a larger number of examples; this could have avoided the combinatorial explosion problems arising from trying all subsets. Follow-on studies could have been performed on the more problematic cases to see whether human participants could handle them well enough.

12.4.4 Effects from the Presence of the RSSE

In most cases, the real-world data that a researcher uses in driving or assessing a simulation was necessarily collected without the RSSE being present. The hope is that the RSSE will not alter the essential decisions that were made, but perhaps allow them to be made faster and with greater confidence.

In the case of Gilligan+Suade, this assumption about the recorded data was challenged. The second simulation phase found that the results from the tool seemed better than predicted by the initial simulation. The presence of the RSSE in the decision process appeared to actually alter nontrivially the decisions made by the "participant." The effect at work could be that developers will make sub-optimal decisions when a complex decision process is not well supported. Thus, the recorded choices were not the "gold standard" that were assumed, but merely good enough for the developers to have completed the task; the presence of Gilligan+Suade apparently improved the decision process. To determine whether this effect was real or an artifact from a biased investigation would require follow-on study.

In the case of the work of Murphy-Hill et al., they point out the fact that their simulation that involved human participants was not completely natural, as a human was giving them the recommendations. Recommendations delivered by an RSSE could be received with less trust, or be deemed annoying if they were delivered at the wrong time. They suggest that social tagging of recommendations be supported as a developer is more likely to pay attention to a recommendation seconded by a trusted colleague.

12.5   Conclusion

Simulation is an important empirical technique used in many areas of science and engineering. Simulation can serve to explore a complex system or to evaluate it. Simulation involves the imitation of some part of a system, in order to avoid the complexities, risks, or costs involved in directly evaluating the system.

We have specifically examined the use of simulation for the evaluation of RSSEs. We have presented a general model of simulation for evaluation of RSSEs that applies to a typical situation in which RSSEs are to be evaluated; this typical situation is analogous to the standard setting of unit testing of software, with drivers and stubs. Variations on this model were mentioned briefly, including the alternative of simulating the RSSE itself to assess developer actions.

Four examples from the literature were described that involved simulation for evaluation of RSSEs. Three of these involved the typical simulation scenario in which the context of the RSSE was simulated to drive the actual RSSE. One of them used the alternative simulation scenario of simulating the RSSE itself as well as its simulation environment.

All empirical methodologies have strengths and weaknesses. A typical simulation has the advantage that a much wider of range of behavior can be examined than could be through user studies, at a lower cost, with greater control, and with greater reproducibility. A typical simulation has the disadvantage that it involves driving a model, which must be assumed to serve as a valid abstraction of the system of interest; when this assumption fails to hold, the conclusions drawn from the simulation may not be valid.

To mitigate this problem, simulations are often used in combination with other forms of evaluation (i.e., in triangulation). Simulations are sometimes used to generalize the results of human-participant studies. Simulations are commonly used as a first step before more expensive, alternative methodologies are pursued.

All the example RSSEs that we have described made use of real-world data to drive their simulations. Real-world data has the advantage that it has not been contrived, so it can be claimed to represent at least some aspect of the real world. Unfortunately, real-world data does not eliminate the need to be cautious in its application. Real-world data has to be collected and recorded and there is no guarantee that this process is free of errors. The data may violate important assumptions of the simulation, despite being "real." The real-world context in which the data was collected could be radically altered were the RSSE added to it, thereby reducing the validity of the results of the simulation. Still, real-world data would generally be more reliable than synthetic data, and thus is highly sought after. The increasing availability of high-quality, real-world data needed to assess the quality of recommendations will only serve to make simulation an even more feasible option on the road ahead.

The future of simulation for evaluation of RSSEs looks bright. An interesting possibility, hinted at in some of the studies described in this chapter, is to directly simulate a limited range of behaviors of developers. From recorded traces of tool interactions, one may be able to extract common behaviors and use these to model the "representative developer" over an extended time. Time will tell if this is more than a dream, but we believe that there is promise.

Overall, simulation is an exciting option with growing importance as an exploration and evaluation technique for RSSEs.

References

1. Avazpour, I., Pitakrat, T., Grunske, L., Grundy, J.: Dimensions and metrics for evaluating recommendation systems. In: Robillard, M., Maalej, W., Walker, R.J., Zimmermann, T. (eds.) Recommendation Systems in Software Engineering, Chap. 10. Springer, New York (2014)
2. Babbage, C.: Passages from the Life of a Philosopher. Longman, Green, Longman, Roberts, & Green, London (1864)
3. Bachmann, A., Bird, C., Rahman, F., Devanbu, P., Bernstein, A.: The missing links: bugs and bug-fix commits. In: Proceedings of the ACM SIGSOFT International Symposium on Foundations of Software Engineering, pp. 97–106 (2010). doi:10.1145/1882291.1882308
4. Bavota, G., De Lucia, A., Marcus, A., Oliveto, R.: Automating Extract Class refactoring: an improved method and its evaluation. Empir. Software Eng. (2013). doi:10.1007/s10664-013-9256-x (in press)
5. Bird, C., Zimmermann, T.: Assessing the value of branches with what-if analysis. In: Proceedings of the ACM SIGSOFT International Symposium on Foundations of Software Engineering, pp. 45:1–45:11 (2012). doi:10.1145/2393596.2393648
6. Collinson, M., Monahan, B., Pym, D.: Semantics for structured systems modelling and simulation. In: Proceedings of the ICST International Conference on Simulation Tools and Techniques, pp. 34:1–34:8 (2010). doi:10.4108/ICST.SIMUTOOLS2010.8631
7. Cossette, B.E., Walker, R.J.: Seeking the ground truth: a retroactive study on the evolution and migration of software libraries. In: Proceedings of the ACM SIGSOFT International Symposium on Foundations of Software Engineering, pp. 55:1–55:11 (2012). doi:10.1145/2393596.2393661

8. Erzberger, C., Prein, G.: Triangulation: validity and empirically-based hypothesis construction. Qual. Quan. **31**(2), 141–154 (1997). doi:10.1023/A:1004249313062

9. Feinstein, A.H., Cannon, H.M.: Constructs of simulation evaluation. Simulat. Gaming **33**(4), 425–440 (2002). doi:10.1177/1046878102238606

10. Foss, T., Stensrud, E., Kitchenham, B., Myrtveit, I.: A simulation study of the model evaluation criterion MMRE. IEEE Trans. Software Eng. **29**(11), 985–995 (2003). doi:10.1109/TSE.2003.1245300

11. Hlupic, V., Irani, Z., Paul, R.J.: Evaluation framework for simulation software. Int. J. Adv. Manuf. Technol. **15**(5), 366–382 (1999). doi:10.1007/s001700050079

12. Holmes, R., Ratchford, T., Robillard, M., Walker, R.J.: Automatically recommending triage decisions for pragmatic reuse tasks. In: Proceedings of the IEEE/ACM International Conference on Automated Software Engineering, pp. 397–408 (2009). doi:10.1109/ASE.2009.65

13. Holmes, R., Walker, R.J.: Customized awareness: recommending relevant external change events. In: Proceedings of the ACM/IEEE International Conference on Software Engineering, pp. 465–474 (2010). doi:10.1145/1806799.1806867

14. Holmes, R., Walker, R.J.: Systematizing pragmatic software reuse. ACM Trans. Software Eng. Methodol. **21**(4), 20:1–20:44 (2012). doi:10.1145/2377656.2377657

15. Holmes, R., Walker, R.J., Murphy, G.C.: Approximate structural context matching: an approach to recommend relevant examples. IEEE Trans. Software Eng. **32**(12), 952–970 (2006). doi:10.1109/TSE.2006.117

16. Hughes, R.I.G.: The Ising model, computer simulation, and universal physics. In: Morgan, M.S., Morrison, M. (eds.) Models as Mediators: Perspectives on Natural and Social Science, No. 52 in Ideas in Context, Chap. 5. Cambridge University Press, Cambridge (1999). doi:10.1017/CBO9780511660108.006

17. Kelley, J.F.: An iterative design methodology for user-friendly natural language office information applications. ACM Trans. Inform. Syst. **2**(1), 26–41 (1984). doi:10.1145/357417.357420

18. Kim, S., Zimmermann, T., Whitehead Jr., E.J., Zeller, A.: Predicting faults from cached history. In: Proceedings of the ACM/IEEE International Conference on Software Engineering, pp. 489–498 (2007). doi:10.1109/ICSE.2007.66

19. Kononenko, O., Dietrich, D., Sharma, R., Holmes, R.: Automatically locating relevant programming help online. In: Proceedings of the IEEE Symposium on Visual Languages and Human-Centric Computing, pp. 127–134 (2012). doi:10.1109/VLHCC.2012.6344497

20. Marcus, A., Poshyvanyk, D., Ferenc, R.: Using the conceptual cohesion of classes for fault prediction in object-oriented systems. IEEE Trans. Software Eng. **34**(2), 287–300 (2008). doi:10.1109/TSE.2007.70768

21. Matejka, J., Li, W., Grossman, T., Fitzmaurice, G.: CommunityCommands: command recommendations for software applications. In: Proceedings of the ACM Symposium on User Interface Software and Technology, pp. 193–202 (2009). doi:10.1145/1622176.1622214

22. Mosteller, F.: A k-sample slippage test for an extreme population. Ann. Math. Stat. **19**(1), 58–65 (1948). doi:10.1214/aoms/1177730290

23. Murphy-Hill, E., Jiresal, R., Murphy, G.C.: Improving software developers' fluency by recommending development environment commands. In: Proceedings of the ACM SIGSOFT International Symposium on Foundations of Software Engineering, pp. 42:1–42:11 (2012). doi:10.1145/2393596.2393645

24. Murphy-Hill, E., Murphy, G.C.: Recommendation delivery: getting the user interface just right. In: Robillard, M., Maalej, W., Walker, R.J., Zimmermann, T. (eds.) Recommendation Systems in Software Engineering, Chap. 9. Springer, New York (2014)

25. Robillard, M.P.: Topology analysis of software dependencies. ACM Trans. Software Eng. Methodol. **17**(4), 18:1–18:36 (2008). doi:10.1145/13487689.13487691

26. Robillard, M., Walker, R.J.: An introduction to recommendation systems in software engineering. In: Robillard, M., Maalej, W., Walker, R.J., Zimmermann, T. (eds.) Recommendation Systems in Software Engineering, Chap. 1. Springer, New York (2014)

27. Robillard, M.P., Walker, R.J., Zimmermann, T.: Recommendation systems for software engineering. IEEE Software **27**(4), 80–86 (2010). doi:10.1109/MS.2009.161

28. Said, A., Tikk, D., Cremonesi, P.: Benchmarking: a methodology for ensuring the relative quality of recommendation systems in software engineering. In: Robillard, M., Maalej, W., Walker, R.J., Zimmermann, T. (eds.) Recommendation Systems in Software Engineering, Chap. 11. Springer, New York (2014)
29. Sánchez, P.J.: Fundamentals of simulation modeling. In: Proceedings of the Winter Simulation Conference, pp. 54–62 (2007). doi:10.1109/WSC.2007.4419588
30. Sebastiani, F.: Machine learning in automated text categorization. ACM Comput. Surv. **34**(1), 1–47 (2002). doi:10.1145/505282.505283
31. Shepperd, M., Kadoda, G.: Using simulation to evaluate prediction techniques. In: Proceedings of the IEEE International Symposium on Software Metrics, pp. 349–359 (2001). doi:10.1109/METRIC.2001.915542
32. Teorey, T.J., Merten, A.G.: Considerations on the level of detail in simulation. In: Proceedings of the Symposium on Simulation of Computer Systems, pp. 137–143 (1973)
33. Tosun Mısırlı, A., Bener, A., Çağlayan, B., Çalıklı, G., Turhan, B.: Field studies: a methodology for construction and evaluation of recommendation systems in software engineering. In: Robillard, M., Maalej, W., Walker, R.J., Zimmermann, T. (eds.) Recommendation Systems in Software Engineering, Chap. 13. Springer, New York (2014)
34. van Rijsbergen, C.J.: Information Retrieval. 2nd edn. Butterworth–Heinemann, London (1979)
35. Winsberg, E.: Simulated experiments: methodology for a virtual world. Philos. Sci. **70**(1), 105–125 (2003). doi:10.1086/367872
36. Ye, Y., Yamamoto, Y., Nakakoji, K., Nishinaka, Y., Asada, M.: Searching the library and asking the peers: learning to use Java APIs on demand. In: Proceedings of the International Symposium on Principles and Practice of Programming in Java, pp. 41–50 (2007). doi:10.1145/1294325.1294332
37. Zimmermann, T., Weißgerber, P., Diehl, S., Zeller, A.: Mining version histories to guide software changes. IEEE Trans. Software Eng. **31**(6), 429–445 (2005). doi:10.1109/TSE.2005.72

Chapter 13
Field Studies

A Methodology for Construction and Evaluation of Recommendation Systems in Software Engineering

Ayşe Tosun Mısırlı, Ayşe Bener, Bora Çağlayan, Gül Çalıklı, and Burak Turhan

Abstract One way to implement and evaluate the effectiveness of recommendation systems in software engineering is to conduct field studies. Field studies are important as they are the extension of laboratory experiments into real-life situations of organizations and/or society. They bring greater realism to the phenomena that are under study. However, field studies require following a rigorous research approach with many challenges attached, such as difficulties in implementing the research design, achieving sufficient control, replication, validity, and reliability. In practice, another challenge is to find organizations who are prepared to be studied. In this chapter, we provide a step-by-step process for the construction and deployment of recommendation systems in software engineering in the field. We also emphasize three main challenges (organizational, data, design) encountered during field studies, both in general and specifically with respect to software organizations.

13.1 Introduction

A *field study* is defined as a study that takes place in the natural environment of the subject of the study rather than in a laboratory environment; it involves observations, experiments, and interactions with participants. Field studies are a well-established

A. Tosun Mısırlı (✉) • B. Turhan
University of Oulu, Oulu, Finland
e-mail: ayse.tosunmisirli@oulu.fi; burak.turhan@oulu.fi

A. Bener • G. Çalıklı
Ryerson University, Toronto, ON, Canada
e-mail: ayse.bener@ryerson.ca; gul.calikli@ryerson.ca

B. Çağlayan
Boğaziçi University, Istanbul, Turkey
e-mail: bora.caglayan@boun.edu.tr

M.P. Robillard et al. (eds.), *Recommendation Systems in Software Engineering*, DOI 10.1007/978-3-642-45135-5_13, © Springer-Verlag Berlin Heidelberg 2014

research methodology in the social sciences. Field studies focus on what really matters in setting the research agenda [22]; in this sense, field studies are critical to understand the problems encountered in practice to come up with solutions that can be turned into action by the practitioners.

This chapter presents a guide for conducting field studies in order to build and evaluate recommendation systems in software engineering. Section 13.2 explains why field studies are important for software engineering research, what their benefits are in the context of recommendation systems, and how field studies should be designed in terms of research worldviews, methodologies and data collection and analysis methods. Section 13.3 provides a recipe for the reader who is interested in building and deploying a recommendation system in a software organization by explaining the main phases to be completed, and considerations regarding each phase. Section 13.4 dives into the phases by discussing potential challenges that can be encountered during each of them and providing solutions used in previous field studies. During the completion of each phase, we explain one or two examples in detail from previous field studies. In Sect. 13.5, we mention potential threats to the validity and reliability of results in a field study. Finally, Sect. 13.6 summarizes the chapter and provides suggestions for future field studies.

13.2 Understanding the Problem in the Field

Software development is a domain that involves complex interactions among the *product*, the *process* that enables the creation of the product, and the *people* who create the product and follow the process that takes place. In this complex environment, there are many uncertainties about which we need to concern ourselves: software continuously changes, and as it changes, it becomes increasingly unstructured; software engineering is difficult, merely because the product is flexible, intangible, and complex [45]. On the other hand, software engineering is one of the rare fields where academic research overlaps with the needs of industry. Depending on the research question, a field study in a software organization may involve observing people or processes, reviewing code or documentation, collecting metrics, interviewing people, and making a qualitative, quantitative, or mixed analysis.

Software engineering is challenging by its nature, and it is the very same nature that makes software engineering a data-rich domain in terms of the artifacts and decisions made daily. Therefore, there are already many recommendation systems to assist software professionals in various activities, and new ones keep emerging to address the needs arising from the ever evolving, complex, and heterogeneous nature of software systems [35, 36]. Recommendation systems in software organizations are built to support decision making under uncertainty and to ease the delivery of a task or a process. The output of a recommendation system is used by all levels of a development team to overcome technical challenges, that is, to efficiently manage/organize technical resources, to improve the quality of the work, and to find and solve problems in the process or in the code itself. As recommendation systems mature, they provide comprehensive insight about the corporate history through various data analysis techniques. In this sense, recommendation systems for software engineering are good examples of field studies in this domain.

Conducting field studies is advantageous both for researchers and software practitioners. With field studies, researchers are able to understand the domain and the main challenges for practitioners during software development, to collect real data, and to propose simple solutions through different types of recommendation systems (depending on the problem). Practitioners, on the other hand, can benefit from field studies, more specifically from the outputs of field studies in the form of recommendation systems, measurement repositories, etc. These systems can address common problems (e.g., code completion [5]), as well as specific problems (e.g., prediction of code fragments that require performance improvement [18]) faced by software practitioners in the field, and guide them in cases where the experience of the user is insufficient to make a justified decision, or the required data processing is intractable/infeasible in terms of time and resources.

In general, the benefit of recommendation systems in software engineering is the reduction of time and effort needed for accomplishing the task at hand. Depending on the specific problem, this saving can vary from a scale of minutes (e.g., API discoverability [14], DebugAdvisor [2]) to months (e.g., performance debugging [18]). In addition to this direct benefit, recommendation systems also have indirect benefits during field usage, for example, increased developer productivity [5], faster development and maintenance cycles [14, 18], improved bug fixing [2], more accurate fault localization [3], and reduced workload and information overload [23].

Designing and conducting a field study needs to follow a consistent process. Below, we briefly explain this process for researchers who would like to initiate a field study in a software organization, as well as for practitioners who are the main participants of a field study in deciding the research methodology and data collection methods.

13.2.1 Research Philosophies

The research process involves deciding on which methodologies and methods to be employed and how a researcher would justify the choice and use of the methodologies and methods. One proposal for a framework has been made that combines methods, methodologies, and epistemologies [10]. *Method* is defined as the techniques or procedures used to gather and analyze data related to research questions or hypotheses. *Methodology* is defined as the strategy, plan of action, process, or design behind the choice and use of particular methods, and linking the choice and use of methods to the desired outcomes. *Theoretical perspective* is the philosophical stance informing the methodology, thus providing a context for the process and grounding its logic and criteria. *Epistemology* is the theory of knowledge embedded in the theoretical perspective and thereby in the methodology. In other words, epistemology will underlie the entire research process and govern the particular theoretical perspective selected. The theoretical perspective will be implicit in research questions, and it constrains the methodology, which is then followed by the usage of methods that are consistent with the methodology.

Some researchers refer to epistemology by using different terms. Some call it "worldviews," meaning "a basic set of beliefs that guide action" [9, p. 6] and [15, p. 17]. These worldviews are often shaped by the discipline area in which the researchers are interested or by past research experiences. The worldviews will lead to embracing a qualitative, quantitative, or mixed approach in the research. Table 13.1 presents different classifications of worldviews, research methodologies, and their corresponding methods. It also presents examples from software engineering for different research designs.

Before any empirical research begins, the researcher needs to decide what worldview should be used depending on the nature of the research question of interest. The researcher then decides which methodology to employ, consistent with the worldview that also embeds the theoretical perspective. Next, the researchers chooses the research methods to be used that are consistent with the methodology. In empirical software engineering research, if a *constructivist* approach is taken, the researcher formulates a hypothesis or question to test, then observes the situation, abstracts observations into data, then analyzes the data, and draws conclusions with respect to the tested hypothesis. In building a recommendation system for software engineering, if a *qualitative* approach is chosen, the researcher would observe how software teams work, attempt to understand the processes, collect data through interviews, interpret the data gathered, and then build a recommendation system to help practitioners determine the project cost or understand the reasons for a defect/issue so that the recommendation system creates an agenda for change in the process or team structure, or both.

There are four types of worldviews: *post-positivist, constructivist, advocacy/participatory*, and *pragmatic* [9]. Post-positivists hold a deterministic philosophy in which the problem reflects the need to identify and assess the causes that influence outcomes. Positivist research is mainly used in the natural sciences and engineering, including software engineering. Factual information in software engineering helps organizations to establish controls, policies, and procedures.

The constructivist worldview, on the other hand, seeks a deeper understanding of the world, and produces subjective and varied outcomes based on interpretations of social systems, that is, people, their actions, and interactions with each other [4].

Advocacy is a research paradigm that aims to address the shortcomings of the constructivist approach to initiate changes in favor of under-represented (marginalized) groups in the society. In other words, the advocacy approach requires that the outcome of research should have an action agenda to change the lives of participants, institutions, and researchers [9].

Finally, pragmatism is problem-centered and derives from the real world's practice-oriented inquires. It is not committed to any one system of reality or philosophy. Researchers believe that the truth is what works at the time and they look both to "what" and "how" to do research [9]. Practices for conducting research based on each of these worldviews are summarized in Table 13.1.

Table 13.1 Research designs as epistemologies, methodologies, and methods [adapted from 9]

Research Design		
Qualitative	Quantitative	Mixed
Epistemology		
Constructivist, Advocacy/ Participatory	Post-positivist	Pragmatic
Methodology		
Phenomenology; grounded theory; ethnography; case study; narrative	Surveys; experiments	Sequential; concurrent; transformative
Method		
Open-ended questions; emerging approaches; text data	Closed-ended questions; predetermined approaches; numeric data	Both open- and closed-ended questions; both emerging and predetermined approaches & both quantitative and qualitative data and analysis
Research practices		
<ul><li>Position the research</li><li>Collect participant meanings</li><li>Affect the study by personal values</li><li>Study the context/ setting of participants</li><li>Validate the accuracy of findings</li><li>Interpret data</li><li>Create agenda for change/reform</li><li>Collaborate with participants</li></ul>	<ul><li>Test and verify theories/explanations</li><li>Identify variables to study</li><li>Interrelate variables in questions/ hypotheses</li><li>Uses standards of validity and reliability</li><li>Observe & measure numerically</li><li>Avoid bias</li><li>Employ statistical methods</li></ul>	<ul><li>Collect quantitative and qualitative data</li><li>Develop rationale for mixing</li><li>Integrate the data at different stages of inquiry</li><li>Present visual representations of the studied methods</li><li>Employ the practices of both qualitative & quantitative research</li></ul>
Example implementations in software engineering research		
Cost/Development effort estimation models; Rule-based models	Predictive models using regression analysis or data mining	Hybrid Bayesian models; Case-based reasoning

13.2.2 Research Methodologies

There are three kinds of research design: *qualitative*, *quantitative*, or *mixed* [9].

Qualitative research is a means to explore and gather in-depth understanding about the phenomena or human behavior [9]. In qualitative research, there is a complex and real-world setting for the research. The subject is a participant in the research process. Research design evolves, and the researcher is inside the setting.

The emphasis is on validity of the research. *Case studies, narrative approaches, grounded theory studies,* and *phenomenology* are research methodologies that follow a qualitative approach (Table 13.1). In software engineering, case studies are popularly used among other qualitative approaches in order to study a contemporary phenomenon in its real-life setting [55]. Case studies require the access to rich and valuable information collected from a variety of data sources so that their outcomes would reflect domain knowledge.

Quantitative research is a means to test theories or examine causal relationships among variables [9]. In quantitative research, there is a controlled setting for research, and the subject is an object of the research. The research design is fixed and the researcher is outside of the setting. The emphasis is on reliability and generalizability of the results. *Experiments* and *surveys* are quantitative research methodologies, both of which are well recognized in software engineering research [55].

Mixed research incorporates the elements of both qualitative and quantitative approaches in order to overcome the limitations of a single research methodology, that is, neutralize or cancel the biases in a single methodology with others [9]. Researchers may identify participants to study or research questions with one method (e.g., a general survey conducted with a large development team), and use the findings to ask the right questions for another method (e.g., a case study via in-depth interviews with a small group). Alternatively, qualitative and quantitative data collection methods can be merged into one database, or analysis can be made to support quantitative data with qualitative findings [9]. *Sequential, transformative,* and *concurrent* are three mixed strategies proposed so far in social sciences.

Field studies in the context of building recommendation systems in software engineering should aim to understand the field in detail, define the problem, and then propose the right solution for the problem at hand. Tight controls as in the case of experiments might be counterproductive in this context. Thus, qualitative approaches—such as case studies—are adopted more than experiments and surveys in software engineering [19] in order to help build local models, so that local insights can be further combined with quantitative approaches, that is, statistics, data mining, to generalize for other settings.

For a more detailed explanation of research methodologies used in software engineering, we suggest examining the book on experimentation in software engineering by Wohlin et al. [55].

13.2.3 Research Methods

Research methods involve data collection, analysis, interpretation, and presentation of results. Depending on the methodology chosen by the researcher, the research method will differ. Quantitative methods require that empirical investigation be based on statistical, mathematical models, and computational techniques. The interpretation of data and its analysis change based on the size of data.

For recommendation systems requiring data mining on large datasets, we recommend reading the explanation by Menzies [30] in Chap. 3; for those using small amounts of data for which heuristics should be utilized in place of online data mining, we suggest reading the explanation by Inozemtseva et al. [21] in Chap. 4. Qualitative methods, on the other hand, are based on observations, interviews, and surveys with open-ended questions to find themes and patterns for interpretation. For a complete list of data collection methods in qualitative research, we recommend examining the article by Seaman [37].

In summary, selecting a particular research design is based on the research problem. If the problem calls for explanation or theory testing, then a quantitative approach is appropriate. If the problem calls for exploration and understanding of the phenomena, then a qualitative approach is appropriate. If the problem is such that one approach alone would not be sufficient to address, then mixed methods are appropriate [9]. Field studies in the context of recommendation systems may employ either research design. In the literature, both quantitative and qualitative research design is employed in building recommendation systems. In many cases, a recommendation system takes quantitative and qualitative data, uses data mining techniques, and predictive analytics, or localized techniques with heuristics to make a recommendation and then the system is further calibrated with expert feedback (qualitative data again). During calibration, the system and expert (developer, tester, manager, etc.) work in collaboration to better deal with the complexities of current systems [39].

13.3   Conducting Field Studies: Step-by-Step Design Process

In a field study, a recommendation system typically goes through several iterations of four steps: (1) planning and negotiation, (2) data collection and analysis, (3) technology development (initial prototype of the recommendation system) and calibration, and (4) deployment. In this section, we describe these steps and how each step evolves in a field study by giving real examples from the literature. Table 13.2 summarizes four main phases for building recommendation systems in software engineering, and important tasks that need to be considered for each phase in conducting field studies.

13.3.1   Phase I: Planning and Negotiation

Field studies are particularly useful in the context of recommendation systems, since the aim is to propose a practical solution to a real challenge in software organizations, and ultimately, to deploy this solution as a tool into existing systems. To accomplish this, the initial steps of a field study identify business goals,

Table 13.2 Main considerations within phases of construction and evaluation of recommendation systems in software engineering

Phase I: Planning and negotiation
- Identify business goals, challenges during software development
- Align objectives of field study with practitioners' expectations
- Define roles and responsibilities of parties
- Initial negotiation between researchers and practitioners on the input, functionality, output of the recommendation system
Phase II: Data collection & analysis
- Select data collection technique(s): Direct, indirect, independent, or mixed
- Select data analysis technique(s) depending on the selection above: Quantitative, qualitative, or mixed
- Involvement of software practitioners into the discussion of data accuracy and analysis
Phase III: Building the recommendation system and local calibration
- Design the system in terms of input, recommendation engine, output
- Implement the recommendation engine
- Select the type of evaluation: Offline, user stories, online
Phase IV: Deployment of the recommendation system
- Integrate with existing systems: Standalone or plug-in
- Improve the system continuously through user feedback: Post-usage calibration

long-term and short-term strategies, and the challenges in a software organization. Then, these business goals should be mapped explicitly to research questions.

During this step, direct interaction with software practitioners is essential. Interactions through brainstorming sessions, formal or informal interviews, and observations of existing development environments that show patterns of activities, goals, and rationales are reasonable to understand the needs of practitioners.

In one longitudinal field study [47], a defect prediction model was built for a large scale software organization in order to improve software quality by effectively allocating testing resources. The researchers initially had project planning meetings (so-called kick-off meetings) with the senior management, project leads, and the members of development team to identify business needs and challenges in the development life cycle. The research goals of the field study were also aligned with management expectations, and the roles and responsibilities of both parties (researchers and practitioners) were clearly defined.

In another field study [31] in a large software development organization, a recommendation system was built to assign people throughout large software development tasks with respect to their expertise. At the beginning, interviews were held with geographically distributed development groups in order to learn the existing problem and their expectations on a recommendation system. Based on the interviews, the researchers realized that the existing techniques for finding experts were highly uncertain and time consuming, and that they imposed a burden on certain individuals (often, the software architects). So, a simple recommendation system to locate the obvious expert was not desired. After initial interviews, the objectives of this recommendation system (called *Expertise Browser*) were set as assigning experts to tasks quickly without imposing a burden on a few individuals, and guiding users to find alternatives when some experts are not available.

After identifying the problem, negotiation with practitioners should be made regarding the input required to feed the recommendation system, functionalities of the system, the output given as a recommendation, and a detailed plan, that is, the time that will be spent for data collection, analysis, and deployment. Field studies require frequent communication between researchers and practitioners in every step, such as data collection, building the recommendation engine, and reporting with an interface. To avoid disappointment or dissatisfaction about the final output, initial project planning meetings should be taken seriously.

13.3.2 Phase II: Data Collection and Analysis

Data Collection Strategies. Different data collection strategies are possible, depending on the research approach selected (qualitative versus quantitative), and research questions defined before conducting a field study. *Direct, indirect,* and *independent* data collection strategies differ from each other in terms of how much contact is required between researchers and practitioners [40].

Direct techniques require a direct, and often the highest amount of, interaction with the practitioners, and hence they require more resources even though the volume of data collected with these techniques is often small to medium [40]. Focus groups, interviews, and questionnaires are three, among many, direct data collection techniques, all of which are commonly used during the construction and evaluation of recommendation systems in software engineering.

Focus groups are very similar to brainstorming sessions, but there is a focus on a particular issue rather than generating as many ideas as possible [40]. Moderators control the groups and make sure that everyone has the opportunity to participate and share their opinions on that particular issue. Interviews are usually more controlled than focus groups because the conversation between the researcher and the respondent are often bounded by a set of questions. Interviews can provide additional information if the researcher follows open-ended questions that allow more interaction with the practitioners. Questionnaires, on the other hand, are administered based on carefully written and ordered sets of questions [40].

Direct techniques are often applied either in Phase I to get general information about the process, the product, and the people involved (see examples in Sect. 13.3.1) or in Phase III to evaluate prototypes of recommendation systems based on the assessment of practitioners (e.g., Sibyl [1]), or during both phases (e.g., Expertise Browser [31]).

Indirect techniques, on the other hand, help researchers to gather data through instrumenting systems that the development team actively uses (e.g., how frequently a tool is used, the timing underlying different activities, the commands developers write). These techniques require very little time from software practitioners and hence, they are appropriate for longitudinal studies.

There are also independent techniques that aim to collect the output and by-products of development without any intervention by software practitioners. Examples of such outputs are source code and documentation, whereas examples of by-products are work requests, change logs, and build and configuration management tools (data repositories). Data collected through independent techniques can be then transformed to inputs of recommendation systems.

Recommendation systems in software engineering have become more popular with the usage of publicly available data, such as source code and other repositories, often collected via indirect and independent techniques [36]. With the adoption of common software development interfaces, such as Bugzilla for issue management, and Eclipse as a development and tool integration platform, it has become easier to adopt indirect and independent techniques during Phase II in field studies. Some examples of recommendation systems for which examples of independent techniques, that is, embedded plug-ins for Eclipse, were used for data collection can be found in Robillard et al. [36].

In field studies, it may be more cost-effective to implement standalone technologies that would seamlessly connect to instrumenting systems and by-products of development in software organizations, and extract required data for the construction of a recommendation system. These technologies help reducing additional communication costs between different plug-ins and tools. *Dione* is an example of a standalone tool that is designed to serve this purpose in software engineering [6]: Dione collects raw data from multiple sources, that is, source code bases, version control systems, and issue repositories, and transforms the data into metrics representing software artifacts related to process, product, and people aspects.

In summary, it is recommended to follow a mixed data collection approach in the construction and calibration of recommendation systems in software engineering. For example, *Sibyl* is a recommendation system that was built in a field study to reduce time and effort required to evaluate the importance or priority of a bug report, and to decide which product component it affects as well as which developer to assign that report [1]. The data used to build initial prototype of Sibyl were collected through a web interface for Bugzilla, and the accuracy and usefulness of recommendations were evaluated based on questionnaires with four development teams. Authors selected questionnaires over interviews due to the fact that there was not much possibility for direct interaction with the teams. Another example for the usage of focus groups to tailor the recommendations based on domain specific information gathered from developers can be seen elsewhere [17].

Data Analysis Techniques. Both qualitative and quantitative data analysis techniques are widely used in conducting any type of empirical software engineering research. Qualitative data analysis techniques are used for exploratory, confirmatory, or grounded theory studies and for visualization [40, Chap. 2], whereas quantitative data analysis techniques can be used for description, comparison, or prediction [40, Chap. 6].

In field studies, depending on research questions and data collection methodology, researchers should choose data analysis techniques that are best suited.

If *direct* techniques are used in the form of interviews, questionnaires, etc., rigorous analysis is necessary and it often requires more time and effort than expected (e.g., transforming all responses in a survey to measurable units). In this case, researchers also have the possibility to perform data analysis in parallel with data collection as soon as significant amount of data has been collected [40]. However, if *indirect* or *independent* techniques are chosen, depending on the research questions and hypotheses formed at the beginning of research, quantitative analysis techniques, such as appropriate statistical tests (considering distributional assumptions of data) and data cleaning algorithms (noise detection or removal) should be used [55].

As a final point, in the context of recommendation systems, it is generally more important and useful to discuss the results of data analysis with practitioners in the field. Practitioners can tell researchers whether analysis results are accurate portrayals of the existing situation or whether there are potential outliers or noise in the original data. This also helps researchers choose appropriate analysis techniques and algorithms when building the systems.

For a more detailed explanation of data analysis, we suggest reading the book by Yin [57] to examine its role in case study research; the books by Wohlin et al. [55] and Shull et al. [40] to study quantitative versus qualitative techniques in software engineering; or the article by Lethbridge et al. [25] to choose a data collection method in field studies and to decide the best analysis techniques by considering the advantages and disadvantages of the selected method.

13.3.3   Phase III: Building the Recommendation System and Local Calibration

Before building a recommendation system in the field, researchers should rigorously work on the design in terms of input provided to the system, the output that will be produced, and the engine that is the core part of the system calculating the recommendations. In this section, we define these dimensions and give examples about their implementation from recommendation systems in the field.

Robillard et al. [36] define input and output dimensions as follows:

- *Input* is the context of a recommendation system that is provided by the user explicitly or extracted from system implicitly.
- *Output* is the recommendation that will be produced by the system, and it can have two types: *pull mode* (for reactive recommenders), that is, producing the output when it is requested by the developer (run only when the user asks for it); or *push mode* (for proactive recommenders), that is, producing continuous output (continuous and up-to-date feedback as new data come).

In a field study, input and output modes are often specified through initial negotiations with practitioners, that is, based on real users' specific needs, how much novelty or risk they are seeking, and in what granularity or frequency they want to get recommendations. However, these can be rough estimates at Phase I, or subject to change during Phase III (calibration) based on practitioners' experimentation with the system and opinions after usage.

The recommendation engine, on the other hand, is the real intelligence provided by the researchers during Phase III. This dimension mainly consists of data gathering and analysis, implementation of a model with predictive power, and selection of a ranking algorithm that systematically lists recommendations from the most valuable to the least. The engine can be evaluated in several ways [38]: *offline, user studies, online*. Selection among these evaluation techniques are based on the availability of necessary data or the infrastructure in a field setting.

Offline. This type of evaluation is done without user interaction, using existing datasets from public data repositories, open source systems, or using a pre-collected dataset from a software organization. The accuracy of the system is initially evaluated during offline experiments. In doing so, researchers assume that the data available are similar enough to what will be provided after the system is deployed. Offline experiments are useful to test a set of candidate algorithms with a lower cost compared to the other ways of experimentation. For example, simulations are held offline to evaluate recommendation systems by using a repository data (preferably real data from an organization) that contain both examples of real queries and the corresponding examples of expected recommendations (Walker and Holmes [54] provide more information on simulation in Chap. 12).

User Studies. These are conducted by selecting a small group of subjects to use the system or a pilot project (component) among many projects (components of a large project) in a software organization. While users perform their tasks, researchers may record users' behaviors, collect statistics, and gather feedback after the usage [38]. For example, a recommender called APIExplorer was evaluated through a pilot study with 32 sessions of participants [14]. APIExplorer was developed as a feature in Eclipse IDE that discovers and recommends methods or types in APIs, which are not directly reachable from the type a developer is currently working with. During the pilot usage, real-life APIs were selected to see how the model would perform, were it deployed, and it was calibrated with both algorithm refinements and user feedback. Other examples of user studies can be found for the selection of a set of components of a large project [47], and for the usage of focus groups to tailor the recommendations [17].

Online. This type of evaluation is done when the system is used by real users that perform real tasks. It is most trustworthy to compare different ranking algorithms online, learn the users' context or evaluate the user interface, yet not very easy to apply with real users in a software organization. Online evaluations are by nature feasible only after the recommendation system is deployed. For example, a code completion recommendation system can incorporate two different algorithms (providing two different recommendations) and randomly switch between them while a developer is using the IDE, and at the same the system can log user interaction, that is, to learn which algorithm's recommendation is useful, for calibration. One example for online experiments is reported by Ye and Fischer [56], in which they proposed a recommendation system called CodeBroker to locate and propose reusable components by using developers' partially written programs. The system builds user models, and implicitly updates them when it observes that software developers reuse a component during programming. Components that have been reused more than X times by a developer are considered well known and they are not recommended to the developer any more.

13.3.4   Phase IV: Deployment of the Recommendation System

Deployment is hard and it requires trust in the recommendation system. Therefore, we have seen very few examples in the literature describing evaluations based on deployed models and real usage after conducting a field study. The main points in the process of deployment can be summarized as follows:

Integration with Existing Systems.   Depending on the design of a recommendation system, it can operate either independently as a standalone application [6] or as a plugin [14, 23] closely attached to development environments or other systems that are actively used in a software organization. In both cases, the system should be fed with data required for operation. Therefore, as the first step before deployment, all systems which a recommendation system communicates with should be clarified by discussing with development teams. Often, this communication has been handled during a pilot study, but scaling up to large systems may need a new design. For example, a recommendation system called *Mylar* was designed to improve the productivity by monitoring programmer's activity through filtered and ranked information that is presented in a development environment [23]. The deployed version of Mylar (renamed Mylyn) has currently been in use by thousands of programmers. During integration, a bridge architecture was designed to handle the communication and interaction between existing systems, historical storage, and Mylyn. The performance of the communication between systems was also improved by generating mechanisms for storing and collapsing interaction logs.

Post-usage Calibration.   Even though a recommendation system is calibrated multiple times during offline experiments and user studies, new requests may arise after deployment. In the case of Mylyn [23], the authors realized that daily usage revealed uncovered tasks and misconceptions about how developers work on related tasks. So, they calibrated the tool by adding clusters to cover related tasks. In other systems, such as DebugAdvisor deployed in Microsoft [2], the tool can be calibrated based on both qualitative feedback gathered from users through surveys and quantitative data collected from usage logs. In DebugAdvisor, the authors let users flag recommendations of the tool as useful or not through a user interface, and the system automatically self-adjusts in future recommendations. As mentioned earlier, online experiments are intended to calibrate a recommendation system in real time, which can only be done after the system is deployed. Thus, data stored in logs as users select, rank, or filter some of the recommendations (e.g., CodeBroker [56]) can be used to calibrate the deployed system simultaneously compared to post-usage feedback in the form of surveys.

13.4   Challenges in Conducting Field Studies

During the step-by-step process required to build a recommendation system in a real setting, researchers can encounter several challenges that may slow down or interrupt the activities. These challenges can be classified into three: *organizational challenges*, *data collection and quality challenges*, and *design challenges*.

In this section, we give examples for these challenges at each step of the recommendation system building process.

13.4.1   Organizational Challenges

Organizational challenges reveal themselves mainly in the form of resistance by software teams to actions needed of them (conducting interviews, surveys with the team, or asking manual work from the team) for building recommendation systems; or in the form of cultural issues, effect of size, or software development methodology used that would affect the process of building such systems.

Phase I

Initial meetings with senior management are essential to define business needs and to negotiate about the recommendation system. However, it is not sufficient to convince only senior management in software organizations. The success of a field study highly depends on the willingness of participants from all levels (e.g., project managers, designers, analysts, developers, and testers) who take part during construction, calibration, and usage of a recommendation system. Technical staff are more likely to know about software artifacts that are actively used during development (e.g., tools, usage logs, documentation, configuration management systems) that are also required to build a recommendation system. Moreover, recommendation systems often target the development team as real users, and hence, their initial motivation and knowledge about the context, process, and possible risks would ease the construction and deployment of these systems. A large kick-off meeting consisting of software engineers, that is, designers, analysts, developers and testers, junior and senior managers as well as researchers is necessary to overcome these challenges in initiating a field study. It is crucial that the recommendation system aims to make life easier for software engineers (e.g., analysts, designers, developers, testers, etc.). Otherwise, it is impossible to integrate the usage of a recommendation system into a company's development lifecycle, even if senior management approves the recommendation system during initial meetings. It is very likely that resistance of developers toward the usage of the recommendation system will affect the decisions of senior management in the long run. Therefore, while building recommendation systems, a "bottom-up" (from development team to managers) approach should be preferred over a "top-down" (from managers to team) approach.

A recommendation system will be useful only if it provides solutions for company's existing and significant software engineering problems. Therefore, identification of these problems is crucial for the success of the field study through interviews, questionnaires, and focus groups. Below, we summarize potential challenges regarding these techniques during Phase I:

Scheduling a Meeting. It is often challenging to schedule a focus group, or one-to-one interviews due to the busy schedules of developers. Managerial support usually helps the researchers to solve such problems. Developers should be informed about the importance of these meetings as a chance to express their needs, and to point out major challenges in their daily tasks. Alternatively, questionnaires can be conducted online, and hence, developers have the freedom to respond to the questions during their spare time.

Meeting Agenda. Initial meetings, or interviews can become too unfocused, unless the moderator is well trained. People may have the tendency toward remembering events that are meaningful to them, or tasks that they spent more conscious effort than others (e.g., [25]), or with which they are more experienced. For instance, according to a test lead, allocation of testing resources may be a more significant issue compared to others. On the other hand, from senior management's point of view, the most significant problem may be the cost estimation of a software project. To avoid general discussions, the main problem that will be addressed in a recommendation system should be clearly specified. Researchers can also employ multiple methods, such as questionnaires, interviews, observation/shadowing, and investigation of quantitative data from work databases, to mitigate potential problems due to biased data, that is, triangulation [40].

Selection of Participants. Another issue arises due to the fact that only a subset of the development team will be able to present in these meetings; this is called *convenience sampling* [55]. Software engineers and managers who are voluntarily involved in these meetings may cause a self-selection bias [25, 40] because they may have different characteristics from the whole population in a software organization. Therefore, problems indicated by these participants may not reflect a company's actual software engineering problems. Conflicts arising due to selection of participants can be resolved through the analysis of company's annual reports, and by consulting senior managers in the organization.

Phase II

Data collection techniques, which are employed to build recommendation systems, generally involve analysis of documents, source code, and history logs that are obtained from work databases and configuration management systems. Yet, there are situations when recommendation systems may also require human intervention, that is, direct or indirect intervention from real users, especially for evaluating the systems or further calibration. In such situations, user opinions can be collected through questionnaires and interviews. However, interviews are costly and time consuming. Prior to interviews, appointments need to be scheduled, and usually the researcher needs to spend a lot of time in the field to collect responses of practitioners. Software engineers, on the other hand, will exhibit resistance to such interviews due to their heavy workloads and tight schedules while rushing for the next release of the software product.

Another issue arising from organizational challenges is the "missing data problem". Data collected to feed the recommendation system might be partially or completely missing in the field, or there might be no defined process inside the development life cycle that force developers to manually enter comments and required information into the company's work databases, such as configuration management systems. For instance, recommendation systems that predict software defect proneness might suffer from lack of information regarding defective files in organizations where changes (commits) in the version management system are not matched with bugs. In such cases, researchers may propose a process change in software development lifecycle in order to handle missing data [47]. However, it is still very likely that development team would not volunteer to increase their daily workload, which may lead to termination of such projects [48].

In large software engineering organizations, the work performed by software engineers is often managed carefully through problem reporting, change requests, and configuration management systems. The rest of the information (e.g., descriptions and comments) needs to be entered into systems manually. When there is little control over the quantity and quality of manually entered information, it is very likely to have empty data-entry forms. Moreover, some fields might be filled in different ways by different developers. Comments entered by developers might contain cryptic abbreviations, which would be expected to form a consistent picture only in the minds of the software engineers who originally wrote them. In such cases, one solution would be to consult the comment owners. However, there are also some situations when a record is old, or the software engineer who worked on it is no longer available. Then, data cleaning techniques should be employed to filter these records from the training data of the recommendation system (see Chap. 3 [30]).

Phase III

A successful recommendation system should align with the goals of the software organization. During Phase III, developers should work with practitioners to ensure this alignment. In this section, we discuss the challenges related to the development methodology, organization size, and culture of the organization that may affect Phases III and IV of a recommendation system.

Software Development Methodologies. In order to align with organizational goals, a recommender should target one or more parts of a development methodology and provide a cost effective alternative by automating or reducing the workload related to those parts. The employed software development methodology provides clues for solving some of the concerns of the organization. It should be noted that the particular implementation of a methodology in an organization may differ significantly from its textbook definition. Therefore, it is beneficial to observe the actual setting, or at least the most relevant phase related to the recommendation system.

Release cycles and development phases change dramatically between iterative/agile and waterfall-like methodologies [45]. In traditional methodologies, design, development and testing are clearly separated at least in theory. In this case, providing detailed reports to guide and increase the efficiency of the next phase may be beneficial. However, in agile development, software phases tend to overlap with each other, and instant recommendations during the iterations may be a better approach compared to recommendations for each phase.

An example of such approaches is RASCAL [29], a recommendation system developed to propose reusable code snippets from the source code repository. The authors initially discussed various shortcomings of the agile methodology, such as lack of support materials and documentation in agile projects. Afterwards, they showed how their recommendation system addresses these shortcomings by proposing reusable snippets in the source code to developers with no support documents.

Organization Size. Size (the number of people involved) is an important characteristic of groups, organizations, and communities in which social behavior occurs. Size is also an indicator about the complexity of an organization [13].

Organization size may affect the organizational needs in several ways. The complexity that emerges with size hinders the capacity of the organization to change fast. Every small change may be politically challenged by cliques that attempt to keep the status quo [12]. These political challenges may complicate getting organizational data to calibrate the recommender and setting up (implementing and integrating) in software organizations. In such cases, trust metrics may be defined for a recommendation system to estimate its real value for an organization [28].

Organizational Culture. Culture is a broad term with different definitions proposed by different sociologists. For instance, Gudykunst et al. [16] defines culture as the systems of knowledge shared by a relatively large group of people.

In order to build a successful recommendation system, one should understand the organization's systems of knowledge, that is, the organizational culture. Organizational culture may affect the knowledge needs and user interface expectations. For this reason, Chen and Pu [8] propose a survey-based approach to understand the key organizational characteristics before building a recommendation system.

Hu [20] defines five dimensions in the organizational culture. Three of the proposed dimensions affect the capacity of a change in an organization:

Term Orientation.   Term orientation is the relative importance of future for an organization. Long-term-oriented organizations attach more importance to the future, and foster pragmatic values oriented toward rewards, including persistence, saving and capacity for adaptation. In short-term-oriented organizations, values promoted are related to the past and the present, such as steadiness and respect for tradition. Long-term-oriented organizations introduce new ideas to the organization, such as a new recommendation system, relatively easier than short-term-oriented organizations. Field studies who successfully implemented a recommendation system in software organizations are often conducted with long-term-oriented organizations, but such organizational characteristics have not been mentioned in many field studies.

Uncertainty Avoidance Index.   Uncertainty avoidance index defines the capacity and willingness of organizations to deal with an uncertain environment. Uncertainty avoidance index may affect the expectation of a company from a recommendation system. Organizations with high uncertainty avoidance index try to minimize the occurrence of unknown and unusual circumstances and to proceed with careful changes step by step by planning and by implementing rules, laws and regulations. In contrast, low uncertainty avoidance organizations accept and feel comfortable in unstructured situations or changeable environments and try to have as few rules as possible.

Power Distance Index (PDI).   Power distance is the extent to which the less powerful members of organizations accept and expect that power is distributed unequally. Organizations with high PDI depend on the decisions of a few influential people. In these organizations, the number of people that must be convinced about the benefit of a recommendation system is low, but if the influential people leave, there is a risk of losing support entirely. On the other hand, organizations with low PDI tend to make the decisions collaboratively. In these organizations, convincing the entire organization about the benefits of a recommendation system is harder, but the risk of employee turnover affecting the support is low.

Phase IV

The main goal of recommendation systems in software engineering is to help developers through decision making by intelligently narrowing down all possible alternatives to solve a specific problem, and providing simple, easy-to-use and actionable recommendations. While doing that, recommendation systems should communicate with existing systems to collect data, analyze patterns, run its prediction engine, store results and report through a user-friendly interface. Unfortunately, due to complexity of the engine and operations, these systems can become too complex and cumbersome.

Besides, these systems often require calibration, in the form of updating the input (data) or adjusting the granularity of the output, at several times during their usage. However, in many software organizations, there is almost no personnel qualified as data analysts, who can understand the underlying mechanism of recommendation systems, evaluate outputs, and decide when to update input data, how to improve the performance, and to take actions accordingly. The combination of lack of experts in software organizations and complex and heavy systems affects not only the deployment phase, but also the post-deployment/usage phase. Possible solutions to these challenges can be to design systems with simple and actionable inputs as well as self-adjustable (automatic calibration) based on new data or user feedback.

Even when the precision of a recommendation system is high and reliable, users in a software organization may not trust the recommendations [32]. Thus, they may not feel like the recommendations are useful to help them solve some of their daily challenges. To increase trust, and hence, usage of these systems, software professionals offered some solutions, such as simulating social interactions between peers in a recommendation system, or giving recommendations based on what peers in development teams do or other experts do [32].

13.4.2 Data Challenges

Data challenges are potential problems that can be encountered while accessing data repositories, or related to the quality or accuracy of data that are extracted from these information sources.

Phase II

"Security and privacy issues" are very likely to arise since building recommendation systems requires access to instrumenting systems and by-products of software organizations, such as source code, documentation, and configuration management systems. Organizations may not be willing to share such data with researchers due to security and privacy issues. Therefore, during initial meetings and discussions, solutions should be found to collect data without violating the company's privacy and security policies. For instance, one or two people from the company's technical staff can be trained to extract required data from available resources to share it anonymously with researchers.

In addition to being related to organizational challenges, the "missing data problem" can also be categorized as a data challenge. Even if organizational challenges are resolved, that is, the development team agrees upon a change in the development process, it will take time to collect enough data to build a recommendation system.

For example, in Tosun et al. [47], the data collection step was problematic at the beginning since changes in the version control systems were not properly matched with bug reports. The researchers called for an emergency meeting with senior managers and the development team to explain the problem and its effects on building a recommendation system to predict pre-release software defects. After this meeting, a process change has been adopted, initially at pilot projects, such that developers have to provide the issue ID and additional comments about the reason of change, when they make a commit to the version control system. However, since data collection would take significant amount of time, in order to minimize time loss, the researchers proposed an alternative solution. This alternative solution was using cross-company (CC) data [50] in order to build a prototype recommendation system. In other words, a two-phase approach was employed: (1) the researchers used imported CC data, which were filtered via the k-nearest neighborhood (kNN) algorithm, to build the recommendation system; and (2) the organization started a data collection program. Phase two commenced when there was enough local data, namely "within company" (WC), to build the final system. During phase two, the organization would switch to new defect predictors learned from the WC data.

In the empirical software engineering literature, some imputation methods have been employed to handle the missing data problem in cost estimation models [7, 33, 46, 51, 52]. Imputing means to fill missing values by considering the underlying missing value mechanism [26]. In many cases, data are missing due to high data collection costs [11]. Expectation maximization methods, such as EMMI and EMSI, are very powerful imputation techniques such that the recommendation systems built with imputed data can still achieve very high accuracy rates [26, 52].

13.4.3 Design Challenges

Finally, design challenges are related to issues—which should be considered before building a recommendation system—affecting the performance, usability, and reliability of its output.

Phase III

There are many potential design challenges during the building phase of recommendation systems. However, very few field studies mention these challenges. In this section, we provide a partial list of common challenges based on prior studies on the design of recommendation systems:

Scaling Challenges.   Large organizations tend to have complex and large software repositories and hence, dedicated specialists for configuration management. Large software repositories provide rich input data to recommendation systems, yet cause different challenges during feeding the system with historical data. A system tested on a 100 kLOC repository developed by 5 people may not work for a 10 MLOC repository with multiple branches and 10+ years of development history developed by 1,000 people. Scalability is an important challenge for recommendation systems just like any other software. Some algorithms scale easily while others fail dramatically when scaled even on the most advanced hardware. On the other hand, data storage needs may get very high in a real usage scenario or number of concurrent users may freeze the system. If the recommendation system runs on a client machine, scalability problems may force the developer to terminate the application rather than wait for a response. It is easier to address possible scalability issues during the design phase of recommendation systems in software engineering. Client–server workload distribution, multimachine scaling availability, and data storage estimation are some of these issues that must be considered in order to avoid scalability problems [27].

Data Privacy Challenges.   Privacy is a common concern for everyone in the digital age. There should be a frank explanation of what the recommendation system can and will do with the extracted data in order to avoid the privacy concerns. If a clear privacy statement is not in effect, people may think of the software as a modern Big Brother microphone even for the most innocent of recommendation systems. Therefore, every recommendation system should have a clear and transparent data privacy policy [34].

Usability Challenges.   Usability is a common issue for software systems. A recommendation system should be easy to configure and should provide actionable outputs. Visualization, live notifications, and a user-friendly interface may dramatically affect the usage of a system. In this regard, observing work patterns of the real users of a recommendation system, and early mock-up designs help researchers to test and improve the usability of the system [24].

Excessive Localization Challenges.   Specific artificial scenarios may overestimate the model performance during beta testing. User trust in a recommendation system may significantly degrade if the system fails in very common, simple scenarios in reality [38].

Phase IV

While the design of recommendation systems in terms of input, output, and the engine was explained earlier, a redesign approach may be needed before deployment. During this process, researchers often come across challenges, such as scalability, privacy, robustness, and adaptivity [38]. Privacy in terms of data and user profiles and scalability have already been discussed in Sects. 13.4.1 and 13.4.2. Robustness is necessary to provide stability in the presence of fake information provided by developers. Sometimes, developers may try to fake such systems to see how they behave in the presence of noisy or wrong data. Another situation can be providing stability of the system under conditions when there are lots of user requests. Before deployment, tests are done with a small set of practitioners, and hence, the system may not operate properly when its client runs on hundreds of developer machines.

Adaptivity is another issue related with rapid changes or shifts in the input data provided to recommendation systems. In general, recommendation systems should adapt themselves to unusual events, like a system recommending news to readers may shift its focus for a short period of time due to a disaster [38]. In software engineering, a large-scale project with many connected components may produce a lot more development logs than usual, and hence it may require different recommendations on topics, such as failure-proneness or reusable components. In such cases, a recommendations system should adapt itself to such large amounts of data through filtering or adjustments in existing algorithms. In some cases, additional offline experiments can also be conducted to compare different algorithms.

13.5   Methodological Issues

In empirical software engineering research, research design should be consistent and follow certain protocols depending on the research methodology. In this section, we mention potential threats that must be addressed in a field study in order to increase the validity and reliability of results. It must be noted that there are many aspects that need to be considered in an empirical research depending on the methodology (e.g., survey in an organization, field experiments for comparing different approaches, multiple case studies), and hence we suggest that the reader study the empirical software engineering literature [e.g., 22, 53, 55].

While building a system, tool, or experimenting on a new technique in the field, it may not be necessary to derive general conclusions. However, depending on the experimentation type (e.g., online experiments, offline experiments, user studies), possible threats to the validity of the results should be considered as early as possible, generally at the planning phase. For example, when an initial prototype of a system is going to be built using offline experiments, internal, construct, and conclusion validity should be considered [55, p. 102]. Or when a qualitative analysis as a case study is conducted to make early analysis on the prototype, case study protocols, hypothesis analysis, and other factors should be considered [57]. If researchers aim to achieve more general conclusions based on multiple case studies or the field usage, external validity issues should be considered [55]. Moreover, research design with cause and effect constructs should be selected by considering replication of the same design on different settings [40, p. 365].

Field studies require involvement of human subjects, in addition to collection of information that can help identifying individuals through examination of software artifacts (e.g., source code and documents). Therefore, ethical issues should be taken into consideration. Researchers who do not follow mandated ethical guidelines, risk losing the cooperation or honesty of participants [41], as well as losing access to funding and other resources [42]. In the empirical software engineering literature, there are some guidelines to help researchers deal with ethical issues while conducting field studies [e.g., 43, 44, 53].

In a field study, there is one major issue affecting the whole process from planning to design of experiments or systems/tools, or from evaluation of results to deployment: researchers. It is very critical to have domain knowledge, that is, characteristics and problems of the domain, experience about organizational dynamics, or to have the ability to observe and interpret activities through qualitative and quantitative data in a field study. Researchers who aim to implement recommendation systems in real settings must combine their knowledge about empirical research methodologies with their previous knowledge about the dynamics of software development, and interpret what they observe to provide useful and practical solutions for practitioners. In addition, researchers must be careful about the impact of their own bias when preparing questionnaires, conducting surveys with practitioners, and interpreting analysis results. Shull et al. [40] briefly defines researcher bias, giving suggestions to avoid this throughout questionnaire construction.

13.6   Conclusion

In this chapter, we have discussed field studies in the context of recommendation systems in software engineering. Our aim is to guide researchers step by step in how to conduct a field study on building recommendation systems. At the beginning of this chapter, we highlighted the importance of having a research thought process and its consistency in order to put field studies into perspective. Then, we highlighted potential challenges throughout this process and suggested solutions to overcome some of these challenges in software engineering. Our research has been on building recommendation systems with industry partners for years. We have conducted many field studies, and deployed recommendation systems in industry. Some of these models/systems were successful, and some were not. The aftermath of our experiences over the years shows that conducting field studies is a rewarding experience both for researchers and practitioners. Software engineering, specifically the area of recommendation systems, is a rare topic where researchers and practitioners can work together to solve problems in the domain. We suggest that recommendation systems should be built for the "men in the field" (analyst, developer, architect, tester) as part of their routine tasks as tool support/plugin [48]. We envision that such a plugin should give reasons regarding causalities that are mapped to business objectives and hence, the output of a recommendation system should be easy to interpret and actionable. Field studies are the only way researchers can understand the domain and propose technical solutions for real needs of practitioners. We have seen that it is easy to overcome technical challenges; however, social, organizational, and cognitive challenges are the ones that make the adoption and usage of recommendation systems difficult [48]. That is why we need to conduct more field studies to explore what is out there, and how we can simplify a problem and propose simple solutions. Field studies will help us understand some of the areas that were overlooked such as modeling people aspects of software development in building recommendation systems, or combining human social interactions with code dependency structure to connect the dots.

Lack of generalizations in field studies is a long debated topic in empirical software engineering. Isolated case studies only show benefits of a recommendation system in a particular context. However, as researchers we can use the synergies of other techniques such as machine learning/data mining to find common patterns and contexts, and to make generalizations from local models. Such a combination of software engineering and machine learning can help decision makers to access enormous amounts of data for analysis and to remove errors in their thinking process. Researchers, by building recommendation systems as tools, would enable practitioners to query a huge database of different contexts and organizations for making recommendations [6, 49]. Recommendation systems should not be built as offline number crunching experiments. In order to build a theory, we need to understand the underlying concepts, and combine them with available data and models [49]. In this sense, field studies are the only way to discover concepts, assumptions, and limitations.

References

1. Anvik, J., Murphy, G.C.: Reducing the effort of bug report triage: recommenders for development-oriented decisions. ACM Trans. Software Eng. Methodol. **20**(3), 10:1–10:35 (2011). doi:10.1145/2000791.2000794
2. Ashok, B., Joy, J., Liang, H., Rajamani, S.K., Srinivasa, G., Vangala, V.: DebugAdvisor: a recommender system for debugging. In: Proceedings of the European Software Engineering Conference/ACM SIGSOFT International Symposium on Foundations of Software Engineering, pp. 373–382 (2009). doi:10.1145/1595696.1595766
3. Bakir, A., Kocaguneli, E., Tosun, A., Bener, A., Turhan, B.: Xiruxe: an intelligent fault tracking tool. In: Proceedings of the International Conference on Artificial Intelligence and Pattern Recognition, Orlando, Florida, USA, July 13–16, pp. 293–300 (2009)
4. Bener, A.B.: Risk perception, trust and credibility: a case in internet banking. Technical Report, Department of Information System, London School of Economics, London (2000)
5. Bruch, M., Monperrus, M., Mezini, M.: Learning from examples to improve code completion systems. In: Proceedings of the European Software Engineering Conference/ACM SIGSOFT International Symposium on Foundations of Software Engineering, pp. 213–222 (2009). doi:10.1145/1595696.1595728
6. Caglayan, B., Misirli, A.T., Calikli, G., Bener, A., Aytac, T., Turhan, B.: Dione: an integrated measurement and defect prediction solution. In: Proceedings of the ACM SIGSOFT International Symposium on Foundations of Software Engineering, pp. 20:1–20:2 (2012). doi:10.1145/2393596.2393619
7. Cartwright, M.H., Shepperd, M.J., Song, Q.: Dealing with missing software project data. In: Proceedings of the IEEE International Symposium on Software Metrics, pp. 154–165 (2003). doi:10.1109/METRIC.2003.1232464
8. Chen, L., Pu, P.: A cross-cultural user evaluation of product recommender interfaces. In: Proceedings of the ACM Conference on Recommender Systems, pp. 75–82 (2008). doi:10.1145/1454008.1454022

9. Creswell, J.W.: Research Design: Qualitative, Quantitative, and Mixed Methods Approaches, 3rd edn. Sage, Beverly Hills (2009)
10. Crotty, M.J.: The Foundations of Social Research: Meaning and Perspective in the Research Process. Sage, Beverly Hills (1998)
11. DeMarco, T.: Controlling Software Projects: Management, Measurement, and Estimates. Prentice Hall, Englewood Cliffs (1982)
12. DeMarco, T., Lister, T.: Peopleware: Productive Projects and Teams, 2nd edn. Dorset House, New York (1999)
13. Dewar, R., Hage, J.: Size, technology, complexity, and structural differentiation: toward a theoretical synthesis. Adm. Sci. Q. **23**(1), 111–136 (1978)
14. Duala-Ekoko, E., Robillard, M.P.: Using structure-based recommendations to facilitate discoverability in APIs. In: Proceedings of the European Conference on Object-Oriented Programming, pp. 79–104 (2011). doi:10.1007/978-3-642-22655-7_5
15. Guba, E.G.: The Paradigm Dialog. Sage, Beverly Hills (1990)
16. Gudykunst, W.B., Ting-Toomey, S., Chua, E.: Culture and Interpersonal Communication. Sage, Beverly Hills (1988)
17. Guo, Y., Seaman, C., Zazworka, N., Shull, F.: Domain-specific tailoring of code smells: an empirical study. In: Proceedings of the ACM/IEEE International Conference on Software Engineering, vol. 2, pp. 167–170 (2010). doi:10.1145/1810295.1810321
18. Han, S., Dang, Y., Ge, S., Zhang, D., Xie, T.: Performance debugging in the large via mining millions of stack traces. In: Proceedings of the ACM/IEEE International Conference on Software Engineering, pp. 145–155 (2012). doi:10.1109/ICSE.2012.6227198
19. Höfer, A., Tichy, W.F.: Status of empirical research in software engineering. In: Basili, V., Rombach, D., Schneider, K., Kitchenham, B., Pfahl, D., Selby, R.W. (eds.) Empirical Software Engineering Issues: Critical Assessment and Future Directions, pp. 10–19. Springer, Berlin (2007). doi:10.1007/978-3-540-71301-2_3
20. Hu, R.: Design and user issues in personality-based recommender systems. In: Proceedings of the ACM Conference on Recommender Systems, pp. 357–360 (2010). doi:10.1145/1864708.1864790
21. Inozemtseva, L., Holmes, R., Walker, R.J.: Recommendation systems in-the-small. In: Robillard, M., Maalej, W., Walker, R.J., Zimmermann, T. (eds.) Recommendation Systems in Software Engineering. Springer, Berlin (2014)
22. Jain, A.K., Murty, M.N., Flynn, P.J.: Data clustering: a review. ACM Comput. Surv. **31**(3), 264–323 (1999). doi:10.1145/331499.331504
23. Kersten, M., Murphy, G.C.: Using task context to improve programmer productivity. In: Proceedings of the ACM SIGSOFT International Symposium on Foundations of Software Engineering, pp. 1–11 (2006). doi:10.1145/1181775.1181777
24. Krug, S.: Don't Make Me Think: A Common Sense Approach to Web Usability, 2nd edn. New Riders, Thousand Oaks (2005)
25. Lethbridge, T.C., Sim, S.E., Singer, J.: Studying software engineers: data collection techniques for software field studies. Empir. Software Eng. **10**, 311–341 (2005). doi:10.1007/s10664-005-1290-x
26. Little, R.J., Rubin Donald, B.: Statistical Analysis with Missing Data, 2nd edn. Wiley, London (2002)
27. Liu, H.H.: Software Performance and Scalability: A Quantitative Approach. Wiley, London (2009)
28. Massa, P., Bhattacharjee, B.: Using trust in recommender systems: an experimental analysis. In: Jensen, C., Poslad, S., Dimitrakos, T. (eds.) Proceedings of the International Conference on Trust Management. Lecture Notes in Computer Science, vol. 2995, pp. 221–235 (2004). doi:10.1007/978-3-540-24747-0_17
29. McCarey, F., Ó Cinnéide, M., Kushmerick, N.: RASCAL: a recommender agent for agile reuse. Artif. Intell. Rev. **24**(3–4), 253–276 (2005). doi:10.1007/s10462-005-9012-8
30. Menzies, T.: Data mining: a tutorial. In: Robillard, M., Maalej, W., Walker, R.J., Zimmermann, T. (eds.) Recommendation Systems in Software Engineering. Springer, Berlin (2014)

31. Mockus, A., Herbsleb, J.D.: Expertise browser: a quantitative approach to identifying expertise. In: Proceedings of the ACM/IEEE International Conference on Software Engineering, pp. 503–512 (2002). doi:10.1145/581339.581401

32. Murphy, G.C., Murphy-Hill, E.: What is trust in a recommender for software development? In: Proceedings of the International Workshop on Recommendation Systems for Software Engineering, pp. 57–58 (2010). doi:10.1145/1808920.1808934

33. Myrtveit, I., Stensrud, E., Olsson, U.H.: Analyzing data sets with missing data: An empirical evaluation of imputation methods and likelihood-based methods. IEEE Trans. Software Eng. 27(11), 999–1013 (2001). doi:10.1109/32.965340

34. Ramakrishnan, N., Keller, B.J., Mirza, B.J., Grama, A.Y., Karypis, G.: Privacy risks in recommender systems. IEEE Internet Comput. 5(6), 54–62 (2001). doi:10.1109/4236.968832

35. Robillard, M., Walker, R.J.: An introduction to recommendation systems in software engineering. In: Robillard, M., Maalej, W., Walker, R.J., Zimmermann, T. (eds.) Recommendation Systems in Software Engineering. Springer, Berlin (2014)

36. Robillard, M.P., Walker, R.J., Zimmermann, T.: Recommendation systems for software engineering. IEEE Software 27(4), 80–86 (2010). doi:10.1109/MS.2009.161

37. Seaman, C.: Qualitative methods in empirical studies of software engineering. IEEE Trans. Software Eng. 24(5), 1–16 (1999). doi:10.1109/32.799955

38. Shani, G., Gunawardana, A.: Evaluating recommendation systems. In: Ricci, F., Rokach, L., Shapira, B., Kantor, P.B. (eds.) Recommender Systems Handbook, pp. 257–297. Springer, Berlin (2011). doi:10.1007/978-0-387-85820-3_8

39. Shull, F.: Research 2.0? IEEE Software 29(6), 4–8 (2012). doi:10.1109/MS.2012.164

40. Shull, F., Singer, J., Sjoberg, D.I.K. (eds.): Guide to Advanced Empirical Software Engineering. Springer, Berlin (2008). doi:10.1007/978-1-84800-044-5

41. Sieber, J.E.: Planning Ethically Responsible Research: A Guide for Students and Internal Review Boards, 1st edn. Sage, Beverly Hills (1992)

42. Sieber, J.E.: Protecting research subjects, employees and researchers: Implications for software engineering. Empir. Software Eng. 6(4), 329–341 (2001). doi:10.1023/A:1011978700481

43. Singer, J., Vinson, N.G.: Why and how research ethics matters to you: yes, you! Empir. Software Eng. 6(4), 287–290 (2001). doi:10.1023/A:1011998412776

44. Singer, J., Vinson, N.G.: Ethical issues in empirical studies of software engineering. IEEE Trans. Software Eng. 28(12), 1171–1180 (2002). doi:10.1109/TSE.2002.1158289

45. Sommerville, I.: Software Engineering, 8th edn. Addison-Wesley, Reading (2006)

46. Strike, K., El Emam, K., Madhavji, N.: Software cost estimation with incomplete data. IEEE Trans. Software Eng. 27(10), 890–908 (2001). doi:10.1109/32.935855

47. Tosun, A., Bener, A.B., Turhan, B., Menzies, T.: Practical considerations in deploying statistical methods for defect prediction: a case study within the Turkish telecommunications industry. Inf. Software Technol. 52(11), 1242–1257 (2010). doi:10.1016/j.infsof.2010.06.006

48. Tosun Misirli, A., Caglayan, B., Bener, A., Turhan, B.: A retrospective study of software analytics projects: in-depth interviews with practitioners. IEEE Software 30(5), 54–61 (2013). doi:10.1109/MS.2013.93

49. Turhan, B., Bener, A.: On combining the scattered knowledge: putting the bricks together. In: Proceedings of the International NSF Sponsored Workshop on Realizing Artificial Intelligence Synergies in Software Engineering in conjunction with ICSE, Zurich, Switzerland (2013)

50. Turhan, B., Bener, A., Menzies, T.: Nearest neighbor sampling for cross company defect predictors. In: Proceedings of the International Workshop on Defects in Large Software Systems, p. 26 (2008). doi:10.1145/1390817.1390824

51. Twala, B.: An empirical comparison of techniques for handling incomplete data using decision trees. Appl. Artif. Intell. Int. J. 23(5), 373–405 (2009). doi:10.1080/08839510902872223

52. Twala, B., Cartwright, M., Shepperd, M.: Ensemble of missing data techniques to improve software prediction accuracy. In: Proceedings of the ACM/IEEE International Conference on Software Engineering, pp. 909–912 (2006). doi:10.1145/1134285.1134449

53. Vinson, N.G., Singer, J.: A practical guide to ethical research involving humans. In: Shull, F., Singer, J., Sjøberg, D.I.K. (eds.) Guide to Advanced Empirical Software Engineering, pp. 229–256. Springer, Berlin (2008). doi:10.1007/978-1-84800-044-5_9

54. Walker, R.J., Holmes, R.: Simulation: a methodology to evaluate recommendation systems in software engineering. In: Robillard, M., Maalej, W., Walker, R.J., Zimmermann, T. (eds.) Recommendation Systems in Software Engineering. Springer, Berlin (2014)
55. Wohlin, C., Runeson, P., Host, M., Ohlsson, M.C., Regnell, B., Wesslen, A.: Experimentation in Software Engineering. Springer, Berlin (2012). doi:10.1007/978-3-642-29044-2
56. Ye, Y., Fischer, G.: Supporting reuse by delivering task-relevant and personalized information. In: Proceedings of the ACM/IEEE International Conference on Software Engineering, pp. 513–523 (2002). doi:10.1145/581339.581402
57. Yin, R.K.: Case Study Research: Design and Methods, 3rd edn. Sage, Beverly Hills (2003)

Part III
Applications

Chapter 14
Reuse-Oriented Code Recommendation Systems

Werner Janjic, Oliver Hummel, and Colin Atkinson

Abstract Effective software reuse has long been regarded as an important foundation for a more engineering-like approach to software development. Proactive recommendation systems that have the ability to unobtrusively suggest immediately applicable reuse opportunities can become a crucial step toward realizing this goal and making reuse more practical. This chapter focuses on tools that support reuse through the recommendation of source code—*reuse-oriented code recommendation systems* (ROCR). These support a large variety of common code reuse approaches from the copy-and-paste metaphor to other techniques such as automatically generating code using the knowledge gained by mining source code repositories. In this chapter, we discuss the foundations of software search and reuse, provide an overview of the main characteristics of ROCR systems, and describe how they can be built.

14.1 Introduction

Although the idea of software reuse is not new, it has yet to take off in practice. The basic problem is that the perceived benefits of systematic software reuse still do not clearly outweigh the effort, risks, and uncertainties involved. Developers are faced with the dilemma of whether to first create a detailed system design and then try to find matching coarse-grained components relatively late in the development process or to invest a great deal of effort discovering what components already

---

W. Janjic (✉) • C. Atkinson
Software-Engineering Group, University of Mannheim, Mannheim, Germany
e-mail: werner.janjic@informatik.uni-mannheim.de; atkinson@informatik.uni-mannheim.de

O. Hummel
Institute for Program Structures and Data Organization, Karlsruhe Institute of Technology, Karlsruhe, Germany
e-mail: hummel@kit.edu

M.P. Robillard et al. (eds.), *Recommendation Systems in Software Engineering*,
DOI 10.1007/978-3-642-45135-5_14, © Springer-Verlag Berlin Heidelberg 2014

exist and then try to tailor and combine them to meet the requirements. In either case, it is not always certain that all system requirements can be fulfilled and that something reusable can actually be found. It is therefore no surprise that the reuse approaches that have recently gained the most attention are *pragmatic reuse* approaches [10] that focus on the non-preplanned reuse of source code assets mainly during implementation.

Regardless of the exact motivation for reuse, researchers and practitioners have traditionally faced three main obstacles to implementing an effective reuse program for mainstream software development:

- The *repository problem* [8, 29], that is, where to find a sufficient amount of reusable material
- The *representation problem* [9], that is, how to optimally store and represent the reusable material
- The *retrieval problem* [25], that is, how to formulate and execute queries for a repository in a simple and precise manner

A great deal of progress has been made in all these areas recently (partly due to the open source "revolution" that made literally millions of potentially reusable files freely available), and new solutions to these problems laid the foundation for a new generation of *internet-scale software search engines*.

Although software search engines are an essential prerequisite for reuse recommendation tools, in their simple (mostly web-based) form they cannot be regarded as recommendation engines since they will only retrieve exactly what they are asked to retrieve. Thus, they are a necessary but not sufficient part of the whole solution; additional features would be needed to move into the realm of practical, large-scale software reuse. An ideal reuse recommendation engine would automate the whole process of searching, adapting, and evaluating reuse candidates as well as validating that they seamlessly integrate into the application under development. Obviously, in general this process becomes more challenging the larger and more complex the reuse candidates.

The main obstacle to software reuse is no longer the lack of components to reuse or the ability to retrieve them efficiently. Many projects have shown that this is feasible with modern technology [3, 11, 14, 27]. The main obstacle is rather the balance between the effort required to evaluate and incorporate components into new applications and the likely benefit (including the risk that a reuse candidate will turn out to be unsuitable). This is where code recommendation tools can come in handy. Their role is to nonintrusively and reliably find and recommend high quality code artifacts leveraging software reuse and to help developers integrate them into their systems with minimal effort.

There are different forms of recommendation system supporting different services and use cases involved in software reuse. Nevertheless, based on the generic definition of a recommendation system from Robillard et al. [28], we can define a reuse-oriented code recommendation system (ROCR[1]) as *any tool that recommends code artifacts of any kind and size for the sake of supporting reuse tasks.* In general, ROCRs are assistant tools for developers, which are seamlessly integrated into the developers' software development process and environment. Based on observations of the pros and cons of example ROCRs, we can identify a minimum set of requirements that have to be met by modern code recommendation tools to make code reuse more convenient. These "best practices" should be standard features of ROCR systems as they contribute to higher acceptance of such systems among users.

Proactive recommendation systems that unobtrusively suggest code with a high likelihood of being beneficial in a given situation provide a promising way of supporting reuse in the implementation phase of software development projects. The artifacts recommended by such systems need not just be functional production code but can include all different kinds of executable software used in the lifecycle of a project such as tests, prototypes, frameworks, libraries, or small code snippets that can be retrieved, recommended, and reused. Furthermore, a code artifact can be reused in different ways ranging from direct inclusion in a new software product to using it as an oracle to drive the software testing process [2, 17].

The remainder of this chapter discusses opportunities, challenges, and techniques associated with the creation of ROCR systems and describes the basic technologies needed to build such a system. Many examples of ROCRs have been produced, including Code Finder [8], CodeBroker [32], Strathcona [11], Prospector [22], Code Genie [21], Code Conjurer [15], and Code Recommenders [5]. Surveying all such tools is beyond the scope of this chapter; two archetypal examples (Strathcona and Code Conjurer) are outlined in Sect. 14.2. Section 14.3 describes the process of software reuse as well as the basic characteristics and range of different search services that state-of-the-art code search engines can provide. Section 14.4 takes a closer look at different forms of code-related reuse that provides the motivation for variants of code recommendation systems with different foci. It then introduces the important characteristics of these variants along with implications for their usage. Building on the provided foundations, Sect. 14.5 focuses on the implementation of a recommendation system using the open source tool Code Conjurer [14] to provide concrete examples for the discussed aspects. Finally, a discussion and some thoughts on the future of reuse recommendation technology—emphasizing open issues and current developments—are presented in the last two sections.

14.2   Introductory Examples

To provide an intuitive introduction to the subject of this chapter, we present two ROCR systems by briefly describing their background and characterizing their features. More detailed information on each of them can be found in the provided

---

[1]The acronym ROCR is meant to be pronounced "rocker."

```
public class MyClass {
  public CompilationUnit createASTFromSource(String source) {
    ASTParser.setSource(source.toCharArray());
  }
}
```

Listing 14.1 Example skeleton used to query Strathcona

literature sources. The first one, Strathcona, is a recommendation system that suggests examples of actual usage scenarios based on information extracted from existing software components, while the second, Code Conjurer, is a "classic" reuse tool that recommends reusable code in a copy-and-paste manner, leveraging a particular code search engine (Merobase).

14.2.1 Code Recommendation for API Usage with Strathcona

Strathcona is an *example recommendation tool* [11]. Instead of following the established source code reuse approaches that target component reuse, the Strathcona recommendation system focuses on the lack of documentation accompanying the wide variety of frameworks and software libraries that are used in modern software systems. The example recommender assists users by recommending usage and invocation examples relevant to the developer's context without imposing new hurdles for users such as learning a new query language. It achieves this by extracting all necessary search parameters directly from the developer's code. An illustrating example that is familiar to most developers who work within the Eclipse IDE is the question of how to create an **abstract syntax tree** (AST) from a piece of source code. A first quick look at the documentation for the **application programming interface** (API) provided by Eclipse suggests that the `setSource(...)` method of the `ASTParser` class would be helpful in achieving this goal, resulting in the developer trying to write an implementation like that in Listing 14.1.

However, the documentation does not describe the three steps necessary to complete the task, namely: (1) the parser needs to be created by using a factory method, (2) the parser needs to be made aware of the source code, and (3) the AST has to be created. Strathcona's client (provided as a plugin for Eclipse) will extract the structure of the **developer context** to identify the class, its parents, method calls, and possibly existing field declarations to form a query for its backend, where different matching heuristics can be applied. The server looks up possible example recommendations and returns the top ten examples to the recommender client; Listing 14.2 gives an example (shown in the source view, one of several presentations provided by Strathcona). The examples serve both to solve the developer's immediate problem, and to provide context about additional issues about which they may be unaware (like the possibility of setting preferences on generating bindings or on fault tolerance, as in this example).

```
public class ASTResolving {
  public static CompilationUnit createQuickFixAST(
      ICompilationUnit compilationUnit, IProgressMonitor monitor)
      {
    ASTParser astParser = ASTParser.newParser(ASTProvider.
        SHARED_AST_LEVEL);
    astParser.setSource(compilationUnit);
    astParser.setResolveBindings(true);
    astParser.setStatementsRecovery(ASTProvider.
        SHARED_AST_STATEMENT_RECOVERY);
    astParser.setBindingsRecovery(ASTProvider.
        SHARED_BINDING_RECOVERY);
    return (CompilationUnit) astParser.createAST(monitor);
  }
}
```

Listing 14.2 Example result (source view without highlighting) delivered by Strathcona

14.2.2 Code Reuse with Code Conjurer

Many developers experience the feeling when implementing a piece of code that "this must have been already implemented by someone else." It is certainly possible to find existing implementations of frequently used components by using a web-based search engine, but this is typically a haphazard process that disturbs the natural workflow of developers and requires the explicit cognitive decision to search for reusable artifacts. In most cases, attempts to use "raw" code search engines either lead to frustration because nothing reusable can be found or to a decrease in productivity since searches take too much time. Moreover, developers often miss possible reuse opportunities because they did not expect reusable artifacts to be available. To support this "classic" code reuse scenario, the Code Conjurer recommendation system nonintrusively suggests reusable artifacts by examining developers' code and autonomously querying the Merobase code search engine for results [14]. As an example, imagine a developer writing a simple text editor that requires the contents of a file to be loaded into a string object and the changes to be written back to the file. Code Conjurer can help to find a routine that does all of this based on the method declarations in the source code. For example, solely relying on the information in Listing 14.3, Code Conjurer will autonomously query Merobase for reusable artifacts without the user noticing.

Upon receiving the search results, the Code Conjurer client will then present the developer with results of the kind shown in Listing 14.4.

This code recommendation may be directly reused in the developer's project via a simple drag-and-drop action, thus imposing no additional effort on the developer related to searching and reusing code. In other words, Code Conjurer seamlessly integrates code reuse into the "natural" workflow of software developers. In addition to that, Code Conjurer integrates reuse with test-driven development: if developers

```java
public class TextDocument {
  public String loadFile(String filename) {
  }

  public void saveFile(String filename) {
  }
}
```

Listing 14.3 Example class stub used by Code Conjurer for code recommendation

```java
private String loadFile(String fName) throws Exception {
    FileReader fr = new FileReader(fName);
    BufferedReader br = new BufferedReader(fr);
    StringBuffer sb = new StringBuffer();
    String line;

    while ((line = br.readLine()) != null) {
        sb.ppend(line);
    }
    br.close();
    fr.close();

    return sb.toString();
}
```

Listing 14.4 Example result delivered by Code Conjurer

write JUnit tests before they write the actual code, Code Conjurer is able to find reusable assets that fulfill the requirements manifested in the test cases and therewith to recommend semantically matching components.

14.3 Foundations

Before a ROCR can be beneficial and reuse can actually be carried out, it is necessary to have a critical mass of potentially reusable artifacts. These artifacts need to be mined for interesting information and an effective search-engine that can efficiently support searches needs to be built. But why do developers actually want to find something reusable? The essential motivation for *software search* and *reuse* is clearly captured by a frequently-cited quotation from Krueger [19] who was strongly opposed to the continuous "reinvention of the wheel" in software development:

> Software reuse is the process of creating software systems from existing software rather than building software systems from scratch. [...] Simply stated, software reuse is using existing software artifacts during the construction of a new software system.

This simple vision was built upon the suggestions made even earlier by McIlroy [23], which are often regarded as the starting point for research in the area of software reuse. Since software reuse depends on the ability to discover reusable artifacts, it is necessary to take a closer look at software search engines that form the "backend" for most ROCR systems. In the past, the development of tools designed to support reuse has usually been preceded or accompanied by the creation of a search engine focused on the particular kind of reuse to be supported. This separation of concerns helped their developers to ensure best quality in both fields: search engines focusing on optimizing the processing of search queries and client systems providing a convenient way for users to benefit from this functionality within their development environments.

Before taking a closer look at the whys and hows of ROCRs, the following section covers the basic foundations on code reuse itself as well as some basic knowledge on software search engines, as a prerequisite for the creation of ROCR systems. In this context, the term *software search engine* is used in a broader sense than for just plain source code search since there are different categories/variants of ROCR systems and not all of them focus purely on code; some also provide automatically generated code recommendations based on the use of sophisticated data mining techniques to harvest the knowledge embedded in existing code.

14.3.1   Software Reuse Process

In the literature, there are numerous publications dealing with software reuse, its foundations, and possible improvements. For example, de Almeida et al. [7] define a comprehensive framework that cleanly describes the key ingredients for software reuse in general. Besides the need for a repository and search infrastructure, they describe a generic software reuse process and various best practices for effective software reuse. As with classical software development, for effective software reuse it is necessary to have a specification of *what* should be built or reused as it forms the foundation for a query to the search backend that looks for reusable candidates. The simplest way to do this in a search engine is the "Google approach" of looking for keywords like "getDistance int" to find a distance calculator, for example. Nevertheless, such a simple hand-crafted query does not convey much information beyond the meaning of names and will most probably lead to poor (i.e., rather imprecise) results [13].

Thus, it is necessary to improve and enrich pure name-matching with additional information from the context of the environment in which the reused asset should be integrated. An overview of the improvements in precision that can be achieved with enhanced query formulation is depicted in Table 14.1, which compares four textual software search techniques. The table illustrates that all techniques except the interface-based search deliver a large number of false-positives. Therefore, they make it hard for developers to identify concretely reusable candidates without the additional effort of examining many useless ones.

Table 14.1 Precision of code retrieval techniques [13]

	signature matching	keyword-based	name-based	interface-based
average precision	0.9%	16.3%	17.2%	53.7%
standard deviation	1.8%	21.9%	19.3%	22.4%

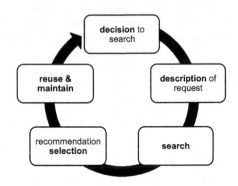

Fig. 14.1 Overview of the microprocess of software reuse. Ideally a software reuse action is followed by a new one

When the search returns a set of candidate results, these are usually not directly *fit for purpose* for various reasons such as missing dependencies or API mismatches. Thus, the process of software reuse involves their examination as well as possibly their reengineering and adaptation to support seamless integration into the developers' software projects. By reusing a previously created piece of code, the lifecycle of the reused asset is tied to that of the whole project. In other words, the incorporated code is subject to modifications or refactoring within its new environment and tests may reveal issue. All these aspects need to be reflected within a ROCR system that ideally supports the full automation of this process as well as the responses to developers' inputs.

A simplified representation of the microprocess of software reuse is depicted in Fig. 14.1. The process itself is generic and applies to manual as well as tool-supported software search and reuse. The particular elements of this process are as follows:

Decision. During a software project, developers decide to actively search for a reusable asset. Therefore, they need to decide what kind of asset they want to reuse. The different kinds of search scenarios/assets that users search for will be described in the subsequent section.

Description. Once a developer has decided to look for reusable assets, a clear description of *what* should be reused needs to be created. This specification ideally should comprise all required information that is necessary to find useful reusable assets.

Search. The description serves as the query to a search engine. Sophisticated algorithms should be able to automatically refine and adapt queries in order to filter out all useless artifacts and ensure that no useful ones are missed. This is almost impossible without tool support, as it would consume a lot of time to create a query, inspect the results, refine and re-issue the query, etc. This cycle may have to be repeated several times and is obviously not very efficient when done manually.

Selection.   From the "raw" set of search results, the developer needs to choose whether any of the results are useful and if there are different candidates that fulfill the given criteria. In that case, the developer has to select the best match from the list, which can be a very tedious task since it may involve trial uses of a large number of possible candidates. If this is carried out manually, it involves to copy of the code from the search engine, look for necessary dependencies, eventually adapt the provided interface of a reused class and finally try it out. This must be performed for every candidate in order to find the best matching one.

Reuse and Maintain.   Once a candidate has been selected for reuse and integrated into the developer's system, the microprocess of code reuse is completed. Nevertheless, the reused candidates are now part of the developer's project development lifecycle and should be subject to all the same actions and processes as the other parts of the system like testing and maintenance.

Although the microprocess of reuse is complete, Fig. 14.1 reflects that reuse should not be a one-off event but should rather be continuously applied throughout project development [e.g., 19].

14.3.2   *Software Search*

A recommendation system's ability to provide reusable code assets to the developer is mainly based on a repository of previously written code, which has been indexed and made efficiently searchable. In the past, there have been many commercial and scientific attempts to provide web-based search engines for code. Examples include Google Code Search, Koders, Krugle, Sourcerer, and Merobase. However, none of them ever reported significant numbers of users comparable to mainstream search engines. In fact, Google even shut down their code search engine in 2012, clearly illustrating that developers need some other form of support for code reuse. This is where ROCR systems become an interesting alternative to web-based search engines as they offer a large range of potential usage scenarios that are very similar to the archetypal usage scenarios of software search described by Janjic et al. [17].

Detailed understandings of the different use cases for software search have only emerged recently through studies and online surveys such as those described by Umarji et al. [30]. A prominent example from this survey is the use of search engines to provide guidance in the use of libraries—a topic that led to the creation of a couple of recommendation systems that have received significant research attention (like, e.g., Strathcona [11]) and their approaches inspired the official Eclipse Code Recommenders project.

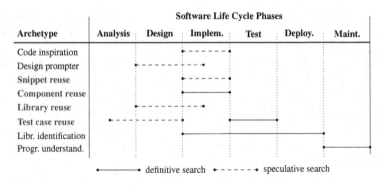

Fig. 14.2 Search scenarios in software engineering [adapted from 17]

Searches motivated by the goal of *reusing code without modification* are subject to the following four categories:

- Code snippets, wrappers or parsers
- Reusable data structures, algorithms and graphical user interface (GUI) widgets to be incorporated into an implementation
- Reusable libraries to be incorporated into an implementation
- A reusable system to be used as a starting point for an implementation

Searches motivated by the goal of *finding reference examples* are categorized by the following four categories:

- A block of code to be used as an example
- Examples for how to implement a data structure, an algorithm or a GUI widget
- Examples for how to use a library
- Looking at similar systems for ideas and inspiration

Figure 14.2 visualizes the eight archetypal search scenarios assigned to the traditional software development life cycle. Searches are grouped into speculative or definitive searches, represented by dashed or solid lines respectively. While the former are likely to occur early during the software development process, giving users an idea about how to solve particular tasks, the latter are more likely to occur late in the design and implementation phases when a concrete specification of a required component is typically available. Since our focus is source code recommendation, the tools presented in this chapter focus on recommending artifacts originating from the following four archetypal usage-scenarios of software search:

1. Snippet reuse
2. Component reuse
3. Library reuse
4. Test case reuse

Having clarified the motivation for software searches and having described concrete use cases in which they are typically applied, we deal with the characteristics of ROCRs in general in the next section.

14.4   Common Characteristics of ROCRs

In this section, we discuss common characteristics of ROCR systems. These criteria were largely distilled from previous research work capturing the "best practices" that should be considered for newly built ROCR systems. It is important to emphasize that the characteristics presented in this section are valid for all the different categories of ROCR systems that we introduce hereafter.

14.4.1   Use Case Characteristics

The term software reuse is usually associated with the integration of existing software (i.e., code) into a project under development utilizing a copy-and-paste approach to reuse [20]. This is also known as *code scavenging* when contiguous blocks of source code are copied to the new system [19]. The underlying goal of these techniques, which are known by different names and are subsumed under the term *pragmatic reuse* [10], is to copy as much code as possible from already existing projects. However, this is not the only kind of reuse that is possible. There are many other forms of software reuse like *design scavenging*, where large blocks of code are reused and subject to major internal changes. This diversity in motivation for reuse leads to different varieties of ROCR systems. ROCR systems were designed to support other forms of reuse than just to copy pre-existing code. For example, some systems recommend automatically created code fragments by leveraging knowledge from pre-existing source code or other software artifacts.

Component Reuse

The most obvious use case for a ROCR system is to present previously written code assets to developers. These artifacts may have different levels of granularity ranging from code snippets, methods, and classes up to whole subsystems and systems. A well known member of this family is Code Conjurer, which offers developers the possibility to find reusable code artifacts from the Merobase component finder [18]. When using this Eclipse plugin in its proactive mode, developers are offered suggestions for reusable methods and classes that fit into their programming context; they can simply drag-and-drop the best match into their project. By offering the possibility of automatic dependency resolution, where classes are accompanied by those classes that they make use of (e.g., by instantiation or method invocation), Code Conjurer even offers the automated reuse of (smaller) systems, which we call components in the sense of component-based software development [1].

Library Reuse

Especially within object-oriented development projects, developers constantly utilize prefabricated building blocks provided in the form of libraries by invoking some of their functionality. This is very convenient at first sight, since libraries form a cohesive piece of software that usually incorporates a lot of reusable objects with their dependencies. Although they can make the development of new software much easier, there are, however, numerous obstacles to their usage that every developer experiences on a regular basis. Questions like "how is this library used," "which objects do I need," "how are they created," and "what sequence of calls do I have to make" arise almost every time a new framework, API, or library is used. Tools like Strathcona [11] or Prospector [22] explicitly address this problem by recommending code snippets that show examples of how libraries can be used or which call sequence is necessary to transform an object from one into another type (e.g., a `File` into an `AbstractSyntaxTree`).

Test Case Reuse

Modern code search engines index vast quantities and varieties of reusable code artifacts. This also includes a large number of test cases along with production code. For instance, JUnit tests are written as plain Java code and can even be built into and shipped with a component. This opens up another form of code recommendation—the recommendation of test code for a newly created system. Appropriate recommendation techniques for JUnit test code were introduced by Janjic and Atkinson [16]. They focus on predicting the best possible "next test" based on a repository of previously written test cases and the knowledge extracted from them. Such systems do not recommend reusable code per se, but generate reusable test code by assembling the previously analyzed knowledge bound up in existing tests and their accompanied production code.

14.4.2   *Design Characteristics*

Building ROCR systems is a challenging task. Users are sensitive to the usability of such systems and the quality of the recommendations they provide. If ROCR systems do not work or behave the way that users expect them to, if they start to annoy developers with too many suggestions—especially if these are useless or incorrect—they can quickly get deactivated or uninstalled. To name an example, a "Clippy-style" intrusive user-interface will most likely cause users to dislike even the best system (see Murphy-Hill and Murphy [26] in Chap. 9), since it disturbs them in their primary tasks and forces them to additional cognitive decisions combined with additional effort (even if this only means to move/click the mouse to hide an unsuitable recommendation). Therefore, the first important characteristic of a ROCR system is how these systems should be integrated into users' development environments.

Integration and Usability

An environment for code reuse (sometimes also called *software reuse environment*) [7] should ensure full integration of the reuse process into developers' personal development processes and IDEs. To be successful, the microprocess of code reuse, which comprises similar tasks to classic software development, has to be non-intrusively adopted and integrated into the development process of the users' software projects. For a ROCR system this means that it should be unnoticeable to the developers unless it has something useful to recommend. And even in the case that the system can be helpful it must make its recommendation as clearly, concisely, and unobtrusively as possible. ROCR systems must also make it easy for developers to reject the recommendation and continue their work with no additional effort should they decide that the suggested recommendations are not of interest.

In Chap. 9, Murphy-Hill and Murphy [26] present the general characteristics of recommendation systems' user interfaces (UIs) in more detail. The characteristics presented there almost fully apply to ROCR systems as well, so we do not repeat them here.

Autonomous Background Agent

One of the key problems of web-based code search engines is that the developers usually have to leave their current working environment (i.e., the active code editor and project), which obviously interrupts their workflow. Moreover, because queries have to be defined in a completely different environment (the web-browser) without access to the immediate context of the user's work, there is very little space to formulate queries that fully match the developer's goal. In addition, developers have to understand how a search engine works to be able to formulate adequate queries that deliver precise results. And, last but not least, developers have to invest a significant amount of effort to manually evaluate and integrate reusable assets into their new applications. In particular, to try out any of the recommendations, users have to switch between (at least) two windows, and may even lose track in the process.

Reuse-oriented code recommendation systems should therefore operate in a completely automatic manner in the background, constantly monitoring the developers' actions. More specifically, an autonomous background agent process is required to observe all changes made to the system under development and to proactively decide when to trigger a search for recommendable artifacts. This should happen without any user involvement. A ROCR system may in fact be much better at timing a search than the user would be, as it can take into account different factors like network and system load, the time necessary for the creation of the recommendations, etc. If a recommendation system needs some time to examine recommendations from a list of search results for fitness for purpose or has to create the recommendations on the fly by extracting information from the search, it makes even more sense that it initiates the recommendation process at the earliest possible moment so that the recommendations are ready should the user request them.

The timing and smartness of the background agent in issuing searches and providing valuable information to the search engine is a key feature of the recommendation system. This proactive behavior therefore needs to be well designed since it plays a major role in determining how a ROCR system is perceived by its users.

Context Awareness

In order to be able to efficiently find potential recommendations, a ROCR system needs to access as much information about the development context as possible. Depending on the kind of recommendation system, context awareness may range from the immediate environment of the cursor to the source code of the whole project. As the ability to analyze context data is an important driver to the proactive behavior of a recommendation system, it should be directly embedded into a developer's working environment with full project access. This enables the aforementioned background agent to autonomously decide, when to issue searches and to deliver recommendations to the system's user.

Traditional code search engines usually offer users a small text field where they can write a short query describing the desired reusable assets. This query can either be in the form of a sequence of keywords or a sophisticated query language to provide a full description of the interface the requested assets should provide. While the former case is quite easy to use, the latter involves additional effort in the formulation of the query. As the evaluations in Table 14.1 show, keyword-based searches tend to be rather imprecise, while the interface-based ones seem to provide more precise search results. Further manual refinements of a query may make the whole searching process more time-consuming and inefficient. This can frustrate the user who, dissatisfied by this experience, might be tempted to revert to "reinventing the wheel" again.

To address this problem, context aware ROCR systems should remove the responsibility for query formulation from developers, instead performing such tasks on their behalf. In conjunction with a background agent, context awareness allows the system to perform search tasks hidden from the users' view. Depending on the kind of code recommendation system, context awareness may have different foci. One application is when a recommendation system aims at simplifying API usage of a framework or library. In this case the recommendation system is usually more interested on the immediate context of the cursor than on other classes in the developers' project. More specifically, it uses the last few lines created to issue a search based on such information as the type of a newly instantiated object (i.e., source type), method invocations associated with that object and the allocation of a method's return value to another new object (target type). Another example of the usage of context awareness can be found in Sect. 14.5 where Code Conjurer [14] is used to illustrate how code recommendation systems can be implemented.

Since the possibilities for investigating the context of the code under development are uncountable and mining it for relevant information during query formulation is a time consuming task, this process has to be carried out automatically if it is to be efficient. In Chap. 3, Menzies [24] provides further insights into the topic of data-mining.

Evaluation and Ranking

To be useful for developers, recommendation systems in general and ROCR systems in particular should not present the raw data acquired from the search backend, but should provide a meaningful ranked overview of the recommendations. The consequences of providing the user with incorrect or unordered recommendations are similar to those mentioned in the section on user-interface characteristics. Furthermore, following the ideas of Brun et al. [6], the users of a recommendation system should not be required to inspect large numbers of options before they (hopefully) find a useful asset. Therefore the IDE should autonomously perform an evaluation of the consequences of the application of the assets within the developers' context. This approach is called *speculative analysis* and it enables ROCR systems to investigate and predict the consequences of the inclusion of any of the suggested options in the developer's project.

Implementing this approach, however, only does half the work since the information obtained through speculative analysis is just a basis for ranking the recommendations. The detailed ranking criteria strongly depend on the focus of the ROCR system and need to be optimized on a domain-by-domain basis. If the reuse system is used in conjunction with a private reuse repository, it is also possible to filter out the classes and types that are in the so-called *reuse-by-memory* space of a developer and thus need not be recommended by the system [31]. This is done by CodeBroker, for instance, where the system removes recommendations well-known to the developer to save time.

Ready on Demand

The introduction to this chapter already mentioned the dilemma of *make-or-reuse* from which code search and reuse considerably suffered in the past. Yet, it is still a challenge to convince developers that this approach can make them more efficient during system development since issuing a query to a search engine typically comes at the price of interrupting their cognitive work on a program. In contrast, ROCR systems do not create this problem since they are integrated into the developers' IDE and have to be ready on demand in order to be successful. Imagine a reuse-oriented recommendation system that is tightly integrated into the code editor and which forces the developer to stop typing while it is performing a time consuming task. This would result in immediate deactivation of the system and adoption of the *make* option described above.

To avoid such situations, ROCR systems have to be ready on demand and must not cause any delays on the developer's work. If they cannot deliver any appropriate recommendations in a particular situation, they need to stay silent and invisible.

Traceability

Recommendation systems in general and code recommendation systems in particular need to be easy to understand and self-explanatory when they are used. The aforementioned requirement of integrating the system into the developer's IDE is a key consequence of this. Thereby a tight integration means as well, that the usage, the "look-and-feel" and the behavior of the recommendation system has to be similar to what developers are used to from their IDE. No new design or usage metaphors should be imposed, as they may impose an extra hurdle to the usage of the system.

Beyond plain UI design criteria, however, it is also important that the recommendations themselves are understandable and reasonable from the developers' point of view. Recommendation systems should present their information in a clean and transparent manner so the users can clearly comprehend their value. This also involves the aforementioned ranking, where users should easily understand why an option outranks others and in the ideal case should also be able to adapt the ranking criteria to their needs. When a recommendation is finally integrated into the system under development, the system should highlight that fact and should not perform any action that cannot easily be undone and observed by users in case that the reused component needs to be removed from the system at a future point in time for unforeseen reasons.

Summary

To sum up the characteristics discussed in this section, imagine a ROCR system as an adviser that provides a developer with an easy to use interface for the most sophisticated search engines and mining tools available. It must silently monitor the developers' activities and present recommendations only when there is a high likelihood that they will actually be useful and fit into the current system in an effective way. "Less is more" is probably also an important motto for a ROCR system, since too much visible activity can easily annoy users and cause them to switch off all or part of the functionality. The subsequent section discusses how to tackle this none trivial challenge from an implementation point of view.

14.5   Implementing ROCRs

After having laid out the basic foundations and having discussed the generic characteristics of ROCR systems, this section focuses on how such systems can be implemented for, and incorporated, into modern IDEs. More specifically, it provides an overview of the architectural organization of a recommender-enhanced IDE and briefly touches on the question of which technologies can be helpful to build ROCR systems.

14.5.1   Architecture of ROCR Systems

A ROCR system is supposed to automate the micro-process of code reuse. Therefore, it is not composed of a single building block, but synthesizes various modules that need to fit together in order to create a ROCR system as illustrated in Fig. 14.3. Let us take a closer look at the individual parts of such an architecture and describe them in more detail by reviewing the process steps outlined previously in Fig. 14.1:

decision $\rightarrow$ description $\rightarrow$ search $\rightarrow$ selection $\rightarrow$ reuse and maintain

While the introduction outlined this process in general terms, the following reflects it in the specific context of ROCR systems.

Decision.   A ROCR system is integrated into the IDE of the developer and includes an autonomous background agent. The system constantly monitors developer actions within the IDE and autonomously decides when it should trigger the process of searching for a recommendation.

Description.   Considering the full context of the developers' projects, the ROCR system collects all relevant information that is necessary to create a description of the current task for which it aims to create a reuse recommendation. The result is the formulation of a query that can be sent to the underlying search engine.

Search.   Utilizing the information gathered from the project, the search infrastructure performs a search for reusable assets. ROCR systems take into account that the results at that stage can only be regarded as raw material (i.e., candidates) for further examination in the subsequent selection process and are by no means ready to use.

Selection.   The selection part of the considered microprocess can also involve a *conversion* step in the context of ROCR systems. Since these are, as discussed before, not solely focused on copy-and-paste reuse of code, in this step they may also generate code recommendations from information contained in the search results. At this stage, the ROCR system automatically evaluates the set of candidates to provide a ranked selection of recommendations. Based on the information gained from this, the system should rank the recommendations and reject those that are presumably not useful to the developer. This ensures that the

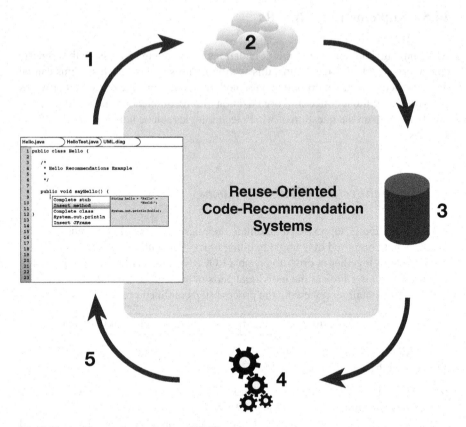

Fig. 14.3 Architectural overview on a ROCR system

users of the system get a precise list of recommendations from which they can
choose the most beneficial for their purposes.

Reuse.   When a recommendation is selected it becomes part of the developer's
system. The recommended asset is integrated into the development lifecycle
of the project and becomes subject to the same quality assurance criteria and
maintenance tasks as the rest of the system under development.

This generic architecture is naturally only an outline of the specific architecture for any single ROCR system implementation tailored to a specific usage
scenario. Possible refinement options may address the inclusion of user feedback
on recommendations, the association of the recommendations with artifacts from
the development context (e.g., for caching purposes), social aspects like reporting
of users' recommendations of reused assets to other users [e.g., 4] and reporting
changes to reused assets back to the original source, etc. Some of these aspects are
addressed in the discussion in Sect. 14.6.

14.5.2   *Implementation Outline*

As with any software system, the implementation of a ROCR system must be driven by the specification of functionality the system should deliver. In our case, this is the recommendation of any form of source code that is automatically derived from previous implementations. The Eclipse plug-in *Code Conjurer* [14] therefore serves as a reference system, which supports the reuse of Java code based on interface-based or test-driven searches. The system utilizes the Merobase code search engine[2] and recommends reusable code assets that fit into the context of the class under development. Developers may choose to integrate only portions of the recommendations into their project (by dragging a method into a class) or to reuse a class with all its dependencies and, if necessary, appropriate adapters.

Background Agent for Search Initiation

The decision when to search for recommendable assets is the responsibility of the autonomous background agent that "intelligently" triggers the recommendation process. In this context, "intelligent" means that it should perform its task in a smart way in that sense that not every event, such as a keystroke, should initiate a search and drain the resources of the development system or the network and search infrastructure.

As Code Conjurer is a Java-based, code-centric tool, its background agent is merely activated when a developer is working in a Java Editor and remains inactive otherwise. If a developer changes any structural property of the class under development, such as any of its interface defining parts, the system switches to a state where it waits for further user action within a given timeframe. If no further user interaction is observed, the system initiates a search in due consideration of the development context. Therefore, Code Conjurer examines the development context looking for tests that accompany the class under development and if it finds any, it accordingly creates a query and issues a search to the search infrastructure.

Thus, the "smartness" of a background agent for ROCR systems has several facets. It must be able to construct a query that goes beyond the information a user would provide to a code search engine, issues queries autonomously (which helps to prevent delays induced by the search infrastructure), and it considers the limitation of resources by incorporating a grace timer for user interaction. This is introduced to prevent the system from initiating too many search requests one after another that would either be carried out in parallel with minimal differences in content or would have to be frequently canceled, both resulting in a waste of resources.

---

[2]The Merobase repository of reusable assets contains approximately 2.5 million Java source files with around 22 million methods [18].

Search Infrastructure

There is an obvious synergy between search engines and recommendation systems. As previously mentioned, on the one hand practically all ROCR systems have user interfaces, which are integrated into an IDE, but need to rely on some kind of search engine (or database) as their source of information. Code search engines on the other hand are good in delivering a large amount of information, but often require relatively complex queries that need to be manually prepared by users. Hence, simply by providing a semi-automatic and context aware way of invoking search engines, recommendation systems already improve the reuse process.

To a certain extent, the creation of search engines nowadays is a straight-forward task and there are many tutorials available that describe this process in detail. Besides the use of relational databases (which, e.g., also underpinned the Sourcerer [21] code search engine), document-driven full-text databases such as Lucene or MongoDB have recently gained a lot of popularity in projects like Code Recommenders [5], Merobase [18], and Sentre [16]. Since it is very important for a recommendation system to be responsive and provide recommendations to users on an ad hoc on-demand basis, it is important that the underlying search infrastructure supports this goal.

The search infrastructure can be distributed in many different ways. If the recommendations are created from a small and static pool of data, it is possible to ship the search infrastructure with the recommendation system itself. This is, however, the least common case, since the code base from which the search indices are created usually changes rapidly (after all, it primarily consists of source code) and search infrastructure should aim to incorporate short update cycles. Therefore, it is helpful to separate the search infrastructure from the ROCR system and to locate it on a centrally maintained and operated server that provides enough resources to store the data and execute the updates as well as the searches. Additionally, another positive effect of this separation is the ability to store user feedback from the reuse process to improve the user experience of all clients.

In our exemplary implementation, Code Conjurer queries the Merobase search engine via a web service in order to receive potentially reusable code assets. Merobase itself is a web application implemented using J2EE utilizing Lucene and runs on a JBoss application server. The queries arriving at the server are translated (parsed) into the Lucene query language in order to use Lucene to drive the code search process [12]. The results of a search (which usually takes less than a second) are immediately returned to Code Conjurer for further analysis.

Selection and Ranking of Recommendations

When receiving the search results, a recommendation system should evaluate and process them before they are presented to the user. This helps to elevate the users' perception of the ROCR system and makes its application more effective and efficient. The context awareness of ROCR systems is one of the key features that make them superior to traditional search engines by enabling them, for instance, to autonomously issue queries or to evaluate the effects of accepting a recommendation before it is actually selected. In the literature, the latter is referred to as *speculative analysis* [6].

Code Conjurer supports speculative analysis, when it comes to the recommendation of JUnit test cases, that is, test code [16]. In general, there are two main ways in which this feature can be implemented for classic code recommendation:

Distance Measure. A naive measure that can be used to rank the results is a distance metric between an issued query and the results delivered by the search backend. It subsumes a comparison of the interface-description provided by the class under development with the interface-description of the elements in the result list. The smaller the deviation of a reuse candidate's interface from the developer's class' interface, the higher the ranking of the particular candidate in the list of recommendations. As an example, consider a generic class that comprises a set of methods with input parameters. If the interface-description of this class perfectly matches the interface-description of a candidate the distance between them is zero and thus the candidate will be ranked highly. However, if only the class names of the query and the candidate match, it is assigned a low ranking.

Test-Driven Reuse. The main difference between code and other (textual) documents is that code is executable. As described in the characterization of the background agent Code Conjurer therefore uses its context awareness and examines the project's workspace in order to look for test cases that have been written for the class under development. If the system is able to identify accompanying tests, they are executed against the reuse candidates and used as a means of evaluating the candidate's fitness for purpose. Thereby a set of running candidates is obtained and the system can distinguish between those that provide an interface that matches the one defined in the test and those that need an adapter for their interface in order to execute tests. In both approaches, additional metrics like LOC, cyclomatic complexity and execution times can also be used to influence the final ranking.

Convenient Integration of Recommendations

In Chap. 9, Murphy-Hill and Murphy [26] discuss the importance of an effective user-interface design and of making recommendation systems as easy to use and access as possible. This applies in particular to ROCR systems, since developers can quickly get frustrated by popup-windows or other UI effects that disturb their creative work and distract them from their main task—the creation of software. Thus, the recommendations should seamlessly integrate into the IDE and be intuitive to use as well as to not use. As mentioned before, an example of how this can be achieved is shown in Fig. 14.4, where the recommendation system is integrated into the auto-completion feature of the IDE.

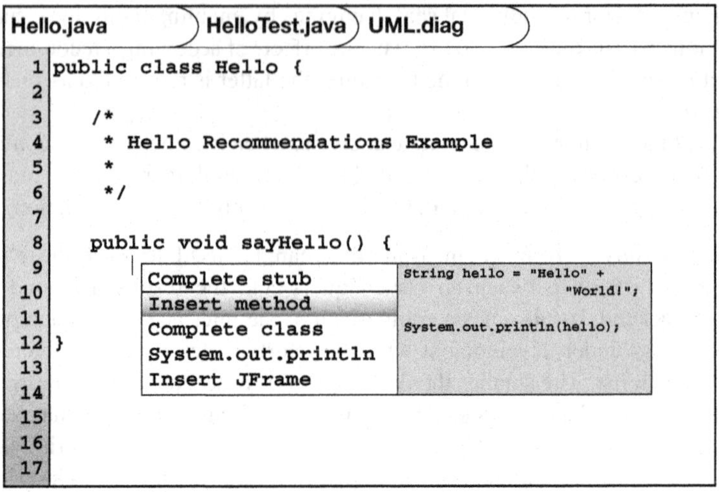

```
 Hello.java          HelloTest.java ) UML.diag

 1 public class Hello {
 2
 3     /*
 4      * Hello Recommendations Example
 5      *
 6      */
 7
 8     public void sayHello() {
 9         |
                Complete stub        String hello = "Hello" +
10                                                      "World!";
                Insert method
11
                Complete class       System.out.println(hello);
12 }            System.out.println
13              Insert JFrame
14
15
16
17
```

Fig. 14.4 Recommendations integrated in the IDE's auto-completion

In this case, the system does not distract the developer with unwanted popup windows and there is no need to activate any special views. Moreover the recommendations themselves can be examined using the arrow keys, and if users want to use the recommendation they can simply integrate it by pressing the enter key. Similarly, discarding the recommendations only involves the pressing of the escape key. This is a very convenient way for developers to interact with the system that takes into account the fact that during the creation of code users usually have their fingers on the keyboard and are not in contact with other input devices.

Code Conjurer also provides a convenient way of integrating reuse candidates in the system under development. If a reusable asset calls some functionality of another class or object, the system tries to automatically resolve this dependency and offers the developer the option of integrating that artifact into the system as well. In addition to that, it automatically adapts search results to the developer's context: if a reuse candidate in test-driven search provides a different interface to the one required by the test, an adapter generator tries to produce the necessary glue code to allow the candidate to be invoked. If this is successful, Code Conjurer supports the automatic integration of the component and the adapter into the developer's Eclipse workspace.

14.6 Discussion

The principles, practices, and examples presented in this chapter provide a basic overview of ROCR systems and their creation. Many of the characteristics described are more or less "best practices" distilled through a constant process of improvement and learning about how these systems can be improved and enriched. This short section is intended to take a look at the implications arising from the usage of ROCR systems and point to possible improvements in future systems.

14.6.1 *Responsibility*

Software development is a labor-intensive task, involving creativity and endurance. It is thus unfortunate that developers continue to invest a huge amount of effort in re-creating similar code over and over again. Software reuse, however, promises to ease this burden on developers and to provide more room for the creation of truly new components. This is, nevertheless, only one side of the coin, since the reuse of code imposes a great deal of responsibility on developers.

Although modern systems are able to perform initial checks on the reused code like filtering malicious code (as it is performed, for instance, with the server-side execution in Code Conjurer) or evaluating the system's state by applying speculative analysis, developers have to ensure that the recommended and reused code does not introduce any (possibly malicious) unwanted behavior into the system under development. Furthermore, they need to inspect the code for any potentially harmful modules and ensure that the quality of the code at least matches that of a "self-made" system.

As explained before, when integrated into the system, the recommended code assets have to adhere to the same process and quality standards as the code written by the project developers themselves. The developers must understand what the reused code does, which beside code-inspection involves reading additional comments and documentation about the component at hand and, as a side effect, identifying possibly superfluous statements, that is, dead code.

An example of how this can be implemented is provided by Code Conjurer, which supports the identification of superfluous parts of code in reuse candidates. During a test-driven search the system inspects the reuse candidates and examines whether dead-code can be removed before compilation. If the reused component executes in the context of the developer's test case, the system allows only the necessary parts of the reuse candidate to be integrated. In addition, it provides dependency resolution when necessary and cleans up imports and declarations after the code has been inserted into the new system.

Although parts of the code inspection and cleanup actions have been considered and partially implemented in contemporary tools, in general the question of quality assurance in ROCR systems has been somewhat neglected in the past.

14.6.2 *Feedback*

In the same way that context awareness is critical to the processes of query formulation and result evaluation, the collection of user created feedback is critical to the quality and improvement of future recommendations provided by ROCR

W. Janjic et al.

systems. This not only involves processing intentional feedback from users like the manual rating of a recommended asset. It also means collecting indirect feedback derived from the users' behavior and interaction with the system under development.

As an example, one aspect of (intentional) user feedback includes ideas from social media and networks. Users may want to tell other developers within their project that a particular piece of code they reused does a great job and that they recommend its reuse. Additionally, this may help to motivate other users in their decision to exploit reuse in their projects. Developers of ROCR systems are therefore encouraged to enable users to share their experience with the system and the code assets it recommends.

Information acquired from automatically collected feedback can help to adjust the process of evaluating and ranking the retrieved results of the search, which usually relies on algorithms that grade the results with the help of a set of weighted criteria. Ideally, when the system offers a list of ranked recommendations to its users, the first item on the list should be the most suitable. It may, however, happen that users pick some other candidate from the list in accordance with their own evaluation criteria. Although this is not likely to be an issue for a small list of recommendations, the users' confidence in the recommendation system would be higher if it learned from their decisions and improved its recommendations accordingly. To achieve this, the system may for instance analyze how the different internal ranking criteria can be re-adjusted to put a user's choice first in the list and store this information in a data model for learning algorithms.

In addition, it is important to keep in mind that the process of code reuse also involves the maintenance of the integrated assets. This means, that users will invariably create new versions of the code recommended by the ROCR system by fixing bugs, improving efficiency, ... These changes can be monitored and processed in order to archive the new version of the code and provide it to other users who reused an older version. In this way the overall quality of the code in software projects applying reuse should rise, since the more often a piece of code is reused the more it will be refined and cleaned of bugs.

14.6.3 Privacy

The overall application of ROCR systems, as well as the specific issue of user feedback, cannot be considered without a look at privacy issues. The following list of issues provides an impression of some problems that may arise.

Query Formulation. Whenever a ROCR system relies on a server-side search infrastructure, the queries extracted from the developer's code are sent to the network and thus potentially exposed to others. Users need to be aware of this and ROCR systems should incorporate mechanisms to establish a trust relationship with developers. The wide range of possibilities includes the anonymization of user-related information (i.e., removal of user-id, client IP, etc.) in the server logs, as well as the usage of secure connections. In addition, the query may contain sensitive data (like the inner design structure of a developer's system) that should not be stored or exposed to others.

Test-Driven Reuse.   With the availability of test-driven reuse, a balance has to be found between the aforementioned privacy rights of the users of a system and the protection against attacks. Since test-driven reuse involves the execution of the user's code (on the server infrastructure in the case of Code Conjurer), it must be possible to track the sources of possibly malicious code and intentional attacks.

Versioning.   Automating the tracking of versions may not be as easy as it seems at first sight. Reused artifacts may become deeply integrated into a developer's system and thus be tightly connected to the intellectual property of the developer and/or owning company. Since not all open-source licenses have a strong copyleft, users might not want to share their valuable code and thus it may be hard if not impossible to track changes just to the reused code without revealing more code from the project.

14.7   Conclusion

Software engineering has benefited greatly from the open source movement, especially the nascent genre of ROCR systems. Without open source it would have been much harder if not impossible to build the ROCR systems described in this chapter since a key prerequisite for them is a large set of source code that can be used as a basis for recommendations. As discussed, the ROCR systems that have been built to date index all kinds of software artifacts ranging from small code snippets, API usage, coarse-grained components and even test cases.

All tools presented in this chapter generally need to support the simplified software reuse process presented in Sect. 14.3.1 that requires developers to carry out five steps: First they need to consciously decide to reuse an artifact. Once this decision has been made they need to describe what they are looking for so that the search tool is able to find candidates for reuse. In most cases, a search will deliver a number of candidate results so that the next step is to select and tailor the most useful artifact. Once it has been integrated into the project, it needs to be maintained and updated like all other artifacts in the developer's code base.

In principle, a full-fledged ROCR system should be able to support all these steps automatically so that the developer is not burdened with them. This means that the system needs to monitor the developer's activities and must be able to independently decide when it is worthwhile to execute a search query. Obviously, it needs to be able to generate an appropriative query for the underlying search engine and rank the results according to their usefulness for a given context. Ideally, the developer then simply needs to choose the most appropriate result and the corresponding artifact is then integrated into the project automatically by the ROCR system. In a perfect world, the ROCR system would keep track of changes to the reused artifact from then on and would at least notify the developer when they occur.

A ROCR system basically consists of two main parts, namely a search engine or repository hosting the code base used to search for recommendations (the back-end if you will) and the actual recommendation engine (the front-end) that is responsible for the user and IDE interaction. If stable, generic, and mature software search engines were available it would be possible to drive several recommender systems from one search engine. However, all ROCR systems created in the last 15 years have been built in the context of academic theses and incorporated their own specialized search engine. As a result, many of them are no longer operational due to the rapid change in the landscape of code search and reuse technologies. Hence, building novel and more sustainable ROCR systems that finally accomplish the transition to a production-ready tool is still a challenge for an upcoming generation of students or industrial developers. We hope this chapter will provide them with the historical context and background knowledge needed to create them.

References

1. Atkinson, C., Bostan, P., Brenner, D., Falcone, G., Gutheil, M., Hummel, O., Juhasz, M., Stoll, D.: Modeling components and component-based systems in KobrA. In: Rausch, A., Reussner, R., Mirandola, R., Plášil, F. (eds.) The Common Component Modeling Example. Lecture Notes in Computer Science, vol. 5153, pp. 54–84. Springer, Heidelberg (2008). doi:10.1007/978-3-540-85289-6_4
2. Atkinson, C., Hummel, O., Janjic, W.: Search-enhanced testing. In: Proceedings of the ACM/IEEE International Conference on Software Engineering, pp. 880–883 (2011). doi:10.1145/1985793.1985932
3. Bajracharya, S., Ngo, T., Linstead, E., Dou, Y., Rigor, P., Baldi, P., Lopes, C.: Sourcerer: a search engine for open source code supporting structure-based search. In: Companion to the ACM SIGPLAN Conference on Object-Oriented Programming, Systems, Languages, and Applications, pp. 681–682 (2006). doi:10.1145/1176617.1176671
4. Begel, A., Phang, K.Y., Zimmermann, T.: Codebook: discovering and exploiting relationships in software repositories. In: Proceedings of the ACM/IEEE International Conference on Software Engineering, pp. 125–134 (2010). doi:10.1145/1806799.1806821
5. Bruch, M., Monperrus, M., Mezini, M.: Learning from examples to improve code completion systems. In: Proceedings of the European Software Engineering Conference/ACM SIGSOFT International Symposium on Foundations of Software Engineering, pp. 213–222 (2009). doi:10.1145/1595696.1595728
6. Brun, Y., Holmes, R., Ernst, M.D., Notkin, D.: Speculative analysis: exploring future development states of software. In: Proceedings of the FSE/SDP Workshop on the Future of Software Engineering Research, pp. 59–64 (2010). doi:10.1145/1882362.1882375
7. de Almeida, E.S., Alvaro, A., Lucrédio, D., Garcia, V., de Lemos Meira, S.R.: RiSE project: towards a robust framework for software reuse. In: Proceedings of the IEEE International Conference on Information Reuse and Integration, pp. 48–53 (2004). doi:10.1109/IRI.2004.1431435
8. Fischer, G., Henninger, S., Redmiles, D.: Cognitive tools for locating and comprehending software objects for reuse. In: Proceedings of the ACM/IEEE International Conference on Software Engineering, pp. 318–328 (1991). doi:10.1109/ICSE.1991.130658
9. Frakes, W.B., Pole, T.: An empirical study of representation methods for reusable software components. IEEE Trans. Software Eng. **20**(8), 617–630 (1994). doi:10.1109/32.310671

10. Holmes, R., Walker, R.J.: Systematizing pragmatic software reuse. ACM Trans. Software Eng.
    Meth. **21**(4), 20:1–20:44 (2012). doi:10.1145/2377656.2377657
11. Holmes, R., Walker, R.J., Murphy, G.C.: Approximate structural context matching: an
    approach to recommend relevant examples. IEEE Trans. Software Eng. **32**(12), 952–970
    (2006). doi:10.1109/TSE.2006.117
12. Hummel, O., Atkinson, C., Schumacher, M.: Artifact representation techniques for large-scale
    software search engines. In: Sim, S.E., Gallardo-Valencia, R.E. (eds.) Finding Source Code on
    the Web for Remix and Reuse. Springer, Heidelberg (2013). doi:10.1007/978-1-4614-6596-
    6_5
13. Hummel, O., Janjic, W., Atkinson, C.: Evaluating the efficiency of retrieval methods for com-
    ponent repositories. In: Proceedings of the International Conference on Software Engineering
    and Knowledge Engineering, pp. 404–409 (2007)
14. Hummel, O., Janjic, W., Atkinson, C.: Code Conjurer: pulling reusable software out of thin air.
    IEEE Software **25**(5), 45–52 (2008). doi:10.1109/MS.2008.110
15. Janjic, W.: Realising high-precision component recommendations for software-development
    environments. Diploma thesis, University of Mannheim (2007)
16. Janjic, W., Atkinson, C.: Utilizing software reuse experience for automated test recommenda-
    tion. In: Proceedings of the International Workshop on Automation of Software Test (2013)
17. Janjic, W., Hummel, O., Atkinson, C.: More archetypal usage scenarios for software search
    engines. In: Proceedings of the Workshop on Search-Driven Development: Users, Infrastruc-
    ture, Tools, and Evaluation, pp. 21–24 (2010). doi:10.1145/1809175.1809181
18. Janjic, W., Hummel, O., Schumacher, M., Atkinson, C.: An unabridged source code dataset for
    research in software reuse. In: Proceedings of the International Working Conference on Mining
    Software Repositories, pp. 339–342 (2013)
19. Krueger, C.W.: Software reuse. ACM Comput. Surv. **24**(2), 131–183 (1992).
    doi:10.1145/130844.130856
20. Lange, B.M., Moher, T.G.: Some strategies of reuse in an object-oriented programming envi-
    ronment. In: Proceedings of the ACM SIGCHI Conference on Human Factors in Computing
    Systems, pp. 69–73 (1989). doi:10.1145/67449.67465
21. Lazzarini Lemos, O.A., Bajracharya, S., Ossher, J., Masiero, P.C., Lopes, C.: A test-driven
    approach to code search and its application to the reuse of auxiliary functionality. Inform.
    Software Tech. **53**(4), 294–306 (2011). doi:10.1016/j.infsof.2010.11.009
22. Mandelin, D., Xu, L., Bodík, R., Kimelman, D.: Jungloid mining: helping to navigate the API
    jungle. In: Proceedings of the ACM SIGPLAN Conference on Programming Language Design
    and Implementation, pp. 48–61 (2005). doi:10.1145/1065010.1065018
23. McIlroy, M.D.: Mass-produced software components. In: Software Engineering: Report on a
    Conference by the NATO Science Committee, pp. 138–155 (1968)
24. Menzies, T.: Data mining: a tutorial. In: Robillard, M., Maalej, W., Walker, R.J.,
    Zimmermann, T. (eds.) Recommendation Systems in Software Engineering, Springer,
    Heidelberg, Chap. 3 (2014)
25. Mili, A., Mili, R., Mittermeir, R.T.: A survey of software reuse libraries. Ann. Software Eng.
    5, 349–414 (1998). doi:10.1023/A:1018964121953
26. Murphy-Hill, E., Murphy, G.C.: Recommendation delivery: getting the user interface just right.
    In: Robillard, M., Maalej, W., Walker, R.J., Zimmermann, T. (eds.) Recommendation Systems
    in Software Engineering, Springer, Heidelberg, Chap. 9 (2014)
27. Reiss, S.P.: Semantics-based code search. In: Proceedings of the ACM/IEEE International
    Conference on Software Engineering, pp. 243–253 (2009). doi:10.1109/ICSE.2009.5070525
28. Robillard, M.P., Walker, R.J., Zimmermann, T.: Recommendation systems for software
    engineering. IEEE Software **27**(4), 80–86 (2010). doi:10.1109/MS.2009.161
29. Seacord, R.: Software engineering component repositories. In: Proceedings of the International
    Workshop on Component-Based Software Engineering (1999)

30. Umarji, M., Sim, S.E., Lopes, C.V.: Archetypal internet-scale source code searching. In: Proceedings of the IFIP World Computer Conference, *IFIP—The International Federation for Information Processing*, vol. 275, pp. 257–263. Springer, Heidelberg (2008). doi:10.1007/978-0-387-09684-1_21

31. Ye, Y.: Supporting component-based software development with active component repository systems. Ph.D. thesis, Department of Computer Science, University of Colorado, Boulder (2001)

32. Ye, Y., Fischer, G.: Supporting reuse by delivering task-relevant and personalized information. In: Proceedings of the ACM/IEEE International Conference on Software Engineering, pp. 513–523 (2002). doi:10.1145/581339.581402

Chapter 15
Recommending Refactoring Operations in Large Software Systems

Gabriele Bavota, Andrea De Lucia, Andrian Marcus, and Rocco Oliveto

Abstract During its lifecycle, the internal structure of a software system undergoes continuous modifications. These changes push away the source code from its original design, often reducing its quality. In such cases, refactoring techniques can be applied to improve the readability and reducing the complexity of source code, to improve the architecture and provide for better software extensibility. Despite its advantages, performing refactoring in large and nontrivial software systems might be very challenging. Thus, a lot of effort has been devoted to the definition of automatic or semi-automatic approaches to support developer during software refactoring. Many of the proposed techniques are for recommending refactoring operations. In this chapter, we present *guidelines* on how to build such recommendation systems and how to evaluate them. We also highlight some of the *challenges* that exist in the field, pointing toward future research directions.

G. Bavota (✉)
University of Sannio, Benevento, Italy
e-mail: gbavota@unisannio.it

A. De Lucia
University of Salerno, Fisciano, Italy
e-mail: adelucia@unisa.it

A. Marcus
Wayne State University, Detroit, MI, USA
e-mail: amarcus@wayne.edu

R. Oliveto
University of Molise, Pesche, Italy
e-mail: rocco.oliveto@unimol.it

M.P. Robillard et al. (eds.), *Recommendation Systems in Software Engineering*,
DOI 10.1007/978-3-642-45135-5_15, © Springer-Verlag Berlin Heidelberg 2014

15.1 Introduction

During software evolution, change is the rule rather than the exception [27]. Continuous modifications in the environment and requirements drive software evolution. Unfortunately, programmers do not always have the necessary time to make sure that the changes conform to good design practices. In consequence, software quality often decreases, resulting in more difficulties in maintaining existing software [45]. Several empirical studies have provided evidence that low design quality is generally associated with lower productivity, more rework, and more effort for developers [7, 17, 21]. *Refactoring* is one solution aimed at restoring or improving the quality of the software.

Refactoring has been defined as *the process of changing a software system in such a way that it does not alter the external behavior of the code yet improves its internal structure* [27]. Different refactoring operations might improve different quality aspects of a system and help in removing *code bad smells* [27] (i.e., symptoms of possible design problems in source code) as well as *antipatterns* [19] (i.e., design flaws in source code).[1] As an example, in object-oriented systems Blob classes (i.e., large classes implementing unrelated responsibilities) can be decomposed by splitting their methods into different classes that group together strongly related responsibilities and are easier to comprehend and maintain (this operation is known as the *Extract Class* refactoring). Typical advantages of refactoring include improved readability and reduced complexity of source code, a more expressive internal architecture and better software extensibility [27]. Refactoring is advocated as a good programming practice to be continuously performed during software development and maintenance [15, 27, 32, 43]. In fact, as explained by Kerievsky [32]:

> By continuously improving the design of code, we make it easier and easier to work with. This is in sharp contrast to what typically happens: little refactoring and a great deal of attention paid to expediently adding new features. If you get into the hygienic habit of refactoring continuously, you'll find that it is easier to extend and maintain code.

Despite its advantages, performing some refactoring operations in large and non-trivial software systems can be very challenging. First, identifying refactoring opportunities in large systems is very difficult, as the design flaws are not always obvious [27]. Second, when a design problem has been identified, it is not always easy to apply the correct refactoring operation to solve it. As an example, splitting a noncohesive class into different classes with strongly related responsibilities (i.e., *Extract Class* refactoring) requires the analysis of all the methods of the original class to identify groups of methods implementing similar responsibilities, which should be grouped together in the new classes to be extracted. This task becomes

---

[1]The main difference between code smells and anti-patterns is that a code smell represents something "probably wrong" in the code, while an anti-pattern is certainly a design problem in source code. In other words, a code smell might indicate an antipattern. As example, a Large Class (bad smell) is one of the symptoms of a Blob Class (antipattern).

harder when the size of the class to split increases and its cohesion decreases. In the end, once the refactoring solution has been defined, the software engineer must apply it without changing the external behavior of the system. All these observations highlight the need for refactoring recommendation systems supporting the software engineer in (1) identifying refactoring opportunities (i.e., design flaws) and (2) designing and applying a refactoring solution.

Regarding the identification of refactoring opportunities, several approaches specialized in the identification of design flaws in source code (e.g., antipattern) have been proposed in the literature. Some of these approaches are manual [65], others apply rules based on software product metrics [33, 42, 48] or other source of information (e.g., design change-propagation [58]). These approaches are out of the scope of this chapter, since they are focused on identifying a code design problem, ignoring how to solve it through an appropriate refactoring operation. The interested reader can find a complete treatment of more recent work in this field in the paper by Moha et al. [48].

On the other hand, approaches recommending how to refactor a design flaw are the focus of this chapter.[2] By analyzing these approaches we will derive a set of guidelines for building and evaluating recommendation systems for supporting software refactoring. In addition, we will also discuss some problems that are still open, which will allow us to start tracing future research directions in the field.

15.2   Recommendation Systems for Software Refactoring

There are more than 90 different refactoring operations defined in Fowler's catalog. Most of the refactoring operations are simple source code transformations aimed at increasing source code comprehension. For example, the *Remove Parameter* refactoring removes a parameter not used anymore by the method. Most research efforts have been focused on providing support to developers when performing more complex refactoring operations, e.g., *Extract Class* [27]. In the following, we discuss the recommendation systems existing in literature classifying them on the basis of the supported refactoring operation(s). Specifically, for each approach we report: (1) the support it provides to perform the refactoring operation(s), (2) the information it exploits from source code, (3) the algorithm used, and (4) the evaluation conducted for it. Table 15.1 summarizes the refactoring operations discussed in this chapter, by classifying them based on the benefits provided to the source code.

---

[2]Note that some of these approaches are also able to identify the design flaw besides suggesting how to solve it.

Table 15.1 Refactoring operations discussed in this chapter

Name	Description	References
Improving code decomposition		
Extract class	Splits a complex and low cohesive class into new classes having a better (focused) defined set of responsibilities.	[9, 12, 25, 63]
Extract package	Splits a package grouping heterogeneous responsibilities into different cohesive packages grouping together classes implementing similar responsibilities.	[10]
Extract method	Splits a method composed by several code fragments performing different actions, into new methods, each one implementing a specific and isolable action.	[1, 67]
Improving names and location of code		
Rename method (field)	Applied when the name of a method (field) does not reveal its purpose, compromising the code comprehension.	[4]
Move method	Moves a method m from its original class to an "envied class", containing responsibilities closer to those implemented by m.	[5, 52, 62, 66]
Move class	Moves a class C from its package to a new package grouping together responsibilities closer to those implemented by C.	[3, 14]
Improving conformance with Object-Oriented programming principles		
Push down field	In a class hierarchy, moves a field only used by some subclasses from the superclass to the subclasses using it.	[51]
Pull up field	In a class hierarchy, moves a field implemented in all subclasses to their superclass.	[51]
Push down method	In a class hierarchy, moves a method only used by some subclasses from the superclass to the subclasses using it.	[51]
Pull up method	In a class hierarchy, moves a method implemented in all subclasses to their superclass.	[51]
Extract hierarchy	When a class is implementing several different behaviors in conditional statements, extract from it a hierarchy of classes, each one representing a special case.	[51]
Collapse hierarchy	Merges together a superclass and the subclass that are very similar.	[51]

15.2.1 Improving Code Decomposition

In this section, we present recommendation systems supporting refactoring operations aimed at improving code decomposition.

Extract Class Refactoring

Extract Class refactoring is used to remove the Blob antipattern [19] from a software system. A Blob is a large and complex class that centralizes the behavior of a portion of a system and only uses other classes as data holders, that is, data classes. Blobs are generally characterized by low cohesion since they implement several different responsibilities. In addition, due to the numerous dependencies with the data classes, Blobs also exhibit high levels of coupling.

Extract Class refactoring is applied to split the responsibilities implemented in a Blob class into different classes with higher cohesion (i.e., grouping together strongly related responsibilities). Blob classes have negative impact on comprehension and maintenance activities, well documented by existing empirical studies [7, 17, 21, 29, 41]. Hence, removing Blobs is a very important design improvement activity. Given the complex nature of Blob classes, performing Extract Class refactoring is a difficult task, as the following steps must be performed:

1. Analyzing the methods of the Blob class (which are often in the hundreds) to understand the main responsibility for each of them
2. Identifying clusters of methods that implement similar and related responsibilities
3. Distributing the attributes of the Blob class among the identified clusters of methods
4. Splitting the Blob class into new classes, which contain the clusters of methods and attributes
5. Ensuring that no changes in the system behavior result from this refactoring

Manual Extract Class refactoring is a difficult and error-prone task, hence research has been devoted to define approaches able to support the developers in performing it.

The Extract class refactoring can be formulated as a cluster analysis problem, where it is necessary to identify the optimal partitioning on methods in different classes. As proposed by Fokaefs et al. [26], structural dependencies between the entities of a class to be refactored (i.e., attributes and methods) can be exploited to guide the clustering process. Specifically, using this information, Fokaefs et al. [26] compute its *entity set* for each attribute (i.e., the set of methods using it). For each method they also compute the *entity set* (i.e., all the methods that are invoked by a method and all the attributes that are accessed by it). The Jaccard distance between all couples of entity sets of the class is computed in order to cluster together cohesive groups of entities that can be extracted as separate classes. The Jaccard distance is computed as follows:

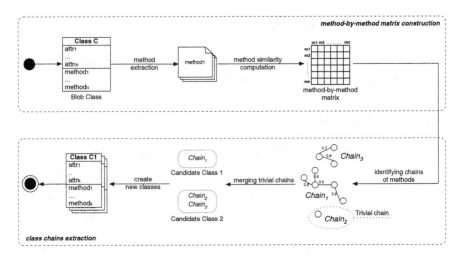

Fig. 15.1 Class extraction process based on the transitive closure of graphs proposed by Bavota et al. [9]

$$\mathrm{Jaccard}(E_i, E_j) = 1 - \frac{\mid E_i \cap E_j \mid}{\mid E_i \cup E_j \mid}$$

where E_i and E_j are two entity sets, the numerator is the number of common entities between the two sets, and the denominator is the total number of unique entities in the two sets.

The approach proposed by Fokaefs et al. [26] has been implemented as an Eclipse plug-in, called JDeodorant. The benefits of JDeodorant have been empirically analyzed. The empirical evaluation indicated that the refactoring operations provided by JDeodorant are meaningful and they approximate the refactoring operations previously performed by three developers with 67 % precision and 82 % recall.

An alternative approach for the identification of Extract class refactoring operations is based on graph theory, and in particular on the concept of a transitive closure [9]. The approach takes as input a class previously identified as a candidate for refactoring. The class is refactored following the process depicted in Fig. 15.1. In the top path of the process the candidate class is parsed to build a *method-by-method* matrix, an $n \times n$ matrix where n is the number of methods in the class to be refactored. A generic entry $c_{i,j}$ of the method-by-method matrix represents the likelihood that method m_i and method m_j should be in the same class. This likelihood is computed as a hybrid coupling measure between methods (which reflects the degree to which they are related) obtained by combining three structural and semantic measures, that is, the structural similarity between methods (SSM) [28], the call-based dependence between methods (CDM) [12], and the conceptual similarity between methods (CSM) [55]. In the SSM measure, the higher the number of instance variables shared by two methods, the higher their likelihood to be in the same class. CDM takes into account the calls performed by the methods, that is, the higher the calls interaction between two methods the higher their coupling. Finally, CSM measures the coupling between methods as their textual similarity. The conjecture is that if developers used similar terms in comments and identifiers of two methods, it is likely that they are "describing" similar responsibilities implemented by the two methods. These three measures are combined through a weighted sum in order to obtain the hybrid coupling measure mentioned before. It is worth noting that the *method-by-method* matrix is just a convenient way of storing a weighted graph representing the Blob class, where each node in the graph represents one of its methods and the weight of the edge connecting two nodes (i.e., methods) represents their coupling.

Using the information in the *method-by-method* matrix, the second part (bottom path) of the refactoring process shown in Fig. 15.1 extracts the new classes from the input Blob. In particular, a filtering step is used to remove spurious links and to split the initial graph represented in the *method-by-method* matrix into disconnected subgraphs. This is done by removing all edges in the graph having a weight lower than a defined threshold named $minCoupling$. Then, the approach identifies the chains of connected methods belonging to the different subgraphs. Each computed chain represents a class to be extracted from the original class. However, some of these chains could have a very short length (trivial chains). To avoid the extraction of classes with a very low number of methods, each trivial chain is merged with the most coupled non trivial chain to obtain the final set of classes to be extracted from the original class. The attributes of the original class are also distributed among the extracted classes according to how they are used by the methods in the new classes, that is, each attribute is assigned to the new class having the higher number of methods using it.

The approach has been implemented as an Eclipse plug-in, called ARIES [9, 11]. To better understand how ARIES works, let us assume that we are interested in refactoring the UserManagement class shown in Fig. 15.2. Given its name and its set of methods, probably the original responsibility of this class was to implement a set of operations that allow to manipulate the User entity in the database. However, during software maintenance, two new responsibilities were added to this class, that is, the management of the Teaching entity and the management of the Role entity. Figure 15.3 shows: (1) the values for the similarity measures used by the approach, that is, CDM, CSM, and SSM, in three separate matrices, and (2) how these values are combined in the *method-by-method* matrix through a weighted sum.

Figure 15.4 shows how ARIES [9, 11] extracts from the UserManagement class three new classes having better defined responsibilities than the original class. The first part of the figure shows the graph that can be obtained from the method-by-method matrix (note that the edges weighted with 0.0, that is, pairs of methods having zero coupling, are omitted), while the second part of the figure shows the connected components obtained after the matrix filtering. In this example, we arbitrarily set *minCoupling* = 0.2. Thus, all the edges having weight lower than 0.2 (that represent spurious relationships between methods) are removed from the graph. The extracted components correspond to the preliminary method chains. The third part of the figure shows the refinement of the method chains. In particular,

```
public class UserManagement {
    private static final String TABLE_USER = "user";
    private static final String TABLE_TEACHING = "teaching";
    private static final String TABLE_ROLE = "role";

    public void insertUser(User pUser){
        boolean check = checkMandatoryFieldsUser(pUser);
        String sql = "INSERT INTO " + UserManagement.TABLE_USER + " ... ";
        ...
    }
    public void updateUser(User pUser){
        boolean check = checkMandatoryFieldsUser(pUser);
        String sql = "UPDATE " + UserManagement.TABLE_USER + " ... ";
        ...
    }
    public void deleteUser(User pUser){
        String sql = "DELETE FROM " + UserManagement.TABLE_USER + " ... ";
        ...
    }
    public void existsUser(User pUser){
        String sql = "SELECT FROM " + UserManagement.TABLE_USER + " ... ";
        ...
    }
    public boolean checkMandatoryFieldsUser(User pUser){
        ...
    }
    public void insertTeaching(Teaching pTeaching){
        boolean check = checkMandatoryFieldsTeaching(pTeaching);
        String sql = "INSERT INTO " + UserManagement.TABLE_TEACHING + " ... ";
        ...
    }
    public void updateTeaching(Teaching pTeaching){
        boolean check = checkMandatoryFieldsTeaching(pTeaching);
        String sql = "UPDATE " + UserManagement.TABLE_TEACHING + " ... ";
        ...
    }
    public void deleteTeaching(Teaching pTeaching){
        String sql = "DELETE FROM " + UserManagement.TABLE_TEACHING + " ... ";
        ...
    }
    public boolean checkMandatoryFieldsTeaching(Teaching pTeaching){
        ...
    }
    public void insertRole(Role pRole){
        boolean check = checkMandatoryFieldsRole(pRole);
        String sql = "INSERT INTO " + UserManagement.TABLE_ROLE + " ... ";
        ...
    }
    public void deleteRole(Role pRole){
        String sql = "DELETE FROM " + UserManagement.TABLE_ROLE + " ... ";
        ...
    }
    public boolean checkMandatoryFieldsRole(Role pRole){
        ...
    }
}
```

Fig. 15.2 UserManagement: an example of a Blob class [9]

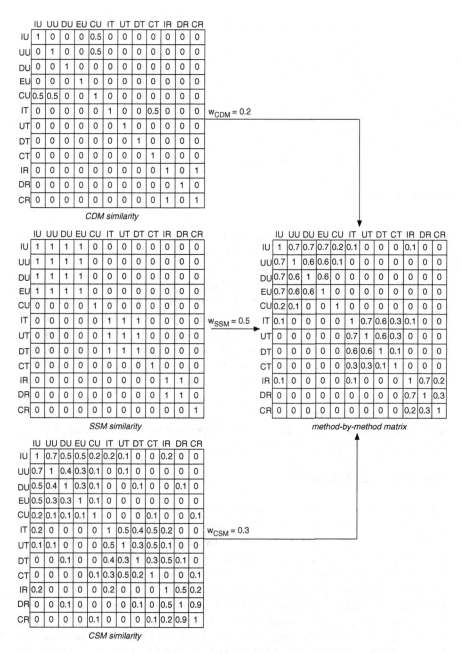

IU = insertUser - UU = updateUser - DU = deleteUser - EU = existsUser - CU = checkMandatoryFieldsUser
IT = insertTeaching - UT = updateTeaching - DT = deleteTeaching - CT = checkMandatoryFieldsTeaching
IR = insertRole - DR = deleteRole - CR = checkMandatoryFieldsRole

Fig. 15.3 Method-by-method matrix construction [9]

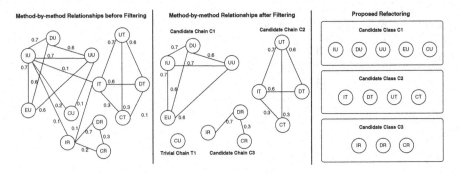

Fig. 15.4 The extraction process followed by ARIES [9, 11]

a trivial chain composed of only one method (checkUser) is added to the most coupled non trivial chain (i.e., C_1). In the end, ARIES recommends splitting the original class into three new classes.

ARIES aims at guiding the developer through the entire refactoring process. In fact, ARIES provides support for: (1) identifying Blob classes candidate for Extract Class refactoring, (2) recommending the refactoring solution (i.e., how to split the Blob class), and (3) applying the refactoring, while preserving the system behavior. The recommended refactoring solutions have been empirically evaluated through quality metrics and user studies [9] and the results show that ARIES's recommendations: (a) strongly increase the cohesion of the refactored classes without leading to significant increases in terms of coupling; (b) are considered useful by developers performing extract class refactoring; and (c) are able to approximate manually performed refactoring operations with 91 % accuracy.

Extract Package Refactoring

Extract Package refactoring is similar to Extract Class refactoring, but it acts at a different level of granularity. As it is possible to have complex classes grouping together unrelated responsibilities (i.e., Blobs), it is also possible to observe the same phenomenon at a higher granularity level: packages grouping together classes implementing unrelated responsibilities. These packages are known as "Promiscuous packages" and usually have low cohesion. The aim of Extract Package refactoring is to split a promiscuous package into different cohesive packages grouping together classes implementing similar responsibilities. Promiscuous packages often implement entire subsystems grouping together hundreds of classes. As with the Extract Class refactoring, in order to perform Extract Package refactoring, the developer needs to analyze all classes in the promiscuous package, understand their responsibilities, and group together in new packages those implementing similar things. This is a difficult and time-consuming task. To provide support for this refactoring, some of the techniques proposed for software re-modularization could be easily adapted [e.g., 47,56]. One way is to consider the classes of the promiscuous package as the entire set of classes to re-modularize and apply one of the approaches existing in literature to organize the classes into new packages (i.e., to split the promiscuous package into new ones).

Alternatively, the approach proposed by Bavota et al. [10] for identifying Extract class refactoring operations can be customized for recommending Extract Package refactoring solutions as well. Using a graph theory-based algorithm (similar to the one used for Extract Class refactoring in ARIES) it is possible to exploit structural and semantic relationship between classes to extracts chains of strongly related classes in the package to be refactored. The classes of the original package are distributed in different packages according to the extracted chains. If the number of extracted chains is one, then no re-modularization is recommended by the tool (this generally happens when the cohesion of the analyzed package is high). Otherwise, based on the extracted class chains, the approach recommends new packages with higher cohesion than the original package. Note that the aim of this approach is to suggest how to split a package (previously identified by the software engineer as a candidate for re-modularization) in smaller, more cohesive packages, while the implementation of the refactoring in the software system is left to the developer. However, it is worth noting that preserving the system behavior for refactoring operations acting at class level (like extract package refactoring) is quite simple, since it is enough to update package declarations and imports in the impacted classes (i.e., the moved ones and those using them). The evaluation of the approach has been performed on five systems. On four of them, original developers have been involved in the evaluation of the meaningfulness of the recommended refactoring operations, while on the fifth one external developers performed the same task. Overall, developers evaluated as meaningful 77 % of the recommended refactoring operations [10].

Extract Method Refactoring

The Extract Method refactoring is generally applied on methods composed by several code fragments performing different actions. In particular, code fragments implementing a specific and isolable action are extracted and grouped into a new method. Smaller methods increase the chance of code-reuse and ease code comprehension.

Identifying Extract Method refactoring opportunities is far from trivial. The analysis of the history of a software system can be worthwhile for supporting such a tasks. The conjecture is that statements in a method that change together are good candidate to be extracted from the original method aiming at creating a new independent method [44]. In order to identify the set of methods that change together, it is possible to use a weighted dependence graph (WPDG) [44], which is an extended program dependence graph (PDG) where edges are weighted based on the modification histories of the methods. Specifically, each node of the graph represents a statement of the method under analysis, while the weight of the edge that connect two statements i and j represents the likelihood that when changing i the developer also changes j. Once the WPDG is obtained, a threshold is used to distinguish which edges ought to remain or vanish. It is worth noting that eliminating edges with a weight lower than the fixed threshold results in splitting the original WPDG in several subgraphs. Then, the new methods are obtained considering every reachable path from the method entry node on the split WPDG [44].

It is clear that when historical information are not available or they are poor, it is not possible to accurately identify Extract Method refactoring operations. An alternative source of information for identify such refactoring operations can be derived by using slicing [69]. A slice is an executable subset of program statements that preserves the original behavior of the program with respect to a subset of variables of interest and at a given program point [69]. It can be computed both statically or dynamically. In the context of refactoring, fine slicing is particularly suitable for identifying Extract Method refactoring operations [1]. Fine slicing is a technique to compute executable program slices and can be used to extract noncontiguous pieces of code and untangle loops [2]. The extracted slices can be used to decompose a long method body into different methods, each with a precise responsibility.

Other than fine slicing, more sophisticated slicing-based techniques can be used to identify Extract Method refactoring operations. As proposed by Chatzigeorgiou [67], Extract Method refactoring solutions can be identified by employing two slicing techniques:

1. *A complete computation slice* is used to identify all the statements in a method affecting the computation of a given variable.
2. *An object state slice* is used to capture the statements affecting the state of a given object.

The proposed approach has been implemented as a fully automated technique in the JDeodorant Eclipse plugin. The evaluation, performed with a designer, shows that the proposed technique is able to capture slices of code implementing a distinct and independent functionality compared to the rest of the original method and thus leads to extracted methods with useful functionality.

15.2.2 Improving Names and Code Location

Other refactoring operations aimed at improving names and code locations. Concerning the former, having meaningful names for methods and fields is essential for easier code comprehension [36]. Thus, *Rename Method* (*Rename Field*) refactoring should be applied when the name of a method (field) does not reveal its purpose, compromising the code comprehension. Abebe and Tonella [4] propose an approach that could be used to support these refactorings. Their technique exploits ontological concepts and relations automatically extracted from the source code to suggest identifiers names. While the approach has not been evaluated in the context of refactoring, it represents a good starting point for *Rename Method* (*Rename Field*) recommendation systems.

Refactorings improving the location of code aim at grouping together similar responsibilities in order to ease code comprehension and maintenance. Examples of such refactoring operations are the Move Method refactoring, Move Field refactoring, and Move Class refactoring. Move Field is applied when a field is used by another class more than the class on which it is defined [27]. However, in this family of refactorings, most researchers focused on Move Method and Move Class refactoring.

Move Method Refactoring

This refactoring is targeted to solve the bad smell known in literature as "Feature Envy" [27]. This smell arises when a method seems to be more interested in a class other (known as envied class) than the one it is implemented in, e.g., the method invokes getter methods of another object many times [27]. Usually, this negatively influences the cohesion and the coupling of the class in which the method is implemented. In fact, the method suffering of feature envy reduces the cohesion of the class because it likely implements different responsibilities with respect to those implemented by the other methods of the class and increases the coupling, due to the many dependencies with methods of the envied class.

By applying the Move Method refactoring, the method is moved to the envied class. Unfortunately, not all the cases are cut-and-dried. Often a method uses features of several classes, thus the identification of the appropriate envied class (as well as the method to be moved) is not always trivial especially in large software systems [66]. For this reason, approaches to support move method refactoring have been proposed by researchers.

A simple way to identify Move Method refactoring operations can be obtained by analyzing the abstract syntax tree (AST) of a software system [5]. Specifically, for each field in a given class it is possible to determine the set of methods referencing the field by traversing the AST. If a foreign method makes too many references to a number of distinct fields, then the method should be moved into the class under analysis. An empirical evaluation of this approach—conducted on ten C++ systems—indicates that 88 % of the recommended refactorings were meaningful. Alternatively, the identification of Move Method refactoring could be formulated as an optimization problem, that is, finding a location for a specific method that optimize some quality metrics, such as cohesion and coupling [62]. Since the search space is huge, meta-heuristic search algorithms, such as Genetic Algorithms (GA), can be used to find a pseudo-optimal solution. An empirical evaluation conducted on an open source system confirms the suitability of GA for identifying Move Method refactoring operations [62].

Note that the two approaches described above are just meant to recommend the refactoring operation to perform and not to apply it on the software system

```
extractMoveMethodRefactoringSuggestions(Method m)
   T = {}
   S = entity set of m
   for i = 1 to size of S
       entity = S[i]
       T = T ∪ {entity.ownerClass}
   sort(T)
   suggestions = {}
   for i = 1 to size of T
       if (T[i] ≠ m.ownerClass ∧ modifiesDataStructureInTargetClass(m, T[i]) ∧
       preconditionsSatisfied(m, T[i]))
           suggestions = suggestions ∪ {moveMethodSuggestion(m→ T[i])}
   if suggestions ≠ ∅
       return suggestions
   else
       for i = 1 to size of T
           if T[i] = m.ownerClass
               return {}
           else if preconditionsSatisfied(m, T[i])
               return {moveMethodSuggestion(m→ T[i])}
   return {}
```

Fig. 15.5 Algorithm used for the extraction of Move Method refactoring operations proposed by Tsantalis and Chatzigeorgiou [66]

(by ensuring behavior preservation). A fully automated approach for move method refactoring has been proposed by Tsantalis and Chatzigeorgiou [66]. The approach, implemented in the JDeodorant Eclipse plugin, is able to identify move method refactoring operations as well as to apply them in the system by preserving the behavior. The algorithm used by their approach is shown in Fig. 15.5. Given a method m, the approach forms a set of candidate target classes where m should be moved (set T in Fig. 15.5). This set is obtained by examining the entities (i.e., attributes and methods) that m accesses from the other classes (entity set S in Fig. 15.5). In particular, each class in the system containing at least one of the entities accessed by m is added to T. Then, the candidate target classes in T are sorted in descending order according to the number of entities that m accesses from each of them ($sort(T)$ in Fig. 15.5). In the following steps, each target class $T[i]$ is analyzed to verify its suitability to be the recommended class. In particular, $T[i]$ must satisfy three conditions to be considered in the set of candidate suggestions: (1) $T[i]$ is not the class m currently belongs to, (2) m modifies at least one data structure in $T[i]$, and (3) moving m in $T[i]$ satisfies a set of behavior preserving preconditions (see Tsantalis and Chatzigeorgiou [66] for the complete description of these preconditions). The set of classes in T satisfying all the above described conditions are put in the *suggestions* set (see Fig. 15.5). If *suggestions* is not empty, the approach suggests to move m in the first candidate target class following the order of the sorted set T. On the other side, if *suggestions* is empty, the classes in the sorted set T are again analyzed by applying milder constraints than before. In particular, if a class $T[i]$ is the m owner class, then no refactoring suggestion is performed and the algorithm stops. Otherwise, the approach checks if moving the method m into $T[i]$ satisfies the behavior preserving preconditions. If so, the approach suggests to move m into $T[i]$. An empirical evaluation conducted on open source systems indicate that the refactoring operations proposed by the approach make sense from the point of view of the designer involved in the evaluation.

The approach described above uses only structural information (e.g., method calls) for identifying Move Method refactoring opportunities. However, analyzing identifiers and comments in the source code can derive "semantic" information that could be combined with structural information aiming at identifying more meaningful Move Method refactoring operations. This is the idea behind Methodbook [52], an approach that analyzes methods to extract words contained in comments and identifiers. Then, a light-weight static analysis is performed to detect: (1) structural dependencies between methods (i.e., method calls and shared instance variables), and (2) the original system design. The extracted structural and semantic information is provided as input to Relational Topic Model (RTM) [20], a probabilistic topic modeling technique representing documents (i.e., methods) as random mixtures over latent topics, where each topic is characterized by a probabilistic distribution over words and is represented by a set of words mostly relevant for explaining the topic. The provided structural information are used by RTM to adjust the probability distribution of each topic taking into account explicit relationships between documents. In Methodbook, explicit relationships between documents (methods) are modeled through (i) the structural dependencies existing among the methods, and (ii) the original design. The same set of behavior preserving preconditions defined by Tsantalis and Chatzigeorgiou [66] are applied in Methodbook, allowing the automatic application of the suggested move method refactorings on the software system. A preliminary evaluation indicates that Methodbook was able to correctly place about 70 % of the analyzed methods.

Move Class Refactoring

Move Class refactoring aims at solving one of the main reasons for architectural erosion in software systems: inconsistent placement of source code classes in software packages [3]. Such a scenario negatively impacts the package cohesion and also increases the number of dependencies (coupling) between packages [35]. In such cases, re-modularization of the system is necessary [27, 50]. While most of the approaches existing in literature focus on proposing a new, system level re-modularizations to the developer [e.g., 30, 40, 56, 71], using Move Class refactoring it is possible to perform a more focused and fine-grained re-modularization, by moving the misplaced class into a more suitable package of the system, that is, one that has classes more functionally related to it than the one it is placed in. Identifying Move Class refactoring opportunities in a large software system is not easy, due to the number of classes contained in it and to the intricate web of relationships existing among them.

Like the Move Method refactoring, the identification of Move Class refactoring operations can be formulated as an optimization problem [3]. Specifically, starting from an initial decomposition, a search-based approach can be adopted for automatically reducing (structural) dependencies between packages of a software system by moving classes between the original packages. An empirical evaluation confirms the benefits of such an approach; by applying the recommended refactoring operations it is possible to achieve improvements in package cohesion together with coupling reduction.

It is worth noting that besides structural information, semantic information can also be used to identify Move Class refactoring operations [14]. Specifically, the analysis of underlying latent topics in source code (acquired via RTM) can be combined with structural dependencies aiming at identifying more meaningful refactoring operations. An empirical evaluation confirms the benefits of such a combination. Specifically, the combined approach provides not only a coupling reduction among the software modules, but also recommendations that are considered by developers meaningful from a functional point of view [14].

Note that, as explained for the Extract Package refactoring, all approaches recommending move class refactoring operations can be easily automated to preserve the system behavior due to the fact that this refactoring acts at class level.

15.2.3 Improving Conformance with Object-Oriented Programming Principles

All refactoring operations aimed at improving encapsulation, inheritance, and polymorphism fall in this category.

For example, Replace Conditional With Polymorphism refactoring is applied when in a class there is a conditional expression choosing a different behavior depending on the type of an object [27]. Applying this refactoring (1) the method containing the conditional expression is converted in an abstract method, and (2) each branch of the conditional expression is moved into an overriding method in a subclass. In this way, it is possible to benefit of all advantages derived by polymorphism.

Encapsulate Field refactoring is used to make private a field, providing getters and setters method to access it from the outside (if needed). This refactoring improves the encapsulation of the code by ensuring that all accesses to a field are managed by explicitly designed methods.

Other refactoring operations improve the inheritance organization of objects. As example, Pull Up Method (Pull Up Field) refactoring is used when two subclasses inheriting from the same class implement exactly the same method (field) while Push Down Method (Push Down Field) refactoring is used when a method (field) implemented in a superclass is of interest only for some of its subclasses [27].

While no techniques have been proposed in literature for supporting Replace Conditional With Polymorphism and Encapsulate Field refactoring, an approach dealing with the improvement of the inheritance organization of objects have been proposed by O'Keeffe and Ó Cinnéide [51]. They formulate the task of refactoring as a search problem in the space of alternative designs. The alternative designs are

generated by applying a set of refactoring operations. In particular, the refactoring
types considered in this work are: push down field, pull up field, pull down method,
pull up method, extract hierarchy, and collapse hierarchy. The search for the optimal
design is guided by a quality evaluation function based on eleven object-oriented
design metrics, that is, the Chidamber and Kemerer [21] (CK) metrics [21] that
reflects refactoring goals. The results achieved in the reported experimentation show
that the presented approach is able to improve the design quality of a given system
from a quality metric point of view.

15.3 Building a Refactoring Recommendation System

When building a refactoring recommendation system there are two critical issues to
deal with:

1. *Capturing relationships existing between code components.* This step is very
   important since the goal of several refactoring operations (e.g., Extract Class,
   Move Method, Move Field, Extract Subclass, Extract Package, Pull Up Method,
   etc.) is to re-organize code components in such a way that related components
   (i.e., those implementing similar responsibilities) are grouped together. There
   are different sources of information that can be exploited to capture relationships
   between the code components object of the refactoring.
2. *Define the algorithm to generate the refactoring recommendation.* Each algorithm has strengths and weaknesses. On the basis of the refactoring operations to
   support, an algorithm ensuring a fair compromise of strengths and weaknesses
   must be chosen.

In the following section, we present some guidelines on how to deal with these
two issues.

15.3.1 Capturing Relationships Between Source Code Components

The analysis of the relationships existing between code components can be made
from different perspectives. Most of the techniques existing in literature exploit
structural information extracted by statically analyzing the source code to capture
different relations between components (e.g., classes), such as, the number of
calls between two entities, variable accesses, or inheritance relations. A second
option is dynamic information, which takes into account call relationships occurring
during program execution. In addition, textual (i.e., semantic) information can be
exploited to capture relations between code components from the code lexicon using

Information Retrieval (IR) techniques [6]. Finally, historical data can be used to identify co-changing code components.

The refactoring approaches existing in literature mostly exploit structural and semantic information and not so much the dynamic and historical information.[3] This is due to the fact that structural and semantic information are easily obtainable from the source code while dynamic and historical ones are very difficult to collect and not always available. Moreover, recent work showed that using only structural and semantic information it is possible to capture almost all relationships captured with dynamic and historical information [13]. Thus, in the following, we only discuss structural and semantic relationships extracted from the source code to support software refactoring.

Structural Relationships

In this section we discuss the sources of information capturing structural relationships (i.e., structural coupling) between code components. Table 15.2 summarizes the sources of information exploited by the approaches in literature.

Method Calls. The most obvious source of information that can be exploited to capture structural relationships between code components is the calls interaction. Method Calls as source of information to capture relationships between code components have been exploited in many refactoring recommendation approaches [3, 5, 9, 12, 14, 25, 51, 52, 62, 63, 66] (see Table 15.2 for details). Methods generally call each other when co-operating in the implementation of some responsibilities. This source of information can be useful for refactoring operations acting at both method (e.g., Extract Class, Move Method) and class (e.g., Extract Package, Move Class) level.

Methods with high call interactions are good candidates to be grouped together when performing refactoring operations acting at method level. As example, this source of information is important for Extract Class refactoring (i.e., which methods of the class to be split should be grouped together), for Inline Method (i.e., which methods co-operate so much that merging one into another would be better to reduce coupling) and so on. A measure capturing method call interactions is the CDM [12]. CDM has values in [0, 1]; the higher the number of calls between two methods, the higher the CDM value and thus, the coupling between methods.

The calls between methods belonging to different classes also represent frequently used information to measure coupling between classes. In fact, it is reasonable to think that classes having many call interactions co-operate to implement the same (or strongly related) responsibilities and thus, are highly coupled. This information is particularly important for refactoring operations aimed at improving

---

[3]The only exception is represented by the approach proposed by Maruyama and Shima [44] that exploits historical information.

Table 15.2 Sources of information exploited in the literature to capture relationships between code components

Reference	Supported refactoring	Method calls	Shared variables	Inheritance relationships	Original decomposition	Semantic similarity
[63]	Extract class	X	X			
[25]	Extract class	X	X			
[12]	Extract class	X	X			X
[9]	Extract class	X	X			X
[5]	Move method	X				
[62]	Move method	X	X			
[66]	Move method	X	X			
[52]	Move method	X	X		X	X
[1]	Extract method		X			
[67]	Extract method		X			
[10]	Extract package	X				X
[3]	Move class	X			X	
[14]	Move class	X			X	X
[51]	Multiple refactorings	X	X	X	X	

the modularization quality of Object-Oriented systems, e.g., Extract Package, Move Class. There are many metrics available in literature to measure the coupling between classes based on their call interactions. Examples are the information-flow-based coupling (ICP) [37] and the message passing coupling (MPC) [38].

Shared Instance Variables. The instance variables shared by two methods are an important source of information for refactoring operations acting at method level (e.g., Extract Class, Move Method). In fact, they also represent a form of communications between methods (performed through shared data). Thus, methods sharing instance variables are more coupled than methods not sharing any data. Shared Instance Variables as source of information to capture relationships between code components have been used in many refactoring recommendation approaches [1, 3, 9, 12, 14, 25, 51, 52, 62, 63, 66, 67] (see Table 15.2 for details).

A measure to capture this form of coupling between methods is the SSM [28], used to compute the cohesion metric ClassCoh [28]. SSM has values in [0, 1]; the higher the number of instance variables the two methods share, the higher the SSM value is and thus, the coupling between methods.

Inheritance Relationships. A source of structural information to capture relationships between classes (and thus useful to refactoring acting at class level) are the inheritance dependencies existing among them. Exploiting this information is mandatory when working on approaches aimed at supporting refactoring operations that modify the class hierarchy, e.g., Extract Subclass, Extract Superclass, Pull Up Method, Push Down Method. Inheritance relationships have been exploited to support refactoring operations dealing with improving class hierarchy [51] (see Table 15.2).

Generally, the measurement of inheritance relationships between two classes is performed through a simple boolean value: *true* if two classes have inheritance relationships or *false* otherwise.

Original Decomposition. A last source of structural information that can be exploited to capture relationships between code components is the original decomposition or, in other words, the choices made by the developers when designing the system. For example, if the developers placed two methods inside the same class it is reasonable to assume that from their point of view these two methods are in some way related. For instance, in case of Move Method refactoring, this information can be used to take into account the choices made by the original developers when suggesting refactoring operations. The same conjecture can be also made at class level: if two classes were implemented in the same package by the developers, it is likely that from their point of view these two classes were in some way related. Information about the original decomposition has been used for Move Method [52] and Move Class [14] refactorings (see Table 15.2).

Semantic Relationships

The semantic relationships between code components are computed by measuring their textual similarity. If the vocabulary of two code components (i.e., methods or classes) is very similar, then it is likely that the developers used similar terms to describe similar responsibilities implemented by the two components. This information can be useful to support all kinds of refactoring aimed at grouping together similar code components, at both method and class level.

IR techniques have been employed to measure the textual similarity between code components. Semantic coupling can be captured at both method and class level. The CSM has been introduced by Marcus et al. [41] to define the conceptual cohesion of classes (C3) and the conceptual coupling between classes (CCBC) [55]. Two methods are conceptually related if their (domain) semantics are similar, that is, they perform conceptually similar actions. In order to compute CSM between two methods, Marcus et al. propose the use of latent semantic indexing (LSI) [23], an advanced IR method that can be used to compute the textual similarity between the two methods. Clearly, the higher the similarity, the higher the conceptual similarity.

Semantic relationships have been exploited in several refactoring recommendation approaches [9, 10, 12, 14, 52] (see Table 15.2 for details).

Table 15.3 Algorithms exploited in the literature to identify refactoring recommendations

Refactoring operation	Approach	References
Extract class	Clustering-based	[25, 63]
	Graph-based	[9, 12]
Move method	Heuristic-based	[5, 52, 66]
	Search-based	[62]
Extract method	Slicing-based	[1, 67]
Extract package	Graph-based	[10]
Move class	Search-based	[3]
	Heuristic-based	[14]
Combination of multiple operations	Search-based	[51]

15.3.2 Define the Algorithm to Generate the Refactoring Recommendations

The choice of algorithm to be applied in order to identify a refactoring solution mainly depends on the refactoring operations that we are interested in supporting. Table 15.3 reports the algorithms reported in literature, classified by the supported refactoring operation. The algorithms fall in five categories: (1) clustering-based, (2) graph-based, (3) search-based, (4) slicing-based, and (5) heuristic-based.

Clustering algorithms are particularly well-suited to support refactoring operations dealing with splitting of complex decomposition units (e.g., Blob classes, promiscuous packages) into simpler ones. In fact, these algorithms have been mainly used to support Extract Class refactoring. The main problem to solve with these algorithms is related to the definition of the number of clusters to form. As example, partitioning algorithms like k-means [31] explicitly require as input the number of clusters to be generated, that is, the number of classes that should be extracted from the Blob in case of Extract Class refactoring. This means that a developer performing Extract Class refactoring should know a priori the number of different responsibilities implemented in the Blob class, which is not a realistic assumption. Heuristics approximating the optimal number of clusters could be applied (e.g., the silhouette heuristic [60]). However, the performance of these heuristics in the refactoring field is currently unknown. Another possibility are hierarchical agglomerative algorithms, successfully applied by Fokaefs et al. [25]. Such algorithms start by placing each entity to be clustered in a single cluster. Then, at each iteration, merge the two most similar clusters, terminating when all entities are contained in a single cluster. The output of hierarchical agglomerative algorithms is represented with a dendrogram, a tree diagram where the leafs of the tree represent the entities to cluster while the remaining nodes represent possible clusters the entities belong to, up to the root representing a cluster containing all the entities. The distance between merged clusters increases with the level of the merger (starting from the leaves toward the root). This means that nodes (i.e., clusters) at a higher level group together entities having higher distance (lower similarity) between them. In fact, the top node, that is, the root of the tree, groups all entities in a single cluster, while the bottom nodes (i.e., the leaves) place each entity in a distinct cluster. Finding the right level where to cut the dendrogram (i.e., determine the clusters) is a difficult problem that has to be solved by applying heuristics (e.g., the one defined by Fokaefs et al. [25]).

Other algorithms used to support refactoring aimed at simplifying complex decomposition units (i.e., Extract Class, and Extract Package) are those based on graph theory. First, a weighted-graph representation of the complex object to decompose is built. Each node in the graph represents one of the entities composing the complex object. For example, these components could be the classes of a promiscuous package in need of Extract Package refactoring. As for the weight on the edge connecting two nodes, it can be used to represent the relationships between them (i.e., how similar they are). Having a graph-based representation, it is possible to apply graph partitioning algorithms in order to split the original graph representing the complex object into subgraphs representing the new simpler objects to extract. Examples are the Max Flow-Min Cut algorithm applied by Bavota et al. [12] that, however, suffers of a strong limitation: it always splits the complex object into two new simpler objects. This means that, for example, each Blob class is always split into two new classes, independently from the different responsibilities implemented in it. Another possibility is to identify disconnected components in the graph, as done by Bavota et al.[9]. However, several different choices can be made by looking at graph theory-based algorithms [64]. Generating a unique refactoring solution using graph-based algorithms is generally easier than adopting clustering algorithms. While the solution generated by using graph-based algorithms is unique, they do not provide to the developer alternative solutions like, for example, the hierarchical agglomerative algorithms.

When the refactoring operation to support is Extract Method, slicing-based algorithms represent the most obvious choice. In fact, slicing algorithms allow to decompose a large method (generally the kind of methods targeted for this refactoring) into different smaller methods, each one represented by a slice. Thus, a slicing algorithm, generally in its static variant, represents the natural solution for this kind of refactoring.

Widely used to support Move Method refactoring are heuristic-based algorithms [5,24,52,66]. When the problem faced by the refactoring operation is to move pieces of code to a more appropriate place, a simple analysis of the dependencies between code components can be enough. For example, to recommend that a method m, implemented in a class C_m, should be moved to a new class C_n:

1. Count the dependencies existing between m and C_m. The dependencies to analyze depend on the sources of information exploited by the approach (see Sect. 15.3.1).
2. Count the dependencies existing between m and C_n.

3. If the dependencies between m and C_n are more than those existing between m and C_m, then recommend moving m in C_n.

Finally, search based algorithms can be applied to all kinds of refactoring operations. Not by chance, they are the only algorithms applied when the goal is to support a combination of multiple refactoring operations, as done by O'Keeffe and Ó Cinnéide [51]. In these algorithms, the task of refactoring is formulated as a search problem in the space of alternative designs. The alternative designs are generated applying a set of refactoring operations supported by the approach. The search for the optimal design is guided by a quality evaluation function, usually based on code quality metrics. The strengths of these algorithms is their generality. On the weaknesses side, given the nondeterministic component of these algorithms, they may recommend a different refactoring solution at each run. Nondeterminism is not a desirable property for a refactoring recommendation system.

15.4 Evaluating a Refactoring Recommendation System

The evaluation of a refactoring recommendation system represents another challenge. This is due to the fact that, unlike other fields (e.g., traceability recovery, bug prediction, etc.), in most cases no oracles are available to evaluate the performance of the recommendation systems. In this section, we report some evaluation strategies that can be useful in the evaluation of refactoring recommendation systems.

15.4.1 Evaluation Based on Quality Metrics

The easiest way to get a first evaluation of a refactoring recommendation system is to exploit quality metrics. In other words, selected quality metrics are measured in a software system before and after the application of the recommended refactoring operations to verify if the internal software quality of the system is improved with the application of the refactoring operations. For instance, there are several quality metrics available in literature that have been demonstrated to capture different aspects of software maintainability. For example, the previously presented MPC metric (see Sect. 15.3.1) directly correlates with the maintenance effort [37], that is, higher MPC values (higher coupling) indicate higher effort in maintaining a software system. Thus, refactoring recommendations reducing the MPC in a software system are certainly preferable to those increasing the MPC. As another example, the CCBC metric (see Sect. 15.3.1) has been used to support change impact analysis. Thus, two classes exhibiting high CCBC are likely to be co-changed during a modification activity performed in a system. Consequently, refactoring recommendations (e.g., Move Class refactoring) able to group in the same software module classes having high CCBC between them could reduce the effort needed by a developer to localize the change. This clearly results in more manageable maintenance activities.

Several empirical studies provided evidence that high levels of coupling and lack of cohesion are associated with lower productivity, greater rework, and more design effort for developers [7,16–18,21]. In addition, lower cohesion and/or higher coupling of classes have been shown to correlate with higher defect rates [29,39,41]. Thus, refactoring recommendation systems should suggest refactoring operations able to improve a software system from the quality metrics point-of-view (e.g., increase cohesion and reduce coupling).

It is important to highlight that, while metrics-based evaluations allow to easily compare different recommendation systems, they are affected by many threats to validity. First, in all the software metrics evaluations there is a risk that the improvements in terms of the quality metrics achieved by applying the proposed refactoring operations are obtained by construction. In fact, the information used by the recommendation systems to identify refactoring opportunities (e.g., method calls, shared instance variables, semantic similarity) are often the same exploited by the quality metrics. For example, all Extract Class recommendation systems exploit information like method calls and shared instance variables to identify cohesive clusters of methods that can be extracted from the Blob class. Since this information is the same used by cohesion metrics (e.g., lack of cohesion of methods [21], which uses information about shared instance variables), the increase of cohesion achieved after performing a recommended Extract Class refactoring is expected. Thus, even if a software metric evaluation is needed to verify that a refactoring technique does not negatively affect the software quality, this kind of evaluation should not be central in the evaluation of a new technique. Besides improving quality metrics it is necessary to show that recommended refactoring operations are meaningful from a developer's point of view. In fact, improvements in quality metrics are not always enough to justify the need to change the original design from the developers' point of view.

Many approaches [3,9,12,14,25,62,66,67] have been evaluated using quality metrics (see Table 15.4). Results of these evaluations generally showed improvements in the values of the chosen metrics. For instance, the Extract Class refactoring approach proposed by Bavota et al. [9] was able to increase the cohesion of the refactored Blob classes of over five times. Other approaches, like those for Move Method refactoring, achieve smaller improvements due to the fact that the applied refactoring is quite circumscribed. For example, the approach by Tsantalis and Chatzigeorgiou [66] was able to improve class cohesion by 3 %, on average.

15.4.2 Evaluation Based on Historical Information

Developers are not always available for evaluating a refactoring recommendation systems. A possible solution to evaluate the recommended refactoring from a developer's point-of-view, without directly involving developers is to simulate

Table 15.4 Evaluations performed in the literature to experiment a refactoring recommendation system

Reference	Supported refactoring	Quality metrics	Historical information	External developers	Original developers
[63]	Extract class				
[25]	Extract class	X			X
[12]	Extract class	X		X	
[9]	Extract class	X	X	X	
[5]	Move method			X	
[62]	Move method	X		X	
[66]	Move method	X			X
[52]	Move method				
[1]	Extract method				
[67]	Extract method	X		X	
[10]	Extract package			X	X
[3]	Move class	X			
[14]	Move class	X		X	X
[51]	Multiple operations			X	

their presence by using as oracle refactoring operations previously performed by developers.[4] These refactoring operations can be obtained by using available tools that able to identify refactoring operations performed among two subsequent version of a software system. For example, the Ref-Finder tool [57] is able to identify 63 different types of refactoring. The tool is not 100 % precise, but the refactoring operations retrieved by it can be manually validated in order to obtain a reliable oracle on which to test the refactoring recommendation system. For example, suppose that we want to evaluate a Move Method refactoring recommendation system. We can identify the move method refactoring operations performed by developers of an open source system S between version 1.0 and version 1.1 of S. Then, we can apply our refactoring recommendation system on the version 1.0 of S and measure (e.g., through precision and recall) to what extent the recommended refactoring operations reflect those performed by the original developers. If the recommendation system is able to propose with a good accuracy the refactoring actually performed by original developers this means that (1) the recommended refactoring operations are (at least by some approximation) meaningful from a developer's point-of-view and (2) the recommendation systems can effectively support the developers in the identification of refactoring solutions.

To date, this type of evaluation has been only exploited in the evaluation of ARIES [9], used for Extract Class refactoring. In this work, the authors use Ref-Finder [57] to mine the history of six open source systems looking for extract

---

[4]For more information on simulation techniques to evaluate recommendation systems, see Walker and Holmes [68] in Chap. 12.

class refactoring operations performed by the original developers. Note that Ref-Finder retrieves Extract Class refactoring operations as a set of Move Method and Move Field operations from the original class to the new extracted classes. Thus, a manual validation has been performed on the sets of Move Method and Move Field refactoring retrieved by Ref-Finder to identify extract class refactoring operations. Then, ARIES has been applied to the classes refactored by the developers to measure how far is the refactoring recommendation from the refactoring performed by the original developers. To this aim, the MoJo effectiveness measure (MoJoFM) [70] has been used. The MoJoFM is a normalized variant of the MoJo distance and it is computed as follows:

$$\text{MoJoFM}(A, B) = 1 - \frac{\text{mno}(A, B)}{\max(\text{mno}(\forall\, A, B))}$$

where mno(A, B) is the minimum number of *Move* or *Join* operations to perform in order to transform the partition A into B, and max(mno($\forall\, A, B$) is the maximum possible distance of any partition A from the gold standard partition B. Thus, MoJoFM returns 0 if a clustering algorithm produces the farthest partition away from the gold standard; it returns 1 if a clustering algorithm produces exactly the gold standard.

ARIES achieved a 0.91 MoJoFM value, on average, for the 11 classes on which it has been applied [9].

15.4.3 Evaluation with Developers

The best scenario for evaluating a refactoring recommendation system is when developers are available to rate the meaningfulness of the recommended refactoring operations (e.g., through a Likert scale [53]).

We distinguish two kinds of studies that could be performed. The first is performed with original developers, that is, the developers evaluate the refactoring operations on systems they developed in the past. The second is performed with external developers, that is, the developers evaluate the refactoring operations on systems they do not know. The evaluations performed with original developers are preferred since external developers do not have a deep knowledge of the design of the subject system under analysis and thus may not be aware of some of the design choices that could appear as suboptimal, but that are the results of a rational choice. However, studies with external developers can complement studies performed with original developers. In fact, even if the original developers have deep knowledge of the system's design, they could be the authors of some bad design choices and consequently could not recognize good recommended refactorings as meaningful. This threat can be mitigated by conducting a study with the external developers.

Several authors have performed evaluations with original developers [25, 66], while external developers have also been involved in several empirical evaluations [5, 12, 51, 62, 67]. Some works have involved both types of developers [10, 14] (see Table 15.4). Generally, the results achieved in such evaluations showed that most of the refactoring suggestions generated by the experimented tools are appreciated by developers that recognize their meaningfulness. For instance, the approach proposed by Bavota et al. [14] to support Move Class refactoring has been evaluated with 48 external developers and 10 original developers. More than 70 % of the suggested Move Class refactoring operations have been judged as meaningful by the subjects.

15.5 Conclusion

Refactoring is an important activity employed to improve the quality of a software system during its evolution. Different refactoring operations might improve different quality aspects of a system. In particular, there are more than 90 different refactoring operations defined in the Fowler's catalog. Most of the refactoring operations are simple source code transformations aimed at increasing source code comprehension. Others are really complex and their application is error-prone and time consuming. This is the reason why in the last decade a lot of effort has been devoted to the definition of approaches able to recommend nontrivial refactoring operations (e.g., Extract Class refactoring).

In this chapter, we have described and analyzed the state of the art, while deriving guidelines for building as well as evaluating a refactoring recommendation system. The analysis of the literature has also allowed to identify some open issues.

Preserving the System Behavior. A first issue is related to the intrinsic definition of refactoring. In theory, a refactoring should not change the behavior of a software system, but only help in improving some of its nonfunctional attributes. In practice, a refactoring might be risky as any other change occurring in a system, causing possible bug introductions. A recent study investigated the extent to which refactoring activities induce bug fixes in software systems [8]. The authors analyzed a total of 12,922 refactoring operations of 52 different types and found that 15 % of the analyzed refactorings likely induced faults in the system. Moreover, the authors found that some specific kinds of refactorings are very likely to induce bug fixes, such as Pull Up Method and Extract Subclass, where the percentage of fixes likely induced by such refactorings is around 40 %.

This result could be partially explained by the survey performed by Kim et al. [34] with 328 Microsoft engineers (of which 83 % developers) to understand (1) the participants' own refactoring definition, (2) when and how they refactor code, (3) if refactoring tools are used by developers, and (4) developers' perception toward the benefits, risks, and challenges of refactoring. Three of their findings are related to the problem of preserving system behavior [34]:

- While developers recognize refactoring as a way to improve the quality of a software, in almost 50 % of the cases *they do not define refactoring as a behavior-preserving operation.*
- 51 % of developers *perform refactoring manually.*
- The *main risk* the developers fear when performing refactoring operations is *bug introduction* (77 %).

Some of these findings are also partially confirmed in the study performed by Murphy-Hill et al. [49]. They analyze eight different datasets trying to understand how developers perform refactoring. Examples of the exploited datasets are usage data from 41 developers using the Eclipse environment, data from the Eclipse Usage Collector aggregating activities of 13,000 developers for almost one year, and information extracted from versioning systems. The paper discusses several interesting findings: (i) developers often interleave refactoring with other programming activities (thus, potentially changing the system behavior), and (ii) most of the refactoring operations (close to 90 %) are performed manually by developers without the help of any tool.

While the fact that developers mostly perform refactoring manually could explain the bugs introduced through refactoring as observed by Bavota et al. [8], Das et al. [22] showed that even automated refactoring performed by Integrated Development Environments could be fault-prone. They propose a possible solution to ensure that refactoring engines (i.e., the tools that apply the refactoring operations) correctly transform the program when applying refactoring operations. In particular, Das et al. [22] proposed an approach to automate the testing of refactoring engines. The technique generates ASTs of the refactored Java programs (to date the only supported programming language) to verify that the behavior of the system remains unchanged after the application of the refactoring operations. Their approach was able to identify 45 previously unreported bugs in Eclipse and NetBeans, two of the most popular refactoring engines for Java [22]. Thus, the approach by Das et al. [22] certainly represent a good way to verify that a refactoring recommendation tool correctly applies refactoring operations.

Solutions to the problem of behavior preservation during refactoring have been also proposed by Overbey and Johnson [54], Schäfer et al. [61], and Mens et al. [46]. However, none of these works have presented a fully generalizable approach that can be applied for every possible refactoring.

Another possibility to ensure that the performed refactoring does not alter the system external behavior is to define strong preconditions that must be verified in order to apply it. An example of this approach is in the technique for Move Method refactoring presented by Tsantalis and Chatzigeorgiou [66]. The Move Method refactoring operation is performed only if the involved code components satisfy all preconditions. However, this "strong preconditions philosophy" has also been criticized in literature [59] since it could avoid the application of desirable refactoring operations just because there is a small price to pay in terms of small adjustments in the source code. The result of this observation has been the *program metamorphosis* approach proposed by Reichenbach et al. [59] that relaxes the behavior-preservation checks by considering them later in the refactoring process: when a refactoring alters the external behavior of the system, the approach allows the user to correct or accept the behavioral changes.

All in all, the problem of ensuring the preservation of the system behavior during refactoring has still to be solved.

Usability of the Refactoring Recommendation Systems. A second open issue is related to the usability of the refactoring recommendation system. In general, recommendations are based only on quality metrics. However, quality metrics do not tell the whole story about the code and may not be able to capture the perception of the developer about refactoring. This could generate refactoring operations that are not usable because the developer is not able to understand why the recommendation system is proposing a specific refactoring operations. In such a situation the developer might lose faith in the recommendation system. A way to overcome such a situation has been recently proposed by Bavota et al. [14]. In particular, the authors analyze underlying natural language topics in classes not only to identify refactoring operations but also to identify their responsibilities and provide some rationale behind the proposed refactoring recommendation. An empirical study conducted with developers has indicated the usefulness of such an explanation in understanding (and, consequently, in accepting or rejecting) a recommended refactoring operation [14]. However, the approach exploited by Bavota et al. [14] represents a first attempt, while more sophisticated techniques could be used to automatically derive the rationale behind a recommended refactoring operation (e.g., by exploiting natural language techniques).

Provide Complete Support to the Developer Performing Refactoring. As of today, there are no approaches that provide simultaneous and integrated support to multiple types of refactoring operations. It would be worthwhile to have tools able to suggest a complete set of refactoring operations of different types able to improve the design of a software system from different points of view (e.g., removal of different types of antipatterns, improved adherence to object-oriented design practices, etc.). This would also allow to integrate in the refactoring tool a wider subset of existing refactoring operations. As example, recommending Rename Method refactoring solutions could be worthwhile if combined with Extract Method recommendations. In fact, automatically assigning a name reflecting the responsibility implemented in the extracted method can save developers' time. Note that in the literature the goal of covering more refactoring operations is accomplished in part in the work by O'Keeffe and Ó Cinnéide [51] where, however, only refactoring operations working on class hierarchies are combined together.

Also, most of the approaches in the literature have not been implemented in IDEs and this does not encourages developers in using them, as revealed in the existing studies [34, 49]. While the integration of refactoring approaches in IDEs is far from trivial for the reasons discussed above (i.e., behavior preservation, usability of the tools), more effort should be spent in this direction.

References

1. Abadi, A., Ettinger, R., Feldman, Y.A.: Fine slicing for advanced method extraction. In: Proceedings of the Workshop on Refactoring Tools (2009)
2. Abadi, A., Ettinger, R., Feldman, Y.A.: Fine slicing: theory and applications for computation extraction. In: Proceedings of the International Conference on Fundamental Approaches to Software Engineering. Lecture Notes in Computer Science, vol. 7212, pp. 471–485 (2012). doi:10.1007/978-3-642-28872-2_32?
3. Abdeen, H., Ducasse, S., Sahraoui, H.A., Alloui, I.: Automatic package coupling and cycle minimization. In: Proceedings of the Working Conference on Reverse Engineering, pp. 103–112 (2009). doi:10.1109/WCRE.2009.13
4. Abebe, S.L., Tonella, P.: Automated identifier completion and replacement. In: Proceedings of the European Conference on Software Maintenance and Reengineering, pp. 263–272 (2013). doi:10.1109/CSMR.2013.35
5. Atkinson, D.C., King, T.: Lightweight detection of program refactorings. In: Proceedings of the Asia–Pacific Software Engineering Conference, pp. 663–670 (2005). doi:10.1109/APSEC.2005.76
6. Baeza-Yates, R., Ribeiro-Neto, B.: Modern Information Retrieval. Addison-Wesley, Reading, MA (1999)
7. Basili, V.R., Briand, L., Melo, W.L.: A validation of object-oriented design metrics as quality indicators. IEEE T. Software Eng. 22(10), 751–761 (1995). doi:10.1109/32.544352
8. Bavota, G., De Carluccio, B., De Lucia, A., Di Penta, M., Oliveto, R., Strollo, O.: When does a refactoring induce bugs?: an empirical study. In: Proceedings of the IEEE International Working Conference on Source Code Analysis and Manipulation, pp. 104–113 (2012a). doi:10.1109/SCAM.2012.20
9. Bavota, G., De Lucia, A., Marcus, A., Oliveto, R.: Automating extract class refactoring: an improved method and its evaluation. Empir. Software Eng. (2013a, in press). doi:10.1007/s10664-013-9256-x
10. Bavota, G., De Lucia, A., Marcus, A., Oliveto, R.: Using structural and semantic measures to improve software modularization. Empir. Software Eng. 18(5), 901–932 (2013b). doi:10.1007/s10664-012-9226-8?
11. Bavota, G., De Lucia, A., Marcus, A., Oliveto, R., Palomba, F.: Supporting extract class refactoring in Eclipse: the ARIES project. In: Proceedings of the ACM/IEEE International Conference on Software Engineering, pp. 1419–1422 (2012b). doi:10.1109/ICSE.2012.6227233
12. Bavota, G., De Lucia, A., Oliveto, R.: Identifying extract class refactoring opportunities using structural and semantic cohesion measures. J. Syst. Software 84(3), 397–414 (2011). doi:10.1016/j.jss.2010.11.918
13. Bavota, G., Dit, B., Oliveto, R., Di Penta, M., Poshyvanyk, D., De Lucia, A.: An empirical study on the developers' perception of software coupling. In: Proceedings of the ACM/IEEE International Conference on Software Engineering, pp. 692–701 (2013c). doi:10.1109/ICSE.2013.6606615
14. Bavota, G., Gethers, M., Oliveto, R., Poshyvanyk, D., De Lucia, A.: Improving software modularization via automated analysis of latent topics and dependencies. ACM T. Software Eng. Meth. (2013d, in press)
15. Beck, K., Andres, C.: Extreme Programming Explained: Embrace Change. Addison-Wesley, Reading, MA (2004)
16. Binkley, A.B., Schach, S.R.: Validation of the coupling dependency metric as a predictor of run-time failures and maintenance measures. In: Proceedings of the ACM/IEEE International Conference on Software Engineering, pp. 452–455 (1998). doi:10.1109/ICSE.1998.671604
17. Briand, L.C., Wuest, J., Lounis, H.: Using coupling measurement for impact analysis in object-oriented systems. In: Proceedings of the IEEE International Conference on Software Maintenance, pp. 475–482 (1999a). doi:10.1109/ICSM.1999.792645

18. Briand, L.C., Wüst, J., Ikonomovski, S.V., Lounis, H.: Investigating quality factors in object-oriented designs: an industrial case study. In: Proceedings of the ACM/IEEE International Conference on Software Engineering, pp. 345–354 (1999b). doi:10.1145/302405.302654
19. Brown, W.J., Malveau, R.C., Brown, W.H., McCormick III, H.W., Mowbray, T.J.: Anti Patterns: Refactoring Software, Architectures, and Projects in Crisis. Wiley, New York (1998)
20. Chang, J., Blei, D.M.: Hierarchical relational models for document networks. Ann. Appl. Stat. **4**(1), 124–150 (2010). doi:10.1214/09-AOAS309
21. Chidamber, S.R., Kemerer, C.F.: A metrics suite for object oriented design. IEEE T. Software Eng. **20**(6), 476–493 (1994). doi:10.1109/32.295895
22. Das, A.S., Datar, M., Garg, A., Rajaram, S.: Google news personalization: scalable online collaborative filtering. In: Proceedings of the International Conference on the World Wide Web, pp. 271–280 (2007). doi:10.1145/1242572.1242610
23. Deerwester, S., Dumais, S., Furnas, G., Landauer, T., Harshman, R.: Indexing by latent semantic analysis. J. Am. Soc. Inform. Sci. **41**(6), 391–407 (1990). doi:10.1002/(SICI)1097-4571(199009)41:6⟨391::AID-ASI1⟩3.0.CO;2-9
24. Du Bois, B., Demeyer, S., Verelst, J.: Refactoring: improving coupling and cohesion of existing code. In: Proceedings of the Working Conference on Reverse Engineering, pp. 144–151 (2004). doi:10.1109/WCRE.2004.33
25. Fokaefs, M., Tsantalis, N., Chatzigeorgiou, A., Sander, J.: Decomposing object-oriented class modules using an agglomerative clustering technique. In: Proceedings of the IEEE International Conference on Software Maintenance, pp. 93–101 (2009)
26. Fokaefs, M., Tsantalis, N., Stroulia, E., Chatzigeorgiou, A.: Identification and application of extract class refactorings in object-oriented systems. J. Syst. Software **85**(10), 2241–2260 (2012). doi:10.1016/j.jss.2012.04.013
27. Fowler, M.: Refactoring: improving the design of existing code. Addison-Wesley, Reading, MA (1999)
28. Gui, G., Scott, P.D.: Coupling and cohesion measures for evaluation of component reusability. In: Proceedings of the International Workshop on Mining Software Repositories, pp. 18–21 (2006). doi:10.1145/1137983.1137989
29. Gyimóthy, T., Ferenc, R., Siket, I.: Empirical validation of object-oriented metrics on open source software for fault prediction. IEEE T. Software Eng. **31**(10), 897–910 (2005). doi:10.1109/TSE.2005.112
30. Harman, M., Hierons, R.M., Proctor, M.: A new representation and crossover operator for search-based optimization of software modularization. In: Proceedings of the Genetic and Evolutionary Computation Conference, pp. 1351–1358 (2002)
31. Hartigan, J.A.: Clustering Algorithms. Wiley, New York (1975)
32. Kerievsky, J.: Refactoring to Patterns. Pearson, London (2004)
33. Khomh, F., Vaucher, S., Guéhéneuc, Y.G., Sahraoui, H.: BDTEX: a GQM-based Bayesian approach for the detection of antipatterns. J. Syst. Software **84**(4), 559–572 (2011). doi:10.1016/j.jss.2010.11.921
34. Kim, M., Zimmermann, T., Nagappan, N.: A field study of refactoring challenges and benefits. In: Proceedings of the ACM SIGSOFT International Symposium on Foundations of Software Engineering, pp. 50:1–50:11 (2012). doi:10.1145/2393596.2393655
35. Lanza, M., Marinescu, R.: Object-Oriented Metrics in Practice: Using Software Metrics to Characterize, Evaluate, and Improve the Design of Object-Oriented Systems. Springer, Berlin (2006). doi:10.1007/3-540-39538-5
36. Lawrie, D., Morrell, C., Feild, H., Binkley, D.: Effective identifier names for comprehension and memory. Innov. Syst. Software Eng. **3**(4), 303–318 (2007). doi:10.1007/s11334-007-0031-2?
37. Lee, Y.S., Liang, B.S., Wu, S.F., Wang, F.J.: Measuring the coupling and cohesion of an object-oriented program based on information flow. In: Proceedings of the International Conference on Software Quality, pp. 81–90 (1995)

38. Li, W., Henry, S.: Maintenance metrics for the object oriented paradigm. In: Proceedings of the International Software Metrics Symposium, pp. 52–60 (1993). doi:10.1109/METRIC.1993.263801
39. Liu, Y., Poshyvanyk, D., Ferenc, R., Gyimóthy, T., Chrisochoides, N.: Modeling class cohesion as mixtures of latent topics. In: Proceedings of the IEEE International Conference on Software Maintenance, pp. 233–242 (2009). doi:10.1109/ICSM.2009.5306318
40. Mancoridis, S., Mitchell, B.S., Rorres, C., Chen, Y.F., Gansner, E.R.: Using automatic clustering to produce high-level system organizations of source code. In: Proceedings of the IEEE International Workshop on Program Comprehenension, pp. 45–52 (1998). doi:10.1109/WPC.1998.693283
41. Marcus, A., Poshyvanyk, D., Ferenc, R.: Using the conceptual cohesion of classes for fault prediction in object-oriented systems. IEEE T. Software Eng. 34(2), 287–300 (2008). doi:10.1109/TSE.2007.70768
42. Marinescu, R.: Detection strategies: metrics-based rules for detecting design flaws. In: Proceedings of the IEEE International Conference on Software Maintenance, pp. 350–359 (2004). doi:10.1109/ICSM.2004.1357820
43. Martin, R.C. (ed.): Clean Code: A Handbook of Agile Software Craftsmanship. Prentice Hall, Upper Saddle River (2009)
44. Maruyama, K., Shima, K.: Automatic method refactoring using weighted dependence graphs. In: Proceedings of the ACM/IEEE International Conference on Software Engineering, pp. 236–245 (1999). doi:10.1145/302405.302627
45. Mens, T., Tourwe, T.: A survey of software refactoring. IEEE T. Software Eng. 30(2), 126–139 (2004). doi:10.1109/TSE.2004.1265817
46. Mens, T., Van Eetvelde, N., Demeyer, S., Janssens, D.: Formalizing refactorings with graph transformations. J. Software Maint. Evol. R. 17(4), 247–276 (2005). doi:10.1002/smr.316
47. Mitchell, B.S., Mancoridis, S.: On the automatic modularization of software systems using the Bunch tool. IEEE T. Software Eng. 32(3), 193–208 (2006). doi:10.1109/TSE.2006.31
48. Moha, N., Guéhéneuc, Y.G., Duchien, L., Le Meur, A.F.: DECOR: a method for the specification and detection of code and design smells. IEEE T. Software Eng. 36(1), 20–36 (2010). doi:10.1109/TSE.2009.50
49. Murphy-Hill, E., Parnin, C., Black, A.P.: How we refactor, and how we know it. IEEE T. Software Eng. 38(1), 5–18 (2011). doi:10.1109/TSE.2011.41
50. Nierstrasz, O., Ducasse, S., Demeyer, S.: Object-Oriented Reengineering Patterns. Morgan Kaufmann, San Francisco (2003)
51. O'Keeffe, M., Ó Cinnéide, M.: Search-based software maintenance. In: Proceedings of the European Conference on Software Maintenance and Reengineering, pp. 249–260 (2006). doi:10.1109/CSMR.2006.49
52. Oliveto, R., Gethers, M., Bavota, G., Poshyvanyk, D., De Lucia, A.: Identifying method friendships to remove the feature envy bad smell. In: Proceedings of the ACM/IEEE International Conference on Software Engineering, pp. 820–823 (2011). doi:10.1145/1985793.1985913
53. Oppenheim, A.N.: Questionnaire Design, Interviewing and Attitude Measurement. Pinter, New York(1992)
54. Overbey, J.L., Johnson, R.E.: Differential precondition checking: a lightweight, reusable analysis for refactoring tools. In: Proceedings of the IEEE/ACM International Conference on Automated Software Engineering, pp. 303–312 (2011). doi:10.1109/ASE.2011.6100067
55. Poshyvanyk, D., Marcus, A., Ferenc, R., Gyimóthy, T.: Using information retrieval based coupling measures for impact analysis. Empir. Software Eng. 14(1), 5–32 (2009). doi:10.1007/s10664-008-9088-2?
56. Praditwong, K., Harman, M., Yao, X.: Software module clustering as a multi-objective search problem. IEEE T. Software Eng. 37(2), 264–282 (2011). doi:10.1109/TSE.2010.26
57. Prete, K., Rachatasumrit, N., Sudan, N., Kim, M.: Template-based reconstruction of complex refactorings. In: Proceedings of the IEEE International Conference on Software Maintenance, pp. 1–10 (2010). doi:10.1109/ICSM.2010.5609577

58. Rao, A.A., Reddy, K.N.: Detecting bad smells in object oriented design using design change propagation probability matrix. In: Proceedings of the International MultiConference of Engineers and Computer Scientists. Lecture Notes in Engineering and Computer Science, pp. 1001–1007 (2008)
59. Reichenbach, C., Coughlin, D., Diwan, A.: Program metamorphosis. In: Proceedings of the European Conference on Object-Oriented Programming. Lecture Notes in Computer Science, vol. 5653, pp. 394–418 (2009). doi:10.1007/978-3-642-03013-0_18
60. Rousseeuw, P.J.: Silhouettes: a graphical aid to the interpretation and validation of cluster analysis. J. Comput. Appl. Math. **20**, 53–65 (1987). doi:10.1016/0377-0427(87)90125-7
61. Schäfer, M., Verbaere, M., Ekman, T., de Moor, O.: Stepping stones over the refactoring Rubicon. In: Proceedings of the European Conference on Object-Oriented Programming. Lecture Notes in Computer Science, vol. 5653, pp. 369–393 (2009). doi:10.1007/978-3-642-03013-0_17
62. Seng, O., Stammel, J., Burkhart, D.: Search-based determination of refactorings for improving the class structure of object-oriented systems. In: Proceedings of the Genetic and Evolutionary Computation Conference, pp. 1909–1916 (2006). doi:10.1145/1143997.1144315
63. Simon, F., Steinbrückner, F., Lewerentz, C.: Metrics based refactoring. In: Proceedings of the European Conference on Software Maintenance and Reengineering, pp. 30–38 (2001). doi:10.1109/.2001.914965
64. Thulasiraman, K., Swamy, M.N.S.: Graphs: Theory and Algorithms. Wiley, New York (1992)
65. Travassos, G., Shull, F., Fredericks, M., Basili, V.R.: Detecting defects in object-oriented designs: using reading techniques to increase software quality. In: Proceedings of the ACM SIGPLAN Conference on Object-Oriented Programming, Systems, Languages, and Applications, pp. 47–56 (1999). doi:10.1145/320384.320389
66. Tsantalis, N., Chatzigeorgiou, A.: Identification of move method refactoring opportunities. IEEE T. Software Eng. **35**, 347–367 (2009). doi:10.1109/TSE.2009.1
67. Tsantalis, N., Chatzigeorgiou, A.: Identification of extract method refactoring opportunities for the decomposition of methods. J. Syst. Software **84**(10), 1757–1782 (2011). doi:10.1016/j.jss.2011.05.016
68. Walker, R.J., Holmes, R.: Simulation: a methodology to evaluate recommendation systems in software engineering. In: Robillard, M., Maalej, W., Walker, R.J., Zimmermann, T. (eds.) Recommendation Systems in Software Engineering, Springer, Heidelberg, Chap. 12 (2014)
69. Weiser, M.: Program slicing. IEEE T. Software Eng. **10**(4), 352–357 (1984). doi:10.1109/TSE.1984.5010248
70. Wen, Z., Tzerpos, V.: An effectiveness measure for software clustering algorithms. In: Proceedings of the IEEE International Workshop on Program Comprehenension, pp. 194–203 (2004). doi:10.1109/WPC.2004.1311061
71. Wu, J., Hassan, A.E., Holt, R.C.: Comparison of clustering algorithms in the context of software evolution. In: Proceedings of the IEEE International Conference on Software Maintenance, pp. 525–535 (2005). doi:10.1109/ICSM.2005.31

Chapter 16
Recommending Program Transformations

Automating Repetitive Software Changes

Miryung Kim and Na Meng

Abstract Adding features and fixing bugs in software often require systematic edits which are similar but not identical changes to multiple code locations. Finding all relevant locations and making the correct edits is a tedious and error-prone process. This chapter presents several state-of-the art approaches to recommending program transformation in order to automate repetitive software changes. First, it discusses *programming-by-demonstration* (PBD) approaches that automate repetitive tasks by inferring a generalized action script from a user's recorded actions. Second, it presents edit location suggestion approaches that only recommend candidate edit locations but do not apply necessary code transformations. Finally, it describes program transformation approaches that take code examples or version histories as input, automatically identify candidate edit locations, and apply context awareness, customization program transformations to generate a new program version. In particular, this chapter describes two concrete example-based program transformation approaches in detail, Sydit and Lase. These two approaches are selected for an in-depth discussion, because they handle the issue of both recommending change locations and applying transformations, and they are specifically designed to update programs as opposed to regular text documents. The chapter is then concluded with open issues and challenges of recommending program transformations.

16.1 Introduction

Recent work observes that software evolution often requires *systematic and repetitive changes*. Developers apply similar but not identical changes to different contexts [23, 24, 34, 45]. Nguyen et al. [45] find that 17 to 45 % of bug fixes are recurring fixes that involve similar changes to numerous methods. Another class of

M. Kim (✉) • N. Meng
The University of Texas at Austin, Austin, TX, USA
e-mail: miryung@ece.utexas.edu; miryung@cs.utexas.edu; mengna09@cs.utexas.edu

M.P. Robillard et al. (eds.), *Recommendation Systems in Software Engineering*,
DOI 10.1007/978-3-642-45135-5_16, © Springer-Verlag Berlin Heidelberg 2014

systematic changes occur when application programming interface (API) evolution requires all the clients to update their code [17] or when developers refactor code to improve its internal structure. Cross-system bug fixes happen frequently among forked software products such as FreeBSD, NetBSD, and OpenBSD, despite the limited overlap of contributors [6, 54]. Manual application of systematic changes is tedious and error-prone. Developers must find all required change locations, rewrite those locations manually, and test the modifications. A failure to systematically extend software may lead to costly errors of omissions and logical inconsistencies.

For example, Fig. 16.1 shows a systematic change example drawn from revisions to org.eclipse.debug.core on 2006-10-05 and 2006-11-06, respectively. The unchanged code is shown in black, additions in blue with a blue"+," and deletions in red with a red"−." Consider methods mA and mB: getLaunchConfigurations (ILaunchConfigurationType) and getLaunchConfigurations(IProject). These methods iterate over elements received by calling getAllLaunchConfig urations(), process the elements one by one, and add it to a predefined list when an element meets a certain condition.

Suppose that Pat intends to apply similar changes to mA and mB. In mA, Pat wants to move the declaration of variable config out of the while loop and to add code to process config, as shown in lines 5 and 7–11 in mA. Pat wants to perform a similar edit to mB, but on the cfg variable instead of config. This example typifies *systematic edits*. Such similar yet not identical edits to multiple methods cannot be applied using existing refactoring engines in integrated development environment, because they change the semantics of a program. Even though these two program changes are similar, without assistance, Pat must manually edit both methods, which is tedious and error-prone.

Existing source transformation tools automate repetitive changes by requiring developers to prescribe the changes in a formal syntax. For example, TXL [8] is a programming language designed for software analysis and source transformation. It requires users to specify a programming language's structure (i.e., syntax tree) and a set of transformation rules. TXL then automatically transforms any program written in the target language according to the rules. These tools can handle nontrivial *semantics-modifying* changes, such as *inserting a null-check before dereferencing an object*. However, it requires developers to have a good command of language syntax and script programming [3, 4, 19].

Refactoring engines in IDEs automate many predefined *semantics-preserving* transformations. When performing a refactoring task (e.g., rename method), developers only need to decide the refactoring type and provide all necessary information (e.g., the old and new name of the method) as input to enable the transformation. Then the refactoring engines automatically check predefined constraints to ensure that the transformation preserves semantics before actually making the transformation. Although some tools allow developers to define new refactoring types, specifying refactoring preconditions and code transformation from scratch is time consuming and error-prone.

Existing interactive text-editing approaches, such as a *search-and-replace* feature of a text editor, can help developers look for edit locations based on keywords or

```
 1  public ILaunchConfiguration[] getLaunchConfigurations
 2    (ILaunchConfigurationType type) throws CoreException {
 3     Iterator iter = getAllLaunchConfigurations().iterator();
 4     List configs = new ArrayList();
 5  +  ILaunchConfiguration config = null;
 6     while (iter.hasNext()) {
 7  -  ILaunchConfiguration config = (ILaunchConfiguration)iter.next
       ();
 8  +  config = (ILaunchConfiguration)iter.next();
 9  +  if (!config.inValid()) {
10  +  config.reset();
11  +  }
12        if (config.getType().equals(type)) {
13           configs.add(config);
14        }
15     }
16     return (ILaunchConfiguration[])configs.toArray
17       (new ILaunchConfiguration[configs.size()]);
18  }
```

a

```
 1  protected List getLaunchConfigurations(IProject project) {
 2     Iterator iter = getAllLaunchConfigurations().iterator();
 3  +  ILaunchConfiguration cfg = null;
 4     List cfgs = new ArrayList();
 5     while (iter.hasNext()) {
 6  -  ILaunchConfiguration cfg = (ILaunchConfiguration)iter.next();
 7  +  cfg = (ILaunchConfiguration)iter.next();
 8  +  if (!cfg.inValid()) {
 9  +  cfg.reset();
10  +  }
11        IFile file = cfg.getFile();
12        if (file != null && file.getProject().equals(project)) {
13           cfgs.add(cfg);
14        }
15     }
16     return cfgs;
17  }
```

b

Fig. 16.1 Systematic edit from revisions of org.eclipse.debug.core [37]. (a) mA_o to mA_n. (b) mB_o to mB_n

regular expressions, and apply edits by replacing the matching text at each location with user-specified text. These approaches treat programs as plain text. Therefore, they cannot handle nontrivial program transformations that require analysis of program syntax or semantics.

This chapter presents several state-of-the art approaches that overcome these limitations by leveraging *user-specified change examples*. First, it discusses *programming-by-demonstration* (PBD) approaches that automate repetitive tasks by inferring a generalized action script from a user's recorded actions. However, these PBD approaches are not suitable for updating code as they are designed for regular text. Second, it presents edit location suggestion approaches that stop at only recommending candidate locations but do not apply necessary code transformations. Thus these approaches still require programmers to edit code manually. Finally, it describes program transformation approaches that take code change examples as input, automatically identify candidate edit locations and also apply context-aware, customized program transformations to generate a new program version. In particular, this chapter describes two concrete techniques in detail, Sydit [36, 37] and Lase [38]. We chose to describe these two in detail because Lase has the most advanced edit capability among the techniques that handle both issues of finding edit locations and applying transformation and Sydit is the predecessor of Lase.

Given an exemplar edit, Sydit generates a *context-aware, abstract edit script*, and then applies the edit script to new program locations specified by the user. Evaluations show that Sydit is effective in automating program transformation. However, the tool depends on the user to specify edit locations.

Lase addresses this problem by learning edit scripts from *multiple examples* as opposed to a single example [38]. Lase (1) creates context-aware edit scripts from two or more examples, uses these scripts to (2) automatically identify edit locations and to (3) transform the code. Evaluation shows that Lase can identify edit locations with high precision and recall.

There are several open issues and remaining challenges in recommending program transformations based on examples. First, it is currently difficult for developers to view recommended program transformations, especially when the recommendation spans across multiple locations in the program. Second, it is difficult for developers to check correctness of the recommended program transformations, because none of the existing techniques provide additional support for validating recommended edits. Third, the granularity of program transformations is limited to intra-function or intra-method edits at large, making it difficult to apply high-level transformations such as modifications to class hierarchies and method signatures. Finally, existing techniques are limited to automating homogeneous, repetitive edits, but leave it to developers to coordinate heterogeneous edits.

16.2 Motivation

Software Evolution Often Requires Systematic Changes. This insight arises from numerous other research efforts, primarily within the domain of crosscutting concerns and refactorings. *Crosscutting concerns* represent design decisions that are generally scattered throughout a program such as performance, error handling, and synchronization [21, 59]. Modifications to these design decisions involve similar changes to every occurrence of the design decision. *Refactoring* is the process of improving internal software structure in ways that do not alter its external behavior. Refactoring often consists of one or more elementary transformations, such as "moving the `print` method in each `Document` subclass to its superclass" or "introducing three abstract `visit*` methods." Another class of systematic changes occur when the evolution of an application programming interface (API) requires all API clients to update their API usage code [17], though the details can vary from location to location [19]. A recent study of bug fixes shows that a considerable portion of bug fixes (17–45 %) are actually recurring fixes that involve similar edits [45]. Another study on code changes finds that on average 75 % of changes share similar structural-dependence characteristics, e.g., invoking the same method or accessing the same data field [23]. These studies indicate that systematic code updates are common and often unavoidable.

Manual Implementation of Systematic Changes Is Tedious and Error-Prone. Purushothaman and Perry [53] found that only about 10 % of changes (in one, large industrial system) involve a single line of code, but even a single line change has about a 4 % chance of resulting in an error; on the other hand, changes of 500 lines or more have nearly a 50 % chance of causing at least one defect. Eaddy et al. [11] find that the more scattered the implementation of a concern is, the more likely it is to have defects. Murphy-Hill et al. [43] find that almost 90 % of refactorings are performed manually without the help of automated refactoring tools. These refactorings are potentially error-prone since they often require coordinated edits across different parts of a system. Weißgerber and Diehl [64] find that there is an increase in the number of bugs after refactorings. Kim et al. [22] also find a short-term increase in the number of bug fixes after API-level rename, move, and signature change refactorings. Some of these bugs were caused by inconsistent refactorings. These studies motivate automated tool support for applying systematic edits.

Systematic Changes Are Generally not Semantics-Preserving and They Are Beyond the Scope and Capability of Existing Refactoring Engines. To investigate the challenges associated with refactorings, Kim et al. [25] conducted a survey with professional developers at Microsoft. They sent a survey invitation to 1,290 engineers whose commit messages include a keyword "refactoring" in the last 2 years of version histories of five MS products; 328 of them responded to the survey. More than half of the participants said they carry out refactorings in the context of bug fixes or feature additions, and these changes are generally not semantics-preserving transformations. In fact, when developers are asked about their own definition of refactoring, 46 % of participants did not mention preservation of semantics, behavior, or functionality at all. During a follow-up interview, some developers explicitly said, "Strictly speaking, refactoring means that behavior does not change, but realistically speaking, it usually is done while adding features or fixing bugs." Furthermore, over 95 % of participants in the study said that they do most refactorings manually; 53 % reported that refactorings that they perform do not match the types and capability of transformations supported by existing refactoring engines. This motivates a flexible, example-based approach for applying systematic program transformations.

16.3 State-of-the Art Approaches to Recommending Program Transformations

This section describes state-of-the art approaches to recommending program transformations, compares these approaches using a unified framework, and discusses their strengths and weaknesses. We first discuss individual approaches and present comparison results in Tables 16.1–16.3. Table 16.1 shows the comparison of existing approaches in terms of input, output, edit type, and automation capability. Table 16.2 describes the comparison of existing approaches in terms of edit capability: the second column shows whether each technique can handle single line or multiple-line edits; the third column shows whether each technique handles a sequence of contiguous edits or non-contiguous edits; the fourth column shows whether it supports only replication of concrete edits or edits that can be customized to individual target contexts; and the last column shows whether the technique models surrounding unchanged code or not. Table 16.3 shows the comparison of existing approaches, in terms of evaluation subjects, programming languages, data set size, and assessment methods.

16.3.1 Programming-by-Demonstration

Programming-by-example [30] (PbE) is a software agent-based approach that infers a generalized action script from a user's recorded actions. SMARTedit [28] automates repetitive text edits by learning a series of functions such as *"move a cursor to the end of a line."* Like macro recording systems, SMARTedit learns the program by observing a user performing her or his task. However, unlike macro-recorders, SMARTedit examines the context in which the user's actions are performed and learns programs that work correctly in new contexts. Using a machine learning concept called *version space algebra*, SMARTedit is able to learn useful text-editing after only a small number of demonstrations. Similarly, Visual AWK [27] allows users to interactively generalize text edits.

Several approaches learn string manipulations or a skeleton of repetitive editing tasks from examples or demonstrations. For example, the Editing by Example (EBE) system looks at the input and output behavior of the complete demonstration [47]. EBE synthesizes a program that generalizes the transformation expressed by text change examples. The TELS system records editing actions, such as search-and-replace, and generalizes them into a program that transforms input into output [65]. TELS also uses heuristic rules to match actions against each other to detect loops in the user's demonstrated program. However, TELS's dependence on domain-specific heuristic rules makes it difficult to apply the same techniques to a different domain, such as editing Java programs. The Dynamic Macro system of Masui and Nakayama [32] records macros in the emacs text editor. Dynamic Macro performs automatic segmentation of the user's actions, breaking up the stream of actions into repetitive

Table 16.1 Comparison of existing approaches in terms of input, output, edit type, and automation capability

Tool	Input	Output	Type	Location	Xform
Visual AWK [27]	Recorded editing actions and text to modify	Modified version of the text	Textual	Semi-automatic	Semi-automatic
EBE [47]	Reference edit in terms of textual differences	Transformation program	Textual	Automatic	Automatic
TELS [65]	Recoded editing actions	A transformation program	Textual	Semi-automatic	Semi-automatic
Dynamic macro system [32]	Edit action log	Text editing macro	Textual	Automatic	Automatic
Cima [33]	Reference edit in terms of old and new versions of changed example(s)	Transformation rule	Textual	Automatic	Automatic
Simultaneous text editing [41]	Demonstration of text editing and text to modify	Modified version of all selected text	Textual	Manual	Automatic
Linked editing [60]	Demonstration of text editing and code clones to modify	Modified version of all linked code clones	Syntactic	Manual	Automatic
CloneTracker [10]	Demonstration of text editing and code clones to modify	Modified version of all linked code clones	syntactic	Automatic	Automatic
Clever [46]	Two consecutive revisions of subject system	Modified version of system	Syntactic	Automatic	Automatic
Trident [19]	Search terms and replacement terms	Modified version of system	Lexical/syntactic	Automatic	Automatic
Program synthesis [13]	Reference edit in terms of old and new versions of changed example(s) and text to modify	Modified version of text	Textual	Automatic	Automatic
Reverb [34, 35]	Demonstration of source editing	Similar locations in the project	Semantic	Automatic	Manual
DQL [62]	DQL query and codebase	Locations matching the query	Semantic	Automatic	Manual
PQL [31]	PQL query and codebase	Locations matching the query	Semantic	Automatic	Automatic
PR-Miner [29]	Codebase	Locations violating extracted general programming rules	Semantic	Automatic	Manual

(continued)

Table 16.1 (continued)

Tool	Input	Output	Type	Location	Xform
HAM [5]	Project's version history	Code changes which are likely to be crosscutting concern	Semantic	–	–
Find-concept [57]	Natural language-based query and codebase	Locations matching the query	Semantic	Semi-automatic	–
FixWizard [45]	Manually identified bug fixes and codebase	Locations in need of recurring bug fixes	Semantic	Automatic	Manual
LibSync [44]	Client programs already migrated to library's new version and those not yet	Locations to update with edit suggestions	Semantic	Automatic	Manual
iXj [4]	Sample code to replace together with abstract replacement code	Visualized transformation program	Syntactic	Automatic	Automatic
ChangeFactory [55]	Recorded editing actions	A transformation program	Semantic	–	–
spdiff [2]	Reference edit in terms of multiple old and new methods	Semantic patch	Semantic	Automatic	Automatic
Coccinelle [48]	Semantic patch and codebase	Modified version of codebase	Semantic	Automatic	Automatic
ClearView [50]	Normal executions and erroneous executions of program	Dynamically patched program	Semantic	Automatic	Automatic
Weimer et al. [63]	Faulty program and test suites	Fixed program	Semantic	Automatic	Automatic
Sydit [36,37]	Reference edit in terms of old and new method and target location	Modified version of target	Semantic	Manual	Automatic
Lase [18,38]	Reference edit in terms of multiple old and new methods and codebase	Modified version of codebase	Syntactic	Automatic	Automatic

Table 16.2 Comparison of existing approaches in terms of edit capability

Tool	Multiple vs. Single	Contiguous vs. non-contiguous	Abstract vs. concrete	Context modeling
Visual AWK [27]	Single	Contiguous	Concrete	No
EBE [47]	Single	Contiguous	Concrete	No
TELS [65]	Single	Contiguous	Concrete	No
Dynamic macro system [32]	Single	Contiguous	Concrete	No
Cima [33]	Single	Contiguous	Concrete	Yes
Simultaneous text editing [41]	Single	Contiguous	Concrete	No
Linked editing [60]	Multiple	Non-contiguous	Concrete	Yes
CloneTracker [10]	Multiple	Non-contiguous	Concrete	Yes
Clever [46]	Multiple	Non-contiguous	Concrete	Yes
Trident [19]	Single	Non-contiguous	Abstract	No
Program synthesis [13]	Single	Contiguous	Concrete	No
Reverb [34, 35]	–	–	–	–
DQL [62]	–	–	–	–
PQL [31]	Single	Contiguous	Abstract	Yes
PR-Miner [29]	–	–	–	–
HAM [5]	–	–	–	–
Find-concept [57]	–	–	–	–
FixWizard [45]	–	–	–	–
LibSync [44]	–	–	–	–
iXj [4]	Single	Contiguous	Abstract	No
ChangeFactory [55]	–	–	–	–
spdiff [2]	Single	Contiguous	Abstract	No
Coccinelle [48]	Single	Contiguous	Abstract	No
ClearView [50]	Multiple	Non-contiguous	Abstract	Yes
Weimer et al. [63]	Single	Contiguous	Concrete	No
Sydit [36, 37]	Multiple	Non-contiguous	Abstract	Yes
Lase [18, 38]	Multiple	Non-contiguous	Abstract	Yes

subsequences, without requiring the user to invoke the macro-editor explicitly. Dynamic Macro performs no generalization and relies on several heuristics for detecting repetitive patterns of actions. The Cima system [33] learns generalized rules for classifying, generating, and modifying data, given examples, hints, and background knowledge. It allows a user to give hints to the learner to focus its attention on certain features, such as the particular area code preceding phone numbers of interests. However, the knowledge gained from these hints is combined with a set of hard-coded heuristics. As a result, it is unclear which hypotheses Cima is considering or why it prefers a certain inferred program over another. In general, these PBD approaches are not suitable for editing a program because they do not consider a program's syntax, control, or data dependencies.

Simultaneous text editing automates repetitive editing [41]. Users interactively demonstrate their edit in one context and the tool replicates *identical, lexical* edits on the preselected code fragments. Simultaneous text editing cannot easily handle

Table 16.3 Comparison of existing approaches in terms of evaluation

Tool	Subjects	Lng.	Data size	Evaluation
Visual AWK [27]	–	–	–	–
EBE [47]	–	–	–	–
TELS [65]	Text	–	3 text editing tasks	Count how many interactions needed between the system and its user to bake a correct transformation program
Dynamic macro system [32]	Text	–	Unknown	Compare results against user experience for 1 year
Cima [33]	Text	–	5 text editing tasks	User study
Simultaneous text editing [41]	Text	–	3 text editing tasks	User study
Linked editing [60]	Text	–	1 code clone linking task and 2 text editing tasks	User study
CloneTracker [10]	5 open source projects	Java	5 clone groups	User study
Clever [46]	7 open source projects	Java	7 open source projects	Compare results against version histories
Trident [19]	1 API migration	Java	1 open source project	Case study
Program synthesis [13]	Text	–	Unknown	User study
Reverb [34, 35]	2 open source projects	Java	2 open source projects	Compare results against manually determined locations
DQL [62]	2 open source projects	Java	4 searching tasks	Compare results against those of a clone detection tool and a text search tool
PQL [31]	6 open source projects	Java	3 searching tasks	Manually check results
PR-Miner [29]	3 open source projects	C	Top 60 reported rule violations	Manually check results
HAM [5]	3 open source projects	Java	Top 50 aspect candidates	Manually check results
Find-concept [57]	4 open source projects	Java	9 searching tasks	User study
FixWizard [45]	5 open source projects	Java	1414 bug fixes	Manually check results
LibSync [44]	6 pairs of API–client open source projects	Java	67 suggested locations together with adaptive changes	Manually check results

iXj [4]	1 open source project	Java	1 program transformation task	User study
ChangeFactory [55]	–		–	–
spdiff [2]	Linux and client programs	C	4 known patches	Compare results against known patches
Coccinelle [48]	Linux and client programs	C	26 known patches	Compare results against known patches
ClearView [50]	Firefox	C	10 known bugs	Test the tool's ability to successfully survive security attacks
Weimer et al. [63]	10 open source projects	C	10 known faulty programs	Run each generated program against the standard test suites
Sydit [36,37]	5 open source projects	Java	56 example method pairs	Compare the results against version histories
Lase [18,38]	2 open source projects	Java	61 program transformation tasks	Compare results against version histories

similar yet different edits because its capability is limited in instantiating a *syntactic*, context-aware, abstract transformation. Linked Editing [60] applies the same edits to a set of code clones specified by a user. CloneTracker [10] takes the output of a clone detector as input and automatically produces an abstract syntax-based clone region descriptor for each clone. Using this descriptor, it automatically tracks clones across program versions and identifies modifications to the clones. Similar to Linked Editing, it uses the longest common subsequence algorithm to map corresponding lines and to echo edits in one clone to other counterparts upon a developer's request. The Clever version control system detects inconsistent changes in clones and propagates *identical* edits to inconsistent clones [46]. Clever provides limited support in adapting the content of learned edits by renaming variable names suitable for target context. However, because Clever does not exploit program structure, when abstracting edits, it does not adapt the edit content to different contexts beyond renaming of variables. Trident [19] aims to support refactoring of dangling references by permitting the developer to specify lexical and syntactic constraints on search terms and replacement terms, locating potential matches and applying requested replacements; an iterative process is supported allowing the developer to back out of a given requested change atomically.

Program synthesis is the task of automatically synthesizing a program in some underlying language from a given specification using some search techniques [13]. It has been used for a variety of applications such as string manipulation macros [14], table transformation in Excel spreadsheets [16], geometry construction [15], etc. The synthesizer then completes the program satisfying the specification [58]. However, these program synthesis approaches do not currently handle automation of similar program changes in mainstream programming languages such as Java because they do not capture control and data flow contexts nor abstract identifiers in edit content.

In summary, the programming by demonstration approaches can learn edits from examples, but they are mostly designed for *regular text documents* instead of *programs*. Thus they cannot handle program transformations that require understanding program syntax and semantics.

In Table 16.1, the top one-third compares the above-mentioned PBD approaches in terms of inputs, outputs, and automation capability. Column **Type** describes the type of edit operations: textual edit vs. syntactic edits vs. semantic edits. Column **Location** describes whether each technique can find locations automatically, semiautomatically, or manually. Column **Transformation** describes whether each technique can apply transformations automatically, semiautomatically, or manually. Table 16.1 shows that most PBD approaches can handle only textual edits or they are very limited in terms of syntactic program editing capability.

In Table 16.2, the top one-third compares the above-mentioned PBD approaches in terms of edit capability. Column **Multiple vs. Single** shows whether each technique can apply multiline or single line edits. Column **Contiguous vs. Non-contiguous** describes whether each technique can only apply contiguous program transformations or also apply transformations separated with gaps. Column **Abstract vs. Concrete** describes whether each technique can apply customized abstract edits to different edit locations or simply apply identical concrete edits. Column **Context Modeling** describes whether each technique models the surrounding unchanged code relevant to edit operations in order to position edits correctly. The symbol "—" is recorded when a technique does not apply any edit automatically. Table 16.2 shows that most PBD approaches handle only concrete edits and are unable to apply edits customized to fit target program contexts.

Furthermore, as shown in Table 16.3, some techniques do not have any user study or only have done a study involving a handful of editing tasks. When the symbol "—" is recorded for **Subjects**, **Data size**, and **Evaluation** means no empirical study is reported. "—" recorded for **Lng.** (Language) means the technique targets plain text instead of any specific programming language.

16.3.2 Edit Location Suggestion

Code matching and example search tools can be used to identify similar code fragments that often require similar edits. Reverb [34] watches the developer make a change to a method and searches for other methods in the project where the syntax and semantics are similar to the original ones of the exemplar; however, it does not apply the transformations. DQL [62] helps developers to locate code regions that may need similar edits; developers can write and make queries involving dependence conditions and textual conditions on the system-dependence graph of the program so that the tool automatically locates code satisfying the condition. PQL [31] is a high-level specification language focusing on specifying patterns that occur during a program run. The PQL query analyzer can automatically detect code regions matching the query. Similarly, PR-Miner [29] automatically extracts implicit programming rules from large software code and detects violations to the extracted programming rules, which are strong indications of bugs. While all these tools could be used to identify candidate edit locations that may require similar edits, none of these tools help programmers in automatically applying similar changes to these locations. There are other tools that are similar to PQL and PR-Miner, such as JQuery [9] or SOUL [40]. While they can be used to find edit locations via pattern matching, they do not have a feature of automatically applying program transformations to the found code snippets. Similarly, Castro et al. diagnose and correct design inconsistencies but only *semiautomatically* [7].

Concern mining techniques locate and document crosscutting concerns [5,57]. Shepherd et al. [57] locate concerns using natural language program analysis. Breu and Zimmermann [5] mine aspects from version history by grouping method-calls that are added together. However, these tools leave it to a programmer to apply similar edits, when these concerns evolve. We do not exhaustively list all concern mining techniques here. Please refer to Kellens et al. [20] for a survey of automated code-level aspect mining techniques. In Chap. 5, Mens and Lozano [39] discuss techniques that recommend edit locations based on mined source code patterns.

FixWizard identifies code clones, recognizes recurring bug fixes to the clones, and suggests edit locations and exemplar edits [45]. Yet, it does *not generate syntactic edits*, nor does it support abstraction of variables, methods, and types. LibSync helps client applications migrate library API usages by learning migration patterns [44] with respect to a partial AST with containment and data dependencies. Though it suggests example API updates, it is *unable* to transform code. These limitations leave programmers with the burden of manually editing the suggested edit locations, which is error-prone and tedious.

In summary, the middle parts of Tables 16.1–16.3 show the comparison of the above-mentioned edit location suggestion techniques. These techniques can be used to find changed locations automatically, but leave it to developers to manually apply necessary transformations. While the evaluation of some techniques involves real open source project data, none evaluates them in the context of a user applying similar program transformations to the found locations.

16.3.3 Generating and Applying Program Transformations from Examples

To reduce programmers' burden in making similar changes to similar code fragments, several approaches take code change examples as input, find change locations, and apply customized program transformations to these locations. These approaches are fundamentally different from source transformation tools or refactoring engines, because users do not need to specify the script of repetitive program transformations in advance. Rather, the skeleton of repetitive transformations is generalized from change examples. This section lists such approaches and discusses their capability.

Sydit takes a code change example in Java as input and automatically infers a generalized edit script that a user can use to apply similar edits to a specified target [36, 37]. Their subsequent work Lase uses multiple change examples as input, automatically infers a generalized edit script, locates candidate change locations, and applies the inferred edit to these change locations [38]. Both Sydit and Lase infer the context of edit, encode edit positions in terms of surrounding data and control flow contexts, and abstract the content of edit scripts, making it applicable to code that has a similar control and data flow structure but uses different variable, type, and method names.

iXj [4] and ChangeFactory [55] provide interactive source transformation tools for editing a program. iXj does not generalize code transformation, though it has a limited capability of generalizing the scope of transformation. ChangeFactory requires a user to generalize edit content and location manually.

To support API migration, Lawall et al. [1, 2, 48] find differences in the API usage of client code, create an edit script, and transform programs to use updated APIs. Their approach is limited in two respects: the edit scripts are confined to term-replacements and they only apply to API usage changes. While it uses control- and data-dependence analysis to model the context of edits [1], the inferred context includes only inserted and deleted API method invocations and control and data dependencies among them. Their context does not include unchanged code on which the edits depend. Thus, when there is no deleted API method invocation, the extracted context cannot be used to position edits in a target method. Sydit is more flexible, because it computes edit context that is not limited to API method invocations and it can include unchanged statements related to edits. Therefore, even if the edits include only insertions, Sydit can correctly position edits by finding corresponding context nodes in a target method.

Automatic program repair generates candidate patches and checks correctness using compilation and testing [50, 63]. For example, the approach of Perkins et al. [50] generates patches that enforce invariants observed in correct executions but are violated in erroneous executions. It tests patched executions and selects the most successful patch. Weimer et al. [63] generate their candidate patches by replicating, mutating, or deleting code *randomly* from the existing program and thus far have focused on single line edits.

In summary, the bottom one-third of Tables 16.1–16.3 summarizes the comparison of the above-mentioned techniques. While these techniques can be used to find edit locations and apply transformations, some can handle only single line edits or contiguous edits. Very few can go beyond replication of concrete edits.

In the next two sections, we discuss two concrete example-based program transformation approaches in detail, Sydit and Lase. These two approaches are selected to discuss in depth for two reasons. First, they are specifically designed for updating programs as opposed to regular text documents. Second, they handle the issue of both recommending edit locations and applying transformations. They also have strengths of modeling change contexts correctly and customizing edit content appropriately to fit the target contexts. We discuss Sydit first, because Lase extends Sydit by leveraging multiple edit examples instead of a single example.

16.4 SYDIT: Generating Program Transformations from a Single Example

This section describes Sydit [37], which generates an *abstract, context-aware* edit script from a single changed method and applies it to a user-specified target. To facilitate illustration, we use Fig. 16.1 as a running example throughout this section.

16.4.1 Generating an Edit Script from a Single Example

There are two phases in Sydit. Phase I takes as input an old and new version of method mA to create an *abstract, context-aware* edit script Δ. Phase II applies Δ to a target method, mB, producing a modified method mB_s.

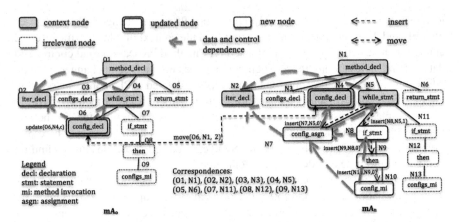

Fig. 16.2 Extraction of a syntactic edit from A_{old} and A_{new} and identification of its context [37]

Phase I: Creating Edit Scripts. Given mA_o and mA_n, Sydit compares their syntax trees using a program differencing tool [12], to create an edit $\Delta_A = [e_1, e_2, \ldots, e_n]$, as a sequence of abstract syntax tree (AST) node additions, deletions, updates, and moves, described as follows:

insert (Node u, Node v, int k)   Insert u and position it as the $(k + 1)^{th}$ child of v.

delete (Node u)   Delete u.

update (Node u, Node v)   Replace u's label and AST type with v's while maintaining u's position in the tree.

move (Node u, Node v, int k)   Delete u from its current position and insert it as the $(k + 1)^{th}$ child of v.

For our example, the inferred edit Δ_A between mA_o and mA_n is shown below.

1. update ("ILaunchConfiguration config = (ILaunchConfiguration)
        iter.next();", "ILaunchConfiguration config = **null**;")
2. move ("ILaunchConfiguration config = **null**;", "**protected** List
        getLaunchConfigurations(IProject project){", 2)
3. insert ("config = (ILaunchConfiguration)iter.next();",
        "**while** (iter.hasNext()){", 0)
4. insert ("**if** (config.inValid()){!", "**while** (iter.hasNext()){", 1)
5. insert ("then", "**if** (config.inValid()){!", 0)
6. insert ("config.reset()", "then", 0)

Figure 16.2 shows the edit in a graphical way. It indexes all nodes to simplify explanation. For each edit, Sydit extracts relevant context from both old and new versions of a changed method using control-, data-, and containment-dependence analysis. Here, the *context* relevant to an edit includes the edited nodes and nodes on which they depend. For instance, since the inserted node N7 is contained by and control dependent on N5, data dependent on N2 and N4, N2, N4, N5, and N7 are

Fig. 16.3 Abstract edit script
derived from Fig. 16.2 [37]

```
1.  ... method_declaration(...){
2.      $T1 $v1 = $m1().$m2();
3.      ...
4.      while($v1.$m3()){
5.  UPDATE: $T2 $v2 = ($T2)$v1.$m4();
6.      TO: $T2 $v2 = null;
7.  INSERT: $v2 = ($T2)$v1.$m4();
8.  INSERT: if(!$v2.$m5()){
9.              INSERT: $v2.$m6();
10.         }
11.     ...
12.     }
13.     ...
14. }
```

extracted as context relevant to the insert operation. The extracted context reflects
the control-, data-, and containment-dependence constraints the exemplar changed
method has on the derived edit. Given a target method, Sydit looks for the context's
correspondence in the method to ensure that all underlying constraints are satisfied.
If such a correspondence is found, Sydit infers that a similar edit is applicable to the
method, ignoring statements irrelevant to the edit.

Sydit then creates an *abstract, context-aware edit script* Δ, by replacing all
concrete types, methods, and variables with unique symbolic identifiers Tx, mx,
and vx, where x is a number, and recalculating each edit operation's location
with respect to its extracted context. This step generalizes the edit script, making
it applicable to code using different identifiers or structurally different code. For
instance, Fig. 16.3 shows a resulting abstract edit script derived from Fig. 16.2. It
abstracts the config variable in mA to $v2. After removing all irrelevant statements,
for the moved ILaunchConfiguration declaration, Sydit calibrates its source
location as a child position 0 of while (i.e., its first AST child node), and target
location as a child position 1 of the method declaration node.

Phase II: Applying Edit Scripts. When given a target method, Sydit looks for
nodes in the method that match the abstract context nodes in Δ and induce one-
to-one mappings between abstract and concrete identifiers. The node mapping
problem can be rephrased as a subtree isomorphism problem, which looks for a
subtree in the target method's AST matching the given context's tree. Sydit uses an
algorithm specially designed to solve the problem [37]. The algorithm establishes
node matches in a bottom-up manner. It first establishes matches for all leaf nodes
in the context tree, and then does so for all inner nodes based on leaf matching
result. If every node in the abstract context finds a unique correspondence in the
target method's tree, Sydit infers that the abstract edit script can be customized to
an edit script applicable to the method. It then establishes identifier mappings based
on the node mappings. In our example, mB_0 contains a subtree corresponding to the
abstract context for Δ, so Sydit can create a concrete edit script for mB_0 out of Δ.
Since Sydit establishes a mapping between the abstract node $T2 $v2 = **null** and
concrete node ILaunchConfiguration cfg = **null**, it aligns the identifiers used
and infers mapping $T2 to ILaunchConfiguration, $v2 to cfg.

Sydit next proceeds to generate concrete edits for the target. With identifier mappings derived above, it replaces abstract identifiers used in Δ with corresponding

concrete identifiers found in the target method, such as replacing $v2 with cfg. With node mappings derived above, it recalculates each edit operation's location with respect to the concrete target method. For example, it calibrates the target move location as child position 1 of mB_o's method declaration node. After applying the resulting edit script to mB_o, Sydit produces a suggested version mB_s, which is the same as mB_n shown at the bottom of Fig. 16.1.

16.4.2 Evaluation

Sydit is evaluated on 56 method pairs that experienced similar edits from Eclipse JDT Core, Eclipse Compare, Eclipse Core Runtime, Eclipse Debug, and jEdit. The two methods in each pair share at least one common syntactic edit and their content is at least 40 % similar according to the syntactic differencing algorithm of Fluri et al. [12]. These examples are then manually inspected and categorized based on (1) whether the edits involve changing a *single* AST node vs. *multiple* nodes, (2) whether the edits are *contiguous* vs. *non-contiguous*, and (3) whether the edits' content is *identical* vs. *abstract* over types, methods, and identifiers. Table 16.4 shows the number of examples in each of the six categories. Note that there are only six categories instead of eight, since non-contiguous edits always involve multiple nodes.

For each method pair (mA_o, mB_o) in the old version that changed similarly to become (mA_n, mB_n) in the new version, Sydit generates an edit script from mA_o and mA_n and tries to apply the learned edits to the target method mB_o, producing mB_s, which is compared against mB_n to measure Sydit's effectiveness. In Table 16.4, "matched" is the number of examples for which Sydit matches the change context learnt from mA to the target method mB_o and produces some edits. The "compilable" row is the number of examples for which Sydit produces a syntactically valid program, and "correct" is the number of examples for which Sydit replicates edits that are semantically identical to what the programmer actually did, i.e., that mB_s is semantically equivalent to mB_n.

The "coverage" row is $\dfrac{\text{"matched"}}{\text{"examples"}}$, and "accuracy" is $\dfrac{\text{"correct"}}{\text{"examples"}}$.

The "similarity" measures how similar mB_s is to mB_n for the examples which Sydit can match learnt context and produce some edits. The results are generated using Sydit's default context extraction method, i.e., one source node and one sink node for each control- and data-dependence edge, in addition to a parent node of each edited node, since the configuration is evaluated to produce the best results. For this configuration, Sydit matches the derived edit context and creates an edit for 46 of 56 examples, achieving 82 % coverage. In 39 of 46 cases, the edits are semantically equivalent to the programmer's hand edit. Even for those cases in which Sydit

Table 16.4 Sydit's coverage and accuracy on preselected targets [37]

	Single node	Multiple nodes	
		Contiguous	Non-contiguous
Identical	SI	CI	NI
examples	7	7	11
matched	5	7	8
compilable	5	7	8
correct	5	7	8
coverage	71%	100%	73%
accuracy	71%	100%	73%
similarity	100%	100%	100%
Abstract	SA	CA	NA
examples	7	12	12
matched	7	9	10
compilable	6	8	9
correct	6	6	7
coverage	100%	75%	83%
accuracy	86%	50%	58%
similarity	86%	95%	95%
Total coverage	82%	(46/56)	
Total accuracy	70%	(39/56)	
Total similarity	96%	(46)	

produces a different edit, the output and the expected output are often similar. On average, Sydit's output is 96 % similar to the version created by a human developer. While this preliminary evaluation shows accuracy for applying a known systematic edit to a given target location, it does not measure the accuracy for applying the edit to all locations where it is applicable because Sydit is unable to find edit locations automatically. The next section describes the follow-up approach (Lase) that leverages multiple examples to find edit candidates automatically.

16.5   LASE: Locating and Applying Program Transformations from Multiple Examples

Sydit produces code transformation from a single example. It relies on programmers to specify *where* to apply the code transformation, and it does not automatically find edit locations. This section describes Lase, which uses multiple edit examples instead of a single example to infer code transformation, automatically searches for edit locations, and applies customized edits to the locations [38].

16.5.1 Why Learning from Multiple Examples?

The edit script inferred by Sydit is not always well suited to finding edit locations for two reasons. First, the mechanism of learning from a single example cannot disambiguate which changes in the example should be generalized to other places while which should not. As a result, it simply generalizes every change in the example and thus may *overspecify* the script. The over-specification may make the extracted edit context too specific to the example, failing to match places where it should have matched. Second, the full identifier abstraction may *over generalize* the script, allowing the extracted edit context to match places that it should not have matched, because they use different concrete identifiers.

Lase seeks an edit script that serves double duty, both finding edit locations and accurately transforming the code. It learns from two or more exemplar edits given by the developer to solve the problems of over-generalization and over-specification. Although developers may also want to directly create or modify a script, since they already make similar edits to more than one place, providing multiple examples could be a natural interface.

We use Fig. 16.4 as a running example throughout the section. Consider the three methods with similar changes: mA, mB, and mC. All these methods perform similar tasks: (1) iterate over all elements returned by values(), (2) process elements one by one, (3) cast each element to an object of a certain type, and (4) when an element meets a certain condition, invoke the element's update() method. Additionally, mA and mB also experience some specific changes, respectively. For instance, mA deletes two print statements before the while loop. mB deletes one print statement inside the while loop and adds an extra type check and element processing.

16.5.2 Learning and Applying Edits from Multiple Examples

Lase creates a *partially abstract, context-aware* edit script from multiple exemplar changed methods, finds edit locations using the extracted context in the edit script, and finally applies the edit script to each location. There are three phases in Lase. Phase I takes as input several changed methods, such as mA and mB, to create a *partially abstract, context-aware* edit script Δ_p. Phase II uses the extracted context in Δ_p to search for edit locations which can be changed similarly, such as mC. Phase III applies Δ_p to each found location and suggests a modified version to developers. Figure 16.5 shows the inferred edit script from mA and mB in Fig. 16.4. The details of Lase's edit generalization, location search, and edit customization algorithms are described elsewhere [38].

```
 1  public void textChanged (TEvent event) {
 2     Iterator e = fActions.values().iterator();
 3  -    print(event.getReplacedText());
 4  -    print(event.getText());
 5     while(e.hasNext()) {
 6  -    MVAction action = (MVAction)e.next();
 7  -    if(action.isContentDependent())
 8  -    action.update();
 9  +    Object next = e.next();
10  +    if (next instanceof MVAction) {
11  +    MVAction action =(MVAction)next;
12  +    if(action.isContentDependent())
13  +    action.update();
14  +    }
15     }
16     System.out.println(event + " is processed");
17  }
```

a

```
 1  public void updateActions () {
 2     Iterator iter = getActions().values().iterator();
 3     while(iter.hasNext()) {
 4  -    print(this.getReplacedText());
 5  -    MVAction action=(MVAction)iter.next();
 6  -    if(action.isDependent())
 7  -    action.update();
 8  +    Object next = iter.next();
 9  +    if (next instanceof MVAction) {
10  +    MVAction action =(MVAction)next;
11  +    if(action.isDependent())
12  +    action.update();}
13  +    }
14  +    if (next instanceof FRAction) {
15  +    FRAction action = (FRAction)next;
16  +    if(action.isDependent())
17  +    action.update();}
18  +    }
19     }
20     print(this.toString());
21  }
```

b

```
 1  public void selectionChanged (SEvent event) {
 2     Iterator e = fActions.values().iterator();
 3     while(e.hasNext()) {
 4  -    MVAction action=(MVAction)e.next();
 5  -    if(action.isSelectionDependent())
 6  -    action.update();
 7  +    Object next = e.next();
 8  +    if (next instanceof MVAction) {
 9  +    MVAction action =(MVAction)next;
10  +    if(action.isSelectionDependent())
11  +    action.update();
12  +    }
13     }
14  }
```

c

Fig. 16.4 A systematic edit to three methods based on revisions from 2007-04-16 and 2007-04-30 to org.eclipse.compare [38]. (**a**) mA_o to mA_n. (**b**) mB_o to mB_n. (**c**) mC_o to mC_n

```
1.  … … method_declaration(… …){
2.     Iterator v$0 = u$0:FieldAccessOrMethodInvocation
                        .values().iterator();
3.     while(v$0.hasNext()){
4.        UPDATE: MVAction action = (MVAction)v$0.next();
5.           TO: Object next = v$0.next();
6.        if(action.m$0()){
7.           … …
8.        }
9.        INSERT: if(next instanceof MVAction){
10.          INSERT: MVAction action = (MVAction)next;
11.          … …
12.       }
```

Fig. 16.5 Partially abstract, context-aware edit script derived from mA and mB [38]

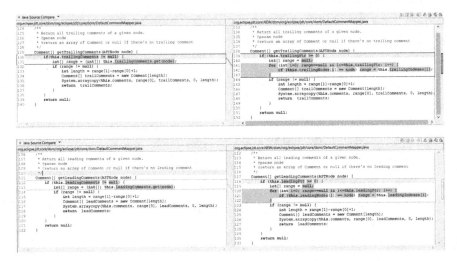

Fig. 16.6 A programmer makes similar but not identical edits to `getTrailingComments` and `getLeadingComments`. While `getTrailingComments` involves edits to `trailing-Comments` and `trailingPtr`, `getLeadingComments` involves edits to `leading-Comments` and `leadingPtr`. The two examples are provided as input to Lase to generate a partially abstract, context-aware edit script [38]

16.5.3 LASE as an Eclipse Plugin

The Lase approach described above is implemented as an Eclipse IDE plugin [18]. Suppose that Bob modifies the code comment processing logic in `org.eclipse.jdt` by updating two methods `getTrailingComments` and `getLeadingComments` in `org.eclipse.jdt.core.dom.DefaultCommentMapper`, shown in Fig. 16.6. In the `getTrailingComments` method, he modifies the `if` condition, modifies an assignment to `range`, and inserts a `for` loop to scan for a given AST node. In the `getLeadingComments` method, he makes a similar edit by modifying its `if` condition, an assignment to `range`, and by inserting a `for` loop. After making these repetitive edits to the two methods, Bob suspects a similar edit may be needed to all methods with a comment processing logic. He uses Lase to automatically search for candidate edit locations and view edit suggestions.

Input Selection. Using the input selection *user interface*, Bob provides a set of edit examples. He specifies the old and new versions of getTrailingComments and getLeadingComments, respectively. He names this group of similar changes as a *comment processing logic change*. He then selects *an edit script generation* option to derive generalized program transformation among the specified examples.

Edit Operation View. For each example, using an *edit operation view*, Bob examines the details of constituent edit operations (*insert, delete, move,* and *update*) with respect to underlying abstract syntax trees. In this view, Bob can also examine corresponding edit context—surrounding unchanged code that is control- or data dependent on the edited code. Figure 16.7a shows edit operations and corresponding context within the AST of the method getTrailingComments. The AST nodes include both unchanged nodes and changed nodes which are the source and/or target of individual insert, delete, move, or update operations. These nodes can be expanded to show more details.

Edit Script Hierarchy View. To create an edit script from multiple examples, Lase generalizes exemplar edits, pair-by-pair. Lase creates a base cluster for each method. It then compares them pair-by-pair. By merging the results of two cluster nodes, Lase generalizes common edit sequences in the edit hierarchy through a bottom-up construction.

For example, by opening the *edit script hierarchy view* shown in Fig. 16.7b, Bob can examine a group of inferred edit scripts at different abstraction levels. By default, Lase uses the top node, i.e., an edit script inferred from *all* examples. By clicking a node in the edit script hierarchy, Bob may select a different subset of provided examples to adjust the abstraction level of an edit script. The selected script is used to search for edit locations and generate customized edits.

Searching for Edit Locations and Applying Customized Edits. Bob begins his search for edit locations with similar context. In this case, when Lase finishes searching for the target locations, Bob sees four candidate change locations in the menu. Two of them are getTrailingComments and getLeadingComments, which are used as input examples and thus match the context of the inferred edit script—this provides an additional confirmation that the edit script can correctly describe the common edits for the two examples.

Bob then examines the edit suggestions for the first candidate method getExtendedEnd using the *comparison view* (see Fig. 16.8). He sees that getExtendedEnd contains the same structure as his example methods. For example, the if statement checking whether trailingComments is set to null and the assignment to range. When viewing the Lase's edit suggestions, Bob notices that the suggested change involves inserting new variables. Lase cannot infer the names of the new variables because there are no matching variable names in the target context. Bob thus chooses

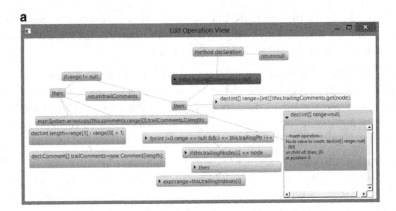

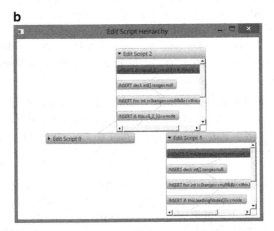

Fig. 16.7 (**a**) Lase visualizes edit operations and corresponding context with respect to the AST. (**b**) Lase learns an edit from two or more examples. Each node in the edit script hierarchy corresponds to an edit script from a different subset of the input examples [38]

Fig. 16.8 A user can review and correct edit suggestions generated by Lase before approving the tool-suggested edit [38]

the names of those variables by replacing $v_1_, $v_2_, and $v_3_ with concrete names. Choosing variables and any other changes Bob wishes to make could be easily done by making direct modifications on the edit suggestion in this comparison view. He applies the modified edits and repeats the process with the other methods.

16.5.4 Evaluation

To measure Lase's precision, recall, and edit correctness, a test suite of supplementary bug fixes [49, 54] was used. (See Walker and Holmes [61] in Chap. 12 about an evaluation method using a change history-based simulation). Precision and recall are regarding identified method-level edit locations and edit correctness measures the accuracy of applied edits to the found method locations. Supplementary bug fixes are fixes that span multiple commit, where initial commits tend to be incomplete or incorrect, and thus developers apply supplementary changes to resolve the issue or the bug. If a bug is fixed more than once and there are clones of at least two lines in bug patches checked in at different times, they are manually examined for systematic changes. Using this method, 2 systematic edits in Eclipse JDT and 22 systematic edits in Eclipse SWT are found.

Meng et al. then use these patches as an oracle test suite for correct systematic edits and test if Lase can produce the same results as the developers given the first two fixes in each set of systematic fixes. If Lase, however, produces the same results as developers do in later patches, it indicates that Lase can help programmers detect edit locations earlier, reduce errors of omissions, and make systematic edits. Lase locates edit positions with respect to the oracle data set with 99 % precision, 89 % recall, and performs edits with 91 % edit correctness. Furthermore, given the test suite, Lase identifies and correctly edits nine locations that developers confirmed they missed.

The number of exemplar edits from which Lase learns a systematic edit affects its effectiveness. To determine how sensitive Lase is to different numbers of exemplar edits, Meng et al. randomly pick seven cases in the oracle data set and enumerate subsets of exemplar edits, e.g., all pairs of two exemplar methods. They evaluate the precision, recall, and edit correctness for each set separately and calculate an average for exemplar edit sets for each cardinality to determine how sensitive Lase is to different numbers of exemplar edits. Table 16.5 shows the results.

Our hypothesis is as the number of exemplar edits increases, precision and edit correctness should decrease while recall should increase, because the more exemplar edits provided, the less common context is likely to be shared among them, and the more methods may be found to match the context. However, as shown in Table 16.5, precision P does not change as a function of the number of exemplar edits except for case 12, where two exemplar edits cause the highest precision because exemplar edits are very different from each other. Recall R is more sensitive to the number of exemplar edits, increasing as a function of exemplars.

Table 16.5 Lase's effectiveness when learning from multiple examples [38]

	Exemplars (#)	P (%)	R (%)	EC (%)
Index 4	2	100	51	72
	3	100	82	67
	4	100	96	67
	5	100	100	67
Index 5	2	100	80	100
	3	100	84	100
	4	100	91	100
Index 7	2	100	83	100
	3	100	84	100
	4	100	88	100
	5	100	92	100
	6	100	96	100
Index 12	2	78	90	85
	3	49	98	83
	4	31	100	82
Index 13	2	100	100	95
	3	100	100	94
	4	100	100	93
	5	100	100	91
Index 19	2	100	66	100
	3	100	94	100
	4	100	100	100
	5	100	100	100
Index 23	2	100	72	100
	3	100	88	100
	4	100	96	100

In theory, edit correctness EC can vary inconsistently with the number of exemplar edits, because it strictly depends on the similarity between edits. For instance, when exemplar edits are diverse, Lase extracts fewer common edit operations, which lowers edit correctness. When exemplar edits are similar, adding exemplar methods may not decrease the number of common edit operations, but may induce more identifier abstraction and result in a more flexible edit script, which increases edit correctness.

16.6 Open Issues and Challenges

This section discusses open issues and challenges of recommending program transformations from examples.

Finding Input Examples. While the techniques discussed in Sects. 16.4 and 16.5 learn a generalized program transformation script from examples, it is still left to developers to provide multiple examples for edit script generation and refinement.

Where do these examples come from? Developers can construct the examples on purpose or carefully pick them out of the codebase they are working on. However, a more efficient way is to automatically detect repetitive code changes. One possibility is to mine software version history for similar code changes [23, 26] by comparing subsequent snapshots of codebase. Another possibility is to observe developers' edit actions to recognize recurring code changes by monitoring the commands or keystrokes a developer inputs.

Granularity. Most approaches in Sect. 16.3 target replication of intra-method edits. For higher level edits, such as modifying a class hierarchy or delegating an existing task to a newly created methods, we need more complicated edit types to define and more sophisticated context modeling approaches to explore. The edit types should handle the coordination of heterogeneous edits, i.e., various edits to different program entities, in addition to replication of homogeneous edits. For instance, an edit type "Rename" includes renaming an entity (i.e., class, method, field, variable) and modifying all references to the entity. The context modeling approaches should correlate a changed code entity with other entities in the same class hierarchy or performing the same task. For instance, if a method is inserted to an interface, all classes directly implementing the class should be included as edit context as they need to add implementations for the newly declared method.

Context Characterization. The effectiveness of example-based program transformation approaches is affected by the amount of dependence information encoded in the abstract change context C derived from an exemplar edit. For example, given a statement inserted in a `for` loop, the edit could be applicable to all `for` loops, resulting in higher recall but lower precision. However, if the approach requires a context with a control-dependence chain that includes an `if` controlling execution of the `for`, then this context will help find fewer candidates and waste less time on testing extraneous cases. Determining a setting for context extraction requires a rigorous empirical study: (1) varying the number of dependence hops k, (2) varying the degree of identifier abstraction for variable, method, and type names, (3) including upstream- and/or downstream-dependence relations, (4) using containment dependencies only, etc.

Edit Customization. While some approaches are able to customize edit content to fit the target context, it is generally difficult to customize edit content in the target context, when it involves inserted code only. For example, in Lase, edits are customized based on mapping between symbolic identifiers and concrete identifiers discovered from a target context. However, such mappings cannot always be found for inserted code that only exists in the new version. For instance, as shown in Fig. 16.9, since `actionBars` only exists in A_{new} and `serviceLocator` only exists in B_{new}, it is difficult to infer `serviceLocator` to use in B_{new} from `actionBars` used in A_{new}. In this case, existing approaches borrow verbatim code, `actionBars`, from the source edit, and add it to the target edit without recognizing naming conversion patterns. As a result, it may produce semantically equivalent code with poor readability: e.g., `IServiceLocator actionBars` instead of `IServiceLocator`

```
1  public IActionBars
2      getActionBars() {
3  +   IActionBars actionBars = fContainer}.getActionBars();
4  -   if (fContainer == null) {
5  +   if (actionBars == null && !fContainerProvided) {
6      return Utilities.findActionBars(fComposite);...
```

a

```
1  public IServiceLocator
2      getServiceLocator() {
3  +   IServiceLocator actionBars = fContainer.getServiceLocator();
4  -   if (fContainer == null) {
5  +   if (actionBars == null && !fContainerProvided) {
6      return Utilities.findSite(fComposite);...
```

b

Fig. 16.9 A motivating example for synthesizing target-specific identifiers [37]. (**a**) A_{old} to A_{new}.
(**b**) B_{old} to $B_{suggested}$

serviceLocator. A better strategy is to synthesize the target-specific identifiers
by inferring naming patterns from the source edit. This requires a natural language
analysis of programs [52], e.g., semantic analysis of identifier names used in the
target context.

Integrated Compilation and Testing. Existing tools suggest edits without checking correctness, so developers need to decide whether the suggestion is correct on
their own. In extreme cases, when tools provide suggestions with many false positive, developers may spend more time examining the tools' useless suggestions than
manually making systematic changes without any tool support. Before suggesting
the edits, a recommendation tool may proactively compile a suggested version and
run regression tests relevant to the proposed edits by integrating existing regression
test selection algorithms. If the suggested version does not fail more tests, a user
may have higher confidence in it. Otherwise, the tool may locate failure-inducing
edits by integrating existing change impact analysis algorithms. This step is similar
to speculatively exploring the consequences of applying quick fix recommendations
in an IDE [42] and can help prevent a user from approving failure-inducing edits.

Edit Validation. During the inspection process, a user may still want to reason
about the deeper semantics of the suggested edits. While this is a program
differencing problem, a naive application of existing differencing algorithms may
not help developers much—by definition, syntactic edits to the source and the target
are the same. A new validation approach is needed to allow developers to focus their
attention to *differential deltas*—differences between the effect of a reference edit
(A_{old} to A_{new}) and the effect of a target edit (B_{old} to $B_{suggested}$). The insight behind this
approach is that developers may have good understanding of a reference edit already
and what they want to know is subtle semantic discrepancies caused by porting a

reference edit to a new context. For example, one may compare the control and data flow contexts of a reference edit against those of a ported edit. Another possible approach is to compare the path conditions and effects involving a reference edit against those of a ported edit in the target context [51]. Such semantic comparison could help developers validate whether there exists behavioral differences.

Edit Script Correction. Before accepting recommendation transformations, a user may want to correct the derived script or suggested edits. After correction, the tool may rematch the modified script and recompute the suggested edits, providing feedback to the user. To detect errors inadvertently introduced by manual edits such as a name capture of a preexisting variable, the tool must check name binding and def-use relation preservation [56].

16.7 Conclusion

Systematic changes—making similar but not identical changes to multiple code locations—are common and often unavoidable, when evolving large software systems. This chapter has described the existing body of knowledge and approaches to address this problem. First, it described PBD techniques designed to automate repetitive tasks and discussed how EBE approaches are inadequate for automating program transformations due to their inability to model program-specific syntax and semantics. Second, it overviewed recommendation techniques that suggest candidate edit locations but do not manipulate code by applying code transformations to these locations. Third, it described *example-based program transformation approaches* that take code change examples as input, infer a generalized program transformation script, locate matching candidate locations, and apply the script to these locations. Existing approaches were compared using unified comparison criteria in terms of required inputs, user involvement, the degree of automation, edit capability, evaluation method, and scale to date. In particular, this chapter summarized two approaches, Sydit and Lase. These approaches were selected for an in-depth discussion because they are the most advanced in terms of their capability to position edits correctly by capturing the control- and data-flow contexts of the edits, and to apply non-contiguous, abstract program edits. These strengths make it possible to apply the inferred script to new contexts in a robust manner. The chapter concluded with a set of open problems and challenges that remain to be tackled to fully solve the problem of automating systematic software updates.

Acknowledgments We thank Kathryn McKinley who contributed to designing and evaluating key algorithms of Sydit and Lase. We also thank her for our fruitful collaboration and numerous discussions on example-based program transformation approaches. We thank John Jacobellis who is a main contributor of developing the Lase Eclipse plugin. This work was supported in part by the National Science Foundation under grants CCF-1149391, CCF-1117902, SHF-0910818, and CCF-0811524 and by a Microsoft SEIF award.

References

1. Andersen, J.: Semantic patch inference. Ph.D. thesis, University of Copenhagen (2009)
2. Andersen, J., Lawall, J.L.: Generic patch inference. In: Proceedings of the IEEE/ACM International Conference on Automated Software Engineering, pp. 337–346 (2008). doi:10.1109/ASE.2008.44
3. Baxter, I.D., Pidgeon, C., Mehlich, M.: DMS: program transformations for practical scalable software evolution. In: Proceedings of the ACM/IEEE International Conference on Software Engineering, pp. 625–634 (2004). doi:10.1109/ICSE.2004.1317484
4. Boshernitsan, M., Graham, S.L., Hearst, M.A.: Aligning development tools with the way programmers think about code changes. In: Proceedings of the ACM SIGCHI Conference on Human Factors in Computing Systems, pp. 567–576 (2007). doi:10.1145/1240624.1240715
5. Breu, S., Zimmermann, T.: Mining aspects from version history. In: Proceedings of the IEEE/ACM International Conference on Automated Software Engineering, pp. 221–230 (2006). doi:10.1109/ASE.2006.50
6. Canfora, G., Cerulo, L., Cimitile, M., Di Penta, M.: Social interactions around cross-system bug fixings: the case of FreeBSD and OpenBSD. In: Proceedings of the International Working Conference on Mining Software Repositories, pp. 143–152 (2011). doi:10.1145/1985441.1985463
7. Castro, S., Brichau, J., Mens, K.: Diagnosis and semi-automatic correction of detected design inconsistencies in source code. In: Proceedings of the International Workshop on Smalltalk Technologies, pp. 8–17 (2009). doi:10.1145/1735935.1735938
8. Cordy, J.R.: The TXL source transformation language. Sci. Comput. Program. **61**(3), 190–210 (2006). doi:10.1016/j.scico.2006.04.002
9. De Volder, K.: JQuery: a generic code browser with a declarative configuration language. In: Hentenryck, P. (ed.) Practical Aspects of Declarative Languages. Lecture Notes in Computer Science, vol. 3819, pp. 88–102. Springer, Heidelberg (2006). doi:10.1007/11603023_7
10. Duala-Ekoko, E., Robillard, M.P.: Clone region descriptors: representing and tracking duplication in source code. ACM T. Software Eng. Meth. **20**(1), 3:1–3:31 (2010). doi:10.1145/1767751.1767754
11. Eaddy, M., Zimmermann, T., Sherwood, K.D., Garg, V., Murphy, G.C., Nagappan, N., Aho, A.V.: Do crosscutting concerns cause defects? IEEE T. Software Eng. **34**(4), 497–515 (2008). doi:10.1109/TSE.2008.36
12. Fluri, B., Würsch, M., Pinzger, M., Gall, H.C.: Change distilling: tree differencing for fine-grained source code change extraction. IEEE T. Software Eng. **33**(11), 725–743 (2007). doi:10.1109/TSE.2007.70731
13. Gulwani, S.: Dimensions in program synthesis. In: Proceedings of the ACM SIGPLAN International Symposium on Principles and Practice of Declarative Programming, pp. 13–24 (2010). doi:10.1145/1836089.1836091
14. Gulwani, S.: Automating string processing in spreadsheets using input–output examples. In: Proceedings of the ACM SIGPLAN Conference on Principles of Programming Languages, pp. 317–330 (2011). http://doi.acm.org/10.1145/1926385.1926423
15. Gulwani, S., Korthikanti, V.A., Tiwari, A.: Synthesizing geometry constructions. In: Proceedings of the ACM SIGPLAN Conference on Programming Language Design and Implementation, pp. 50–61 (2011). http://doi.acm.org/10.1145/1993498.1993505
16. Harris, W.R., Gulwani, S.: Spreadsheet table transformations from examples. In: Proceedings of the ACM SIGPLAN Conference on Programming Language Design and Implementation, pp. 317–328 (2011). doi:10.1145/1993498.1993536
17. Henkel, J., Diwan, A.: CatchUp!: capturing and replaying refactorings to support API evolution. In: Proceedings of the ACM/IEEE International Conference on Software Engineering, pp. 274–283 (2005). doi:10.1145/1062455.1062512

18. Jacobellis, J., Meng, N., Kim, M.: LASE: an example-based program transformation tool for locating and applying systematic edits. In: Proceedings of the ACM/IEEE International Conference on Software Engineering, pp. 1319–1322 (2013). doi:10.1109/ICSE.2013.6606707

19. Kapur, P., Cossette, B., Walker, R.J.: Refactoring references for library migration. In: Proceedings of the ACM SIGPLAN Conference on Object-Oriented Programming, Systems, Languages, and Applications, pp. 726–738 (2010). doi:10.1145/1869459.1869518

20. Kellens, A., Mens, K., Tonella, P.: A survey of automated code-level aspect mining techniques. In: Rashid, A., Aksit, M. (eds.) Transactions on Aspect-Oriented Software Development IV. Lecture Notes in Computer Science, vol. 4640, pp. 143–162. Springer, Heidelberg (2007). doi:10.1007/978-3-540-77042-8_6

21. Kiczales, G., Lamping, J., Menhdhekar, A., Maeda, C., Lopes, C., Loingtier, J.M., Irwin, J.: Aspect-oriented programming. In: Proceedings of the European Conference on Object-Oriented Programming. Lecture Notes in Computer Science, vol. 1241, pp. 220–242 (1997). doi:10.1007/BFb0053381

22. Kim, M., Cai, D., Kim, S.: An empirical investigation into the role of API-level refactorings during software evolution. In: Proceedings of the ACM/IEEE International Conference on Software Engineering, pp. 151–160 (2011). doi:10.1145/1985793.1985815

23. Kim, M., Notkin, D.: Discovering and representing systematic code changes. In: Proceedings of the ACM/IEEE International Conference on Software Engineering, pp. 309–319 (2009). doi:10.1109/ICSE.2009.5070531

24. Kim, M., Sazawal, V., Notkin, D., Murphy, G.: An empirical study of code clone genealogies. In: Proceedings of the European Software Engineering Conference/ACM SIGSOFT International Symposium on Foundations of Software Engineering, pp. 187–196 (2005). doi:10.1145/1081706.1081737

25. Kim, M., Zimmermann, T., Nagappan, N.: A field study of refactoring challenges and benefits. In: Proceedings of the ACM SIGSOFT International Symposium on Foundations of Software Engineering, pp. 50:1–50:11 (2012). doi:10.1145/2393596.2393655

26. Kim, S., Pan, K., Whitehead Jr., E.E.J.: Memories of bug fixes. In: Proceedings of the ACM SIGSOFT International Symposium on Foundations of Software Engineering, pp. 35–45 (2006). doi:10.1145/1181775.1181781

27. Landauer, J., Hirakawa, M.: Visual AWK: a model for text processing by demonstration. In: Proceedings of the IEEE International Symposium on Visual Languages, pp. 267–274 (1995). doi:10.1109/VL.1995.520818

28. Lau, T., Wolfman, S.A., Domingos, P., Weld, D.S.: Learning repetitive text-editing procedures with SMARTedit. In: Lieberman, H. (ed.) Your Wish is My Command: Programming by Example, pp. 209–226. Morgan Kaufmann, Los Altos, CA (2001)

29. Li, Z., Zhou, Y.: PR-Miner: automatically extracting implicit programming rules and detecting violations in large software code. In: Proceedings of the European Software Engineering Conference/ACM SIGSOFT International Symposium on Foundations of Software Engineering, pp. 306–315 (2005). doi:10.1145/1081706.1081755

30. Lieberman, H. (ed.): Your Wish Is My Command: Programming by Example. Morgan Kaufmann, Los Altos, CA (2001)

31. Martin, M., Livshits, B., Lam, M.S.: Finding application errors and security flaws using PQL: a program query language. In: Proceedings of the ACM SIGPLAN Conference on Object-Oriented Programming, Systems, Languages, and Applications, pp. 365–383 (2005). doi:10.1145/1094811.1094840

32. Masui, T., Nakayama, K.: Repeat and predict: two keys to efficient text editing. In: Proceedings of the ACM SIGCHI Conference on Human Factors in Computing Systems, pp. 118–130 (1994). doi:10.1145/191666.191722

33. Maulsby, D., Witten, I.H.: Cima: an interactive concept learning system for end-user applications. Appl. Artif. Intell.: Int. J. **11**(7–8), 653–671 (1997). doi:10.1080/088395197117975

34. McIntyre, M., Walker, R.J.: Assisting potentially-repetitive small-scale changes via semi-automated heuristic search. In: Proceedings of the IEEE/ACM International Conference on Automated Software Engineering, pp. 497–500 (2007). doi:10.1145/1321631.1321718

35. McIntyre, M.: Supporting repetitive small-scale changes. MSc thesis, University of Calgary (2007)
36. Meng, N., Kim, M., McKinley, K.S.: Sydit: creating and applying a program transformation from an example. In: Proceedings of the European Software Engineering Conference/ACM SIGSOFT International Symposium on Foundations of Software Engineering, pp. 440–443 (2011a). doi:10.1145/2025113.2025185
37. Meng, N., Kim, M., McKinley, K.S.: Systematic editing: generating program transformations from an example. In: Proceedings of the ACM SIGPLAN Conference on Programming Language Design and Implementation, pp. 329–342 (2011b). doi:10.1145/1993498.1993537
38. Meng, N., Kim, M., McKinley, K.S.: LASE: locating and applying systematic edits by learning from examples. In: Proceedings of the ACM/IEEE International Conference on Software Engineering, pp. 502–511 (2013). doi:10.1109/ICSE.2013.6606596
39. Mens, K., Lozano, A.: Source code based recommendation systems. In: Robillard, M., Maalej, W., Walker, R.J., Zimmermann, T. (eds.) Recommendation Systems in Software Engineering. Springer, Heidelberg, Chap. 5. (2014)
40. Mens, K., Wuyts, R., D'Hondt, T.: Declaratively codifying software architectures using virtual software classifications. In: Proceedings of the International Conference on Technology of Object-Oriented Languages and Systems, pp. 33–45 (1999). doi:10.1109/TOOLS.1999.778997
41. Miller, R.C., Myers, B.A.: Interactive simultaneous editing of multiple text regions. In: Proceedings of the USENIX Annual Technical Conference, pp. 161–174 (2001)
42. Muşlu, K., Brun, Y., Holmes, R., Ernst, M.D., Notkin, D.: Speculative analysis of integrated development environment recommendations. In: Proceedings of the ACM SIGPLAN Conference on Object-Oriented Programming, Systems, Languages, and Applications, pp. 669–682 (2012). doi:10.1145/2384616.2384665
43. Murphy-Hill, E., Parnin, C., Black, A.P.: How we refactor, and how we know it. IEEE T. Software Eng. **38**(1), 5–18 (2011). doi:10.1109/TSE.2011.41
44. Nguyen, H.A., Nguyen, T.T., Wilson Jr., G., Nguyen, A.T., Kim, M., Nguyen, T.N.: A graph-based approach to API usage adaptation. In: Proceedings of the ACM SIGPLAN Conference on Object-Oriented Programming, Systems, Languages, and Applications, pp. 302–321 (2010a). doi:10.1145/1869459.1869486
45. Nguyen, T.T., Nguyen, H.A., Pham, N.H., Al-Kofahi, J., Nguyen, T.N.: Recurring bug fixes in object-oriented programs. In: Proceedings of the ACM/IEEE International Conference on Software Engineering, pp. 315–324 (2010b). doi:10.1145/1806799.1806847
46. Nguyen, T.T., Nguyen, H.A., Pham, N.H., Al-Kofahi, J.M., Nguyen, T.N.: Clone-aware configuration management. In: Proceedings of the IEEE/ACM International Conference on Automated Software Engineering, pp. 123–134 (2009). doi:10.1109/ASE.2009.90
47. Nix, R.: Editing by example. In: Proceedings of the ACM SIGPLAN Conference on Principles of Programming Languages, pp. 186–195 (1984). doi:10.1145/800017.800530
48. Padioleau, Y., Lawall, J., Hansen, R.R., Muller, G.: Documenting and automating collateral evolutions in Linux device drivers. In: Proceedings of the ACM SIGOPS/EuroSys European Conference on Computer Systems, pp. 247–260 (2008). doi:10.1145/1352592.1352618
49. Park, J., Kim, M., Ray, B., Bae, D.H.: An empirical study of supplementary bug fixes. In: Proceedings of the International Working Conference on Mining Software Repositories, pp. 40–49 (2012). doi:10.1109/MSR.2012.6224298
50. Perkins, J.H., Kim, S., Larsen, S., Amarasinghe, S., Bachrach, J., Carbin, M., Pacheco, C., Sherwood, F., Sidiroglou, S., Sullivan, G., Wong, W.F., Zibin, Y., Ernst, M.D., Rinard, M.: Automatically patching errors in deployed software. In: Proceedings of the ACM Symposium on Operating Systems Principles, pp. 87–102 (2009). doi:10.1145/1629575.1629585
51. Person, S., Dwyer, M.B., Elbaum, S., Pǎsǎreanu, C.S.: Differential symbolic execution. In: Proceedings of the ACM SIGSOFT International Symposium on Foundations of Software Engineering, pp. 226–237 (2008). doi:10.1145/1453101.1453131

52. Pollock, L.: Leveraging natural language analysis of software: achievements, challenges, and opportunities. In: Proceedings of the IEEE International Conference on Software Maintenance, p. 4 (2012). doi:10.1109/ICSM.2012.6405245
53. Purushothaman, R., Perry, D.E.: Toward understanding the rhetoric of small source code changes. IEEE T. Software Eng. **31**(6), 511–526 (2005). doi:10.1109/TSE.2005.74
54. Ray, B., Kim, M.: A case study of cross-system porting in forked projects. In: Proceedings of the European Software Engineering Conference/ACM SIGSOFT International Symposium on Foundations of Software Engineering, pp. 53:1–53:11 (2012). doi:10.1145/2393596.2393659
55. Robbes, R., Lanza, M.: Example-based program transformation. In: Proceedings of the International Conference on Model-Driven Engineering of Languages and Systems. Lecture Notes in Computer Science, vol. 5301, pp. 174–188 (2008). doi:10.1007/978-3-540-87875-9_13
56. Schaefer, M., de Moor, O.: Specifying and implementing refactorings. In: Proceedings of the ACM SIGPLAN Conference on Object-Oriented Programming, Systems, Languages, and Applications, pp. 286–301 (2010). doi:10.1145/1869459.1869485
57. Shepherd, D., Fry, Z.P., Hill, E., Pollock, L., Vijay-Shanker, K.: Using natural language program analysis to locate and understand action-oriented concerns. In: Proceedings of the International Conference on Aspect-Oriented Software Deveopment, pp. 212–224 (2007). doi:10.1145/1218563.1218587
58. Solar-Lezama, A., Arnold, G., Tancau, L., Bodik, R., Saraswat, V., Seshia, S.: Sketching stencils. In: Proceedings of the ACM SIGPLAN Conference on Programming Language Design and Implementation, pp. 167–178 (2007). doi:10.1145/1250734.1250754
59. Tarr, P., Ossher, H., Harrison, W., Stanley M. Sutton, J.: N degrees of separation: multi-dimensional separation of concerns. In: Proceedings of the ACM/IEEE International Conference on Software Engineering, pp. 107–119 (1999). doi:10.1145/302405.302457
60. Toomim, M., Begel, A., Graham, S.L.: Managing duplicated code with linked editing. In: Proceedings of the IEEE Symposium on Visual Languages and Human-Centric Computing, pp. 173–180 (2004). http://dx.doi.org/10.1109/VLHCC.2004.35
61. Walker, R.J., Holmes, R.: Simulation: a methodology to evaluate recommendation systems in software engineering. In: Robillard, M., Maalej, W., Walker, R.J., Zimmermann, T. (eds.) Recommendation Systems in Software Engineering. Springer, Heidelberg, Chap. 12. (2014)
62. Wang, X., Lo, D., Cheng, J., Zhang, L., Mei, H., Yu, J.X.: Matching dependence-related queries in the system dependence graph. In: Proceedings of the IEEE/ACM International Conference on Automated Software Engineering, pp. 457–466 (2010). doi:10.1145/1858996.1859091
63. Weimer, W., Nguyen, T., Le Goues, C., Forrest, S.: Automatically finding patches using genetic programming. In: Proceedings of the ACM/IEEE International Conference on Software Engineering, pp. 364–374 (2009). doi:10.1109/ICSE.2009.5070536
64. Weißgerber, P., Diehl, S.: Are refactorings less error-prone than other changes? In: Proceedings of the International Workshop on Mining Software Repositories, pp. 112–118 (2006). doi:10.1145/1137983.1138011
65. Witten, I.H., Mo, D.: TELS: Learning Text Editing Tasks from Examples, pp. 183–203. MIT, Cambridge, MA (1993)

Chapter 17
Recommendation Systems in Requirements Discovery

Negar Hariri, Carlos Castro-Herrera, Jane Cleland-Huang,
and Bamshad Mobasher

Abstract Recommendation systems offer the opportunity for supporting and
enhancing a wide variety of activities in requirements engineering. We discuss
several potential uses. In particular we highlight the role of recommendation
systems in online forums that are used for capturing and discussing feature requests.
The recommendation system is used to mitigate problems introduced when face-to-
face communication is replaced with potentially high-volume online discussions.
In this context, recommendation systems can be used to suggest relevant topics to
stakeholders and conversely to recommend expert stakeholders for each discussion
topic. We also explore the use of recommendation systems in the domain analysis
process, where they can be used to recommend sets of features to include in new
products.

17.1 Introduction

Requirements engineering covers a variety of different activities focused on the
discovery, analysis, specification, validation, and management of software and
systems requirements [30, 42, 45, 51]. The primary goal of the discovery process is
to elicit and identify stakeholders' needs, wants, and desires for the software system.
This can be somewhat challenging, especially when stakeholders are geographically
distributed and unable to physically gather together for face-to-face meetings.
Different groups of stakeholders also have differing perspectives and goals for
the system, which can create conflicts and inconsistencies. This is particularly

N. Hariri (✉) • J. Cleland-Huang • B. Mobasher
School of Computing, DePaul University, Chicago, IL, USA
e-mail: nhariri@cs.depaul.edu; jhuang@cs.depaul.edu; mobasher@cs.depaul.edu

C. Castro-Herrera
GOOGLE, Chicago, IL, USA
e-mail: ccastro@google.com

M.P. Robillard et al. (eds.), *Recommendation Systems in Software Engineering*,
DOI 10.1007/978-3-642-45135-5_17, © Springer-Verlag Berlin Heidelberg 2014

troublesome if important stakeholders are missing from the requirements elicitation and negotiation process [18].

Robertson and Robertson [45] prescribe a rigorous upfront domain analysis and requirements trawling process which involve identifying and engaging stakeholders, observing users performing tasks in their natural work environments, and conducting interviews, surveys, and group brainstorming meetings. These activities are designed to discover, analyze, and prioritize requirements, to specify use-cases and business rules, and in some cases to propose and evaluate candidate design solutions. All of these activities are highly collaborative and people-intensive.

Several recent trends have significantly impacted the way we think about requirements. The move towards the globalization of software development and the dispersion of stakeholders across multiple geographical locations [13] makes communication and coordination more difficult and introduces challenges caused by diversity in language and culture, lack of engagement in the requirements discovery process, loss of informal communication between stakeholders, a reduced level of trust caused by the lack of face-to-face communication, difficulties in managing conflicts and achieving a common understanding of the requirements, ineffective decision-making meetings, and process delay introduced by the time zone differences [17].

The popularity of open source software development has also affected the requirements process. The collaborative and transparent nature of open source projects has popularized the notion of opening up the requirements elicitation process to allow a far broader set of stakeholders to contribute their ideas and suggestions using an online forum [48]. The impact has been felt even in more traditional projects.

Finally, the broad adoption of agile approaches has impacted the way in which we define requirements. As a community, we now embrace the idea that software requirements may emerge incrementally as the project progresses. This is particularly true in software-intensive projects as opposed to more traditional systems engineering projects. In this chapter we therefore focus more on the ongoing discovery of ideas and features as opposed to the specification of more traditional requirements.

Recommendation systems can potentially address many of the challenges involved in the elicitation process. In general, a recommendation system [1] identifies items of potential interest to a given user based on that user's preference profile (see Ying and Robillard [53] in Chap. 8 for more details on user profiles) or observed behavior. It is not difficult to conceive of stakeholders or even products as the target of recommendations, and users, topics, or features as the recommendable items.

In this chapter we provide an overview of several areas of the requirements process which could potentially benefit from the use of recommendation systems. We then describe two diverse applications of recommendation in greater detail. The first uses a recommendation system to support requirements discovery in online discussion forums by helping to manage and organize stakeholders' discussions, recommending discussion threads to stakeholders, and recommending knowledgeable stakeholders for specific topics. The second application leverages the availability of detailed product information on publicly accessible websites such as Softpedia and then uses this data to learn association rules and to construct a recommendation system capable of recommending domain-specific features for a product. Both applications leverage growing trends towards moving the requirements process online through adopting social networking tools.

17.2 Recommendation Systems in Requirements Engineering

While a significant body of prior work has focused on making recommendations to support more general software engineering tasks such as finding experts to help with development tasks [37, 39, 40], keeping developers informed of stakeholders working on related tasks [52], or supporting the build process [49], there has been far less thought on how to utilize recommendation systems within the requirements discovery process. Felfernig et al. [24] presented a visionary perspective of a "Recommendation and Decision Support System," which would support individual and group activities through recommending stakeholders for quality reviews, prioritizing requirements, suggesting relevant requirements for a current task, identifying dependencies among requirements, proposing changes that could be made to a requirements artifact to maximize group agreement, and identifying sets of requirements for a future release. In other words, they envisioned a system that could assist in a wide array of tasks related to requirements engineering.

Similarly, Maalej and Thurimella [34] proposed a research agenda for recommendation systems in requirements engineering. They envisioned potential uses of recommendation systems which included recommending traceability links, relevant background information, artifacts that have changed, templates to use, past rationale decisions, requirements from previous systems, vocabulary to use, people to collaborate with, status of activities and artifacts, and priorities, among others.

In this chapter we focus on recommendation systems which have been actually implemented and evaluated in the requirements engineering domain. We avoid discussing systems which have the look-and-feel of a recommendation system, but which are purely search based and therefore do not leverage the core concepts that define a recommendation system. For example, in the requirements engineering field, researchers have developed techniques for generating (or retrieving) trace links between various artifacts, such as between requirements and source code, or between requirements and regulatory codes [3, 15, 20, 29]. However, while the end result is a ranked listing of candidate links, which may appear to take on the form of a recommendation, to the large part these approaches leverage basic information retrieval and machine learning techniques instead of the core recommendation algorithms that are the focus of this book.

Another interesting application of a recommendation system was proposed by Lim et al. [32, 33]. They developed a tool called StakeNet, which used social networking techniques to generate recommendations of project stakeholders. Based upon an early definition of the project, they identified an initial set of stakeholder roles and associated stakeholders. They then utilized their tool to invite each of the identified stakeholders to recommend additional stakeholders and to provide a salience measure that captures the influence, legitimacy, and urgency of the recommendation. Finally they used social networking metrics to prioritize candidate stakeholders for inclusion in the project. StakeNet is unique in the way it generates recommendations. Unlike other systems, StakeNet elicits recommendations directly from users and then filters them using social network metrics. It is these filtered recommendations which are presented to the users.

17.3 Recommendation Systems in Online Forums

Wikis and forums provide community-based portals that support collaborative tasks and knowledge management activities. There are many benefits in using online forums to support requirements discovery. For example, forums create a broadly inclusive environment in which geographically distributed stakeholders can collaborate asynchronously in a virtual meeting place to explore, discuss, and specify requirements [21,47,48]. Noll [41] observed that almost all the requirements for Firefox 2.0 were discovered through online forums, wikis, and bug tracking systems. Christley and Madey [14] also pointed out that many activities that take place in open source development are supported by online forums. Laurent and Cleland-Huang [31] explored the way vendor-led open source projects conducted requirements engineering tasks using online forums. They found forums to be very effective for including large numbers of stakeholders; however, they also found that the sheer mass of data collected in the forums created a number of challenges. For example, it was often difficult for new users to find relevant discussion threads. Similarly, project managers found it difficult to extract and manage feature requests from within the forums, in order to identify specific stakeholder roles, and to understand and document feature priorities.

To better understand the challenges of using social networking tools for requirements elicitation, we analyzed discussion threads and topics in the forums of several open source projects and found a high percentage of discussion threads consisting of only one or two feature requests. For example, as shown in Fig. 17.1, 59 % of Poseidon threads, 48 % of Open Bravo threads, and 42 % of Zimbra threads included only one or two posts [16]. The presence of so many small threads suggests either that a significant number of distinct discussion topics exist or that users tend to initiate redundant threads without first searching for related discussions. This phenomenon hinders the overarching goal of the forum, which is to emerge project requirements by facilitating topic-based discussions between stakeholders with similar interests. Without some sort of structuring and support, online forums tend to degenerate into question and answer style venues or, even worse, to contain large numbers of posts which lack any response or related discussion. These

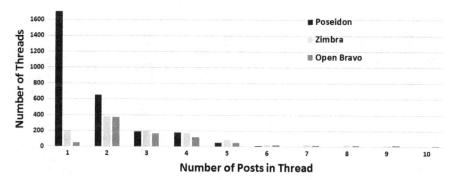

Fig. 17.1 Discussion thread sizes. Forums are characterized by numerous small threads and a couple of very large threads

problems create a rich opportunity for utilizing recommendation systems to improve stakeholder collaboration.

The idea of utilizing recommendation systems in online forums is certainly not new. Spertus et al. [50] developed a system for recommending user-created discussion groups in the Orkut social networking site. They used a collaborative filtering approach based on the k-nearest neighbors (kNN) strategy and compared multiple similarity metrics. Chen et al. [12] also recommended communities in the Orkut social networking site, but their approach differed from Spertus et al. in that they used multiple input sources: users' community memberships and users' textual contributions. Freyne et al. [26] explored the effect that generating early personalized recommendations had on social networking sites. In their work they generated two kinds of recommendations: recommending people to be added to a social network and recommending enhancements to a person's profile. They found that the users who received early recommendations became more engaged in the social network. Guy et al. [27] explored the recommendation of "social software items" within a social networking site. The recommended items included webpages, blog entries, wiki pages, and user communities. They experimented on moving beyond the concept of *user similarity*, to the idea of *user familiarity*, where neighborhoods were created using the user's social network. They discovered that familiarity worked better, and that it provided richer explanations for the recommendations.

17.3.1 Recommending Topics

Recommendation systems can be used to help manage the requirements process in online forums. For example, they can be used to address the problem in which stakeholders with similar interests fail to "find each other" in the forum, meaning that topic discussions are dispersed across multiple threads, preventing full and

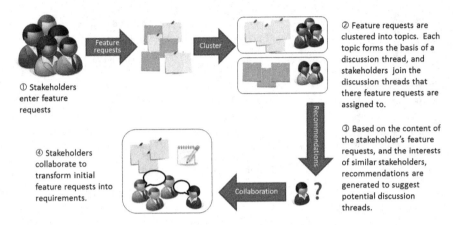

Fig. 17.2 OPCI: Organizer and promoter of collaborative ideas

rigorous exploration of specific issues. In addition, recommendation systems can be used to address the problem of unexplored topics by recommending expert stakeholders for a topic.

As an example, consider the recommendation system OPCI (Organizer and Promoter of Collaborative Ideas) [5, 7–10]. OPCI provides support for recommending stakeholders and topics and optional support for managing the actual discussion threads. If thread management is used, then OPCI proactively helps to maintain a more cohesive set of discussion topics. New posts are analyzed in order to determine if one or more existing and relevant discussion threads already exist. If so, OPCI presents these threads to the user so that they have the option of posting their feature request or comment to one of the existing threads. Furthermore, OPCI also monitors discussions in existing threads, determines when the discussion diverges into a new topic, and makes appropriate suggestions for spawning new threads. We do not elaborate on these features of OPCI further, as they are not central to the application of recommendation systems in a requirements forum. The recommendation systems described in the remainder of this section can be applied to either user-defined or automatically clustered discussion threads.

It is interesting to note that a discussion topic represents both a clustering of feature requests and a grouping of stakeholders. In the remainder of this chapter we refer to a *topic* and *discussion thread* synonymously. The general process is summarized in Fig. 17.2 which shows that OPCI assumes stakeholders' needs are collected in a web-based tool such as a wiki, forum, or bug tracker. The feature requests are then placed into discussion threads either by the users themselves or by a tool such as OPCI. A variety of recommendation algorithms are then used to generate recommendations to project stakeholders, thereby enhancing the quality of the online requirements discovery process.

OPCI uses both content-based and collaborative-based recommendation systems. The content-based recommendation utilizes the content of the discussion threads to initially recommend similar topics to a stakeholder while the collaborative recommendation creates additional recommendations by identifying stakeholders with similar interests, and then using these similarities to generate recommendations. Content-based recommendation systems, which are particularly useful for keeping similar feature requests collocated in a single thread, are discussed in more detail later in the chapter. In the following section we focus on describing the use of collaborative recommendations. These serve the important role of cross-pollinating discussions with contributions from stakeholders with related concerns.

17.3.2 Creating User Profiles

A basic introduction to collaborative recommendation algorithms is provided by Menzies [36] in Chap. 3. The standard kNN-based algorithm with Pearson correlation assumes that each entry in the user profile represents the degree of interest that a user has in a particular item to be recommended.

In order to create a forum-based recommendation system, we construct a *user-by-discussion-thread* matrix R which captures the interest each user has in a particular discussion topic. There are two primary ways to represent this matrix. The first approach represents the degree of interest a user has in each topic, by depicting the number of posts a user has in a thread, and also the extent to which those posts represent core concepts of the thread, i.e., the similarity between the user's posts and the central theme of the thread. This results in a matrix R containing a set of continuous values [10].

Alternately, a binary matrix R can be used, in which a membership score of 1 means that the user has engaged in the discussion thread while a score of 0 means that they have not. However, we cannot assume that a score of 0 means that the user is not interested in the topic.

Switching to a binary representation of the R matrix requires a few additional changes to the similarity and prediction formulas of kNN, mainly because the concept of *average ratings* does not make sense in a binary profile. There are several binary similarity metrics available [50]; one of the most accepted formulas is the binary equivalent of the cosine similarity metric ($\cos'$), defined in Eq. (17.1).

$$\cos'(u_a, u_b) := \frac{|R_{u_a} \cap R_{u_b}|}{\sqrt{|R_{u_a}| \times |R_{u_b}|}}, \tag{17.1}$$

where R_u is the set of rated items of user u; more specifically, the membership (yes or no) of the user in the discussion threads.

Equation (17.2) has been shown to consistently return good recommendations.

$$\hat{r}'_{u,i} := \frac{\sum_{n \in nbr(u)} \text{userSim}(u, n) \times r_{n,i}}{\sum_{n \in nbr(u)} \text{userSim}(u, n)} \tag{17.2}$$

Table 17.1 Characteristics
of the main datasets

Dataset	# Threads	# Posts	# Users
Second Life	50	3392	2120
Student	29	223	36
Sugar CRM	60	885	523
Railway	55	1652	132

17.3.3 Profile Augmentation with Requirements Metadata

In addition to using a binary profile, major improvements can also be achieved
[7] by augmenting the user profiles with additional known attributes about the
users. This metadata can be incorporated into the ratings matrix, such that $R =
(r_{u,i})_{|U| \times (|A| + |I|)}$, where the first A columns indicate that a user has an interest in
a known attribute a of the domain. This approach is feasible in the requirements
engineering domain, where the role of specific stakeholders is often known or easily
elicited. Examples of user attributes include the roles of the users in the project (e.g.,
a developer or project manager), their interest in system qualities (e.g., security
or usability), or their interest in key functionalities or modules (e.g., calendaring
functionality or payroll module). These additional attributes can be used to augment
the user profile and to generate the neighborhoods of similar users.

17.3.4 Evaluation

One of the common ways to evaluate a recommendation system is based on
the standard leave-one-out cross-validation experimental design. In this style of
experiment, we systematically remove one known interest for each user and
then evaluate the recommendation system's ability to successfully recommend
it back. To illustrate the effectiveness of the three variants of recommendation
systems discussed in previous sections, we present experimental results achieved
by generating recommendations using the datasets described in Table 17.1.

"Second Life" is an Internet-based virtual world game in which users create
avatars to explore, and interact in, a "virtual world." "Student" is a small dataset of
feature requests and user interests created by 36 graduate level students at DePaul
University for an Amazon-like student web portal where the students could buy
and sell books. "Sugar CRM" is an open source customer relationship management
system that supports campaign management, email marketing, lead management,
marketing analysis, forecasting, quote management, case management, and many
other features. Finally, "Railway" is a dataset of requirements and stakeholder
roles mined from the public specifications of two large-scale railway systems, the
Canadian Rail Operating Rules and the Standard Code of Operating rules published
by the Association of American Railroads.

Results from four kNN-based variants are shown in the hit ratio graph depicted in
Fig. 17.3 [7]. A hit ratio graph is particularly useful for evaluating a recommendation

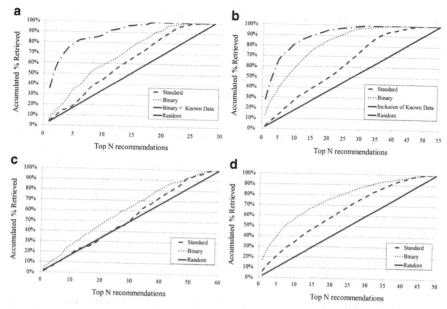

Fig. 17.3 Collaborative recommendation results using standard, binary kNN, and the augmented profiles on four datasets. (**a**) Student dataset. (**b**) Railway dataset. (**c**) Sugar dataset. (**d**) SecondLife dataset

system when the results are presented as a ranked list. Hit ratio curves plot the accumulated percentage of correctly retrieved results against the number of recommendations made. In other words, for the items that were recommended back, it shows how many were ranked as the first item shown to the user, how many were ranked as the second item, and so on. This is typically plotted in a graph and compared against a random recommendation (represented as a diagonal line). The ideal hit ratio graph for a good recommendation will show a sharp improvement over the random case for the early recommendations, indicating that those were indeed items that the user had an interest in.

In this application, binary recommendations tend to outperform the non-binary approach. Furthermore, adding additional information also significantly improves the quality of the generated recommendations, primarily because the additional knowledge increases the density of information in the users' profiles, making the selection of neighbors more reliable.

17.4   Recommending Expert Stakeholders

In addition to using recommendation systems to help stakeholders find relevant discussion threads, recommendations can be made at the project level to identify stakeholders with expertise in specific areas. These recommendations address the commonly occurring problem of unanswered posts. In most open source projects, a significant percentage of posts never receive responses. From a requirements elicitation perspective, this suggests that certain ideas go unexplored and represents lost opportunities for truly understanding and meeting the users' needs.

The same recommendation algorithms, described in the previous sections, can be used to identify three groups of stakeholders [5, 6]:

Direct Stakeholders. Represent users who have directly contributed ideas to the topic. In other words, these are the users whose posts have been clustered together into a topic.

Indirect Stakeholders. Represent users who have contributed ideas to related topics. These stakeholders are discovered through measuring the similarity between the topics (clusters), and selecting users who have posted to closely related discussion threads.

Inferred Stakeholders. Represent users who have exhibited patterns of interest which suggest that they could potentially be interested in the topic. These users are found by a collaborative recommendation, the same binary kNN described in Eqs. (17.1) and (17.2).

While different approaches are possible, it can be particularly effective to use a hybrid recommendation system to identify and recommend expert stakeholders. In the hybrid approach, the text of the unanswered posts is first analyzed and then a content-based recommendation system is used to recommend users that contributed posts with similar content. This is achieved by clustering posts and then identifying stakeholders whose posts are placed in the same cluster (i.e., topic) as the unanswered post. The identified stakeholders are then used as the input to a collaborative recommendation algorithm so that additional users, who might be able to respond to the post, are identified. For this, the binary kNN algorithm described in Sect. 17.3.2 can be used.

The effectiveness of the hybrid recommendation system is illustrated through an experiment that simulates unanswered posts by examining each discussion thread in turn, identifying the first post of the thread, temporarily removing all other posts, and then running the hybrid recommendation to see if the authors (stakeholders) of the removed responses could be identified and recommended back.

Table 17.2 and Fig. 17.4 show the results of this experiment in terms of precision, recall, F_2 measure, and hit ratio graphs (for the collaborative part), compared to a random recommendation. There are several interesting observations. First, the content recommendation returns fairly good precision, recall, and F_2 values and clearly outperforms the random recommender. Second, the collaborative recommender outperforms the content-based recommender in terms of recall but achieves low precision. This is explained by the fact that the collaborative recommendation system outputs a much larger list of suggested users. Because a human user is not interested in so many recommendations, it is important to evaluate the ranking of the recommended users. This is depicted in the hit ratio graphs in Fig. 17.4, which show that the correct users tend to be returned before the incorrect ones. Furthermore, there is a limit to the number of users who can be identified through

Table 17.2 Performance of the recommendation of relevant users in terms of precision, recall, and F_2-measure for six open source forums

Dataset	Content Based recommendation				Collaborative Based recommendation				
	Observed		Random		Observed		Random		
	Prec.	Recall	Prec.	Recall	Prec.	Recall	Prec.	Recall	F_2
7-Zip	39.11%	48.14%	1.55%	1.90%	3.16%	71.77%	0.81%	18.36%	0.03
Alliance l	9.53%	27.01%	0.62%	1.77%	2.19%	42.13%	0.46%	8.78%	0.02
KeePas	23.87%	42.93%	1.20%	2.15%	3.50%	75.51%	0.69%	14.83%	0.03
MiKTe.	15.60%	26.27%	1.11%	1.86%	4.15%	78.11%	0.82%	15.39%	0.03
Notepad	20.50%	37.14%	0.80%	1.45%	2.60%	70.61%	0.50%	13.68%	0.02
phpMyAd	23.15%	49.04%	0.79%	1.69%	5.69%	76.45%	0.41%	5.46%	0.02
RSS Ban	13.79%	14.29%	2.23%	2.31%	13.89%	10.42%	1.92%	1.44%	0.02

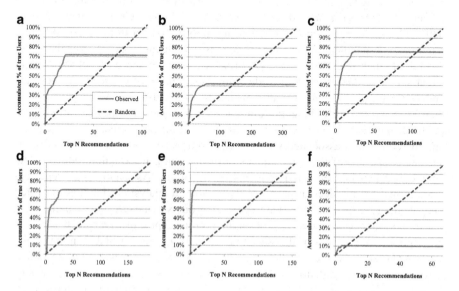

Fig. 17.4 Performance of the recommender of relevant users in terms of hit ratio for six open source forums. (**a**) 7-Zip. (**b**) Alliance. (**c**) KeyPass. (**d**) NotePad++. (**e**) PHP My Admin. (**f**) RSS Bandit

collaborative recommendations (shown as the gap between the two lines in the hit ratio graph at the maximum number of recommendations). This occurs because the collaborative recommendation was constrained to only make recommendations to users who belonged to at least three discussion threads. This restriction ensures the quality of the recommendations but also highlights the problem that we are trying to address: the fact that some users create a post that never gets answered and as a result stop participating in the open source project. A more detailed explanation of these experiments and results can be found in the related work of Castro-Herrera [5].

17.5 Feature Recommendation

The second type of recommendation system we explore in this chapter is designed for use in the **domain analysis** process [19]. Domain analysis is conducted in early phases of a project and involves analyzing existing software systems from the same domain in order to better understand their common and variable parts. Domain analysis supports requirements discovery processes by identifying features commonly included in software products operating in a specific domain.

Domain analysis techniques require analysts to review documentation from existing systems in order to manually, or semi-manually, extract, organize, and model features in the domain. For example, the Domain Analysis and Reuse Environment (DARE) [25] uses semiautomated tools to extract domain vocabulary from text sources and then identifies common domain entities, functions, and objects, by clustering around related words and phrases. Chen et al. [11] manually constructed requirements relationship graphs (RRGs) from several different requirements specifications and then used clustering techniques to merge them into a single domain tree. Alves et al. [2] utilized the vector space model (VSM) and latent semantic analysis (LSA) to determine the similarity between requirements and generate an association matrix which is then clustered. A merging step is then executed to create the entire domain feature model. The primary limitations of these approaches are their reliance upon existing requirements specifications and the constraints associated with mining features from only a small handful of specifications. All of these techniques have one thing in common, which is the need for an existing set of requirements specifications. As requirements represent closely guarded intellectual property, these domain analysis techniques are often only available to organizations with existing products in the targeted domain.

On the other hand, the advent of online product repositories means that partial descriptions of hundreds of thousands of products are now available in the public domain. These product descriptions can be used in place of actual requirements to construct a recommendation system. In this section we explain how hundreds of thousands of partial product descriptions can be used to learn association rules and generate feature recommendations.

The approach utilizes data mining and machine learning methods to mine software features from online software product repositories and to infer relationships among those features. The inferred affinities are then used to train a recommender system which generates feature recommendations for a given project.

Figure 17.5 represents the overall process, consisting of an initial training phase followed by a usage phase. In the training phase, features are extracted from online product descriptions and the feature recommender is trained, while in the usage phase, the trained system makes recommendations based on an initial description of the product provided by a requirements analyst or other users of the system.

The training phase involves mining product specifications from online software product repositories. For example, feature descriptors could be retrieved from Softpedia which contains a large collection of software products. In the second step, the raw feature descriptors are fed to a clustering algorithm which groups them into features and generates an appropriate name for each feature. Finally, in the third step, a product-by-feature matrix and a feature itemset graph (FIG) based on the relationships between products and the mined features are both constructed.

The trained recommender system can be used to generate recommendations based on an initial textual description of the product provided by the requirements

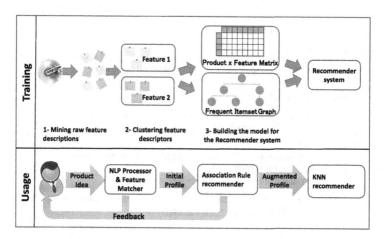

Fig. 17.5 Feature extraction and recommendation

or domain analyst. Basic information retrieval methods are used to match this description to a set of related features in the product-by-feature matrix. These features are presented to the user for confirmation. The quality of the final recommendations can be improved through utilizing a two-phase process. In the first phase, association rule mining, as discussed by Menzies [36] in Chap. 3, is used to augment the initial product profile. This is particularly effective given that we have found that association rules tend to produce relatively accurate, but incomplete recommendations. Finally, the augmented profile is used in a standard kNN approach to generate an additional set of feature recommendations. As we will later show, recommendations produced from the association rule recommender are usually complementary to the features recommended by the kNN recommender, and furthermore, augmenting the initial sparse product profile helps the kNN recommender to produce more accurate recommendations.

Figure 17.6 illustrates a feature recommendation scenario for an anti-virus product. An initial product description is first mapped to four features in the recommender's knowledge base related to *spam detection, disk scans, virus definitions*, and *virus databases*, which serve as seeds for generating feature recommendations. The product profile is then augmented by association rule mining with recommended features such as *network intrusion detection* and *real-time file monitoring*. Finally (although not shown in the figure), the kNN recommender system makes an additional set of recommendations.

17.5.1 Feature Mining

Features must initially be mined from product specifications. For the examples presented in this chapter, we utilized 117,265 different products from 21 Softpedia

---

Step # 1: Enter initial product description

The product will protect the computer from viruses and email spam. It will maintain a database of known viruses and will retrieve updated descriptions from a server. It will scan the computer on demand for viruses.

Step # 2: Confirm features

We have identified the following features from your initial product description. Please confirm :

☑   Email spam detection
☑   Virus definition update and automatic update supported
☑   Disk scan for finding malware
☑   Internal database to detect known viruses

We notice that you appear to be developing an Anti-virus software system. Would you like to ***browse the feature model?***

Step # 3: Recommend features

Based on the features you have already selected we recommend the following three features. Please confirm:

☑   Network intrusion detection   *Why?*
☑   Real time file monitoring   *Why?*
☑   Web history and cookies management   *Why?*
Click here for more recommendations   ***View Feature Model***

Fig. 17.6 An example usage scenario

categories. Product descriptions are parsed into sentences to form *feature descriptors* and then preprocessed using standard information retrieval techniques such as stemming and stop-word removal. Each feature descriptor is then transformed into a vector space representation using the TF–IDF approach.

As many products contain similar features, and these features are described in slightly different ways, the descriptors must be clustered into coherent clusters such that each cluster corresponds to a software feature.

The similarity of a pair of feature descriptors can be measured by computing the cosine similarity of their corresponding TF–IDF vectors. This similarity measure can be used by any conventional clustering algorithm such as K-means [35], K-medoid [35], or spherical K-means [22] to group similar feature descriptors. In our system we used the *incremental diffusive clustering* (IDC) approach [23] to group the feature descriptors into 1,135 clusters. This algorithm uses a heuristic approach to determine the number of clusters. Based on our previous studies, this algorithm tends to outperform other algorithms, including K-means, spherical K-means, and latent Dirichlet allocation (LDA) [4] for clustering requirements [28].

It is important to present a comprehensible recommendation to the user. To this end, each feature needs to be meaningfully named. One approach uses the *medoid* as the name. The medoid is defined as the descriptor that is most representative of the feature's theme. The medoid is identified by first computing the cosine similarity between each descriptor and the centroid of the cluster and then summing up the different weighted values in the descriptor's term vector for all values above a certain threshold (0.1). Both scores are normalized and then added together for each descriptor. The descriptor scoring the highest value is selected as the feature name. This approach produces quite meaningful names. As an example, a feature based on the theme of *updat, databas, automat, viru* might subsequently be named *Virus definition update and automatic update supported.*

17.5.2 Feature Recommendation Algorithm

The goal of the feature recommendation module is to provide recommendations for a project with a given set of initial features. The feature recommender can be trained by creating a binary product-by-feature matrix, $M := (m_{i,j})_{P \times F}$, where P represents the number of products (117,265), F is the number of identified features (1,135), and $m_{i,j}$ is 1 if and only if the feature j includes a descriptor originally mined from the product i. Having this matrix, various collaborative filtering methods, including neighborhood-based techniques such as user-based kNN and item-based kNN as well as matrix factorization approaches such as BPRMF [43], can be exploited to produce recommendations. For a new product p with a set of features F_p, the recommendation algorithm computes a recommendation score for each of the features which are not in F_p and presents to the users the top N (where N is the number of recommendations) features with the highest recommendation scores.

To compare different recommendation algorithms, we describe the results of applying a fivefold cross-validation experiment [44]. For each product p in the test data, $L = 3$ features are randomly selected and used to represent the product profile. One of the remaining features, f_t, is randomly selected as the target feature, and each recommendation algorithm is evaluated based on its predictive power in recommending the target feature.

Hit ratio results for three algorithms at different sizes of recommendations are shown in Fig. 17.7. As can be seen, although BPRMF returns good performance when $N > 45$, it does not perform well at higher ranks. Assuming that the user is likely to look at the first ten recommendations, user-base kNN returns the best performance in comparison with the other two methods.

17.5.3 Addressing the Cold Start Problem

One of the problems frequently experienced with typical recommender systems, including systems based on collaborative filtering, is the product cold start problem which occurs when not enough is known about a product to make useful personalized recommendations. This situation can typically arise when the user's description of a product matches very few features in the database. This makes it difficult to find

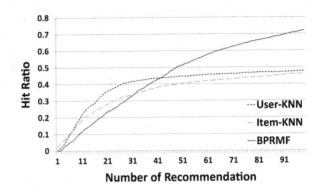

Fig. 17.7 Hit ratio comparison of different recommendation algorithms

a good neighborhood for the product, and as this neighborhood is the basis for the prediction of item scores, the recommendations accuracy is negatively affected. The solution to this problem usually involves a form of bootstrapping to enrich the initial product profiles. In the feature recommendation system, *association rule mining* can be used to enhance the initial product profile and then the discovered rules can be integrated into a hybrid recommendation framework using the kNN. Given an initial small profile for a target product, a preliminary set of recommendations are generated through association rule mining. These features are then shown to the user, and those accepted by the user are added to the product profile. The standard kNN approach is then applied on this augmented profile to generate additional recommendations.

Association rule mining is described in more detail by Menzies [36] in Chap. 3. Association rules identify groups of items based on patterns of co-occurrence across transactions. In this context each product is viewed as a "transaction," and association rules are generated among sets of features that commonly occur together among a significant number of products. The sets of features that satisfy a predefined support threshold are generally referred to as *frequent item sets*; however, in the context of domain analysis we refer to them as *frequent feature sets*.

Association rules are used to address the cold-start problem by augmenting an initially sparse profile. When a partial profile is matched against the antecedent of a discovered rule, the items on the right-hand side of the matching rules are sorted according to the confidence values for the rule, and the top ranked items from this list form the recommendation set. In order to reduce the search time, the frequent item sets can be stored in a directed acyclic graph, called a frequent itemset graph (FIG) [38, 46].

The graph is organized into levels from 0 to k, where k is the maximum size among all discovered frequent item sets. Each node at depth d in the graph corresponds to a frequent item set I of size d and is linked to item sets of size $d+1$ that contain I at the next level. The root node at level 0 corresponds to the empty

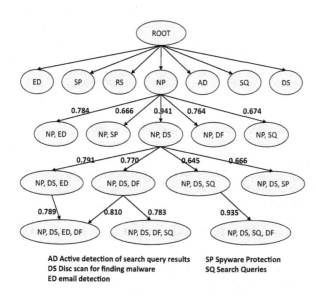

AD Active detection of search query results   SP Spyware Protection
DS Disc scan for finding malware   SQ Search Queries
ED email detection

Fig. 17.8 A subset of a frequent itemset graph for the *Network Intrusion Protection* augmented with confidence scores

items set. Each node also stores the support value of the corresponding frequent item set.

Given an initial profile comprised of a set of features f, the algorithm performs a depth-first search of the graph to level $|f|$. Each candidate recommendation r is a feature contained in a frequent itemset $f \cup \{r\}$ at level $|f + 1|$. For each such child node of f, the feature r is added to the recommendation set if the support ratio $\sigma(f \cup \{r\})/\sigma\{f\}$, which is the confidence of the association rule $f \Rightarrow \{r\}$, is greater than or equal to a pre-specified minimum confidence threshold. This process is repeated for each subset of the initial itemset f, and conflicting candidate recommendations are resolved by retaining the highest confidence values. The recommended features corresponding to rules with highest confidence are shown to the user, and those accepted by the user are added to the product profile.

Figure 17.8 shows a small subset of frequent feature sets mined from the anti-virus software features. The displayed itemset graph shows features associated with *network intrusion detection*. For example, one rule specified in this graph states that if *network intrusion detection* (NP) and *disk scan for finding malware* (DS) features are found in a product, then we have a confidence of 0.791 that the product will also contain an *email detection* feature.

The effect of association rule mining on the performance of the system can be shown experimentally. For illustrative purposes we conducted a fivefold cross-validation experiment. In each of the five runs, one of the folds served as a testing set while the frequent itemset graph was generated from the remaining folds. For each product in the test set, $L = 3$ features were selected and the remaining features are removed from the profile. The frequent itemset graph was then used to

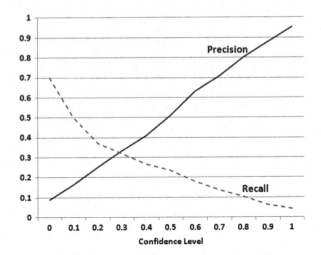

Fig. 17.9 Precision and recall at different levels of confidence

generate recommendations, and those recommendations with confidence scores of 0.2 or higher were recommended to the user. The produced recommendations can be evaluated in terms of precision and coverage, where precision is defined as the fraction of recommended items that are originally part of the product profile, and coverage as the fraction of profiles which receives recommendations.

Figure 17.9 shows the precision and recall for different levels of confidence. For example, at a confidence level of 0.2, the precision of the generated recommendations is 25 % and recall is 37 %. The association rule approach can therefore achieve high precision in its recommendations, but at the cost of lower recall. These observations support our earlier claims that association rule mining can be useful for identifying a small set of previously unused features with a high degree of precision.

To simulate the step in which the user evaluates the initial recommendations, the correct recommendations can be automatically accepted, and the incorrect ones rejected based on the known data stored in the product-by-feature matrix. These accepted recommendations are then used to augment the initial product profile of size $L = 3$, and the augmented profile is given as input to the kNN recommender to generate more recommendations. We label this hybrid method as kNN+.

The hybrid recommender can also be evaluated using the cross validation experiment, with the small modification that the left-out item is selected from the set of features that are not part of the augmented profile. Figure 17.10 compares the hit ratio results of the user-based kNN approach with the kNN+ method. As can be seen, the quality of recommendations is significantly improved when association rules are used to augment the product profile before running the kNN algorithm. This difference represents a 0.1 improvement in hit ratio at rank of 20.

These results demonstrate the viability of using recommendation systems to recommend features during the domain analysis process.

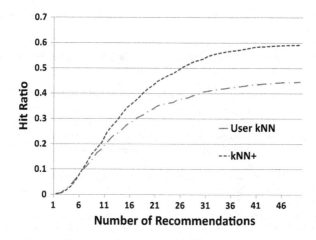

Fig. 17.10 Comparison of hit ratio for the hybrid method and the user-based kNN

17.6 Conclusion

In this chapter we have highlighted two specific applications of recommendation system in the requirements engineering domain. However, as pointed out earlier by Felfernig et al. [24] and Maalej and Thurimella [34] the potential exists for a far broader set of applications. The requirements engineering process has many of the characteristics of fields in which recommendation system technology has had significant impact. Its people-intensive upfront activities, and large quantities of data in the form of formal requirements, feature requests, and other very informal discussion posts, create an environment which can clearly benefit from social media tools such as recommendation systems. As such, the two in-depth examples we have described in this chapter serve as a proof of concept for the potential that exists to use recommendation systems to support a wide range of requirements-related activities in the future.

References

1. Adomavicius, G., Tuzhilin, A.: Toward the next generation of recommender systems: a survey of the state-of-the-art and possible extensions. IEEE T. Knowl. Data En. **17**(6), 734–749 (2005). doi:10.1109/TKDE.2005.99
2. Alves, V., Schwanninger, C., Barbosa, L., Rashid, A., Sawyer, P., Rayson, P., Pohl, K., Rummler, A.: An exploratory study of information retrieval techniques in domain analysis. In: Proceedings of the International Software Product Lines Conference, pp. 67–76 (2008). doi:10.1109/SPLC.2008.18
3. Antoniol, G., Canfora, G., Casazza, G., De Lucia, A., Merlo, E.: Recovering traceability links between code and documentation. IEEE T. Software Eng. **28**(10), 970–983 (2002). doi:10.1109/TSE.2002.1041053

4. Blei, D.M., Ng, A.Y., Jordan, M.I.: Latent Dirichlet allocation. J. Mach. Learn. Res. **3**, 993–1022 (2003)
5. Castro-Herrera, C.: A hybrid recommender system for finding relevant users in open source forums. In: Proceedings of the International Workshop on Managing Requirements Knowledge, pp. 41–50 (2010). doi:10.1109/MARK.2010.5623811
6. Castro-Herrera, C., Cleland-Huang, J.: Utilizing recommender systems to support software requirements elicitation. In: Proceedings of the International Workshop on Recommendation Systems for Software Engineering, pp. 6–10 (2010). doi:10.1145/1808920.1808922
7. Castro-Herrera, C., Cleland-Huang, J., Mobasher, B.: Enhancing stakeholder profiles to improve recommendations in online requirements elicitation. In: Proceedings of the IEEE International Requirements Engineering Conference, pp. 37–46 (2009a). doi:10.1109/RE.2009.20
8. Castro-Herrera, C., Cleland-Huang, J., Mobasher, B.: A recommender system for dynamically evolving online forums. In: Proceedings of the ACM Conference on Recommender Systems, pp. 213–216 (2009b). doi:10.1145/1639714.1639751
9. Castro-Herrera, C., Duan, C., Cleland-Huang, J., Mobasher, B.: Using data mining and recommender systems to facilitate large-scale, open, and inclusive requirements elicitation processes. In: Proceedings of the IEEE International Requirements Engineering Conference, pp. 165–168 (2008). doi:10.1109/RE.2008.47
10. Castro-Herrera, C., Duan, C., Cleland-Huang, J., Mobasher, B.: A recommender system for requirements elicitation in large-scale software projects. In: Proceedings of the ACM SIGAPP Symposium on Applied Computing, pp. 1419–1426 (2009c). doi:10.1145/1529282.1529601
11. Chen, K., Zhang, W., Zhao, H., Mei, H.: An approach to constructing feature models based on requirements clustering. In: Proceedings of the IEEE International Requirements Engineering Conference, pp. 31–40 (2005). doi:10.1109/RE.2005.9
12. Chen, W.Y., Zhang, D., Chang, E.Y.: Combinational collaborative filtering for personalized community recommendation. In: Proceedings of the ACM SIGKDD Conference on Knowledge Discovery and Data Mining, pp. 115–123 (2008). doi:10.1145/1401890.1401909
13. Cheng, B.H.C., Atlee, J.M.: Research directions in requirements engineering. In: Proceedings of the Future of Software Engineering, pp. 285–303 (2007). doi:10.1109/FOSE.2007.17
14. Christley, S., Madey, G.: Analysis of activity in the open source software development community. In: Proceedings of the Hawaii International Conference on Systems Science, pp. 166b:1–166b:10 (2007). doi:10.1109/HICSS.2007.74
15. Cleland-Huang, J., Czauderna, A., Gibiec, M., Emenecker, J.: A machine learning approach for tracing regulatory codes to product specific requirements. In: Proceedings of the ACM/IEEE International Conference on Software Engineering, vol. 1, pp. 155–164 (2010). doi:10.1145/1806799.1806825
16. Cleland-Huang, J., Dumitru, H., Duan, C., Castro-Herrera, C.: Automated support for managing feature requests in open forums. Commun. ACM **52**(10), 68–74 (2009). doi:10.1145/1562764.1562784
17. Damian, D., Zowghi, D.: The impact of stakeholders' geographical distribution on managing requirements in a multi-site organization. In: Proceedings of the IEEE Joint International Conference on Requirements Engineering, pp. 319–330 (2002). doi:10.1109/ICRE.2002.1048545
18. Davis, A.M., Tubío, Ó.D., Hickey, A.M., Juzgado, N.J., Moreno, A.M.: Effectiveness of requirements elicitation techniques: empirical results derived from a systematic review. In: Proceedings of the IEEE International Requirements Engineering Conference, pp. 176–185 (2006). doi:10.1109/RE.2006.17
19. Davril, J.M., Delfosse, E., Hariri, N., Acher, M., Cleland-Huang, J., Heymans, P.: Feature model extraction from large collections of informal product descriptions. In: Proceedings of the European Software Engineering Conference/ACM SIGSOFT International Symposium on Foundations of Software Engineering, pp. 290–300 (2013). doi:10.1145/2491411.2491455
20. De Lucia, A., Fasano, F., Oliveto, R., Tortora, G.: Enhancing an artefact management system with traceability recovery features. In: Proceedings of the IEEE International Conference on Software Maintenance, pp. 306–315 (2004). doi:10.1109/ICSM.2004.1357816

21. Decker, B., Ras, E., Rech, J., Jaubert, P., Rieth, M.: Wiki-based stakeholder participation in requirements engineering. IEEE Software **24**(2), 28–35 (2007). doi:10.1109/MS.2007.60
22. Dhillon, I.S., Modha, D.S.: Concept decompositions for large sparse text data using clustering. Mach. Learn. **42**(1–2), 143–175 (2001). doi:10.1023/A:1007612920971
23. Dumitru, H., Gibiec, M., Hariri, N., Cleland-Huang, J., Mobasher, B., Castro-Herrera, C., Mirakhorli, M.: On-demand feature recommendations derived from mining public product descriptions. In: Proceedings of the ACM/IEEE International Conference on Software Engineering, pp. 181–190 (2011). doi:10.1145/1985793.1985819
24. Felfernig, A., Schubert, M., Mandl, M., Ricci, F., Maalej, W.: Recommendation and decision technologies for requirements engineering. In: Proceedings of the International Workshop on Recommendation Systems for Software Engineering, pp. 11–15 (2010). doi:10.1145/1808920.1808923
25. Frakes, W.B., Prieto-Diaz, R., Fox, C.J.: DARE: domain analysis and reuse environment. Ann. Software Eng. **5**(1), 125–141 (1998). doi:10.1023/A:1018972323770
26. Freyne, J., Jacovi, M., Guy, I., Geyer, W.: Increasing engagement through early recommender intervention. In: Proceedings of the ACM Conference on Recommender Systems, pp. 85–92 (2009). doi:10.1145/1639714.1639730
27. Guy, I., Zwerdling, N., Carmel, D., Ronen, I., Uziel, E., Yogev, S., Ofek-Koifman, S.: Personalized recommendation of social software items based on social relations. In: Proceedings of the ACM Conference on Recommender Systems, pp. 53–60 (2009). doi:10.1145/1639714.1639725
28. Hariri, N., Castro-Herrera, C., Mirakhorli, M., Cleland-Huang, J., Mobasher, B.: Supporting domain analysis through mining and recommending features from online product listings. IEEE T. Software Eng. **39**(12): 1736–1752 (2013). doi:10.1109/TSE.2013.39.
29. Hayes, J.H., Dekhtyar, A., Sundaram, S.K.: Advancing candidate link generation for requirements tracing: the study of methods. IEEE T. Software Eng. **32**(1), 4–19 (2006). doi:10.1109/TSE.2006.3
30. Hull, E., Jackson, K., Dick, J.: Requirements Engineering. 2nd edn. Springer, Heidelberg (2005). doi:10.1007/b138335
31. Laurent, P., Cleland-Huang, J.: Lessons learned from open source projects for facilitating online requirements processes. In: Proceedings of the International Working Conference on Requirements Engineering. Lecture Notes in Computer Science, vol. 5512, pp. 240–255 (2009). doi:10.1007/978-3-642-02050-6_21
32. Lim, S., Quercia, D., Finkelstein, A.: StakeNet: using social networks to analyse the stakeholders of large-scale software projects. In: Proceedings of the ACM/IEEE International Conference on Software Engineering, pp. 295–304 (2010). doi:10.1145/1806799.1806844
33. Lim, S.L., Damian, D., Ishikawa, F., Finkelstein, A.: Using Web 2.0 for stakeholder analysis: StakeSource and its application in ten industrial projects. In: Maalej, W., Thurimella, A. (eds.) Managing Requirements Knowledge, Chap. 10, pp. 221–242. Springer, Heidelberg (2013). doi:10.1007/978-3-642-34419-0_10
34. Maalej, W., Thurimella, A.: Towards a research agenda for recommendation systems in requirements engineering. In: Proceedings of the International Workshop on Managing Requirements Knowledge, pp. 32–39 (2009). doi:10.1109/MARK.2009.12
35. Manning, C.D., Raghavan, P., Schutze, H.: Introduction to Information Retrieval. Cambridge University Press, Cambridge (2008)
36. Menzies, T.: Data mining: a tutorial. In: Robillard, M., Maalej, W., Walker, R.J., Zimmermann, T. (eds.) Recommendation Systems in Software Engineering. Springer, Heidelberg, Chap. 3 (2014)
37. Minto, S., Murphy, G.C.: Recommending emergent teams. In: Proceedings of the International Workshop on Mining Software Repositories, pp. 5:1–5:8 (2007). doi:10.1109/MSR.2007.27
38. Mobasher, B., Dai, H., Luo, T., Nakagawa, M.: Effective personalization based on association rule discovery from web usage data. In: Proceedings of the ACM Workshop on Web Information and Data Management, pp. 9–5 (2001). doi:10.1145/502932.502935

39. Mockus, A., Herbsleb, J.D.: Expertise browser: a quantitative approach to identifying expertise. In: Proceedings of the ACM/IEEE International Conference on Software Engineering, pp. 503–512 (2002). doi:10.1145/581339.581401

40. Moraes, A., Silva, E., da Trindade, C., Barbosa, Y., Meira, S.: Recommending experts using communication history. In: Proceedings of the International Workshop on Recommendation Systems for Software Engineering, pp. 41–45 (2010). doi:10.1145/1808920.1808929

41. Noll, J.: Requirements acquisition in open source development: Firefox 2.0. In: Proceedings of the IFIP World Computer Conference, IFIP: International Federation for Information Processing, vol. 275, pp. 69–79. Springer, Heidelberg (2008). doi:10.1007/978-0-387-09684-1_6

42. Pressman, R.: Software Engineering: A Practitioner's Approach. 7th edn. McGraw-Hill, New York (2009)

43. Rendle, S., Freudenthaler, C., Gantner, Z., Schmidt-Thieme, L.: BPR: Bayesian personalized ranking from implicit feedback. In: Proceedings of the Conference on Uncertainty in Artificial Intelligence, pp. 452–461 (2009)

44. Ricci, F., Rokach, L., Shapira, B., Kantor, P.B. (eds.): Recommender Systems Handbook. Springer, New York (2011). doi:10.1007/978-0-387-85820-3

45. Robertson, S., Robertson, J.: Mastering the Requirements Process. Addison-Wesley, Reading, MA (1999)

46. Sandvig, J.J., Mobasher, B., Burke, R.: Robustness of collaborative recommendation based on association rule mining. In: Proceedings of the ACM Conference on Recommender Systems, pp. 105–112 (2007). doi:10.1145/1297231.1297249

47. Scacchi, W.: Understanding the requirements for developing open source software systems. IEE Proc. Software **149**(1), 24–39 (2002). doi:10.1049/ip-sen:20020202

48. Scacchi, W.: Free/open source software development: recent research results and emerging opportunities. In: Companion Papers to the European Software Engineering Conference/ACM SIGSOFT International Symposium on Foundations of Software Engineering, pp. 459–468 (2007). doi:10.1145/1295014.1295019

49. Schröter, A., Kwan, I., Panjer, L.D., Damian, D.: Chat to succeed. In: Proceedings of the International Workshop on Recommendation Systems for Software Engineering, pp. 43–44 (2008). doi:10.1145/1454247.1454263

50. Spertus, E., Sahami, M., Buyukkokten, O.: Evaluating similarity measures: a large-scale study in the Orkut social network. In: Proceedings of the ACM SIGKDD Conference on Knowledge Discovery and Data Mining, pp. 678–684 (2005). doi:10.1145/1081870.1081956

51. Thayer, R.H., Dorfman, M.: Software Requirements Engineering. 2nd edn. Wiley, New York (1997)

52. Xiang, P.F., Ying, A.T.T., Cheng, P., Dang, Y.B., Ehrlich, K., Helander, M.E., Matchen, P.M., Empere, A., Tarr, P.L., Williams, C., Yang, S.X.: Ensemble: a recommendation tool for promoting communication in software teams. In: Proceedings of the International Workshop on Recommendation Systems for Software Engineering (2008). doi:10.1145/1454247.1454259

53. Ying, A.T.T., Robillard, M.: Developer profiles for recommendation systems. In: Robillard, M., Maalej, W., Walker, R.J., Zimmermann, T. (eds.) Recommendation Systems in Software Engineering. Springer, Heidelberg, Chap. 8 (2014)

Chapter 18
Changes, Evolution, and Bugs

Recommendation Systems for Issue Management

Markus Borg and Per Runeson

Abstract Changes in evolving software systems are often managed using an
issue repository. This repository may contribute to information overload in an
organization, but it may also help in navigating the software system. Software
developers spend much effort on issue triage, a task in which the mere number of
issue reports becomes a significant challenge. One specific difficulty is to determine
whether a newly submitted issue report is a duplicate of an issue previously reported,
if it contains complementary information related to a known issue, or if the issue
report addresses something that has not been observed before. However, the large
number of issue reports may also be used to help a developer to navigate the software
development project to find related software artifacts, required both to understand
the issue itself, and to analyze the impact of a possible issue resolution. This
chapter presents recommendation systems that use information in issue repositories
to support these two challenges, by supporting either duplicate detection of issue
reports or navigation of artifacts in evolving software systems.

18.1 Introduction

As software systems evolve, modifications due to discovered defects or new feature
requests are inevitable. Typically, projects manage change requests and defect
reports in issue repositories [21, 43, 50]. In large software engineering projects,
the number of issue reports reaches several thousands and challenges engineers'
ability to overview the content [4, 23]. Also, distributed development—in terms of
both geographical and organizational distances—intensifies the need for efficient
management of archived issue reports. Further, issue reports can constitute junctures

M. Borg (✉) • P. Runeson
Department of Computer Science, Lund University, Lund, Sweden
e-mail: markus.borg@cs.lth.se; per.runeson@cs.lth.se

M.P. Robillard et al. (eds.), *Recommendation Systems in Software Engineering*,
DOI 10.1007/978-3-642-45135-5_18, © Springer-Verlag Berlin Heidelberg 2014

for several other software artifacts, with pointers to, for example, requirements, test cases, and code components that are involved in the resolution of the issue.

The relationships between issue reports and other software artifacts implies challenges in managing the large amount of information. On the other hand, it also brings opportunities in using the link information to support software developers in their tasks. Networks of software artifacts can be an actionable input to a system recommending related information for the task at hand. With proper tool support, archived issue reports can be harnessed to support developers in tasks such as issue triage and change impact analysis.

Issue management in software engineering is similar to task management in general, for example, in a service organization. Issue reports are similar to the baton in a relay race: different actors (e.g., developers, testers, quality assurance, customers) contribute to solving the task, and the issue management system is the central node that dispatches subtasks to the actors. Issue reports may originate from several sources, within the development organization or from outside customers or sub-contractors. Issues may be pure defect reports, but may also contain change requests and proposals.

An issue repository is typically a database where issue reports (i.e., defect reports and change requests) are stored and maintained over time [21, 43]. The Bugzilla open source issue repository [38] is probably the best known, although several open source and proprietary alternatives exist. Existing issue repositories have features for storing and dispatching issue reports to actors as well as statistical functionality for management reporting. In Chap. 6, Herzig and Zeller [19] elaborate further on issue management.

To support the management and resolution of issues in software development, recommendation systems in software engineering (RSSEs) have been proposed. Figure 18.1 shows the two basic approaches to RSSEs, content-based filtering and collaborative filtering, in the context of issue reports. In an RSSE based on content-based filtering, each issue is represented by a set of features. In previous work, issues have typically been represented by textual features, that is, the terms in their descriptions. Apart from the textual content of the issue reports, issues can be represented by features such as severity, submission date, responsible developer, impacted source code, etc. [35]. The RSSE then compares the features of the given issue to all other issues in the issue repository to recommend the most similar issues. Section 18.2 presents several examples of how RSSEs have been used to recommend duplicate issue reports, as well as results from empirical evaluations.

Collaborative filtering, on the other hand, relies on a crowd of developers in the organization. In a narrow sense, algorithms for collaborative filtering identify users with similar preferences to produce recommendations for the information seeker [48]. In an RSSE for issues, this would mean matching the profile of the information seeker with the other developers. When the peers most similar to the information-seeking developer have been identified, the RSSE can recommend the issues with which these peers most often interact. The user profiles could be based on either previous interaction with issue reports or by features such as role, team, location, etc. (further discussed by Ying and Robillard [51] in Chap. 8).

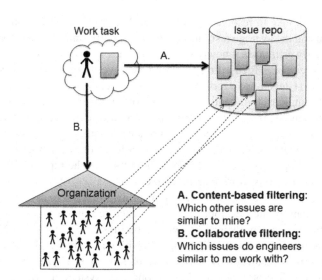

Fig. 18.1 Main principles of an RSSE for issues, content-based and collaborative filtering. The two approaches can also be combined in a hybrid system

In a wider sense, collaborative filtering can be used to refer to all social recommendation systems. One approach is to reuse the "trails" in the software engineering information landscape, that is, following in the footsteps of previous work. This type of collaborative RSSE identifies patterns in data, produced by developers as part of their normal work tasks. This approach can also be referred to as social data mining [48]. The idea is to aggregate the decisions from previous work and make it explicit, with the purpose to support future decision making. Section 18.3 presents two applications of this approach related to navigation from issue reports to other artifacts during software evolution.

18.2   Supporting Issue Triage Using RSSEs

Issue triage—analyzing a new issue report and deciding how to react to it—requires a lot of effort in large software projects [11]. Questions that are typically asked include: Has this issue been reported before? Should this issue be fixed? Who should fix this issue? Where should this issue be fixed? When debugging large software systems, answering the last question is easier if the developer is aware of all relevant reported pieces of information; thus, similar issue reports are also of interest.

Software engineering research has addressed several aspects of issue triaging. Examples include work by Guo et al. [18] on predicting which reported issues get fixed at Microsoft. Based on this information, developers could more easily prioritize issues during triage, for example, to decide which bugs should be closed or migrated to future product versions. A related but more specific consideration is how long it will take to resolve a given issue. Both Weiss et al. [50] and Raja [37] report that using the average resolution time of textually similar issue reports can be used as an early estimate for newly submitted issues.

Several researchers focused on assessing the severity of issue reports. Menzies and Marcus [31] developed a tool that alerts developers when the manually assigned severity is anomalous. Lamkanfi et al. [27] report promising results from automated severity assignments in a study on three issue repositories used in development of open source systems (OSSes). Another approach to identify severe issue reports was presented by Gegick et al. [16]: with a research focus on security-critical software development, they successfully identified about 80 % of the reported issues related to security on a large software system from Cisco.

Another challenge in large software engineering projects is to assign issue reports to the most appropriate developer [11], to reduce resolution times and minimize reassignment of bug reports also known as "bug tossing". Anvik and Murphy [2] trained a classifier to automatically assign incoming issue reports to developers and reported promising results on five OSS projects. Jonsson et al. [22] did similar work and evaluated their prototype on a large proprietary system at Ericsson, reporting performance comparable to manual assignment by human experts.

The rest of this section presents work on duplicate detection of issue reports to aid issue triage. When searching for related or duplicate issue reports, part of the problem lies in defining what counts as a duplicate. Duplicates can be categorized as either those that describe the *same failure* and those that describe two *different failures with the same underlying fault* [40]. These two kinds are inherently different in that the former type, which describes the same failure, generally uses similar vocabulary. The latter type, on the other hand, which describes two failures stemming from the same fault, may use different vocabulary. RSSEs relying on content-based filtering based on textual features are thus better suited for addressing duplicates of the former type. In this section we refer to the first submitted issue report on a specific fault as the *master report*, and subsequent reports as *duplicate reports*.

18.2.1 Duplicates: Burden or Asset?

During the lifecycle of large software systems, maintenance activities account for a majority of the development costs [5]. In many software projects, the management of the maintenance work revolves around issue reports in an issue repository. However, the inflow of issue reports often requires significant effort to address them, typically exceeding the available resources [20]. This challenge is further intensified in open source projects, where the software users directly report issues to an open issue repository. Anvik et al. [1] highlighted the continuous inflow of new issue reports in the Mozilla community as challenging already in 2005, when the average number of daily submitted issue reports was about 300.

One reason for the daunting inflow of issue reports is that the same issues are reported in multiple reports. Previous studies have shown that the number of duplicate issue reports in issue repositories can be considerable. Sureka and Jalote [47] report that 13 % of the issue reports in the Eclipse project (among 205,242 issue reports) were duplicates, while Anvik et al. [1] studied an earlier stage of the Eclipse project and found that the duplicate fraction in 2005 was 20 % (among 18,165 issue reports); they also studied the issue repository used in development of Mozilla Firefox, observing that it contained 30 % duplicate reports (among 2,013 issue reports). Another study on Mozilla software, not restricted to Firefox, was conducted by Jalbert and Weimer [20]. They observed that 26 % of the issue reports were duplicates (among 29,000 issue reports). While a majority of studies on issue management have addressed open source development, the challenge of duplicate issue reports have also been reported from proprietary contexts. Runeson et al. [40] showed that the phenomenon exists also at Sony Ericsson Mobile Communications (SEMC), where practitioners acknowledged the extra effort caused by duplicates. At SEMC, practitioners estimated that 10% of the issue reports were duplicates.

On the other hand, based on results from a survey on duplicate issue reports among open source developers, Bettenburg et al. [4] present another view on the matter. While a majority of the respondents had experienced duplicate reports, few of them considered it to be a serious problem. On the contrary, the respondents stressed that multiple issue reports related to the same issue often provide additional information, thus decreasing resolution times. Furthermore, Bettenburg et al. present empirical evidence confirming that additional information is present in duplicates, in the context of the Eclipse project. Their findings show that duplicates are most often submitted by other users, and that duplicates provide different perspectives and additional information, for example, additional steps to reproduce the issue and supplementary stack traces. Consequently, duplicate detection enables merging of issue reports, a feature that can support bug triaging.

As already indicated, providing duplicate recommendations can be meaningful at different points in time in a software development project. First, a tool can support detection of duplicate issue reports on the submitter side. At submission time, only the information entered by the submitter is available, typically limited to basic system information and a natural language description of the observed software behavior. As such, the tool can rely on content-based filtering using text retrieval techniques to recommend the most similar issues reports among the ones already existing in the issue repository. With this type of support, the submitter can decide whether to (1) submit a new issue report, (2) add additional information to an already open issue report, or (3) skip submitting the issue report if all information is already available in the issue repository. Making the right decision at submission time has the potential to speed up the issue triage on the developer side. On the other hand, Runeson et al. [40] report that it might be hard to make authors of issue reports use the tool in such ways. When people take the time to write a full issue report, they will most likely submit it regardless of the outcome of a duplicate detection, as that action requires the least effort.

Second, a tool can support an engineer on the receiving side of the issue repository. When the developer first receives the issue report, again the only information available is typically a natural language description of the issue and some basic

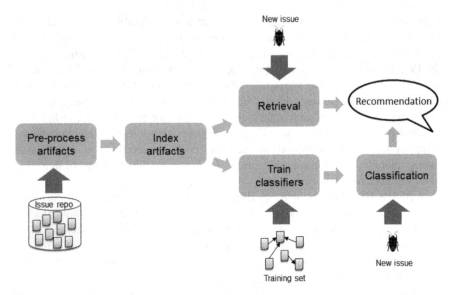

Fig. 18.2 Overview of RSSEs for duplicate detection. The steps in the *top track* show an RSSE based on the IR approach, while the *bottom track* displays a classification-based approach

system information. Thus, the same options regarding decision making based on the output of a content-based filtering recommender is available. However, as the developer probably is more knowledgeable than the submitter, the decision might not be the same. Being aware of the duplicate status can be used both to avoid double triaging, and to support issue resolution by aggregating all available information. In an interview with developers on the receiving side, Runeson et al. [40] found support for the feasibility of issue duplicate detection in a proprietary context.

18.2.2 RSSEs for Duplicate Detection

Current best practice on RSSEs for duplicate detection is based on content-based filtering, and has reached a level of maturity to allow a transition to some well-established software engineering tools. For instance, both HP Quality Center and Bugzilla implement automatic comparisons between newly submitted issue reports and previously reported issues, and this functionality is also used in the marketing of both tools. Also SuggestiMate for JIRA offers this feature. Two general approaches to duplicate detection based on content are used in RSSEs for duplicate detection, either treating it as an information retrieval (IR) problem, or a classification problem. Both approaches have mostly relied on analyzing the textual content in the issue descriptions, thus they share several steps, as presented in Fig. 18.2. However, while an indexed document space of issue reports is enough to deploy an IR-based approach, a duplicate detector based on classification requires also a classifier trained on an annotated subset of issue reports. This section presents some experiences from implementations of duplicate detection for issue reports, and summarizes evaluation results and lessons learned.

The accuracy of a tool for duplicate detection can be evaluated in several ways. The most commonly reported measure in the literature is average recall when considering the top-k recommendations (recall at k), for example, how many of the duplicates do I find within the top 1, 2, 3, ..., 10 recommendations. As we assume that each duplicate report has exactly one master report, recall at k shows the fraction of duplicate reports with their corresponding master reports presented among the top k recommendations [29]. Another possible perspective is to consider sets of duplicate issue reports, that is, considering a network of issue reports with undirected edges representing duplicates [8]. Since a majority of previous work applies the first perspective, we use it as the basis for our discussions, more specifically recall at 10.

18.2.3 Duplicate Detection as an IR Problem

The detection of duplicate issue reports can be treated as an IR problem, for example, implementing classical algebraic IR models. IR is defined as *"finding material (usually documents) of an unstructured nature (usually text) that satisfies an information need from within large collections (usually stored on computers)"* [29]. Thus, IR deals with analyzing large collections to retrieve the most relevant to a given information need. In the context of duplicate detection, this transforms into "given this issue report, which other issue reports are most likely to be duplicates?" The system then returns a ranked list of potential duplicates to the user of the tool.

As depicted in Fig. 18.2, an IR-based RSSE for duplicate detection implements three main steps. The first step, after the issue reports are extracted from the issue repository, is to *preprocess* their textual content. The most common preprocessing steps are:

Normalization. Converting all text to lowercase. Removing special characters. Pruning white spaces from the text, keeping only single whitespaces between terms.

Stop Word Removal. Filtering out words that are not suitable as textual features, as they appear in most texts. Examples of such words that capture no semantics of an issue report include "the," "is," "at," "and," "one," "which," etc. Freely available lists of stop words can be found on the web. Also, stop word functions can be used in combination with lists, that is, a function that filters out all words containing fewer characters than a given threshold.

Stemming. Reducing inflected words to their stem. This step addresses grammatical variation such as conjugation of verbs and declension of nouns. Stemming should reduce "crash," "crashes," and "crashing" to the same stem, converting them to identical terms. In software engineering, Porter's stemmer [36] is the most commonly applied stemmer for English.

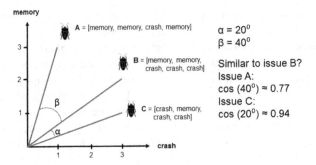

Fig. 18.3 Duplicate detection based on the VSM. In the example, applying raw term weights and cosine similarities, the two most similar issue reports are issue B and issue C

The second step in Fig. 18.2 depicts *indexing* the preprocessed issue reports. RSSEs for duplicate detection typically consider the issue reports as a bag-of-words, a simplifying assumption that represents a document as an unordered collection of words. The standard technique is to apply the *vector space model* (VSM), representing all issue reports as feature vectors of their contained terms [29]. All terms after preprocessing are stored in a document–term matrix that represents each issue report based on the frequencies of the terms contained in their respective description. Thus, the VSM represents the issue reports in a high-dimensional space where each term constitutes a dimension. An entry in the matrix denotes the weight of a specific term in a given issue report. While term weights can be both binary (i.e., existing or nonexisting) and raw (i.e., based on term frequency (TF)), usually some variant of *term frequency–inverse document frequency* (TF–IDF) weighting is applied. TF–IDF is used to weight a term based on the length of the document and the frequency of the term, both in the document and in the entire document collection. Further details on representing text using the VSM is presented by Menzies [30] in Chap. 3.

When VSM is used for IR, document relevance is assumed to be correlated with textual similarity. Thus, when looking for possible duplicates of a given issue report, its similarities to all other indexed issue reports are calculated. When a new issue report arrives, it must first be preprocessed and represented in the same vector-space as was used for indexing the issue repository. The most common similarity measure applied is the cosine similarity, calculated as the cosine of the angle between feature vectors, as presented in Fig. 18.3. As no entries in the document–term matrix are negative, the resulting similarity value is bounded in [0, 1]. Furthermore, calculating cosine similarity is efficient in sparse high-dimensional spaces as only nonzero dimensions need be considered. As presented as the final step in the top track in Fig. 18.2, the most similar issue reports are *retrieved* and used as recommendations.

Runeson et al. [40] were the first to propose extracting textual features from issue reports and applying the VSM to find duplicates. They considered the textual content in the title and description of the issue reports, and applied the standard preprocessing steps stop word removal and stemming. The resulting textual features were then weighted according to $TF = 1 + \log(\text{frequency})$ before the issue reports were represented as feature vectors in the vector space.

Runeson et al. evaluated their system on data from Sony Ericsson Mobile Communications, a large company where a software product line is used for developing mobile phones. At the company, about 10 % of the issue reports were signaled as duplicates. In this context, Runeson et al. evaluated their RSSE for duplicate detection, and explored a number of variations of their system: (a) the length of the stop word list; (b) adding a thesaurus to deal with synonyms in the issue reports; (c) adding a spellchecker to auto-correct misspelled terms; (d) considering the textual content of an additional field in the issue repository, that is, "project name"; (e) up-weighting textual features in the title, to make them more important than the content in the description; (f) different similarity measures (apart from cosine similarities, also Dice's coefficient and the Jaccard similarity coefficient were evaluated); and (g) filtering duplicates according to timeframes. However, while some modifications had a small effect on the performance, for example, adding extra weight to terms in the title, they conclude that little was gained from such finetuning. About 2/3 of the duplicates could be identified using their system, and they achieved a recall at 10 of 40 %. This result was well-received among practitioners at the company, who confirmed the potential to save effort.

Wang et al. [49] considered in addition to the textual content of the issue report (title and description), the stack traces attached to an issue report, and represented the features in two separate VSM models. They preprocessed text using stop word removal and stemming, and then they applied TF–IDF feature weights. Wang et al. also proposed to represent stack traces in a vector space, and let each invoked method constitute a dimension. As such, each issue report was represented both in a vector space of textual features, and a vector space of invoked methods. Then, the combined similarity was calculated by treating both vector spaces as equally important. If a similarity above a defined threshold was detected in any of the vector spaces, they classified a report as a duplicate. The authors used machine learning to establish suitable values for these thresholds. Wang et al. calibrated their system on a small set containing 220 issue reports from the Eclipse project, and then they evaluated their approach on a larger dataset, containing 1,749 issue reports, collected from the issue repository used for the development of Firefox. They conclude that complementing textual descriptions with stack traces improved performance, as did relying on the aforementioned thresholds. Either having two issue reports with highly similar stack traces attached, or two issue descriptions that share a high degree of its content, was a strong indication of duplicates in the Firefox dataset. Moreover, they confirmed Runeson et al.'s finding that up-weighting terms in the title can be beneficial. Wang et al. reported that their system reached a recall at 10 as high as 93 % on the Firefox dataset.

Sun et al. [45] proposed a more advanced model for duplicate detection, including both categorical issue features as well as more advanced weighting of textual features. Initially, they performed the same preprocessing operations as in previous work, that is, they stemmed the content in the title and description and they removed all stop words. However, thereafter they calculated textual similarities, both for unigrams (single terms in isolation) and bigrams (sequences of two terms), using the BM25F model, a state-of-the-art IR model for probabilistic retrieval [39] (an alternative to the algebraic VSM). Furthermore, the authors also considered three nominal features (product, component, and type), and two ordinal features (priority, and version). Finally, to tune the weighting of all parameters in the similarity function, they applied machine learning to tune the feature weighting, that is, they applied learning-to-rank ranking in their IR-approach [28].

Sun et al. evaluated their system using issue reports extracted from three open source contexts: OpenOffice, Eclipse, and the Mozilla community. Moreover, they compared the results with output from their previously implemented RSSE for duplicate detection, implementing a classification-based approach (presented in Sect. 18.2.4). In all experimental runs they obtained better results (recall at 10 consistently between 65 % and 70 %), also they reported major improvements concerning execution times. Again, their empirical results showed that the textual content of the title was the single most important feature. However, the results showed that also the product and version information were important features when recommending duplicate issue reports.

Sureka and Jalote [47] presented a different approach to textual similarities, focusing on characters rather than terms. They proposed a character n-gram model to calculate textual similarities between issue reports. They did not perform any language specific stemming and stop word removal, and thus their approach allow also cross-language recommendation of duplicates. Sureka and Jalote applied a feature extraction model that extracted all n-grams of sizes 4 to 10 from the titles and descriptions of issue reports. They evaluated their approach on a random sample of 2,270 issue reports, and obtained the best results when computing textual similarities based on titles only (recall at 10 of 40 %).

18.2.4 Duplicate Detection as a Classification Problem

Duplicate detection can also be considered a classification problem. Given a newly submitted issue report, an RSSE can classify it as either a duplicate or a non-duplicate based on the previously submitted issue reports. As presented in the bottom track in Fig. 18.2, a classification-based RSSE for duplicate detection typically involves four steps. The first two steps are shared with the IR-based approach. First, the issue reports are *preprocessed*, and then the issue reports are *indexed* by the remaining terms, for example, as feature vectors in the VSM as presented in Fig. 18.3. Third, machine learning is used to *train classifiers*, either multiple binary classifiers or a multi-class classifier. A major difference between the classification approach and the IR approach to duplicate detection is thus that the former normally requires *supervised learning*, that is, learning from an annotated training set containing both positive and negative examples (Table 18.1).

Table 18.1 Summary of studies on IR-based duplicate detection, sorted chronologically

Study	Retrieval model and features used	Dataset (# issue reports)	R@10	Lessons learned
Runeson et al. [40]	VSM. Word unigrams from title and description with TF weights. Categorical feature: project.	SEMC (undisclosed "large")	40 %	Fine tuning had little effect. However, best results for (a) short stop word list, (b) using thesaurus and (c) spell checker, (d) considering the project field, (e) doubling the weight of terms in the title, and (f) applying a 50-day filter for issue reports.
Wang et al. [49]	VSM. Word unigrams from title and description with TF–IDF weights. Invoked methods from stack traces with binary weights.	OSS project: Firefox (1,749)	93 %	Combining textual features and stack traces improve performance, especially when independent thresholds are applied. Doubling the weight of terms in the title beneficial.
Sureka and Jalote [47]	Character n-grams from title and description ($4 \leq n \leq 10$).	OSS project: Eclipse (2,270)	40 %	Acceptable results without preprocessing, thus cross-language detection possible. Character n-grams in titles most useful.
Sun et al. [45]	BM25F. Word unigrams and bigrams from title and description with TF-IDF weights. Categorical features: product, component, type, priority, version.	OSS projects: OpenOffice (31,138), Eclipse (209,058), Mozilla (75,653)	OpenOffice: 65 %, Mozilla: 65 %, Eclipse: 70 %	Textual content of title most important feature, followed by product and version information. Faster and more accurate than [46].

"R@10" = recall at 10

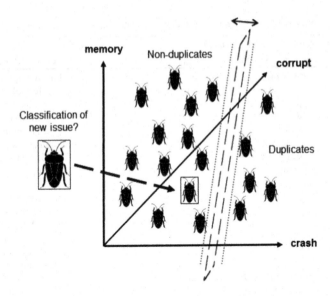

Fig. 18.4 Duplicate detection based on SVM. In this example, the three terms memory, corrupt and crash constitute the dimensions in the vector space. An individual SVM classifier, trained for a specific issue report, predicts that a newly submitted issue report is a nonduplicate. An optimal separating hyperplane, a maximum margin separator, is shown to the *right*

The standard IR approach on the other hand, uses the existing information only, without any learning process. In this section, we focus on describing an approach proposed by Sun et al. [46]. They trained an individual classifier for each existing issue report in three large issue repositories, and used the classifiers to predict whether a newly submitted issue report is a duplicate or not. Fourth, when a new issue report is submitted to the prototype of Sun et al., all classifiers answer the question: "How likely is this newly submitted issue report a duplicate of this master issue report?".

A frequently used approach for "off-the-shelf" supervised learning is to apply *support vector machines* (SVMs), when training classifiers in a new domain [41]. The SVM model maps all issue reports as points in space, where different terms can constitute the dimensions as in the VSM, and individual issue reports are typically represented as the endpoints of their corresponding feature vectors. SVMs then construct a maximum margin separator, a hyperplane that divides the positive and negative examples with a gap as wide as possible (as illustrated in Fig. 18.4), thus creating two classes: duplicates and nonduplicates with respect to a given master issue report. As the fourth and final step, newly submitted issue reports are mapped to the same space, and depending on which side of the hyperplane they belong, the classifier predicts whether the issue reports are duplicates or not. When all SVM classifiers have made their predictions, the classification-based RSSE can *recommend* potential duplicates. Further details on SVMs are presented by Menzies [30] in Chap. 3.

The classification-based RSSE implemented by Sun et al. [46] uses a hash-map-like *bucket structure*. Each bucket contains a master report as the key, and all its duplicate reports as values. Then, an SVM classifier is trained for each bucket, using the duplicate reports as positive examples, and the others as negative examples. When a new issue report is submitted, all classifiers report a probability value given by the distance to the separating hyperplane. The probability values are then used to rank the output, used to recommend potential master issues of a submitted issue report. Sun et al. used a rich set of textual features to train their classifiers. The high number of features originate from considering three different bags-of-words (title, description, and title+description) independently, allowing three different calculations of inverse document frequencies (as IDF weights are calculated based on frequencies in the entire collection). Moreover, they considered both unigrams and bigrams. In total, 54 different textual similarities were calculated between each pair of issue reports, 27 features based on unigrams and 27 features based on bigrams.

Sun et al. [46] evaluated their system on issue reports from three open source projects: OpenOffice, Firefox, and Eclipse. Furthermore, they implemented three previously proposed systems for duplicate detection for comparison (Runeson et al. [40], Wang et al. [49], and Jalbert and Weimer [20]). On all three datasets, they showed that their system outperforms the others. Sun et al. reported recall at 10 of 60 % for both Firefox and Eclipse, and recall at 10 of 55 % for OpenOffice. They also reported that the execution time of their system was longer than what was required in previous work.

Jalbert and Weimer [20] also did work on duplicate detection that they refer to as classification-based. While their approach is based on IR techniques, they extended it by also training a classifier based on linear regression. First they considered textual content in the title and the description as two separate bags-of-words, and preprocessed them using stop word removal and stemming. Through experimentation they showed that considering IDF did not improve performance in their context. Instead, they found it the most useful to consider only term frequencies and weigh the textual features as $TF = 3 + 2 \times \log_2(\text{frequency})$. All issue reports were represented as feature vectors in the VSM, and they calculated cosine similarities to induce a graph of issue reports, connecting issue reports by undirected edges if two issue reports were more similar than a certain threshold. Jalbert and Weimer then applied a graph clustering algorithm developed for social network analysis [33], to generate a set of possibly overlapping nodes in the graph, that is, potentially duplicated reports. Furthermore, they considering a set of ordinal and nominal surface features: severity, operating system, and the number of associated patches or screenshots. They used all the features to train a linear regression model, and to find a corresponding output value cutoff that distinguishes between duplicates and nonduplicates. The linear regression model could then be used for newly submitted issue reports, to perform classifications against each existing issue report.

Table 18.2 Summary of studies on duplicate detection based on classification

Study	Classifier and features used	Dataset (#issue reports)	R@10	Lessons learned
Jalbert and Weimer [20]	Linear regression model. Word unigrams from title and description with TF weights. Categorical features: severity, operating system, nbr attached patches or screenshots.	OSS projects from Mozilla (29,000)	45 %	Performs comparably to Runeson et al. [40]. Through simulation they show that their system realistically could save effort. Also, they show that the textual content in the title is the most important feature.
Sun et al. [46]	SVM. Word unigrams and bigrams from title and description with several TF-IDF weights (in total 54 textual features).	OSS projects: OpenOffice (12,723), Eclipse (44,652), Firefox (47,704)	~60 %	Outperforms Runeson et al. [40], Wang et al. [49], and Jalbert and Weimer [20]. While the high number of textual features leads to better results, more execution time is required.

Jalbert and Weimer evaluated their system on 29,000 issue reports from the Mozilla community, containing reports from several development projects. They report that their system is at least as good as the approach of Runeson et al. [40], and achieved a recall at 10 of 45 % (Table 18.2). By conducting leave-one-out analysis on their textual features, they concluded that the textual content of the title was the most important, followed by the description. While other features also brought value, they all contributed less to the linear model. Also, Jalbert and Weimer simulated the performance of their system over 16 weeks using the submission dates of the issue reports in their dataset, that is, they reported how their tool would have performed if it was deployed in the Mozilla context. They used the chronological first half of the dataset as the training set, and evaluated their work on the second half. Their fully automated system correctly filtered 8 % of all possible duplicates, while allowing at least one report for each real issue to reach developers. The authors estimate that this could have saved 1.5 developer-weeks of triage effort over 16 work weeks (assuming that each manual issue triage would on average require 30 min).

18.3 Navigating from Issue Reports in Evolving Software Systems

Software development typically involves managing large amounts of information, that is, formal and informal software artifacts, that evolve in response to environmental changes and user needs. In traditional software engineering, the software is systematically progressed through analysis, specification, design, implementation, verification, and maintenance. However, the increase of formalized knowledge-intensive activities tend to increase the number of artifacts maintained in a project [52]. When software evolution accumulates changes, made by many different developers over time and possibly from different development sites, it is a challenge to stay on top of all information.

A different development context, also highly challenging in terms of information access, is the development of *open source systems* (OSS). Mature software such as Android, Eclipse, and Mozilla Firefox have successfully adopted OSS development practices. Development of OSS is often characterized by globally distributed workforces and rapid software evolution. As most collaboration is online, communication within the team must be smooth, and all available information must be easily accessible. Open source projects typically rely on simple techniques such as discussion forums and mailing lists for communication, complemented by advanced version control systems for managing source code and supporting artifacts [12]. While the number of artifact types are typically lower than in traditional software development, quick and concise access to information is essential as teams cannot rely on face-to-face communication.

Thus, both large traditional projects and OSS projects risk being threatened by *information overload*, a state where individuals do not have the time or capacity to process all available information [15]. Knowledge workers frequently report the stressing feeling of having to deal with too much information [14], and in general spend a substantial effort on locating relevant information [24]. Thus, an important characteristic of a software development context is the *findability* that it provides, defined as "the degree to which a system or environment supports navigation and retrieval" [34]. A prerequisite to developing an RSSE for navigation support is to properly understand the context of the work task that is to be supported.

This section presents two separate examples of RSSEs supporting software evolution, where issue reports are used as "hubs" in generating traces between information items. First, we present Hipikat [12], an RSSE targeting software evolution in open source projects, specifically aiming at helping project newcomers. Second, we introduce ImpRec, an RSSE supporting safety-critical change impact analysis in a company with rich development processes. Both RSSEs are based on knowledge reuse from previous collaborative effort in projects complemented by textual analysis of artifact content, and rely on artifact usage rather than explicit ratings provided by engineers.

We present both Hipikat and ImpRec using a four-step model, shown in Fig. 18.5. The development of the RSSEs starts by *modeling the information space*, to create

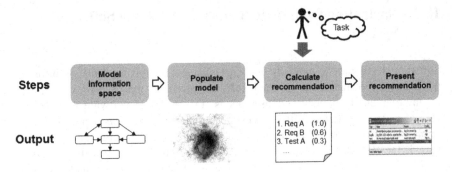

Fig. 18.5 Four step model for development of an RSSE for navigation support

a schema that can be used to represent the involved software artifacts. Second, the developed model is *populated* by historical data from the corresponding projects, and stored in an actionable data structure. Also as part of this step, textual content of artifacts are preprocessed and indexed. When the historical data has been processed, the RSSEs are ready to *calculate recommendations*. This can either be initiated by the developer explicitly, or implicitly based on the work task the developer pursues at a given time. The final step in the model covers how the *recommendations are presented* to the developers.

Hipikat and ImpRec are not the only approaches supporting navigation in large software engineering projects. Begel et al. [3] developed Codebook, a framework for connecting engineers and their software artifacts. It was developed to support mining various software repositories, and to capture relations among people and artifacts in a single graph structure. Codebook was evaluated by implementing portal solutions at Microsoft, helping developers discover and track both colleagues and work artifacts in a large software project. Seichter et al. [42], also inspired by the social media revolution, addressed the management of artifacts software ecosystems by creating "social networks" with artifacts as first-class citizens. The explicitly visible network of artifacts supported maintaining relations between artifacts and enabled personal "news feeds" for involved developers, containing recommendations for relevant changes, possible dependencies, etc. Gethers et al. [17] proposed automated impact analysis from textual change requests, an approach that is reused in ImpRec. Their tool combined IR techniques, analysis of software evolution using data mining, and execution information via dynamic analysis to recommend an initial set of impacted methods in the source code of four OSS systems.

18.4 Hipikat: Helping a Project Newcomer Come Up-to-Speed

Hipikat was developed by Čubranić et al. to build a project memory to support newcomer software developers by using information about past modifications to the project. The aim is to help them perform modification tasks to the system

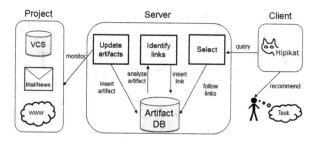

Fig. 18.6 Client–server architecture of Hipikat [adapted from 12]

more effectively [10, 12]. Hipikat has mainly been studied in the context of the Eclipse OSS community. The main Eclipse project is the Eclipse Platform, a mature integrated development environment (IDE) written in Java, known for its extensible architecture and many third-party plug-ins.

For software developers joining the Eclipse Platform project, the first contact with the heterogeneous information space of the project can be discouraging: there are several thousands of files, issue reports, documentation, and discussions. In a traditional project, the developer would join a team and gain knowledge through mentoring [44]. An experienced team member would work closely with the newcomer and orally impart the information structure and help him becoming productive. However, in OSS projects such lightweight interaction is typically not possible as the developers are globally distributed. Thus, it is challenging for a project newcomer to come up-to-speed and learn a new software system, for example, navigating source code and finding issue reports relevant to the work task at hand.

Hipikat is implemented as a client–server architecture, as depicted in Fig. 18.6. The server maintains the *project memory*, a semantic network of artifacts and relations, formed during development and updated as the target system evolved. Developers interact with Hipikat clients, which can be implemented in various ways, such as the Eclipse plug-in developed by Čubranić et al. [12]. The server and the clients communicate over a SOAP RPC protocol, and the server provides recommendations to the clients in an XML format [10]. Sections 18.4.1–18.4.2 present Hipikat according to the structure in Fig. 18.5.

18.4.1   Step 1: Modeling the Hipikat Project Memory

Čubranić et al. developed Hipikat with the ambition to provide a project newcomer recommendations of source code, accompanying information, and stored developer communication relevant to an issue report. Figure 18.7 displays the five artifact types represented in the project memory, and the relations among them. Four of the types

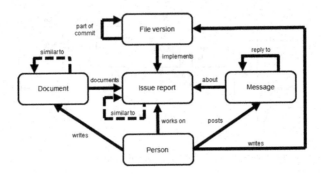

Fig. 18.7 Entity–relation diagram of the software artifacts in the Hipikat project memory [adapted from 12]

correspond to artifacts commonly created in OSS projects. The central entity is the *issue report*. Source code *file versions* implement resolutions to issues described in issue reports, and might be related to other file versions in the same commit. Project *documents* represent accompanying information posted on the project website, for example, design documentation, and such artifacts might document aspects relevant to an issue report. Another artifact type in the model is the project *message* (e.g., in discussion forums or mailing lists) that might contain information about an issue report. Messages might also be related to each other as they might be posted as responses, that is, "reply-to" links. Furthermore, the Hipikat model also covers implicit relations between documents and between issue reports respectively, modeling that these artifacts might have outgoing "similar to" relations if artifacts share much content (represented by dashed edges in Fig. 18.7). Finally, the scheme of the project memory represents *persons*, who might work on issue reports, post messages, and write documents and source code file versions.

18.4.2 Step 2: Populating the Hipikat Project Memory

The Hipikat server is responsible for populating the Hipikat project memory. The server has three functions, implemented in three subsystems as seen in Fig. 18.6. The *update artifacts* subsystem monitors the project information space for additions and changes during the OSS evolution. Čubranić et al. distinguish between three categories of artifacts in the Eclipse Platform development project: *immutable* (e.g., source file revisions), *modifiable but not deletable* (e.g., issue reports in Bugzilla), and *changeable* (e.g., webpages). The update subsystem has separate modules for the following project information sources: CVS (the version control system), Bugzilla (the issue repository), www.eclipse.com (the webpage), Usenet newsgroups, and Mailman (the archive of email messages). *Change listeners* in the subsystem are notified as the information space changes, and new and modified artifacts are inserted in the artifact database (see Fig. 18.6). More specifically, the artifact database stores mostly artifact metadata, for example, ID, author, path and creation date, but also natural language content is stored such as commit comments, issue descriptions and email body text.

Apart from the artifacts stored in the project memory, a vital aspect of the project memory is the relations among them. Some explicit relations are directly available in the artifact metadata, for example, authors and dates. However, Hipikat also implements several modules that independently analyze artifact content to deduct additional links. Moreover, Hipikat creates links with different *confidence*, a measure of trustworthiness that is used when presenting recommendations to the developer. The four link types "implements," "part-of-commit," "reply-to," and "similar-to" (see Fig. 18.7) are identified in the *identify links* subsystem using the following five modules [10]:

Log Analyzer   Uses regular expressions to identify commit comments containing issue IDs to insert high confidence "implements" links.

Activity Matcher   Searches for commits by a developer that occur shortly before the *same* developer changes the status of an issue report to resolved. Inserts implements links between source code file version and issue reports to the project memory with confidence reflecting the time span.

CVS Commit Matcher   Identifies file versions checked in within a few minutes. "Part-of-commit" links are added if they have the same author and commit comment.

Thread Matcher   Identifies both conversation threads of newsgroup postings and email threads by looking for specific headers in the stored messages. "Reply-to" links are inserted accordingly.

Text Similarity Matcher   Predicts relations among documents and among issue reports (see Fig. 18.7) based on the similarity of the textual content. This is implemented in the same manner as the IR-based duplicate detection described in Sect. 18.2.3. All textual content is preprocessed using stop word removal and stemmed using Porter's stemmer, then indexed using the VSM. Hipikat uses the log-entropy model for feature weighting. As an additional step, the vector space is transformed using latent semantic indexing [13] (further described by Menzies [30] in Chap. 3), an approach that aims to remove noise and to deal with synonymy. Finally, cosine similarities are calculated and "similar-to" links are added to the project memory.

18.4.3   Step 3: Calculating Recommendations in Hipikat

The third subsystem developed in the Hipikat server, *Select* (see Fig. 18.6), calculates recommendations by using the relationship links in the project memory. Hipikat recommendations are always calculated in response to a query, either explicitly initiated by the user, or implicitly as the user performs work tasks [12]. An implicit query identifies the artifact from which the query originates, and that might also contain additional context options. For explicit queries, Hipikat searches

Table 18.3 Summary of links followed in the Hipikat project memory

Module	Type of link	Confidence	Link source	Link target
Log Analyzer	Implements	High	Commit	Issue report
Activity Matcher	Implements	Low, Medium, Medium high, High	Commit	Issue report
CVS Commit Matcher	Part-of-commit	Medium low, Medium, Medium high, High	Commit	Commit
Thread Matcher	Reply-to	—	Message	Message
Text Similarity Matcher	Similar-to	Cosine similarity	Document	Document
Text Similarity Matcher	Similar-to	Cosine similarity	Issue report	Issue report

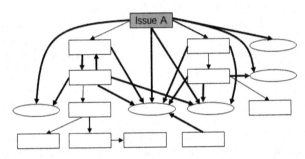

Fig. 18.8 Example of Hipikat recommendation trails, in this case items in the project memory related to Issue A. Issue reports are represented as boxes, and source code file versions as ovals. All edges are directed, and have a confidence value as indicated by the edge weights [adapted from 10]

for the artifact the developer specifies in the query. The Select subsystem locates that artifact in the project memory, and follows relationship links to generate a set of recommended artifacts for the developer to consider in his current work task.

The Select subsystem contains modules that correspond to the five identification modules described in Sect. 18.4.2. As the modules recommend artifacts, they also provide rationales for their choices as well as Hipikat's confidence for the recommendations. Before the final recommendations are presented to the developer, the output from the modules is merged. If multiple modules recommend the same artifact, only the one with the highest confidence will be kept. Table 18.3 lists the link types that are followed by Hipikat, to enable the RSSE to detect recommendation trails in the project memory. Figure 18.8 shows an example of such trails, originating from a study on the Avid visualizer, a Java tool for visualizing the operation of a Java system [10].

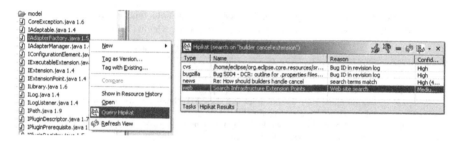

Fig. 18.9 The Hipikat user interface. To the *left*, querying Hipikat from a context menu. To the *right*, presentation of Hipikat recommendations [reproduced, with permission from the original developers, from 10]

18.4.4   Step 4: Presenting Recommendations

The Hipikat client is available as an Eclipse plugin, which means it is integrated in the IDE. The goal of Čubranić et al. was to develop an unobtrusive client, so the user interaction is kept simple. Primarily, the developer explicitly queries Hipikat for recommendations from context menus. "Query Hipikat" is an available menu item in the context menus of several entities in Eclipse, for example, version controlled files either in the workspace Navigator or opened in the Java editor, files in Repository view, revisions in the Resource History view and Java classes in the Outline or Hierarchy views.

As a response to queries from the Hipikat client, the Hipikat server returns a list of recommended artifacts as presented in Sect. 18.4.3. The list is presented in a Hipikat *Results view*, where each recommended artifact is displayed together with its type, why it is recommended and the confidence of the recommendation. The recommended articles are grouped by artifact type. Double-clicking on an artifact opens them for viewing, either directly in Eclipse, or in a web browser. Moreover, the developer can also initiate new Hipikat queries from the context menus of the artifacts in the Results view (Fig. 18.9).

Developers using Hipikat can also provide feedback on the recommendations. For each recommended artifact, a developer can select "like" or "dislike". Dislikes clean the list of recommendations, that is, disliked artifacts are removed from the list. Liked recommendations, on the other hand, move to the top of the list. To better use the developer feedback is one out of several improvements that Čubranić [10] outlined to further improve Hipikat; however, the RSSE is not actively developed anymore.

Table 18.4 Impact analysis template. Questions in bold fonts require explicit trace links to other artifacts. Based on a description by Klevin [26]

	Impact Analysis Questions for Error Corrections
Q1	Is the reported problem safety critical?
Q2	In which versions/revisions does this problem exist?
Q3	How are general system functions and properties affected by the change?
Q4	**List modified code files/modules and their SIL classifications, and/or affected safety related hardware modules.**
Q5	**Which library items are affected by the change? (e.g., library types, firmware functions, HW types, HW libraries)**
Q6	**Which documents need to be modified? (e.g., product requirements specifications, architecture, functional requirements specifications, design descriptions, schematics, functional test descriptions, design test descriptions)**
Q7	**Which test cases need to be executed? (e.g., design tests, functional tests, sequence tests, environmental/EMC tests, FPGA simulations)**
Q8	**Which user documents, including online help, need to be modified?**
Q9	How long will it take to correct the problem, and verify the correction?
Q10	What is the root cause of this problem?
Q11	How could this problem have been avoided?
Q12	**Which requirements and functions need to be retested by product test/system test organization?**

18.5 ImpRec: Supporting Impact Analysis in a Safety Context

The goal of ImpRec is to support artifact navigation in a development organization in a large multinational company, active in the power and automation sector. The development context is safety-critical embedded development in the domain of industrial control systems, governed by IEC 61511[1] and certified to a Safety Integrity Level (SIL) of 2 as defined by IEC 61508.[2] The targeted system has evolved over a long time, the oldest source code was developed in the 1980s. A typical project has a duration of 12–18 months and follows an iterative stage-gate project management model. The number of developers is in the magnitude of hundreds, distributed across sites in Europe, Asia and North America.

As specified in IEC 61511, the impact of proposed software changes should be analyzed before implementation. In the case company, this process is integrated in the issue repository [6]. As part of the analysis, engineers are required to investigate the impact of a change, and document their findings in an *impact analysis report* according to a project specific template. The template is validated by an external certifying agency, and the impact analysis reports are internally reviewed and externally assessed during safety audits.

A slightly modified version of this template is presented in Table 18.4. Several questions explicitly ask for trace links (6 out of 12 questions). The engineer is required to specify source code that will be modified (with a file-level granularity),

---

[1] Functional safety—Safety instrumented systems for the process industry sector.

[2] Functional safety of Electrical/Electronic/Programmable Electronic safety-related systems.

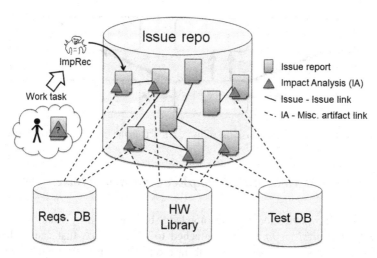

Fig. 18.10   Impact analysis supported by ImpRec. Trace link structure created by collaborative effort. Trace links among defects and from impact analysis reports to requirements, HW descriptions, and test cases

and also which related software artifacts need to be updated to reflect the changes, for example, requirement specifications, design documents, test case descriptions, test scripts and user manuals. Furthermore, the impact analysis should specify which high-level system requirements cover the involved features, and which test cases should be executed to verify that the changes are correct once implemented in the system. In the addressed software system, the extensive evolution has created a complex dependency web of software artifacts, thus the impact analysis is a daunting work task.

Figure 18.10 shows an overview of the ImpRec recommendation approach. To the left, a developer is about to conduct a new impact analysis as part of a defect correction, that is, answering Q1–Q12 of the impact analysis template in Table 18.4. First, content-based filtering is used to find issue reports with descriptions similar to the current issue report stored in the issue repository. The same techniques as presented in Sect. 18.2.3 on detection of duplicate issue reports using IR approaches are applied. Then, originating from the most similar issue reports, the collaboratively constructed trace link network, the "trails of previous developers in the information landscape" is used to recommend which trace links the developer should consider specifying in the impact analysis report. As such, the new impact analysis work task is seeded by the pre-existing traceability from past impact analysis reports. The network of collaboratively created trace links is referred to as the *knowledge base*, a concept corresponding to the project memory in Hipikat. Note that the current scope of ImpRec is limited to recommend noncode artifacts relevant to an issue report, as these are considered more challenging in the case company.

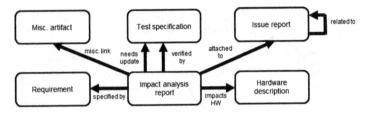

Fig. 18.11 Entity–relation diagram of the software artifacts in the ImpRec knowledge base

18.5.1 Step 1: Modeling the ImpRec Knowledge Base

Figure 18.11 shows the model of the knowledge base as an entity–relation diagram. The *impact analysis report* that is attached to *issue reports* that cause changes to safety-critical source code is the hub in the model. An impact analysis report can contain trace links to several different artifact types, specifying relationships from individual issue reports (Q4–Q8 and Q12 in Table 18.4). *Requirements* (e.g., system requirements, safety requirements, and functional descriptions) can specify functionality that is impacted by the problem described in an issue report. *Test specifications* can verify functionality that is described in an issue report. Also, making the changes required to resolve an issue report might force updates to test specifications as well. The changes might also impact *hardware specifications*. Finally, an issue report can be related to other issue reports, a relation that is explicitly specified by developers in the issue repository (presented also in Fig. 18.10). Furthermore, as the type of artifacts cannot always be deduced by ImpRec, *miscellaneous artifacts* and *miscellaneous links* are also included in the model.

18.5.2 Step 2: Populating the ImpRec Knowledge Base

To aggregate the trace links from previous developers, ImpRec mines the issue repository [7]. In the studied case, 4,845 out of the 26,703 issue reports in the issue repository contain impact analysis reports. As a first step, the issue reports in the issue repository were exported to an extended comma-separated-value (CSV) format, a format specified by the vendor of the issue repository, and transformed to XML. Thus, the overall information of the issue reports were well structured; however, the attached impact analysis reports were stored as text elements. On the other hand, the textual information in the text elements were semi-structured according to the structure in the impact analysis template in Table 18.4.

Then, regular expressions were used to extract *trace links from the impact analysis reports*. Due to the fixed format of artifact IDs, this method could extract all correctly formatted trace links. To determine the type of the extracted trace links, two heuristics were used. Thanks to the structure of the impact analysis template, each trace links corresponded to a specific question. As such, in the context of

Table 18.5 Types of links extracted from the issue repository. All links have an issue report as source. "IA" = impact analysis

Trace link type	Description	Classification strategy	Count
related to	Link to another issue report that has been signaled by an engineer as related. The link is not bidirectional by default.	Separate field in issue report	18,835
specified by	Link to a specific requirement. Used to signal that a requirement needs to be updated, or requires verification.	Format of requirement IDs	3,996
verified by	Link to a test case description that needs to be executed, or a requirement that requires verification.	IA template, Q8 and Q12	2,297
needs update	Link to a software artifact that needs to be updated.	IA template, Q7 and Q9	1,106
impacts HW	Link from an IA report to a hardware description that is impacted by the issue or its implemented resolution.	IA template, Q6	1,221
miscellaneous link	Trace links from an IA report to an artifact, but the meaning of the link could not be deduced.	Default choice	775

Table 18.6 Types of nodes extracted from the issue repository. "IA" = impact analysis

Trace artifact type	Description	Classification strategy	Count
issue report	An individual issue report.	Separate item in issue repository	26,703
impact analysis report	A documented impact analysis.	Attached to an issue report	4,845
requirement	An individual requirement. The requirements are organized in requirement specifications.	Separate ID format	572
test specification	A document that contains test case descriptions.	IA template, Q8 and Q12	243
HW description	An artifact that describes the behavior of hardware	Separate ID format	1,106
miscellaneous artifact	An artifact whose type could not be deduced.	Default choice	376

Q8 and Q12 it could be deduced that the meaning of the links was related to verification, Q7 and Q9 deal with document updates, and Q6 refers to impact on hardware descriptions. Second, as requirement IDs have a distinguishable format in the company, also requirements specifications could be identified.

Next, explicit *trace links between issue reports* in the issue repository were extracted [8]. Each defect in the issue repository has a field "Related issues" used by engineers to manually signal other issues as related, by adding their issue IDs. Finally, the two extracted networks were combined into a single network, the ImpRec *knowledge base*. The knowledge base, consisting of 29,000 nodes and 28,230 edges, is represented as a semantic network expressed in GraphML [9]. Tables 18.5 and 18.6 summarize the different types of extracted trace links and trace artifacts.

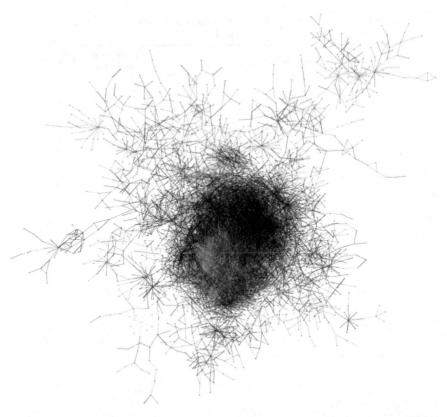

Fig. 18.12 A visualization of the knowledge base, displaying the largest component (10,211 artifacts and 23,078 relations)

Note that this only contains artifacts actually pointed out by the previous impact analysis reports, and that the total number of artifacts in the content management systems in the company is much higher. However, while the extracted traceability is a partial view, this is the traceability associated with the most volatile parts of the system to date, and thus a pragmatic starting point for future impact analyses.

Figure 18.12 shows an overview of the largest interconnected component of the knowledge base, comprising 36.2 % of the nodes and 81.7 % of the edges, created in the graph editor yEd [32] using an *organic layout*. The graph nodes are treated like physical objects with mutually repulsive forces. The edges on the other hand are considered to be metal springs attached to nodes, producing repulsive forces if they are long and attractive forces if they are short. By simulating these physical forces, the organic layout finds a minimum of the sum of the forces emitted by nodes and edges. Output from organic layouts typically show inherent symmetric and clustered graph structures, useful for finding highly connected backbone regions in a graph. Although the primary purpose of the knowledge base is not to enable visual analytics, visual representations of complex information might enable additional insights [25]. Regarding the knowledge base, we can make some general observations. First, Fig. 18.12 shows that there is a highly interconnected central region containing thousands of artifacts, rather than several distinctive clusters. This region displays a high link density, and while "specified by" (i.e., links to requirements) dominate the central region, all link types are present. This implies that changes to an artifact in this region could impact a high number of artifacts. In general, the complex link structure displayed in Fig. 18.12 suggests that much traceability information about artifact relations in the software system has been captured in the knowledge base.

18.5.3 Step 3: Calculating Recommendations in ImpRec

When the knowledge base is represented as a semantic network, ImpRec calculates recommendations in three steps:

1. Retrieval of likely related issue reports, based on their textual *content*
2. Search for artifacts that previously were marked as impacted, based on the *collaboratively* created knowledge base
3. Ranking the identified artifacts based on textual similarities and network structure

First, ImpRec uses content-based filtering, based on the textual content of the issue reports, to identify starting points in the knowledge base. Both terms in the title and description of issue reports are considered, after stemming and stop word removal. Then the remaining textual features are assigned TF–IDF weights before representing them in the VSM. ImpRec then calculates cosine similarities between the given issue report and all others, and finally rank them accordingly. This work is in line with previous work on IR-based duplicate detection presented in Sect. 18.2.3. ImpRec considers the top five issue reports, corresponding to the five highest non-zero cosine similarity values, as *starting points 1–5* in the knowledge base. Moreover, the similarity values of the five issue reports are re-normalized between 0 and 1 (SIM_i) for later ranking purposes.

Originating from the starting points, ImpRec performs breadth-first searches in the knowledge database to find artifacts (ART_x) that previously have been pointed out as impacted. First, impacted artifacts linked from starting points are identified, then issue reports connected to the starting points are considered. ImpRec searches for impacted artifacts up to three levels away from starting points (*LEVEL*), that is, a maximum of three "related issue" links from a starting point are followed. The searches from each starting point results in an *impact set* of possibly impacted artifacts (SET_i), which are then used as input to the ranking engine.

In the knowledge base, ImpRec calculates centrality measures for each artifact ($CENT_x$). As the artifacts ImpRec recommends are only link targets, that is, they have no outgoing links themselves, only the number of incoming edges are

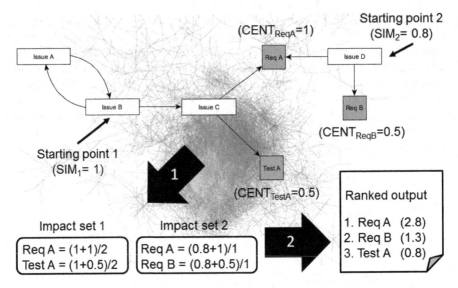

Fig. 18.13 Example calculation of impact recommendation in a simplified knowledge base

considered for this calculation. The resulting *in-degree centralities* are normalized between 0 and 1 and also used as input to the ranking engine.

The ranking of the artifacts in the set of recommendations is based on their individual weights. The general equation for calculating the weight of a recommended artifact, weight(ART_x), is the following:

$$\text{weight}(ART_x) = \sum_{\substack{ART_x \in SET_i \\ 1 \leq i \leq 5}} \frac{a \times SIM_i + b \times CENT_x}{c \times LEVEL} \quad (18.1)$$

where SIM_i is the similarity of the issue report that was used as starting point when identifying ART_x, $LEVEL$ is the number of related issue links followed from the starting point to identify ART_x, and $CENT_x$ is the centrality measure of ART_x in the knowledge base. The constants a, b, and c permit tuning for context-specific improvements.

Figure 18.13 illustrates the calculation of an example recommendation in a simplified knowledge base where $a = b = c = 1$. First, content-based filtering based on textual features finds two starting points in the network, with normalized similarity values equal to 1 and 0.6, respectively. Starting point 1 (Issue B in the figure) does not have any direct links to any impacted artifacts; however, a breadth-first search identifies Req A and Test A through Issue C. Both Req A and Test A are added to Impact set 1. Starting point 2 (Issue D in the figure) on the other hand has direct links to impacted artifacts; thus, Req A and Req B are both added to Impact set 2. The weight of the individual artifacts in each impact set is then calculated according to (18.1), considering textual similarities ($SIM_1 = 1$ and $SIM_2 = 0.8$), node centralities ($CENT_{ReqA} = 1$, $CENT_{ReqB} = 0.5$, and $CENT_{TestA} = 0.5$), and the

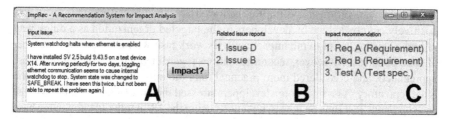

Fig. 18.14 Prototype user interface for ImpRec. A is used for inputting the natural language issue report. Output is presented to the *right*, possibly related issues in B, and suggestions for impacted software artifacts in C

number of links followed between issue reports (2 for artifacts in Impact set 1 and 1 for artifacts in Impact set 2).

Finally, the weights of the artifacts in the two impact sets are summarized (presented in the lower right part of Fig. 18.13). Req A is included in both Impact sets 1 and 2; thus, its final weight in the list of ranked recommendations is $1 + 1.8 = 2.8$. The weights of Req B and Test A are lower, 1.3 and 0.8, respectively, which results in lower rankings for them.

18.5.4   Step 4: Presenting Recommendations

The developers at the case company all work in an Microsoft Windows environment; thus we have not considered ImpRec for multiple platforms. The current version of ImpRec is written as a lightweight standalone tool in .NET, supporting basic user interaction. Figure 18.14 shows the ImpRec user interface. The leftmost frame is used to input the description of the issue report for which the developer is conducting an impact analysis. Based on the textual content in the text box, recommendations are calculated when the developer clicks the "Impact?" button.

The center and rightmost frames in ImpRec are used to present the calculated recommendations. In the center frame, the issue reports ImpRec recommends a developer to investigate are presented, that is, similar to how RSSEs for duplicate detection (see Sect. 18.2) typically report candidate duplicates. In the rightmost frame, ImpRec lists the most likely impacted artifacts. The content in both the frames are sorted, to ensure the recommendations with the highest confidence are presented first.

For ImpRec to be truly integrated in the impact analysis process, the tool needs to be integrated in the working environment of the developers. As the impact analyses are conducted with issue reports as starting points, and the outcome is stored as attachments to issue reports, the natural approach is to develop an ImpRec plugin to the issue repository used in the organization.

Early evaluations using 90 % of the dataset for training and the last 10 % as a test set show that about 40 % of the previous impact could be identified by ImpRec. The highest possible recall for this dataset is thus relatively low. However, the ranking function appears promising as ImpRec achieved a recall at 5 of 30 %. This result was positively acknowledged by developers in the targeted organization as a quick way to find a starting point in the impact analysis work task with a manageable number of false positives. Moreover, recommendations regarding related issue reports were appreciated, and considered more practical than the current search function in the issue repository. As a final note, developers stressed the need to keep the knowledge base updated. Test runs on new issue reports using the 18-month old knowledge base in the prototype revealed that ImpRec's recommendations did not reflect the latest work in the organization. While this finding is not surprising due to the dynamics of software engineering, it highlights the need for future work both on how to automatically update the knowledge base and how to identify obsolete content.

18.6   Conclusion

Issue reports are primarily used as "batons" in the communication between different actors in the software development process, whether in-house or open source. This chapter demonstrates that there are several aspects to issue reports that benefit from recommendation systems. First, we presented different approaches to recommending duplicate issue reports, either for reducing information overload by merging duplicates, or to provide more information of the issue at hand, for example, for other recommendation systems. Evaluations indicate recall of 40–93 % when considering the top 10 recommendations. While the results are promising, further research is needed to understand variations and tailoring to specific contexts. Second, we presented two approaches to recommending traces to software engineering artifacts, using issue reports as an information "hub," implemented in the tools Hipikat and ImpRec. Both approaches have shown potential of being useful for practitioners to help navigating a continuously expanding software project. Still, they have to be better integrated into development environments, and heuristics for the search methods have to be improved to make them feasible for everyday practice.

Acknowledgments This work was funded by the Industrial Excellence Center EASE—Embedded Applications Software Engineering. Thanks go to the developers of Hipikat for providing related material.

References

1. Anvik, J., Hiew, L., Murphy, G.: Coping with an open bug repository. In: Proceedings of the Eclipse Technology eXchange, pp. 35–39, San Diego, CA, USA, 16–17 October 2005. doi:10.1145/1117696.1117704
2. Anvik, J., Murphy, G.C.: Reducing the effort of bug report triage: Recommenders for development-oriented decisions. ACM Trans. Software Eng. Meth. **20**(3), 10:1–10:35 (2011). doi:10.1145/2000791.2000794

3. Begel, A., Phang, K.Y., Zimmermann, T.: Codebook: Discovering and exploiting relationships in software repositories. In: Proceedings of the ACM/IEEE International Conference on Software Engineering, pp. 125–134, Cape Town, South Africa, 1–8 May 2010. doi:10.1145/1806799.1806821
4. Bettenburg, N., Premraj, R., Zimmermann, T.: Duplicate bug reports considered harmful … really? In: Proceedings of the IEEE International Conference on Software Maintenance, pp. 337–345, Beijing, 28 September–4 October 2008. doi:10.1109/ICSM.2008.4658082
5. Boehm, B., Basili, V.: Software defect reduction top 10 list. Computer **34**(1), 135–137 (2001). doi:10.1109/2.962984
6. Borg, M.: Findability through traceability: A realistic application of candidate trace links? In: Proceedings of the International Conference on Evaluating Novel Approaches to Software Engineering, pp. 173–181, Wroclaw, Poland, 29–30 June 2012.
7. Borg, M., Gotel, O., Wnuk, K.: Enabling traceability reuse for impact analyses: A feasibility study in a safety context. In: Proceedings of the International Workshop on Traceability in Emerging Forms of Software Engineering, pp. 72–78, San Francisco, CA, USA, 19 May 2013a
8. Borg, M., Pfahl, D., Runeson, P.: Analyzing networks of issue reports. In: Proceedings of the European Conference on Software Maintenance and Reengineering, pp. 79–88, Genova, Italy, 5–8 March 2013b. doi:10.1109/CSMR.2013.18
9. Brandes, U., Eiglsperger, M., Lerner, J., Pich, C.: Graph markup language (GraphML). In: Tamassia, R. (ed.) Handbook of Graph Drawing and Visualization, Chap. 16, pp. 517–542. Chapman and Hall/CRC, London (2013)
10. Čubranić, D.: Project history as a group memory: Learning from the past. Ph.D. thesis, University of British Columbia (2004)
11. Čubranić, D., Murphy, G.C.: Automatic bug triage using text categorization. In: Proceedings of the International Conference on Software Engineering and Knowledge Engineering, pp. 92–97, Banff, Anbert, Canada, 20–24 June 2004
12. Čubranić, D., Murphy, G.C., Singer, J., Booth, K.S.: Hipikat: A project memory for software development. IEEE Trans. Software Eng. **31**(6), 446–465 (2005). doi:10.1109/TSE.2005.71
13. Deerwester, S., Dumais, S., Furnas, G., Landauer, T., Harshman, R.: Indexing by latent semantic analysis. J. Am. Soc. Inform. Sci. **41**(6), 391–407 (1990). doi:10.1002/(SICI)1097-4571(199009)41:6⟨391::AID-ASI1⟩3.0.CO;2-9
14. Edmunds, A., Morris, A.: The problem of information overload in business organisations: A review of the literature. Int. J. Inform. Manag. **20**(1), 17–28 (2000). doi:10.1016/S0268-4012(99)00051-1
15. Eppler, M., Mengis, J.: The concept of information overload: A review of literature from organization science, accounting, marketing, MIS, and related disciplines. Inform. Soc. Int. J. **20**(5), 325–344 (2004). doi:10.1080/01972240490507974
16. Gegick, M., Rotella, P., Xie, T.: Identifying security bug reports via text mining: An industrial case study. In: Proceedings of the International Working Conference on Mining Software Repositories, pp. 11–20, Cape Town, South Africa, 21–28 May 2010. doi:10.1109/MSR.2010.5463340
17. Gethers, M., Dit, B., Kagdi, H., Poshyvanyk, D.: Integrated impact analysis for managing software changes. In: Proceedings of the ACM/IEEE International Conference on Software Engineering, pp. 430–440, Zurich, Switzerland, 2–9 June 2012. doi:10.1109/ICSE.2012.6227172
18. Guo, P.J., Zimmermann, T., Nagappan, N., Murphy, B.: Characterizing and predicting which bugs get fixed. In: Proceedings of the ACM/IEEE International Conference on Software Engineering, vol. 1, pp. 495–504, Cape Town, South Africa, 1–8 May 2010. doi:10.1145/1806799.1806871
19. Herzig, K., Zeller, A.: Mining bug data: A practitioner's guide. In: Robillard, M., Maalej, W., Walker, R.J., Zimmermann, T. (eds.) Recommendation Systems in Software Engineering, Chap. 6. Springer, New York (2014)
20. Jalbert, N., Weimer, W.: Automated duplicate detection for bug tracking systems. In: Proceedings of the International Conference on Dependable Systems and Networks, pp. 52–61, Anchorage, Alaska, USA, 24–27 June 2008. doi:0.1109/DSN.2008.4630070

21. Johnson, J., Dubois, P.: Issue tracking. Comput. Sci. Eng. **5**(6), 71–77 (2003). doi:10.1109/MCISE.2003.1238707
22. Jonsson, L., Broman, D., Sandahl, K., Eldh, S.: Towards automated anomaly report assignment in large complex systems using stacked generalization. In: Proceedings of the IEEE International Conference on Software Testing, Verification and Validation, pp. 437–446, Montreal, QC, Canada, 17–21 April 2012. doi:10.1109/ICST.2012.124
23. Just, S., Premraj, R., Zimmermann, T.: Towards the next generation of bug tracking systems. In: Proceedings of the IEEE Symposium on Visual Languages and Human-Centric Computing, pp. 82–85, Herrsching am Ammersee, Germany, 15–19 September 2008. doi:10.1109/VLHCC.2008.4639063
24. Karr-Wisniewski, P., Lu, Y.: When more is too much: Operationalizing technology overload and exploring its impact on knowledge worker productivity. Comput. Hum. Behav. **26**(5), 1061–1072 (2010). doi:10.1016/j.chb.2010.03.008
25. Keim, D., Mansmann, F., Schneidewind, J., Thomas, J., Ziegler, H.: Visual analytics: Scope and challenges. In: Simoff, S., Böhlen, M., Mazeika, A. (eds.) Visual Data Mining: Theory, Techniques and Tools for Visual Analytics. Lecture Notes in Computer Science, vol. 4404, pp. 76–90. Springer, Berlin Heidelberg (2008). doi:10.1007/978-3-540-71080-6_6
26. Klevin, A.: People, process and tools: A study of impact analysis in a change process. Master thesis, Lund University (2012). URL http://sam.cs.lth.se/ExjobGetFile?id=467
27. Lamkanfi, A., Demeyer, S., Giger, E., Goethals, B.: Predicting the severity of a reported bug. In: Proceedings of the International Working Conference on Mining Software Repositories, pp. 1–10, Cape Town, South Africa, 2–3 May 2010. doi:10.1109/MSR.2010.5463284
28. Liu, T.Y.: Learning to Rank for Information Retrieval. Springer, Berlin, Heidelberg (2011). doi:10.1007/978-3-642-14267-3
29. Manning, C.D., Raghavan, P., Schutze, H.: Introduction to Information Retrieval. Cambridge University Press, Cambridge (2008)
30. Menzies, T.: Data mining: A tutorial. In: Robillard, M., Maalej, W., Walker, R.J., Zimmermann, T. (eds.) Recommendation Systems in Software Engineering, Chap. 3. Springer, New York (2014)
31. Menzies, T., Marcus, A.: Automated severity assessment of software defect reports. In: Proceedings of the IEEE International Conference on Software Maintenance, pp. 346–355, Beijing, China, 28 September–4 October 2008. doi:10.1109/ICSM.2008.4658083
32. Mierswa, I., Wurst, M., Klinkenberg, R., Scholz, M., Euler, T.: YALE: Rapid prototyping for complex data mining tasks. In: Proceedings of the ACM SIGKDD Conference on Knowledge Discovery and Data Mining, pp. 935–940, Philadelphia, PA, USA, 20–23 August 2006. doi:10.1145/1150402.1150531
33. Mishra, N., Schreiber, R., Stanton, I., Tarjan, R.: Clustering social networks. In: Proceedings of the International Workshop on Algorithms and Models for the Web-Graph. Lecture Notes in Computer Science, vol. 4863, pp. 56–67, San Diego, CA, USA, 11–12 December 2007. doi:10.1007/978-3-540-77004-6_5
34. Morville, P.: Ambient Findability: What We Find Changes Who We Become. O'Reilly, Sebastopol (2005)
35. Pol, M., Teunissen, R., van Veenendaal, E.: Software Testing: A Guide to the TMap Approach. Pearson, Reading (2002)
36. Porter, M.F.: An algorithm for suffix stripping. Program **14**(3), 130–137 (1980). doi:10.1108/eb046814
37. Raja, U.: All complaints are not created equal: Text analysis of open source software defect reports. Empir. Software Eng. **18**(1), 117–138 (2013). doi:10.1007/s10664-012-9197-9
38. Reis, C.R., Fortes, R.P.d.M.: An overview of the software engineering process and tools in the Mozilla project. In: Proceedings of the Workshop on Open Source Software Development, pp. 155–175, Orlando, FL, USA, 2002
39. Robertson, S., Zaragoza, H.: The probabilistic relevance framework: BM25 and beyond. Found. Trends Inform. Retrieval **3**(4), 333–389 (2009). doi:10.1561/1500000019

40. Runeson, P., Alexandersson, M., Nyholm, O.: Detection of duplicate defect reports using natural language processing. In: Proceedings of the ACM/IEEE International Conference on Software Engineering, pp. 499–510, Atlanta, Georgia, USA, 5–9 November 2007. doi:10.1109/ICSE.2007.32
41. Russell, S.J., Norvig, P.: Artificial Intelligence: A Modern Approach, 3rd edn. Prentice Hall, Englewood Cliffs, NJ (2009)
42. Seichter, D., Dhungana, D., Pleuss, A., Hauptmann, B.: Knowledge management in software ecosystems: Software artefacts as first-class citizens. In: Companion to the European Conference on Software Architecture, pp. 119–126, Copenhagen, Denmark, 23–26 August 2010. doi:10.1145/1842752.1842780
43. Serrano, N., Ciordia, I.: Bugzilla, ITracker, and other bug trackers. IEEE Software 22(2), 11–13 (2005). doi:10.1109/MS.2005.32
44. Sim, S.E., Holt, R.C.: The ramp-up problem in software projects: A case study of how software immigrants naturalize. In: Proceedings of the ACM/IEEE International Conference on Software Engineering, pp. 361–370, Kyoto, Japan, 19–25 April 1998. doi:10.1109/ICSE.1998.671389
45. Sun, C., Lo, D., Khoo, S.C., Jiang, J.: Towards more accurate retrieval of duplicate bug reports. In: Proceedings of the IEEE/ACM International Conference on Automated Software Engineering, pp. 253–262, Lawrence, KS, USA, 6–10 November 2011. doi:10.1109/ASE.2011.6100061
46. Sun, C., Lo, D., Wang, X., Jiang, J., Khoo, S.C.: A discriminative model approach for accurate duplicate bug report retrieval. In: Proceedings of the ACM/IEEE International Conference on Software Engineering, pp. 45–54, Cape Town, South Africa, 1–8 May 2010. doi:10.1145/1806799.1806811
47. Sureka, A., Jalote, P.: Detecting duplicate bug report using character N-gram-based features. In: Proceedings of the Asia–Pacific Software Engineering Conference, pp. 366–374, Sydney, Australia, 30 November–03 December 2010. doi:10.1109/APSEC.2010.49
48. Terveen, L., Hill, W.: Beyond recommender systems: Helping people help each other. In: Carroll, J.M. (ed.) Human–Computer Interaction in the New Millennium. Addison-Wesley, Reading, MA (2001)
49. Wang, X., Zhang, L., Xie, T., Anvik, J., Sun, J.: An approach to detecting duplicate bug reports using natural language and execution information. In: Proceedings of the ACM/IEEE International Conference on Software Engineering, pp. 461–470, Leipzig, Germany, 10–18 May 2008. doi:10.1145/1368088.1368151
50. Weiss, C., Premraj, R., Zimmermann, T., Zeller, A.: How long will it take to fix this bug? In: Proceedings of the International Workshop on Mining Software Repositories, Minneapolis, MN, USA, 19–20 May 2007. doi:10.1109/MSR.2007.13
51. Ying, A.T.T., Robillard, M.: Developer profiles for recommendation systems. In: Robillard, M., Maalej, W., Walker, R.J., Zimmermann, T. (eds.) Recommendation Systems in Software Engineering, Chap. 8. Springer, New York (2014)
52. Zantout, H., Marir, F.: Document management systems from current capabilities towards intelligent information retrieval: An overview. Int. J. Inform. Manag. 19(6), 471–484 (1999). doi:10.1016/S0268-4012(99)00043-2

Chapter 19
Recommendation Heuristics for Improving Product Line Configuration Processes

Raúl Mazo, Cosmin Dumitrescu, Camille Salinesi, and Daniel Diaz

Abstract In mass customization industries, such as car manufacturing, configurators play an important role both to interact with customers and in engineering processes. This is particularly true when engineers rely on reuse of assets and product line engineering techniques. Theoretically, product line configuration should be guided by the product line model. However, in the industrial context, the configuration of products from product line models is complex and error-prone due to the large number of variables in the models. The configuration activity quickly becomes cumbersome due to the number of decisions needed to get a proper configuration, to the fact that they should be taken in predefined order, or the poor response time of configurators when decisions are not appropriate. This chapter presents a collection of recommendation heuristics to improve the interactivity of product line configuration so as to make it scalable to common engineering situations. We describe the principles, benefits, and the implementation of each heuristic using constraint programming. The application and usability of the heuristics is demonstrated using a case study from the car industry.

19.1 Introduction

Product line engineering (PLE) is a viable and important reuse-based development paradigm that allows companies to realize improvements in time to market, cost, productivity, quality, and flexibility [8]. According to Clements and Northrop [9], PLE is different from single-system development with reuse in two aspects. First, developing a family of products requires "choices and options" that are optimized from the beginning and not just a single product specification that evolves

R. Mazo (✉) • C. Dumitrescu • C. Salinesi • D. Diaz
Université Paris 1 Panthéon-Sorbonne, Paris, France
e-mail: raul.mazo@univ-paris1.fr; Cosmin.Dumitrescu@malix.univ-paris1.fr;
Camille.Salinesi@univ-paris1.fr; Daniel.Diaz@univ-paris1.fr

M.P. Robillard et al. (eds.), *Recommendation Systems in Software Engineering*,
DOI 10.1007/978-3-642-45135-5_19, © Springer-Verlag Berlin Heidelberg 2014

over time. Second, product lines imply a preplanned reuse strategy that applies across the entire set of products rather than ad hoc or opportunistic reuse. The product line strategy has been successfully used in many different industry sectors, and in particular, in software development companies [9, 27]. Many different kinds of artifacts can be reused: including requirements, to model fragments, code, test data. These artifacts can be embodied as patterns, libraries of classes and meta classes, services or parameterized components. Reuse can be achieved in many different ways: instantiation, integration, composition or setting up parameters.

The product line (PL) is often so complex that it is not even possible to make an extensive list of all possible products. One example is the vehicle product line of the French manufacturer Renault, which can lead to 10^{21} configurations for the "Traffic" van product family [3]. On the one hand, in Internet applications, it is important to ensure short response times and support multiple users (e.g., the online Renault car configurator). On the other hand, engineering applications need to support the specification and configuration of large product line models. Due to their complexity and size, it becomes difficult for the engineer to parse and configure these models. This is where recommendation techniques can improve some of the shortcomings of product line configuration of large models. This chapter presents an application of recommendation heuristics to the configuration of product line models. It discusses the advantages of each of these heuristics in respect to experiments on a model of a family of parking brake systems.

In Sect. 19.2, we present background information related to the configuration of product lines and variability modeling. This is also where introduce an industrial case based on the configuration of an automotive electric parking brake (EPB) system. In Sect. 19.3, we introduce the set of heuristics for the configuration of product lines. In Sect. 19.4, we present a practical "hands-on" experience for transforming the product line OVM model to a GNU Prolog constraint model, followed by the implementation of heuristics in GNU Prolog. Finally, in Sect. 19.5, we discuss the usage and advantages of each heuristic and explain the context where each of them should be applied.

19.2 Background

PLE explicitly addresses reuse by differentiating between two kinds of development processes [27]: domain engineering and application engineering. The aim of the domain engineering process is to manage the reusable artifacts participating in the PL and the dependencies among them.

The reusable artifacts, called domain artifacts (e.g., requirements, architectural components, pieces of processes, methods, and tests), are related in a model representing the legal combinations of the reusable artifacts (called product line model). The aim of the application engineering process is to exploit the product line model in order to derive specific applications by reusing the domain artifacts. To generate new products, PLE takes into account the customer requirements but also the constraints of the PL domain.

The specification of requirements in the context of PLs is called a configuration process. In PLE, a configuration process is a step-wise process, with the objective to deliver configurations that both satisfy the domain constraints, provided by the product line model, and the stakeholders' requirements, which can be specified too [13]. Dealing with PL constraints in domain and application engineering has been the subject of extensive literature that suggests different approaches, mostly based on constraint and satisfiability (SAT) problem solving [25, 28]. Configuration requirements can be completely specified (i.e., to have a complete configuration, otherwise called completely defined configurations in which all variables have a value) or partially specified (i.e., to have partial configuration, in other words, configurations in which some decisions remain to be achieved). Once a complete or a partial configuration is specified, it evolves in its own project with the aim to become a new product.

The main requirement of people using these models is to support the navigation of the large models. While some approaches suggest to handle the configuration process in advance, either in the PL specification itself [11] or in addition to it [1], recommendation is clearly a track that has been overlooked by the literature and that still needs to be considered.

In Chap. 2, Felfernig et al. [16] introduce two categories of knowledge-based recommendation approaches: case-based recommendation [7] and constraint-based recommendation [32]. Broadly speaking, case-based recommendation treats recommendation as a similarity-assessment problem and constraint-based recommendation as a process of constraint satisfaction. In this chapter, we consider a third category of knowledge-based recommendation that we call heuristics-based recommendation. We classify this technique as a knowledge-based technique as it is based on a set of knowledge sources that were implemented as heuristics to recommend what element(s) to configure during product line model (PLM) configuration processes. There are no a priori limitations on how the heuristics presented in this chapter can be combined or the field in which they can be applied.

During the configuration process, it is possible to make the distinction between three types of recommendation: recommendation based on the PLM, recommendation based on a set of predefined heuristics and trace-based recommendation:

Recommendation based on the product line model.   Allows the user to perform choices according to his requirements by navigating through the available alternatives at any given moment. Most of the approaches in the product line literature deal with this type of recommendation by only taking into account explicitly defined information in the product line (variability) model.

Heuristics-based recommendation.   Suggests choices that shorten the configuration time, leading to valid configurations, based on a set of heuristics. The contribution of this chapter focuses on this type of recommendation.

Trace-based recommendation.   Suggests choices based on previous (logged) configurations and the current stage and context of each project. This type of recommendation is out of the scope of this chapter.

19.2.1   Configuration of Product Line Models

An interactive product configurator is a tool that allows the user to specify a product according to his specific requirements and the constraints of the product line model to combine these needs. This process can be done interactively—that is, in a step-wise fashion—and guided—that is, proposing the resolution of certain requirements before others and automatically proposing a valid solution when there is only one possible choice in the solution space. To be useful in the e-commerce context, a configurator must be complete (i.e., to ensure that no solutions are lost), allow order-independent selection/retraction of decisions, give short response times and offer recommendation to maximize the possibilities to have one satisfactory configuration. Solution techniques applied to the interactive configuration problem have been compared by Hadzic and Andersen [17] and Hadzic et al. [18]. They mainly distinguish approaches based on propositional logic, on the one hand, and on constraint programming, on the other hand. When using propositional logic based approaches, configuration problems are restricted to logic connectives and equality constraints [18, 31]. Arithmetic expressions are excluded because of the underlying solution methods. These approaches have two steps. First, the feature model is translated into a propositional formula. In the second step the formula is solved by appropriate solvers, in particular SAT solvers [25], and solvers based on binary decision diagrams (BDDs) [18, 30]. BDD-based solvers translate the propositional formula into a compact representation, the BDD. While many operations on BDDs can be implemented efficiently, the structure of the BDD is crucial as a bad variable ordering may result in exponential size and, thus, blow up in memory.

Feature models can be naturally mapped into constraint systems in order to reason (e.g., perform configuration) on them, in particular into communicating sequential processes (CSPs) [5, 10, 30]; into constraint programs over finite domains (CPs) [21]; and into constraint logic programs (CLPs) [24].

There are several academic tools dealing with configuration of product line models (e.g., SPLOT, FaMa, VariaMos [22], Feature Plug-in [2]), but very few have looked at PL tools and their ability to answer industry needs [3].

Jiang et al. [19] propose a constraint-based recommendation technique that gives to stakeholders a minimal set of repair actions in situations where no solution can be found for their configuration choices. Their approach also takes into account the preferences of a customer community to include collaborative recommendation. Authors deal with the situation where no solution can be found for the customers' configuration as a constraint satisfaction problem. Authors use a well-known collaborative recommendation technique consisting in calculating the contribution

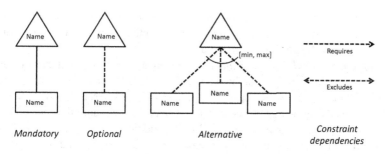

Fig. 19.1 Legend for the OVM representation of variability

of each configuration choice in terms of reliability, economy, and performance by means of a utility function—such as multi-attribute utility theory (MAUT) by von Winterfeldt and Edwards [34]. The utility term of von Winterfeldt and Edwards denotes the degree of fit between a feature of the product and the given set of customer requirements.

19.2.2 Variability Modeling

In the automotive industry, reuse is a core asset that allows car manufacturers to develop products faster and stay competitive. One of the most promising ways to manage reuse is by means of a product line approach. In the PL approach, the valid combinations of reusable artifacts are represented by means of a product line model. There are several notations used in industry to represent their product line models; for instance, the orthogonal variability model (OVM) notation [27], the DOPLER notation [11], and the constraint-based notations [3, 23]. Since the industrial case used in this chapter is originality presented in the OVM notation, we will use this formalism to illustrate the application of the approach. OVM is a language to document variability though variants, variation points, and variability dependencies among them.

The term variant used in this chapter is specific to product lines and is somewhat different from the same term used throughout the book. According to Pohl et al. [27], *variants* are associated to the different shapes of an artifact available at the same time. The term is thus associated to variability in the space of the product family artifacts, in opposition to variability in time, which according to Pohl et al. is defined as "the existence of different versions of an artifact that are valid at different times."

Figure 19.1 illustrates the concrete syntax of OVM. As the figure shows, decision points are represented as triangles, and variants as rectangles attached to them. The figure also shows the five types of variability dependencies that can be used in OVM to specify how variants of a product line must or can be selected: mandatory, optional, alternative, requires, and excludes.

- A *mandatory variability dependency* between a variation point and a variant describes that this variant must always be selected when the variation point is considered for the configuration at hand.
- An *optional variability dependency* between a variation point and a variant describes that this variant can be selected but does not need to be selected.
- An *alternative choice* is a specialization of optional variability dependencies. An alternative choice group comprises at least two variants that are related to a variation point by optional variability dependencies. The [min, max] bounds define that at least min and at most max variants can be selected for the product at hand.
- *Additional dependencies* between variation points and variants, for example, to enforce that two variants of different variation points cannot be selected together.

19.2.3   Industrial Case

In this section, we present our industrial case, from the automotive industry, that corresponds to the electric parking brake (EPB) system by means of an OVM model, as well as some of the problems encountered in the traditional configuration strategy and observable on this particular model.

The orthogonal variability model enables the derivation of SysML models covering all system aspects from system requirements to physical implementation. The systems engineering process requires that the engineering activities are performed in a certain order, enabling documentation, traceability of assets and providing deliverables at different project milestones. Our configuration strategy takes into account two common scenarios:

- Following the systems engineering analysis phases, with partial configurations for each phase. Each partial configuration has an impact on specific system model items [15]. The main concern is to follow the systems engineering approach, providing partial models for document generation at each project milestone. However, a second concern is to minimize the number of steps to reach each valid partial configuration.
- Direct (quick) configuration of a system model. In this case, the concern is to minimize the number of steps required to reach the valid desired configuration.

In both of these cases, the traditional approach for an interactive configuration may present the following problems: a non-valid configuration can be reached as a result of the user sequence of choices, and the number of steps required to reach the configuration may not be minimal and require extra time and effort from the user.

Furthermore, psychological studies [26] have shown that in a configuration process of complex products users do not exactly know their preferences when confronted with a set of alternatives, about which they do not possess solid previous knowledge. This may lead to delays for the exploration of alternatives at certain stages of the configuration process. It is particularly in this kind of situation that the approach presented in this chapter can useful. The OVM notation allows the variability of this industrial example to be represented with a concrete syntax that facilitates the understanding and presentation of this case of a complex system. The Electric Parking Brake (EPB) system is a variation of the classical, purely mechanical, parking brake that ensures vehicle immobilization when the driver brings the vehicle to a full stop and leaves the vehicle. We have chosen this case because it satisfies the following requirements: (1) it represents an industrial case of reduced complexity; (2) it does not pose confidentiality concerns; and (3) it contains enough variability for exploring our research questions.

Figure 19.2 presents the main variations that were identified in the design of this system. The variability of the electric parking brake system is explained according to the viewpoints specific to a systems engineering process: customer, context, design, internal behavior, and physical architecture.

- *Customer visible variability* corresponds to the variability stemming from the vehicle level by the product division. The EPB proposes three types of service: *Manual, Automatic,* and *Assisted.*[1] The *Manual* brake is controlled by the driver either through the classical lever or a switch. The *Automatic* parking brake system variant may enable or disable the brake itself depending on the situation: for example, when the driver turns off the engine and leaves the vehicle, the parking brake is activated. The *Assisted* brake brings extra functions that aid the driver in other situations: such as assistance when starting the car on a slope. In all operational scenarios, except for the manual variant, the system can decide to lock the parking brake. This is, for instance, the case when the driver exits the car, the engine is stopped, and the vehicle starts on a slope. Thus the behavior of the system is given by the two variation points: *BrakeLock* and *BrakeRelease*, where variants that involve automatic actions are mutually exclusive with the Manual type of parking brake. Hill start assistance is also a customer option, but the function can be allocated and implemented through different vehicle systems: through the electric parking brake itself (*EPBEnabled* variant) or through the classic braking system (*ESCEnabled* variant).
- *The context viewpoint* contains different facets of the system context, such as: system boundary variability, enabling systems and vehicle environment. In the EPB example, variants in the context refer to gearbox type. The gearbox and the presence of certain types of trailers (*VehicleTrailer* variation point) have a direct impact on the internal behavior of the EPB system. The presence of a trailer, for example, may require the hill start assistance functionality to be disabled, or to adapt to the new total weight conditions.
- *The design alternatives viewpoint* specifies design decisions that impact the whole or parts of the technical solution. The design decisions viewpoint includes: the main solution alternatives (*ArchitectureDesignAlternatives*), choices on how

---

[1]The variability presented here does not necessarily use the same names and expose the same options as online vehicle catalogs.

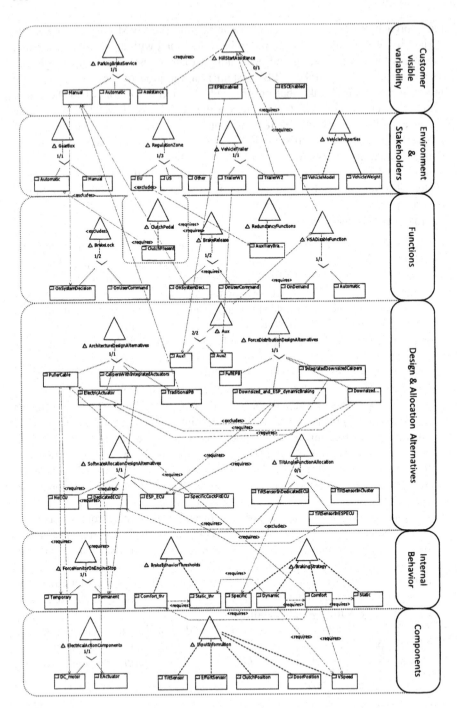

Fig. 19.2 OVM of the electric parking brake system

Fig. 19.3 Main design alternatives of the electric parking brake system (*PullerCable* and *ElectricActuator* variants)

to distribute the effort among the EPB and the main hydraulic braking system (*ForceDistributionDesignAlternatives* variation point), the decision on software allocation to hardware (*SoftwareAllocationDesignAlternatives* variation point), and the allocation of the slope angle detection function (*TiltAngleFunctionAllocation* variation point). Allocation of this last function to a specific computer would obviously require that the computer (ECU) already exists.

- *The variability entailed by the system internal behavior* viewpoint impacts the states and transitions of the system physical and software components. In the EPB, the braking strategy can vary depending on the deriving conditions. Each strategy requires specific information: Comfort and Dynamic require vehicle speed information (*VSpeed*) and the specific strategy for hill start assistance requires that there is a tilt angle sensor. Braking pressure is monitored after the vehicle has stopped for a certain amount of time (*Temporary*) for the single DC motor, puller cable solution, and permanently monitored (Permanent) for the other solutions

- *The variability entailed by the physical architecture* specifies variability in component decomposition, through optional or replaceable components, as well as physical interfaces variability between components. Physical variability of the EPB consists in the presence of different means of applying the brake force: electric actuators mounted on the calipers or single DC motor and puller cable much like the traditional mechanical parking brake. Also, the type of sensors available may vary depending on the configuration and needs.

In addition to variation points and dependencies, the variants' attributes were associated to the different variants, in order to specify supplementary needed information regarding the impact of PL configuration on performance (braking force dissymmetry, response time on brake), reuse (vehicle range coverage), or cost increase in respect to a reference configuration of the system (extra engineering cost). These attributes are numerical variables that play a role during the derivation process and help the engineers make the right choices by assessing the impact of their choices on the system configuration and as the basis for supplementary constraints.

Figure 19.3 presents two examples of physical configurations of the EPB system. The instance on the right corresponds to a "puller cable" technical solution (*ArchitectureDesignAlternatives: PullerCable*), while the instance on the left corresponds to the solution based on "electric actuators" (*ArchitectureDesignAlternatives:*

ElectricActuators). While system models can heavily rely on reuse for both of these configurations, only physical designs based on modular structures can further leverage the reuse of components in different configurations on this level.

19.3   Recommendation Heuristics in the Product Line Configuration Process

In an industrial context, letting the customers express their requirements that they want, while considering the constraints imposed by the product line model, entails a cumbersome and error-prone configuration process. Evidence of these difficulties are multiple. For instance, in Business-to-Consumer commerce (B2C) in France, 60 % of the shopping baskets in e-commerce are abandoned before purchase, because the customer does not find a satisfactory configuration. The conversion rate visitor/buyer rarely exceeds 15 %, according to the Fédération e-commerce et vente à distance (FEVAD). This difficulty is even more critical when the e-catalog contains a huge number of items, as is the case when the products to be sold are highly customized (e.g., computers or vehicles). One possible answer to this difficulty can be an interactive configuration process that recommends customers the best configuration alternatives to follow. When configuration is done interactively, the user specifies the characteristics of the product step-by-step according to his requirements, thus, gradually shrinking the search space of the configuration problem. This interactive configuration process is supported by a software tool (called the configurator) that is intended to recommend to customers the best configuration alternatives that lead them to a satisfiable product in a minimum number of steps.

The main contributions of this chapter are a collection of heuristics that are intended to (a) help customers specify the characteristics of their products step-by-step according to their requirements, and (b) to avoid useless or inefficient decisions. The collection of heuristics were designed to improve the configurators' interactivity and thereafter successfully contribute to a faster and less error-prone configuration process. A detailed description of the implementation of these heuristics is presented using Constraint Programming. This formalism was chosen because it can be implemented in a straightforward way and because it can be used to formalize any product line whatever notation was initially used to specify it [23,24]. The application of the heuristics is demonstrated using our electric parking brake systems case.

19.3.1   Principle of Heuristics-Based Configuration

The objective of the application of heuristics to the configuration process is to increase the chance of success and to reduce the configuration time: (1) either by

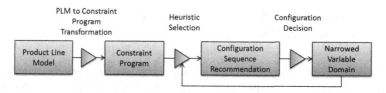

Fig. 19.4 Configuration workflow for product line heuristics-based recommendation

reducing the number of configuration steps or (2) by optimizing the computation time required by the solver to propagate configuration decisions.

Configuration is an interactive and iterative process. The user makes choices by assigning values to configuration variables. A step in the configuration process consists of a user choice and propagation of configuration decisions by the solver, if the value is valid, or of going back to the previous configuration state otherwise. Each value assignment can affect other variables. As a result, the order of value assignments has an impact on the overall number of steps of the process. Finally, the computation time of each configuration step is influenced by the complexity and size of the product line model.

A generic configuration process iteration is presented in Fig. 19.4 as a flow of activities. Activities (e.g., selection, transformation, decision making) are represented as triangles, while assets, used in the configuration process (e.g., product line model, configuration sequence), are presented as rectangles. The asset may be the input of an activity, if it is on the left of that activity, or the produced output if it is placed on the right. Finally, the arrows link the graphical elements and point to the direction of the activity flow. Each configuration iteration consists of the following activities:

PLM transformation.   The product line model, described using OVM, is transformed to a constraint program. We use the GNU Prolog language [12] to represent the constraint program and the GNU Prolog solver [12] as the engine to solve it. The configurator consists of a frontend (e.g., online interface) and a solver. The solver propagates the configuration decisions and ensures they are valid with regard to the product line model. The transformation from OVM to GNU Prolog, for the Electric Parking Brake case, is described in Sect. 19.3.2.

Heuristic selection.   The user can change the heuristics taken into consideration for future configuration steps, in respect to the desired objective. The appropriate context and advantages for each heuristic are discussed in Sect. 19.5.

Variable prioritization.   The configurator recommends variables to be configured, ordered in respect to the applied heuristics.

User choices.   The user can follow the recommendations or can continue to assign values to other variables of interest.

19.3.2   Representing Orthogonal Variability Models as Constraint Programs

Alternative choices with cardinalities $< m..n >$, optional, mandatory, requires and excludes dependencies are represented as constraint programs as follows (further details are provided in Mazo et al. [23]).

Alternative Choices. An alternative choice is a dependency between a variation point and a collection of variants. Variation points are represented in constraint programming as Boolean variables and variants are represented as finite domain integers. The semantics of this dependency can be represented by the following collection of GNU Prolog constraints:

$$(Variant_1 > 0) <=> Bool\_Variant_1 \, ,$$

$$(Variant_i > 0) <=> Bool\_Variant_i \, ,$$

$$VariationPoint * m =< Bool\_Variant_1 + \ldots + Bool\_Variant_i \, ,$$

$$Bool\_Variant_1 + \ldots + Bool\_Variant_i =< VariationPoint * n \, .$$

For instance, the $< 1..1 >$ alternative choice of the variation point *ParkingBrake-Service* is represented in GNU Prolog as follows:

$$(PBSManual > 0) <=> Bool\_PBSManual \, ,$$

$$(PBSAutomatic > 0) <=> Bool\_PBSAutomatic \, ,$$

$$(PBSAssistance > 0) <=> Bool\_PBSAssistance \, ,$$

$$ParkingBrakeService = Bool\_PBSManual + Bool\_PBSAutomatic$$

$$+ Bool\_PBSAssistance \, .$$

Optional Dependencies. Optional dependencies relate variants and variation points in the following manner:

$$(Variant > 0) ==> VariationPoint \, .$$

For instance, the optional dependency between the variation point *ClutchPedal* and the variant *ClutchPres* is represented by the GNU Prolog constraint:

$$(ClutchPres > 0) ==> ClutchPedal \, .$$

Mandatory Dependencies. Mandatory dependencies relate variants and variation points in the following manner:

$$(Variant > 0) <=> VariationPoint \, .$$

For instance, *VehicleWeight* should be configured each time its parent variation point (*VehicleProperties*) is configured in a product. The semantics of this dependency can be represented as follows in GNU Prolog:

$$(VehicleWeight > 0) <=> VehicleProperties$$

Requires-Type Dependencies. When a *Variant$_1$* requires a *Variant$_2$*, the semantics of this kind of dependencies can be represented by the following constraint:

$$(Variant_1 > 0) ==> (Variant_2 > 0) .$$

When a *VariationPoint$_1$* requires a *VariationPoint$_2$*:

$$VariantPoint_1 ==> VariationPoint_2 .$$

For instance, when the variant *IntegratedDownsizedCalipers* is selected in a configuration, the variant *ElectricActuator* should also be selected. This can be represented as follows in GNU Prolog:

$$(IntegratedDownsizedCalipers > 0) ==> (ElectricActuator > 0) .$$

Excludes-Type Dependencies. When two variants (*Variant$_1$* and *Variant$_2$*) exclude each other, the semantics of this kind of dependencies can be represented as follows:

$$Variant_1 * Variant_2 = 0 .$$

When two variation points (*VariationPoint$_1$* and *VariationPoint$_2$*) exclude each other:

$$VariationPoint_1 * VariationPoint_2 = 0 .$$

For instance, the fact that *BLOnSystemDecision* and *PBSManual* cannot be together in the same product is represented by the following constraint in GNU Prolog:

$$BLOnSystemDecision * PBSManual = 0 .$$

19.3.3 Configuration Heuristics

Configuration of variability models enables the realization of consistent system specifications from requirements at the domain level. However, as diversity plays a major role in automotive industry competitiveness, it is often difficult to manage the large number of variations that a vehicle system includes.

While users can express their priorities in a free configuration order, the configurator should choose the order that best optimizes its computational task and complete the configuration of the product line models based on the users decisions. The configurator completeness should ensure that no solutions are lost. Besides, backtrack-freeness [17] should guarantee that the configurator only offers decision alternatives for which solutions remain, and the configurator should guarantee a short response time compatible with an interactive usage (e.g., with a web-based configuration). By defining a set of heuristics for product line configuration we intend to address the issue of decision ordering in order to allow the user to have access to pertinent choices and optimize the number of steps required to reach a complete configuration and the response time of the solver. The heuristics presented here are:

Heuristic 1.   Variables with the smallest domain first
Heuristic 2.   The most constrained variables first
Heuristic 3.   Variables appearing in most products first
Heuristic 4.   Automatic completion when there is no choice
Heuristic 5.   Variables required by the latest configured variable first
Heuristic 6.   Variables that split the problem space in two first

It is worth noting that there is no predefined order to use the heuristics. Indeed, the configuration heuristics that can be suitable to be used at configuration time t can be different from the configuration heuristics that the user will want to use at $t + 1$. There are several heuristics that the user can select together for one or several configuration steps. In the case that users select several configuration heuristics, the configurator will propose a collection of candidate variables to configure according to the selected heuristics. For instance, if the users want to configure first the variables with the smallest domain (Heuristic 1) and the variables with the largest variability factor (Heuristic 3), the configurator will recommend them to configure the variables with the smallest domain decreasingly sorted by the variability factor. These heuristics are discussed below.

Heuristic 1: Variables with the Smallest Domain First

Principle. This heuristic recommends to choose first the variable with the smallest domain. The domain of a variable is the set of possible values that the variable can take according to its domain definition and the constraints in which the variable is involved. This strategy is known as "first fail principle" [6] and can be explained as "to succeed, try first where you are most likely to fail."

Rationale. This could be counter-intuitive since configuring first the variable with the biggest domain reduce the search space the most. However, this decreases the possibility of obtaining a valid product at the end because that constrains the solver's possibilities to choice a particular domain value that satisfies the set of constraints. Thus, even if setting first the variables with the largest domains reduces faster the solution space to be analyzed by the solver than setting first variables with small domains, it also decrease the possibility of having a valid product at the end of the configuration process. Of course, we prefer the latter choice. If all the variables have the same number of domain values (e.g., all variables are Boolean), the user can choose other heuristics to improve the configuration process.

Example. For instance, let us consider the variables:

$$V_1 = ForceDistributionDesignAlternatives \text{ and } V_2 = ElectricalActionComponents.$$

They have enumeration domains with different cardinalities, where $card(V_1) > card(V_2)$, thus the second variable has the smaller. The choices associated to the first variable decide about the way brake force generation should be shared between the electric parking brake electrical actuators and the classic vehicle hydraulic system. The second variable decides about the physical architecture: single DC motor or two electric actuators attached to the vehicle calipers. The solver should propose variable *ElectricalActionComponents* first, according to the proposed heuristic.

Advantages. This heuristic avoids unnecessary evaluations (e.g., when variable V_2 is set to a particular value of its domain, the solver does not need to check for other values of V_2) and increases the possibility to succeed the configuration process (i.e., configuring first the variables where the constraint program is most likely to fail, we increase the possibilities of the solver to succeed).

Heuristic 2: The Most Constrained Variables First

Principle. Another heuristic that can be applied when all variables have the same number of values is to choose the variable that participates in the largest number of constraints (in the absence of more specific information on which constraints are likely to be difficult to satisfy, for instance). This heuristic follows also the principle of dealing with hard cases first.

Rationale. In industrial languages like constraint networks [3] where there are no root artifacts to guide the configuration process, this heuristic allows identifying the variables that mostly reduce the number of choices in a configuration process.

Example. In the EPB model, the *PullerCable* variant is one of the most constrained in this model, being linked to the way force is distributed among braking systems (*ForceDistributionDesignAlternatives*), internal system behavior (*ForceMonitorOnEngineStop*) and physical implementation (*DC_motor*). In consequence, it reduces other choices in the configuration process, directly linked to the initial variable.

Advantages. By setting first the variable related with the largest number of other variables the solver would automatically propagate the user's choice to the largest number of other variables. In that way the space of the solution is considerably reduced after each choice, which reduces the number of configuration steps (user's choices) and the average configuration time (solver's inference time).

Heuristic 3: Variables Appearing in Most Products First

Principle. This heuristic proposes configuring first the variables that have an impact on all potential products. To avoid the generation of all products of the PL, which is usually impossible in very large models [4, 23], we propose two steps: (1) configure first the core variables and (2) configure the rest of variables once ordered according to their impact on the solution space. To implement the first step, we use the *computing the core elements* operation that is fully automated in the VariaMos tool [22]. To avoid generation of all solutions in order to calculate the core elements as proposed by Schneeweiss and Hofstedt [29], we evaluate if each variable can take the *null* value (e.g., the 0 value on Boolean variables) in at least one correct configuration. If a variable cannot take its *null* value, the variable does not become part of the core variables of the product line model because this can never be omitted from any product. To know if a variable can take the *null* value in a valid configuration takes only few milliseconds even in the largest product line models available in literature. Details of this algorithm, its improvements, implementation, and evaluation can be found in Mazo et al. [24]. The second step is implemented thanks to the operation of computing the variability factor of a given variable, and fully automated in our tool VariaMos [22]. This variability factor of a given variable corresponds to the ratio between the number of products in which the variable is present and the number of products represented in the product line model.

Rationale. The heuristic can be applied when the user needs to reach a valid configuration with as little input as possible. Fixing the values of the core variables (usually approximately 2/3 of the variables of the product line model [8]) decreases the size of the problem space in the same proportion, avoiding unnecessary input from the user. This also makes feasible the calculation of the variability factor of the remaining variables. The variables with a higher variability factor reduce the path to a valid product and the need for user input.

Example. In products where the customer requirements do not include assistance (*ParkingBrakeService = Assistance*) from the system, other than for parking brake situations, the option for hill start assistance and for disabling the hill start assistant function are excluded. As a consequence, the definition of these variables does not appear in all products, and according to this heuristic should not be proposed before core variables.

Advantages. This heuristic is useful because (1) it avoids wrong users' configurations in the sense that core variables cannot be configured with *null* values, and (2) the order proposed in this technique decreases the solver's inference in finding satisfactory configurations.

Heuristic 4: Automatic Completion When There Is No Choice

Principle. This heuristic provides a mechanism to automatically complete the configuration of variables where only one value of their domain is possible.

Rationale. Due to the fact that the aim is to eliminate, in the domains of variables yet to be instantiated, the values that are not consistent with the current instantiation, this heuristic also works when a variable has several values on its domain but only one is valid. This heuristic is automatically provided by most constraint solvers available on the market, with at least, three algorithms that implement it: Forward Checking, Partial Look-Ahead, and Full Look-Ahead.

Example. We consider variable $V_1 = HillStartAssistance$, $V_2 = BrakeLock$ and $V_3 = ParkingBrakeService$. Setting the values $V_1 = EPBEnabled$ and $V_2 = OnSystemDecision$ excludes all values for V_3, except $V_3 = Automatic$, in which case this single possible value should be selected automatically.

Advantage. The automatic assignment of values to variables, once there are no more alternative solutions, avoids the possibility of invalid configurations due to wrong values requested by the user. Therefore, it contributes to the success of the configuration process.

Heuristic 5: Variables Required by the Latest Configured Variable First

Principle. Another heuristic consists in choosing the variable that has the largest number of constraints with the past-configured variables.

Rationale. This heuristic has a particular application during configuration of engineering artifacts, where choices often represent engineering decisions linked by causality relations. A choice may not be reached before a previous choice has been performed. In this particular context, following related variables (that serve for the reuse of engineering artifacts) would mean advancing in the design space towards a more detailed description of the system being configured.

Example. In the case of the EPB system, we can find logical implications that have their origin in technical constraints or problem solving logic. For example, the system needs to be able to disable the hill start assistant function (*HSADisableFunction*), if a trailer is used (when the function is not able to adapt to the change of weight of the vehicle). In this case it is convenient to propose variable *HSADisableFunction* once variable *VehicleTrailer* = *TrailerW1* has been set, both for the user (logical flow of ideas), but also to avoid potential future conflicts in the configuration.

Advantages. This heuristic allows conflicts to be identified as soon as possible (with regards to the number of configuration steps) in a configuration process. Hence, this increases the possibility to fix the configuration conflicts and the possibility to succeed in the configuration process.

Heuristic 6: Variables That Split the Problem Space in Two First

Principle. Breaking a problem into sub-problems is a powerful tool in many domains. This heuristic consists in setting first the variables splitting the problem space in two. Due to the fact that these variables have most potential to reduce the solution space, the application of this heuristic naturally reduces the number of configuration choices.

Rationale. This is due to the fact that after one choice, the solver will have a reduced solution space to exam and the user will have fewer configurations to do. Several product line modeling languages (e.g., Feature models) are inspired by this principle and propose the use of a root element with two of more choices related by OR or XOR operators that divide the problem space in branches that can be easily removed from the solution space. To achieve this we need to search for variables that divide the problem space in roughly similar parts, searching the decision trees have almost the same depth for each of the values of the variable.

Example. In the case of the parking brake system, the choice concerning the presence of the hill start assistance function splits the decision tree in roughly similar parts.

Advantages. Setting first the variables that break the problem in two equal parts, reduces the computation time of future choices and increases the chances of reaching a completely defined product in a reduced number of steps.

19.4 Application to the Configuration of a Parking Brake System

One particular question that can be raised about the configuration heuristics that have been presented in this chapter is *are they useful?* Although only long-term experience will provide a definitive answer to this question, one might be interested in looking for its implementation and its application in a real case. To do that, we have (1) implemented our collection of heuristics in the constraint logic programming solver GNU Prolog [12], and (2) applied these heuristics in typical configuration processes of our industrial case. For each heuristic, we measure the time required by the solver to generate X products; then, we compare these results with the ones obtained when we do not use any heuristics or use a contra-sense approach in the same configuration process. The industrial case was developed in the broader context of introducing product line techniques in model based systems engineering [14]. Our electric parking brake (EPB) systems model (Fig. 19.2) is represented by means of the OVM notation [27] and is composed of 19 variation points, 46 variants, 16 alternative choices, 1 mandatory and 7 optional variability dependencies, and 28 additional dependencies (21 requires-type, 5 excludes-type, and 2 non-classified dependencies [23]). To present the feasibility of our approach and conclude what heuristics should be recommended for use during a product line configuration process, we first transform our EPB model into an automatically exploitable language, then we explain how to implement each heuristic and we compare the results gathered from their application to our industrial case.

Once our EPB model is represented as a GNU Prolog constraint program, we can apply our collection of heuristics to configure different EPB systems and measure the results obtained each time and compare them with the results obtained when no heuristic is used.

Heuristic 1: Variables with the Smallest Domain First

The GNU Prolog predicate `fd_labeling(Vars, Options)` assigns a value to each variable of the list `Vars` according to the list of labeling options given by `Options`. `Vars` can be also a single finite domain variable. This predicate is re-executable on backtracking. `Options` is an optional list of labeling options that specifies the heuristic to select the variable to enumerate. When no option is specified, the solver selects the leftmost variable in the list of variables (`Vars`) to enumerate in the configuration process.

This heuristic is already implemented in the GNU Prolog solver and can be used in a configuration process by means of the following predicate:

$$fd\_labeling(Vars\ , [variable\_method(ff)])\ ,$$

where `Vars` is the list of variables of the constraint program (variation points and variants of our model) and `variable_method(ff)` is the GNU Prolog predicate offered by the solver to call the *ff* (first fail) heuristic in the current configuration process (i.e., in the current `fd_labeling`).

Heuristic 2: The Most Constrained Variables First

To implement Heuristic 2 in GNU Prolog, we just need to sort the list of variables (`Vars`), where the first variables in the list are those that are more constrained, and then use the predicate `fd_labeling(Vars)` in our configuration process. In our industrial case,

```
Vars = [PullerCable, ESPECU, PBSManual, ElectricActuator,
    HillStartAssistance, Static, TrailerW1, Permanent,
    DownsizedAndESPDynamicBraking, VSpeed, HSADisableFunction,
    TraditionalPB, DCMotor, DownsizedAndExtratorqueESP,
    AuxiliaryBrakeRelease, EU, BROnSystemDecision,
    BROnSystemDecision, TiltSensorIn1, TiltSensorIn2, TrailerW2,
    EPBEnabled, Comfort, CalipserWithIntegr, EActuator,
    PBSAssistance, FullEPB, Temporary, ClutchPres, DedicatedECU,
    Dynamic, BLOnSystemDecision, IntegratedDownsizedCalipers,
    GBAutomatic, \dots]
```

all the other variables appear one time in the constraints of the model.

Heuristic 3: Variables Appearing in Most Products First

Considering the explanation given, to implement Heuristic 3 in GNU Prolog we just need to calculate the variability factor of each variable of the model (this function is fully implemented in VariaMos [22]) and sort the list of variables (Vars) according to the variability factor, being the first on the list those variables that have largest variability factor. Then, we use the predicate fd_labeling(Vars) in our configuration process to constraint the solver to use first the variables of Vars with the largest variability factor in the configuration process. The ten variables with largest variability factor in our industrial case are: ClutchPosition, DoorPosition, InputInformation, Static, ElectricalActionComponents, DCMotor, BrakingStrategy, VehicleTrailer, TrailerW2, and ForceMonitor OnEngineStop.

Heuristic 4: Automatic Completion When There Is No choice

Partial lookahead [33] is about propagation on the min and max values of the variables' domains. Partial lookahead is configured by default in GNU Prolog. For instance, given the following constraint expressed in GNU Prolog: X#= 2*Y + 3, X#< 10 (where "#" before each constraint symbol forces the solver to apply a partial look-ahead propagation technique in the corresponding constraint and "," means a logic AND) the solver will define the following domain for both variables involved: $X = (3..9)$ and $Y = (0..3)$. Indeed, when the solver uses the partial look-ahead propagation technique, it only considers the border values to define the new domain of each variable after propagation. On the contrary, full lookahead [33] allows operations about the whole domain in order to also propagate the "holes". Thus, if we use this technique in our constraint, that is, X#= 2*Y + 3, X#< 10 the solver will define a more precise domain: $X = (3 : 5 : 7 : 9)$ and $Y = (0..3)$. It is worth noting that to use full lookahead in GNU Prolog, we just put "#" at the end of operations that will use full propagation.

Heuristic 5: Variables Required by the Latest Configured Variable First

Because of this heuristic helps identify configuration conflicts as soon as possible in an interactive configuration process, it cannot be implemented by means of static list of variables sorted in a certain order as we did for the other ones. Conflicts that can be identified with this heuristic look like "a configuration with TraditionalBP and an DownsizedAndESPDynamicBraking in a same product is not possible". This kind of configuration conflicts can, in certain situations, be avoided if people who configure the variant DownsizedAndESPDynamicBraking follow the requirements of this variant (e.g., the variant ESP_ECU) and not just the intuition or hazard to define the next variables to configure. Thus, the use of this heuristic is highly recommended to use in interactive and guided configuration environments.

Heuristic 6: Variables That Split the Problem Space in Two First

This heuristic can be implemented as follows. First, it is necessary to find variables in which a configuration dichotomy must be done, that is, assuming that one variable, belonging to the collection of variables to be configured in a certain configuration stage has a domain value of 10, the dichotomy consists of computing the number of results when the variable is less than 5, computing the number of results when the variable is greater than or equal to 5, compare both results and classify this variable according to its ability to divide the solution space. The difficulty while implementing this heuristic is to build this list of variables at each configuration step. A good choice in the context of product line models that are represented by graph like or tree like formalisms (e.g., Feature Models) is to begin the configuration process by the root feature and then navigate the tree structure to define what are the variables that most divide the solution space of the product line being configured. Since our industrial case is modeled in the OVM notation, where the notion of a single root does not exist. We will then need to consider all the variation points of our EPB model as roots. Thus, to implement this heuristic when the EPB model is represented as a GNU Prolog constraint program, the list L of variables corresponding to the constraint program is constituted in the following way: $L = [VP_1, VP_2, \ldots, VP_n, V_1, V_2, \ldots, V_n]$ where the collection of variables $VP_1, VP_2, \ldots, VP_n$ corresponding to the variation points of the EPB model are placed at the beginning of the list, and the collection of variables $V_1, V_2, \ldots, V_n$ corresponding to the variations of the model are placed at the end of the list. One or several of these decision points can be configured from the beginning of the configuration process by means of a partial configuration and the rest will be left to be configured by the solver (in the order defined by the list L) through the mechanism of propagation. In our industrial case, the configuration list L should look like

```
L = [ParkingBrakeService, BrakeLock, BrakeRelease,
    HillStartAssistance, HSADisableFunction, RegulationZone,
    GearBox, VehicleTrailer, ArchitectureDesignAlternatives,
    ForceDistributionDesignAlternatives,
    SoftwareAllocationDesignAlternatives,
    TiltAngleFunctionAllocation, ElectricalActionComponents,
    BrakingStrategy, ForceMonitorOnEngineStop, InputInformation,
    ...] .
```

The rest of L is composed of variables corresponding to the variants of our OVM industrial case.

19.5   Discussion

We used two partial configurations to test our approach. The first partial configuration gives a value to the variables with the largest domain: *DCMotor*, *Static*, and *FullEPB* (DCMotor #= 10, Static #= 50, FullEPB #= 1000).

The second partial configuration used to test our approach is typical for vehicles equipped with an automatic parking brake (ParkingBrakeService #= 1, BrakeRelease #= 1, ForceDistributionDesignAlternatives #= 1, HSAAutomatic #= 0, GBAutomatic #= 1, DCMotor #= 10, Comfort #= 90, FullEPB #= 1000).

We used the industrial case (see Sect. 19.2.3) to test our approach and get some insight on the improvements brought to the configuration process, by using the heuristics presented in this chapter. In order to do that, we used a typical configuration in automotive industry, where variables *ParkingBrakeService*, *BrakeRelease*, *ForceDistribution*, and *GBAutomatic* are set to 1 to indicate that the reusable components corresponding to these variables are present into the cars that we intend to configure. In addition, the variable *HSAAutomatic* is set to 0 to indicate that the design alternative for disabling the hill start assistance will be not present in the product(s) that we intend to configure. Also, variable *DCMotor* is set to 10 to indicate the maximum power for the electric motor (design decisions), *Comfort* is set to 10 to indicate that when the system should switch to this braking strategy while the vehicle is in motion (design decisions regarding system behavior), and *FullEPB* is set to 1,000 for the maximum allowed braking force.

Table 19.1 summarizes the results and provides comments on each heuristic. We learned from the tests that Heuristics 1 (variables with the smallest domain first) and 3 (variables appearing in the most products first) are very useful when users need to get a fast feedback from the solver (this is the case, for instance, of online product configurators). In particular, we recommend to use Heuristic 1 because, in our case, it allows to reduce the time spend by the solver to propagate the configuration choices (feedback time). Also, we recommend using Heuristic 3 because, in our case, it allowed to reduce by 10 %, on average, the feedback time.

Combining Heuristics 1 and 3 reduces even more the feedback time, which improves a lot the configuration process of large product line models. To be precise, this combination reduced, in our industrial case, by fourth the feedback time compared with the case when no heuristic is used in the configuration process. Nevertheless, we also recommend using Heuristic 2 combined with Heuristic 1 to reduce the computation time of the solver by half (on average, in our running case) the time spend by the solver to propagate our configuration preferences compared with the case where no heuristic is chosen.

The use of Heuristic 4 with application of the full lookahead algorithm (used by default in GNU Prolog to implement Heuristic 4) takes much more time than all the other tests; however, the configurations proposed by the solver after propagation of the configuration choices on the product line model are more accurate. Thus, using this algorithm, the solver never proposes an option that in reality the user cannot select later. This characteristic is very important in an iterative product line configuration process where the idea is to prevent false expectations about configurations that will in reality be impossible. Thus, we recommend the use of Heuristic 4 in configuration process where prevent the user mistake, his frustration and the subsequent abandon of the process is a more important issue compared with the long time spend by the solver to effectuate propagation and give a feedback.

Table 19.1 Advantages of heuristics after experiments

H	Advantages	When to use	Comments
H1	• Avoids unnecessary evaluations • Reduces the solver inference time • Increases the success rate of the configuration	• The size of the domain of variables varies a lot • The user needs a fast feedback from the solver (e.g., configurators on the Internet)	The solver reduces the time spent to propagate the configuration choices by 50% on average. Further investigation is needed to understand how much this heuristic increases the success rate of the configuration.
H2	• Reduces number of configuration steps	• The PL modeling technique does not involve the presence of root artifacts (e.g., OVM)	It should theoretically reduce the number of configuration steps, but further research is necessary to understand the extent of its impact.
H3	• Avoids wrong configuration of core variables • Decreases the time needed by a solver to configure products	• The user requirement is to reach a valid configuration fast • The users don't have any other preferences regarding the configuration sequence • The user needs a fast feedback from the solver (e.g., configurators on the Internet)	The solver reduces the time spent to propagate the configuration choices by 10% on average.
H4	• Increases the success rate of the configuration	• The solver used to automate the constraint propagation has built-in support • In all the interactive configurators to prevent input of erroneous values (because of the invalid user choices) • Preventing user frustration is more important than the computation time (e.g., some Internet applications)	By using the full-look ahead algorithm to implement this heuristic, the solver (i) never proposes, to users, options that in reality they cannot select later, and (ii) increases the time spend to propagate the configuration choices by 37% on average.
H5	• Allows identifying conflicts as soon as possible • Increases the success rate of the configuration (by fixing existing conflicts)	• Appropriate in engineering, where there is causality relation between artifacts • Follows an existing, implicit configuration sequence, related to constraint dependencies	The experiments confirm that this heuristic: (i) guides the user to continue the configuration process when no other preference exists, and (ii) enables testing the configurations at design-time of the PL model.
H6	• Reduces the computation time of future configuration choices • Increases the chances of reaching a completely defined product in a reduced number of steps	• The user requirement is to reach a valid configuration with a minimum number of choices • The users don't have any other preferences regarding the configuration sequence	This heuristic reduces the feedback time of the solver by 8% on average. Further research is necessary to know how much the number of configuration steps is reduced.

From a usability point of view, the experiment shows that Heuristic 5 is useful in two cases: (1) to guide the users to continue the configuration process when they do not know how to continue the configuration process (i.e., they do not know which variables to consider next in the configuration process), and (2) to test configurations at design-time when engineers are calibrating the product line model. Heuristic 5 recommend setting first the variables required by the latest configured variable and in that way it helps identifying configuration conflicts as soon as possible in a configuration process (and not to reduce time spent in configuration as Heuristics 1–3). Heuristic 5 makes sense when it is applied in an interactive configuration process to recommend users the next variables to configure without loosing the configuration sequence.

Our experiment also shows us that Heuristic 6 (variables that split the problem space in two first) only reduces the feedback time by 8 % on average. This heuristic is implicit in the tree-like configuration processes like the one used by people that guide the configuration process by a feature-like product line model [20]. Even if this heuristic allows us to structure the product line configuration processes by means of a predefined order, this is not always the best strategy (in terms of time and accuracy) to guide the configuration processes of industrial (often very large) product line models.

In our particular industrial case, we recommend to use Heuristic 3 combined with Heuristic 1 in order to reduce the computation time of the solver in the configuration process because this combination reduces by fourth the computation time compared with the case when no heuristics are used. Application of Heuristic 1 alone is also a good recommendation to improve computing time in our industrial product line configuration process. In that regards, we also recommend to use Heuristic 2 combined with Heuristic 1 to reduce the computation time of the solver because it is reduced by half when these two heuristics are applied with an initial configuration of the most restrictive variables. It is worth noting that the use of Heuristic 4 with application of the Full Look-Ahead algorithm has taken much more time than all the other tests; however, partial configurations proposed by the solver are more accurate, that is, using this algorithm, the solver never proposes an option that the user cannot select later. This characteristic is very important in an iterative product line configuration process where the idea is to prevent false expectations about impossible configurations and thus prevent user mistakes, frustration and the subsequent abandon of the process. The other heuristics should be further evaluated to determine in which configuration situations and in which kind of models they should be recommended to use.

19.6 Conclusion

The purpose of the heuristics was to improve the configuration process by (1) reducing the number of configuration steps or (2) reducing the computation time required by the solver to test the validity of the product line. The configuration of variables is done interactively by the user. Thus the order depends on their preference. By prioritizing choices, and recommending certain configuration variables before others, it is possible to improve these two aspects of the configuration process.

However, other questions may be raised: Which heuristics are better to improve the quality and pertinence of the solutions? Against what other criteria can we compare the collection of heuristics presented in this chapter? How to classify the heuristics according to their pertinence in certain situations? What kind of systematic recommendation should be presented to a user during a product line configuration process? How to apply and even combine the collection of heuristics presented in this chapter, in an interactive and incremental configuration process? In conclusion, the application of these heuristics on other product line models, specified with different formalisms can be implemented using the same principles, but may need further evaluation.

References

1. Abbasi, E., Hubaux, A., Heymans, P.: A toolset for feature-based configuration workflows. In: Proceedings of the International Software Product Lines Conference, pp. 65–69, Munich, 22–26 August 2011. doi:10.1109/SPLC.2011.41
2. Antkiewicz, M., Czarnecki, K.: FeaturePlugin: Feature modeling plug-in for Eclipse. In: Proceedings of the Eclipse Technology eXchange, pp. 67–72, Barcelona, March 2004. doi:10.1145/1066129.1066143
3. Astesana, J.M., Cosserat, L., Fargier, H.: Constraint-based vehicle configuration: A case study. In: Proceedings of the IEEE International Conference on Tools with Artificial Intelligence, vol. 1, pp. 68–75, Arras, France, 27–29 October 2010. doi:10.1109/ICTAI.2010.19
4. Batory, D., Benavides, D., Ruiz-Cortés, A.: Automated analysis of feature models: Challenges ahead. Comm. ACM **49**(12), 45–47 (2006). doi:10.1145/1183236.1183264
5. Benavides, D., Trinidad, P., Ruiz-Cortés, A.: Automated reasoning on feature models. In: Proceedings of the International Conference on Advanced Information Systems Engineering, *Lecture Notes in Computer Science*, vol. 3520, pp. 491–503. Springer, Heidelberg (2005). doi:10.1007/11431855_34
6. Boussemart, F., Hemery, F., Lecoutre, C., Sais, L.: Boosting systematic search by weighting constraints. In: Proceedings of the European Conference on Artificial Intelligence, pp. 146–150, Valencia, Spain, 22–27 August 2004
7. Burke, R.: Knowledge-based recommender systems. Encyclopedia of Library and Information Science **69**(32), 180–200 (2000)
8. Clements, P., Northrop, L.M.: Software Product Lines: Practices and Patterns. Addison-Wesley, Reading, MA (2002)
9. Clements, P., Northrop, L.M.: A framework for software product line practice (2007). URL http://www.sei.cmu.edu/productlines/frame_report/introduction.htm. Version 5.0
10. van Deursen, A., Klint, P.: Domain-specific language design requires feature descriptions. J. Comput. Inform. Technol. **10**(1), 1–17 (2002)
11. Dhungana, D., Grünbacher, P., Rabiser, R.: The DOPLER meta-tool for decision-oriented variability modeling: A multiple case study. Int. J. Autom. Software Eng. **18**(1), 77–114 (2010). doi:10.1007/s10515-010-0076-6
12. Diaz, D., Codognet, P.: Design and implementation of the GNU Prolog system. J. Funct. Logic Program. **2001**(6), 6:1–6:29 (2001)

13. Djebbi, O., Salinesi, C.: RED-PL: A method for deriving product requirements from a product line requirements model. In: Proceedings of the International Conference on Advanced Information Systems Engineering, *Lecture Notes in Computer Science*, vol. 4495, pp. 279–293. Springer, Heidelberg (2007). doi:10.1007/978-3-540-72988-4_20

14. Dumitrescu, C., Mazo, R., Salinesi, C., Dauron, A.: Bridging the gap between product lines and systems engineering: An experience in variability management for automotive model based systems engineering. In: Proceedings of the International Software Product Lines Conference, pp. 254–263, Tokyo, Japan, 26–30 August 2013a. doi:10.1145/2491627.2491655

15. Dumitrescu, C., Tessier, P., Salinesi, C., Gérard, S., Dauron, A.: Flexible product line derivation applied to a model based systems engineering process. In: Proceedings of the International Conference on Complex Systems Design & Management, pp. 227–239. Springer, Heidelberg (2013b). doi:10.1007/978-3-642-34404-6_15

16. Felfernig, A., Jeran, M., Ninaus, G., Reinfrank, F., Reitererand, S., Stettinger, M.: Basic approaches in recommendation systems. In: Robillard, M., Maalej, W., Walker, R.J., Zimmermann, T. (eds.) Recommendation Systems in Software Engineering, Chap. 2. Springer, Heidelberg (2014)

17. Hadzic, T., Andersen, H.R.: An introduction to solving interactive configuration problems. Tech. Rep. TR-2004-49, The IT University of Copenhagen (2004)

18. Hadzic, T., Subbarayan, S., Jensen, R.M., Andersen, H.R., Møller, J., Hulgaard, H.: Fast backtrack-free product configuration using a precompiled solution space representation. In: Proceedings of the International Conference on Economic, Technical and Organisational Aspects of Product Configuration Systems, pp. 131–138, Copenhagen, Denmark, 28–29 June 2004

19. Jiang, Z., Wang, W., Benbasat, I.: Multimedia-based interactive advising technology for online consumer decision support. Commun. ACM **48**(9), 92–98 (2005). doi:10.1145/1081992.1081995

20. Kang, K.C., Cohen, S.G., Hess, J.A., Novak, W.E., Peterson, A.S.: Feature-oriented domain analysis (FODA) feasibility study. Tech. Rep. CMU/SEI-90-TR-21, Carnegie Mellon University, Software Engineering Institute (1990)

21. Mazo, R., Lopez-Herrejon, R.E., Salinesi, C., Diaz, D., Egyed, A.: Conformance checking with constraint logic programming: The case of feature models. In: Proceedings of the IEEE International Computer Software and Applications Conference, pp. 456–465, Munich, Germany, 18–22 July 2011a. doi:10.1109/COMPSAC.2011.66

22. Mazo, R., Salinesi, C., Diaz, D.: VariaMos: A tool for product line driven systems engineering with a constraint based approach. In: Proceedings of the CAiSE Forum, *CEUR Workshop Proceedings*, vol. 855, pp. 147–154, Gdansk, Poland, 28 June 2012a

23. Mazo, R., Salinesi, C., Diaz, D., Djebbi, O., Lora-Michiels, A.: Constraints: The heart of domain and application engineering in the product lines engineering strategy. Int. J. Inform. Syst. Model. Des. **3**(2), 33–68 (2012b). doi:10.4018/jismd.2012040102

24. Mazo, R., Salinesi, C., Diaz, D., Lora-Michiels, A.: Transforming attribute and clone-enabled feature models into constraint programs over finite domains. In: Proceedings of the International Conference on Evaluating Novel Approaches to Software Engineering, pp. 188–199, Beijing, China, 8–11 June 2011b

25. Mendonca, M., Wasowski, A., Czarnecki, K.: SAT-based analysis of feature models is easy. In: Proceedings of the International Software Product Lines Conference, pp. 231–240, San Francisco, CA, USA, 24–28 August 2009

26. Payne, J.W., Bettman, J.R., Johnson, E.J.: The Adaptive Decision Maker. Cambridge University Press, Cambridge (1993)

27. Pohl, K., Böckle, G., van der Linden, F.J.: Software Product Line Engineering: Foundations, Principles and Techniques. Springer, Heidelberg (2005). doi:10.1007/3-540-28901-1

28. Salinesi, C., Mazo, R., Diaz, D., Djebbi, O.: Using integer constraint solving in reuse based requirements engineering. In: Proceedings of the IEEE International Requirements Engineering Conference, pp. 243–251, Sydney, NSW, Australia, 27 September–1 October 2010. doi:10.1109/RE.2010.36

29. Schneeweiss, D., Hofstedt, P.: FdConfig: A constraint-based interactive product configurator. Tech. Rep. arXiv:1108.5586 (2011)
30. Subbarayan, S.: Integrating CSP decomposition techniques and BDDs for compiling configuration problems. In: Proceedings of the International Conference on Integration of AI and OR Techniques in Constraint Programming for Combinatorial Optimization Problems, *Lecture Notes in Computer Science*, vol. 3524. Springer, Heidelberg (2005). doi:10.1007/11493853_26
31. Subbarayan, S., Jensen, R.M., Hadzic, T., Andersen, H.R., Hulgaard, H., Møller, J.: Comparing two implementations of a complete and backtrack-free interactive configurator. In: Proceedings of the Workshop on CSP Techniques with Immediate Application, pp. 97–111, Toronto, Canada, 27 September 2004
32. Thompson, C.A., Göker, M.H., Langley, P.: A personalized system for conversational recommendations. J. Artif. Intell. Res. **21**(1), 393–428 (2004)
33. Van Hentenryck, P.: Constraint Satisfaction in Logic Programming. MIT Press, Boston, MA (1989)
34. von Winterfeldt, D., Edwards, W.: Decision Analysis and Behavioral Research. Cambridge University Press, New York (1986)

Glossary

Abstract syntax tree The syntactic structure of source code represented as a graph (specifically, as a tree) in which vertices represent syntactic entities and edges represent the containment relationship. As syntax is language-specific, abstract syntax trees are also language-specific. A *concrete syntax tree* (or *parse tree*) is a similar representation constructed during the parsing of source code, e.g., by a compiler; it will contain redundant information and will fail to distinguish structures that differ due to semantic context. In software engineering, all such representations are typically referred to as abstract syntax trees, without this differentiation.

Accuracy [*Within information retrieval*] For binary classification of items, the percentage of the items available that are either correctly recommended or correctly not recommended. It can equivalently be interpreted as a probability, rather than a ratio. The measure is defined as

$$\frac{TP + TN}{TP + TN + FP + FN};$$

see confusion matrix for the definition of these quantities.
[*Within science and engineering generally*] The degree of closeness of measurements of a quantity to that quantity's actual value. Compare precision.

Adaptability A property of a system that indicates its ability to adapt automatically to changing conditions.

Adaptivity See adaptability.

Anomaly detection A data mining technique in which items are detected that do not conform to other patterns in the data, or in which patterns are detected that do not conform to expected patterns.

Antecedent See association rule.

Application programming interface The specification of how external agents should access functionality programmatically.

API See application programming interface.

Argument See validity [within mathematics].

M.P. Robillard et al. (eds.), *Recommendation Systems in Software Engineering*,
DOI 10.1007/978-3-642-45135-5, © Springer-Verlag Berlin Heidelberg 2014

Association rule A relation between two sets of items (*itemsets*), called the *antecedents* and *consequents*, in which the presence (equivalently, their truth, their relevance, etc.) of the antecedents implies the presence of the consequents.

Association rule mining Any mechanical process in which association rules are inferred within a dataset. Such a process operates atop a finite set of real data, in which transactions occur involving multiple items; if the same items frequently occur together, an association rule can be inferred. As the inferences of such a process may be false and may need to deal with anomalous cases, two concepts can be used in considering the quality of the mined rules: *support* and *confidence*. The support for an itemset is defined as the proportion of commits that contain the itemset. The confidence of an association rule is defined as the proportion of commits in which the antecedent is true for which the rule is correct, and hence the consequent is also true.

AST See abstract syntax tree.

Attribute A characteristic of a class of entities, whose specific value sometimes varies between instances of the class. In some circumstances, the instances themselves are described as possessing individual attributes.

Availability The ability of a user to obtain or access a system. This may be affected by factors such as system load, network connections, or the monetary cost of accessing the system.

Balanced F-score See F-measure.

Benchmark A standardized point of reference for a measurement.

Benchmarking The process of comparing something against standardized points of references in order to identify a best practice.

Bias The tendency to preferentially produce an outcome despite the existence of alternatives that are equally or more valid. This results in a *systematic error* in empirical data. Threats to validity can produce bias.

Binary classification See classification.

Bug See issue.

Bug report See issue report.

Case study A descriptive or explanatory analysis of an instance of a situation or phenomenon, useful as an exemplar of that instance and for the generation of hypotheses about other instances.

Changeset See commit.

Classification The assignment of items to two or more sets. Classification refers to both the process by which the assignment is created and the result. The special case of *binary classification* utilizes only two sets that are typically called true and false, with reference to whether the items in them are deemed relevant or not in some context. Comparison of actual classifications (arising from some form of real-world knowledge) and predicted classifications (arising from a mechanical interpretation of a model, called a *classifier*, such as a recommendation system) is an important means of assessing the quality of a classifier. Note that such an assessment may be invalid if the assumptions of the actual classifications are based on false premises. See confusion matrix.

Classifier See classification.

Clickable link A kind of navigation aid in which hypertext links are displayed, e.g., in an integrated development environment to allow the user to jump directly to corresponding code.

Cluster analysis The task of partitioning a set such that the items within a partition (called a *cluster*) are more similar in a defined sense than items in different partitions. It is an important method in exploratory data mining.

Cold start problem An issue arises when a recommendation system requires data to make its recommendations, e.g., extracted from a historical repository, but no such data yet exists.

Collaborative filtering A technique for generating recommendations in which the similarity of opinions of agents on a set of existing issues is used to predict the similarity of opinions of those agents on other issues. *Social tagging*, in which users label items as interesting, liked, recommended, etc., is one such technique.

Commit [*Within RSSEs*] A set of resources whose changes are added to a version control system together. For version control systems that do not support explicit commits of multiple resources, an inferred commit can be reconstructed where individually committed resources possess the same author and comment metadata, and the timestamps are in close proximity. Note that commit and *changeset* are synonymous under most situations, except where a distinction is needed between the resources changed contemporaneously and the resources added to a version control system together (e.g., when the author of the changeset differs from the author of the commit).

[*Within data management more generally*] A set of tentative changes that have been made permanent, typically at the end of a *transaction*.

Confidence See association rule mining.

Configuration An arrangement of parts and/or their parametrization by concrete values to obtain specific, well-defined instances that are interrelated in a well-defined manner.

Confusion matrix A means of categorizing the correctness of the mechanical classifications of a set of items. Confusion matrices are usually 2×2 (for binary classification), though larger sizes and higher dimensionality are both possible. In both dimensions of the table are listed the possible classifications of the items under consideration; one dimension represents the actual or true classifications while the other represents the predicted or expected classifications from a classifier (e.g., a recommendation system). Each cell of the table records the number of items that have the corresponding combination of predicted and actual classifications. A perfect classifier will always agree with the actual classifications. In the special case of binary classification, the four cells of the table are given special names. *True positive* items *TP* are those that are correctly predicted by the classifier as true (equivalently, as yes, on, OK, of interest, etc.); *true negative* items *TN* are correctly predicted as false (equivalently, as no, off, not OK, not of interest, etc.). Cases where the classifier disagrees with reality are termed *false positives FP* (the classifier predicts true, but the actual classification is false) and *false negatives FN* (the classifier predicts false, but the actual classification is true). In many circumstances, the multiple values of

the confusion matrix are replaced by a smaller set of measures that combine
the individual cell values in various ways; note that this replacement necessarily
loses information. In statistics, false positives are known as *type I errors*, and
false negatives as *type II errors*. See precision, recall, F-measure, accuracy, false
negative rate.

Consequent See association rule.

Content-based recommendation system A recommendation system that makes
recommendations based on items' content and profiles of users' interests.

Context The situation in which a system operates. The sense is usually limited
to what is both visible and deemed relevant. Thus, a context could involve the
physical location of a device, the characteristics of a task, the goals of a user, etc.

Context awareness A property describing a system that can sense its context and
react accordingly.

Corpus A large collection of examples, systems, or other entities from which
patterns can be inferred or recommendations can be drawn.

Correctness Usually, an imprecise term used in a situation where an item can be
assessed as "right" or "wrong" (or sometimes as a fuzzy, intermediate value) to
indicate the property of being "right." It implies that an independent means of this
assessment is available that possesses greater validity if not absolute validity.

Coverage The percentage of items available to a recommendation system for
which it is capable of making recommendations.

Critiquing-based recommendation system A knowledge-based recommendation system that supports a simple form of articulating preferences (e.g., higher
performance, lower price, etc.).

Cross-validation A technique for model validation in which a set of pairs of
queries and recommendations are repeatedly partitioned into training and test
data, and the performance of the model is characterized over the different
partitions. Variations exist for selecting the partitions, such as *k-fold cross-
validation*, in which the dataset is partitioned into k equal sized subsamples;
each subsample is then used as the validation data against which to evaluate the
model that has been trained on the other $k - 1$ subsamples. A related idea is
k-tail evaluation, in which a sequence of data is partitioned into a suffix of k
data items and a prefix of the remainder; the prefix is used as the training set and
the suffix is used as the testing set. k-tail evaluation has less statistical validity,
as the same data sequence would be repeatedly partitioned, leading to a lack of
independence.

Customization The process of adaptation of an item for the sake of accommodat-
ing differences between individual contexts and/or users.

Data cleaning The process of detecting and correcting/removing data items that
are corrupt or otherwise inaccurate. Also called *data cleansing* or *data scrubbing*.

Data mining The mechanical discovery of patterns within a (large) dataset. The
term is often abused to mean any form of large-scale data processing. See
association rule mining, cluster analysis, anomaly detection, machine learning.

Density A measure for characterizing datasets in which ratings have been made by users or inferred from users. It represents how many of the data items have been rated, as a percentage, per user, or overall, according to the circumstances.

Developer A human that interacts with the internal representations of software systems, such as source code or system designs. A developer acts as the user of various software tools, including integrated development environments and recommendation systems in software engineering. Developers are also known as *programmers* and *software engineers*. In our situation, we include *managers* who may know nothing about the programmatic entities within the software system.

Developer context The context in which the developer is working at a particular point in time, such as when a recommendation is generated.

Developer profile A set of attributes deemed useful for describing a developer, typically that will possess similarities to and differences from profiles of other developers.

Diversity A property of a set of recommendations wherein the recommendations are not considered trivial variations on each other.

Domain analysis The process of analyzing common terminology, problems, and solutions over a range of systems that share a common purpose.

Edit location Individual locations within an entity (typically the source code for a software system) that are modified by a developer to achieve some purpose. A high-level transformation (such as a refactoring) will be enacted as changes at individual edit locations, either automatically by a tool or manually by a developer.

End-user A human that uses a software system through a non-programmatic interface. The term is used to distinguish users who are not developers.

Enhancement See issue.

Extensibility A property of an item (typically, a programmatic entity) representing the ease with which it can be extended.

Evaluation An examination of a thing to assess its merits.

Execution trace A record of the execution of a program, typically listing the methods executed in the order in which they were executed. An execution trace may also record details of the objects and values passed, as well as metadata about the execution such as the time at which a method was entered and left and the thread in which the execution occurred. Statement-level execution traces are also common.

Expected recommendation The recommendation that ought to be obtained for a given input from a "perfect" RSSE. In many situations, the expected recommendation must be assumed based on an independent source of information (like real-world data).

Experiment A disciplined procedure to test a hypothesis, usually under (partially) controlled conditions. Or the act of following such a procedure.

Explanation A description of why an RSSE has chosen to produce a recommendation, generally presented to the user on demand and in context of that recommendation.

Exploration A collection of information about a previously unknown (physical or conceptual) space. Or the act of collecting such information.

Failure The externally visible evidence of a bug within a software system. A bug may never cause a failure if the bug is never executed. A failure may occur long after the execution of a bug.

Fallout The probability that a recommendation system will recommend a false item. It is equivalent to $1 -$ true positive rate. See confusion matrix for a general overview.

False negative See confusion matrix.

False negative rate For binary classification of items, the percentage of the items predicted to be irrelevant that are actually relevant. It is used as a measure of quality of classifiers. It can equivalently be interpreted as a probability, rather than a ratio. The measure is defined as

$$\frac{FN}{FN + TN};$$

see confusion matrix for the definition of these quantities.

False positive See confusion matrix.

False positive rate For binary classification of items, the percentage of the irrelevant items that are predicted to be relevant. It is used as a measure of quality of classifiers. It can equivalently be interpreted as a probability, rather than a ratio. The measure is defined as

$$\frac{FP}{TN + FP};$$

see confusion matrix for the definition of these quantities.

Feature A distinguishing characteristic of an entity, intended to be positive in its target context.

Feature request See issue.

Field study A study conducted in a real-world setting, as opposed to an artificial one, such as a laboratory. A field study avoids control but merely observes phenomena, in the hope of minimizing influence on the phenomena and obtaining a richer set of observations.

F-measure A single measure that combines precision and recall. (Note that this necessarily loses information.) The *general F-measure* F_β is defined (for real, non-negative values of β) as

$$(1 + \beta^2) \times \frac{\text{precision} \times \text{recall}}{\beta^2 \times \text{precision} + \text{recall}}.$$

More typically, β is set to the value of 1, producing the F_1 *measure* (also called the *traditional F-measure* or *balanced F-score*); it is defined as

$$2 \times \frac{\text{precision} \times \text{recall}}{\text{precision} + \text{recall}}.$$

The F_1 measure is typically called the F-measure for simplicity.

F_1 **measure** See F-measure.

F_β **measure** See F-measure.

Frequent itemset See association rule mining.

Functional requirement A kind of requirement that focuses on the functionality aspects of a system, as opposed to the quality properties.

Fuzzy set A set of items for which a special function called a *membership function* is defined. The membership function maps each item to a value in the interval [0, 1] that represents the probability that that item is a member of the set.

General F-measure See F-measure.

Generalizability A property of an empirical result representing how well it would apply to situations other than those explicitly evaluated.

Ground truth Data collected from direct assessment as opposed to indirectly or remotely, i.e., "on the ground." This matters as the validity of data collected through a series of inferences, or indirect interpretation is threatened at each step. On the other hand, ground truth data is often avoided due to high costs or risks associated with its collection.

Group recommendation system A recommendation system whose recommendations are aimed at a group as a whole, rather than individuals.

Heuristic A technique or value derived from experience, experimentation, or intuition from which a problem can be solved with no expectation of optimality. Heuristics are often used in situations where execution time is an important factor and suboptimal solutions are expected to suffice.

Heuristics-based recommendation An approach used in knowledge-based recommendation systems that uses heuristics in order to derive recommendations.

Human–computer interaction See user interface.

Hybrid recommendation system A recommendation system that combines two or more recommendation approaches in forming its recommendations, e.g., collaborative filtering, content-based, group, knowledge-based.

IDE See integrated development environment.

Information retrieval "Finding material (usually documents) of an unstructured nature (usually text) that satisfies an information need from within large collections (usually stored on computers)" [30].

Integrated development environment A software application that provides a set of software tools for the development of other software. These software tools are typically integrated by sharing their internal representations of data (e.g., source code) and may also communicate directly with each other to reuse their functionality or to announce events to one another. Integrated development environments are typically intended to be extensible to new software tools. Integrated development environments aim to support the developer in their development tasks, focusing on usability for those tasks.

Interaction data Data collected from the users of a software system as they perform events with that system. Such data may be low level, recording keystrokes and mouse clicks at certain coordinates; or high level, recording presses of graphical button widgets, bringing a specific text editor to the foreground, or browsing for information. This data often consists of a description of the event that has occurred along with metadata such as the timestamp of the event. Inferring high-level interaction data from low-level interaction data is a nontrivial operation. *Navigation data* is a special form of interaction data in which the interactions (of interest) consist solely of moving between or within items, such as source code classes.

Invalid See validity [within mathematics].

Issue Constitutes two classes of entities: *bugs* and *enhancements*. A bug is a defect in a software system. An enhancement (or *feature request*) is a change that is desired to alter the system for reasons other than repairing a bug, such as extending functionality. These are grouped together under the generic label "issue" when it is not known or not important whether one is dealing with bugs or enhancements specifically. Bugs are also called *defects* and *problems*. Enhancements are also called *changes* and *problems*. Issues are also called *problems*. See issue report, issue repository, issue management system.

Issue management system A system that permits the recording of an *issue report*, as well as supporting the process of triaging, assigning, prioritizing, merging, and closing issue issues (i.e., the management of issues). An issue management system operates atop an issue repository.

Issue report Generally a structured report either describing a bug within a software system or requesting that a change be made; in other words, an issue report reports an issue. Issue reports are generally managed together, regardless of whether they constitute reports of bugs or enhancement requests. Issue reports typically collect metadata about the issue and about the management of the issue. See issue repository, issue management system.

Issue repository A collection of issue reports, stored in a specific manner, such as in a relational database. An issue repository is used by an issue management system to permit issues to be reported and managed through the process of addressing them.

Issue triage The lightweight analysis of a novel issue report to decide how to react to it, for example, to label it as a duplicate or of high priority.

Itemset See association rule.

k-**fold cross-validation** See cross-validation.

k-**furthest neighbors** A recommendation algorithm that recommends the k items that are least similar to a specified one (e.g., users that are dissimilar to the current user).

k-**nearest neighbors** A recommendation algorithm that recommends the k items that are most similar to a specified one (e.g., users that are similar to the current user).

k-**tail evaluation** See cross-validation.

Knowledge capture A process of explicitly recording in a tangible representation the knowledge possessed by a user.

Knowledge-based recommendation system A recommendation system that models knowledge about users and items in order to reason about which items meet a user's requirements. See critiquing-based recommendation system.

Learner See machine learning.

Machine learning A technique whereby a program (called the *machine learner* or simply the *learner*) can adapt according to the data it receives.

Macroevaluation A means of evaluating the quality of a recommendation system in which individual confusion matrices are populated with the results from individual recommendation trials. Each confusion matrix can then be summarized with standard measures, and measures of central tendency (such as the mean) can then be calculated over the individual measures.

Manager See developer.

Metric [*Within software engineering*] A measure of some specified property of entities within a defined set. Often, a given metric is intended to have greater meaning than its definition would automatically give it. A *validated metric* is thus a metric for which this greater meaning has been empirically validated to hold. For example, using a person's shoe size as a metric of intelligence would only be valid if we could demonstrate high correlation (or perfect correlation) between the two.
[*Within mathematics*] A function generalizing the notion of distance. A metric must conform to a certain set of properties: non-negativity, identity of indiscernibles, symmetry, and the triangle inequality.

Microevaluation A means of evaluating the quality of a recommendation system in which a confusion matrix is populated with the results from multiple recommendation trials without differentiating them. The confusion matrix can then be summarized with standard measures.

Natural language processing The automated interpretation of human language. This is more complex than the processing of programming languages due to a much greater presence of ambiguity and context-sensitivity in human languages.

Navigation data See interaction data.

Network analysis An analysis of a graph representing a set of entities and some relationship between them. This can be performed to characterize the overall shape of the network, to identify local properties, or to make decisions about the underlying entities or processes that the graph represents.

Noise Random data that does not carry information content but that can obscure the information content around it.

Non-functional requirement A kind of requirement that focuses on the quality aspects of a system, as opposed to its functionality.

Novelty The experience of discovering an item that is significantly different from others already known. Compare diversity and serendipity.

Ontology [*Within computer science*] The set of concepts that exist within a domain, and the relationships between those concepts. Note that a taxonomy is an ontology restricted to only include the subsumption relation (i.e., parent/child).

Overfitting Use of a statistical model to describe noise in a dataset rather than the relationship obscured by the noise. This can occur when the number of parameters in a model is close to the number of datapoints being fit, or when there has been no differentiation between the data used to derive the model and the data used to validate the model.

Personalization The delivery of different information (i.e., recommendations) depending on the target user.

Persuasiveness The capability of a recommendation system to influence a user's attitude, decisions, or behavior.

Positive predictive value See precision.

Precision [*Within information retrieval*] For binary classification of items, the percentage of the items predicted to be relevant that are actually relevant. It is used as a measure of quality of classifiers. It can equivalently be interpreted as a probability, rather than a ratio. The measure is defined as

$$\frac{TP}{TP + FP};$$

see confusion matrix for the definition of these quantities. A synonymous term used in other areas is *positive predictive value*. When the set of items predicted to be relevant is restricted to those above some threshold n (such as above some value of similarity) or the size of this set is constrained to n, we can speak of *precision at n*.

[*Within science and engineering generally*] The degree to which repeated measurements of the same quantity under unchanged conditions agree. Compare accuracy.

Prediction A statement about the state of some entity derived only in part from the information possessed about it. Predictions often focus on the future state of an entity based on its current state and some model of change. Recommendations implicitly or explicitly predict the utility of the recommended item/action to the user.

Privacy The ability of an individual or group to selectively reveal information about themselves, when and if they so choose.

Proactive recommendation A recommendation that is presented to the user when the recommendation system deems it appropriate, without waiting for the user to request it.

Program transformation Any alteration or act of alteration of a program, usually conceived at the level of source code, but that could operate at higher or lower levels of abstraction.

Programmer See developer.

Quality An imprecise term denoting the fitness for purpose of a product or process. It may involve both objective and subjective elements, resulting in significantly different opinions of quality from different stakeholders.

Reactive recommendation A recommendation that is presented to the user only when the user requests it.

Reactivity The ability of a recommendation system to provide good quality recommendations in real-time according to some specified time threshold criterion.

Recall For binary classification of items, the percentage of the items that are actually relevant that are predicted to be relevant. It is used as a measure of quality of classifiers. It can equivalently be interpreted as a probability, rather than a ratio. The measure is defined as

$$\frac{TP}{TP + FN};$$

see confusion matrix for the definition of these quantities. Synonymous terms used in other areas are *true positive rate* and *sensitivity*. When the set of items predicted to be relevant is restricted to those above some threshold n (such as above some value of similarity) or the size of this set is constrained to n, we can speak of *recall at n*.

Recommendation An information item estimated to be valuable in a given context. When the "estimate" is universally accurate, the information item is not a recommendation, but the correct answer.

Recommendation box The area wherein recommendations are displayed on an online surface.

Recommendation system A software application that provides information items estimated to be valuable for a task in a given context, i.e., recommendations. If the "estimate" is universally accurate, the system is not a recommendation system, but a system for computing the correct answer.

Recommendation system in software engineering A software application that provides information item estimated to be valuable for a software engineering task in a given context. If the "estimate" is universally accurate, the system is not an RSSE, but a system for computing the correct answer.

Refactoring Restructuring software to alter its internal structure without altering its external behavior. Such changes are typically performed in order to improve the internal properties of the software (such as its understandability or extensibility) without breaking external software agents or making end-users aware of the changes. Refactoring is both the general notion of such changes and specific transformations, especially when standardized (e.g., a *rename refactoring*).

Reinforcement [*Within RSSEs*] A heuristic measure defined by the Suade tool [10] for the likelihood of the relevance of an entity given its relationship with other elements, some of which are known to be relevant. According to the intuition of reinforcement, structural neighbors that are part of a cluster that contains many elements already in the set of interest are more likely to be interesting because they are the "odd ones out" in the cluster of elements related to the set of interest.

Relevance The value of an item to a specific user in completing a specific task at a specific time.

Reporter The user who has reported an issue.

Representativeness A property of a data item or sample that allows it to stand in for other items or the general population of interest. Representativeness can only be defined relative to a specific property or set of properties of interest. In mathematical terms, a sample could be considered representative if it is an element of an equivalence class under a pertinent equivalence relation. True representativeness is often difficult to assess when the population characteristics are not known.

Reproducibility The ability of an evaluation to be repeated in order to arrive at the same conclusions. The term is often meant more narrowly as the ability for an experiment to be repeated by different researchers to arrive at the same results. An irreproducible evaluation is generally not seen as valuable due to the possibility that it was conducted incorrectly and thus that the conclusions are not supported.

Requirement A condition or capability that must be met by a software product or software development process.

Requirements elicitation/negotiation A collaborative process, involving multiple stakeholders, of identifying requirements. As stakeholders' opinions may conflict as to the importance or value of individual requirements, negotiation is used to resolve conflicts.

Response time The time taken by a system to react to an input.

Robustness The ability of a system to cope with faults and failures.

Root-mean-squared error A measure comparing the values predicted by a model (i.e., a recommendation system) and the values actually observed. It is defined as

$$\sqrt{\frac{\sum_{i=1}^{n}(x_i - \hat{x}_i)^2}{n}},$$

where each x_i is the predicted value and each $\hat{x}_i$ is the actual value.

RSSE See recommendation system in software engineering.

Satisfiability [*Within mathematics*] The problem of determining if there exists an interpretation that satisfies a logical (Boolean) expression.

Scalability The ability of something to accommodate growth reasonably, or to be adapted in order to accommodate growth reasonably. For example, this can mean that the growth in execution time does not exceed some bound relative to the input size. In principle, scalability should also support shrinkage at reasonable reduction in resource usage, but for many contexts, it is only the growth characteristic that is deemed important.

SCoReS See source code-based recommendation system.

Sensitivity See recall.

Serendipity The experience of finding an unexpected and fortuitous item. Compare novelty.

Simulation An imitation of the behavior of some process, usually for the purpose of studying that process. Equivalently, an imitation of the functioning of one system by another, usually simpler one.

Social network A graph consisting of actors (the vertices) and their relationships (the edges) in which the actors have a social existence (i.e., they will generally be humans) and their represented relationships will have a social significance.

Social tagging See collaborative filtering.

Software configuration management system See version control system.

Software engineer See developer.

Software product line A set of software systems that share a common, managed set of features, as opposed to possessing copies of those features.

Software quality metrics Any set of metrics used to measure the quality aspects of software products, projects, and/or processes.

Sound See validity [within mathematics].

Soundness See validity [within mathematics].

Source code-based recommendation system A recommendation system that produces recommendations principally by analyzing the source code of a software system.

Specificity [*Within RSSEs*] A heuristic measure defined by the Suade tool [10] for the likelihood of the relevance of an entity given its relationship with other elements, some of which are known to be relevant. According to the intuition of specificity, structural neighbors that have few structural dependencies are more likely to be interesting because their relation to an element of interest is more unique.
[*Within information retrieval*] See true negative rate.

Speculative analysis A dynamic analysis technique in which a range of possible actions are automatically tried, and the estimated quality of the results is used to rank the possibilities.

Stakeholder An entity (typically a person, but sometimes a group or organization) with an interest in the process or outcome of a project.

Support See association rule mining.

Systematic error See bias.

Taxonomy A classification of concepts or entities within a domain, and their parent/child relationships. See ontology.

Test-driven development A software development process in which an automated test case is written prior to the functionality that that test case is intended to exercise. The idea has been promoted in various agile software development methodologies for its potential to define the conditions for completion, and to avoid writing test cases that immediately pass rather than checking for correct behavior, which can happen due to the phenomenon of "debugging blindness."

Text link A kind of navigation aid consisting of textual references, such as corresponding files and line numbers, e.g., see Chap. 5.

Threat to validity See validity [within evaluation].

Traditional F-measure See F-measure.

Transaction See commit.

Transparency A property of a recommendation that permits the user to understand why the recommendation has been made.

Triangulation [*Within evaluation*] Conducting multiple evaluations, typically via different methods and/or on different data sources, in order to improve the generalizability of the findings. Since each method and data source will have its own threats to validity, the intent is that the different methods/data sources will differ in their threats to validity, and thus, some threats can be shown to exist or not exist.

True negative See confusion matrix.

True negative rate For binary classification of items, the percentage of the items that are actually not relevant that are predicted to be not relevant. It is used as a measure of quality of classifiers. It can equivalently be interpreted as a probability, rather than a ratio. The measure is defined as

$$\frac{TN}{TN + FP};$$

see confusion matrix for the definition of these quantities. A synonymous term from other areas is *specificity*. When the set of items predicted to be relevant is restricted to those above some threshold n (such as above some value of similarity) or the size of this set is constrained to n, we can speak of *true negative rate at n*.

True positive See confusion matrix.

True positive rate See recall.

Trust Reliance on the actions of an entity, such as a recommendation system. Trust can be established transitively through a recommendation by trusted entity, or directly through repeated observation of reliable actions. Trust can be lost by observation of unreliable actions. Believable explanations of behavior can help to establish trust.

Type I error See confusion matrix.

Type II error See confusion matrix.

Understandability A property that assesses a user's ability to correctly interpret the meaning of an item. It necessarily depends on the knowledge, experience, and skills of the user.

Usability A property that assesses a user's ability to easily use an item. This generally includes aspects of understandability.

User An agent external to a software system that makes use of that system. A user is usually a human being in the software engineering context, but in some other areas, software agents are also deemed to be users or other software entities. In the context of recommendation systems in software engineering, the user is usually a developer; for example, an RSSE residing within an integrated development environment would target a developer. The generic term *user* is taken to include both developers and end-users.

User history See interaction data.

User interface The portion of a software system that supports interaction with a user.

User satisfaction The extent to which a user is supported in their task by a recommendation.

Valid See validity [within mathematics].

Validity [*Within evaluation*] The extent to which the findings of an evaluation are well founded and correspond to reality. Every empirical method and every data source possesses one or more properties (called threats to validity) that may render findings derived therefrom to lack validity.

[*Within mathematics*] A property of a logical argument. A *valid argument* is one in which the truth of the premises necessitates the truth of the consequences, regardless of whether the premises are actually true; an argument that lacks validity is called *invalid*. This contrasts with a *sound argument*, which is one that is also valid, but whose premises are known to be true. *Soundness* is the analogous property that deals with the question of whether an argument is sound or not sound.

Variant See version.

VCS See version control system.

Version Given an entity (such as an entire software system), a version of that entity constitutes a particular set of changes to it from its original form. Different versions may coexist to support different purposes, or they may sequentially supplant older versions, or both. Synonymous terms are *revision* and *variant*. Specifically coexistent versions are also called *variants*.

Version control system A software system used to record incremental changes to resources, along with metadata describing those changes, such as the author, timestamp when the change was added, and a comment made by the developer who added the change. Version control systems can be subsumed more generally by the term *software configuration management systems*.

Wizard of Oz experiment An experiment in which apparently automated responses/recommendations are being faked, either hard-coded in the software being used to mediate the experiment or manually entered by an experimenter (usually in secret) during the experiment. (The name derives from a fictional character in American literature who was pretending to have great magical powers but was actually operating special effects from a hidden location.)

Index

Note: Italicized page references point to (explicit or implicit) definitions.